Confucian China and Its Modern Fate

Joseph R. Levenson

CONFUCIAN CHINA
AND ITS
MODERN FATE

A TRILOGY

University of California Press

BERKELEY AND LOS ANGELES 1968

University of California Press

Berkeley and Los Angeles, California

Library of Congress Catalog Card Number 68-23033

First Combined Edition

Printed in the United States of America

ROSEMARY MONTEFIORE LEVENSON

GENERAL PREFACE

Problems, problems. How does one introduce this kaleidoscopic theme? Perhaps I should tackle the "problem of intellectual continuity" in my own studies, and find the point of departure for *Confucian China and Its Modern Fate* in *Liang Ch'i-ch'ao and the Mind of Modern China*. In the middle and end of that work, I related the early Jesuit to the later Reformist Confucian-Western syncretism. These syncretistic efforts (the first in the seventeenth century, the second in the 1890's) were comparable, but not analogous:

The intervening centuries of decline and fall had made the difference. In the Jesuit episode, a syncretism was necessary to western thought to effect its entrance into the Chinese mind; when Liang wrote, a syncretism was necessary to the Chinese mind to soften the blow of the irresistable entrance of western thought. In the first case, the Chinese tradition was standing firm, and the western intruders sought admission by cloaking themselves in the trappings of that tradition; in the second case, the Chinese tradition was disintegrating, and its heirs, to save the fragments, had to interpret them in the spirit of the western intrusion . . .

When orthodox Confucianists of the nineties saw the Reform Movement simply as a new phase of a traditional battle between the Confucian "rule of virtue" and the Legalist "rule of law," when they identified western invasions with the earlier, "traditional," barbarian invasions, their wisdom was but the knowledge of dead secrets. A new civilization was flooding into China, and Liang had known, in his early years, that Confucius must either preside over the process or be drowned in it.

But the Jesuits had known that, as for their intrusion, Confucius would either preside over it or block it. Somewhere, then, in the course of the years between Matteo Ricci and Liang Ch'i-ch'ao, Confucianism had lost the initiative. The orthodox Confucianists, standing still, had been moving towards oblivion. In the beginning, their idea was a force, the product and the intellectual prop of a living society. In the end it was a shade, living only in the minds of many, treasured in the mind for its own sake after the society which had produced it and which needed it had begun to dissolve away . . .

That was a way of putting it — not very satisfactory. We could sum it up (moving from *Liang* to *Confucian China*) in a dull old pair of words: Confucianism moving from "objective" to "subjective" significance. As the world changed, the world view lost its wholeness and contemporary relevance. Confucianists had always been historical-minded; now they became historical themselves. Modern men could still voice Confucian thoughts, but the complexity of a Confucian system was gone. Fung Yu-lan, the philosopher, still talks about *jen* in the midst of Communist China — "human kindness" (humankind-ness), "benevolence", in the midst of Communist "struggle." The idea (one hopes) is eternal; but is it being *perpetuated* in China, with its associations in the old high culture? Or is it rather being *preserved,* precisely because its currency is past? Fung sides with Mencius while Mao Tse-tung confronts him. If he thinks Mao is wrong (understandably enough, he does not quite say Mao is wrong), then he thinks — he is driven to think — that Mencius is right.

And Mencius, and Fung, may well be right. But "thought" and "thinking," "truth" and "life" need not be identical. Living history is full of "error," and death and truth are far from incompatible. Something logically plausible may be psychologically uncongenial. Something theoretically defensible may be historically undefendable. That is what we mean when we say that history is not a morality tale, and when we feel the poignancy of a lost cause — the loss of objective mastery — not just coldly clock the passing, changing years.

At the end of Volume One, I speak of intellectual history as the history, not of thought, but of men thinking. "Thought" is constant, ideas or systems of ideas forever meaning what they mean in themselves, as logical constructions. But "thinking," a psychological act, implies context (changing), not disembodiment, and men mean different things when they think thoughts in different total environments. Therefore, as studies of intellectual history, these volumes, even when they seem most rarefied, at least imply the social context. *Monarchical Decay*, with its "institutional" theme, is properly the centerpiece. The "amateur ideal," so prominent a motif in Confucian China and in *Intellectual Continuity*, was institutionalized as well as conceptualized. Indeed, paying respect to the good Confucian "one-ness of knowledge and action," I cannot separate the one from the other. It is no use waving a cheerful good-bye to Imperial China, as though the bureaucratic monarchy were inessential (or the Communist regime were preserving its essence), and pretending that Confucianism is essentially undisturbed. A set of Confucian attitudes, even if one could deem them uncorroded, does not sum up the *gestalt*. Intellectual history, after all, is only a type of the history men write, only a method, an avenue of entry, not an end. "Out there," in the history men make, the web is never rent, and intellectual, social, political, economic, cultural threads are interwoven. In the specialized approach, one tampers with the unity of nature; but the end is, to restore the whole in comprehensible form.

Accordingly, when I conjure up dichotomies — objective/subjective, intellectual/emotional, history/value, traditional/modern, culturalism/nationalism, Confucianist/Legalist, and the like — these are offered, not as stark confrontations really "there" in history, but as heuristic devices for explaining (not conforming to) the life situation. Only categories clash, categories of explanation. What they are used to explain is the overlapping, intermingling, noncategorical quality of minds, situations, and events. Antitheses are abstractions, proposed only to let us see how, and why, their starkness in definition is mitigated in history.

Thus, when the early Jesuits faced those early modern

Confucianists who still retained the initiative and "objective significance," Confucianists repelled them with "value" objections, anti-Christian ideas that might have come from Descartes or the Enlightenment. Certainly these were universalistic ideas, not just particular, "historical" reactions. But there were psychological satisfactions in wielding these weapons of logic. A tradition can always be attacked or defended on intellectual grounds. Yet, the emotional feeling for native ground is always there. "History" and "value" (as an example of antithesis) are always — together — there.

I do not suggest, then, that some ("emotional") Chinese minds were attached purely to history, as against some ("intellectual") minds attached purely to value: "traditionalists" with the first attachment, "iconoclasts" with the second. Wherever men stood on the traditionalist-iconoclast spectrum, concern for history and concern for value suffused their formulations.

Even when the world was upside down, and attacks on Christianity helped Chinese to desert Confucianism, not to defend it, the history/value dichotomy was relevant. Intellectual disenchantment with the great Chinese tradition had emotional repercussions; and the emotional drive was translated into intellectual terms (was Darwin the answer? Dewey? Kropotkin? Marx?). *Some* alternative had to attract if Confucianism repelled them. For the rejection of what had once been defended in a cool Cartesian spirit could not be cool. Even when clearing the ground, Chinese wanted desperately to own the ground they stood on. They wanted to continue making *Chinese* history even when — or rather, by — making the products of Chinese history . . . *history.*

From writing *Liang,* to writing *Confucian China,* to reading Benjamin Schwartz's masterly *In Search of Wealth and Power: Yen Fu and the West* — at least the last step supports the battered theory of progress. In Yen's life (1853-1921), and in Schwartz's life of Yen (the famous translator of Huxley, Spencer, Montesquieu, and others) , there is plenty of modern fate, and one can infer there a good deal of what my trilogy is about. Unlike the "self-strengtheners," middle and late nineteenth-century officials who bungled the industrial effort, Yen reasoned as though both *yung* and *t'i*, material function *and* spiritual essence, could be traced to western sources. But if Yen was farther gone in defection from the Confucian tradition than any of these predecessors, he was not *déraciné*, as so many of his younger readers and successors would seem to be. The stamp of tradition on his personal culture was indelible. And he adapted traditional fragments (a Confucian *personal* culture was itself a fragment of a personal-public whole) to his genuine anti-Confucianism. The half-way house was his natural place — neither at home with Confucian tradition, nor in the utterly strange lands of revolution. He deliberately sought out early Chinese intimations of his new intellectual values — Hsun-tzu for Spencer, Lao-tzu for Darwin, for example. But in both what Yen inherited from Chinese history and in what he discerned in it, he never claimed and did not exemplify the persistence of "Chinese essence." Chinese thought, before his, might be seen as full of suggestive *aperçus*, analogous to or anticipating certain modern universal conclusions. But the systems of thought that drove these conclusions home were western; and it was in the light of these systems, especially eighteenth-century French and nineteenth-century English, that the *aperçus* could be perceived.

Herbert Spencer, not Confucius or any Confucianist, persuaded Yen that China was an organism, and it was to this organism's survival and growth, not to any Way divined at a stage in its past, that Chinese individuals ought to be committed. Yen, conservatively, saw a place for Confucianism as a moral preservative while roads to evolutionary advance were being prepared. It would militate against racialism, revolution, irresponsible libertarianism, which he saw as blind alleys to helplessness. But this was Confucianism as social cement, not truth. The morality of the "moral preservative" was instrumental, not final. As the product of a stage of evolution, and a tool during another stage that was well before the last, it was sure to be superseded, to be ultimately undefendable and therefore indefensible.

To say that something is indefensible because undefendable is the ultimate immorality. What led Yen, not entirely comprehending, to this equation (or to positions from which it had to be inferred) was the social Darwinism that convinced him about stages of evolution. Social-Darwinist determinism is nothing if not a solvent of morality. Where Spencer attempted to reconcile a Darwinian blind self-assertiveness with an innate moral sense, this was incongruous. But Yen did not see it. On the issue of liberty he was ready to see Spencer as a moralist (with Spencer himself, against all logic) — and to see Mill as a statist (against Mill's intentions). It made it easy for Yen to break with the Confucianist within himself without unequivocally confronting him.

Here, with this problem of the tension within Yen, exemplified sometimes in his idiosyncratic interpretations of western thinkers, sometimes in his facile acceptance of their own idiosyncracies, we face a problem of interpretation. How important was "the Confucianist within himself?" That part of Yen that resented China's apparent lack of success responded to demands to make it new. But a part of Yen (and of many others) resented the West's apparent success, too, and this part spoke for the Chinese past, or waited to speak, against the compulsions to scuttle it. To the World-War and post-War Yen, the Darwinian "struggle for existence" became, on Western military form, a moral excrescence, and evolution a failure. An organic definition of societies could authorize a traditionalistic particularism ("national essence"), a psychological rather than a practical conservatism, quite as directly as a taste and hope for evolutionary change. And Yen ended his days closer to this conservatism than to that of the period

of his great translations. This was still not authentic Confucian commitment; he was fundamentally "modern" and
could never really go home again. But had he really always been longing for what only the War gave him; a
chance to see Chinese values as defendable, hence defensible, once more?

For Yen and other Chinese intellectuals of his generation were tinged with a malaise. Overtly, Yen wrote about
China, patient, not agent, able only to be acted upon, not
to act, because it lagged in wealth and power. But he was
writing about himself, too. Translating and expounding
Montesquieu, Mill, Huxley, Spencer, he felt himself to be
dealing with intellectual actors, men who had changed
history. But Yen was a reactor. The fact that he had to go
to them to find his affirmations — even though he
changed them in the process — meant that anyone translating and expounding Yen would be explaining Chinese
history, not going to Yen for *his* affirmations. Darwin and
even his epigones were intrinsically, supra-historically,
interesting. Yen was interesting for what he made of them.
What was weak about modern China was not simply what
Yen detected with his social Darwinist vision; it was what
he reflected, too, in depending on that vision. What China
lacked — and what drove Yen to an intellectual life that
exemplified the lack — was more than wealth and power,
conventionally understood. It was power to launch a Yen
Fu into universal significance, instead of holding him
down, just historically significant, while he made a particular, Chinese record by reacting to what he considered
universal.

By the time Yen died, in 1921, "scientism" (the assumption that all aspects of the universe are knowable through
the methods of natural science) was permeating the Chinese intellectual world. As D.W.Y. Kwok describes it in
Scientism in Chinese Thought 1900-1950, scientism,
though triumphant, proved emotionally charged and intellectually flat. But the "spiritual" efforts to counter it
were even more jejune. The total picture is drab, as

though to confirm Yen Fu's malaise and the depressed state of modern China — the very state that provoked so many thinkers to put themselves in the picture in the first place. What was weak about modern China was not just the paucity of science which the scientism coterie detected. It was what the scientism reflected, as something ostensibly universal, but merely historically significant in the end: too banal as disembodied *thought* to be anything more than an index to Chinese *thinking*. Anyone interested in Chinese history can profit from Kwok's discussion of the 1923 debate on "Science and Metaphysics." Anyone interested in science and metaphysics need not give it another glance.

Yet, one's interest in Chinese history now is of a universal order, the interest of cosmopolitans in a burgeoning cosmopolitanism, which was rising from the ashes of cosmopolitanism. The very iconoclasm of "scientism," its dismissal of Confucian "spirit," was a ticket-of-leave from a Chinese world to a China *in* the world. The Chinese world had had its own provincials within it while Confucian sophisticates ruled. It was when this world faded, and a nation began to emerge, that the old sophistication began to fail. Cosmopolitan in the Chinese imperial world, Confucianists struck a provincial note in the wider world of the nations, and they passed out of history, into history. Confucian ideas may live. There is hope for *jen*, for example, in a new cosmopolitan complex, in the extra-historical life-in-death which Whitehead terms "out-of-time-ness," or immortality. But Fung Yu-lan, *jen* and all, is fairly out of the Confucianists' time. In the manner of their passing they bequeathed their particular world (universal, to them), where they had been historians in particular, to historians in general.

It is not only Fung, confronting Mao, who may seem to stand for a still vital Confucianism. Mao himself, requiring the "sinification of Marxism," has been seen as a typical ruler with perennial Chinese purposes. But when

xvi

Mao salts his pronouncements with classical citations, these appear, as much as any Reformist classical reference of Liang in the nineties, just subjectively significant. The early Jesuits had found that Confucian authority could not be safely flouted: there was a world (*the* world, for confident Confucianists) that had to be taken, on Confucian terms, as objectively existing. Today, however, in the world in which Mao has to operate while claiming universality, the Classics are irrelevant, and the citations, if anything, only undermine the claim. The only possible universal in the current Chinese way is the model of revolution, a political and economic model. Culturally — with reference to specific, historical Chinese culture — Mao has no message for the world. Old China claimed to be exemplary because others were different and therefore lower. New China claims to be exemplary because it identifies affinities, a common plane of victimization and a common destiny, so that the Chinese mode of liberation should meet the needs of others.

Or, the way back is the way out: these classical citations may Sinify, but they do the reverse of Confucianize. For in a genuinely Confucian China, a China that *was* the world, to cite the Classics was the very method of universal speech. The Confucian Classics were the repositories of value in the abstract, absolute for everyone, not just Chinese values relevant to China alone. When the Classics make China particular instead of universal, it is a China *in* the world — still China, but really new, even as it invokes (indeed, precisely as it invokes) what connects it to the old.

The volumes of the trilogy were first published jointly by Routledge & Kegan Paul and the University of California Press in 1958, 1964, and 1965; details about the publication history of each are included in the individual prefaces.   J.R.L.

VOLUME ONE

THE PROBLEM OF INTELLECTUAL CONTINUITY

PREFACE FOR VOLUME ONE

ALTHOUGH its themes may seem separate and miscellaneous at first and the chronological line irregular, this book deals with one continuous process of change. This is the change: during much of Chinese history new ideas, to be acceptable, had to be proved compatible with tradition; in more recent times tradition, to be retainable, has had to seem compatible with new, independently persuasive ideas. Chinese values have continued to be prized, but by minds that seem more 'traditionalistic' than traditional—modern minds with nostalgia for the past, not minds with the past's authentic intellectual colour. And other minds, of course, have abandoned many of the older Chinese values.

The intellectual history that all these minds have made has sweep and depth, a sweep of change from major point to point, and a depth of change beneath the points themselves. That is why, when we seem to be sailing nicely from nineteenth to twentieth century, describing a transition from *t'i-yung* to *chin-wen* emphasis or from early nationalism to communism, we may take sudden dips of a few centuries or so; for the account of a modern transformation of an old idea adds an important dimension to the account of its modern abandonment. Politically nationalistic criticism of traditional Chinese culture, for example, is a story of recent decades. Change in connotations of the Chinese terms traditionally used to correlate political and cultural questions is a story of many centuries. But the stories point to the same conclusion and they ought to be put together, at whatever cost to the narrative ideals of smooth progression and never looking back.

Any writer of intellectual history has to face a challenge from sceptical 'populists': do the literary remains of an educated fringe really relate to the history of a total society? A recent critic has brushed off a collection of studies of formal Chinese thought as really relevant only to a 'mandarin sub-culture'. But just because 'Boxer' masses in 1900 show a peasant hostility to western innovations, shall we conclude that intellectual Confucian 'self-strengtheners' and 'reformers', with their various commitments to one or another degree of western innovation, were playing a fancy philosophical game, quite removed from the basic stuff of Chinese history? On the contrary—'mandarin' intellectual currents are as relevant as can be to the fate of Chinese society, right down to its most illiterate and least-recorded strata. And the intellectual historian believes this, not because he assumes, as a simple article of faith, that the spirit of the literary documents naturally permeates the whole society, even to minds incompetent to express it, but (to limit the case to China) because the Chinese intelligentsia has had a traditional role as exemplar in Chinese society. In their growing iconoclasm, literati cannot abandon that role and open a gulf in sentiment between themselves and apparently motionless masses (who traditionally had expected literati to embody their own conventional aspirations), without radically changing not only a 'sub-culture' but the map of the Chinese world.

The plan of the book and a good deal of the content were hammered out for the First and Second Conferences on Chinese Thought in 1952 and 1954. I am especially grateful to Arthur Wright and John Fairbank (the directors, respectively, of the Conferences), to all the participants, to Mary Wright, and to H. F. Schurmann for their criticisms and suggestions. But there is plenty of room for disagreement about the matter of the book, and one should by no means assume that my conclusions must be acceptable to the friends who have helped me.

Parts of the book in different form have been published in *Studies in Chinese Thought*, ed. Arthur F. Wright (University of Chicago Press: Chicago, copyright 1953 by the University of Chicago), *Chinese Thought and Institutions*, ed. John K. Fairbank (University of Chicago Press: Chicago, copyright 1957 by the University of Chicago), *The Far Eastern Quarterly*, *Pacific Affairs*, *Sinologica*, and *Asiatische Studien*. I wish to thank the publishers and editors for permission to use this material here.

I am also very grateful to James Cahill, of the Freer Gallery in Washington for his help in suggesting and locating some of the pictures used in the Anchor edition to illustrate interpretations in Chapter II, although these interpretations are, of course, my own.

J.R.L.

Contents

CONTENTS

Part Two: Chinese Culture in Its Modern Metamorphoses: The Tensions of Intellectual Choice

CONTENTS

CONTENTS

Introduction:
The Special and General
Historical Quests

> A traveller, who has lost his way, should not ask,
> 'Where am I?' What he really wants to know is, Where
> are the other places? He has got his own body, but he
> has lost them.
>
> Alfred North Whitehead, *Process and Reality*

WITH the passing of time, ideas change. This statement is ambiguous, and less banal than it seems. It refers to thinkers in a given society, and it refers to thought. With the former shade of meaning, it seems almost a truism: men may change their minds or, at the very least, make a change from the mind of their fathers. Ideas at last lose currency, and new ideas achieve it. If we see an iconoclastic Chinese rejection, in the nineteenth and twentieth centuries, of traditional Chinese beliefs, we say that we see ideas changing.

But an idea changes not only when some thinkers believe it to be outworn but when other thinkers continue to hold it. An idea changes in its persistence as well as in its rejection, changes 'in itself' and not merely in its appeal to the mind. While iconoclasts relegate traditional ideas to the past, traditionalists, at the same time, transform traditional ideas in the present.

This apparently paradoxical transformation-with-preservation of a traditional idea arises from a change in its world, a change in the thinker's alternatives. For (in a Taoist manner of speaking) a thought includes what its thinker eliminates; an idea has its particular quality from the fact

xxvii

that other ideas, expressed in other quarters, are demonstrably alternatives. An idea is always grasped in relative association, never in absolute isolation, and no idea, in history, keeps a changeless self-identity. An audience which appreciates that Mozart is not Wagner will never hear the eighteenth-century *Don Giovanni*. The mind of a nostalgic European medievalist, though it may follow its model in the most intimate, accurate detail, is scarcely the mirror of a medieval mind; there is sophisticated protest where simple affirmation is meant to be. And a harried Chinese Confucianist among modern Chinese iconoclasts, however scrupulously he respects the past and conforms to the letter of tradition, has left his complacent Confucian ancestors hopelessly far behind him.[1]

Vocabulary and syntax, then, may remain the same, late and soon, but the statement changes in meaning as its world changes. Is there another postulate, besides the postulate of the changing world, which confirms this change in meaning, as time passes, in the statement whose literal content remains unchanged?

There is such a postulate, the logical principle which states that 'a body of knowledge consists not of "propositions", "statements", or "judgments" . . . but of these together with the questions they are meant to answer.'[2] By this token, a proposition's meaning is relative to the question it answers.[3] A change, then, in the question behind an idea, like a change in the alternatives beside it, imposes change on the persisting positive content of the idea itself.

Let us consider, for example, European acknowledgment of the worth of Asian civilizations. In both the eighteenth and nineteenth centuries, there were Europeans who denied the doctrine of western superiority to China. But this denial, this freedom from parochialism, was quite a different idea in the eighteenth century than in the next one; for in the first case it was essentially an expression of rationalism, while in the second, it was anti-rationalistic.

Voltaire's admiration of China derived from his deism, a universalist disbelief in particular revelation. His denial of European pretensions was a negative answer to the question,

'Is possession of Christianity the criterion of cultural excellence?' But nineteenth-century opponents of Europocentrism derived not from Voltaire but from Herder, with his romantic principle that every age and every people has its own particular genius. Rationalism, with Turgot and Condorcet, had developed a theory of stages of progress of civilization and had turned from uncritical admiration of the non-European world to uncritical condemnation; Condorcet lowered China in the scale of nations to the level of the primitive agricultural state of society. 'Civilization', to the rationalists, now meant exclusively European civilization. The romantics, therefore, in their denial of European pretensions, meant to answer, negatively, the question, 'Is "secular progress" the criterion of cultural excellence?' Thus, successive 'same' ideas, western expressions of cosmopolitan sympathies, change as the questions behind them change.[4]

An idea, then, is a denial of alternatives and an answer to a question.[5] What a man really means cannot be gathered solely from what he asserts; what he asks and what other men assert invest his ideas with meaning. In no idea does meaning simply inhere, governed only by its degree of correspondence with some unchanging objective reality, without regard to the problems of its thinker.

In nineteenth-century China, the problems of thinkers imposed changes on earlier Chinese ideas. Most thinkers, with a strongly Chinese (if not generally human) predisposition towards the offerings of their own particular culture, continued to ascribe to them a universal validity. But some thinkers did not, and more and more of them failed to do so as the decades passed, and western society proved socially subversive in China, and western ideas alluring. In these circumstances of material change and iconoclastic challenge, tenacious traditionalists seem to have become not simply men believing in intellectually compelling ideas, which by chance were the products of Chinese history, but Chinese having a will to believe, an emotional need to feel the intellectual compulsion, just because the ideas in question came down from a Chinese past. When Confucian traditionalism comes to be accepted not from a confidence in its universal validity but from a *traditionalistic* compulsion to profess that confidence, Confucianism is transformed from a primary, philosophical commitment to a secondary, romantic one, and traditionalism from a philosophical principle to a psychological device. [6]

And then this inner change in a persisting idea, this change which works through the thinker's loyalty, furthers the trend to the other type of intellectual change in time—alienation.

Modern Chinese intellectual history, the period of western influence, may be summed up as two reciprocal processes, the progressive abandonment of tradition by iconoclasts and the petrifaction of tradition by traditionalists. But both of these processes—not only the traditionalistic, but the iconoclastic as well—show a Chinese concern to establish the equivalence of China and the West. Many different intellectual choices have been made in modern China, but the choosers' considerations were not, nor could they have been, entirely intellectual; always, along with the search for right answers, or ideas acceptable to anyone, there continued a search for ideas that *Chinese* could accept. Commitment to the general, commitment to the special, and a sequence of intellectual expedients to make these commitments seem to coincide—these appear to me to characterize the thought of modern China.

In pre-modern China, respect for precedent was one of the prime Confucian attitudes that pervaded intellectual life. In modern China—perhaps as one of the signs of the western intrusion on Chinese culture—precedent began to be treated not exclusively as a Confucian issue, but as an issue familiar enough in a western context: to what degree, if any, should precedent preclude man's free exercise of reason? May the products of one history be judged by reference to the products of any other? The issue is a real one for would-be cultural innovators. That is why eighteenth-century European rationalists, intending to criticize, by purely objective standards, anomalies and flaws in western culture, felt they must burst the confines of their own special history and invented a host of literary visitors—Turks, Persians, Moroc-

cans, Hurons, Iroquois, Peruvians, Siamese, Chinese—to do
the job.[7] Uninvolved in western history, they could presumably evaluate its fruits, they could deal abstractly, unhistoric-
ally, in universals.

An opposing view sees history as organic, not to be
modified at will. A man makes choices not as a member of a
bloodless, universal humanity ('The constitution of 1795 is
... made for men. But there is on earth no man as such ...'),
but as a member of his proudly particular, vibrant people,
with its own national spirit ('I have seen in my life French-
men, Italians, Russians ... but I declare that never in my
life have I seen a man ...').[8] 'Those who have only the
world's outlook without the requisite Burmese outlook,' says
a premier of Burma, 'are like those who long for distant aunts
over the heads of their own mother.'[9] For a people (Hegel,
for one, especially stresses this point) is, in this relativistic
view, an organization which pre-exists its members.[10]
Montaigne, hating dogmatism, expressed this aversion in his
sense of cultural relativism or historical contingency; this
he felt, was the concrete refutation of reason's pretensions to
create an order outside history, ideal states of philosophy in
neither time nor place.[11] Though Montaigne characteristically did not push this idea too far, its implications were
fully historicist; more reasonable than the mystagogic Hegel
but no more rationalistic, he left history, in effect, to
be autonomous, engulfing man, since human efforts to
divert the stream towards freely chosen ends were so dis-
countenanced.

If an intellectual choice which contravenes 'the spirit of
the people' is impious or impossible (and, depending on its
thoroughness, historicism makes it one or both), then the
individual thinker, his scope determined for him in a world
he never made, can have no standards which make him free
to judge what his people's history offers him. Yet, in fact,
history is made of his judgments, for a completely binding
traditionalism would keep a people forever at the post, never
moving into history. Some tempering of traditionalism by
judgment must occur, or histories would be frozen by the law
that nothing can be added to a way of life, if it seems a

departure from what has gone before. Absolute traditionalism is a completely hypothetical, self-destructive concept; a
sense of the past can never develop if an original unmitigated
reverence for 'what is' precludes its ever becoming past.

Traditionalism, that is, can take its subjective tone only in
a world in which alternatives to the worship of the 'eternal
yesterday' have been sharply presented. A traditionalist may
insist that 'mine or yours?', my history or your history, is the
only relevant question which a man may ask before making
a choice among cultural elements. But the conscious will to
narrow the vision (and this will, not the blind plodding in the
footsteps of the past, is the essence of traditionalism) can
never exist apart from the realization that another question
is always being asked: 'true or false?'

The modern Chinese commitment to the general, of which
I have spoken, is the commitment to seek the answers that are
'true'; these thinkers' commitment to the special is their need
of answers that are somehow 'theirs'. The first commitment
brings many men to intellectual alienation from Chinese
tradition, while the second leaves them with an emotional tie
to it. And intellectual alienation and emotional tie intensify
each other. As the former proceeds, the continued attribution
of general validity to special inheritances stems more and
more from the thinker's emotional need to harmonize his
commitments, less and less from a genuine intellectual conviction that he has the best of both worlds. Finally the tie is
snapped. No idea commended solely by the special imperative that it must be true and not at all by an unclouded
general confidence that it *is* true can persist.

The reverse of that situation, however, is equally impossible. Values depend, in the last analysis, on their natural
sources in particular places and times.[12] A man may be
ready to reject the institutions, science, morality, or aesthetics
which his history offers him, but he knows that whatever he
does accept has its place in someone's history. And no one is
so ethereal, so cleanly delivered from native soil and the
limited culture which formed him, that he can see its relative
disqualification with perfect equanimity. Man is not a
neutral machine, calmly recording right answers; if a foreign

answer is to be intellectually accepted as right, the native culture's emotional claims must somehow be squared.

I believe that an understanding of this principle makes the chronological sequence in modern Chinese history logically comprehensible. As traditional ideas change in losing their unquestioned intellectual acceptability, and traditionalists fail thereby to maintain the harmony of special and general, 'mine' and 'true', iconoclasm thrives. But iconoclasts, of the mildest or the deepest hue, face the danger of the same failure, and their ideas change—in a series of acceptance, rejection, and acceptance of something new—as they seek a formula which will keep the psychological peace. The quest for this formula has been the common ground of all the new currents of Chinese thought since the Opium War. How can the thinker scrap Chinese ideas which the western impact has made to seem inadequate, while he preserves his confidence of Chinese equivalence with the West? How shall he see himself as modern man and modern Chinese together?[13]

Was the posing of this question in modern China really inescapable? Such would be the case only if there was a marked distinction between earlier and recent values held in China, and if western influence could account for the transition while indigenous trends in Chinese history could not. Before one may suggest, then, that the great problem for Chinese thinkers in the last century has been the problem of reconciliation of their general intellectual avowals and their special Chinese sentiments, he must reflect on the history of early-modern, 'pre-western' Chinese thought. For if that history was a history of burgeoning modern values (a growing spirit of science, for example—such a major strain in modern thought), then a later nagging doubt about Chinese continuity was unnecessary; if, on the other hand, the modern values cannot be traced to pre-western roots in Chinese history, such a doubt was unavoidable.

Let us put the question.

Part One

THE TONE OF
EARLY-MODERN CHINESE
INTELLECTUAL CULTURE

CHAPTER I

The Abortiveness of Empiricism in Early Ch'ing Thought

IN Sung and Ming intellectual life, idealist philosophies came to the fore. Later, in the seventeenth and eighteenth centuries, to a number of Chinese thinkers, that predominance of idealism seemed a disaster, and they formally disavowed it. What does the existence of these early materialists mean? Does it indicate that the seemingly stable, traditionalistic Chinese society was likely to develop under its own power, without a catalytic intrustion of Western industrialism, into a society with a scientific temper?

1. THE CRITIQUE OF IDEALISM

In the natural world described in the neo-Confucian philosophy of Chu Hsi (1130–1200), a thing exists as a complex of *li* and *ch'i*, ideal form and mutable matter. To *ch'i*, which is perceptible, *li* is the regulative principle; to *li*, which is intelligible, *ch'i* is the medium in which it manifests itself. *Li* is the universal which the intellect apprehends and the senses never reach, and the metaphysical order is from universal to particular, from Being to individual things.

Already in the Sung and Ming periods, there were thinkers who saw grave limitations in Chu Hsi's *li-hsüeh*. But the criticism came from the far side of idealism, from the subjective-idealist *hsin-hsüeh* of Lu Hsiang-shan (1139–93) and

3

Wang Yang-ming (1472–1529). Chu Hsi was an idealist in his search for an unmoving reality behind phenomena, but in his view, at least, reality had an objective existence, outside the mind which sought to apprehend it. For the Lu-Wang school, however, mind itself was the world of truth, and intuition the key to it. According to *li-hsüeh* neo-Confucianism, man's error was his failure to press on to absolutes (and finally to the Absolute, the *li* of *li*, the *t'ai-chi*) through phantasms of sense-experience. According to *hsin-hsüeh* neo-Confucianism, man's error was his very consciousness of these phantasms, or of the illusory distinction between subject and object which is the first condition of any sense-experience at all.[1]

In the seventeenth century, voices began to be raised against both these speculative tendencies to disparage the sensible as compared to a hypothetical transcendent. 'Between heaven and earth', wrote Huang Tsung-hsi (1610–95), 'there is only *ch'i* (matter), there is not *li* (form, idea, "law"). The names *li* and *ch'i* are devised by man. . . . One really existing thing (*wu*) has two names, not two really existing things one essence.' Thus, Huang considers *li* to be merely *ming*, or name, not *shih*, or actual fact.[2] Huang's contemporary, Wang Fu-chih (1619–92), also emphasized the primacy of the tangible, concrete fact over the abstract, generic classification. *Ming* derives from *shih*, he said,[3] name from fact, i.e. the general formal term from particular cognizable examples. And Li Kung (1659–1733), similarly, in a move to vindicate the earthy, observable particular thing against the idealists' attitude of rarefied concern with higher, invisible realms, declared, 'It is said in the *Shih-[ching]*: "there are things, and there are rules for them"; apart from things, where is *li*?' And he charged the *li-hsüeh* philosophers with the error of seeking *li* apart from actual things.[4]

It was in such a fashion that Ch'ing critics of Sung idealism defended the metaphysical priority of the world of sense-perception. They shored up their materialistic position by asserting also that *ch'i* was not morally second to *li*, as their Sung adversaries would have it. Desire, the subjective correlative of *ch'i*, or matter, is good, said Wang Fu-chih, and Yen Yüan (1635–1704), and Tai Chen (1724–77). Only Buddhism, said Wang, not genuine Confucianism, separates Heaven's Law from human desire.[5] It is Buddhist or Taoist (and therefore wrong), said Yen, to teach that man is endowed with evil *ch'i*, as the allegedly Confucian Sung philosophers taught; that was what Buddha meant when he called the ears and eyes and mouth and nose 'six villains'.[6] And Tai agreed, condemning as Buddhist or Taoist the neo-Confucianist Chou Tun-i (1017–73), for preaching the need to annihilate physical desire.[7]

If there were men like these who attacked the *li-hsüeh* from a materialistic standpoint, it must, of course, follow that the *hsin-hsüeh*, an even more uncompromising idealism than the other neo-Confucianism, should also be attacked. Dualistic philosophers who emphasized the importance of objective matter—either explicitly, by denying the reality of forms, or implicitly, by defending subjective desire (whose object is something sensible)—naturally put under their ban Wang Yang-ming's monistic emphasis on mind and intuition. According to Wang Fu-chih, the subjective-idealist *hsin-hsüeh* was 'outside, Confucian; inside, Taoist',[8] or '*yang*, Confucian; *yin*, Buddhist'.[9] Huang Tsung-hsi, the foe of mysticism and 'airy vagueness', found the fatal stain of Zen on Lu and Wang.[10] Ku Yen-wu (1613–82) concurred,[11] and besides, in order to cite an example of one man's changing the course of history, he arraigned Wang Yang-ming for causing, almost single-handed, the decline and fall of the Ming empire.[12]

What was the prescription of these opponents of idealism for stopping the rot? *Tao* and *te*, the Way and Virtue, are inseparable from practicality, said Huang Tsung-hsi.[13] Recording empty words is not the equivalent of observing action, said Ku Yen-wu,[14] and he said, too, that the superior man studies in order to 'assist the world'.[15] The learning of the ancients was in practical matters, said Tai Chen.[16] Chinese thinkers, they all meant, should abandon world-denying quietism, and get away from abstractions and down to things.

5

2. SCIENCE AND CH'ING EMPIRICISM: THEIR DEGREE OF COINCIDENCE

How relevant to science are these injunctions to look without and not within, and to dwell on things and not on essences? They are relevant, we may say, in the sense that they are *compatible* with the development of modern science as the issue of a struggle against an anti-empirical, or rationalistic, metaphysics. The scientist must assume, like the Ch'ing denouncers of the *hsin-hsüeh*, that the material world is not a state of mind. And the scientist also assumes, like the Ch'ing critics of Chu Hsi's *li-hsüeh*, that the way to begin to acquire useful knowledge is to characterize material instances instead of groping for ethereal Ideas. For the question as to the essence of things (in neo-Confucian terms, the question of *li*) can produce nothing but tautological answers; 'Burrow down and still further down,' it has been said, 'and God will still be only godly, man only human, and the world only worldly.'[17] But a scientific statement has a true predicate. It begins, as the anti-*li-hsüeh* Ch'ing materialists would begin, with the thing, and then predicates something as a quality, a property, or an attribute of the thing.

Science, it is true, does not end with this predication of qualities to individual things. Indeed, it deals as seriously as philosophical idealism with the *type*, and the predicate which it considers meaningful, as a contribution to logical understanding, is the one which affirms of the single instance what is true of all its kind. But the scientist's type is his own construction, a generalization which he makes from a detailed experience of the behaviour of individual things; as a scientist, an inductive empiricist, he cannot explain that behaviour by the generalization. As Locke put it, species and genera are the 'workmanship of the understanding', not the mind's discovery.[18]

Kant, in his *Critique of Judgment*, has made perhaps the clearest distinction between Platonic or neo-Confucian idealism and the empirical theory of their respective early modern opponents. The *intellectus archetypus*, he says, is a form of reason 'which being, not like ours, discursive, but intuitive, proceeds from the synthetic universal (the intuition of the whole as such) to the particular, that is, from the whole to the parts'. Such a reason, according to Kant, lies outside human possibilities. The reason peculiar to man is the *intellectus ectypus*, which is restricted to taking in through the senses the single details of the world as such and constructing pictures of their totalities, but these pictures have only a hypothetical character and claim no reality for themselves. 'Our understanding has this peculiarity as concerns the judgment, that in cognitive understanding the particular is not determined by the universal and therefore cannot be derived from it.'[19]

By Kant's criterion, then, of a reason possible to man, a reason that can win for man some knowledge of nature, Huang Tsung-hsi's statement that *li* is 'name, not fact', Li Kung's sceptical question, 'apart from things, where is *li*?' —taken utterly seriously—are subsumed in any genuine expression of the scientific spirit.

3. SCIENCE AND CH'ING EMPIRICISM: THEIR NON-IDENTITY

But that is the most we can say. The empirical attitudes of these early Ch'ing thinkers, while in harmony with the scientific critique of idealism, are neither scientific themselves nor necessarily conducive to the birth of science. In European history, divergence from idealism could take the form of the pre-scientific nominalism of Peter Abelard (1079–1142) as well as the form of Francis Bacon's (1561–1626) inductive empirical science; our Chinese thinkers seem, on the whole, more like Abelard than like Bacon.

Abelard's nominalism (or rather, his so-called 'conceptualism', a somewhat disguised version of his teacher's, Roscelin's, nominalism) denied the objective existence of universals. Rejecting the extreme Augustinian 'realism', which regarded the individual material thing as simply the shadow of an eternal idea, he held that universals were created by the mind by means of abstraction, and that the true reality was the object and not the idea, not the 'name'.[20] Wang Fu-chih and his Chinese colleagues said as much.

7

Bacon, however, said more. He went beyond simply ascribing ultimate reality to the world of phenomena instead of to a hypothetical realm of pure Being. He meant not merely to define the real world but to encroach upon it. It was not enough for him to banish abstractions, which can only be contemplated, in favour of tangibles, which can be observed, for observation was not enough. One had to observe with a method and a purpose. Bacon's method was induction from experimentally verified 'irreducible and stubborn facts', his purpose the eliciting of general laws for the organization of facts into science.[21]

It has already been suggested that the Ch'ing empiricists were not so ambitious. Let there be practical action in the real phenomenal world—that was the sum of their challenge to contemplative idealists, and their practical ethic implied for them a simple epistemology, a common-sense opinion that knowledge comes to the mind when the mind is put in compresence with facts. But according to Bacon (and also, Descartes), what makes a natural scientist is not his knowledge of facts about nature but his ability to ask questions about nature; knowledge comes only by answering questions, and these must be the right questions, asked in the right order.[22]

Our Chinese critics of idealism could agree with Bacon that 'the wit and mind of man, if it work upon matter . . . worketh according to the stuff and is limited thereby; but if it work upon itself, as the spider worketh his web, then it is endless and brings forth indeed cobwebs of learning . . . of no substance or profit'. They might say, too, with Bacon, that their method was 'to dwell among things soberly. . . .' But although they might pride themselves, like Ku Yen-wu, on looking around them and 'testing books with facts', they rarely asked questions systematically which might make them see the essential relevance of some orders of facts to others, they never aspired, as Bacon did, 'to establish for ever a true and legitimate union between the experimental and rational faculty'.[23] Though he might go as far as the Renaissance scientist in deprecating search for the universal, eternal form of particular things, the empirically-minded Ch'ing

8

Confucianist had a temper predominantly nominalist, unembarrassing to scientific spirit, but by no means its equivalent nor its guaranteed precursor.[24]

4. PROTEST AND STABILITY: THE REMINISCENCE OF AN EARLIER AFFIRMATION

It appears, then, that the early Ch'ing empiricists need not be seen as budding scientists. This conclusion—that their thought was not necessarily a sign of any indigenous Chinese trend towards the establishment of science in its modern intellectual pre-eminence—suggests a positive corollary. We must acknowledge that these philosophers were genuinely critical of their prestige-laden Sung and Ming predecessors, critical enough so that some historians have delighted to call them scientific. But was the dissidence perhaps *within* the world of Chinese tradition, and witness to its stability, not a sign of its transformation irrespective of the West?

Bacon expressed his distrust of traditional authority and his faith in science in these words: 'He that would begin in certainties shall end in doubts; but if he be content to begin with doubts and have patience a while he shall end in certainties.'[25] The Ch'ing empiricists expressed doubts of a sort, but they began in certainty, the traditional Chinese certainty that modern opinion, if legitimate, conforms to the truths in the classics of Confucian antiquity. There is more than rhetoric, there is serious acceptance of Confucian authority, in the reams of Ch'ing denunciation of the earlier *li-hsüeh* and *hsin-hsüeh* Confucianists (the latter especially) for their alleged Buddhist and Taoist deviations. Tai Chen was particularly keen against Taoists and Buddhists in Confucians' clothing,[26] and even with Tai, the latest and most independent of the thinkers we consider, there is no question, I think, of subterfuge, no reasonable suspicion that he may be making an oblique attack on Confucian authority itself. Before he would come to conclusions about contemporary needs and expedients, he demanded contemporary evidence; but always, he said, to be finally certain of his conclusions, he required corroboration from antiquity.[27]

Tai was a traditionalist, then, in accepting a traditional check on his own researches. And the outer, social end of his studies made them traditional, too. He and the other empiricists were taking a time-honoured stand, for a matter-of-fact approach, in the running, traditional Chinese conflict between practical and mystical intellectual tendencies.

The obvious, historic Confucian alternative to anti-intellectual mysticism was textual scholarship. Some of the Ch'ing scholars, notably Yen Yüan and Li Kung, had such an antipathy to mysticism that they were unequivocal in their commitment to empiricism, and they disparaged in-ordinate textual study as another deterrent to practical observation. Two of the three grave flaws which Yen Yüan saw in contemporary scholars were 'absorption in phraseo-logy' and 'fascination with commentaries' (the other was 'carelessness about false doctrines', the Buddhist and Taoist miasmas).[28] He pointed with alarm to the scholars of the Han and Chin periods, busying themselves with 'sentences and phrases' while society went to ruin.[29] Li Kung distinguished between 'paper' and 'affairs of the world', and deplored the fatal triumph during the Sung and Ming periods of 'pen and ink' over the spirit of 'capacity to govern'.[30]

But the school of the 'Han Learning' (of which Ku Yen-wu was a leading member), not the Yen-Li school, was the really prominent foe of the Sung Learning. And for the Han Learning, empiricism, practical observation, seems to have been less a positive philosophy than a symbol of opposition to mystical introspection; the true emphasis of the Han Learning was on another classic alternative to introspec-tion—on that most fundamental of Confucian practices, the study of texts. The Han Learning could attack *mind* (where truth exists for subjective idealism)—in the name of *nature* (where truth exists, though perhaps unattainably, for science) —in the interests, really, of *books* (where truth exists for Con-fucian literati).

Now, was this a sign of disruption, a fresh challenge to the Sung Learning *in toto*, or was it a sign of stability, in effect a restatement of an old challenge from one of the wings of the Sung Learning to the other? Chu Hsi himself, after all, in distinguishing his objective-idealist *li-hsüeh* from the contemplative *hsin-hsüeh*, had urged *ko-wu*, 'investigation of things'; and this quasi-empiricist appeal, which, like the later one, denied the *hsin-hsüeh* philosophy in one manner, only swept the field clear for Chu Hsi's fixing of a textual orthodoxy, which denied the *hsin-hsüeh* in another way. Chu Hsi, we know, was no hero to the scholars of the Han Learning. Yet, though they rejected his *li-hsüeh* metaphysics, it is hard to see from its consequences how their 'practicality' was more of a challenge to bibliolatry than Chu Hsi's *ko-wu* had been. Ku Yen-wu's avowed purpose in 'investigating things' was not the neo-Confucian purpose of divining their *li*, but he came to a neo-Confucian end, a traditional Chinese celebration of the Confucian classics. From the standpoint of the development of science, it was as dead an end as any.

It is sometimes suggested that Ch'ing philological scholarship (e.g. the efforts of Ku Yen-wu and others to find out the ancient pronunciations of Chinese characters) is evidence of an indigenous Chinese commitment to scientific method. Nevertheless, however favourably Ch'ing philology may compare with the eighteenth- and nineteenth-century 'scientific philology' of Sir William Jones, Max Müller, and other Europeans, it can hardly be seen as subversive of Confucian anti-scientism. Strictly speaking, scientific method is in fact as applicable to the study of language as to the study of stars. But in general usage, where there is perhaps a proper feeling for the historical priorities, the adjective *scientific*, used in connection with such studies as philology, is essentially metaphorical, and the metaphor is drawn from natural science; natural science is the point of reference which gives meaning to the adjective when it is applied in other fields. One might proceed, as European scholars did, from contemplating natural science to thinking 'scientifically' about philological problems, but we have no grounds for turning the metaphor inside-out, and expecting that the Chinese would have necessarily proceeded from sound philology to the point of thinking 'philologically' about the basic fields of natural science. If the most successful intellectual explorations of the early Ch'ing period—so successful that they have earned our modern accolade, 'scientific'—were, indeed, in the field of philology, which is so near to Confucian concern with texts and history, this very fact shows how far early Ch'ing thinkers were from any deep concern with the riddle of nature.

However, when modern science did at last begin to commend itself in China, there was a role of a sort for the Han Learning. But it was not the role which one might expect if he read too much into Ku Yen-wu's empiricism. The Han Learning was exploited by the so-called *chin-wen* reformers of the later nineteenth century (of whom more will be said below), who admired modern science but were troubled by its foreign auspices, and who had to tamper with the orthodox classical canon—the Sung canon of Chu Hsi—since it failed to lend itself to a modernistic interpretation. Thus, it was not its crusade against idealism but its concern with textual authenticity which linked the Han Learning, through the Reform Movement, with modern science in China. And the link existed not because the early-Ch'ing anti-Sung critical scholarship pointed the way itself, but because it seemed possible to wring from this scholarship the sanction of Confucius for the scientific convictions which men arrived at by submitting to other authority.

A number of historians in modern China have tried to find an impressive Chinese pedigree for modern science; their efforts seem, paradoxically, a subjective response to the fact that none exists. In so far as science, whose prestige and progressive development came from the West, has been intellectually forced on Chinese minds in the last century, an emotional need has developed, a need to defend the intellectual history of China against any suggestion of failure. Liang Ch'i-ch'ao (1873–1929), Hsiao I-shan (1902–), and others, over-interpreting Ch'ing empiricism, occasionally imply that a modern Chinese scientific consciousness is a natural product of Chinese history, and that western example and western disruption of traditional China were never indispensable.[31] But these protestations arise, perhaps, from the situation whose existence they contest, a Chinese cultural situation of fractured continuity.

5. CONCLUSION

There was important scientific achievement in China before the modern period; recent research has begun to show us just how extensive it was.[32] But on the whole the Confucian literati were consistently uninterested, and the intellectual affinities of science were mainly Taoist and unorthodox. As Needham says, science had no social prestige, and it would never have occurred to traditional Chinese scholars that kudos were to be gained from claiming discoveries or inventions.[33]

When this did occur to modern Chinese scholars, it was the steady advance of a western tradition of science that furnished criteria for reappraisal of the Chinese intellectual past. Chu Hsi's philosophy, from the vantage point of twentieth-century science, may well be seen not as the idealism which the Ch'ing empiricists disputed but as an organic philosophy of nature, closely resembling the point of view which scientists have reached in the West after three centuries of mechanical materialism.[34] And yet, it is the three centuries of mechanical materialism which endow the organic philosophy with its content, everything implied in the upsetting of those centuries' conclusions. This was the tradition of cumulative inquiry which could not be found in China, and therefore had to be sought. In its universal persuasiveness it impelled the search for a Chinese parallel; it provided the touchstones for identification; and, in being set against the subsequent Chinese findings, it distinguished these as a brilliant cluster of scientific *aperçus*, but not a coherent tradition of science flowing into the universal stream.

What is at issue here, of course, is not ability but taste. If Chinese in modern times have been forced to wonder where science belongs in their heritage, it is not because their forbears were constitutionally unable to nurture a growing tradition of science, but because they did not care to; early Ch'ing empiricists were not aiming at science and falling short, but living out the values of their culture. There can be no presumptuous western question of 'failure' in Chinese civilization—only recognition of a Chinese taste for a style of culture not the style of the modern West, nor of modern China.

This pre-western Chinese style had other ingredients besides a tepid concern for science. A whole pattern of cultural preferences hung together, all appropriate to one another and to a specific social order, which was to fall into jeopardy soon. Many apparently narrow avenues could lead us into that whole coherent, precarious intellectual world. We shall try the road of inquiry into Chinese painting.

CHAPTER II

The Amateur Ideal in Ming and Early Ch'ing Society: Evidence from Painting

The master said, 'The accomplished scholar is not a utensil.'

Lun-yü II, xii

Another common and important feature of these functions is their *political* character; they do not demand particular, special knowledge, but a *savoir-vivre* and a *savoir-faire.* . . .

Etienne Balázs, 'Les aspects significatifs de la société chinoise', *Asiatische Studien* 6 (1952), 83

WHILE the alien Mongols ruled in China (Yüan dynasty, 1279–1368), Confucian literati were at one of their relatively low points of social importance. The Ming dynasty raised them high again, and as a ruling intelligentsia they naturally cherished an ideal of social stability.[1] As a corollary, in matters of taste they deprecated the idea of change and the quest for originality.[2] By and large, the literati were classicists, like Jonathan Swift in England, and in Swift's defence of the ancients against the moderns, in his vast preference for the humanities over the natural sciences, and in his patrician uneasiness with material utility as the touchstone of value, we see the pattern of literati culture with significant clarity.[3]

Swift died in savage indignation and derangement. The

moderns were taking his world and he knew it. Science, progress, business, and utility, the combination he deplored, would soon be leading themes in modern western culture. But in Ming and early Ch'ing China, the China of the four or five centuries before westerners came in force, science was slighted, progress denied, business disparaged and (with possibly increasing difficulty) confined; and with these three went the fourth of Swift's desiderata, an anti-vocational retrospective humanism in learning. Artistic style and a cultivated knowledge of the approved canon of ancient works, the 'sweetness and light' of a classical love of letters—these, not specialized, 'useful' technical training, were the tools of intellectual expression and the keys to social power.[4] These were the qualities mainly tested in the state examinations, which qualified the winners for prestige and opportunities.[5]

The *élite*, in short, were not permitted (as Balázs puts it) to 'impoverish their personalities in specialization'.[6] The Ming style was the amateur style; Ming culture was the apotheosis of the amateur.

I. THE MING STYLE, IN SOCIETY AND ART

i. In Society

Probably more in the Ming period than ever before, as the extreme aestheticism of the Ming eight-legged essay suggests, Chinese officials were amateurs in office. They were trained academically and (for the most part) tested by written examinations, but they were not trained directly for tasks to be undertaken; whatever the case among aides in official yamens, mere hirelings without the proper Confucianist's claim to leadership, the higher degree-holding members of the bureaucracy—the ruling class *par excellence*—were not identified with expertise.[7] The prestige of office depended on that fact. The scholar's belle-lettristic cultivation, a type of learning divorced from the official tasks for which it qualified him, was essential—not to performance of official functions with technical efficiency (there it was rather inhibiting), but to the cultural celebration of those functions.

If the knowledge characteristic of officials had been a vocational, technical, 'useful' knowledge, then it would have been only a professional means, with no intrinsic quality to dignify the bureaucratic end. But when office could be taken to symbolize high culture, knowledge for its own sake, the terminal values of civilization, then office-holding was clearly superior to any other social role. No other sort of success (commercial, military, technological, or the like), which might be assumed to depend on a body of professional knowledge devised as a logical means to produce it, could compete in prestige with success in winning office; for the peculiar preparation for the latter success, by its aesthetic independence, its very irrelevance, logically, to the bureaucratic end —at least in a specialized, technical sense, if not in a broadly moral one—made of that end the end of life.[8] A course in classical letters might train the official ideally to rule by virtuous example—to be himself, as it were, the finest product of art and thought, radiating harmony to society—but it was far from a training in special techniques for effecting social harmony, not by magical sympathy, but by logical consequence.

In China, of course, because of the nature of its institutions, this aesthetic brand of knowledge really was for the sake of something: office. But it was a symbolic, not a logical qualification. To see the genuine significance of this distinction, let us compare the Ming situation with the modern English one, for in England, too, classical training has frequently given entrée to civil office. A recent tribute to a British civil servant, after praising his classical scholarship, attempted, rather defensively, it seems, to make an ordinary logical reference of his classical training to his official role:

He read classics at Malvern and became a humanist. . . . Then in 1932, like many a classical scholar before him, he entered the Home Civil Service. . . . He is certainly a great civil servant, and I have no doubt whatever that he owes his quality to his humanism. It is that which gentles his will and disciplines his mind to the delicacies of human relationships.[9]

Living, as he does, in a highly specialized society, in which the amateur yields to the expert almost all along the line, a society in which 'amateur' as a term, in fact, has developed rather its connotation of imperfect skill than of disinterested love, the writer here must strike us as quasi-apologetic (which no Ming classicist, in a similar case, would ever have been) in making such a 'professional' plea for the classical curriculum: he writes as though he feels that his public—a practical, vocationally-minded public with a common-sense indifference to educational frills—must be doubting the genuine relevance of antique studies to modern professional tasks. He cannot simply assume a general public acceptance of an obvious affinity between classical education and a managerial office. The prestige of letters, it is true, has lent a greater prestige to the higher bureaucracy in England than it has to its western counterparts. But in England—and here it has differed from China—the bureaucracy, though thus enhanced, has not been able to reflect its glory back to the source. For while the social facts of Chinese history made bureaucracy the central point of power, the social facts of English history have relegated bureaucracy to a role of service to other powers in the English state. Socially, the rise of 'business' (which Swift had seen with such distress), with its anti-traditional, anti-humanist bias, put bureaucracy in the shade, while intellectually it forced the classics from their solitary eminence. To be sure, the nineteenth-century Oxford and Cambridge ideal, like the Confucian, was the educated gentleman, prepared for the world of affairs and his place in the governing class by a course in humane letters, with nothing crudely purposive about it; but this ideal in the Victorian age has been called 'almost the sole barrier against an all-encroaching materialism and professionalism'.[10] In England, instead of the splendid, symbolic Ming alignment of the highest cultural values with the highest social power, we finally find bureaucracy rather more just a useful employment, while the classics, in so far as they preserve vestigial links with power, tend to be justified as a logically useful means to an end which is only a means itself.

Culture, 'the best that has been thought and known' (as Matthew Arnold paraphrased 'sweetness and light'),[11] has a bad time in a world of utilitarians. When the 'yahoos' and 'philistines' of Swift and Arnold dominate society, the defence of culture may tend to lean on philistine criteria. An amateur's love of the liberal arts, his belief that they justify themselves, may be complicated by society's insistence that he find a professional point in their cultivation. But in China, the men of social consequence in the Ming and early Ch'ing periods were hardly cultural philistines; the professional point in their humanistic studies was in their failing to have any specialized professional point. They were amateurs in the fullest sense of the word, genteel initiates in a humane culture, without interest in progress, leanings to science, sympathy for commerce, nor prejudice in favour of utility. Amateurs in government because their training was in art, they had an amateur bias in art itself, for their profession was government.

Long before, in the Sung dynasty, Wang An-shih (1021–86) had tried, among other things, to make the civil-service examinations more practical than aesthetic. Although Wang was unquestionably a dedicated Confucianist, trying to revive in Confucianism its primal concern with political science, his finest official and scholarly contemporaries, who began by largely sharing his convictions, finally turned away, and ordinary Confucianists never forgave him. Was it only impracticability they saw in his sweeping programme, or disputable points in his classical exegesis, or an immediate material challenge to their perquisites; or did they also sense that a Confucian landed bureaucracy would rule as intellectual amateurs, or not at all? Had Wang struck a false note, a possible knell for the omnicompetent, socially superior sophisticates, who were no mere scribes in a feudal state, nor professional civil servants in a business one?

Su Tung-p'o (1036–1101), one of the foremost serious opponents of Wang An-shih, seems to have been the first painter to speak of *shih-ta-fu hua*, the 'officials' style' in painting, a term which became in the Ming era one of the several interchangeable terms for the 'amateur style'.[12]

ii. In Painting

By the end of the Ming dynasty, one rule had been firmly established in the world of painting: officials themselves were painters, and they liked their painting best. Painters *by profession* were disparaged. The Ming emperors had revived the court academy of painting (*Hua-yüan*), associated mainly with the names of Hui-tsung (*regn.* 1101–26, the last real emperor of the Northern Sung) and his Southern Sung successors.[13] But the Ming academy differed from the Sung in that the latter had merely honoured painters with official titles, while their Ming counterparts were genuinely court-painters, working to specifications.[14] Accordingly, the Ming academy, unlike Hui-tsung's, was never put on an equal footing with the *Han-lin yüan*, the highest circle of literary scholars, and Ming *Hua-yüan* painters by no means had the rank or prestige of *Han-lin* literati.[15] There were court painters in the Imperial Guard—a surprising place for them, on the face of it, but not so surprising when one reflects that the Imperial Guard was a catch-all for non-bureaucratic types, and that it represented the emperor and his personal corps of eunuchs in their character as rivals to the civil-official interest.[16]

Wen Cheng-ming (1470–1567), a scholar who had the *Han-lin* rank, and a famous painter as well, clearly expressed the amateur's creed. 'The cultivated man,' he said, 'in retirement from office, frequently takes pleasure in playing with the brush and producing landscapes for his own gratification.'[17] Or for the gratification of his cultivated friends—like the gentleman-painter Shen Shih-t'ien (1427–1509), a model of leisurely, exquisite taste; he identified a stray ink-landscape in his hall as the calling-card of one of his fellow-spirits, who had splashed it playfully on a bit of silk that was lying at hand, and whom Shen recaptured and kept as his guest for a casual matter of three months.[18] Mo Shih-lung, a very important late-Ming critic, highly approved of some earlier artists for looking at painting as a joy in itself, not as their profession.[19] His friend, Tung Ch'i-ch'ang (1555–1636), echoed Mo in praising one of the fourteenth-century Yüan masters as the first to make the painter's pleasure as well as expression the end of his art.[20] Tung himself, painter and calligrapher as well as the foremost critic of his time, was perfectly careless about what became of his own productions. It was said of him that if a person of station asked directly for some of his work, the petitioner might be fobbed off with anything—Tung's signature, perhaps, or a poem from his brush, on a painting by somebody else. If people wanted a Tung original, they learned to seek it from the women of his household, for whom he would frequently, idly, paint or write.[21]

Tung had, quite simply, a contempt for professionalism. One of its connotations, he felt, was narrowness of culture. The true *wen-jen*, the 'literary man', the amateur, had a feeling for nature and a flair for both painting and poetry.[22] It was a familiar thing for painters to deprecate their special talents by offering themselves as rounded personalities; the sixteenth-century painter Hsü Wei, for example, said of himself (though critics disagreed) that his calligraphy came first, poetry second, prose composition next, and painting last.[23] The Ch'ing scholar Shen Tsung-ch'ien (*fl. ca.* 1780?) summed up the persisting amateur's bias against narrow specialization: 'Painting and poetry are both things with which scholars divert their minds. Generally, therefore, those who can participate in the writing of poetry can all take part in painting.'[24]

The amateur's scorn of professionals had an aspect, too, of patrician contempt for the grasping climbers who were not the gentry's sort. There were overtones of anti-commercial feeling in the scholar's insistence that the proper artist is financially disinterested. Mi Fu (1051–1107), the famous intuitive Sung artist who was a classical hero to the Ming amateur school, had written, 'In matters of calligraphy and painting, one is not to discuss price. The gentleman is hard to capture by money.'[25] That was the finding of the hapless nobleman who came to Lu Chih (1496–1576) with a letter from one of Lu's friends, secured a picture on the strength of it, and then committed the horrible gaffe of offering sums of money; there is something almost mythic in the account of Lu's passionate act of rejection, as though a vital nerve of a culture had been touched.[26] Much later, the 'Mustard-seed Garden' manual (*Chieh-tzu yüan hua chuan*), an encyclopedic instruction book for painters, appearing in several parts between 1679 and 1818 (though its earliest stratum was late Ming), made the same equation between professionalism and a falling short of literati standards of gentility. 'When one has the venal manner,' it loftily proclaimed, 'one's painting is very vulgar.'[27] And the Ch'ing painter Tsou I-kuei (1686–1772) laid down the rule that the *shih-ta-fu* painter, the amateur painter-official, 'is not acquisitive in the world, nor does he distract his heart with considerations of admiration or detraction'.[28]

In short, in the amateur's culture of the Ming and early Ch'ing, officials as critics commended officials as painters to officials as connoisseurs. 'Wang Yü, tzu Jih-ch'u, hao Tung-chuang Lao-jen painted landscapes and grasped in them the very marrow of the Vice President of the Board of Revenue's art.'[29] A remark like this, ordinary enough in its own day, will joyously strike the modern reader as comically incongruous; he could hardly sense more vividly the individual quality of the culture which knew it as commonplace.

2. THE PARADOX OF AN ACADEMIC ANTI-ACADEMICISM

i. *The 'Northern' and the 'Southern' Schools of Painting*

Since they were intellectual leaders and social leaders at the same time, the painting *élite* formed a school of thought as well as a league of amateurs. By the end of the Ming dynasty an aesthetically expressive term, *nan-hua*, 'southern painting', had become assimilated to *wen-jen hua* and *shih-ta-fu hua*, sociologically expressive, equivalent terms for the painting of the 'gentleman'. Not its inventor, but the scholar who made the distinction between northern and southern styles a canon of connoisseurship, was the anti-professional Tung Ch'i-ch'ang, the acknowledged doyen of calligraphers, painters, and critics in late Ming times, 'master of a hundred generations in the forest of art', whose reputation as the arbiter of elegance had spread as far as Liu-ch'iu and Korea.[30]

He traced the northern and southern schools through various masters, from the T'ang dynasty's Li Ssu-hsün (651–716 or 720) and Wang Wei (698–759), respectively, down to his own day. The names 'northern' and 'southern' referred, not to a geographical distribution of painters, but to two T'ang dynasty schools of Ch'an (or Zen) Buddhism, whose philosophical principles were said to colour the two aesthetics.[31] However, the term *Ch'an-hua*, Ch'an painting, came to be reserved for the southern style, as a term contrasting with *yüan-hua*, academic painting of the northern school.[32] The idealist landscape of the southern school was inspired by the artist's 'sudden awakening' (a concept usually called in the West *satori*, from the Japanese Buddhist terminology), the shock of intuition of the nature of reality; and Tung considered that paintings in this style were superior to those of the northern school, which was intellectual rather than intuitive, more meticulous in detail, and interested rather in the formal relations of objects than in their spirit. 'True classic elegance', he said, 'does not lie in exact and punctilious execution.'[33]

This sort of caveat against painstaking, conscious workmanship was the first commandment in the southern aesthetic. According to theory, the literati-painter, without design, hurled his inner conception of landscape on the silk.[34] Spontaneity was all, and the elliptical phrase *ch'i-yün*, 'spirit-consonance', from the first of the famous 'six laws' of painting of Hsieh Ho (*fl. ca.* 500), was taken over as the southern concept of intuitive communion of the painter with his subject; intellectual apprehension was 'academic', and despised. ' . . . *ch'i-yün* is the result of something that is inborn; the more skill is applied, the further *ch'i-yün* recedes,' said Tung Ch'i-ch'ang,[35] and while Mo Shih-lung would allow that the academic style was *ching-miao*, refined and subtle, he found it correspondingly deficient in *tzu-jan*, the priceless spontaneity.[36] 'There are painters', he said, 'who take the old masters as teachers. But whoever wants to make forward strides himself must choose Heaven and Earth as teachers.'[37]

Hsiung-chung i-ch'i, 'spirit flashing into the mind', was the motto professed in the *wen-jen hua*[38]—not cool knowledge, but searing insight.

ii. *The Confucianist Choice of a Buddhist Aesthetic*

A question now arises of momentous importance for the understanding of Ming culture: how could Ming Confucian intellectuals, the most academic of men in their literary practice, committed to the preservation of recorded wisdom —and a wisdom, at that, which referred in the main to human relations in civilization—how could such a group reject a theory of painting which they associated with learning, and prize instead an anti-intellectual theory of mystical abstraction from civilized concerns? One might expect that Confucian traditionalists, who looked for the gradual education of man in society, would feel an affinity with the academic northern aesthetic and oppose the southern Ch'an; for the latter, after all, in its original emphasis on the sudden enlightenment of man in nature, challenged the whole Confucian view of life and culture. A purely aesthetic explanation of the literati-school's disparagement of the Academy, like the partisan suggestion that the Ming and Ch'ing authorities just failed to grasp the spirit and value of *Hua-yüan* art,[39] raises more questions than it answers. For, even entertaining the hypothesis of simple lapse in taste, how shall we account for this *wen-jen* blind spot?

Yet, what is logically curious is sociologically comprehensible. An idea's meaning, we have observed, depends not only on what a thinker affirms but on what he denies, and for Ming Confucianists, with their amateur leanings, the intuitive Ch'an need not mean—as it could not mean to such bookish custodians of an intellectual tradition—anti-intellectualism;[40] *anti-professionalism* would fill the bill. A flash of intuitive insight is nothing if not 'natural', and how could a professional painter, who worked to order, be natural? How could the academic be natural, planning his strokes and carefully painting them in?[41] The very idea of a special vocation of 'fine arts' was equally distasteful to Ch'an mystics and Confucian literati; 'natural' is opposed to 'artistic', and the latter word has a queasy, professional sound.[42]

The southern aesthetic, then, took hold in literati circles not because they were *philosophically* committed, committed to inspiration over tradition, but because they were *socially* committed, committed to genteel amateurism over professionalism. More than one writer has suggested that it was practical compulsion, especially in early Ch'ing times, which made the officials such southern enthusiasts; deep literary culture was obligatory, painting could only come second, as an amateur's pastime, and the scholars made a virtue of necessity, opting for intuition since a really rigorous painter's training was impossible.[43] Such a view is doubtless inadequate—many literati-painters, after all, were exquisitely accomplished virtuosi—but nevertheless, though for reasons less practical than symbolic (and not philosophical at all), an anti-academic aesthetic was the popular choice of the amateur. The Ch'an of the Ming Confucianists was not serious.

Buddhism in general had ceased to be serious for Confucian literati as long ago as the Sung period. The intellectual synthesis of Chu Hsi was a Confucian raid on Buddhism and a blunting of its point as an intellectual rival; and organized Buddhism—ecclesiastical, iconological, and always repellent socially to the gentry-official class—was relegated to the peasant masses and finally lost its one-time intellectual lure. Ch'an ideas, which were anti-ecclesiastical, anti-iconological, and thereby divorced from an anti-Confucian social organization, remained in the gentry's world and animated its landscape painting (Buddhist figure painting, once an important branch of Chinese art, languished almost completely in the Ming phase of the church's decline and the amateur-painter's rise).[44] But this last shred of Buddhism was not a foreign body in the gentry's Confucian environment. The Ch'an intuitive nature-cult of the Ming painters was not an antithesis to Confucian humanism, but a tame, learned element in the Confucian humane culture—not a bold challenge to didacticism, but a cultural possession of didactically educated men.

iii. The Routinization of Intuition

An ostensibly Buddhist doctrine, once embraced in that Confucian spirit, must be changed in itself. The real paradox of the Ming aesthetic was not in the harmonizing of two warring creeds, but in the self-contradiction of one of them. Peace was easy to arrange when one of the pair of rivals denied itself. In the last analysis, the conventionally learned *shih-ta-fu* painter felt quite at ease in the southern school of individual inspiration—because the southern school had conventional rules for manufacturing inspiration. An anti-academicism which was socially vital to the amateur gentry-officials, but intellectually alien, was safely academicized.

Ambivalence was built into the Ming intuitive southern theory, for it was a theory not intuited but learned. Sung literati, predecessors of the Ming in the Confucian taming of Buddhism, had already made the basic statements of the credo which the Ming called southern. The academic use-lessness of the imitation of outward form, the indispensable oneness of immediate perception and immediate execution, the impossibility of learning *ch'i-yün*, that 'spirit-consonance' which man derives solely from innate knowledge—all these were Sung lessons to Tung Ch'i-ch'ang and his fellow-critics of the Ming and Ch'ing.[45]

And behind the Sung was Hsieh Ho, whose six principles were handed down (especially the first: 'spirit-consonance, life-movement') as prescriptions for the unprescribable, binding rules for untrammelled intuitive genius. 'In painting there are six canons . . .', a Ming treatise flatly began.[46] That was the law—all the rest was commentary. Wang Yü (*fl. ca.* 1680–1724), whose painting was said to betray him as 'a parasite on others', solemnly preached about quite unconscious creative activity.[47] His aesthetic, opposed to stereotype, was a stereotype as an aesthetic; his painting, failing to follow it, was consistent with it.

There was no getting around it. The free, natural southern souls of literati-amateurs were pervaded with traditional-ism. It was said of Tung Ch'i-ch'ang (who may be found, incidentally, on a Ch'ing list of select Ming masters of the eight-legged essay)[48] that he copied the works of the old masters—especially those of his Sung namesake, the Ch'an artist, Tung Yüan—with such a zeal that he forgot to eat and sleep.[49] A late Ming source reported that a wonderful scroll by Shen Shih-t'ien had been executed, in the true amateur spirit, as a gift for a friend on his travels; that the scroll was modelled completely after Tung Yüan; and that it later became the outstanding treasure of a most famous connoisseur.[50] Obviously, with the anti-academic Ming and Ch'ing critics, no painting failed of an accolade just for its being patently derivative. It was right and proper to imitate the ancients—because the ancients were spontaneous.

This is why, in the Ming and early Ch'ing China of the gentry-scholar-official, who was anti-professional in his outlook but never anti-traditional, the implications of anti-academicism were so far from what they were in the West. By definition, anti-academicism anywhere depends on a common conception of genius: that genius, a general quality, is shared only by artists who spontaneously choose their individual ways to express it. 'A good work of art must be *mehr gefühlt als gemessen*[51] . . . he that imitates the divine *Iliad*, does not imitate Homer[52] . . . the men who have reduced locomotion to its simplest elements, in the trotting wagon and the yacht *America*, are nearer to Athens at this moment than they who would bend the Greek temple to every use. . . .'[53]

Pronouncements on genius like these seemed to be made in China as in the West. The warning against missing Homer by hitting the *Iliad* was paraphrased, in effect, by Wang K'en-t'ang, a *chin-shih* of 1589: 'If one paints water, mountains, trees, and stones and roams "only thus" with the brush, such is not the old method.'[54] Yün Shou-p'ing wrote in the seventeenth century about the intuitive southern technique of *hsieh-i*, the representation of the idea, the immanent form, of visible objects:

It was said in the Sung period: 'If one can reach the point where he creates unconsciously, like the ancients, this is called *hsieh-i*. . . . If the artist creates unintentionally, then he attains the unconscious creativity of the ancients.'[55]

And Ou-yang Hsiu (1007–72), perhaps the very Sung spokesman to whom Yün referred, had begun a poem in the following way: 'In ancient painting, they painted *i*, the idea, not *hsing*, the (mere) outer appearance.'[56] Presumably then, by this token, only a spark of intuitive insight, not a copyist's talent, could bring an artist close to the works of ancient genius.

But in the West these reflections were arguments of an *avant-garde*; in China they were arguments of traditionalists. Given the social context in China of anti-academicism, its intellectual sequence was twisted around. Spontaneous creativity was as much the prize in one society as in the other. Yet it became in China not the means of reaching the ancient end of genius, but the end reached through the ancient means of genius. The very words which acclaimed the Chinese ancients for their spontaneity were really acclaiming spontaneity for its ancient embodiment. In the poem of Ou-yang Hsiu, the 'mere-ness' of *hsing*, or outer appearance, in comparison with *i*, the idea, was conveyed by the linking of *ku-hua*, ancient painting, with *i*.

In western anti-academicism, then, fidelity to the inner voice of genius justified abandonment of ancient outer appearances. In Chinese anti-academicism, it was fidelity to the outer voice, the voice of antiquity, speaking through outer appearances, which justified fidelity to the inner voice. Small wonder that southern theory seemed to chase itself in circles, and that Tung Ch'i-ch'ang appealed to master-models, while he solemnly intoned that genius could not be taught.

How could anti-academicism in Ming China take the form it did in the West, where an *avant-garde* in the arts, straining against the conventional taste of an outside public, was part of a generally vaguely displaced intelligentsia, iconoclastically restless in a world it could not dominate? In China, where the intelligentsia (artists among them) did dominate, as gentry-officials, disdain of the elders and contempt for the public were unlikely, to say the least. The easy western association of anti-academicism with youthful individualism was impossible there. No higher praise could be meted out, by Tung Ch'i-ch'ang or any other southern critic, than to say of a painter that he entered completely into the spirit of some old master.[57]

It was not that he should copy his master directly; that would be pedantic, academic, entirely unsuitable. Nevertheless, as a Ch'ing literati-painter significantly put it, he had to copy old examples in a certain fashion, as the student of literature must thoroughly examine the productions handed down from the past.[58] He was supposed to copy in a manner called *lin-mo*, which would divine the spirit of the master-work, not repeat the letter. One Ming critic mentioned four great painters who had studied a painting of Tung Yüan, copied it in the *lin-mo* way, and produced works quite dissimilar among themselves. If 'vulgar men' (i.e. academics, professionals, not literati) had been set this task, the critic said, their works would all have been quite the same as the original model.[59]

What has happened here? Unmistakably, the field for Buddhist artistic intuition has been subtly transferred by Confucian literati from nature to art itself. The academic is still condemned. Careful surface copying of visible phenomena is properly anathematized, in accordance with southern principles. But communion with masters in a great tradition (a congenial Confucian idea) has superseded the Buddhist communion with nature. It was not the persistence of the old landscape themes which compromised the amateurs' creed of anti-academicism. Chinese painters from Wang Wei on (at least those whom the *wen-jen* mainly honoured) had forsworn individualism in subject-matter in order to ignite and reveal their individuality of soul, their personal intuition of an already existing beauty.[60] But to the traditional subjects, Ming literati-painters come to adapt traditional insights. A painter's 'spirit-consonance' need not be with mountains, but with a classic painter of mountains. The southern artist's immersion in nature through landscape-painting is not a Ch'an rejection of cultural sophistication, but a Confucian extension of it.

Once art had been thrust between the artist and nature, the quest for intuitive knowledge was flatly compromised. Unless an act of cognition is a directly experienced *knowledge of . . .*, it is not intuitive; the only alternative form of cognition, relational *knowledge about* . . ., is intellectual, and it disrupts the single whole of experience which theoretically the southern aesthetic envisaged.[61] In the true artist of 'sudden enlightenment', art and contemplation are indistinguishable, what he sees is not external, he becomes what he represents.[62] The object of such enlightenment is a 'thing-in-itself', a super-sensible reality, beyond sensation; for thing-in-itself, the non-ephemeral ideal, is implied in intuitive understanding with absolute necessity, and can only be grasped, as Kant put it, by 'art's free conformity to rule'. The 'imposition of rules on art' is not intuitive, and Cézanne, who affirmed this completely, proclaimed a significant corollary: 'les causeries sur l'art sont presques inutiles.'[63]

But the Ming and early Ch'ing period was the great age of *causeries*, treatises which precisely did impose rules on art.[64] In the foreword to the last section (1818) of the *Mustard-seed Garden*, the painter's manual which epitomized the movement, the author made the fatal promise that genius could be taught, 'spirit-consonance' and 'life-movement' distilled in explanation. 'Thus can he [the reader] enter the "divine class" and the "skilled class", and follow in the steps of painters like Ku K'ai-chih and Wu Tao-tzu.'[65]

It was another passage in the same foreword, but from a different hand, which plainly exposed the intellectual corruption of the intuitive process. In a dialogue, a question was raised about portraiture. Why was there no manual for this most difficult form of art, when there seemed to be a manual for everything else? The answerer stated that everything else—mountains, rivers, grasses, trees, birds, beasts, fish, insects—had fixed forms. If one studied them assiduously, one could reach the point of reproducing them by rules. But the human face had most varied forms, not lending themselves to stereotyping, and it was hard to convey these forms in words.[66]

Fixed forms, then, were presumably easy to convey in verbal formulas. But fixed forms remind us of things-in-themselves, ideals beneath the sensible surface of phenomenal life. The very concept of the type-form is correlated essentially with the concept of intuitive apprehension. And this is the antithesis of intellectual apprehension, which is the fruit of didactic exposition, or just what artists were invited to find in the *Mustard-seed Garden*.

In itself, of course, the mere will to deal with technical problems of execution, and to study their resolutions, need not bar intuitive penetration. Every art has a technical language, upon which even the most personal of artists depends for communication, and even, perhaps, for seeing. Freed from concern with the hand when technique is automatic, the mind may be free for vision, and a codification of technical knowledge can assist in this liberation.

Accordingly, the role of technique in Chinese painting, intellectually formulated and transmitted, has occasionally been compared with the creative musician's standard equipment in harmony or fugue.[67] For the most part, however, Ming-Ch'ing painters' technical mystery tends to seem a larger part of their art than that, as another analogy drawn from music illustrates: 'When a Chinese artist reproduces a composition of an old master or paints in his style, it is no more plagiarism than when Horowitz plays a composition by Brahms.'[68] Such a statement quite properly reduces any 'moral' question about *lin-mo* representation to absurdity. But in the realm aesthetic of questions, if Ming is to Sung as pianist to composer, then Ming knowledge of technical rules, vocabulary of typeforms, and the like is not a simple pre-condition of creativity, but an interpreter's key to what was once created. The later landscapist's technical lore opened the way not directly from mind to nature, but to earlier sudden meetings of nature and mind. Insight into silence, for music which must be there, is not the same as insight into music.

The sum of the matter is this: Ming and early Ch'ing aesthetic anti-academicism was academically perpetuated. While thus inconsistent internally, as 'thought', it was appropriate to its thinkers, who were part of a dominant social class, traditionalistic, humanistic, and essentially opposed to specialization. No other society had an aesthetic ostensibly more favourable to genius, the foe of the academy; and no other society was less likely to practise what it preached—or even to preach what it said it did. This society, which had come to its anti-academicism naturally, not philosophically logically but socio-logically, was the home of authority, prescription, and routine, restraints on genius but spurs to conventional learning. Matthew Arnold, who took from Swift, the Ming scholar-gentleman *manqué*, his definition of culture as 'sweetness and light', said what the Ming scholar-gentleman-painters could never say, though in practice they proved it—that cultural continuity depends on intelligence, which is more transferable than genius, and which academies cause to thrive.[69]

iv. Bureaucracy and the Stereotyped Aesthetic: a Negative Confirmation of the Link

In the seventeenth century, three eccentric painters flourished whose devotion to Ch'an was much more freely given than that of the ordinary southern painter, and whose work was far less stereotyped than their contemporaries'. They were the Buddhist priests Shih-t'ao (Tao-chi), Shih-ch'i, and Pa-ta-shan-jen.

It was said of the two Shih, in awe, that they were *san-seng ju-sheng che*, beings for whom no space of time existed between their leaving the priesthood and entering sagehood.[70] They were painters, that is, who had reached the heights not step by step, with progressive learning, but in a leap of sudden enlightenment. 'Only so might I paint landscapes,' Shih-ch'i wrote on a painting, 'so, as if I conversed with mountains.'[71] He was said to have been 'naturally intelligent' (*su-hui*, a Buddhist phrase) from early youth, and to have read no Confucian books.[72]

'Knowledge is secondary, natural gifts are primary, and acquired gifts are not gifts,'[73] Shih-t'ao wrote, and 'I am I, and in me there is only I!'[74] Schools and models were death to art. What he longed to establish was a method of painting so natural that it would prove to be no method.[75] 'Shih-t'ao loved a wild manner in painting bamboo,' wrote Cheng Pan-ch'iao (1693–1765), 'almost disordered, without rule;

but rule lay naturally prepared within it.'[76] (' . . . art's free conformity to rule'.)

He felt a real affinity with Pa-ta-shan-jen, and unconventionally praised him as unprecedented: 'In his manner of calligraphy and painting, he stands ahead of earlier men; and his eye has none in antiquity to compare with it, to a height of more than a hundred generations.' [77] Whenever Pa-ta-shan-jen had the passionate urge to paint (wrote another near-contemporary), he bared his arm and snatched his brush and scattered everything all around, while he uttered loud cries like a crazy man.[78] Pa-ta-shan-jen was of Ming royal lineage and became a priest after 1644. One day he wrote 'Dumb' on his door, and never spoke a word again to anyone. 'His brush was very free and did not adhere to rules.' [79]

It is surely no accident that these free spirits, whose southern aesthetic was straight and undistorted, should have led peculiar civil lives. They were not of the normal intelligentsia, conventional Confucian officials (like Tung Ch'i-ch'ang), or retired gentlemen (like Shen Shih-t'ien) who owed their cultured ease to their official affiliations and whose Apollonian temperaments were hardly attuned to frenzy. If their theory and practice of painting had an uncommon logical consistency, they themselves had an uncommon sociological status. As deviants in society and deviants in art, they confirm the correlation between the gentry-scholar's domination and an amateur, unadmitted academicism.

These early Ch'ing eccentrics, then, had no unsettling influence in the world of painting, for the Manchu conquest left the *shih-ta-fu*, *wen-jen* position socially unimpaired. Many scholars in the first generation of Manchu rule, it is true— the so-called 'Ming remnants' (*i-lao* or *i-ch'en*), who declined or were denied office—were disturbed and disaffected. Among them were some of the empiricists we have met, who, in their opposition to idealist introspection, skated close to the edge of literati anti-vocationalism and urged that practical, technical problems of agriculture and water-works and military tactics and weapons be subjects of serious study.

They called also for *applied* historical and classical research. And of all this welter of topics, only literary scholarship survived in the mainstream of education, once the conquest-situation had shaken down and the bureaucratic society, with its appropriate cultural ideals, had shown its persistent quality.[80] A few partisans of the Ming, disillusioned, like Pa-ta-shan-jen, might leave the great world and reflect their resignation in their painting. But the main body of the literati accepted the Ch'ing as the conventional type of dynasty it was, kept their careers with their sense of proportion, and maintained, with all its implications for their southern style of painting, their anti-professional, traditionalistic cultural continuity.

Indeed, the independence of even these painting rebels may be over-estimated. Shih-t'ao, for one, like quite the literatus, frequently used phrases of Li Po, Tu Fu, and other early writers in his own poetic inscriptions on his paintings.[81] And in any case, if he really did revive the pure southern spirit, his own and subsequent generations of undisturbed traditionalists failed to understand. His antipathy to 'rules', his intuitive sentiments about 'method', were echoed in the *Hua-hsüeh ch'ien-shuo* of Wang Kai, another seventeenth-century painter ('The summit of method is the return to no method'),[82] and Wang was none other than the teacher of elementary method in the *Mustard-seed Garden*, the queen of rulebooks. And, 'How could he [Shih-t'ao] have attained such deep merit and strength', asked an early nineteenth-century scholar, 'if he had not absorbed all the masters of T'ang and Sung in his heart and spirit . . . ?'[83]

3. ECLECTICISM AND CONNOISSEURSHIP

i. The Softening of Partisan Lines

Tung Ch'i-ch'ang's aesthetic distinction between south and north implied tension between intuition and intellect, nature and books. But since southern intuitive theory was compromised by the social commitments of its highly intellectual adherents, north–south tension was inevitably relaxed.[84] For all his southern sympathies, Tung believed that a fusion of northern and southern procedures was possible, that reality, to some extent, could be not merely seized upon but learned about. 'If one has studied ten thousand volumes, walked ten thousand li, and freed one's mind from all dust and dirt, beautiful landscapes will rise quite naturally in the mind. . . .'[85]

Even Shih-ch'i, one of the intensely southern Buddhist painters of the seventeenth century, injected a northern note in an inscription on a painting: ' . . . In peace we discussed the ideas of the Buddhists and the fine points of the six laws [of Hsieh Ho]. Whoever wishes to say anything about them must have absorbed a great deal from books and history, and must climb mountains, to push on to the essence of the sources.'[86] And Yün Shou-p'ing, his contemporary, also reflected on the need to harmonize intuition and intellect. He repeated a saying of Ni Tsan (1301–74), one of the four Yüan masters who were heroes of the southern school. Ni had said, 'Making a picture is nothing other than drawing one's inner spontaneity.' Yün went on, 'This remark is most subtle'—and, after this genuflection to the approved concept of intuition—'and yet, one must speak with cognoscenti.'[87]

This flexibility in theory was matched by a certain catholicity in taste. Tung Ch'i-ch'ang found himself admiring a scroll by the Emperor Hui-tsung, the arch-northern founder of the Sung academy. Somewhat embarrassed at seeing his preference outrun his principles, he questioned the attribution.[88] But Mo Shih-lung, professedly just as sternly discriminating as Tung—and equally the architect of the system of discrimination—sometimes frankly owned to his basically eclectic taste. Theoretically he rejected the northern school; in practice, when he was faced with actual productions of great painters whom he called northern, like Li T'ang of the Sung and Tai Chin of the Ming, he simply commended them.[89]

But the low temperature of aesthetic controversy in the Ming and early Ch'ing period was indicated not only by relaxed discrimination but by confused discrimination. A

Ch'ing note on the Ming painter, Hu Chung-hou, reported both that he had great skill in *ch'ing-lu* (blue-green) landscape (an unequivocally academic province) and that his master in brush-method was Tung Yüan (one of the Sung masters whose southern credentials were most impeccable).[90] Lan Ying (*fl. ca.* 1660), always classified as a painter of the *Che* (Chekiang) school, a perpetuator of the northern traditions of the Sung academy, was said to resemble Shen Shih-t'ien, one of the great literati-painters of the *Wu* (Wu-hsien, modern Soochow—by extension, Kiangsu) school, which was considered safely southern. The fact of the matter was that Lan Ying, like hosts of others, eluded rigid classification. The north–south dichotomy, a formal abstraction imposed on the history of Chinese painting for extra-aesthetic reasons, could prove suggestive for identification of differing elements of style, but it could not be fitted to the body of work of individual artists. Lan Ying did, in fact, range in his painting all the way from Che to Wu. He and so many others, by abstract southern standards, were eclectics.[91]

More famous than Lan Ying were his predecessors, Ch'iu Ying (*fl.* 1522–60) and T'ang Yin (1470–1524). They, too, were usually numbered among the academics and sometimes among the angels of the southern school.[92] For they could be labelled as northern, southern, and syncretic in turns. Ch'iu Ying, in particular, was felt to have magnificent talents in *lin-mo* copying, which he exercised especially in reinterpreting the masterpieces of the renowned Yen collection. It was said that of the famous brushes of T'ang, Sung, and Yüan, there were none, whatever their tendencies, whose essence he could not grasp.[93] Essentially uncommitted stylistically, he produced, for example, a picture-book of sixteen paintings, illustrations of T'ang poems, in which he exhibited various methods. Both northern style and southern style, according to the canons of the later critics, were represented, and types of line both 'thick and turbid', as the experts called it, and 'pure and elegant'.[94] T'ang Yin, too, changed methods and models according to impulse.[95] And Wen Cheng-ming, universally considered a paladin of the Wu school, the southern stronghold, roamed like the others through a wide variety of Sung and Yüan styles and was said to have mastered them all.[96]

Eclecticism, however, meant more than divided loyalties between the northern and southern styles; it meant the fusion of them in individual works. For instance, one of the Ch'iu Ying paintings in his album of T'ang illustrations shows an emperor's visit to a newly-built mansion. This is executed in the right foreground in a meticulous academic style, while in the background and on the left suggestively misty pale-wash mountains taper off towards southern infinity.[97] Such stylistic complexities were common. The late Ming painter, Sheng Mao-yeh (*fl. ca.* 1635), was described by connoisseurs as painting northern pines, detailed and stylized, among southern rocks and mountains.[98]

The movement towards the joining of the two styles culminated in Wang Hui (1632–1717), celebrated during his lifetime as the *hua-sheng*, the painter-sage, and later on as the greatest genius among the 'six great masters' of the early Ch'ing. All question of trends and schools aside, Wang Hui beyond a doubt was a superb painter, one of the most compelling figures in art history, but the grounds on which he was first admired more truly expressed his age than his own individual mastery did. An accepted proof of his merits, his claim to special appreciation, was this: 'In painting there were northern and southern schools; Wang Hui brought them together.'[99] He was avowedly an eclectic, drawing on legions of the old masters (Yüan for the use of brush and ink, he recommended, Sung for mountains and rivers, T'ang for expression of the spirit), and his favourite model, significantly enough, was the earlier many-sided eclectic, T'ang Yin.[100]

The eclecticism of T'ang Yin has been described as that of a transitional figure, standing midway in time between the domination of the Che school (which, led by Tai Chin [*fl. ca.* 1664], the 'modern Ma Yüan', had early Ming imperial favour for its revival of the style of the Southern Sung imperial academy) and the Wu school, citadel of the amateurs.[101] If this was so of T'ang Yin, Wang Hui's eclecticism was of a different order, with special implications. Whether or not T'ang Yin should really be seen as an unconscious figure, adrift in a process of qualitative change between one vogue and another, Wang Hui can only be seen as a deliberately syncretic figure, reintegrating the first vogue into the second, consciously striving for harmony and an end to conflict (however unspirited) which might have led to renewal of process, and change.

ii. Virtuosi and Connoisseurs

Syncretism is not by definition (and unquestionably not in Wang Hui) a source of artistic sterility. It is certainly possible to express a genuine aesthetic insight by combining techniques which were once exploited to different ends. But the late Ming, early Ch'ing syncretism came not from an arrival at a new insight to which earlier techniques were adapted, but from a virtuoso's fascination by techniques.

The techniques of painting which syncretists pieced together had each existed, in the first instance, because the painter had seen his subject in a certain way and had used the brush in a manner contrived to convey it. In the eclectic spirit which had come by the seventeenth century to dominate Chinese painting, however, interest in the brushwork itself transcended interest in the subject, the aesthetic vision which brushwork might presumably have been intended to realize. 'No brushwork method at all,' an eighteenth-century Chinese artist said of western painting, and he therefore dismissed it in the typical wen-jen manner: it was only chiang, or artisanship.[102] To the connoisseur, variety of brush-strokes became an important criterion of value, and critics were as ready to analyse single strokes as to contemplate a composition as a whole. They expressed their refined discriminations in vague and elusive language ('his brushwork manner was exceedingly elegant and smooth, fine and close, but it was slightly weak'), as if to imply the exquisite subtlety of their aesthetic appreciations.[103]

The spirit which invested this eclectic connoisseurship —whether one's principles were supposed to be southern, northern, or in between—was the traditional Chinese inclination to follow early models. We have observed how artists like Ch'iu Ying had diverted the painter's efforts from divining the spirit of nature to divining the spirit of previous paintings. It became a virtue, really, to have no stylistic commitment; all styles were simply like natural features, whose essence the genius captures. Tung Ch'i-ch'ang, with his practically canonical pronouncements, made this vogue of *ni-ku*, imitation of the ancients, all-prevailing, and he approved the methods of eclectics who sought to make masterpieces by synthesizing details from the works of different masters.[104] It was a virtuoso's task, and a connoisseur's delight.

Upon request the late Ming, early Ch'ing painter, Lan Ying, produced for his friend, the governor of Shansi, whose connoisseurship he admired, a painting combining the different manners of Tung Yüan, Huang Kung-wang, Wang Meng, and Wu Chen.[105] The manners were different, but all were southern; which meant that one needed a nice sense of discrimination to blend and yet distinguish them, and that such intellectual subtlety transcended intuition in importance (even the intuitions that the connoisseurs were subtle about), and that southern models could serve a northern painter—Lan Ying, it may be remembered, was supposed to follow the *Che* tradition—for a sophisticated amateur's pastiche.

When the painter's emphasis was on fidelity to models instead of on fidelity to vision—which is what animated the men who created the models—there was no stylistic, aesthetic reason why various techniques developed in the past could not be mixed. And so the modern painter could throw everything into the pot, all the technical elements devised by men who had been aesthetically serious, committed to some end behind their technical means. By late Ming times, the end of the approved painter was the demonstration of his mastery of means. Style became a counter in an artist's game of self-display, while gentry-literati-officials and their set were the self-appreciative happy few who recognized the rules and knew the esoterica.[106]

4. CONCLUSION: MODERNIZATION AS THE CORROSION OF THE AMATEUR IDEAL

i. The Relativity of Judgments of 'Decadence'

Historians of the arts have sometimes led their subjects out of the world of men into a world of their own, where the principles of change seem interior to the art rather than governed by decisions of the artist. Thus, we have been assured that seventeenth-century Dutch landscape bears no resemblance to Breughel because by the seventeenth century Breughel's tradition of mannerist landscape had been exhausted.[107] Or we are treated to tautologies, according to which art is 'doomed to become moribund' when it 'reaches the limit of its idiom', and in 'yielding its final flowers' shows that 'nothing more can be done with it'—hence the passing of the grand manner of the eighteenth century in Europe and the romantic movement of the nineteenth.[108]

How do aesthetic values really come to be superseded? This sort of thing, purporting to be a revelation of cause, an answer to the question, leaves the question still to be asked. For Chinese painting, well before the middle of the Ch'ing period, with its enshrinement of eclectic virtuosi and connoisseurs, had, by any 'internal' criteria, reached the limit of its idiom and yielded its final flowers. And yet the values of the past persisted for generations, and the fear of imitation, the feeling that creativity demanded freshness in the artist's purposes, remained unfamiliar to Chinese minds. Wang Hui was happy to write on a landscape he painted in 1692 that it was a copy of a copy of a Sung original;[109] while his colleague, Yün Shou-p'ing, the flower-painter, was described approvingly by a Ch'ing compiler as having gone back to the 'boneless' painting of Hsü Ch'ung-ssu, of the eleventh century, and made his work one with it.[110] (Yün had often, in fact, inscribed 'Hsu Ch'ung-ssu boneless flower picture' on his own productions).[111] And Tsou I-kuei, another flower-painter, committed to finding a traditional sanction for his art, began a treatise with the following apologia:

When the ancients discussed painting, they treated landscape in detail but slighted flowering plants. This does not imply a comparison of their merits. Flower painting flourished in the northern Sung, but Hsü [Hsi] and Huang [Ch'üan] could not express themselves theoretically, and therefore their methods were not transmitted.[112]

The lesson taught by this Chinese experience is that an artform is 'exhausted' when its practitioners think it is. And a circular explanation will not hold—they think so not when some hypothetically objective exhaustion occurs in the art itself, but when outer circumstance, beyond the realm of purely aesthetic content, has changed their subjective criteria; otherwise, how account for the varying lengths of time it takes for different publics to leave behind their worked-out forms? There were Ch'ing experiments in western-style perspective, but these remained exoticisms; suspicion of sterility in modern Chinese painting, embarrassment about the extent of traditional discipleship (instead of a happy acceptance of it) began in China only late in the nineteenth century, when Chinese society began to change under western pressure and along western lines, and when modern western value-judgments, accordingly—like praise of 'originality'—were bound to intrude their influence. We have seen how the amateur commitments of the literati-official class in early-modern China brought Chinese painting to its late Ming, early Ch'ing condition. A reassessment of that condition never came until a change in role was thrust on the official class, and a change in its education, and a change in the general currency of its amateur ideal.

ii. *Nationalism: Culture-change and the Professionalization of Bureaucracy*

The world of painting in early-modern, pre-western China issued from and reflected a broader world of social institutions. Behind the amateur painter and the southern critic was the anti-professional official, whose socially high estate was the mark of his deeply respected humanistic culture, not a technically specialized one. It was felt, of course, that Confucian moral learning was especially appropriate to government-service, since administration was supposed to be less by law than by example. Still, the official's education failed to make him professional, it was not vocational, for this important reason: his learning was not just valuable for office, but happened to be *the* body of learning, artistic as well as moral, which was valuable in itself, and which lent itself more easily, for examination purposes, to aesthetic exposition than to practical implementation. It was this intimate association of bureaucracy with the mastery of high culture which was cracked by modern western pressure and its concomitant, Chinese nationalism.

When the Chinese nation began to supersede Chinese culture as the focal point of loyalty,[113] sentiments grew for changing, and finally for abandoning, the examination system (this was done in 1905). An education sacrosanct in the old heyday of the amateurs when 'the accomplished scholar was not a utensil', came to be criticized more and more, towards the end of the nineteenth century, as being far too predominantly literary—as failing, that is, to equip officials with specialized, useful knowledge for the national defence.[114] The Chinese state was changing its identity, from that of a world, an environment in which the officials' culture flourished, to that of a nation, whose needs should colour its bureaucracy's educational purposes. It meant the end of the 'aesthetic value' and self-sufficiency of the bureaucratic Confucian 'princely man', which had been at opposite poles (as Weber saw it) from the Puritan—and capitalist—'vocation'.[115]

With the pressure, then, of modern western industrialism (and those attendant concepts—science, progress, business, and utility—unhonoured, we have noticed, in the Ming literati culture) on Chinese society and Chinese consciousness, the charge of formalism came to be levelled at the official examinations and at the intellectual ideals which the latter sustained. But objectively, at the time such censure began to be effective, the examinations were not essentially more formalistic than in Ming and early Ch'ing times, when the 'eight-legged essay', such a scandal to the moderns, was perfected and prescribed.[116]

Only then (almost, only now) was the scholar-official's emphasis on form, on the subtleties of style, in the literati-painting as in the literary essay, generally felt to be the symptom of a weak concern with content.[117] Earlier, the idea had occurred to a few individuals: in the seventeenth century Ku Yen-wu had called the eight-legged essay more harmful than the ancient burning of the books, since it led, in effect, by the prominence given to formal technique, to the destruction of books through their not being read.[118] To rationalistic, insufficiently historically-minded moderns, to whom such criticism appeared incontrovertible, the fact that Ku's views had not prevailed seemed a bad accident or a Manchu Machiavellian achievement. But a less desperate or question-begging explanation than these lies in one's awareness of the amateur ideal as a long-continued condition of Chinese thought. Only when the modern West impinged on China and undermined the position of the gentry-literati-officials, who had set the styles in art and expression as they set the rates in taxes and rents—only then did the concept of 'amateur' slide into its modern sense of something less than 'specialist', and what had once been precious to tradition-alists and classicists seem mainly preciosity to a new youth in a new world of science and revolution.

Interlude: Confucianism and the End of the Taoist Connection

WHERE are the Taoists of yesteryear in modern Chinese history? As the amateur ideal and the world that made it faded, Confucian institutions and loyalties still persisted. But Confucianism changed in its persistence, and one of the signs of its transformation was the fact that men who abandoned it appraised it by novel western standards, not by Taoist ones. When, arising from affirmations about science, progress, business, and utility, doubts were voiced about official careerism and its typical intellectual background, these were allegations against one form of action and education, not (in the Taoist vein) against action itself and education in the abstract.

In earlier times, as the old saw has it, a man might be 'a Confucianist in office and a Taoist out'—indulge with part of his being a Confucian passion for the ordering of social life, and with the other part seek, or affect to seek, the Taoist harmony of man immersed in nature, as distinct from the Confucian harmony of men among masses of men. Together, Confucianism and Taoism made the whole man, the one implying a testimonial to civilization and the values and goals of social life, the other, release from society and social concerns. The common thread of harmony tied them together, and a Taoist intuitive aesthetics made a precedent for Ch'an in the high art of Confucian ruling circles (as the Taoist spirit of detachment favoured the Confucianist-amateur's coolness to professional commitment). But the opposing emphases on nature and society made Taoism potentially, especially at times of crack-up in the society's

44

bureaucratic structure, more of an alternative to Confucianism than a complement. As popular Taoism, it could mean peasant rebellion, like the late Han revolt of the Yellow Turbans against landlord-Confucianist-officialdom. As sophisticated Taoism, it could mean literati withdrawal from social action into third-century A.D. 'pure-talk' (*ch'ing-t'an*), or the euphoria of the 'Seven Sages of the Bamboo Grove', or the T'ang poet's nostalgia for men

> . . . whose hearts are without guile.
> Gay like children. . . .[1]

That is how, traditionally, the Confucian-official role would be disparaged.

But rebels tended to reconstitute the Confucian state, and the sophisticated critics implicitly, in the escapist form of their censure, rendered to Confucianism, Confucianism alone, the real world of social life and action. How different the modern censure has been—neither Taoist blind protest nor Taoist world-denying quietism, but conscious revolution, and rejections of Confucianism in the nineteenth and twentieth centuries which were not at all rejections of the great world, but a choosing of other ideals for action in society. The tone of Chinese culture was changed; intellectual life was newly strained. For the new choices were not easy to make, and the new defence of the old was difficult, too.

Part Two

CHINESE CULTURE IN ITS MODERN METAMORPHOSES: THE TENSIONS OF INTELLECTUAL CHOICE

CHAPTER III

Eclecticism in the Area of Native Chinese Choices

1. CONSIDERATIONS OF TIME BECOME CONSIDERATIONS OF SPACE

IN intellectual controversies within the Confucian tradition, each school tried to score a point by claiming for itself a sort of apostolic succession from the sages. Opponents would almost invariably be accused of deviation from a right path laid down in antiquity. The old was prized over the new, and seventeenth- and eighteenth-century critics of Sung and Ming thought charged primarily not that it failed to meet needs of the present, but that it strayed from truths of the past.

Ku Yen-wu, for example, criticizing the Ming-Ch'ing school of Wang Yang-ming, charged that this school was really a revival of the ill-famed fourth-century *ch'ing-t'an* (pure talk) school, but that, whereas the original *ch'ing-t'an* was frankly Taoist, their modern descendants masqueraded as Confucianists. In truth, said Ku, they were far from the thought of Confucius and Mencius. They 'dwelt upon the surface (lit. "coarseness") without reaching the essence (lit. "fineness") [of the sages]'. They 'never asked about the great principles of the master's sayings on learning and government'.[1] Lu Shih-i (1611–72) also stated that many of his contemporaries in the intellectual world were really like the *ch'ing-t'an* school, which had been so injurious in the Chin period. As empty speculators, he charged, they were guilty of straying from the path of Confucius, in whose *Lun-yü* (Analects) Lu discerned a call to practical action.[2] Prominent Ch'ing critics of the neo-Confucian 'Sung Learning', we may recall, were known as the school of the 'Han Learning', not as the school of the 'Ch'ing Learning'. Such was the zeal of Chinese thinkers to sally forth under ancient colours.

The pedigree, then, of an intellectual position was one of the main criteria of its value or truth. This was true for traditional thought before the western intrusion, and it was true after it. But in the nineteenth century, with antiquity still a Chinese criterion of value, the West forced revision of Chinese judgments on the older contending philosophies. Petty distinctions and conflicts between Chinese schools paled into insignificance before the glaring contrast of western culture to everything Chinese. Grounds for discrimination between Chinese schools were blurred when a new western alternative existed for them all, a more genuine alternative than they afforded one another. Chinese thought was shocked into a semblance of unity; when the West was a serious rival, Chinese rivals closed their ranks. The question 'new or old?' as a test of value continued to be asked, but the question was removed from a Chinese world to the larger world of the West and China. As a first effect of their comprehending that western culture had to be taken seriously, the Chinese schools became less contentious about which of them was old. They all were old (having existed before the West came) and the West was new.

Why was it the nineteenth-century West that first offered a sufficiently strong alternative to press the Chinese schools together? Why did the seventeenth-century West, revealed to China by the scholarly Jesuit missionaries, miss having this effect? For one thing, of course, the Jesuits were far fewer than their modern successors as representative westerners, and the earlier exposition of western culture was bound to seem less strident. However, difference simply in the weight of western numbers is probably not the whole story behind the difference, during these two encounters, in relative Chinese awareness of intellectual challenge. To some extent, to be sure (as we shall consider at a later stage of the book), the Jesuits used their western learning as a calculated irritant, but on the whole they used it to establish themselves as educated gentlemen, qualified to mingle with Confucian literati. The Jesuits largely satisfied Confucian expectations as to the likely course of intelligent foreigners in Chinese society: they gave their actions a Chinese cast and tried, in great measure, to accommodate their own ideas to Chinese civilization. But Europeans in the nineteenth-century treaty-ports, after the Opium War (1839–42), were independent spirits, unconcerned with Chinese susceptibilities. Where the early Jesuits extended to China a graceful invitation to embellish and enrich its existing civilization, which was universally respected, later Europeans exposed to China an uncompromisingly foreign alternative.

The Jesuits were culturally conciliatory because Chinese society, in their day, was stable, and they would receive a hearing more or less as candidates for membership or not at all. But the Chinese who heard them were only casually interested in such frankly western knowledge as the Jesuits offered. For, since seventeenth-century Europe was unable to jeopardize the stability of Chinese society, western knowledge was superfluous to the Chinese literati; it had no relevance to power or success. A mastery of traditional Chinese learn-ing was not only necessary but sufficient—at least, to the extent that intellectual factors counted—to enable a Chinese to get the most out of Chinese life and the Chinese state.

Traditional Chinese learning, that is, was the intellectual substance of the state examinations; the examinations were the conventional and the only really approved path to the mandarin-bureaucracy; and the bureaucracy was the radi-ating çentre of the highest social and economic power. The Jesuits, bringing only European ideas, with no European military or economic force behind them, made no dent at all in the prevailing bureaucratic system of power, so that the examination-road remained the usual road of ambition, and classical literary culture remained the core of education. For, whatever its intrinsic validity or its piquant surface attractive-ness, the Jesuits' intellectual offering was mainly scientific and technological (even in art, it was the geometrical illusionism of Renaissance perspective which gave the Jesuits' oil paintings their degree of interest in Chinese eyes). And nothing had happened socially to make the Chinese literati either unable or unzealous to guard their amateur standing. They were of the type of humanistic gentleman, whose characteristic quest is the mastery of an already ordered culture, an inheritance in the liberal arts; on the face of it, science was uncongenial to them, and in its heart as well— for the scientific spirit could only be subversive of traditionalism, which came so naturally to them in their social personalities and was so explicit intellectually in their formal Confucian code.

Thus western science, which ideally, potentially, was a threat to Confucian letters in the seventeenth and eighteenth centuries, was not yet actually a threat, and this was because the social position of Confucian officials, while ideally, potentially threatened by business power (whose growth in the West was parallel to growth in the fields of science),[3] had not yet been actually threatened. Business values, like scientific values, were still overshadowed. Business is never secure without a system of abstract, impersonal legal relationships. The Confucian official, his moralistic bias militating against such a system, still ruled the roost, without western interference, in a rent and tax economy. He was still able, by a combination of threat (bureaucratic squeeze) and lure (the somewhat imperfectly open examination system, highway for social mobility), to render abortive any revolutionary impulse in proto-capitalist elements. In this society of bureaucratic dominance, Confucian learning was, not utilitarian, but supremely useful—and utterly demanding.

After the Opium War, however, European industrialism and commercial enterprise began to act as a catalyst in traditional Chinese society. Before the establishment of treaty-ports in 1842, with their provision for the operation of western law on Chinese soil, there had already arisen a Chinese group of commercial intermediaries, the 'compradores', who were associated with western business firms. They became the nucleus of a new Chinese business community, déclassé from the point of view of the older Chinese society, but relatively protected from the consequences, political and economic, of the mandarin's disapproval. The treaty-ports became havens of personal and commercial security, where funds could be safe from the depredations of powerful officials, and where the commercial climate and the legal code encouraged reinvestment of business profits in business, instead of perpetuating the traditional flight of capital into land, the traditional hunger of business families for bureaucratic gentility. At the very moment that the western powers, by their physical assault, were contributing to the demoralization of the Ch'ing regime and therefore making problematic the advantages of an official career in its service, western political penetration was pointing the way to unorthodox alternatives.

It was a small beginning in the middle of the nineteenth century, small in numbers and small in noise. Confucianism, the examinations, the civil service, and the imperial state still had a reasonable life to run and kept prestige in the ports, and it would be wrong to suggest that even today the Confucian mentality has been finally superseded. But the conditions for corrosion were established with the treaties. In the eighteen-sixties, after the Taiping Rebellion (1850–64) had been put down, when the classical examinations were reinstituted in the Shanghai region, troubled Chinese observers noted that candidates were inordinately few.[4] And Shanghai was the centre of the western business network.

Thus, new roads to power for Chinese, roads smoothed by western knowledge, had come to be dimly seen. A challenge was offered to the usefulness of Chinese thought, and when the question of its usefulness could be raised, the question of its truth came alive. Chinese thought, all schools of it, had a genuine, serious western rival.

2. THE ECLECTICISM OF TSENG KUO-FAN

The tendency to turn away from purely Chinese intellectual disputes was characteristic of those who were really aware of the western intrusion. But facts, of course, may run well ahead of awareness, and in the nineteenth century, particularly in its earlier decades, there were many parochial minds which persisted in treating China as the world and in analysing Chinese thought according to its traditional refinements. T'ang Ching-hai (1778–1861), for example, in his *Ch'ing Ju-hsüeh-an hsiao-shih* (Short history of the intellectual situation of Ch'ing Confucianism), published in 1845, made a systematic and thoroughly partisan classification of Ch'ing philosophers. He exalted the *li-hsüeh* of the Sung neo-Confucianists Ch'eng I and Chu Hsi and disparaged the *hsin-hsüeh* of Lu Hsiang-shan and Wang Yang-ming, of the Sung and Ming dynasties, respectively.[5]

Tseng Kuo-fan (1811–72), however, the most powerful governor-general during the Taiping Rebellion and the T'ung-chih reign (1860–74), was implicated in dealings with the West and exposed to western ideas as few of his contemporaries among the Chinese literati could be. He remained certain of the universality of Chinese spiritual values; nevertheless, his Chinese ethnocentrism was not that of a man whose complacency had never been challenged, but of one who has known a rival claim and disposed of it. And though Tseng flatly rejected the rival western claim (and condemned the anti-Confucian, pseudo, Christian Taiping rebels of mid-century for seemingly accepting it), Tseng's very facing it affected his view of the heritage he defended.

He came to admire the practical techniques of the West and to feel, correspondingly, that the peculiar excellence of China (which he always affirmed) need not be assumed to characterize traditional Chinese practice in that sphere of practical techniques. And in the sphere of ultimate values of civilization—the sphere which was left to Tseng for the indulgence of his pride in being Chinese—he became more of a composite Chinese, an antithesis to westerners, and less of a partisan sectarian, an adherent of one pre-western Chinese school against another. As a loyal Chinese, but a Chinese among westerners, he seemed to lose the will to dwell on intramural distinctions. An eclectic in the larger sense, ready to infuse something of western civilization into Chinese civilization, he was comprehensive, too, in the field of native Chinese choices, and sought to impose a peace on traditional Chinese enemies.

He would synthesize the best points of all systems of thought, he asserted. The various philosophers of the late Chou period were not as great as Confucius because they were biased or one-sided. But if the biases could be rectified and the deficits made up, if these philosophers could lend themselves to a composite—with Lao-tzu's and Chuang-tzu's doctrine of emptiness and tranquillity for relaxing the mind, and Mo-tzu's doctrine of industry and frugality for regulating the self, and Kuan-tzu's and Shang Yang's doctrine of severity and orderliness for unifying the people—then all of them would be worth following and indispensable.[6]

To combine the industry and frugality of Emperor Yü and Mo-tzu with the tranquillity and emptiness of Lao-tzu and Chuang-tzu—is not this the art of simultaneously accomplishing self-cultivation and group-regulation?[7]

By gratifying oneself with the way of Chuang-tzu and restricting oneself with the way of Hsün-tzu, may not one be a princely man attaining the Way?[8]

Coming to classical Chinese conflicts in this conciliatory spirit, Tseng had similar views about more recent intellectual controversies. (And so, indeed, had his properly filial son, Tseng Chi-tse, 1839-90, who scorned the fashionable Ch'ing criticism of Lu-Wang idealism, and intimated, in his father's vein, that modern writers liked to dwell on comparisons between Chu Hsi and Lu Hsiang-shan just for the joy of sectarianism.)[9] The elder Tseng wrote approvingly of both the Sung Learning and of its later rival, the Han Learning, which dismissed the tradition of the 'five Sung philosophers' as 'loosely fanciful'. The scholars of the Han Learning had been attacked in turn, as 'renegade', and accused of 'splitting the classical tradition into fragments and causing the true path such harm as would never come to an end'. Yet, according to Tseng Kuo-fan, the peace-maker, there was little distinction between them, and he urged their adherents not to be inflexible. Their differences could be easily adjusted and the schools could fit together. Why should the two denounce each other?[10] For himself, Tseng subscribed to the catholic motto of Yao Nai (1731–1815), founder of the so-called *T'ung-ch'eng p'ai*, a moribund school of thinkers (named after a place in Anhui province) whose intellectual influence Tseng revived: '*I li* (the Sung learning's ethics and metaphysics), *k'ao-chü* (the Han learning's textual study), *tz'u-chang* (their literary expression)—these three equally important.'[11]

It was his philosophy of *li-hsüeh* (the classic *li* of 'rites', not the neo-Confucian *li* of archetypical 'forms'),[12] Tseng maintained, which would bring about the unification of the Han and Sung schools and put an end to intellectual warfare.[13] The *li-hsüeh* was indeed a philosophy of wholeness, drawing together complementary pairs of classical concepts, all of them ancient expressions of a working dichotomy of 'inner' and 'outer'. There are *t'i* and *yung*, substance and function, what one is and what one does; and there are *sheng* and *wang*, the sage in spirit and the king in action, whose *t'i* is evinced in *hsiu-chi*, his inner cultivation of the self, and whose *yung* is evinced in *chih-jen*, the governing of men in the outer world. *Li* is the common noumenon underlying the self-nurturing, world-pacifying sage-king's being and activity; without *li*, from the standpoint of the inner there is no *tao* or *te*, metaphysical truth or rightness, and from the standpoint of the outer there is no *cheng-shih*, no governing.[14]

In the eyes of Tseng Kuo-fan, Chinese philosophical factions stood, at worst, for parts of the whole Confucian conception. But the *li-hsüeh* embraced them all, for the *li-hsüeh* recaptured the whole.

When Tseng referred to this whole in contrasting it with western principles (whether these were being expressed by Europeans or by Chinese peasant Taiping rebels), he called it *ming-chiao*, the teachings of the sages, a definition of civilization which was in the broadest sense Chinese. Hellmut Wilhelm has called it characteristic of Tseng that he did not use the term for Confucianism (*ju-chiao*) or for orthodoxy (*cheng-chiao*), by which usually Sung Confucianism was understood.[15] Another time, noting with some satisfaction the Protestant-Catholic schism in Christianity, Tseng oversimplified the history of Confucianism, making it, in comparison, a steadily standing monolith, with no cracks and no decay.[16]

When western conceptions were seen as alternative, the Chinese creed for a man like Tseng had to be close to all-inclusive.[17]

3. THE ENCROACHMENT OF 'CHINA' ON GENERAL JUDGMENTS OF VALUE

Why, with Tseng and others like him, was there a waning of discrimination between Chinese alternatives, while to their predecessors and their less worldly-wise contemporaries, such discrimination was both natural and important? The positive content of the Sung Learning and the Han Learning, for example, had not changed. But some change had occurred —a redefinition of the Chinese ideas in terms of new alternatives, and a consequent reordering of the psychology of Chinese thinkers. When Tseng, unlike some others, declared such Chinese controversy intellectually insignificant, perhaps he did so, in part, because for him, at least, it was emotionally undesirable.

For all his consistently serene Chinese self-confidence, he knew the West as a rival, a rival so formidable that he felt compelled to encourage an infusion of western material culture into Chinese civilization. This recommendation, this implied deference to the West as a centre of value, was wrapped in a saving rationalization, which preserved the claims of China to a basic superiority. If, then, in this broad eclecticism (which we shall shortly examine), we find Tseng unable to accept the western value simply, as a matter of intellectual persuasion, but find him concerned instead, out of considerations irrelevant to a general intellectual quest, to make it seem legitimate for a *Chinese* to accept, may not this same special commitment have a place in his narrower, indigenously Chinese eclecticism? It is easy to see how such eclecticism would indulge the will of Chinese traditionalists, of whatever stamp, to hold their own against western rivals who raise the spectre of doubt among them all. For agreement might seem to shore up defences of the Chinese intellectual world. Literati who could recognize, even dimly, the western onslaught for what it was, could have little stomach for civil war. It was more than unjustifiable—it was unwelcome. However freely they had indulged themselves in the luxury of dissension in the safe old days, now, when the West had challenged Confucius himself, all the bickering claimants of the mantle of Confucius were in real danger, and they were in it together.

Yet, in so far as acceptance of Chinese ideas was beginning to be more and more emotionally willed, it became less and less intellectually forced. When attachment to Chinese inheritances, with their latent emotional associations, had not been threatened (before Chinese society seemed in danger of being torn), the quest for intellectually acceptable answers had been undertaken freely, and Chinese philosophies had been worked out as distinct serious efforts to describe the way of the world. But when Chinese philosophers, defensively ranged against the West, came to be rather indiscriminate in their Chinese intellectual tastes and to sip at all the flowers, their eclecticism was an intellectually delicate thing; for the flowers would never have existed, had serious thinkers of earlier times not cultivated individual gardens and developed their own ideas by marking them off from the others.

Therefore, as considerations of special tie to China intrude on considerations of general judgment in the Chinese approach to Chinese ideas, western ideas, to some extent, are forced on reluctant Chinese minds. And Sino-western syncretisms, inspired by that force and that reluctance, pre-empt the field of Chinese intellectual history.

CHAPTER IV

T'i *and* Yung—
'Substance' and 'Function'

I. THE RATIONALIZATION

BEGINNING slowly in the eighteen-forties, after the British show of technical prowess in the Opium War, and picking up speed by the end of the century, numbers of faithful Confucianists spoke out in favour of change in Chinese culture. Paradoxically, they insisted on change because they had a traditionalistic bias against it. They parted company with unshakable traditionalists not over the question of ends—the ascription of value to Chinese civilization —but over the question of the means to preserve it. To admit innovation in certain areas of life, declared the bolder spirits, was the only means.

Uncompromising anti-westernizers had an attitude of radical simplicity: the way to stay Chinese was to stay Chinese in all the aspects of culture. But the cautious eclectics, protesting their perfect loyalty to the basic Chinese values, believed that immobility would be a self-defeating tactic and an impossible ideal. The only alternative to outright destruction of Chinese civilization by foreign conquerors was selective innovation by dedicated Chinese traditionalists. To justify their proposal in the special sense, to satisfy their will to believe that Chinese superiority was still unchallenged, they emphasized that these areas of innovation from the West were areas of only *practical* value, not of essential value. Western knowledge would be used only to defend the core of Chinese civilization, and it would not impinge upon it.

59

If there should be argument on this point, if some traditionalists should doubt that western ideas could be sterilized just by Chinese rhetoric, or be turned into passive instruments simply by decree, any one of this school of westernizers would respond, in effect, like Li Hung-chang (1823–1901), cutting off discussion with the blank, apodictic apologia: 'If one knows oneself and knows one's opposite number, in a hundred battles one will have a hundred victories.'[1]

This rationalization, whereby something of western culture could have a place in China and yet be kept in its place, was an article of faith for a whole school of Confucian-official westernizers, the 'self-strengtheners', from Lin Tse-hsü (1785–1850) to Chang Chih-tung (1837–1909). It was Chang, a great advocate of railroads and heavy industry, who made the most explicit philosophical statement of what they all assumed—that since elements of western culture would be introduced only for use, condescension could be heaped on 'practicality', and China could seem, not beggarly, but even queenly in borrowing western methods. Taking his terminology from Chu Hsi, he advocated Chinese learning for *t'i* ('substance', 'essence') and western learning for *yung* ('function', 'utility'). In the general excellence of its cultural product, China could still seem more than equivalent to the West. Special Chinese ties need not be strained.[2]

2. THE FALLACY

Why should this rationalization not serve its purpose? Why should the Chinese not be able to rest on this middle ground? The *t'i-yung* dichotomy might well appear to fit the conditions of Chinese self-awareness, as a psychologically suitable camouflage for the infiltration of foreign value—at least in the field of science. In that field, considered apart from other areas of civilization, the modern Chinese had the least hope of linking their special and general quests, of making an emotional Chinese particularism intellectually convincing. For valid conclusions of science, the sphere of the empirically demonstrable, finally enforce their claims to acceptance, regardless of their cultural origins. But scientific values are distinguished from moral and aesthetic values not only by being empirically demonstrable but by being widely and obviously 'useful'. Now, since the Chinese were forced to accept modern science, which ripened in the West, what could be more plausible than that they accept it in the spirit of Chang Chih-tung, emphasizing not that western science was more valuable than Chinese science but that western science was less valuable than Chinese morals and aesthetics, less valuable because of its usefulness? As something useful, it was a means, and a means is less than an end.

Yet, this rationalization, which was meant to compromise the differences between the *avant-garde* and the obscurantists, was attacked in both these quarters, and with considerable cogency. Both stubborn traditionalists and impatient innovators came to feel that the needs for special and general assurance, the *meum* and *verum*, were not really welded together by the *t'i-yung* formula. Since that formula seemed to fail to justify innovation, traditionalists rejected innovation and innovators sought a new formula.

The failure of the *t'i-yung* rationalization to consolidate Chinese devotion to Chinese culture in the modern world of western techniques can be explained in its own terms: Chinese learning, which was to be the *t'i* in the new syncretic culture, was the learning of a society which had always used it for *yung*, as the necessary passport to the best of all careers. Western learning, when sought as *yung*, did not supplement Chinese learning—as the neat formula would have it do— but began to supplant it. For in reality, Chinese learning had come to be prized as substance because of its function, and when its function was usurped, the learning withered.[3] The more western learning came to be accepted as the practical instrument of life and power, the more Confucianism ceased to be *t'i*, essence, the naturally believed-in value of a civilization without a rival, and became instead an historical inheritance, preserved, if at all, as a romantic token of no-surrender to a foreign rival which had changed the essence of Chinese life.

'Officials read Confucian writings now, but what they assiduously seek out is the foreign learning':[4] Yü Yüeh

(1821–1907) resentfully saw it, the coming eclipse of the Confucian *tao*, lingeringly preserved *pro forma* while another way took over the title of necessary knowledge.

T'i-yung westernization began in China, as one might expect, with emphasis on the bare means of military defence —ships and guns—'to drive away the crocodile and to get rid of the whales', to control the barbarians through their own superior techniques.[5] Soon the list of indispensable superior techniques lengthened, to cover industry, commerce, mining, railroads, telegraphs . . ., and essential traditional attitudes were almost casually dissipated by seekers after the useful techniques which were to shield the Chinese essence. Feng Kuei-fen (1809–74) was ready to trade the *chü-jen* and *chin-shih* literary degrees for artisanship at least equal to the foreign.[6] Hsüeh Fu-ch'eng (1838–94), one of those ostensibly only-material innovators whose ideal in matters of spirit was *wan ku pu i* (unchanged from time immemorial),[7] betrayed an enthusiasm for commerce, as a contributor to the national health and as an index of it, which ill accorded with the old Confucian bureaucratic, gentlemanly temper. In three essays celebrating the publication, during the T'ung-chih reign (1860–74), of Imperial Maritime Customs statistics—in itself, a western-sponsored procedure, since the Customs, firmly established by treaty in 1858, was a foreign bureaucracy in its higher strata—Hsüeh said that the figures on duties levied were a mirror reflecting the degree of seclusion or accessibility of the land, poverty or wealth of the people, flourishing or declining of material well-being, and swelling or shrinking of revenues.[8]

This infection of spirit by techniques, of *t'i* by *yung* (in the terms of those who thought the two could be sealed apart), was a consequence of the novelty, in Chinese experience, of the type of foreigner who brought these techniques to China. Chinese had learned from history to expect of their foreign conquerors (if the latter came to rule and not simply to raid) some effort, in varying degree, to become Chinese. The traditional Chinese attitude of self-defence against foreign invaders was a variation on a bit of homely popular wisdom

—'if you can't lick them, join them'—or, more precisely here, 'make them join you'. But the Chinese problem with nineteenth-century Europeans was not the same as with earlier Turks or Manchus; for western conquerors, who could not be beaten by the Chinese devices which lay at hand, were able, with their own industrial and commercial devices, to manipulate China to their own advantage *from a distance*. The bases of their power to perpetuate their power in China remained outside of China. They had no need to become Chinese in any degree whatever.

Hence the only recourse for a traditionally-minded Chinese, anxious to maintain Chinese autonomy by either conversion or dispersion of the foreigners, fitting them in or throwing them out, was to give up on the chances of the former,[9] and to try to develop safe new material devices to defend China by force—safe, that is, from implications of spiritual apostasy. With earlier recalcitrant foreign conquerors, like the Mongols of the thirteenth century, who were more unwilling than most to join the Chinese, the latter could not retaliate by trying to turn the secret of the Mongols' conquest against them; for their secret, the Mongols' successful technique, was nothing less than their tribal-nomadic militant way of life, and the spread of that culture at the expense of Chinese sedentary culture was just what the literati wished to preclude. (The Ming did try border horse-raising, but the ultimate Ch'ing tack was to change the *Mongol* culture, through religious and political policies aimed at pinning the Mongols down, in sedentary fashion, to permanent localities.) But while the source of Mongol military strength was thus quite obviously culturally taboo, western techniques—supposedly tame machines—could offer the illusion of exploitability. The very devices which made it unnecessary for conquerors to meet Chinese at least half-way and become a Chinese dynasty (one of the early Chinese recourses) gave Chinese the fatal vision of the other recourse, development of the means of self-defence, western learning for *yung*, a treacherous 'mere utility'.

Positivistic historians have been criticized for imagining a vain thing, that they can 'appease a new discovery by fitting it into an old world, not allowing it to transform the whole of that world'.[10] The *t'i-yung* dichotomists had just such a misconception. If a man read Mencius and an engineering manual, they felt, Mencius would speak to him just as he had to his father, who read Mencius and Tu Fu. But they were wrong, for the meaning of Mencius changed in his new context, the questions changed which Mencius was taken to answer, and the western ideas accepted as *yung* were not tame, nor dead, but dynamic. For,

> Whatever we know, we know as a whole and in its place in our whole world of experience . . . The process of knowledge is not a process of mere accretion. To speak of 'adding to knowledge' is misleading. For a gain in knowledge is always the transformation and the recreation of an entire world of ideas. It is the creation of a new world by transforming a given world. If knowledge consisted in a mere series of ideas, an addition to it could touch only the raw end . . . But, since it is a system, each advance affects retrospectively the entire whole, and it is the creation of a new world.[11]

What was the 'new world' in China? Not the Confucian intellectual world with western technical interests pasted on, but the Confucian world transformed by the western interests, the Classics paling into functional insignificance. This is the intellectual side of what we have seen already in social terms—the rise of business (historically associated with the rise of '*yung*-ian' science), under western aegis, to a point of possible rivalry with Confucian-official status. Western *yung*, embraced by literati, corrupted the literati's way of thought, ultimately sapping the fullness of their conviction of the Confucian learning's indispensability; and western *yung*, wielded by westerners, put a challenge to the literati's way of life, by encouraging a social alternative, the commercial-industrial way of life, which likewise made the Confucian learning seem more and more irrelevant—and Confucian sanctions (like those behind the family-system) more and more impossible.[12]

3. THE PHILOSOPHICAL ATTENUATION OF THE *T'I-YUNG* CONCEPT

The *t'i-yung* argument for innovation, then, suggested that the heart of Chinese civilization, its spiritual values, would be defended, not jeopardized, by Chinese 'self-strengthening' in the merely practical spheres of life where westerners had their eminence. However, this psychologically appealing formula failed to produce what it promised. No clean line could mark off a material segment of culture from a spiritual segment, and the modern *t'i-yung* dichotomy, for all its traditional Confucian pedigree, was really a cover for essential change and the waning of tradition.

But it was not simply that traditionalists, with the best of Confucian wills, used *t'i-yung* to ease a catalyst, western industrialism, into their world and thereby prepared the way for iconoclasm; there was more to the paradox than that. For *t'i-yung*, in its nineteenth-century usage, not only had Confucian breakdown as an outer consequence but Confucian breakdown in its inner core. The Confucian formula which failed to contain industrialism also failed to express an authentic Confucianism. *T'i-yung*, as Chang Chih-tung invoked it, was a vulgarization of a Sung Confucian principle. The traditionalist tried to assure himself that western machines were tame, but when the terms he used for reassurance were so strangely warped from their orthodox meanings, the ravages of western intruders were exemplified, not belied.

In the Sung neo-Confucianism of Chu Hsi which Chang implied he was perpetuating, *yung* might be described as the functional correlative of *t'i*. Both an essence and a function inhered in the single object; *t'i* and *yung* were two modes of identification of being, while the existing object of identification was one. This *t'i-yung* correlation was a fairly ordinary proposition, and one can find the sense of the neo-Confucian usage in non-Chinese philosophies. With perhaps differing degrees of stress, Goethe's definition of function as 'existence conceived in activity',[13] Whitehead's concept of functional activity ('that every actual thing is something by reason of its activity')[14] seem suggestions of *yung* as Chu Hsi understood it. And Aristotle and the great Aristotelians in effect described *t'i* when they spoke of that which is present in an individual as the cause of its being and unity,[15] or of a name —that which is signified in a definition,[16] or of the object of intuition, the scientifically undemonstrable apprehension of the intellect alone.[17] A thing *is*, and it *does*. Essence, or substance—*t'i*—inexorably implies action, or function—*yung*; and Aquinas, perhaps, was close to Chu Hsi when he wrote that a thing has a disposition towards an operation proper to the thing. '. . . no thing is lacking in its proper operation.'[18]

Chu Hsi's similar sense of the correlation between the quiddity of a thing and its proper operation is apparent in his analyses of classical Confucian qualities. For example, interpreting in a dialogue with his disciples the *Lun-yü* phrases, '*Li chih yung ho wei kuei*',[19] he treated the *yung* of the passage as establishing the functional tie of *ho*, 'harmony' or Legge's 'natural ease', to *li*, the principle of ordered human relationships. He held that *li* became manifest in the production of *ho*. The existence of *ho* was the outer test of the existence of *li* (the inner core of *li* was *ching*, 'reverence'); if *li* was really in being, the operation of *ho* was naturally, necessarily implied.[20]

This absolute naturalness of the correlation between inner essence and outer manifestation was insisted upon by Chu Hsi. Where Mencius, in listing the attributes of the great man, used the phrases, 'to dwell in the wide house of the world', 'to stand in the correct seat of the world', and 'to walk in the great path of the world',[21] Chu Hsi gave as equivalents *jen* ('human-heartedness'), *li* ('propriety'), and *i* ('right conduct'), respectively, and continued:

In the case of the first and second phrases, 'dwelling in the wide house' is *t'i*, 'standing in the correct seat' is *yung*. In the case of the second and third phrases, then 'standing in the correct sea' is *t'i*, 'walking in the great path' is *yung*. If one knows how to dwell in the wide house of the world, he naturally can stand in the correct seat of the world and walk in the great path of the world.[22]

The 'naturally' (*tzu-jan*) in this passage underscores the necessity of the tie between *t'i* and *yung*, and in this case between *jen* and *li* and *i*, the first bringing the second two in its train, since a *yung* may be also a *t'i* and have its own *yung* inevitably as a correlative. In the Mencius passage, it would seem that these qualities were cumulating to make the great man, but in the *t'i-yung* thinking of Chu Hsi the qualities were considered unequivocally not as independent and added to one another, but as interdependent and expressive of one another, inconceivable without one another.[23] Thus, *ai* ('love'), as an emotion (*ch'ing*), is the necessary projection into action—the *yung*, in short—of a human being's innate nature or predisposition (*hsing*); the innate nature which points toward *ai* is *jen*. Or, *ai* is *yung* to *jen*, one of the functional correlatives which Chu Hsi saw as implicitly bound to this particular *t'i*.[24]

This authentically neo-Confucian interpretation of *t'i-yung* was still preserved in the thought of Tseng Kuo-fan. Tseng was a powerful advocate of western technical achievement for China, along the line of reasoning to which the *t'i-yung* dichotomy would soon be misapplied; but Tseng, still an early figure in the history of Chinese westernization, reserved this terminology for his *li-hsüeh*, an attempted synthesis of Chinese philosophies, and thus kept both concepts in the realm of 'spirit' instead of allotting one to the realm of 'matter'. Tseng's *li*, as we have seen, was supposed to pervade the linked worlds of 'inner' and 'outer' and symbolize their union. Sageliness and kingliness, virtue and statesmanship were knit together in the one fabric, substance-and-function.[25]

For Tseng Kuo-fan, then, *t'i-yung* was still an orthodox, neutrally equivalent substance-and-function, not a normatively differentiated end-and-means. The idea that *yung* was *merely yung*, as means are *merely* means in relation to a cherished end, was Chang Chih-tung's ominous note of departure from the neo-Confucian world in which Tseng had still lingered. Western technology, something useful for the material defence of the home of Chinese spiritual values, was the *yung* that Chang accepted for the sake of superior *t'i*. Chu Hsi would never have recognized it.

For Chu Hsi had a word for such an instrument, a means, not end—and the word was not *yung*, but *ch'i*. Commenting on *Lun-yü* II, xii ('The master said, "The accomplished scholar [*chün-tzu*] is not a utensil [*ch'i*]" ',[26] Chu Hsi said that a *chün-tzu* had *te* ('virtue') as his *t'i* and *ts'ai* ('talent') as his *yung*. Man fell short of being a *chün-tzu* and hence remained a mere utensil (*ch'i*), when the *t'i* appropriate to a *chün-tzu* (i.e. *te*) was only approached, so that its *yung*, or manifestation in action, was incomplete.[27] With Chu Hsi, then, in this example, it was not the existence of *yung* but the *incompleteness* of *yung* that made an object, seen under these categories of *t'i* and *yung*, a utensil, means, or instrument. *Yung* here was clearly a different concept from what Chang Chih-tung made of it; it was not an equivalent of 'instrument' but a necessary antidote to instrumentalization.

Chang Chih-tung, seeking a material shield for spiritual values, told Confucianists more conservative than he that *t'i* and *yung* belonged together. To that extent, he sounded like Chu Hsi, who had once condemned the Buddhists for allegedly defending 'empty stillness' (*k'ung-chi*) or '*t'i* without *yung*', i.e. complete abstraction.[28] Chang might see himself as deriving from Chu in his activist insistence that *t'i* was not enough, that the classics *and* railroads were needed in China, but when he seemed to suggest that *t'i* and *yung* were where one found them, and that he found *t'i* in Chinese learning and *yung* in western, he showed how little the neo-Confucian logic met his case. For Chang's sum of a *t'i* from here and a *yung* from there never added up to be Chu Hsi's indivisible entity, a *t'i*—in—*yung* or *yung*—in—*t'i*. Chang was pleading for a coupling of concepts on the authority of an imprecise analogy with an earlier dichotomy, which had really referred to a natural, internal symbiosis, not to a contrived, external aggregation.

In short, Chang Chih-tung, without a conscious acknowledgment of what he was doing, changed the significance of the *t'i-yung* dichotomy in a very important way. Chu Hsi's emphasis had been metaphysical: *t'i* and *yung*, substance and function, jointly defined the one object. But Chang Chih-tung's emphasis was sociological. He was concerned not with the nature of things but the nature of cultures, and *t'i* and *yung* were separate in objective embodiment (as they were not for Chu Hsi) and fused only in mind. Man, that is, had something (Chinese) for *t'i* and something (western) for *yung*; while according to Chu Hsi, all 'somethings' had both *t'i* and *yung*.

Such, then, was Chang Chih-tung's use of an orthodox formula to characterize his effort, by a Sino-western syncretism, to preserve orthodoxy. It betrays a traditionalist's contribution to the wearing away of tradition. In fact, orthodoxy was not preserved by Chinese action taken under cover of the *t'i-yung* sanction; and an orthodoxy had to be mishandled, so that, in fancy, a belief in its preservation might still be entertained.

As an easy, conventional conceit in Chinese thinking, the prescription of Chinese spirit plus western matter has never quite lost its appeal since Chang Chih-tung expressed it in his *t'i-yung* terminology. (Some western observers, too, are still setting China to rights with a bit of easy phrase-making —e.g. 'the grafting of the new scientific culture on the old stock of literary tradition . . .') [29] But in more rigorous, formal thought, the self-destructive implications of a *t'i-yung* defence of Chinese culture were soon exposed. There were thinkers who came to hold that if there was any *t'i* involved in combination with the *yung* of western applied science, it was western pure science, and western philosophy, literature, and art, not their Chinese counterparts. Or, in a further refinement, the applied science and industrialism which were *yung* from the standpoint of scholarship were *t'i* from the standpoint of general social reform. [30] This was how the catalytic power of science and industrialism, which Chang had ignored when he asked them in to protect his spiritual heritage, came to be recognized; and the very recognition of that power was one of the latter's subversive effects.

4. REJECTION OF *T'I-YUNG* AND REJECTION OF INNOVATION: WO-JEN

The traditionalists who in the very beginning, in the middle of the nineteenth century, failed to be persuaded by the official westernizers recognized the *t'i-yung* dichotomy for what it was, a formula for self-deception about the implications of innovation. If the western learning were let loose in China, the Chinese learning would not stay safely screened off and unsullied. And if the western learning came in because the Chinese deluded themselves that there could be two separate components to a culture, the western learning would speedily end the separation and expose the delusion—the new *yung* would become also the new *t'i*.

Wo-jen (d. 1871), one of the most inflexible anti-westernizers in a position of influence in nineteenth-century China, would not defend Chinese culture by accepting western culture as a complement, a *yung* to a *t'i*; he defended it by rejecting western culture as a rival, an alternative *t'i* to the traditional one. That is why we see Wo-jen tracing the origin of western values (which others wish to admit as *yung*) to Chinese history, and saying, in effect, that they had had their chance to become Chinese *t'i* and had been rejected.

In other words, he denied any conflict or, rather, any distinction between the specially Chinese and the generally valid by alleging that all possible value-choices had already been posed and settled in Chinese history; he maintained that the Chinese inheritance was good, and that it ought to be sustained not just because of its particular 'Chinese-ness' but because of its universal rightness. His ideas accorded with comprehension that if elements of western culture were admitted, eventually the grounds for clinging to Chinese culture would seem more and more exclusively particularistic, and the *t'i-yung* rationalization, which was supposed to keep the sense of Chinese identity unspoiled by foreign mentality, would only make that vitiation certain.

Thus, while Chang Chih-tung assumed a radical separation in the conditions of origin of the western and Chinese learning, Wo-jen assumed their identity. For Chang, western learning was a foreign development, a promising candidate for Chinese acceptance as *yung*; for Wo-jen, 'western' learning was a domestic development, a discredited candidate for Chinese acceptance as *t'i*. While Chang thought western learning could be accepted as means, Wo-jen feared it would usurp

Chinese learning's prerogatives as end, and he condemned the western learning, therefore, as an end already judged and rejected in the course of Chinese history. The western scientist, in Wo-jen's view, could not be an aide to Confucius—he was a fallen angel cast out by Confucius, and the relation between them was not collaboration but struggle.

So Wo-jen emphasized the distinction, the incompatibility, between the Chinese ideal of the 'human heart' and the western ideal of 'techniques'. He explicitly disavowed any effort to bring them together as complementary partners, for the Chinese had had the techniques and had let them go. It was a disgrace, he said, for Chinese scholars to study mathematics and astronomy, and, even if this were not the case, foreign teachers should not be used, since Chinese knew as much about these subjects as anyone else.[31] He and like-minded literati delighted to maintain that ancient China had known the prototypes of that scientific learning which the westernizers so uncritically admired. Astronomy and mathematics, it was alleged, derived from the *Chou-pi suan-ching* (a book which was thought to be of Chou Dynasty authorship) and the *Ch'un-ch'iu*. Chemistry derived from the *Shu-ching*, especially the *Hung-fan* ('The great plan') section, and from the Taoist Huai Nan-tzu. The part of physics which covers problems of solids, liquids, and gases was outlined in the *K'ang-ts'ang tzu* (a book by an eighth-century Taoist, Wang Shih-yüan, though it purported to be Chou). Mineralogy was expounded in the *Shu-ching*, optics and mechanics by Mo-tzu, and electricity was explained by Kuan-yin tzu, a Taoist supposed to have been a disciple of Lao-tzu.[32]

Wo-jen's intellectual position, of course, was shaped by social considerations. When he declines to exempt western science from the ban of the conservative Chinese, one hears not Wo-jen the abstract logician speaking, but Wo-jen the head of the *Han-lin yüan*, the spokesman for the most honoured masters of the ancient learning, men whose prestige and careers depended on the discrediting of the western learning, a potential rival. It was just this social sensitivity to the cold blast at the back, perhaps, which accounts for Wo-jen's feeling for the weakness of the *t'i-yung* rationalization. The social position of the Confucian gentry-literati-officialdom was tightly linked with the intellectual pre-eminence of Confucianism; no formula, embroidered with whatever Confucian pieties, which threatened to break the Confucian intellectual monopoly could expect general support from the old bureaucracy.

All question of vested interest aside, western 'matter' could not, in fact, be broken to the service of Chinese Confucian 'spirit'. And the intellectual inadequacy of the *t'i-yung* formula as a principle for a viable syncretism is no better illustrated than by its general rejection among the pillars of the old society. For to say that Wo-jen saw the logical fallacy in the *t'i-yung* rationalization is only to say that he saw its social perils; if the literati, whose pre-eminence was as traditionally *Chinese* as the classics they guarded, were really imperilled by innovation according to a *t'i-yung* formula, a formula which ostensibly protected tradition, then the formula was illogical indeed.

In their opposition to modern technology, were literati like Wo-jen (or, for that matter, less literate poor people, like the mass of Boxers in 1900) really any different from Oxford dons with rural sympathies or Luddite labourers, deploring in their various ways the industrial revolution in nineteenth-century England? In other words, do we need to find, in and around the *t'i-yung* controversy, a constant sensitivity to cultural rivalry, a brooding awareness of alien menace to the autonomy of Chinese civilization? Perhaps it is enough to explain away the opposition to material innovation as nothing especially Chinese, nothing involving a conflict of civilizations, but as simply a local specimen of a ubiquitous type of reaction or nostalgia. And if that is so, then the cardinal avowed assumption of *t'i-yung* reasoning is sound: when western techniques are brought to China, as *yung*—no matter how much, in the natural course of events, they shock the obscurantists who are always with us, for whom novelty is always unsettling—these techniques will not compromise the individuality of the Chinese essence. If Europe was not less European for the spread of railroads, notwithstanding the fact that some Europeans lamented Arcadia or feared for their pigs, then China would not be less Chinese for the spread of railroads, the opposition of some Chinese, elegant literati or fearful peasants, equally notwithstanding.

There is, of course, a good deal of truth in this. Some of the early Chinese hostility to machines was simply a plausible reaction of pre-industrial people to the spectacle of industrialism, not necessarily a Chinese reaction to the threat of westernization. Fears were freely expressed, and not peculiarly Chinese fears, of the stimulation of social unrest by the substitution of machines for men in many occupations; and rationally conceived attacks were made on the value of railroads (e.g. scouting the claims of 'self-strengtheners' that railroads would aid the national defence, and suggesting rather that they might turn out to be royal roads for invaders), without the emotional implications of the history of railroads being allowed to intrude in the argument.[33] The existing Chinese culture was certainly due to be shaken up by modern industrialism, but western culture had been fed into the same machines in recent times and been almost indescribably transformed as well. It would seem, on the basis of this comparison, that *t'i-yung* theory should not be seen as defensive rationalization, since Chinese had no need to feel, even vaguely, that western culture was one-up.

And yet, how convincing is the answer which convincingly explains that the question never needed to be asked? The question of whether China was submitting to westernization cannot be exorcized in this way. It stubbornly existed; it *was* asked. For, even though much opposition to innovation can be accounted for in general anti-modernist terms, *defence* of innovation always did more than just meet that general protest. *T'i-yung* and other, later syncretisms, as we shall see, were Chinese apologetics (including demonstrations that Chinese need not apologize) in a dialogue with the West.

To speak of apologetics is not to suggest that Chinese thinkers, in vindicating the worth of Chinese culture against western pretensions, were saying anything untrue. What is true is no less true because apologists insist upon it. But apologists are no less apologetic because what they insist upon is true; it is the insistence that counts.

In short, we can call the *t'i-yung* rationalization a fallacy, as we have suggested, because the *yung* of modern techniques could not defend the Chinese *t'i*, as advertised, but only change society so that the old *t'i* would have a rival instead of a shield; and we can call this fallacy a rationalization, an explanation of cultural borrowing which explains away the attendant sense of indebtedness, by referring still to this 'live' quality of ostensibly dead material things. For industrialism had social implications behind it as well as before it. There had to be a proper social matrix for the inception of industrialism, and this the West had provided, never China, where the bureaucratic structure, with its anti-scientific and anti-capitalist intellectual aura, had never, like western feudalism, been undermined from within. Because the West could nurture industrialism, the shock of its change at the monster's hands was less emphatic than the Chinese shock or was absorbed, at least, with different questions asked, along with some of the same.

Both Wo-jen and Swift—to reach back for an example—could claim, each for his own culture, that experimental science was not a high traditional value. But only Wo-jen could hope to support his protest (and thus inevitably did so) by describing the eventual acceptance of this putative value as something contrived from the outside. The anti-modernist Swift, however he might decry the fact, could hardly deny that the West itself had finally hatched that wretched enthusiasm for scientific achievement; whatever else scientists had to contend with in Europe, they were necessarily spared any serious allegation, of a xenophobic nature, that science came with the stamp of alien culture. Wo-jen, however, while wryly claiming the scientific achievement, could plausibly, in the name of indigenous Chinese culture, disavow the enthusiasm. And Wo-jen's foes, who felt this enthusiasm in some measure, had to reject his disavowal and claim legitimate Chinese standing for scientific practice. The question of its foreignness could not be waved away.[34]

Thus, the widespread use of the *t'i-yung* formula in China

as an intellectual cloak for industrialization suggests that the ground had not been prepared within, in Chinese social history, for industrialization's acceptance as a value. This lack of preparation, and the social factors behind it, are the reasons for failure of material 'self-strengthening' in nineteenth-century China. Chinese officials, *t'i-yung* enthusiasts as well as sceptical conservatives, made a shambles of their modernizing efforts, by and large, even in their primary field of military power, as the Chinese fiasco in the war with Japan, 1894–5, attested.

And so *t'i-yung* was a fallacy in a twofold sense. The halting persistence of Chinese *t'i* inhibited the Chinese acceptance of *yung*, which was supposed to help the *t'i* to persist without a halt; and the grating injection of western *yung*, though it pointed to social chaos instead of to a smooth new industrial social order, doomed the indigenous social order which was the base of the Chinese *t'i*.[35] But it was not the fallacy in intellectual theory which made a mockery of social hopes; it was rather the Chinese social condition which required that some theory be devised, and which made it certain that the first one, at any rate, would promise an easy syncretism that could not be brought about.

5. REJECTION OF *T'I-YUNG* AND SEARCH FOR A NEW RATIONALIZATION: THE CLASSICAL SANCTION

Wo-jen, refusing to settle for a syncretism of Chinese ends and western means, tried to save Chinese tradition by staking everything on it. Anything, he felt, which westerners were presumptuous enough to offer and westernizers blind enough to accept as a complement to Chinese civilization had already been found wanting by that civilization; and, indeed, the latter could hardly expect to be unaffected in admitting scientific techniques, when it had taken its present spiritual form by frankly demeaning them.

Now, Wo-jen's devising of a Chinese precedent for modern western science is more familiar to us as a tactic of the opposite camp, the syncretists. No theme is more hackneyed in modern Chinese intellectual history than that of proud discovery of modern western values in pre-modern Chinese history. Chinese thinkers have found this by all odds the easiest way to acknowledge the prestige of certain western values, when they feel they must, without thereby casting reflections on Chinese history. Sun I-jang (1848–1908) for example, a traditionalist who nevertheless bowed to the persuasiveness of western science, believed, as Wo-jen did, that Mo-tzu's ideas were very close to modern conceptions of physics,[36] and Hsüeh Fu-ch'eng discoursed with pleasure on Chinese priority in astronomy, mathematics, and various inventions.[37]

When *t'i-yung* innovators resorted to this searching for precedent, they were less consistent in their reasoning than the Wo-jen school of obscurantists in two ways. First, in supporting their case for innovation by maintaining that western science was really Chinese anyway, they tripped themselves up; for their basic argument, of course, was that science, non-Chinese but manageable by Chinese, could be accepted by Chinese without embarrassment because it was merely utilitarian. And second, the miscellaneous character of the specimens which the precedent-seekers retrieved favoured the reactionaries rather than the progressives. If Chinese examples were a scattered lot, and found mainly in the odd by-ways of Chinese thought, this would be consistent with Wo-jen's assertion that they lacked value and were found out early. But when westernizers, on their side, were forced to scour Chinese history for their discoveries (some of which were obviously painfully worked-at), they had to explain away the difficulty of their search, while their opponents could rest their case on it. Why, one might ask (and nineteenth-century Chinese did so), if western ideas are commended to Chinese minds by their Chinese lineage, should this lineage be so hard to trace? If science was valuable, as the westernizers admitted, and if ancient China had known this value, as the westernizers tried to establish, then it was embarrassingly obvious that the Chinese critical faculty had become terribly dulled somewhere along the way. Why else would China in the nineteenth century have to make such a new beginning?

The *t'i-yung* rationalizers, if they diluted their reasoning with appeals to precedent, could never answer that question. And on their own proper ground, they had less feeling than the reactionaries for the ominous potentialities of western methods imported solely 'for use'. Nevertheless, although the reactionaries might well plume themselves for sensing the logical inadequacies of that particular rationalization for innovation, their conclusion—that the innovation must be stopped, rather than the rationalization changed—was unsound. For they were obscurantist in failing to realize that innovation was inevitable, and that some rationalization, logical or not, was a psychological necessity. This may not have been crystal-clear in the eighteen-sixties, when stand-patters like Wo-jen were harrying 'self-strengtheners' like Tseng Kuo-fan, whose premises Chang Chih-tung was later to systematize. But by the eighteen-nineties, after years of bitter lessons, it was hard to deny that drastic changes, under foreign auspices if not Chinese, were on the way for China.

Among those who saw this clearly were the late nineteenth-century reformers of the *chin-wen* ('modern text') school of K'ang Yu-wei (1858–1927), who undertook to attain the goal of the *t'i-yung* school—westernization with honour—while avoiding the basic fallacy in the *t'i-yung* formula. The *chin-wen* school made no attempt to separate *t'i* from *yung* (and thereby doom China to the drain of Chinese *t'i* into western *yung*) but tried, rather, to link *t'i* and *yung* in the Chinese learning. The reformers would not leave the Chinese learning alone as *t'i*, with nothing of *yung* about it, and thereby condemn it; they would rather reinvigorate it, making the values of the modern West not a complement to the Chinese tradition but an integral part of it. In short, K'ang Yu-wei would keep western values (which Wo-jen would not do), but would find them *inside* Confucianism (which Chang Chih-tung would not do).

Instead of saying, like the obscurantists, that Chinese tradition should dispense with western values, or saying, like the *t'i-yung* school, that Chinese tradition should be supplemented with western values, the *chin-wen* school said that

Chinese tradition should possess western values. And it does possess them, said the *chin-wen* reformers, as the Chinese would realize if they only went back to their *authentic* Confucianism, which had long and sadly been under eclipse.

CHAPTER V

The Chin-Wen *School*
and the Classical Sanction[1]

I. NEW VALUES INJECTED INTO CHINESE HISTORY: K'ANG YU-WEI

ALTHOUGH K'ang's reformers believed as little as the obscurantists that a Sino-western civilization would be cleanly partitioned between Chinese essence and western utility, they shared with the official westernizers of the *t'i-yung* school a willingness to proceed towards some such civilization. Indeed, they improved on that willingness. On the spectrum of attitudes toward westernization in nineteenth-century China, *chin-wen* stood as a mean not between implacable anti-westernizers and *t'i-yung* Confucian officialdom, but between the latter and the Protestant missions.[2]

The officials saw themselves as padding their civilization, a pearl of great price, with useful western ideas. China was still alone, they felt, in possessing intrinsic value. The missionaries, however, while perfectly ready to spread useful ideas, were far from ready to accept these Chinese strictures on the culture of the West as a whole. Religious missionaries, after all, could hardly agree that the West was simply materialistic, that practical techniques were the only respectable products of western history. If Confucian officials disparaged western values in the non-material sphere, Christian educators returned the compliment. Not only science, they insisted, but western political and ethical values must come into China and displace their Chinese counterparts.

Between these two groups, there stood the reformers. Before their brief moment of political influence in the summer of 1898, when they prepared decrees for the Emperor to issue (and the Empress-dowager soon to rescind), they conducted school and study-projects neither official nor Christian, though some aid came to them from both those quarters.[3] The reformers disparaged neither the western spirit nor the Chinese spirit, but prized them both and tried to believe them identical. Intellectually alienated from much of what passed for Chinese ideals, yet invincibly Chinese themselves, they strained to establish that mind and heart, in spite of appearances, had not been divided in China by the meeting of East and West.

The reformers, it must be apparent, had more disaffection to explain away than had the liberal, *t'i-yung* officials. The latter, in their confidence of the value and staying-power of the 'essentials' of Chinese civilization, were only a shade less complacent than the outright reactionaries. Old school modernizers felt simply that China was weak; and the weakness was only relative to an evil western strength. But once they had taken 'self-strengthening' to be a Chinese ideal, properly Chinese because supposedly harmless to the Chinese essence, the essence itself became subject to criticism if it seemed to inhibit the programme designed to protect it. And so a younger generation, no more anxious than their elders to break the tie of history, but even more sorely troubled by the gathering wave of disasters, diplomatic and military, which China suffered in the later nineteenth century, came to a paradoxical conclusion: to preserve the Chinese spirit, they must change the spirit as well as the tools of their Chinese civilization. Even before the *chin-wen* school became influential, this necessity had come to be dimly seen. As early as 1878, Kuo Sung-tao (1818–91), the first Chinese minister to England, had observed that overseas students from Japan seemed to be emphasizing political over scientific studies; and he fluttered the ranks of his staid official contemporaries by suggesting that there was more to *yung* than ships and soldiers, and that self-strengthening might have to apply to the Chinese polity (which was presumably an expression of the Chinese spirit) as well as to the world of base material techniques.[4]

The only way in which the reformers could reconcile their traditionalism with their condemnation of the Chinese way of life was to strip from the latter its cloak of tradition. China was not only somehow weak, they felt, but somehow wrong. To escape the consequences of this admission, they tried to show that it was not the genuine principles of Chinese culture which were wrong. These had been perverted, distorted, or suppressed. And if these true principles were asserted again, China could have what the West had, and still be true to itself. The values which the missionaries saw as the issue of European progress and Christian faith, K'ang Yu-wei would make Chinese.

All Chinese traditionalists, whatever their opinions on westernization, had to agree that Confucius was the sage of Chinese culture, and Confucianism its very essence. But if the tables could be turned on the self-deceptive, ostensibly Confucian despisers of the West, and contemporary Chinese culture be described as un-Confucian, then innovations in a wholesale measure, by no means simply in the material sphere, might not discredit the Chinese essence but make for its rediscovery. Accordingly, when K'ang recommended sweeping changes in Chinese society, he presented his views in three great works of Confucian exegesis. In the *Hsin-hsüeh wei-ching k'ao* (On the false classics of the Hsin learning), he challenged the authenticity of certain texts of the Confucian canon (especially the *Tso-chuan*), texts which he wished to see superseded by others more 'exploitable' (especially the *Kung-yang chuan*, one of two long-overshadowed alternatives to the *Tso-chuan* as the key to the meaning of the *Ch'un-ch'iu*, the 'Spring and Autumn Annals'). In the *K'ung-tzu kai-chih k'ao* (On Confucius as a reformer), he drew on his revised Confucian canon to interpret Confucius as a progressive, not a conservative, in his own day. And in the *Ta-t'ung shu* (Book of the great harmony), he made Confucius the prophet of progress to a utopian Confucian future, towards which the West, with its modern values, was also on its way. K'ang set a course for Chinese history in the stream of western optimism, and he called it a Chinese stream. When K'ang, building on the foundation of the 'Han learning' of the seventeenth and eighteenth centuries, seemed to discredit the *ku-wen* ('ancient text') classics of the orthodox Confucian canon, among which the *Tso-chuan* was included, as forgeries by Liu Hsin (d. 23 B.C.), and when he heavily over-interpreted the early Han *chin-wen* ('modern text') classics like the *Kung-yang chuan* ('Kung-yang school' and '*Chin-wen* school' were familiarly interchangeable tags) which he believed he had rehabilitated, all the impressive western values fell into their Chinese places.[5] And science, the twin of progress, was a special favourite which would make the Gobi a part of China, the mountain-top a city, and banish the pains of illness and of toil.[6] Here was no foreign-spawned, patronizingly accepted *yung*, but the life's-blood of a professedly Confucian system.

2. PASSING OF THE *CHIN-WEN* SANCTION

Another eclectic utopian, inspired by the visions of K'ang Yu-wei, was T'an Ssu-t'ung, one of the 'six martyrs' to the reform movement who died in September, 1898, after the 'hundred days of reform'. T'an attempted to syncretize Christianity, the Buddhism of the *Hua-yen* (Lotus) Sutra, and *chin-wen* Confucianism. If man approached social questions with Christian love—in its Chinese form *jen-hsin*, benevolence—then the 'great peace' envisaged in the *chin-wen* school's favourite classic text, the *Kung-yang chuan*, would come into being, with freedom and equality, no differentiation between peoples, and no separation of nations from one another.[7] Like K'ang, T'an leaned a bit to the Chinese side in his universalism, and in the *Jen-hsüeh* (Study of benevolence), T'an's major work, he saw an all-encompassing Buddhism leading the way to unification of the world's religions, and the ancient *ching-t'ien* or 'well-field' idea doing the same for the world's polities, and the non-phonetic Chinese script, which could be all sounds to all men, making for a single world of learning.[8]

In this work, T'an set up a striking parallel between western and Chinese histories. The Papacy killed Christianity in the West, he said, and Luther revived it. Confucianism, done to death in China by the false scholarship of authoritarians, needed a Luther, too.[9] This suggestion that the Chinese reformers had had their western counterparts recurred frequently in reformist writings, and Liang Chi'-ch'ao, in his biographical tribute to K'ang written in 1901, expressed it with simple clarity: 'My teacher is the Martin Luther of Confucianism.' [10]

But the invocation of K'ang as the Chinese Luther was an ambiguous argument, which the *chin-wen* Confucian reformers pointed first at their conservative opponents, and then turned in on themselves. On the one hand, it supported metaphorically the essential position of the *chin-wen* school; for, as Luther claimed to be only restoring the pure Christianity of the Gospels and the Fathers, which had long been distorted by its self-styled representatives, so K'ang could maintain that he, also, had cut through the fog of centuries and restored the doctrine of the real Confucius of the earliest days. And if K'ang's Confucius, the prophet of progess, was the genuine article, then the fruits of progress, which had seemed to be solely western fruits, could spring from the roots of Chinese tradition.

But, on the other hand, the K'ang-Luther analogy could suggest the equivalence of China to Europe in quite a different manner. Instead of forcing the Chinese to contemplate western success, and to find its principle, through tortuous reasoning, in an 'authentic' Chinese past, it could lead him to dwell on western failure, the age of darkness before Luther came, and to feel that China, not unrespectably, develops in parallel fashion. In other words, there need be less emphasis on Chinese deviation from the right way and more on the Chinese advance towards it, an advance which Europeans, with their own dark ages, had been forced to make painfully, too. And K'ang could be a Chinese Luther, not as a rediscoverer of an ancient truth, but as a hero of freedom of thought, who breaks the grip of a smothering, mindless orthodoxy.[11]

This analogy of stages of progress remained, when the

classical sanction lost its force, to cover a Chinese sacrifice of traditional Chinese values. If the West had once been benighted like China, and 'Reformation' and 'Renaissance' were all that were asked of China, then there was an implication of parallel histories and of China redeemed from the tense conflict of special Chinese attachments and the force of generally compelling ideas. Neither intellectually stubborn, out of concern for the dignity of Chinese history, nor flatly submissive to Europe, China could grow into modern times with self-respect. The idea of progress was both a break with conventional Confucian conceptions and a means of explaining the break away.

T'an died before the doctrine of social progress—with Confucian orders to that effect no longer being relevant—was clearly extracted from the *chin-wen* reasoning. And K'ang, as long as he lived, never lost his *chin-wen* convictions: that the stages of progress were Confucian stages, and that the values of progress, modern values, were really values because the sage had once conceived them. But with Liang we see Confucianism trailing off to its twentieth-century ruin; for he comes to accept the second meaning of the K'ang-and-Luther analogy, and insists that what China needs, and can have with no indignity, is *not* a commitment to a pure Confucianism, but a break with it.[12]

Historical evolution, in the basic principle of the *chin-wen* Confucianists, was a universal progress from the 'age of chaos' (as Confucius called it) to the 'great peace' or the 'great harmony'. Confucius, it seemed, had licensed China to listen to new ideas. But the new ideas were so many, and so clearly subversive of the stable Confucian society, that it soon was merely fanciful for moderns to claim the Confucian imprimatur.

And so the classical sanction seemed only for a moment to deny the conflict between home and the world in modern China. But it gave a new direction to the Chinese search for a formula which might succeed. Since Confucianism could neither exclude nor absorb western ideas, since neither *t'i-yung* nor *chin-wen* could really save the Chinese *t'i*, then Chinese thinkers must cease to feel that equivalence with the

West was staked on it. And a new possible defence for China, a new sanction for innovation, could be salvaged from the *chin-wen* doctrine. For if evolution is the way of the world, as the *chin-wen* school had taught, an ancient *t'i* is properly superseded. Men may turn, if they lose the heart to compare the values of Europe and China, to comparing their histories, and see a morphological analogy between the life of China and the life of the West. These may seem to evolve with similar sequences, as the dismal stages of their pasts are succeeded by stages to a brighter future, as their bondage to intellectual orthodoxies gives way to intellectual freedom.

CHAPTER VI

The Modern Ku-wen Opposition, Reactionary and Revolutionary, to Chin-wen Reformism

I. THE REACTIONARY *KU-WEN* ATTACK

THE *chin-wen* school, as its name indicates, was not eclectic in the field of Chinese choices. Though even more aware of western incursions than Tseng Kuo-fan had been, the reformers failed to respond as he did, and, far from burying an ancient domestic intellectual conflict, they revived it. Han dynasty scholarship had finally accepted the so-called *ku-wen* Classics as the really authentic texts, and the rival *chin-wen*, in the third century A.D., went into eclipse. The Han Learning of the early Ch'ing, to a large extent, reversed this judgment, and K'ang Yu-wei, for his generation, kindled the conflict anew.

Yet, K'ang's truculence was not inconsistent with the peaceable eclecticism of Tseng Kuo-fan. For Tseng saw the West as a common rival of all the Chinese schools, and meant to distinguish the West from China as matter is distinguished from spirit. But K'ang had no hopes of separation, and preferred to see peace between civilizations, with the West and China sharing common values. With peace abroad, a battle at home was possible. And for a semblance of peace abroad, a battle at home was necessary. Orthodox Confucianism of

86

the *ku-wen* school could never appear to shelter western values.

It was the need to accommodate western values, then, which impelled the reformers to revive the *chin-wen* scholarship. Since that was the case, since the reformers' scholarship was hardly 'pure', it was impervious to attack by the pure scholarship of *ku-wen* conservatives. When the classical sanction faded, when Chinese rebels ceased protesting that Confucius was their master, it was not the *ku-wen* scholars who effected that development. For the issues now were not the same as in the *ku-wen–chin-wen* conflicts of earlier centuries. Social facts, not textual critics, were the damaging antagonists of the modern *chin-wen* school.

The serious question for these latter-day *chin-wen* scholars was whether their doctrine was really compatible with western experience. They had seized on the *chin-wen* scholarship not as simple Confucianists, who wanted only to know the truth about what their sage had said; they had acted rather as westernizers, for whom the *chin-wen* doctrine *had* to be true if they were to be Confucianists at all. Western values possessed the younger minds, and the harder they found it to cram their new knowledge into K'ang's Confucianism, the less they cared about any Confucius, either the one who spoke through the *ku-wen* texts or the one who spoke through the *chin-wen*.

Thus, when the reactionary *ku-wen* traditionalists attacked the reformers on textual grounds, they were engaging in an irrelevant battle. 'Irrelevant' does not mean unsound. On textual issues, for assertions such as these—that Confucius composed the Six Classics, that Liu Hsin forged the *Tsochuan*—the *chin-wen* scholarship was certainly open to grave indictment.[1] But K'ang's mistakes were more important than other men's corrections, and the indictment had no significance for future Chinese history. For the *ku-wen* critics never answered the real question which the *chin-wen* school was asking: not, 'What does Confucius say?' but, 'How can we make ourselves believe that Confucius said what we accept *on other authority?*'

Therefore, although the lines were drawn as at earlier

times, there was an air of unreality about the textual conflict. For *chin-wen* Confucianism was a different idea before
and after the western invasion of China. And a hostile *ku-wen*
argument, which might have been telling against an eighteenth-century *chin-wen* scholar of the Han Learning, was an
answer later to a dead question. The Confucian canon was
simply not the issue. Liang Ch'i-ch'ao attested to this in 1902,
when he abruptly ceased, in his reformist writings, to exhort
his readers to care about the Classics.[2] And the keener members of the *ku-wen* camp realized this as well. Yeh Te-hui
(1864–1927), brushing past the question of what Confucius
said, seized quite certainly on what K'ang meant, though
K'ang himself was always in the dark:

K'ang Yu-wei, secretly proposing to be a 'reforming Luther'
in his own life, desired to clear away the Six Classics, and
composed first the *Wei-ching k'ao*; and he desired to stir up the
imperial regime, and went on to compose the *Kai-chih k'ao*.[3]

2. THE REVOLUTIONARY *KU-WEN* ATTACK

The *chin-wen* school was reformist in political action, never
anti-dynastic, and it blamed Chinese for distortion of the
genuine Chinese tradition. But other dissidents in the last
years of the empire were revolutionaries. For them, the
Manchu usurpers of Chinese power were fair game, in cultural attacks as well as political. If it had to be acknowledged
that the contemporary West, intellectually and politically,
was far in advance of China, the blame could be heaped on
the Manchus, and the Chinese spared.[4]

Therefore, anti-Manchu revolutionary nationalists had no
need to arraign Confucian 'heretics' for Chinese ills and
every reason to consider that K'ang's diagnosis was counter-
revolutionary. In his *Po K'ung-chiao i* (Refutation of the
'Confucian Religion'), Chang Ping-lin (1868–1936), a viru-
lently anti-Manchu revolutionary, skilfully defended the *ku-
wen* Classics against the *chin-wen* textual criticism.[5]

Yet, though *ku-wen* scholarship may seem proper in revolutionary circles, as a symbol of the denial of reformism, the
great majority of *ku-wen* scholars were consistent conserva-

tives, whose loyalty to the orthodox *ku-wen* canon was an affirmation of the *status quo*; and there was a peculiar complexity about Chang Ping-lin's position. For he came by his *ku-wen* opinions honestly, as a cultural conservative himself, defending the old literary style and the traditional materials of the old imperial examinations.[6] He was an important contributor to the Shanghai monthly *Kuo-sui hsüeh-pao* (1904–11), which defended the Chinese cultural heritage against the 'European wind and American rain', the storm of western ideas, and inveighed against 'ignorant, illiterate self-styled scholars' who puffed up the West and contemned China.[7] He did not derive his conservative views in classical scholarship from his revolutionary political views. He seems, rather, to have derived the latter from his concern to save the 'Chinese essence'. And in this, he parted company with most of his fellow traditionalists.

He saw more clearly than they that change must come to the Chinese scene; and if traditionalism was not to be sentimentality alone, and intellectually indefensible, he must hold, he knew, a rational theory which would keep the Chinese past from seeming discredited by the change. But he was wrong to think that Manchu-baiting was a serviceable theory in the twentieth century. It could seem to protect the reputation of traditional Chinese culture, but it would help to end its existence.

For the institution of the monarchy, the ultimate target of the anti-Manchu revolutionary movement, was as traditionally Chinese as Confucianism itself. The *chin-wen* school, it is true, in attacking the accepted Confucian canon, was culturally subversive, opening the way for cultural drift; when the Classics could be doubted, anything could be doubted. But it was hardly striking a blow for tradition to reject the *chin-wen* heresy and to spare the Classics by condemning the throne. When the imperial system could be doubted, anything could be doubted. Who could be sure of any rule, when almost the oldest rule of all was broken?

My older uncle was drunk, and angry about the revolution most of the time. . . . He would stare at the relatives, and say ironically: 'But, excuse me, we have the revolution.

What difference does it make who is the oldest in the family?
What can I have to do with the marriage of my brother,
Tan Tsi-pu?' [8]

3. THE CLASSICS AND HISTORY

In the last analysis, did Chang Ping-lin even spare the Classics? He felt that he did, of course, as he reaffirmed the
authenticity of the *ku-wen*, orthodox canon and proclaimed
his respect for the Han scholar, Liu Hsin, whom K'ang Yu-
wei and his *chin-wen* followers had vilified as the arch-
forger.[9] The *ku-wen* Classics, Chang loyally insisted, were *history*, not fiction, and *history*, not elliptical, mystical prophecy
—as the Classics became in the rival interpretation. The
Kung-yang chuan, the central text for the *chin-wen* school,
which chose it in preference to the *Tso-chuan*, was philosophically exegetical in character and bore little obvious relation to any course of events; but the *Tso-chuan* was formally
an historical narrative.[10]

'The Classics are all abstract ⸳⸳⸳ds and not real history',
said Liao P'ing (1852–1932), the last and perhaps most
fanciful of the *chin-wen* Confucianists, who revered Confucius
as a visionary, not as a scrupulous traditionalist.[11] Liao
P'ing considered the Classics so far from history that he
treated the *Ch'un-ch'iu* not at all as it appeared, a chronicle
of the ancient state of Lu, but as a vision of the modern world,
with Cheng standing for China, Ch'in for England, Lu for
Japan, and Duke Ai of Lu for the Emperor Meiji.[12] But,
'The Six Classics are all history', Chang countered,[13] deploring (as orthodox scholars had done since later Han times)
chin-wen invocation of Han apocrypha, the esoteric *wei-shu*, as
keys to the Classics' alleged character of prophetic revelation.[14] He scouted the *chin-wen* claim that Confucius composed (not transmitted) the original Classics, and even the
Ch'un-ch'iu, he said, the 'Spring and Autumn Annals', the
one Classic which all Confucianists had always ascribed to
Confucius himself, was not constructed by Confucius *de novo*
but based on the records of Tso Ch'iu-ming, the historian
of Lu.[15]

'*Liu ching chieh shih*', 'The Six Classics are all history.' . . . A traditionalist in so many things, Chang was traditional in his choice of words: this phrase was not his own. And yet, however little he willed it, when Chang Ping-lin repeated these words of Chang Hsüeh-ch'eng (1738–1801),[16] he made them part of the history of the dissipation of Confucianism. For *ching* and *shih*, the Classics and history, had a delicately adjusted relationship in traditional Chinese thought, and what one said about them in earlier times, even if later it was literally repeated, had a different ring in the different modern context.

The study of history had been the most characteristic Confucian intellectual activity. 'Among all branches of scholarly investigation, only in history is China developed to the utmost; among all countries of the world, only in China is history developed to the utmost'—thus Liang Ch'i-ch'ao, with some rhetorical licence, has emphasized the paramount importance of historical thinking in Chinese culture.[17] But this thinking was concerned typically not with process but with permanence, with the illustration of the fixed ideals of the Confucian moral universe. Su Hsün (1009–66), father of the famous poet, painter, and statesman, Su Shih (1036–1101), expressed it very well. How do *shih* and *ching*, he asked, history and the Classics, differ?

Ching stresses the underlying Way and fixed principles (*tao* and *fa*); *shih*, facts and words. Without assimilating history to itself (*te shih*), the classical canon cannot make evident its [standards of] praise or blame; without assimilating the Classics to itself, history cannot decide its course of appreciation and disparagement. A Classic is not a matter-of-fact record of a particular age, and history is not a changeless design for all generations. Different in essence, they are actually supplementary in function.[18]

History, then, by this reckoning, is a record from which a universal, timeless, abstract morality is distilled from particular, temporal, material events. The classical canon is the respository of those abstract principles which make such a reading of history possible. Su Hsün, whose treatise on this subject was in the form of inquiry into the nature of history, obviously had to call *shih* and *ching* correlative, not identical: not all histories were Classics. But if the nature of the Classics had been his point of departure, as it was later for Chang Hsüeh-ch'eng in discussing this relationship, Su Hsün would have found 'The Six Classics are all history' an admissible statement. For he, no less than Chang Hsüeh-ch'eng, saw the Classics as eternal principles *made manifest*, in action (history), not couched in 'empty words'. The idea of *shih* was indispensable to the idea of *ching*; and the idea of *ching*, as the ancient fountain-head of critical judgment—and not, therefore, subject to its appraisal—was indispensable to Confucian intellectual life. Before the twentieth century, to call the Classics history was never construed as a limitation on the Classics, but as philosophical description.

History, then, in the pre-western Confucian context, was regarded without ambiguity; it was the form in which absolute wisdom was cast, and not yet the clothing of relativism. Accordingly, Chang Hsüeh-ch'eng, in the eighteenth century, was not reducing the Classics to 'historical significance' (in the modern relativist terminology) when he emphasized their historical character, but was defining the way in which eternal truth was conveyed. The *tao* cannot be abstracted from its material realization, he said, and Confucius could not state in words the '*tao* of the ancient kings' but could only illustrate it through their history and their documents.[19] The Classics were made of historical material, but the Classics themselves were not simply materials for the history of an age; they were texts for the ages.[20]

In a day when that conviction of the permanent significance of the Classics went virtually unchallenged in Chinese intellectual circles (whatever the quarrels about exegesis), the problem of Classics and history could be taken up without calling into question the canonical character of Classics. Chang Hsüeh-ch'eng affirmed it; and Kung Tzu-chen (1792–1841), who was attracted to *chin-wen* opinions and appropriately, therefore, attacked Chang for his 'Six Classics are all history' pronouncements,[21] affirmed it, too. But when K'ang Yu-wei took up the *chin-wen* thesis and freighted it with western values, which then slipped out of their Confucian casing and openly won adherents·on their own, the old counter-cry, that the Classics were history, was worse than ineffectual in restoring classical loyalties—it compounded the damage *chin-wen* claims had done them. For, once there was .a readiness to listen to foreign voices, without concern for their qualifications by any Confucian standards, the Classics-history equation assumed an ominous ambiguity. If the Classics were not supreme arbiters in modern times, they were not for the ages; and to say, then, that the Classics were history was not to fix their character in eternity, since their title to eternity was spurious. It was, instead, to pin the Classics to the age of their composition, that age alone, and to read them rather as documentation of a stage of a history in process of change, than as final truths which were anciently established and immanent in events and which thereby divested the idea of history of the very connotation of process.

Chang Ping-lin in his later years bitterly conceded that the Classics had been reduced from persistent guide to historical source, that they could no longer be taken to dominate men throughout time, but had to submit instead to the scrutiny of men who allowed them only one time in history. The modern *chin-wen* scholarship, he said, though dying itself in the republican era, had been the fatal source of a still increasing corruption. The veracity of the ancient records had been impugned, such classical figures as Yao, Shun, and Yü were all supposed to have been invented by Confucian scholars, and the Chinese people were forgetting their origins.[22]

Thus Chang held that the great heresy was the denial, by *chin-wen* Confucianists and their inevitable successors, the emancipated non-Confucianists, that the Classics told historical truths; and he, still proclaiming that the Six Classics were all history, was the lonely defender of the faith. In thinking this, he separated himself a bit too clearly from the modern Confucian debacle. For Ku Chieh-kang (b. 1893), a young scholar in the nineteen-twenties who exemplified the heresy, set himself to demonstrate that the Classics, to a large extent, had been contrived by controversialists to express their own ideas, religious and political, and not to render honestly the actual history of ancient China;[23] and Ku confessed a debt to Chang Ping-lin. True, he confessed a debt to K'ang Yu-wei as well.[24] Thus Chang, who had meant to annihilate K'ang, was harried into his company. Their classical theories must have been given a new construction indeed.

Chang Ping-lin and K'ang Yu-wei, the *ku-wen* and *chin-wen* Confucian champions, had milled around an old field—and both had lost the war. Their positive contentions went unheeded; what the post-Confucianists found in both was a negative value. Ku Chieh-kang was inspired by K'ang to see in the classical canon a tendentious myth-making spirit, where an objective historical spirit had been imagined. But, unlike K'ang and the *chin-wen* school, Ku did not propose to criticize 'false Classics' in order to peel down to 'true Classics' of timeless transcendent importance. K'ang's *chin-wen* predecessor, Kung Tzu-chen, who 'read the Classics for their "great principle" ', had protested that *ch'uan-ch'i*, tales of fiction, ought not to be called *ching*, Classics;[25] and while Ku Chieh-kang could appreciate this eye for forgeries, he rejected the implication that somewhere underneath lay an irreducible stratum of supra-historical truth.[26] That is where Chang Ping-lin came in to contribute to Ku's unorthodox detachment. For, while K'ang was right, thought Ku, in pointing out that the accepted Classics, by and large, were doubtful history, Chang was right in suggesting, nevertheless, that the Classics *were* history of a sort, rich though sometimes recalcitrant sources of real data about ancient China, not prophetic texts of a binding religious nature. The *ku-wen* school had won a faded laurel—the Classics were all history, all right—but (to put it another way) the Classics were not classics any more.

CHAPTER VII

The Role of Nationalism in the Disowning of the Past

I. THE ATTACK ON THE MANCHUS

WHEN nationalism swept the Chinese student world, in the first years of the twentieth century, inevitably the Manchus felt the blast of hatred. They were such obvious targets, and on two counts—as usurpers of the Chinese power, and as rulers of China in a bleak age of national degradation. But anti-Manchu feeling was only an effect of nationalism, only a manifestation, not its cause or its core.

The cause of Chinese nationalism, and the core of its content, was intellectual alienation from traditional Chinese culture.[1] Nationalism, as a meaningful concept on the Chinese scene, had not only a positive but a negative significance; in accepting the nation as the proper object of Chinese loyalty, the nationalist rejected the historic alternative, the 'culturalistic' reverence for the 'Chinese way of life', above and beyond all other loyalties. Theoretically, nationalists were free to make any intellectual choice, however unorthodox in terms of Chinese culture, if only it were nationally useful. Chinese civilization lags extraordinarily, European civilization must be adopted—such was the burden of a memorial, in 1894, to the powerful senior official, Li Hung-chang, from the *Hsing Chung hui*, the first political society of the nationalist, Sun Yat-sen.[2]

By the twentieth century, the Manchus were almost

impervious to attack on a culturalistic basis, for they had become the champions of the Chinese way of life. In the seventeenth century they may have seemed to pose a cultural threat to China (though in fact, even by the time of the conquest, in 1644, their Chinese education was far advanced). But as time passed, western culture became the only dangerous alternative. What survived of Manchu cultural peculiarities was mainly contrived, prescribed to keep the Manchus alive and distinct enough to enjoy the power which their cultural deference in larger matters had helped to preserve for them;[3] as long as the Manchus were anti-western Chinese culturalists could rally around the Ch'ing. And where their predecessors had flaunted the slogan, '*Fu Ming, mieh Ch'ing*' (uphold the Ming, destroy the Ch'ing), the 'Boxers' of 1900, xenophobic and culturalistic, rose to the cry, '*Fu Ch'ing, mieh yang*' (uphold the Ch'ing, destroy the foreigner).[4]

Thus, the Manchu cause and the traditional cause had become the same. But there was a brand of Chinese traditionalists, not sublimely confident, like the Boxers, but defeatist, like Chang Ping-lin, who chose to believe that the Ch'ing had thwarted the Chinese genius. It was a straw to clutch at, something to keep them from sweeping along to either cold iconoclasm or arid traditionalism. And so, as a gesture of respect for Chinese culture, they called themselves nationalists, and they re-issued, as supposedly nationalistic fare, seventeenth-century, long-outmoded culturalistic invectives against the Manchus.[5]

Chang condemned K'ang Yu-wei's invocation of a *Shih-chi* passage to indicate the allegedly common ancestry of the Chinese and the ancient Hsiung-nu (by extension, 'men of the north', Manchus). Chang accepted neither the Manchu —Hsiung-nu identification nor the Hsiung-nu—Chinese. And he rejected K'ang's Ch'ing—Ch'u analogy, whereby Ming-period Manchus and *Ch'un-ch'iu* people of Ch'u— racially akin to the Chinese, supposedly, but still culturally barbarian—were completely sinified in Ch'ing times and Han times, respectively. K'ang had hoped to score a point here, since the very founder of the Han dynasty, that first great imperial line which gave its name to the Chinese people for all subsequent generations, was a man of Ch'u. But Chang, on the one hand, was impossible to persuade that Han emperors and Ch'ing emperors had the same relation to the Chinese people they came to rule; and, on the other hand, he was unwilling to accept the Han—even if this imperial parallel could have been constructed—as *bona fide* patrons of the genuine Chinese spirit. He tried to give a racist interpretation of early Confucianism and claimed (for all the world like his *chin-wen* opponents, pushing another thesis) that China had lost *true* comprehension of the *Ch'un-ch'iu* in the Han period, when the racially exclusive national idea was filtered out of Confucianism, and foreigners like the future Manchus were authorized to sun themselves in the light of mistaken Confucian universality.[6]

Yet, right or wrong, the version of Confucius which had really mattered to China throughout her imperial history was a Confucius who distinguished between barbarism and barbarians; the former was irredeemably rejected, the latter —because men were educable—it was possible to redeem. Chang's racist attack on the Ch'ing dynasty of Manchus, who had long ago made the grade as a Chinese dynasty by the traditional cultural, if not the revolutionary national criterion of Chinese-ness, was no vindication of the Chinese past, but repudiation.

Rigorous nationalists like Liang Ch'i-ch'ao, who since 1902 had been proclaiming the need for a 'new people', opposed the specious nationalism of the easy anti-Manchus, for the latter seemed to proclaim (or their conclusions tended to encourage the belief) that the old people was good enough, if only the Manchu incubus could be taken off its neck. Therefore, although the ruin of the Manchus was certain if nationalism spread, as Liang intended it should, he refused to accept his own anti-Manchu conclusions, because the 'official', republican anti-Manchu appeared to reject his premises. Nevertheless, the new state, the republic of 1912, belongs in the history of the new people. Chang Ping-lin was iconoclastic and Liang was revolutionary, each in spite of himself.

2. CULTURALISM AND NATIONALISM AS COMPETITORS FOR LOYALTY

When nationalism began to flourish in Chinese intellectual circles in the earliest years of the twentieth century, it represented a bold attempt to sweep away the cant which had become all too obvious in the usual apologia for Chinese tradition. The dilemma posed by intellectual alienation from tradition and emotional tie to it still existed. But the nationalist dispensed with the effort to end the dilemma by somehow justifying Chinese tradition. He still hoped to establish the cultural equivalence of China with the West; but his ingenious way of accomplishing this was to deny that culture was the proper unit of comparison.

That unit was the nation. When the Confucian efforts of the *chin-wen* school subsided, and yielded the figure of 'parallel histories' for the syncretist to work with, the Chinese nation became his first concern. The ideas of progress and freedom of thought were his new possessions, but these, by themselves, were useless to guide him in intellectual choice. 'Progress to what, thought about what?' he must ask, before tampering with the Chinese tradition. To what end should change take place?

The end of change, he must answer, is the strengthening of the nation. For if the nation, not the culture, has the highest claim on the individual, then the abandonment of traditional values, if they seem to be indefensible, is a cheerful duty, not a painful wrench. And the laws of evolution, not Confucian now but social-Darwinist, exalt the nation as the highest unit in the struggle for existence, and proclaim that the past must die and should never be lamented.[7] The growing Chinese acceptance of the existence and authority of a Chinese nation worked a Nietzschean 'transvaluation of values' in Chinese culture.

We have seen that in the seventeenth century, Chinese had criticized the dominant metaphysics of the day without being philosophically revolutionary in their criticism. They had been critics also of the state of contemporary society, but here, too, as social critics, they were thoroughly Confucian: men had strayed from the fixed ideals of Chinese civilization. Their China was a world, a *t'ien-hsia*, in which traditional values claimed authority. But in the early twentieth century, anti-Confucian critics of the Chinese *status quo* traced disaster not to the flouting of fixed ideals but to blind and slavish respect for them, to the fixity itself; their China was a nation, a *kuo*, in which traditional values were impugned as tyranny.

This changing fortune of a civilization, this vast and perplexing history, was caught in miniature in the changing relation between the concept *t'ien-hsia* and the concept *kuo*. *T'ien-hsia* and *kuo* were time-honoured co-ordinates in Chinese political thinking. And co-ordinates they remained, while ever-increasingly heirs to Chinese history called its values into question.

T'ien-hsia signifies 'the (Chinese) Empire'—alternatively, 'the world'; as *t'ien-hsia*, China *is* the world. And *kuo* is a local political unit, a part of 'the Empire' in classical times, and in the modern world, 'the nation'. But the respective meanings of *t'ien-hsia* and *kuo* are not really revealed in these simple, self-sufficient English equivalents; for at either end of this history, the definition of either term implies a reference to the other, a comparison with the other. In the earlier time it was its contrast with *kuo*, the regime of power, which defined the *t'ien-hsia* as the regime of value. But the claims of value are absolute, and if their justice comes to be doubted, respect for these claims will seem the mark of servility, not civilization. It was its contrast, then, with *t'ien-hsia*—preconception, dictation—which defined the *kuo*, at the later date, as an area of untraditional free inquiry. Just as China persists but changes, the link between *t'ien-hsia* and *kuo* persists while something changes their connotations and the degree of esteem accorded to each.

What works these changes is something unchanging itself: the Chinese need of a China which no defeat may compromise. In the seventeenth century, the Manchus had conquered the Chinese political power, so China as *t'ien-hsia*, unimpeachable, civilization in the abstract, was the China which the vanquished exalted. But China came, in time, to face a new kind of conquest while still subject to the old. To many Chinese, by the turn of the nineteenth and twentieth centuries, China seemed to be losing her title to *t'ien-hsia*, her dignity as a culture. Abandon a hopeless claim, they urged, strengthen political power by changing cultural values, and from a Chinese defeat as *t'ien-hsia* snatch a victory as *kuo*.

Here is a brief excursus, then, into the traditional Chinese past of the subversive concept 'nation'.

i. The Tradition

The meaningless power of sheer egoism is braked by civilization, for every civilization has values, ends to be served. In traditional Chinese civilization the monarch, the *T'ien-tzu*, the Son of Heaven, had an end to serve, an ideal above him, and the anti-Manchu scholar, Huang Tsung-hsi, in his *Ming-i tai-fang lu* (1662), reminded him what it was:

At the beginning of life, each man acted for himself, each man planned for his own well-being. If there was public well-being in the empire (*t'ien-hsia*), he did not try to extend it; if there was public injury, he did not try to expunge it. The princely man emerged, who did not consider his own personal well-being to be the only well-being there was but endowed the empire with its well-being, who did not consider his own personal injury to be the only injury there was but set the empire free of its injury. . . .

Those who later became monarchs were not like that. They considered that the power of bringing well-being or injury to the empire issued entirely from them. They coolly accepted the idea that well-being in the empire devolved wholly upon them and injury in the empire devolved wholly upon others. They kept the men of the empire from venturing in their own interests, from venturing for their own well-being, and they considered their own aggrandizement to be success for the empire. At first there was a sense of shame, but at length there was equanimity, and they looked on the empire as a vast business enterprise to be handed down to their sons and grandsons to receive and enjoy unlimitedly. . . .

The ancients had held that the empire came first and the

monarch second. In general, a monarch's occupations throughout his lifetime were for the empire. Now, it was held that the monarch came first and the empire second. It was because of the monarch that nowhere in the empire was there peace. While he had not yet attained it (the empire), he scattered the sons and daughters of the empire, in order to further his own individual enterprises. He was never sorry, and said that naturally he had undertaken his projects for his sons and grandsons.

When he had already attained it, he clubbed and flayed the bones and marrow of the empire, and he scattered the sons and daughters of the empire, in order to provide for his own individual sensual pleasure. He deemed it natural, and said that this was the profit from his own business. If it was so, then he who encompassed the great injury of the empire was the monarch, and, were there no monarch, men all could attain their own private ends, men all could attain their own well-being. Alas, can this really be the way to establish a monarch?[8]

It could hardly be the way, not in a Confucian China; and Huang Tsung-hsi, with such searing phrases, hurls the imperative of morality at the ruler of *t'ien-hsia*, 'the empire', under-Heaven, the Chinese world. For the gauge of the *t'ien-hsia*'s peace or chaos is the joy or sorrow of its myriad people, not the rise or fall of its ruling house.[9]

Ku Yen-wu concurred in these views and published similar ones in 1670. But he sounded a more deeply philosophical note. For morality, in Ku's *Jih-chih lu*, is more than an attribute of the ideal ruler of the *t'ien-hsia*; it is the distinguishing mark, the *sine qua non*, of *t'ien-hsia* itself.

T'ien-hsia contrasts with *kuo* ('country', 'nation'). The latter connotes not only land and people but protection by military force. But *t'ien-hsia* is a conception of civilized society; it means far more than just a political unit held by *de facto* power. 'There being *t'ien-hsia*,' says Ku, 'it is desired to broaden the people's lives and to straighten the people's virtue.' [10]

There is destruction of *kuo* and destruction of *t'ien-hsia*. Between destruction of *kuo* and destruction of *t'ien-hsia* what distinction should be made? 'Change the surname, alter the style' (*i-hsing kai-hao*)—this is a description of the destruction of *kuo*. The widespread dominion of benevolence and righteousness (*jen* and *i*) decayed into the rule of beast-eat-man, men, leaders, eating each other—this is a description of the destruction of *t'ien-hsia*. . . .[11]

Culture and morality, then, the whole world of values, belong to *t'ien-hsia*. If men have a stake in *kuo* at all, it is only a political stake—'Those who defend the *kuo* are its monarch and its ministers; this is the design of the wealthy. . . .' But civilized man as man, by the very fibre of his human being, must be committed to *t'ien-hsia*—'but as for defending the *t'ien-hsia*, the mean common man shares responsibility'.[12] The civilization, not the nation, has a moral claim on man's allegiance.

This is good classical Chinese doctrine. A hundred generations have known, says Ku, that 'no one without benevolence has ever attained the *t'ien-hsia*'.[13] Mencius had said that first, and had said this before it: 'There have been men without benevolence who have attained a *kuo*.'[14] This, from Mencius —however much it might seem just a counsel of prudence, a warning to covetous rulers of *kuo*, ambitious of 'the empire', that tyranny would carry them only so far—could be more a statement of the ends of life than of the truths of political science. The implication was there, for later men to ponder, that men bent to power or men bent to standards. If they did the first, they were nondescripts living in a *kuo*; if they did the second, they were Chinese living in a Chinese way, in their *t'ien-hsia*, which was the world.

Ku Yen-wu understood this well when he echoed Mencius naturally, without acknowledgment, as he did in the phrase which has just been quoted, and when he wrote, himself, as follows:

When the superior man attains station, he desires to work out the *tao*, the Way; when the small man attains station, he desires to serve his own interests. The desire to work out the Way manifests itself in making *t'ien-hsia* of *kuo-chia*; the desire to serve one's own interest manifests itself in wounding men and destroying things.[15]

To '*t'ien-hsia* the *kuo-chia*', the passage says, to take a political power-unit and make it, with values, a civilization—or to take life, as the Confucianist wishes who knows that *t'ien-hsia* and China are one, and make it ideally Chinese.

Political China is *Chung-kuo*, the central *kuo*. But 'central in what?' is the classical question. And the traditional answer —whether the world was narrow, as in classical times, or vaguely wide, as in Ku's century—was *t'ien-hsia*, a world of standards, which the Chinese ideally upheld, to which barbarians ideally aspired. 'The ancient sons of heaven commonly lived in Chi-chou,' wrote Ku. 'Later men for this reason came to give Chi-chou the name of *Chung-kuo*.' And he quotes statements of the ancients that Chi-chou was central in the *t'ien-hsia*.[16] The world that was *t'ien-hsia* then, the total China of all the *kuo*, was *Chung-kuo* now in a larger world. And *t'ien-hsia* ideally still existed, the larger China of all that world, as long as the people of '*Chung-kuo*' deserved to be central, as faithful servants, not careless masters, of the ideals of civilization. Chinese in their *kuo* were barbarians among barbarians unless they took the yoke of an ideal way, the Chinese way, and set the styles for others. Then the world could be *t'ien-hsia*, not a congeries of *kuo*.

Huang Tsung-hsi and Ku Yen-wu could tell a Chinese emperor what he should do and a Chinese empire what it should be. The ideal was fixed, and Confucian reformism could go no farther than plead that it be adhered to. But the nineteenth century brought outside *kuo* forcefully into China, and some Chinese minds began to stir. Perhaps the Chinese empire should be something other than what traditional standards ordained. Perhaps new criteria had a higher claim, those of western success and Chinese necessity. Should not, perhaps, the vision of *t'ien-hsia* fade away, so that China might survive its fading traditional culture?

ii. The Transformation

In large part the intellectual history of modern China has been the process of making *kuo-chia* of *t'ien-hsia*. The idea of *t'ien-hsia* had indeed been identified with a Way, the

Confucian way, the major indigenous Chinese tradition, and when, for one reason and another, modern Chinese turned to foreign ways for China, the exaltation of nation over culture, of *kuo-chia* over *t'ien-hsia*, was one of their manoeuvres. Culture should be changed, they said, if the change would serve the nation. Such a criterion was intellectually and emotionally helpful. Using it, one could feel both justified in calling for a break with tradition and soothed while contemplating the tradition's decay.

And so Liang Ch'i-ch'ao, for one, in the early twentieth century, urged China to become new and to become a nation, to cease to be old and cease to pay homage exclusively to its culture. The literati had taken the culture as their preserve, and under their influence, said Liang, the Chinese had come to think of China as *t'ien-hsia*, the world, in which no other high culture existed, rather than as *kuo-chia*, a nation, which had a great deal to learn. Nationalism, patriotism, had been destroyed.[17] China, in short, must deem itself not a world but a unit in the world. Unless it chose to come down from its pedestal, its view of itself as *t'ien-hsia*, and to stand as a *kuo* among *kuo*, it would be smashed. And as a *kuo*, it had no standards thrust upon it. A given civilization adheres to certain values or it becomes something else; but a nation's choice is free, if the choice but help it live. Nationalism invades the Chinese scene as culturalism hopelessly gives way.

Thus, if *t'ien-hsia* meant fixed standards, a traditionally accepted ideal of civilization, as, from Mencius to Ku and beyond him, Confucianists had thought it did, then free choice and a pragmatic sanction, the denial of all that *t'ien-hsia* meant, came in with the *kuo* to which *t'ien-hsia* had always been in contrast. And that is how the old order changed, with an old cloak for the new content, the antiquity of the alternatives covering the newness of the choice. *T'ien-hsia* was challenged in the name of *kuo*, Chinese tradition was challenged; but the logic of the battle was a rigorous logic in traditional Chinese terms. For the old Confucianists and the new eclectics shared this one conviction—that culture stood with *t'ien-hsia*, and that culture changed in *kuo*.

3. THE REINTEGRATION OF TRADITION INTO NATIONALISM

When nationalism developed in China as the denial of culturalism, the latter changed in itself; for culturalism now, in its turn, had Chinese nationalism as something new to deny. Chinese culturalism had defined itself formerly as the alternative to foreign barbarism. But now, with the rise of nationalism, when the weight of intellectual opinion was making Chinese 'barbarism' the real alternative, a calculated intemperance seemed to replace the old complacency of spokesmen for tradition. 'Better to see the nation die than its way of life change,' said Hsü T'ung (1819–1900); and Ku Hung-ming (1857–1928), for whom, as for Hsü, the Boxers' practically ideal anti-foreignism in cultural matters outweighed their political hopelessness, protested that footbinding should be sacrosanct, as an important element in the Chinese spirit.[18] One can sense a note of defiance here, a willingness to shock, and a grim decision to stand on principle, though the principle be out of fashion.

Such men as these were quite correct in believing that nationalism and culturalism were irreconcilable, and that the rise of nationalism was somehow linked with the disintegration of Chinese civilization. But there is a complication in the picture.

We have ascribed to nationalism freedom to dispense with the cultural loyalties which are the sum and substance of culturalism. Nationalism thus becomes, it appears, the basis of a cool iconoclasm; without feeling tied by a special cord to earlier Chinese values, a restive modern Chinese generation can abide by what it conceives of as general standards, which lead it to western examples. For the traditional culture need not be protected. Its claims have been explained away. When nationalism follows culturalism, necessity, not precedent, has the right to govern choice.

Yet, if we examine the actual content of nationalistic expression in China, we see that this definition is too abstract.[19] An absolute breach between the *chiao* and the *min*, doctrine and people, 'essence' and nation, is not ruthlessly enforced. On the contrary, there are nationalists who insist on loyalty to the old. They prescribe fidelity to what history has established as Chinese. They will never admit that a Chinese who is careless of Chinese tradition can be a Chinese nationalist. Yen Fu (1853–1921), for example, objected to nationalistic opinion which damned the traditional family as a bad influence on Chinese society and as the nation's rival for loyalty. Yen declared flatly, in 1914, that love of country derived from familism (*chia-ting chü-i*), and that the latter's basic principle was *hsiao*, filial piety, one of the cardinal Confucian virtues and a witness to the abiding place of the old values in the national spirit.[20]

Traditionalism, then, retains a place in nationalism. But in that case, where is the nice distinction between Chinese nationalism and Chinese culturalism? When loyalty to the past is so clearly one of its features, can nationalism really contribute to a deliverance from the past? How do the following sentiments, from a Chinese Nationalist (Kuomintang) handbook of 1934 (a year when Confucian sacrifices were officially reinstated), clash with the culturalism of Chang Chih-tung?

A nation must always remain faithful to its own history and its own culture in order to maintain an independent existence on earth. For a people to keep faith with itself and progress courageously, it ought not to renounce its own old civilization lest it become like a river without a source or a tree without roots. While wishing to assimilate the new knowledge of western civilization, we ought to give it for a base the principles of Confucius. The whole people must learn the doctrine and conform to the thoughts of Confucius.[21]

That statement, with its apparent reaffirmation of the culturalistic *t'i-yung* philosophy, actually shows the difference between the *nationalism* which celebrates a traditional way of life and the *culturalism* which does the same. For Chang Chih-tung was an absolutist, not a relativist, in his convictions about Confucius as a base for western knowledge. He saw value, absolute value, in the Chinese *t'i*. In his inherited way of life (or in that part of it which he cordoned off, yielding to the West the world of 'practical utility'), he found not only the appeal of affinity but the appeal of assurance.

It was not just *his*—it was right. And it was its rightness which justified the allegiance he was moved to assert. Chang, like all true culturalists, did not see the *t'i-yung* formula as universally applicable, *mutatis mutandis*; not just *any* nation's national essence, its *t'i*, was entitled to preservation, with a foreign *yung*, perhaps, to shield it. The Chinese learning, for Chang, had more than mere traditionalism to enjoin its preservation.

Thus, Chang retained a philosophical attachment to Confucianism, the heart of the Chinese *t'i*. But nationalists had a romantic attachment, not a primary belief in Confucianism, but a belief in the need to profess belief. The nationalistic passage quoted above, so near on the surface to culturalism, which attributes absolute value to the culture to which it refers, is really a statement of cultural relativism; and the latter is a tenet of romanticism, which denies the contention of rationalists that abstract value should be the sole criterion in intellectual choice. Romanticism insists indeed (as one writer has put it), on the possibility of valid difference without necessarily approaching or receding from a single norm of excellence.[22]

One must note the anonymity in that Kuomintang pronouncement. Who should remain faithful to its own history and its own culture? 'A nation'—i.e. every nation. As a nationalist literary group, closely linked with the Kuomintang, insisted in 1930, a work of art must emphasize the 'vital conscience of the race'.[23] China must be loyal only as other nations must, each to its own culture.

This note of relativism, so unfamiliar to Chinese minds in the halcyon days of the Empire, was sounded clearly by Liang Ch'i-ch'ao, writing as a nationalist in 1915. It was disastrous, he said, for a nation to break with its past. It must act in keeping with its national character, which is manifested in language, literature, religion, customs, ceremonies, and laws. For a nation dies when its national character is obliterated. That happened, said Liang, to Korea and Annam. So many Chinese elements entered their cultures that their national characters could never be more than half-developed. Hence, they fell into subjection.[24]

It is easy to see the distinction between such an appeal for traditionalism and the earlier, culturalistic one. It had been the assumption of Chinese civilization, in the old days, that if Annam and Korea adopted a certain amount of it, to that degree were they civilized. Traditionalism had not been a blind charge on the Chinese, not an imperative (*'we must'*), but an axiom (*'how could a reasonable man think otherwise?'*). For modern nationalists, however, traditionalism was no longer necessary in the primary sense of the word, as axiomatic, but in the hortatory sense: it must exist if an end is to be achieved. Traditionalism was no longer an end in itself, self-justified.

Its end is nationalism. It must exist in nationalism, shorn of its claim to value as it is, in order that nationalism may exist. The sense of community which is essential to nationalism depends on people's acknowledgment of a common past. And the common past must be prized if a man is to let it forge a bond between himself and his fellow-nationals. Otherwise, why should it matter?

Yet, the fact that traditionalism had to be 'worked at' in Chinese nationalism, instead of exerting a natural charm, reminds us why nationalism swept into favour. The reason was that the tradition had lost its natural charm; Chinese thinkers, however reluctantly, had lost their faith in its continuing value. And nationalism justified emotionally the departure from tradition, which was already justified, only too well, by intellectual conviction.

Chinese nationalism, therefore, began as a paradox, a doctrine with increasingly obvious internal tensions. The nationalist protected tradition so that he might *be* a nationalist and be able to attack it. And a tradition requiring protection instead of compelling belief became increasingly open to attack. In the search for a credo in modern China to bring special and general needs into one intellectual line, to keep the irreplaceable and irrefutable from drastic confrontation, simple nationalism failed to provide the final resting place; for nationalism, which tried to preserve the authority of the waning Confucianism which it had attacked and succeeded, was not at rest itself.

CHAPTER VIII

Emphasis on General Validity:
(1) As a Defence of Tradition

I. 'SELECT THE BEST IN EAST AND WEST'

CHINESE nationalism came into being with two prescriptions for the Chinese thinker which were hard to reconcile. He was to have a special sympathy for the Chinese past, and he was to review the Chinese past with a disinterested critical honesty. A decision to combine the best which the West and China offered seemed the most suitable way to meet the requirements of this complex point of view. The willingness to pool the resources of the two civilizations was to be a genuine willingness, without the reservation of the culturalistic *t'i-yung* westernizers, who always grudgingly added that the western best was a poor one.

This formula seems to call into play the iconoclastic potentialities of nationalism. Ostensibly, value alone shall be the concern of the thinker. This is clear from the fact that 'best', a culturally neutral value-term, describes the object of the thinker's search. The importance of tradition as an influence on judgment seems completely denied, for whatever part of the Chinese heritage which a western 'best' displaces is just as commendable on traditional grounds as what remains.

Nevertheless, just as the past retains significance in Chinese nationalism, though the latter was designed to deny it, so it intrudes in this formula, making the 'best' equivocal. In the apparent need to specify the origins of values, a continuing conflict between universal and particular is tacitly admitted though outwardly denied. Men are to choose, of course, solely according to the dictates of universal reason; but the suggestion is insistently offered that our objective thinker will doubtless find the East as well as the West a repository of values from which he may draw.

Now, if value-judgment were being rigorously applied in a simple, impartial search for the best, such insistence that the West *and* China shall inspire the brave new culture would be irrelevant. For the traditional Chinese values which a modern could reaffirm would be those which conformed to his own standards, i.e. those to which he would subscribe even if he knew nothing of tradition. Therefore, the only motive which a Chinese could have in celebrating the beauty of blended values would be a desire—entirely foreign to the world of value—to see China and the West as equal partners. The supposed commitment to value alone, to the generally acceptable, masks a concern with its special, historical origins.

2. EXAMPLE: TS'AI YÜAN-P'EI

For the first two decades of the twentieth century, an important educator, Ts'ai Yüan-p'ei (1867–1940), was an influential advocate of values-across-the-sea. His fundamental conviction was that truth has no national boundaries. Truth, that is, belongs to the man who knows it, who may be and should be Chinese, even though a particular article of truth has perhaps been discovered in Europe. Value, being universal, is *a fortiori* Chinese; if the Chinese only 'select the best', they are true to themselves.

Ts'ai, then, asking only for an appreciation of truth, was ready to settle for a composite culture based, ostensibly, on a commitment exclusively to abstract validity. Yen Fu, the conservative translator of many philosophical western works, went only so far as to say that if the ancient sages could have survived to modern times, they would have dismissed neither western learning and culture nor the Chinese ideals of 'investigation of things' and 'extension of knowledge.'[1] But in Ts'ai's appeal for syncretism, he meant truth to be absolutely its own sponsor. It was unnecessary for the 'sages' to grant it the freedom of China; truth had its freedom naturally, and Ts'ai had no scruples in 1918 against introducing John Dewey to a Chinese audience as a 'greater thinker than Confucius'.[2]

Therefore, when Ts'ai stressed the importance of the principles of the French Revolution, liberty, equality, and fraternity, it is particularly significant that he related liberty to the classical principle of Righteousness (*i*), equality to the principle of Reciprocity (*shu*), and fraternity to Benevolence (*jen*); and that for liberty he pieced together a mosaic of gems from Confucius and Mencius—for equality, Confucius, Tzu-kung, and the *Ta-hsüeh*—for fraternity, Confucius, Mencius, the Sung neo-Confucianist, Chang Tsai, and assorted sage-emperors and sage-ministers from the *Shu-ching*.[3] For his philosophy, unlike the *chin-wen*, did not demand of him that he legitimize cultural borrowing by a reference to the Classics. He sought only the best from East and West—but with a wish to see the East as a genuine partner.

One can see that desire, too, behind his advocacy of 'world education', something broad enough, he urged, to allow expression to the best in man.[4] Though there were political frontiers, scholarship, he said, a web of interrelations, was public; there were no intellectual frontiers.[5] Living in a particular culture, he implied, was too severely limiting. Implying this, he simultaneously attacked both Chinese ethnocentrism and Chinese self-abasement. For, if China ought to throw her values into a common pool, so ought the West, whose culture was just as limited. And in this spirit he envisaged the 'world-citizen', a man with rights and duties, tempering Nietzsche's egoism with Mencius' and Mo-tzu's altruism.[6] The middle course was the road to take, the best in each culture must be chosen and brought together.[7]

Was this a traditional Chinese appeal for 'harmony' or the recourse of one who saw his tradition imperilled? I think the latter, that Ts'ai's zeal for universality, his eagerness to see both the West and China sacrifice their individualities, was a balm for cultural defeatism. If general validity was all, then reflections were cast on no one's history by intellectual

choices, no culture won or lost. China could choose selectively
from the storehouse of its past or from the storehouse of the
West, without lapsing into either a petrifying imitation of its
own manners or a soul-destroying imitation of western
manners.

But there was a flaw in the premises of Ts'ai's appeal for
the reign of sweet reason. He was magnanimously willing to
sacrifice what the West had already killed—the power of
traditional Chinese culture to contain the Chinese mind. The
westernization of China was becoming a fact; the 'sinification' of Europe was out of the question. Ts'ai had proclaimed
that the cultures should meet, but he meant halfway. The
West had to sacrifice, too. Westerners were supposed to
acknowledge the value of Chinese things, and acknowledge
value not just with their critical faculties, as the western
collectors of Sung landscapes did, but with their creative
faculties, as the Chinese did who went to Paris to learn to
paint like Matisse. Yet, the West would be obliged to
sacrifice only if a significant amount of the Chinese heritage
was universally commendable to modern minds. Values
acceptable to general modern humanity *had to be* found in the
special Chinese past. The lack of concern with anything but
quality, broadly conceived—the emancipation from the less
than broad individual history—was an illusion.

Thus, when Ts'ai described the modern age as the age for
blending eastern and western cultures, and spoke of China
as naturally adopting the 'strong points' of the West, he
went on to couple his appeal for a 'western' point of view
in contemporary Chinese painting with an obviously balancing reference to a (hypothetical) Chinese inspiration for
early western art (' . . . If those western artists were able to
adopt our virtues, shall we, withdrawn, be unable to adopt
the westerners' virtues?').[8] Two points are of interest in this
single simple argument—first, the quest for a Chinese
counterweight to the modern western weight in the scales of
value; second, the turn in the quest to western antiquity, not
to modern times.

Ts'ai's theory, then—'best in East and West'—with its
surface commitment to general validity alone, but its inner,

perhaps defeatist commitment to a share in validity for the historically Chinese, was an incantation which some nationalists used to stave off suspicion that traditional Chinese civilization was petering out, and in no condition to set the terms of its modification. As such, it hastened the day when the tradition's ruin could no longer be concealed. For compulsion *a tergo* to admire a heritage, even the compulsion of one's own nostalgia, instils a doubt that the heritage attracts on its own merits. As their reassertion of old values became thoroughly deliberate and smacked of artifice, Chinese were driven to make other adjustments to the modern world, or were confirmed in them.

The trouble was not, of course, that in traditional Chinese culture there was nothing worth admiring. No suggestion could be more outlandish. To speak of a culture's modern transformation is not to deny the lustre of its great past achievements nor even the discovery of permanent truths in its past. It means only that a new generation finds it impossible to govern action by its own precedents, though the precedents may be honoured, and that as traditionalists, in these circumstances, become more self-conscious, their commendation of past values seems ever less convincing. The fact is, simply, that a European who admired traditional Chinese achievements remained just a European with cosmopolitan tastes, not the synthetic Sino-European whom Ts'ai envisaged; while the Chinese who admired western achievements might pass through cosmopolitanism and synthesis together and become a western convert. It is a matter of difference of tone. When Toulouse-Lautrec or Gauguin made a painting in an oriental vein, it was pastiche, a foreign-dialect story. But when a painter who signs himself Zao Wou-ki (b. 1920) paints a Paul Klee, it is a token of serious commitment, a story in a foreign language.[9] Neither the westerners nor the Chinese use the Esperanto which Ts'ai commends, so hopefully.

Like the *t'i-yung* recipe for synthesis of Chinese and western civilizations, the pure-value formula, 'select the best in East and West', has a persistent emotional appeal which age cannot wither nor custom stale. The more Chinese thinkers are forced to operate in a western intellectual atmosphere, the more the illusion of freedom—the freedom implicit in value-judgment—is insisted upon, in some quarters, to compensate for the reality of force. In a world in which balance is actually lost, the sense of balance may perhaps be recovered by an expression of will, a free construction of a morally pleasing eastern-western symmetry. Thus, Fung Yu-lan (b. 1895) speaks of bringing rationalism (European) and mysticism (Chinese) to the melting point together, so that a universal philosophy may be compounded out of two particular, historical ones, with the strength of each as remedy for the weakness of the other.[10]

Now, with Fung as a Chinese philosopher, represented by this fragment, where does the emphasis lie? Is he primarily the philosopher, seeking peace between mysticism and rationalism? Or is he more profoundly the Chinese, sensitive to an ever-increasing cultural penetration and seeking peace between China and the West? In a man of Fung's superb philosophical attainments, such a drastically oversimplified comparison of Chinese and western philosophies must be culturally significant. It is the Ts'ai Yüan-p'ei mentality still, striving to consolidate an embattled historical China by diffusing it into the neutral air of universal value.

In a contemporary writer more crudely obvious than Ts'ai or Fung, we see this mentality in its fullest condition of strain and paradox. The quintessence of wisdom, political, economic, and cultural, ancient and modern, Chinese and foreign, is not only commended to China—it is attributed to China, and to China alone, in the form of Sun Yat-sen's 'Three People's Principles'.[11] So the universal synthesis redounds to the credit of an individual China, which ostensibly had lost itself in that very universal.

3. 'MATTER' AND 'SPIRIT': THE *T'I-YUNG* RATIONALIZATION *IN EXTREMIS*

For many Chinese, the first World War deferred or ruled out any realization that evaluative eclecticism, however judicious and intelligent, was simply verbalism, not a practical deflection of the western cultural tide. On the level of value, the West fell open to devastating scrutiny; and there seemed such a sharp improvement in China's chances, before any value-selection board, for a mighty share in the synthetic ideal that the problem of western invasion could seem to be solved, by possibly valid denunciation, when the problem was really still intractable. For history is just not made by selection-boards. Western culture might lie exposed in the depths so often assigned to it, and Chinese traditions still not escape a transformation under western influence.

However that may be, Chinese traditionalists were immensely cheered by the western debacle. A mass of post-war Chinese apologetics is summed up in the gloating statement of the erstwhile evolutionist, Yen Fu, in his stubbornly classical style, that three hundred years of European progress had brought only 'profit self and kill others, diminish incorruptibility and banish shame'.[12] But the revival of confidence among Chinese traditionalists could not dispel the modern challenge. To recapture his assurance that whatever was happening ought not to be happening might redeem a traditionalist from failure of nerve, still without affecting its ultimate, outer cause.

Nevertheless, in the nationalists' dedication to an impartial search for the best in East and West, it was refreshing to seem able to be impartial on the Chinese side. Before the War, many of the nationalists who insisted most firmly that China and the West had equal title to whatever was best for modern men had disowned their past more in sorrow than in anger. After the War, they were more than pleased to rediscover it and, instead of defensively pleading 'no contest', to proclaim again their triumph over the mechanistic West. In the early 'twenties, in a sprawling debate on 'science and the philosophy of life', many scholars belaboured one another, making science king, or cutting it down to size as a false pretender, dangerous in its falseness, to absolute dominion. To the Opposition, the West was matter—China, spirit.[13]

Matter could be used, spirit was essential, and *t'i-yung*

analysts were abroad again in the land. Their finest flowers appeared in the writings of Ch'en Li-fu (b. 1900) and in the *China's Destiny* attributed to Chiang Kai-shek where the West was loftily authorized to disclose the secrets of merely material power, while China was beatified for its spiritual achievement in traditionally neglecting the search.

We have already suggested, however, that nationalistic eulogies of the Chinese essence were only a counterfeit of culturalistic confidence in it. The nationalist-traditionalist impulse was for Chinese to be Confucian because Confucius was Chinese, not because he told the simple truth. If nationalists, with latter-day *t'i-yung*, still made absolute claims of general validity for their special Chinese spirit (commending it, as it were, to all mankind), their descent from culturalism was nevertheless exposed in the simultaneous relativism of their pleas for the *national* essence, their emphasis, in a time of foreign borrowing, on *China's* obligations towards what had been proved Chinese. It was a particular urge for balance with the intrusive, seductive West, described by them as materialist, which impelled conviction (quasi-culturalist, or universal) about Chinese spirit—not conviction which led to balance.

Thus, the *t'i-yung* formula of men like Ch'en Li-fu and Chiang Kai-shek differed in meaning, because it differed in context, from the *t'i-yung* formula of Chang Chih-tung. The latter, in urging that western learning be introduced as material *yung*, had addressed himself to traditionalists, who seriously doubted that western learning would really protect the Chinese *t'i*. And they were right to be sceptical. For when the nationalists at a later time revived the *t'i-yung* rationalization, they were forced to confront iconoclasts, the 'new youth' of the 'Chinese Renaissance', who doubted that the *t'i* deserved protection.

CHAPTER IX

Emphasis on General Validity: (2) As an Attack on Tradition

I. CONFUCIANISM, CHRISTIANITY, AND CHINESE SELECTIVITY

THE most aggressive school of Chinese thought in the nineteen-twenties was not *t'i-yung* traditionalism, which distinguished science from Chinese spirit, but iconoclasm, which touted science as the proper basis of a new spirit for modern man. For all their anti-Confucianism, the iconoclasts were no less committed to a special Chinese context of thought than their opponents, hostile critics of western civilization. However grudgingly, most of the latter were reconciled to science and modern technology, and they meant to preserve the balance of cultures by including (or indeed, by emphasizing) the Chinese spiritual inheritance in their combinations of the best from East and West. And rebels against this Chinese spiritual inheritance meant to preserve the balance of cultures, too; but their balance was one of inadequacies, not goods. If with their anti-Confucianism they paid their bitter respects to old China, they scored off the West with anti-Christianity. The whole story of the growth of iconoclasm in modern China, of how it came to be possible for Chinese minds to drift away from historical Chinese values, is implied in the modern history of the Christian Church in China.

i. The Christian Failure to Infiltrate a Living Confucianism

Coming at the end of the sixteenth century to a proud, exclusive Confucian China, Christianity, for all its ecumenical pretensions, had been compromised by its character as a western institution. Ever since the days of Matteo Ricci, who died in Peking in 1610, many spokesmen for Christian claims of general validity have tried to break through the opposition which special Chinese attachments interposes—or not to break through but to will them away, denying significance to the particular origin, the discolouring, compromising, particular source, of the universal. Absolute reason, they imply, transcends historical relativities, and the Church is strange to no one. Europe has no claim on the Church and China no set against it. When the Church has no cultural bias, it should meet no emotional bar. For no Chinese is called to a western creed; man is called to the truth.

So Maritain says today that the Church knows no single civilization, 'no nation has pure hands'.[1] And the Sacred Congregation of the Propaganda, three centuries ago, instructed the Catholic missionary

. . . not to seek for any reason to persuade peoples to change their customs, as long as they are not openly contrary to religion and morality. Indeed, what could be more absurd than to transplant France, Spain, Italy, or some other part of Europe to China? It is not that which you are to import, but the Faith, which neither repulses nor scorns the usages and customs of any people, as long as they are not perverse, but which desires that they be guarded with all the respect which is their due.[2]

One Christian assumption, then, has been that any particular cultural wrapping can cover the core of a universal truth. Yet, this assumption, which should have precluded any Chinese emotional need to balk at Christian foreignness, was but a net to catch the wind. It was meant to persuade a Chinese that the truth belonged to everyone, but the assumption could simply confirm the Chinese in his predisposition to see truth in what belonged to him.

Thus, the early Jesuits in China, in their fear, for their

religion, of its fatal indictment as a western, passing thing, hopefully expressed it as a sort of 'perennial philosophy'. Its truths were supposed to be evident even in the Chinese Classics, if the Chinese would only look. Revelation, the emphasis on what was *sui generis* to the religion, was deliberately shadowed in mysticism, in the insistence that truth is free of temporal, historical context. And this tactic, though born of a sound instinct that some sort of tactic was necessary, was self-defeating; in effect, it authorized the potential convert to see in the foreign church-organization, and in its foreign-composed Scriptures, at best vessels of the truth which must also exist in his own historical inheritance. It is hardly surprising, then, that a seventeenth-century Jesuit should have to record such a Chinese view as this—a friendlier Chinese view than most but not, for the Church, more promising:

. . . men who are most nearly perfect, either by the goodness of their nature or by their industry, best represent the universal nature of the first principle, and their excellence is to be one with it. Whence one must conclude that it is Jesus for Europe, Confucius for China, and Buddha in the Indies . . . Your law is like that which was given to us by Confucius . . .[3]

In summary, then, of the initial Christian problem: A claim of general truth is brought from the West to China. But the westerners see that the Chinese feeling for a special historical Chinese identity, unless it is made irrelevant, will inhibit Chinese acceptance of an outsider's general claim; for men do not change their minds just for the flooding light of allegedly abstract reason. And so the Christians insist that western history, though in some sense, clearly, a Christian history, is just an embodiment (not *the* embodiment) of a supra-historical value. Chinese history, the westerners say, embodies it just as much. Now, eager to harmonize truth and tradition, hating a breach between general and special intellectual appeals, a Chinese may welcome this invitation to keep the peace between them; but this very proposition, he feels, this very plea for Christianity on grounds of its general immanence, makes him justified in preferring the *status quo*. If it is the nature of universals to be immanent in particulars, if the essence of particulars is not their surface-characteristics but oneness of noumenon beneath phenomena, then the Chinese particular, Chinese history, *before the intrusion of the Christian universal*, must have that value in Chinese garb, without Christian colouration. Christian cultural relativism is a poor servant, in the last analysis, to the Christian religious absolute. When, to make his religion proof against Chinese ethnocentrism—to make it, in short, essential—the westerner sees his western culture as fleeting and superficial, the Chinese notes the sacrifice, and accepts it, and stands pat. There is no conversion, no outward turning. If he looks at all for what the westerners see as truth, he looks within.

ii. The Christian Failure to Succeed a Dying Confucianism

Though Christians might deny, then, that Christianity was intrinsically western, the Church did no better in China for that. But if the Christian religion would not be allowed to make its peace with Chinese culture, there was yet one recourse left to the western Christian spokesmen. They could cease to conciliate. Instead of trying nervously to keep Christianity culturally antiseptic (so as not to clash with historic Chinese loyalties), they could openly flaunt their 'foreign' stigma, accept the Chinese tradition as the implacable foe it was, and contribute to and rejoice in its destruction. If Chinese culture blocked them, Chinese culture-change, perhaps, would sweep away the bars.

The compulsion to choose between these tactics—an attack on Chinese culture or an attempt to plant the Christian message within it—has haunted the Christian effort in China through all its modern history. The inadequacies of each suggest the other. Thus, in the very beginning, we find Matteo Ricci, pioneer spokesman for a Christian-Confucian syncretism (which should appease the Chinese historical conscience), trusting not only to that device; he tried, too, to blast the Chinese pretension that Chinese culture had unquestionable general validity, to force the Chinese intellectually to acknowledge—with whatever emotional reluctance

—the higher value of western culture, and of Christianity, coming in tow as a part of it. Ricci, first, explaining his religion in Confucian terms, admits the prestige of Chinese civilization and smuggles Christianity into it. But Ricci, on the other hand, vaunting the western arts and sciences, shakes the Chinese bias against anything foreign and makes it possible for Christianity not to be pre-judged. 'Do not begin with religious polemics', ran a friendly Chinese counsel, he reports. 'Your mathematics alone', they said to him, 'will take away all credit from the fabulous fantasies they (the Chinese) hold on natural phenomena . . .; and how shall they put confidence, for affairs of the other world, in those who are so grossly deceived in the affairs of this life?' [4]

Why has this expectation—that secular westernization in China would smooth the path for a western religious message—been disappointed, up to now? Why should anti-Christian feeling have become particularly marked in the nineteen-twenties, and particularly in the ranks of those most disaffected with Chinese traditional ways? At a disadvantage, admittedly, in the seventeenth century, when traditional Chinese society was yet unimpaired, Christianity should have benefited, presumably, from the later assault on traditional society and from the anti-Confucian iconoclasm attending it. But when Christianity could no longer be damned as foreign (for modern China accepted so much that was foreign), why was it still its fate to be rejected? 'Considering the vast amount of money, personnel, thought, and devotion that has gone into the Christian schools and colleges in China,' wrote a western Christian missionary, surveying the wreck of missionary efforts in the hour of communist triumph, 'our intellectual failure is remarkable.' [5]

Several factors may have had a part in this, but there is one reason sufficient, perhaps, to account for it. Christianity has failed thus far in any general sense to succeed Confucianism, I suggest, because restless Chinese, for all their turning to western ways, still felt a compulsion to own the ground they stood on. Iconoclasm was impossible unless it left unweakened the Chinese sense of cultural equivalence with the West. Only if its old rival, western Christianity, were dispatched with it, could Chinese Confucianism be thrown to the modern western lions.

Culture embraces all the fields of human choice, both those involving value-judgments and those involving scientific judgments. Valid conclusions of science (as remarked already, in another connection) are empirically demonstrable, hence ultimately irresistible. But the necessary supplanting, in the main, of modern Chinese scientific practice by modern western scientific practice—which is the key to the West as *industrial civilization*—leads Chinese to seek compensation in another test of alternatives. In a field where general judgments cannot be empirically proved, where choice is still possible, the special Chinese commitment shows itself; since Christianity (the West as *Christian civilization*) is rejectable, Christianity is rejected.

Confucianism must go. But if Christianity, expendable Christianity, is singled out as its western analogue, then Chinese history need not suffer in comparison with western; when Christianity alone is Confucianism's opposite number, then a surrender of Confucianism to industrialism need not seem a surrender of China to the West—if Christianity only surrenders too. In rejecting Christianity, the modern Chinese, even as he abandons the central tradition of his own history, wills that the central western tradition be comfortably drained as well. For when Chinese Confucianism and western Christianity are packaged together and consigned to oblivion, China can seem redeemed.

Science, then, industrialism—as 'modern' civilization, not as 'western'—may seem to wait in the end, a universal fate, for both a superseded Confucian China and a superseded Christian Europe. And if the fate is really universal, it is properly Chinese. For all the newness of general convictions, the special feeling for China is not outraged, after all.

Chinese hostility to Christianity in the nineteen-twenties often appeared in a context of nationalism, as an identification of missionary activities with foreign political pressure. Nationalism involved an important degree of rejection of Chinese tradition, the 'anti-imperalist' attack implied the association of Christianity with the West: there is nothing here to confuse the picture of Chinese 'spirit' and western 'spirit' balanced in rejection, with Chinese equilibrium as the longed-for concomitant. And the modern swing to Christianity on the part of some Chinese traditionalists corroborates the picture, too. Resisting the secular modernism of the iconoclasts, whose growing power they recognize with growing concern, such traditionalists tend to accept what their opponents had long been establishing as the definition of alternatives for moderns—scientific materialism on the one hand, Christianity and Confucianism, with little discrimination, on the other. As long ago as 1902, an erstwhile Confucianist had appealed for freedom of thought in this revealing fashion:

Whence comes the movement to preserve the Confucian doctrine? It comes from the fear of the incursions of Christianity and a belief that this is the way to resist it. To my way of thinking, this anxiety is out of date. . . . As the strength of science daily waxes, the strength of superstition daily declines. As the frontiers of freedom daily expand, the frontiers of religious domination daily contract. Today the strength of Christianity in Europe is only one or two-tenths of what it was in centuries past.[6]

iii. In Summary

In the seventeenth century, Chinese opposed Christianity as un-traditional. In twentieth-century China, especially after the first World War, the principal anti-Christian cry was that Christianity was un-modern. In the early instance, then, Christianity was criticized for not being Confucian; this was a criticism proper to Chinese civilization. In the later instance, Christianity was criticized for not being scientific; and this was a criticism from western civilization.

Thus, the changing character of Chinese opposition to Christianity reflected the progressive disintegration of traditional Chinese civilization. But it did more than indicate the fact of disintegration, it exemplified the process. After an unimpressive beginning in the early modern period, Christianity assumed a great and important role in Chinese history

—important, but vicarious. Chinese came to require it, not as something to be believed in, but as something to be rejected. Modern Christian missionaries have made outstanding contributions to the westernization of China, but in this, their secular, secondary success, their religious cause was lost, at least for a time, at least as long as waning traditions survive enough to be regretted. For men do not change their intellectual commitments coolly. When Chinese traditionalism crumbles into iconoclasm, it costs the Chinese dear; and he prefers, as far as possible, to pay in a foreign coin.

It may appear that Christianity here has been represented as a problem only for Chinese intellectuals, whether steadfast or delinquent in their expected Confucian loyalties. Would these considerations seem academic to the Chinese masses? After all, when peasants (as distinct from literati) expressed anti-Confucian sentiment during the Taiping Rebellion, their leaders taught a garbled Christianity, a travesty of the original, to be sure, but still not *anti*-Christianity as a hostage for anti-Confucianism.

It is true that, throughout history, for Chinese in conscious social conflict with a Confucian ruling group, an intellectual parallel tended to be constructed; rebellions were often ideologically coloured by the going alternative—Taoist, Buddhist, or Christian—to the Confucian professions of the masters jointly of high culture and high estate. But if Christianity's chances in China for sweeping penetration were of this symbolic character, depending on fission in Chinese society, then the chances were dimmed by the intellectuals' dilemma. For because of their peculiarly strategic position in Chinese society, the desertion of intellectuals from the ruling order was probably more essential to a successful revolution in China than to revolution anywhere else, and an anti-Confucian, hence anti-Christian leadership descended on the anti-Confucian, hence potentially Christian twentieth-century rebels from below. And the potential Christianity had not burgeoned very much. A Christian symbol of social protest had possibly always been less appealing than the promise of radical substance that issued from certain intellectual circles, from the years of the first World War, the Russian Revolution, and the May Fourth movement, 1919, in China.

2. THE PRESSURE OF ICONOCLASM AGAINST NATIONALISM

We have seen that there were nationalists who were willing to innovate, but whose earnest desire was to let the tradition down gently. Nationalism also sheltered a group which felt it possible, under nationalism's auspices, to spare the tradition nothing. If a man would see things honestly, they felt, in the clear, cold light of universal judgment, his release from tradition was unconditional.

Ch'en Tu-hsiu (1880–1942), a leader and mentor of the young intellectuals who gathered under such meaningful banners as *Hsin ch'ing-nien* (The new youth) and *Hsin ch'ao* (The new tide, or 'Renaissance'), was an iconoclast with the best of them. Although something may come down from the ancients, he said, though it be approved by sages, imposed by the government, and accepted by the people—if it is impractical it is without value and should be suppressed; and with this as his general principle, Ch'en cut a wide swathe through Chinese culture, solemnly indicting his fellow-countrymen, and demanding correctives, for servile obedience, lethargy, uncombativeness, ignorance and superstition.[7]

But as an enthusiast for European qualities, Ch'en refused to accept his release from Chinese tradition at the hands of nationalism. He was wary about nationalism as a foe of tradition, for he feared that nationalism would let tradition in by the back door.[8] Many of his students and disciples, however, did combine political nationalism and cultural iconoclasm in the May Fourth movement of 1919 (which politically was a surge of feeling against the Japanese expropriators of Shantung province, etc., their World War allies, and their Chinese official creatures—and culturally, against the temper and institutions of China, which had allegedly made her such easy, helpless game). And in later periods of political crisis, student-patriots continued to link these nationalistic political and iconoclastic strains of thought. In the decade of the nineteen-thirties, in anti-Japanese student circles, the old education was stigmatized as 'poison left over from feudalism'.[9]

This brand of patriotism was unpopular with official nationalists, who suspected a student affinity with communism. The suspicion was well-founded. For the desertion to communism of the younger generation of Chinese intellectuals was apparent during the war against Japan, and signs of it had been noticeable in the nineteen-twenties.

In so far as nationalists really thought as Ch'en did about Chinese tradition, they overloaded their nationalism with iconoclastic content and became quasi- or actual communists. For communism, as we shall see, appeared to be able to absorb a higher degree of anti-traditionalism than simple nationalism was able to do, and yet justify a Chinese, emotionally, or historically, in breaking intellectually with his Chinese past. And there, in communism, they met Ch'en Tu-hsiu, one of the founders of the Communist Party of China. He had refused the sanction of nationalism for his anti-traditionalism, but he could not, as a Chinese, do without any sanction at all.

3. THE SOCIAL COMPULSION ON NATIONALISM, BOTH TO CONTRIBUTE TO AND DENY THE STERILITY OF TRADITION

As long as an iconoclast could believe that nationalism sanctioned iconoclasm unreservedly, as a prerequisite to the strengthening of the nation, he could remain a nationalist. But when he observed that nationalism seemed to encourage the preservation of tradition as a museum-piece, he was forced to re-think his position. One thing was clear—nationalists killed tradition in one way or another, whether they cast it out or congealed it. Why, then, the iconoclasts must ask, should men as modern as they themselves pay lip-service to a tradition in which all nationalists must really have lost their confidence?

Actually, in their diagnosis of sterility in the traditional thought and art which persisted in a nationalistic China, the iconoclasts implied a decision about its causes. The charge of sterility suggested that the new traditionalists had no primary intellectual or aesthetic commitment to what they were doing, but only a social commitment; this was the reason why what they produced lacked value, and equally the reason why they continued to praise and produce it, its aesthetic or intellectual weakness notwithstanding.

The practice of ascribing a role in class struggle to the traditional classical literature goes back at least to the wartime periodical *Hsin ch'ing-nien*, with its slogan of 'opposition to feudal aristocratic literature, approval of popular realistic social literature'.[10] The association of adjectives here shows that realism had become not an aesthetic but a social issue. The zeal for the written use of colloquial language (*pai-hua*) which characterized the *Hsin ch'ing-nien* group was evidence of this; it was largely zeal to make fresh ideas, which the social crisis called for, the matter of literature—ideas which ordinary language would communicate unobtrusively but which literary, classical language would wall off in a separation of art from life. Ch'en Tu-hsiu spoke with scorn of modern practitioners of classical styles as having skill only in 'imitating the old and deceiving men', their works being 'eight-legged', or without content, completely unrelated to the society or the culture of the present day.[11] But new language (new, that is, in the claims made for it as the proper medium for serious literature) was put to the service of new themes, appropriate to the quest of a new society. Hardly had Hu Shih (b. 1891) issued his *pai-hua* manifesto, through *Hsin-ch'ing nien* in 1916, than poems began to appear like *Jen-li-ch'e fu* (Rickshaw boy), by Ch'en Yin-mo, injecting modern social content into a literature anti-classical in form.[12]

Incisive iconoclasts, then, like Lu Hsün (1881–1936), the most highly regarded Chinese writer of the twentieth century, used social analysis in directing the battle in the nineteen-twenties between a morally-motivated naturalism in the arts and what they condemned as 'art for art's sake', traditional Chinese art in particular. Elaborate concern for style was interpreted as a denial of the importance of content and a refusal to say what had to be said about the desperate problems of society. Science (said Mao Tun, b. 1896), the spirit of the modern age, impelled the writer to the search for social truth.[13] Traditional expression in the modern context, it was charged, was socially significant as an effort to establish form as a rival of content, not aesthetically significant as an effort to maintain that traditional form was the best vessel for content. Thinkers and artists must speak out, said the naturalists, and when thinkers and artists with a traditionalistic bias remonstrated that speaking out was vulgar, they were speaking out themselves. In their aesthetic purity, they took a stand on the social issues which they disclaimed as proper subjects of their concern.[14]

In believing that cultural traditionalism in modern China had a social purpose, the iconoclasts were surely right. But the fostering of tradition was hardly just a cynical manoeuvre in social policy. Traditionalism was, indeed, socially useful to nationalists in so far as they were anti-communists. It was also, however, psychologically necessary to nationalists in so far as they were non-communists, barred by their social requirements from the communist means of renouncing a moribund system.

Socially, nationalism was a formula for denying that class-warfare should exist. Chinese must all have solidarity as Chinese, the nationalist could say, and an affirmation that Chinese culture had a universal claim on Chinese loyalty would be a sign of solidarity. Since iconoclasm was linked with social protest (and who knew it better than the nationalists, emerging as critics of the gentry-literati from treaty-port positions of power, outside the control of the traditional society?), traditionalism, successfully nurtured, would be a palliative. This nationalist traditionalism, as we have already suggested, was not universalist, like the older Confucian traditionalism, but relativist and romantic; and in this (to borrow Mannheim's characterization of the romantic traditionalism of Burke, and of other Europeans for several decades after the French Revolution) it was a conscious, reflective counter-movement to a systematic, anti-traditional 'progressive' movement.[15]

Accordingly, having thus been circumscribed in their range of intellectual choices by the social conflict between Chinese and Chinese, non-communist nationalists had to make the most of traditionalism in the cultural conflict between China and the West. Nationalist enough to feel alienation from their traditional culture, they had nowhere to go for compensation but socially impossible communism. Therefore, their only way to treat the malaise which alienation engendered was to deny the alienation. They had to try to believe in the contemporary value of Chinese tradition, and believe sincerely, not as a tactic. Modern Chinese traditionalists have been, not political manipulators in a smoke-filled room, but self-persuading devotees of a culture drying up.

4. THE CHARGE OF STERILITY AGAINST CREATIVE EFFORTS IN THE TRADITIONAL SPIRIT

There should be no mistake: this culture was nothing detached from the devotees, no autonomous abstraction growing old within itself, independent of the human beings who chose to live it. It was the very living it that withered it, that forced men to transform ideas even as the latter persisted. For other men, sensing a new tide of ecumenical and renovating industrial civilization, meant to abandon older Chinese ideas and to supplant them with a new learning, in an education which was not so much a basis for the family's prestige, as in the old Confucian-examination days, but a means of emancipation (a revolutionary freedom) from the family. Living in this changing social setting, with the iconoclasts' creed as alternative and the iconoclasts' questions as the spur to answers, traditionalists failed to keep tradition green. Back again in the world of painting, we can see the sands encroaching.

When science, though disparaged, was admitted under the *t'i-yung* or matter-spirit sanctions, care had to be taken that China should, in fact, preserve its traditions in the realm of spirit. In the field of painting, for example, a revolutionary group had founded an academy in Shanghai in 1913, dedicated to painting in oils by western rules. Since they boldly undertook not only *plein air* and still life but the nude, for the first time in Chinese painting (outside the subterranean realm of erotica), traditional artists could cry scandal with extraordinary vigour and even prompted a few arrests. But traditionalists knew that more was at stake than public morals. For the offending painters of nude models were emphasizing the main point in an anti-traditional manifesto. They were calling for painting after nature rather than the characteristic painting after masters, to which they imputed the decadence of Chinese art.[16]

In an effort to counteract such sentiment, which stabbed into Chinese culture more intimately and ruthlessly than any feeling for factories or steamships seemed to do, the *Chung-kuo hua-hsüeh yen-chiu hui* (Society for the study of Chinese painting) was founded in Peking in 1919, under the sponsorship of Hsü Shih-ch'ang, a political figure of scholarly and traditionalistic bent.[17] Its animating spirit was conveyed quite clearly by a somewhat later writer, in a sarcastic attack on universal criteria; he contended that the individual, historically bequeathed Chinese artistic techniques were a necessary corollary of the Chinese people's individuality:

Recently we have seen men who have made a bit of study of Chinese and western painting and thereupon rejoice to change the face of Chinese painting and make it resemble western painting; they advertise themselves as 'modern Chinese painters' or 'revolutionary Chinese painters', and they strongly condemn the defects of Chinese painting's emphasis on brush and ink, forgetting, on the other hand, that, given a world in which there already are Chinese people of such and such an aspect, then there must be Chinese painting of such and such an aspect. It is a pity that they can change the aspect of Chinese painting in its characteristic features and make it like western paintings, but they cannot change their own aspects and make themselves like western men—the revolution is not thorough—what an eternal shame![18]

What happens to a traditional aesthetic when it is perpetuated as a symbol of something outside its field? The painter Wu Hu-fan (b. 1894), a devotee of the art of Sung, Ming, and early Ch'ing, has left us some useful testimony. He has taken no interest, he says, in new or western techniques of painting because he feels that new things can grow only out of old. They must have roots.[19]

This statement is unexceptionable. It is clearly true, as Sapir has remarked, that an individual is helpless without a cultural heritage to work on:

> He cannot, out of his unaided spiritual powers, weave a strong cultural fabric instinct with the flush of his own personality. Creation is a bending of form to one's will, not a manufacture of form *ex nihilo* . . . the creator from out of a cultural waste gives us hardly more than a gesture or a yawp . . .[20]

In undertaking to work within a tradition, then, Wu made a legitimate decision, and one, moreover, with more promise of value than the undisciplined eclecticisms which other modern artists have embarked upon. We are all familiar with that sort of social coloration of aesthetic purposes which has led so many Chinese painters to do their bit to select the best from East and West, thus to redeem China from either sterile imitation of its own past or servile imitation of the West.[21] ('I then picked out the finest points in western art and applied them to my Chinese techniques . . . thereby blending the East and West into a harmonious whole. . . .')[22]

But Wu Hu-fan himself, it becomes clear, was far from free from social motivations, which led him to see in his traditional forms something quite different from what his traditional masters had seen in them; he emerges as a spokesman for just that course of sterile imitation which has driven other contemporary painters to their hopeless symbolic syntheses, and still others to outright rebellion. For, although his concern with 'roots' implies an interest in development and in the relation between past and present, Wu's interest is in the past itself, a past which he sees as sharply distinct from the present.

One of his paintings is a landscape, with a girl dressed in

ancient Chinese costume in the foreground. When asked why the girl could not have been dressed as Chinese women dress today, he replied.

If I did that, the style would change and in a few years the picture would look old-fashioned and ridiculous. My pictures are not painted for people of today only, but for those who will look at them during a thousand years.[23]

A credo like this reveals the ravages which the West has wrought in traditional Chinese art and, by implication, in traditional Chinese thought in general. Creativity requires, as Whitehead says, a combination of reverence for the society's symbols with freedom of revision;[24] it presupposes a state of tension between a fresh imagination and the weight of tradition, a tension which leads to development within a tradition. 'Even while the hand makes its alterations, the ear hearkens to the deeps of the past. . . .'[25] But how was there to be development within the Chinese artistic tradition when the West stood across its path? The West, it seemed, had anticipated the possible new departures, and Chinese painters who might have been tempted to apply their fresh imaginations to Chinese tradition, and to create their own ideals of value within a stream of invincibly Chinese cultural history, were caught up short when they recognized that now their results might testify to Chinese cultural abdication. Back in their groove, where once they had generally valued tradition as the spur to creativity, now they set a general value on tradition because only there could they find their special Chinese bearings, and special associations and general assurance had to seem united.

The search for roots, then, really meant the search for the old flowers. Development, and with it the hope of creativity, were sacrificed to an idealization of the past, and one undertaken for reasons not solely aesthetic. Wu Hu-fan's statement on costume seems totally illogical unless one sees that the past is idealized and far removed from the plane of the present. For if a change in the fashion tomorrow would be sufficient to render ridiculous the painting of a woman in the costume of today, what principle, except the idealization of the past, could authorize the painting of the costume of yesterday? The present must be ephemeral, and the past, the ancient past of the authentic China, eternal.

When traditionalists lost the will to develop tradition, and sought instead to repeat it, they changed its content. They no longer saw it, with a spontaneous aesthetic vision, as a world of beauty which could pique them to new discoveries. They saw it rather as an antithesis to the West, and development could only weaken it in that capacity. The strength which tradition should have brought them was lost, for they put themselves under the ban:

An automatic perpetuation of standardized values, not subject to the constant remodelling of individuals willing to put some part of themselves into the forms they receive from their predecessors, leads to the dominance of impersonal formulas. The individual is left out in the cold; the culture becomes a manner rather than a way of life, it ceases to be genuine.[26]

Therefore, when western pioneers appeared to be astride all avenues of development, Chinese traditional thought went stale. Traditionalists, seeking to avoid a conflict between historical affection and acknowledgment of value, drained the contemporary value from what they perpetuated. The conflict grew sharper, and it became inevitable that some Chinese should try a course of outright iconoclasm ('. . . We meet poets of this kind at the end of any age, poets with a sense of the past only, or alternatively, poets whose hope of the future is founded upon the attempt to renounce the past . . .')[27] and see where it took them. It took them, in some numbers, to communism.

CHAPTER X

Communism

1. COMMUNISM'S APPEAL TO THE RACKED CHINESE INTELLECTUAL

WHEN conservative Chinese nationalists felt the social compulsion to use their traditional legacy for all it was worth, they weakened its claim to intellectual persuasiveness and made western intellectual alternatives more compelling than ever. But raw intellectual conviction had never been enough to sustain a western-oriented Chinese iconoclasm, and if nationalism was unable to cover a ruthless rejection of traditional Chinese values, the step to communism would be taken by those who were socially free to do so. The very western origin of the communist call to revolt, instead of putting a psychological hurdle in the way of Chinese acceptance, smoothed the path, for it guaranteed that the pre-communist West, the West which had impinged on China, was as firmly rejected by its own critics as by the most hidebound Chinese traditionalist. A Chinese who wishes to be confident, then, of the equivalence of China and the West need not fall back on a desperate traditionalism, since anti-traditionalism, under communist aegis, would serve his purpose. Instead of being the laggard, following in western footsteps, a communist China, with Russia, could seem at the head of the queue.

2. RESIDUAL TRADITIONALISM

But the communists found that a complete disavowal of old China was psychologically impossible even for them. Occasional statements attest to this. The poet Ai Ching remarks that the May Fourth movement went too far in destroying the images of the past.[1] The philosopher Ai Ssu-chi calls for a search for evidence of dialectical materialism in traditional Chinese philosophy.[2] And the important party-statesman Liu Shao-chi, writing that the thought of Mao Tse-tung is the best expression of Marxism applied to a given nation, adds, 'It is as Chinese as it is thoroughly Marxist.' [3]

In saying this, Liu seems to show some private leaning, unconnected with the force of publicly plausible argument. For the statement does not issue logically from a communist assumption, affirmed by Liu himself, according to which the 'Chinese-ness' of Chinese communist doctrine, its particularity, is irrelevant as long as its Marxism, its universal truth, is established.

The assumption which Liu states and which makes Mao's 'Chinese-ness' irrelevant is the frequent assumption, familiar to us, of men who reveal their special involvement in the issue of conflict of cultures by their very disavowing of the issue: only general validity matters. For Liu says:

As regards historical heritages, whether Chinese or foreign, we neither accept nor reject them without discrimination, but accept critically what is valuable and useful and discard what is valueless and inapplicable, basing ourselves on Marxist dialectical materialism and historical materialism.[4]

Now, this is roughly the principle behind the dutiful Chinese response to Comintern manifestos of cultural cosmopolitanism, and in 1952 commemoration of the 'four cultural giants', Avicenna, Leonardo, Hugo, and Gogol, was carried on in Peking, even as in Warsaw or Prague.[5] But in 1953, when the annual chorus of cultural giants had a Chinese in the line, the ancient poet, Ch'ü Yüan (*patriot*-poet, always, in communist appreciations), there was a noticeably greater Chinese fervour in this supra-national celebration.[6] With a similar mingling of universal and particular strains, Chou Yang, a contributor to a symposium at the First All-China Conference of Writers and Artists, in July, 1949, had said that communists respect and humbly welcome the fine, useful legacy of all native and foreign traditions.[7] But here, too, although the general specification 'useful' supersedes the special commendation of tradition, he went on wilfully to reintroduce a special tie to China; for any foreign forms, he said, once they had been used to depict Chinese struggles and been accepted by the masses, would have inevitably changed into a Chinese national and people's form of art.[8]

3. CONCESSION TO TRADITIONALISM: RATIONAL TACTIC OR EMOTIONAL COMMITMENT?

Should such concern for the 'Chinese spirit' be explained not as a kind of emotional manifestation but simply as a tactic to lure the people, the less-advanced thinkers?

We must note at the outset that a concern with what is viable does enter indeed into the communists' analysis of problems of innovation. Chou Yang observes that the old-form drama ('the main pillar of feudal literature') still commands a huge audience. This drama is an important legacy of Chinese national art, he remarks. It is closely linked with the masses, who know it and love it, and yet the old ruling class has used it as a tool to deceive and drug the masses. It is the communist duty, therefore, both to preserve and revise it. As the political consciousness of the masses increases, their liking for the old-form drama will diminish, but the watch-word in revision must be practicality.[9]

Here, then, is a seemingly clear statement that old forms have *ipso facto* no claim on Chinese, but, for tactical reasons, the communists should preserve them and sweeten their content. The old-form drama, it is suggested, can be used to give the masses, not the interpretation of history generally contained in it, one 'saturated with the ideology of a feudal ruling class', but a new and scientific interpretation[10] (just as an old tale, that of Wu Sung, the tiger-killer, is told in a popular 'egg-book' for the peasants—to illustrate Mao's warning that 'imperialism is like a revenging tiger which we must destroy, or it will destroy us').[11]

Elsewhere, the same writer reports that the Liberated Area literature most popular with the masses is that which preserves close ties with national and popular-traditional literature.[12] And Chou En-lai is another who holds that traditional forms have their communist uses. If any form of the old literature or art has taken root among the masses, it has a claim to survive and deserves communist reform. Any attempt to eliminate and replace the old forms of expression, he believes, would surely fail.

Chou is not of the opinion that everything in the old literature and art is good and should therefore be preserved. He is far from suggesting that all Chinese should be conservative admirers of the past. But neither does he think that everything in the old literature and art is bad and should therefore be discarded. Such an attitude, he says, is one which totally disregards the Chinese national traditions and the sentiment of the Chinese people and which is therefore wrong. It is wrong in the sense that it would keep the communists from their primary objective of popularizing literature and art.

Thus, Chou seems to indicate that the communist concession to traditionalism is after all no more than a conscious stratagem. But he goes on to dispel that illusion. For he holds that unsparing denunciation of the old is wrong also in a second sense: it does not fit in with the Chinese communists' historical point of view.[13]

Chinese communist theory, then, is not something to which, intrinsically, the claims of tradition are extraneous. We cannot interpret the communists' tenderness to the particular claims of the Chinese past simply as an artful manipulation of traditionalistic sentiments, to the end of eventually drawing the people past them to a coldly utilitarian iconoclasm. On the contrary, on Chou En-lai's testimony, communist theory demands concessions to the Chinese past not in the interests of its success but as a condition of its existence. The theory is concerned with tradition in its own right, not as a sop to the feelings of the backward.

4. CLASS-ANALYSIS

Communism in China, like simple nationalism, permits iconoclasm while sheltering an impulse to restore a tie with the past. But it is a source of strength to Chinese communism that this impulse is not an embarrassment to it, something either to be smothered or uneasily tolerated, with a nagging sense of inconsistency. As Chou En-lai has indicated, communist theory does not merely suffer the restoration of such a tie, it demands it.

In the communist explanation of history in terms of class-struggle, ideas are represented as ideologies, not compelling acceptance for their abstract value but themselves compelled into existence as expressions of class-interest. Chinese communism, then, can authorize the rejection of the content of an historical heritage while it preserves the urge to inherit. *The* Chinese tradition can be scrapped; but a Chinese tradition exists which can be prized.

The anti-gentry and anti-Confucian Taiping rebels (active 1850-64), whom the communists regard with critical affection as precocious children, but immature,[14] tentatively came to class-analysis of Chinese society and introduced the idea, or the feeling, that Confucian tradition was not Chinese tradition but gentry tradition. With this in mind, Taipings could advocate the introduction of steamships, railroads, and other such products of western material culture without resorting to the *t'i-yung* type of doctrine which appealed to some of the intelligentsia of the same period, the Confucian official self-strengtheners. The latter, understandably not acknowledging any schism in Chinese society, saw the cultural alternatives as Chinese or barbarian and agreed to a supplement for Confucian culture, a western material shield for Chinese spirit. But the rebels, alienated, ready to reject Confucian culture, saw the alternatives as Chinese or gentry, a people to which they belonged or a class from which they were barred, and could feel that what they were shedding was not of themselves.

One index of change in Chinese culture since the rebellion is the degree in which the intelligentsia has moved over to the Taipings' position and made it explicit. An aggressive note of social grievance, not the regretful one of intellectual disenchantment, has been sounding most clearly in expressions of anti-traditionalism. When Confucian tradition (and so much else that goes with it) is consigned to a class, then China, a nation, not a class, has no necessary historical commitment to it. China's natural historical commitment is to its own history.

Who is China? The gentry is not China, say the communists; it is a class, and the gentry-culture is a class-culture. In the feudal society of the past two or three thousand years (runs a rather loose communist analysis), thought had two poles, Confucian and Taoist. Confucian thought was an educational tool of the governing class and therefore emphasized rites. Taoist thought was escapist, a way out for failures in the feudal society.[15] In Chinese literature (according to another communist statement), the true tradition is popular; it does not lie in the court literature or the literature of the leisure class, which has passed for traditional.[16] For China is the non-gentry, comprising all those whom the communists loosely designate as 'the people', who, by their numerical predominance, can identify China with themselves. The tradition which is China's, which is to be appreciated and not disowned and which iconoclasm cannot touch, is the tradition of the non-gentry, one which has always existed but has always been submerged and scorned, or its meaning falsified, as long as the social and cultural domination of the gentry persisted.

Thus, the 'new, correct interpretation' of Chinese history makes the T'ang poet, Po Chü-i, a mainstay of the 'people first' tradition which always existed in China, though it was sometimes obscured.[17] An older poet, Hsi K'ang, one of the 'Seven Sages of the Bamboo Grove' of the third century A.D., is edited by Lu Hsün in the twentieth and acquires the patent of popularity ('feudal era . . . tyrannical government . . . Confucian dogma/patriotic poet . . . spirit of the people . . .', runs the citation, by one of Lu Hsün's admirers).[18] And farthest back of all is the *Shih-ching*, the traditional Classic of Odes or 'Book of Songs', now dismantled as a Classic in the old sense but reconstituted in the new, with popular novels, not ritual codes, joining it in a canon. It is as a gem of people's literature that a communist sees it, with its sense of struggle and indignation; he, despite the calculated insensitivity of Confucian interpreters, finds the saving mark of popular protest in poems reflecting opposition to buying and selling in marriage, to the 'feudal religion of rites', etc.[19] Certainly Mao Tse-tung is not above referring to the *Shih-ching*—as in this bucolic reference to China's need of friends, in Mao's tribute to Stalin, 1939 (the occasion being the sixtieth birthday of that sentimental gentleman from Georgia): 'It is said in the Book of Odes, "When the birds coo, they are seeking friendship". That is exactly the predicament we are in.'[20]

The people's tradition, then, is the Chinese past which can be reclaimed, while what had been represented as the Chinese past (when it was only gentry) is freely disowned or suffers a *C*-change. The Taipings themselves become for the communists a part of a living Chinese tradition which supplants the spurious Chinese tradition of the official spokesmen for gentry China.

And like the world of social protest, the world of science is a natural one for communist raids on the Chinese past. Ancient Chinese inventions or suggestions of the future, like versions of the compass, seismograph, distance-measurement gauge, and armillary sphere, have been proudly emphasized as national achievements.[21] And the lore of Chinese medicine is especially combed for the enrichment of western medical science.[22] This is a people's tradition in the course of construction. For science, so little esteemed in the Confucian official tradition, was 'people's' by default.

5. 'ICONOCLAST-NATIVIST' SYNTHESIS

Such is the formula which the communists use to keep special and general commitments together. An alternative Chinese tradition intervenes between the classical Chinese tradition, which they excoriate, and the western tradition; for the latter would rush in to fill the vacuum left by the removal of traditional (gentry) China, if this 'people's China' were not unearthed to fill it. The class-analysis which disposes of traditional Chinese values as 'gentry' or 'feudal' disposes of a prospective successor, western values, as 'bourgeois'.

The communists seek, in effect, to find a synthesis to displace the western antithesis to the rejected Confucian thesis. China should embrace neither the traditionally celebrated Chinese values nor the modern western ones in whose name the former were first attacked. Thus, the well-known literary figure Kuo Mo-jo speaks critically both of Chinese feudal scorn for the novel as a literary medium and of bourgeois appreciation of the novel when capitalist civilization entered into it, after the May Fourth movement of 1919.[23] The influence of 'obsolete, semi-imperialist and semi-feudal' literature and art is to be exterminated.[24] The May Fourth movement remains a glorious tradition, but its revolutionary thought must be distinguished from its 'reactionary' thought, such as Hu Shih's and Ts'ai Yüan-p'ei's ideas[25]—ideas, that is, of liberal intellectuals, whose anti-traditional critiques (acceptable enough in themselves, perhaps, to their communist former colleagues in the movement) might be represented as mere surrender to western 'cultural aggression', the counterpart of imperialism, in the communist view of the world. Chou Yang states the communist theory clearly. Formerly, he says, Chinese considered the forms of the feudal literature as old. This is correct, but to consider those of the bourgeois literature as new is an error. The latter concept originated from an inclination to worship the West blindly, and this inclination, to put it bluntly, was a reflection of semi-colonial ideas.[26]

In the fine arts, similarly, there is condemnation of complete traditionalists and complete westernizers. Traditional Chinese painting is called 'shih-ta-fu', literati-official (the term is used tendentiously here, not as a scholarly classification aiming at technical precision), and associated with pa-ku, or 'eight-legged essay', that symbol of all that was stylized and stereotyped in the old imperial China.[27] And the modern movement in western art is called the product of a capitalist-class ideology, whose basic tenet is that no such thing exists, that fine arts, literature, philosophy, and science are 'spiritual' manifestations, having no relation to the material conditions of society.[28]

Mao Tse-tung has told us (and he was not the first) what communists think of such a contention. In 1942, in an address which has been accepted as practically an official directive in aesthetic matters, he declared:

All culture or all present-day literature and art belong to a certain class, to a certain party or to a certain political line. There is no such thing as art for art's sake, or literature and art that lie above class distinctions or above partisan interests. There is no such thing as literature and art running parallel to politics or being independent of politics.[29]

It is this approach which enables the communists to 'see through', as they would put it, or be liberated from, as an observer may conclude, both traditional China and the modern West. For it is precisely in the name of the purity of art, says the communist critic, that Chinese perpetuate traditional Chinese art ('imitate Sung, resemble Yüan', he quotes the slogan of this school) or chase after the European moderns.[30]

After the May Fourth movement (the argument runs), 'capitalist painters' either displayed an extreme 'revive-the-old' spirit, in order to quash the revolutionary movement, or (running dogs of the impressionists?) surrendered to the art of capitalist countries. The reactionary spirit was especially strong in the two decades after the Kuomintang coup of 1927. 'Sung Yüan chia fa' (the rule of the Sung and Yuan masters) were widely advocated; in communist opinion, the great monument to this tendency was the Burlington Art Exhibition of 1936, sponsored in London by the Chinese government. As for the surrender to the West, the founding of the T'ien-ma hui, a society to advocate impressionism, in Shanghai in 1921 is cited. In 1931, a passion for post-impressionists, fauves, and surrealists swept the art circles in the big Chinese cities, but this phase petered out when the patriotic fervours of the anti-Japanese resistance movement began to take hold.[31]

As it steers between these two shoals, then, which class-analysis helps it to mark out and avoid, what does the Chinese communist aesthetics value? It has only contempt for the eclectics who use traditional Chinese brush-technique for realistic pictures or who try to paint 'atmospheric life-movement' pictures in oils. These painters, who imagine that they produce a new art, neither Chinese nor western, are simply mired down, it is charged, in the futile *t'i-yung* reformism.[32] This is not the compromise which the communists seek.

What they value in painting is realism.[33] Realism has the virtue, for modern Chinese, of seeming to be a mediant between the idealistic values of the classical Chinese painting most honoured in the traditional canons of criticism and the non-representational, architectural values (among others) of the modern movement in the West. Dispensing the benison of 'realism', communists can retrospectively bleach selected classical art into people's art, which is obviously non-western and can be called 'non-feudal'. Sometimes the urge to see 'socialist realism' as the culmination of the great tradition of Chinese painting makes a communist critic generous with the purifying stream, and Chinese landscape paintings in general are said to exemplify fundamental realism, or strivings towards it, at least.[34] But the redemptive quality of realism may (probably characteristically) be ascribed more selectively, as in one writer's tribute to the 'northern' tradition of the Sung academy—the emperor Hui-tsung himself is praised—as the inspiration of a precious heritage of realistic masterworks.[35] Now, the academic painters had indeed been more detailed than others in their representations of objects. But both the northern school and the southern school of pre-modern Chinese painting had, in actual fact, subordinated realism to formal considerations. For the academics, while less absorbed than their intuitive 'southern' colleagues in transcendence of detail, in problems of immanent form in nature, arranged their detailed natural objects without naturalistic intent, in patterns of formal abstraction, in which the closely observed figures had the effect of setting off the formalizing qualities of the empty space around them. The Hui-tsung sort of 'realism', then, was surely a far cry from the 'socialist realism' of modern representationalists. But there was a sense in which this court tradition could be salvaged for the people: its traditional opponents (at least theoretically —we have seen how eclectic catholicity could mitigate their judgments) had been *shih-ta-fu* painters—'literati-painters'— gentry.

There is a more direct way to pluck this flower, the people, from the nettle of the past; the work of craftsmen, with the blessed anonymity of the humble, may be singled out as the main line of tradition.[36] It is in this connection that the famous frescoes (from Northern Wei to T'ang) in the rock-cut Buddhist temples of Tun-huang have been given the full communist devotional treatment, including commemoration in two sets of postage stamps (in the 'Our Great Motherland' series) of the most widely used denomination.[37] The painter, Hsü Pei-hung, who had gone earlier to Tun-huang for painting inspiration,[38] elicits admiration on interesting grounds: he has fought, it is said, against formalistic or abstract art from abroad, and against the dead hand of the literati-painters of China.[39]

Among art-forms less ambitious than painting, woodcuts of homely scenes have been given tremendous encouragement; their popularity had mushroomed during the war, especially among young artists who were moving away from the Chinese tradition and were influenced not by Sung examples of the woodcut, but by Soviet.[40] The communists have also fostered simpler peasant arts, techniques called 'scissors-cuts' and 'knife-cuts', silhouette designs of flowers, birds, insects, people, or scenes from well-known stories. And the judgment passed on them by one communist critic is this: 'The decadence of China's old-style literati or of the so-called "modernists" has not touched them.'[41]

This compulsion to find a middle-ground in art between old Cathay and new Paris symbolizes a general compulsion in modern China. The need to find a new tradition at home and a new principle of critical selectivity abroad shows that it costs something for a Chinese to scrap the old tradition at home and invite in the West, costs something to the Chinese communist as well as to any other. The need for compensation implies an attachment to the old tradition, an attachment on the part of communists which is not belied but evinced in their repudiation of that tradition. They introduce class-analysis, not joyously to kill the traditional Chinese culture, but in the latest of a series of efforts, all of which have previously failed, to exorcize the spectre of decay.

Communism in China can hardly be defined as a rarefied intellectual refuge from an introspective despondency; earthy social protest is behind it. But the breakdown of traditional Chinese society is the result of the western impact, the same western incursion that ruffled and finally ruined Chinese confidence in China's intellectual self-sufficiency. The question of cultural loyalty comes alive only with the question of social upheaval.

To suggest, therefore, that Chinese communism has a role to play as a device for an intelligentsia in its effort to escape an intellectual dilemma is not to deny but to confirm the fact that Chinese communism has come to the fore because of awesome social pressures. Alienation from Chinese tradition is inseparable from restlessness in Chinese society; and a revolutionary effort to cure the malaise which alienation engenders is the inescapable counterpart, in intellectual history, of the effort, by revolution, to pass through social restlessness to a social equilibrium.

CHAPTER XI

Western Powers and Chinese Revolutions: the Political Side of Culture-change

THE West which drew intellectual responses from China in the course of the last hundred years or so provoked political responses as well. Treaty ports both established the cultural conditions of Chinese nationalism and served as its political targets. And the Chinese path to nationalistic communism has been a long march from a point of self-sufficiency, both intellectual and political, through a deepening slough of western double dominance, to what is hoped to be a point of release to equal standing, or more than equal, with the West again. But the past is not recaptured, experience of the western intrusion can never be blotted out. The present point of Chinese politics and Chinese culture is new. For what emerges now is not the traditional order, but a sense of compensation for its loss.

In pre-Treaty days, Chinese literati had established an attitude towards western thought, but they failed to stabilize it, and in the western century, from the eighteen-forties on, the corrosion of Chinese cultural tradition gradually led to a phase of communist thought. Chinese literati had also established a position against western power, but this, too, gave way, and the enforced change in their diplomatic practice led to a phase of communist polity. This diplomatic practice of Chinese leaders had formed a part of their cultural tradition. The change in one was part of the change in the other. China's becoming a 'people's republic', in alliance with communist Russia against the political power of western nations and erstwhile Chinese leaders, was the same process as Chinese culture's becoming a 'people's culture', ranged against western intellectual power and the Chinese literati tradition. This was the political side of Chinese culture-change.

It is said that the ancient Roman triumvir Crassus had both a private fire department and a private arson squad, and that he made many talents out of using the two in judicious combination. To an interesting degree, western powers in China, and perhaps elsewhere, appear to have played the part of Crassus in the last century. Their material interests seemed best secured when the Chinese government had a fire lit under it, the fire of at least partly western-inspired domestic rebelliousness; for in such a precarious situation, no matter how much they would ordinarily wish to withhold concessions from foreigners, Chinese rulers would have to make concessions, or confirm them, in order to qualify for the foreign aid which alone could save them at home. For both sides, there was one condition to the smooth working of this protection-system: the Chinese government should not become so helpless before its domestic foes that effective foreign aid must overtax the foreigner or over-encumber the Chinese client; the former will not dispense more than his stake is worth, the latter will not repay more than he stands to lose.

In its ideal form, as a point of reference for our comprehension of later modifications, the system was established in 1860. The Taiping Rebellion against the Ch'ing dynasty had already been raging for ten years. Nevertheless, the Manchu government had tried quite naturally, in the ancient manner, to be successfully anti-foreign and anti-rebel at the same time, and it had been reluctant to extend or even confirm the foreign privileges in China granted in the eighteen-forties, in the wake of the Opium War. But though the traditional Chinese world may have seemed the best of all worlds to the ruling group in China, it was no longer a possible one. For when the government was defeated by the

Anglo-French forces in the second western war against China (1856–60), and thereby weakened in its resistance to the rebellion, it was established for the next century that either domestic dissidents or foreign intruders had somehow to be accommodated. Both internal threats and external threats of despoliation could not be fought off at once.

Since in 1860 the foreigners sought only the dynasty's capitulation, while the Taipings sought its extirpation, the dynasty's one recourse was to suffer the evil of foreign aggrandizement at China's expense, and to try to turn the loss to account; when it was hammered home to the Ch'ing that they had no hope of two victories, they became grudgingly reconciled to accepting the one defeat (and the lesser one) which could be put to use in staving off the other. New treaties, more favourable to foreign interests than the old ones, were concluded with western nations in 1860, and thus the latter, especially Britain, were bound to the service of the Chinese government by virtue, in effect, of their owning shares in it. British intervention in the civil war was soon forthcoming. It was worth the while of a western power to preserve the government which at last it had taught to be tractable.

The Taipings, who had never been allies of the foreigners even when they shared the same Manchu enemy, now served the foreign interest by persisting in their enmity while the West abandoned hers. For the British, however easily, perhaps, they might have crushed the Ch'ing forces themselves and even taken over the government, were better suited by a client government—dependent, yet able to play the larger part in its own defence—than by the prospect of wars against a possibly unified, anti-foreign nation-in-arms. No Chinese government would yield bounty to foreigners unless pressures were being exerted upon it. The British had exerted their share (and would do so again, when usable rebels lay not so close to hand), but once their point had been made, it seemed more politic and probably more profitable to let the task of pressing the Ch'ing devolve on the excellent Taipings, who were usefully dangerous but far from invulnerable, and whom the dynasty could never conciliate except by conniving at its own destruction. The British, therefore, by a relatively small expenditure in the form of aid to a Chinese agent, instead of a large expenditure in the form of suppression of Chinese independence, could work their will in China. The Ch'ing regime, in its Taiping-induced extremity, sold out to foreigners what it once had fought to keep.

The situation, then, concerning the foreign stake in China may be summarized, *in a preliminary fashion*, as follows:

Foreign claims in China may be honoured by unpopular governments, which can be used, or by popular (i.e. generally accepted) governments, which must, however, be menaced or forced. For a government representing a general Chinese will would have to oppose foreign intrusion, but an unpopular government would be relatively docile, since acquiescence is the only key to acquiring from foreign sources the force that is needed to counter the force of opposition at home. Therefore, liberal western nations, often providing the inspiration for Chinese protests against Chinese rulers, tend to support discredited Chinese regimes; to see a regime discredited, then to step in as its only hope—that is the way to buy it. The West drains power from the Chinese ruling circles so that the West, for a *quid pro quo*, can give it back to them.

This is the ideal pattern for the western use of leverage against Chinese governments (a pattern depending on the logic of events, not on assumptions of flawlessly rational, cunning forethought in foreign chancelleries). But the pattern dissolves with the passing of time, for the situation is never static. Either the Chinese government, using its bought protection to good advantage, becomes domestically less in jeopardy, hence less inclined to continue to pay for protection; or on the other hand, the jeopardy grows, precisely on account of the government's possession by foreigners, and there is no longer a sort of tame loyal opposition, a steady but moderate resistance to the regime, which the powers can easily and perpetually exploit. They prefer to invest in a Chinese government which is always a little off balance. But either the government eventually tries to dispense with the

West and to right itself (e.g. the Boxer movement, 1900), or it threatens to lose its balance completely and require more western succour, lest it fall, than its services seem to its western sponsors to warrant.

The latter description applies to warlord-foreign relations during the 'Nationalist Revolution' of the nineteen-twenties. From the foreign point of view, Chinese political forces were in an uneasy equilibrium. Chinese hostility to the Peking regimes of puppet warlords was indispensable to ensure their dependence on foreign powers, for the warlords had to replenish abroad the support they squandered at home. However, especially after May 30, 1925, nationalist hatred of the Peking cliques fed on the foreign support of them, and the hatred increased out of all proportion to the foreign aid lent to Peking to counteract it.

Obviously, for the powers, this had reached the point of diminishing returns. The foreigners might well find themselves the receivers of an entirely bankrupt regime, faced by a solid phalanx of Chinese opposition, so that only a total foreign commitment to war against the Chinese nation could protect the West's prerogatives. The ground the warlords stood on might vanish to a pinhead, and foreigners, instead of enjoying the favoured position of arbiter in a civil war, would find themselves faced with a full-fledged national war.

Some foreigners were willing to face this prospect. They saw China as it appeared in the middle nineteen-twenties, a land of two camps: nationalist or 'Bolshevik' (i.e. Kuomintang and communist parties together in an anti-imperialist, nationalist united front), and anti-nationalist. Seeing no hope for themselves in the first camp, the united front, these foreigners stood ready to bail out the warlords, whatever the cost. Other foreigners, assuming, like their compatriots, that Chinese nationalism was implacable, doubted it could be thwarted by the essentially limited western forces which properly might be charged with such a task. As long as Chinese nationalism was so gloomily assessed, as solid and inflexible—as long, that is, as the *North China Herald* continued to inveigh against the raging Bolshevik, Kuomintang leader Chiang Kai-shek—the foreign community could see indeed only two alternatives: either invade China properly, or cut losses and get out.

But by the spring of 1927, when the insight was gained that not all nationalists were Bolsheviks—in short, to put it coldly, when the foreigners realized that civil war was still a possibility—a third, the old and the best, alternative emerged. The West could support a Chinese government strong enough to bear some of the burden of its own support, yet threatened enough from within to need foreign aid. When the Kuomintang, with foreign connivance, broke with the communists in 1927, the western powers had a new agent, neither uselessly weak, as the warlords had become, nor solidly, nationally secure (hence very hard to deal with), as Chiang Kai-shek had seemed to be becoming.

Yet, the arrangement between Chiang and the West was not precisely the old one. The foreigners had to settle for a *faute de mieux*, retention of their treaty rights, but with some infringements and promise of others. There was not simply a change in hirelings, with the foreigners turning from one to another internally-jeopardized regime (as they had done in 1912, for instance, when the Chinese Republic was born). For Chiang was authentically a nationalist, and in the course of its struggle against warlords and foreigners, Chinese nationalism, in these twentieth-century parlous times for Chinese culture, had acquired so strong a position as a moral imperative that a new regime had to appear to be following its dictates. The foreigners were either changing an impossible control-system or they were not. If they were, they had to give their Chinese government such concessions as would prevent the communists simply capturing the title to nationalism. If they were not, they would make of the Kuomintang government just such an isolated, dependent warlord regime as those they had abandoned as bankrupt.

The West could mitigate the anti-foreignism of Chinese rulers by declining, otherwise, to bolster them against Chinese dissidents; that was like old times. But Chinese rulers could force the reduction of foreign pretensions by declining, otherwise, to break their alliance with dissidents (the most intransigent of anti-imperialists), an alliance which could prove for the foreigners a most expensive mischief; that was new. In effect, the West held up the spectre of communism to curb the Kuomintang, and the Kuomintang held up the same spectre to curb the West.

The Kuomintang's terms and the foreigners' terms were figuratively spelled out, each to the other. Implied the foreigners to the Kuomintang: 'If you want to get anything, stop trying to get everything, hence break with the left extremists; or we will block you ourselves with all our strength, or leave you, at best, with no aid from us, to your ultimate communist reckoning.' Implied the Kuomintang to the foreigners: 'If you want to keep anything, stop trying to keep everything, thus forcing us into our communist alliance, which threatens to cost you dear.' In February, 1927, retroceding their concession at Hankow, far up the Yangtze, the British seemed to be heeding the other's warning. In March, at Nanking, nearer the sea, the Kuomintang seemed to be doing the same, as it dissociated itself from what it described as communist violence against foreign nationals. In April, at Shanghai, the foreign stronghold and the nationalists' goal, where a clear-cut decision had to be made, the Kuomintang and the foreigners met, extremes were softened, and the communists, by joint agreement, ruined.

A communist remnant survived, becoming a serious force again in the next decade. The Kuomintang government fought communist rebels, but in 1937 these factions formed their second united front. For a Japanese threat had intervened, a foreign menace of such proportions that civil war could not lend itself to foreign exploitation, but could only be set aside.

The British, principal targets of Chinese nationalism from 1925 to 1927, had hoped at best to hold their own in China, and would never really have ventured, at that late date in Sino-British relations, on full-scale war. Therefore, they could be reached by the Kuomintang, a bargain struck, and Chinese nationalism to some extent politically indulged, at the expense of its solidarity. But when the Japanese, not the

British, posed the challenge to Chinese nationalism, a Kuomintang-foreign bargain was hardly possible. Since Japan was fully prepared to war on China and to monopolize power, not to share it, Chinese nationalism could be indulged not by bargaining but only by resistance; and real resistance precluded civil war. The British and Chiang Kai-shek had had something to offer each other—relief from the prospect of communist expropriation. But the Japanese and Chiang had nothing to offer each other. Chiang could not force the Japanese to any self-denial, since whatever he had to sell they were ready to seize without incurring obligation. And the Japanese had no leverage on Chiang, since whatever part of his power they might save from communist raids they meant to pre-empt themselves.

Therefore, though the Japanese blatantly used the communist threat as a blackmail weapon to force Chiang to their side, in the end they lost him because they changed the rules for intervention in Chinese revolutions. What they wanted (and found in other quarters) was a Chinese agent to facilitate a wartime foreign conquest and the exercise of nakedly foreign rule, not a Chinese agent to facilitate a peacetime foreign remote-control. Chiang, in order to save the chance to break the communists in his own interests (not Japan's) in a later bout, had to join with the communists to clear the ring of the Japanese. As an anti-communist nationalist, he had to keep Japan from handing over the patriotic cause to the Chinese communists, from making nationalism and communism synonymous in China.

In short, Chiang's dearest wish was to eliminate both communists and Japanese from China. He deferred his pursuit of one of these satisfactions in order to seek the other, whose postponement would be fatal.

But with the entrance of the United States into the war against Japan, both of these ends for the first time seemed attainable together. A breach of the united front would no longer of necessity deliver Chiang to Japan, nor must it compromise his nationalism fatally, since the national objective, Japan's defeat, would presumably be provided for. So in the nineteen-forties civil war was prepared again for

China, even before the end came to the general, national war.

Like other modern Chinese civil wars and pressures of dissent on the central government, this civil war was relevant to the preservation of a foreign stake in China. But the situation was complicated, in that the stake was more political now than economic. With Japan's defeat, the United States emerged as the strongest western power in the Far East, and what the United States wanted was the political support of a dependable Chinese government. By American definition, that meant a non-communist government.

But when such support was the prize the United States sought, no manner of aid to the embattled national government could guarantee that the prize would be delivered. To Chiang Kai-shek, because of the difference in kind of the foreign stakes involved, the United States seemed to lack what Britain had held in leverage against him in 1927—the priceless option to withhold the aid with which he could break the left. It had been entirely possible for Britain to utter a plague on both their houses in the early nineteen-twenties, when communists and Kuomintang had seemed equally ready to confiscate the British assets. But it was inconceivable that the United States, whose treasure in China was of a different kind, could abandon Chiang to the communists.

Therefore, it was easy for Chiang to withstand American pressure for Kuomintang reforms. For the Chinese revolution which reform was supposed to block was just as dark a *bête noire* to the United States as to the rulers of China; and the latter, then, rather than dissipate through reform the advantages they wished to save against revolution, assumed that sufficient foreign support would always be forthcoming, no matter how much the need increased as domestic corruption strengthened the rebels' hand.

And so the Kuomintang, in its capacity as a foreign instrument, went the way of the Peking governments of some twenty years before, forfeiting popularity until the only strength it could offer its foreign sponsor was the strength the latter gave it. But this time there was no place for the foreigner to jump, no other possible Chinese protégé, and the opposition to the West's candidate got out of hand. The United States aided the only contender whose triumph would serve her purpose—a contender, however, whose chances of triumph were hopelessly prejudiced by the very inevitability of American aid.

By 1950 the wheel had come full circle. The West had exploited domestic threats to Chinese governments so as to redress the domestic balance and receive a *quid pro quo*. But domestic threats, partly because of the western intervention, grew so strong at last that rebels became the government, while the erstwhile government, with its American ally, became the threat. The Kuomintang, or the United States looming behind it, was converted into the ominous threat which made inevitable Russian aid to China for a time, as a prop to the threatened regime, and equally inevitable the Chinese payment of a *quid pro quo*—a phase of political submission, if nothing else—no longer to the West, but to Russia.

Conclusion: a New Vocabulary or a New Language?

PERHAPS the warlords of the early Republican period were only recent versions of the end-of-Han or end-of-T'ang warlords. Perhaps the Nanking government of Chiang Kai-shek was the Ch'in or Sui type of unifying, ephemeral dynasty which paves the way for a longer-lived bureaucratic centralized regime. Maybe China is forever China, as the saying is, absorbing everyone, and nothing has been new in a crowded century except ephemeral detail, spilling over a changeless paradigm of Chinese history.

If such assumptions held, then the Chinese communists would be not simply somewhat traditionalistic, but traditional; and while being traditionalistic by no means necessarily implies the continuing vitality of rooted values (it may mean the opposite, as we have seen), being traditional implies just that. Chinese civilization may have been broadened (according to this reading of history), its vocabulary enriched in the course of the dialogue between modern China and the modern West, but Chinese civilization remains its old self, still expressed in its own language.

Yet, if it is only the Chinese vocabulary which has been affected, only the detail and not the style of intellectual life, then the effects of the meeting of China and Europe would be the same for each in quality; for cultural diffusion has worked both ways, and Europe as well as China has accepted ideas from the other. But something is wrong with such a conclusion—I think we must feel it. When Needham, in a work pointing out the richness of science in pre-modern China, states the problem of modern culture literally in terms of language ('. . . while the progress of the world has forced Chinese scientists and technologists to be bilingual, the converse has proved so little true . . .'),[1] the metaphor of language is suggested irresistibly: what the West has probably done to China is to change the latter's language—what China has done to the West is to enlarge the latter's vocabulary.

I. VOCABULARY CHANGE IN EUROPE AND CHINA: ART AND IDEAS

Modern Europe has absorbed Far Eastern elements into its art history, either as exoticisms or as assimilations, without giving itself away to any strong external attraction. Rembrandt in his painting in a Rajput manner or Toulouse-Lautrec in his 'Japanese' prints may seem to be swallowing whole an Asian style, but really such exotic works depend for effect on traditions native to the artist; the point of these productions is in their novelty, their piquant revelation of virtuosity, not in their purely aesthetic qualities as they might have been judged in their own milieus where work in these genres was not a sport. In the more important category of assimilation, the great school of French impressionism was strongly influenced by the Oriental print, represented in Europe by the Japanese *ukiyoe*, whose ideals of draughtsmanship and dramatic portrayal were filtered down through Degas (with Hokusai behind his ballet scenes) to the Goncourts, Manet, and Whistler.[2]

Yet, impressionism was undeniably European. That is, the development of its aesthetic and its vogue in Europe were expressions of a European dialogue. In the background were the suggestive pronouncements, the productive conflicts of taste of classicists, romanticists, realists. The line to impressionism ran through Ingres, Delacroix, and Courbet, while the *ukiyoe* was a branch feeder, supplying impressionists with assimilable ideas which helped them to extend a European history.

This was turn-about and fair play. Hokusai had been touched by western influence in perspective and chiaroscuro.[3] But Japanese art was not *bouleversé* by Hokusai. With some western-derived vocabulary, he spoke the language and developed the theses of Chinese and Japanese aesthetics. And as in Tokugawa Japan, so in early-modern China, where a few Chinese artists borrowed western practices, some for exotic effect and some for enrichment, and went on about their business of being Chinese artists, cut off from the widespread unseen roots which had thrown up these surface, amusing ideas. 'Having had talks with the western scholar, Lang Shih-ning, I can now make Chinese drawings in the foreign style.'[4] It was the enjoyment of an obvious trick amidst the accepted Chinese order, not conversion to the underlying, not so accessible, foreign aesthetic purpose.

Similarly, in the realm of general ideas, we find Voltaire acknowledging the influence of Confucian secularism, as strained through the Jesuits' reports on China, but Voltaire's anti-clericalism was a western issue; his Chinese evidence weighed in a conflict whose lines were drawn already in European history.[5] And on the other side of the coin, in so far as Matteo Ricci's Christianity was congenial to the Chinese literati to whom he appealed, it was usually accepted as confirmation of Confucian dispraise of the Buddhists. Like Voltaire's Chinese, Ricci, to many of his admirers, was the honest broker, the impartial witness from outer space, who enlivened a native contest.[6]

2. LANGUAGE CHANGE AND THE PROBLEM OF CONTINUITY

There is a common feature in all these cases of western influence on China and Japan up to a century ago, and of Chinese and Japanese influence on the West in any century: the contacts were predominantly intellectual, not social as well. The effect of ideas in diffusion, the degree of their disarrangement of their fresh intellectual environment, depends, it seems, not on their disembodied character as abstract ideas but on how much of their mother societies they drag with them to the alien land. As long as one society is not being conclusively shaken up by another, foreign ideas may be exploited, as additional vocabulary, in a domestic intellectual situation. But when foreign-impelled social subversion is fairly under way (and that has been so in China, not in the West, and in China only in the nineteenth century and after), then foreign ideas begin to displace domestic. This change of language in a society may be described objectively as new choices made under conditions of total invasion, not of purely intellectual insinuation. It may be described subjectively as new choices made under conditions of increasing intellectual strain, the strain of efforts by main force to naturalize the alien truth and rationalize the native inheritance, the strain of steady divergence between general and special intellectual quests.

If this strain has been more rending in modern China than in modern Japan, and if accordingly Japanese modernization has been far less inhibited than Chinese, this may well confirm a connection between the disruptive impact of a total foreign society and the shattering psychological effect (when such it is) of foreign intellectual penetration. For feudal Japanese society, evolving into indigenous capitalism, was perhaps rather fired by the West than derailed; while the bureaucratic Chinese society, with a lesser potential for capitalist development on its own (and, correspondingly, with its political leaders less flexible intellectually than the Japanese, whose feudal origins made their status rest on assumptions of birth rather than on assumptions of possession of a given intellectual corpus), was struck a blow from the side.

Before the Opium War and the subsequent growing Chinese apprehension about the encroachment of western society, western ideas might certainly run foul of the more-than-ordinary Confucian suspicion of novelty, or of the simply different standards of value of literati in their own society, as yet unreconstructed. However, if western ideas got past these hazards, they were accepted calmly, as worthwhile borrowings, detached from their context of origin and perfectly assimilable to the Chinese inheritance. This is precisely the expressed ideal of many modern Chinese borrowers. But the very expression of the ideal, reiterated so often, belies its modern fulfilment—this is one indication that Chinese society is not, in fact, in its old situation, untampered with, when intellectual agitation at the occasional innovation could be less acute.

In the old situation, innovations from the West, like seventeenth-century cannon or effective western naval vessels or Copernican astronomy, could be slipped into the Chinese language as simply new vocabulary. But in the nineteenth century, when western society hovered close behind the intrusive western science and technology, Chinese admirers of the latter seemed to fear a change of language, and to allay the fear they sometimes invoked the seventeenth-century precedents.[7] These famous precedents, however, had themselves been permitted to exist without elaborate invocation of precedent (Ku Yen-wu's *Jih-chih lu*, with none of the urgency of later statements acknowledging foreign values, said simply, concerning astronomy, that men of the western regions were good at it and had been so from ancient times; their techniques, Ku quietly remarked, were not the same as the ancient Chinese methods but were more effective and therefore widely employed in recent times).[8] Indeed, it was this easy acceptability of the precedents in that safely and soundly authentic Chinese past which enabled the worried innovators of the nineteenth-century's China to say that their minds were at rest.

They were, in fact, restlessly torn, held by the warmth, repelled by the confinement of home. Before the total western invasion, value-change could be vocabulary-enrichment, without requiring historical justification.[9] And this pre-invasion era, then (being perfectly Chinese, borrowings and all), could be a storehouse of historical justification for a later day, when society and language were changing together and foreign offerings had to be admitted as valuable, while purged as far as possible of their alien connotations.

It is a difference in social conditions, therefore, which determines the different psychological conditions of borrowing. That is why it is inexact—yet understandable—to weigh off an ancient Chinese statement of some intellectual principle against the modern western statement of the principle. Western recognition of the Chinese statement and

Chinese recognition of the western have different sorts of repercussions. Interested, perhaps, with his cultural horizons broadened, but his attention steadily fixed on the problems of knowledge at hand—problems coming down to him from his own, non-Chinese intellectual history—a western scientist may hear that the modern 'complementarity principle' (whereby two diametrically opposed statements can validly be made about the same thing) was exemplified in Chi-tsang's (549–623) Theory of Double Truth.[10] But a modern Chinese thinker, if he is moved at all to note an affinity between complementarity and the Double Truth, is unlikely just to be interested in cultural correspondences. He will have been persuaded of the prestige of a modern discovery and of the non-Chinese intellectual tradition in which it takes its place. His cultural horizons have not been broadened, but removed to another plane.

And that is why, too—change in language and enrichment of vocabulary being such quite different processes—it would seem mistaken to base any predictions about modern Chinese communism on the experience of Six Dynasties and T'ang Buddhism. The Indian homeland of Buddhism had not impinged on China socially; the contact was only intellectual. Chinese society had some throes of its own in Buddhism's early Chinese centuries, from the end of the Han to mid-T'ang, and the foreign creed seemed there a serious threat to Confucianism, which was appropriate to a normally operating Chinese bureaucratic society. But the revival of this normal operation confirmed Chinese Confucianism as the master of an originally Indian Buddhism, which settled into a modified but invincibly Chinese background.[11] Communist ideas, on the other hand, come to China from a western world which unmistakably has impinged socially on China, and the old saw about China's absorbing everything should be buried once and for all. Modern China, with industrialism pressing from without and planted within, seems frankly implausible in the role of unmoved mover.

Some compulsion seems to exist in many quarters to see Chinese communism not, indeed, as a foreign creed tamed down to traditional Chinese specifications (and certainly not as a foreign creed untamed and successfully destructive), but as Confucianism with another name and another skin but the same perennial spirit. Canonical texts and canonical texts, bureaucratic intellectual élite and bureaucratic intellectual élite—nothing has changed, allegedly—except, possibly, everything.

For the substance of the respective orthodoxies must count for something, and Confucian harmony is not Marxist struggle, Confucian permanence is not Marxist process, Confucian moralism is not Marxist materialism. And the rationalizations of the intelligentsias' power count for something, and Mencius' cool account of the way of the world— that those who work with their hands always support those who work with their heads[12]—is not the pious Maoist profession that the workers inspire the intellectuals who, simply by chance of their having education in a society still largely illiterate, necessarily take the official posts at first in a complicated system. Nor is the educated man's prestige as an amateur in Confucian society the prestige of the technically specialized product which Chinese communist education is seeking. Marxist classics, communist bureaucracy, even Huai River water-control are not so suggestive of old China exclusively that all Chinese history since the Opium War, with its social upheavals and intellectual agonies, should be reckoned just sound and fury. The categories of Chinese communist thought are not traditional. This is the salient fact. And it is belied neither by some communist taste for traditional achievement (Tun-huang frescoes or the odd phrase from a Confucian classic), nor by some communist casting in traditional roles.

Observers who tend to emphasize the traditional character of the Chinese communist regime often wish to refute the claim that communism has simply been thrust on China by foreign force and connivance. It is the continuity of Chinese history which they mean to assert, quite rightly, against theories of Moscow gold or American professors as the makers of modern China. Yet, the continuity of Chinese history, including its current communist phase, can be affirmed without our explaining the latter as the Confucian eternal return. Revulsion against the landlord system, the family system, the Confucian education has been building up for a long time in China, certainly not just since yesterday in doctrinaire directives. Though communists in power have helped such ideas along, their sources are deep in a century and a half of unplanned western action on the earlier social structure that was offered up to the contact. And what of the intellectual side of Chinese continuity? Old forms with genuinely new content (like the *t'i* and *yung*, *t'ien-hsia* and *kuo*, *ching* and *shih* dichotomies) establish continuity convincingly, at least as well as new forms with allegedly old content would do—and convey the reality of change better. If, as I have meant to do throughout this narrative, one interprets intellectual history as a history not 'of thought', but of men thinking, one will not see a bloodless Confucianism imposing itself by identity on a similarly abstract communism, but Confucian generations giving way, living, feeling and easing the strains. The Confucian tradition, transformed and abandoned, has led directly to the communist version of Chinese change of mind, not by preserving itself immanent in communist doctrine, but by failing in self-preservation, leaving its heirs bereft and potentially strange in their own land, and thus commending that latest doctrine as an answer to a need.

Notes

INTRODUCTION

1. Cf. the discussions of 'prehensions' (whereby everything somehow absorbs what is outside itself into its own being) and of the 'fallacy of simple location' (i.e. 'the belief that it is adequate, in expressing the spatio-temporal relations of a bit of matter, to state that it is where it is, in a definite finite region of space, and throughout a definite finite duration of time, apart from any essential reference of the relations of that bit of matter to other regions of space and to other durations of time'), in Alfred North Whitehead, *Science and the Modern World* (New York, 1937); *Process and Reality* (New York, 1929); and *Adventures of Ideas* (New York, 1933), *passim*. Elsewhere, in *Modes of Thought* (New York, 1938), 26, Whitehead says of every 'actual thing' that 'its nature consists in its relevance to other things, and its individuality consists in its synthesis of other things so far as they are relevant to it'.

2. R. G. Collingwood, *An Autobiography* (Harmondsworth, 1944), 25.

3. *Ibid.*, 27. Cf. Susanne K. Langer, *Philosophy in a New Key* (New York, 1948), 1–2: 'A question is really an ambiguous proposition; the answer is its determination. . . . Therefore a philosophy is characterized more by the *formulation* of its problems than by its solution of them. Its answers establish an edifice of facts; but its questions make the frame in which its picture of facts is plotted. . . . In our questions lie our *principles of analysis* and our answers may express whatever those principles are able to yield.'

4. For this distinction between Voltaire and Condorcet as rationalists, see Duncan Forbes, 'James Mill and India', *The Cambridge Journal*, V, No. 1 (Oct. 1951), 20–1. For Herder, see Ernst Cassirer, *The Problem of Knowledge* (New Haven, 1950), 203–4.

5. Collingwood, who defends the concept of the question-answer synthesis as the substance of ideas, also states the complementary concept, the definition of ideas in terms of alternatives.

NOTES: INTRODUCTION, *pp.* xxx–xxxi

See *An Essay in Philosophical Method* (Oxford, 1933), 106–9, where he states that every philosophical statement is intended to express rejection of some definite proposition which the person making the statement regards as erroneous. A philosophical assertion, whenever it affirms something definite, also denies something definite. '. . . if we cannot understand what the doctrines were which a Plato or a Parmenides meant to deny, it is certain that to just that extent we are unable to grasp what it was that he meant to affirm.'

6. Cf. Anthony Thorlby, 'The Poetry of Four Quartets', *The Cambridge Journal*, V, No. 5 (Feb. 1952), 298: 'The critical dilemma of this generation was nicely expressed by Mr. Allen Tate when he repeated the Christian Creed in answer to the question of what he believed, and added that the real question was what it meant to believe this.'

7. Paul Hazard, *European Thought in the Eighteenth Century, from Montesquieu to Lessing* (New Haven, 1954), 4–6.

8. Quoted passage by de Maistre, cited in Karl Mannheim, 'Conservative Thought', *Essays on Sociology and Social Psychology* (New York, 1953), 148–9.

9. Kingsley Martin, 'Rangoon Reflections', *The New Statesman and Nation*, XLV, No. 1142 (Jan. 24, 1953), 84–5.

10. Jean Hippolyte, *Introduction à l'étude de la philosophie de l'histoire de Hégel* (Paris, 1948), 20. Cf. Oswald Spengler, *The Decline of the West* (New York, 1934), 105: '. . . history is not the mere sum of past things without intrinsic order or inner necessity but . . . an organism of rigorous structure and significant articulation, an organism that does not suddenly dissolve into a formless and ambiguous future when it reaches the accidental present of the observer. Cultures are organisms, and world-history their collective biography.'

Cf. also Cassirer, *The Myth of the State* (New Haven, 1946), 73, where he compares Hegel as a spokesman for traditionalistic historicism and Plato as the founder of the opposing philosophical school in western thought. Hegel maintains, 'The striving for a morality of one's own is futile and by its very nature impossible of attainment. In regard to morality the saying of the wisest men of antiquity is the only true one—to be moral is to live in accordance with the moral traditions of one's own country.' Plato's view is that tradition follows rules that it can neither understand nor justify; implicit faith in tradition can never be the standard of a true moral life.

Elsewhere, too, in *The Problem of Knowledge*, 13, Cassirer sees history as a particularistic category, when he links Descartes' 'unhistorical temper' to his achievement in conceiving a *mathesis universalis*.

11. Herbert Luthy, 'Montaigne, or the Art of Being Truthful', *Encounter*, I, No. 2 (Nov. 1953), 43.

12. Richard McKeon, 'Conflicts of Values in a Community of Cultures', *The Journal of Philosophy*, XLVII, No. 8 (April 13, 1950), 203.

13. See Franz Boas, *The Mind of Primitive Man* (New York, 1938), 236–8, 249, where he writes of the ubiquitous tension between conscious rationality, implied in readiness to change, and emotional tenacity, implied in resistance to change. This is the tension between (in our terms) general and special commitments, which comes when men are confronted with the fact that certain ideas exist for which they cannot give any explanation except that they are there. Boas refers to the 'mental agonies that accompany the freeing of the mind from traditional opinions that have a sentimental value'. 'We try to justify our adherence to inherited or otherwise conditioned principles by trying to convince ourselves that these principles are the correct ones.'

James Baldwin, in *Notes of a Native Son* (Boston, 1955), 6–7, 165, writes movingly of the same problem from a slightly different point of approach; he describes not so much the shock of realization that one's history may not culminate in rationally chosen values, but the disturbing, irrepressible consciousness that what one values may lie outside his history. When one's own historical associations seem unchoosable, choices seem alien: '. . . I was forced to recognize that I was a kind of bastard of the West; when I followed the line of my past I did not find myself in Europe but in Africa. And this meant that in some subtle way, in a really profound way, I brought to Shakespeare, Bach, Rembrandt, to the stones of Paris, to the cathedral at Chartres and to the Empire State Building a special attitude. These were not really my creations, they did not contain my history; I might search in vain forever for any reflection of myself. I was an interloper; this was not my heritage. . . .'

'For this village, even were it incomparably more remote and incredibly more primitive, is the West, the West onto which I have been so strangely grafted. These people cannot be, from the point of view of power, strangers anywhere in the world; they have made the modern world, in effect, even if they do not know it. The most illiterate among them is related in a way that I am not, to Dante, Shakespeare, Michelangelo, Aeschylus, Da Vinci, Rembrandt, and Racine; the cathedral at Chartres says something to them that it cannot say to me, as indeed would New York's Empire State Building, should anyone here ever see it. Out of their hymns and dances come Beethoven and Bach. Go back a few centuries and they are in their full glory—but I am in Africa, watching the conquerors arrive.'

CHAPTER I

1. See Siu-chi Huang, *Lu Hsiang-shan, a Twelfth Century Chinese Idealist Philosopher* (New Haven, 1944), for a comparative discussion of these schools and for bibliographical references in Chinese and in translation.

2. T'an P'i-mu, *Ch'ing-tai ssu-hsiang shih-kang* (Historical outline of Ch'ing thought) (Shanghai, 1940), 10–11.

3. Hou Wai-lu, *Chin-tai Chung-kuo ssu-hsiang hsüeh-shuo shih* (Intellectual history of modern China) (Shanghai, 1947), I, 5.

4. T'an, 53.

5. *Ibid.*, 33.

6. Yen Yüan, 'Ts'un hsüeh pien', *Chi-fu ts'ung-shu* (1879), *ts'e* 275, 1.12.

7. Tai Chen, 'Meng-tzu tzu-i su-cheng', *An-hui ts'ung-shu*, 6th Ser. (Shanghai, 1936), *ts'e* 10, 1.11.

8. Hou, 8.

9. Liang Ch'i-ch'ao, 'Chung-kuo chin san-pai nien hsüeh-shu shih' (History of Chinese scholarship in the last three hundred years), *Yin-ping-shih ho-chi* (Shanghai, 1936), *chuan-chi*, XVII, 6. [Hereafter, YPSHC: CC.]

10. Ch'ien Mu, *Chung-kuo chin san-pai nien hsüeh-shu shih* (History of Chinese scholarship in the last three hundred years) (Chungking, 1945), 20.

11. Ku Yen-wu, *Jih-chih lu* (Shanghai, 1933), I, 18, 108, 114.

12. *Ibid.*, 121.

13. T'an, 1.

14. *Ibid.*, 2.

15. Ku, I, author's preface, 1.

16. T'an, 1.

17. Franz Rosenzweig, 'The New Thinking', *Franz Rosenzweig,*

His Life and Thought, trans. Nahum Glatzer (Philadelphia, 1953), 192.

18. R. I. Aaron, *The Theory of Universals* (Oxford, 1952), 25. For an interesting reference to this relation between generalization and particular instance, made by the musicologist, Donald Tovey, in terms of the musical 'form' and the musical 'work', see Aaron Copland, *Music and Imagination* (Cambridge, 1952), 63.

19. Ernst Lehrs, *Man or Matter* (London, 1951), 65–6.

20. Cf. George Sarton, *Introduction to the History of Science* (Washington, 1931), II, 194; A. C. Crombie, *Augustine to Galileo* (London, 1952), 11; Paul Sandor, *Histoire de la dialectique* (Paris, 1947), 65. It should be noted that there is a question in the minds of some recent scholars about the degree of nominalism in Abelard's thought. However, for our purposes here, the important thing is to define pre-Baconian nominalism, not to attribute it to any particular thinker, and Abelard may still be cited for purposes of illustration.

21. John U. Nef, 'The Genesis of Industrialism and of Modern Science, 1560–1640', *Essays in Honor of Conyers Read,* ed. Norton Downs (Chicago, 1953), 217; Whitehead, *Science and the Modern World,* 62.

22. Collingwood, *An Autobiography,* 22.

23. For Bacon, see Basil Willey, *The Seventeenth Century Background* (London, 1950), 25; for Ku, see Hou, I, 181, 186.

24. The example of Bacon has been introduced into the discussion not because his standing as a philosopher of science is secure, but because he gave the critique of idealism a turn towards science. He is, therefore, a fit subject for comparison with the Chinese thinkers who, like him, rejected the idealism of intellectual predecessors, but who failed to proceed in his direction. Scientific thinking has, of course, left Bacon far behind. It has been pointed out that he was notoriously wide of the mark in his illustrations of scientific method in the *Novum Organum* [Lawrence J. Henderson, *The Order of Nature* (Cambridge, 1917), 27], and Einstein implicitly criticizes the extremes of Baconian induction when he speaks of a 'philosophical prejudice'—the faith that facts by themselves can and should yield scientific knowledge without free conceptual construction [Albert Einstein, 'Autobiographical Notes', *Albert Einstein: Philosopher-Scientist,* ed. Paul Arthur Schilpp (Evanston, 1949), 49]. But we may cite Whitehead's moderate estimate of Bacon to confirm the latter in his place as an immediately post-idealist spokesman for science, as distinct from

the Ch'ing empiricists: 'The explicit realization of the antithesis between the deductive rationalism of the scholastics and the inductive observational methods of the moderns must chiefly be ascribed to Bacon. . . . Induction has proved to be a somewhat more complex process than Bacon anticipated. . . . But when you have made all the requisite deductions, Bacon remains as one of the great builders who constructed the mind of the modern world' [Whitehead, *Science and the Modern World*, 62–3].

25. Margaret L. Wiley, *The Subtle Knot, Creative Scepticism in Seventeenth Century England* (Cambridge, 1952), 18.

26. For examples, see note 7, above; 'Meng-tzu tsu-i su-cheng', Preface, 1b; 'Tung-yüan wen-chi', *An-hui ts'ung-shu*, 6th Ser., *ts'e* 10, 8.13.

27. Tai, 'Tung-yüan wen-chi', *ts'e* 35, 9.9.

28. Yen, 4.8b.

29. *Ibid.*, 1.1b.

30. T'an, 55.

31. E.g. Liang, 'Tai Tung-yüan sheng-jih ni-pai nien chi-nien hui yüan-ch'i' (The origins of the conference to commemorate the two hundredth anniversary of the birth of Tai Tung-yüan), *Yin-ping-shih ho-chi, wen-chi*, XIV, 40.38 *et seq.* [hereafter, YPSHC: WC], where Tai's affinity with modern science is proclaimed. Liang also related the Yen-Li school to the pragmatism of James and Dewey, which was associated with the use of scientific method; see Liang, 'Yen-Li hsüeh-p'ai yü hsien-tai chiao-yü ssu-ch'ao' (The Yen-Li school and the contemporary educational thought-tide), *ibid.*, 41.3. Hsü Shih-ch'ang (1858–1939) made a more extreme statement of the eternal and universal significance of the Yen-Li teachings; see Mansfield Freeman, 'Yen Hsi Chai, a Seventeenth Century Philosopher', *Journal of the North China Branch of the Royal Asiatic Society*, LVII (1926), 70.

Hsiao I-shan, *Ch'ing-tai t'ung-shih* (General history of the Ch'ing period) (Shanghai, 1927), I, 763 and 797, finds a spirit very similar to that of modern science in Ch'ing scholarship, especially in Ku Yen-wu and the Han Learning. Hou Wai-lu, I, 165, similarly finds a strong tendency towards modern science in Ku and the Yen-Li school.

32. Joseph Needham, *Science and Civilization in China*, 7 volumes, in process of publication.

33. Needham, I (Cambridge, 1954), 43.

34. So seen by Needham, I, 4.

CHAPTER II

1. Cf. Plato's *Republic*, a consistent model for a timeless, permanent social order. Plato held that philosophy, as soon as it turned from the study of nature to set up standards for human things, was at war with the state, potentially; and to banish the chance of conflict between the state, which has the authority, and philosophers out of office, he made the philosophers rulers of the Republic. See Werner Jaeger, *Paideia: the Ideals of Greek Culture* (New York, 1943), II, 71.

2. For the link between constancy of the social structure and constancy of taste, see Levin L. Schücking, *The Sociology* of *Literary Taste* (New York, 1944), 64.

3. For Swift's humanistic attack on 'originality', see the famous passage about the 'modern' spider (bringing dirt and poison, spun and spat wholly from himself) and the 'ancient' bee (pretending to nothing of his own, but ranging through nature to make honey and wax, or sweetness and light), in *An Account of a Battel between the Antient and Modern Books in St. James' Library* (first published in 1704). For his antipathy to science, see *Gulliver's Travels*, Part III, Chapter V ('The Grand Academy of Lagardo'), directed against the Royal Society, the citadel of science, which was challenging the humanities as an intellectual fashion. The conflict between science and letters was already established as a literary theme, e.g. in Shadwell's seventeenth-century play, *The Virtuoso* (i.e. scientist), in which the rhetorician Sir Samuel Formal remarks of Sir Nicholas Gimcrack: 'He is an enemy to wit as all Virtuosos are'; see C. S. Duncan, 'The Scientist as a Comic Type', *Modern Philology*, XIV, No. 5 (Sept. 1916), 92. For the necessarily ephemeral quality of a *combined* literary and scientific amateurism in that century and the next (because of the complexity, on the one hand, of Newtonian physics, which heralded the end of scientific communication between the generally cultivated humanist and the necessarily specialized natural scientist; and because of the philosophical implications, on the other hand, of Newtonian physics, which rendered the gentleman's tribute to Newton a tribute not so much to science as to order), see B. Ifor Evans, *Literature and Science* (London, 1954), 22-5, 72, and J. Bronowski, *William Blake, 1757–1827* (Harmondsworth, 1954), 145. For Swift's distaste for utilitarian criteria, and the contrast on this issue between Swift and such anti-traditionalistic 'moderns' and devotees of science as Bacon and Locke, see Miriam Kosh Starkman, *Swift's Satire on*

Learning in 'A Tale of a Tub' (Princeton, 1950), 72, 9, and Walter E. Houghton, Jr., 'The English Virtuoso in the Seventeenth Century' (part 2), *Journal of the History of Ideas*, III, No. 2 (April 1942), 215; and, for his corollary disdain of the business interests, Bronowski, 40. As a confirmation of the coherence of these various antipathies, see W. Arthur Lewis, *The Theory of Economic Growth* (London, 1955), 70–1, for an analysis of the stimulation of specialization by trade, of intellectual diversity (with attendant individual narrowness) by specialization, and of communal intellectual progress by intellectual diversity.

4. Cf. Fei Hsiao-tung, *China's Gentry: Essays in Rural-Urban Relations* (Chicago, 1953), 75: 'In Chinese traditional society, the intelligentsia have been a class without technical knowledge. They monopolized authority based on the wisdom of the past, spent time on literature, and tried to express themselves through art.'

5. It should be noted that the formalistic 'eight-legged essay', with its strong emphasis on rhetorical skill and literary culture, became a prominent feature of the examination system in the early Ming period. It was Ku Yen-wu's opinion that it took its final form some time after the *Ch'eng-hua* period (1465–87), but an essay of 1385 has been preserved which has all the features of the developed form. See Suzuki Torao, 'Kobun hihō no zenku' (The development of the forms of *pa-ku wen*), *Shinagaku*, IV, No. 1 (July 1926), 35–7; for specimens of the style, *ibid.*, 30–1, 35–6; and for T'ang and Sung predecessors, *Tz'u-hai*, I 325.

6. Etienne Balázs, 'Les aspects significatifs de la société chinoise', *Asiatische Studien*, VI (1952), 84.

7. Albert Chan, in his unpublished Harvard doctoral dissertation, *The Decline and Fall of the Ming Dynasty, a Study of the Internal Factors* (Oct. 1953), 113–14, notes that sub-officials, *li*, were a class quite distinct from that of officials, *kuan*. *Li* were employed by *kuan* to look after public works, among other things. In the *Yung-lo* period (1403–24), sub-officials were forbidden to take the examinations for metropolitan degrees.

8. On this suggestion that the cultural prestige of office in China (its economic value is another subject) depended on the external associations of bureaucracy, cf. C. Wright Mills, *White Collar: the American Middle Classes* (New York, 1951), 247: 'The rationalization of office and store undermines the special skills based on experience and education. It makes the employee easy to replace by shortening the training he needs: it weakens not

only his bargaining power but his prestige. It opens white-collar positions to people with less education, thus destroying the educational prestige of white collar work, for there is no inherent prestige attached to the nature of any work; it is, Hans Speier remarks, the esteem the people doing it enjoy that often lends prestige to the work itself.'

9. Kenneth Bradley, 'Personal Portrait: Sir Andrew Cohen', *London Calling*, No. 745 (Feb. 11, 1954), 13.

10. Noel Gilroy Annan, *Leslie Stephen: His Thought and Character in Relation to His Time* (Cambridge, 1952), 36–8. The opinion is G. M. Young's.

11. Matthew Arnold, *Culture and Anarchy* (London, 1920), 31.

12. Victoria Contag, 'Tung Ch'i-ch'ang's *Hua Ch'an Shih Sui Pi* und das *Hua Shuo* des Mo Shih-lung', *Ostasiatische Zeitschrift* (hereafter, OZ), IX, Nos. 3–4 (May–August, 1933), 86. The term, *shih-ta-fu*, derives from the title of certain clerical aides to the aristocracy in antiquity.

13. The *Han-lin t'u hua yüan*, to give it its full Sung title, was actually founded by the minor dynasty of the Southern T'ang (923–36). See Taki Seiichi, 'Shina e no ni dai chōryū' (The two main currents of Chinese painting), *Kokka*, 458 (Jan. 1929), 3. It should be noted, however, that A. G. Wenley has expressed doubts that a *hua-yüan*, by that name or by variants of it, in fact existed in the Sung dynasty, although various contemporary and near-contemporary sources refer to it. Mr. Wenley infers from a study of the *Sung-shih* that not a *yüan*, or official academy, independent of other government departments, but *hsüeh*, or schools, under various superior departments, existed then. See A. G. Wenley, 'A Note on the So-called Sung Academy of Painting', *Harvard Journal of Asiatic Studies*, VI, No. 2 (June 1941), 269–72.

14. Contag, 92.

15. Osvald Sirèn, *A History of Later Chinese Painting* (London, 1938), I, 24.

16. Charles O. Hucker, 'The "*Tung-lin*" Movement of the Late Ming Period', *Chinese Thought and Institutions*, ed. John K. Fairbank (Chicago, 1957), 137–8. For an account of a Ming court painter (Liu Chieh, 1522–66) whose style was that of the Sung Academy and who was appointed an officer in the Imperial Guard, see Sirèn, *Early Chinese Paintings from the A. W. Bahr Collection* (London, 1938), 91.

17. Hu Man, *Chung-kuo mei-shu shih* (History of Chinese art) (Shanghai, 1950), 151.

18. Herbert A. Giles, *An Introduction to the History of Chinese Pictorial Art* (London, 1918), 181. For Shen Shih-t'ien as the very embodiment of the refined 'Wu taste' in sixteenth-century and subsequent opinion, see Tempō Imazeki, 'Shin Sekiden jiseki' (Biographical note on Shen Shih-t'ien), part 1, *Kokka*, 457 (Dec. 1928), 349–50.

19. Contag, 88.

20. Sirèn, *Later Chinese Painting*, I, 7.

21. *Ku-kung shu-hua chi* (Palace Museum collection of painting and calligraphy) (Peiping, 1930), *ts'e* 1, plate 15.

22. Contag, OZ, IX, 5 (Oct. 1933), 178.

23. Sirèn, *A. W. Bahr Collection*, 103.

24. Sheng Tsung-ch'ien, 'Chieh-chou hsüeh hua pien', *Hua-lun ts'ung-k'an* (Collection of treatises on painting), ed. Yü Hai-yen (Peiping, 1937), *ts'e* 3, 2.1.

25. Tanaka Toyozō, *Tōyō bijutsu dansō* (Discussions on Far Eastern art) (Tokyo, 1949), 69. For Tung Ch'i-ch'ang's admiration of Mi Fu, see *Ku-kung shu hua chi, ts'e* 1, plate 15, and Contag, 'Schriftcharakteristeken in der Malerei, dargestellt an Bildern Wang Meng's und anderer Maler der Südschule', OZ, XVII, No. 1–2 (1941), 49.

26. 'Lotus Flowers, by Liu (sic) Chih', *Kokka*, 315 (Aug. 1916), 38 (in English). In Giles, 187, there is a very similar story involving Wen Cheng-ming and a merchant.

27. Raphael Petrucci, tr., *Encyclopedie de la peinture chinoise* (Paris, 1918), 48. See introduction, vi–viii, for dating of the work.

28. Tsou I-kuei, 'Hsiao-shan hua-p'u', *Ssu t'ung ku chai lun hua chi k'o*, ed. Chang Hsiang-ho (Peking, 1909), *ts'e* 3, 2.4b.

29. Sirèn, 'An Important Treatise on Painting from the Beginning of the Eighteenth Century', *T'oung pao*, XXXIV, No. 3 (1938), 154. The reference is to Wang Yüan-ch'i (1642–1715).

30. For these references to the high standing of Tung Ch'i-ch'ang, see Naitō Konan, 'Tō Kishō Sai Bunki ezō' (Tung Ch'i-ch'ang's portrait of Ts'ai Wen-chi), *Tōyō bijutsu* (Far Eastern art), I (April 1929), 64, and Tajima Shiichi, ed., *Tōyō bijutsu taikan* (General View of Far Eastern art), XI (Tokyo, 1912), plate 16.

31. The *locus classicus* for the origins of the north–south dichotomy in Chinese painting is Tung Ch'i-ch'ang, *Hua Ch'an shih sui-pi*, ed. Wang Ju-lu (Peking, 1840), 2.14b–15. This passage has been quoted or paraphrased in almost every serious modern history of Chinese art. One can see Tung's identification of the southern style with the amateur style in a slightly earlier passage

in the same work, where he states that *wen-jen chih hua*, literati-painting, began with Wang Wei (*ibid.*, 2.14). The earliest extant appearance of the term *wen-jen hua*, as a synonym first for *shih-ta-fu* (or *shih-fu*) *hua* and later also for *nan hua*, seems to be in the *Hua-p'u* (Treatise on painting) of T'ang Yin (1466–1524), where it is recorded as an expression of Wang Ssu-shan, of the Yüan period; see Ise Senichirō, *Ji Ko Gaishi shi Kei Kō Shina sansuiga shi* (History of Chinese landscape painting from Ku K'ai-chih to Ching Hao) (Kyoto, 1933), 147.

For a discussion of the growing post-Sung correlation between painting style and personal status of the painter, and of Tung Ch'i-ch'ang's friend, Mo Shih-lung, as the original theorist about northern and southern schools and their beginnings, see Yoshizawa Tadashi, 'Nanga to bunjinga' (Southern painting and literati painting), part 1, *Kokka*, 622 (Sept. 1942), 257–8.

The following are among the major pre-Ming painters who were later identified as representative figures in one or the other school: *Northern*—the colourist landscapists Chao Po-chü and his brother Chao Po-su, and the academicians Liu Sung-nien, Li T'ang, Ma Yüan, and Hsia Kuei, all of the Sung dynasty; *Southern*—the Sung painters Li Ch'eng, Fan K'uan, Tung Yüan, and Chü-jan, and the 'four masters' of the Yüan dynasty, Huang Kung-wang, Wu Chen, Ni Tsan, and Wang Meng. See T'eng Ku, 'Kuan-yü yüan-t'i hua ho wen-jen hui chih shih ti k'ao-ch'a' (An examination of the history of 'academic' and 'literati' painting), *Fu-jen hsüeh-chih*, II, No. 2 (Sept. 1930), 68.

32. Taki, 'Shin Keinan *Kudan kinga satsu* ni tsuite' (On the picture-album *Chiu-tuan chin-hua-ts'e*, by Shen Ch'i-nan), *Kokka*, 495 (Feb. 1932), 33.

33. Contag, 'Schriftcharakteristeken', 49.

34. Contag, 'Tung Ch'i-ch'ang', OZ, IX (3–4), 96.

35. Sirèn, *Later Chinese Painting*, I, 182.

36. Yoshizawa, part 3, *Kokka*, 624 (Nov. 1942), 346. *Ching-miao* seems to have become a fairly standard term of qualified praise for academics. A Ch'ing continuation of a Yüan treatise says of Lan Meng, a seventeenth-century painter usually ascribed to the academic Chekiang school (see below), that he was expert in painting landscapes with Sung and Yüan models, and that there were none which were not *ching-miao*; see Hsia Wen-yen, *T'u-hui pao-chien*, ed. Chieh-lu ts'ao t'ang, 7.29.

37. Contag, *Die Beiden Steine* (Braunschweig, 1950), 37.

38. Ise, 'Bunjinga—nanga yori bunjinga e no suii' (Literati

painting—the transition from southern painting to literati painting), *Tōyō bijutsu,* III (Sept. 1929), 7.

39. Shih Yai, 'Sung-li Han-lin t'u-hua yüan chi hua-hsüeh shih shih hsi-nien' (A chronology of notable historical data and works of the Hanlin painting academy of the Sung dynasty), *Chung-kuo wen-hua yen-chiu hui-p'an* (Bulletin of Chinese Studies, Chengtu), III (Sept. 1943), 327.

40. This description holds true even for most of the scholars in the prominent *Lu* (Hsiang-shan)—*Wang* (Yang-ming) tradition, which was more introspective than the examination-sanctioned Chu Hsi tradition, but which was still in the world of conventional cultural standards, whatever the allegations made by orthodox critics of its anti-social implications. What happened to the relatively rare Ming literatus who embraced Ch'an as though he really meant it, with all its aura of apostasy from Confucian morality and rejection of its textual underpinnings, is suggested by Charles Hucker's account of the persecution of Li Chih; see Hucker, 144–5. Obviously, the authoritative exponents of a southern aesthetic in painting met with no such strictures.

41. For the tendency among members of the Academy to make preparatory series of sketches, see Aschwin Lippe, 'The Waterfall', *Bulletin of the Metropolitan Museum of Art,* XII (Oct. 1953), 60.

42. For the disparagement of the concept of fine arts because of its connotation of conscious planning, cf. the late sixteenth century scholars Kao Lien and T'u Lung, quoted in Contag' 'Tung Ch'i-ch'ang's', IX (3–4), 95.

43. Ch'in Chung-wen, *Chung-kuo hui-hua hsüeh shih* (History of Chinese painting) (Peiping, 1934), 150; 'I Fukyū hitsu: sansui zu' (Landscape, by I Fu-chiu), *Kokka,* 174 (Nov. 1904), 108 and plate V.

44. P'an T'ien-shou, *Chung-kuo hui-hua shih* (History of Chinese painting) (Shanghai, 1935), 161–2; Liu Ssu-hsün, *Chung-kuo mei-shu fa-ta shih* (History of the development of Chinese art) (Chungking, 1946), 98. It is true that, especially in the early Ming period, some fine Buddhist figure paintings were executed; but these seem to have derived rather from the early Ming passion for imitating T'ang works than from Buddhist religious commitment.

45. For these as Sung concepts of Su Tung-p'o *et al.,* see, respectively, J. P. Dubosc, 'A New Approach to Chinese Painting', *Oriental Art,* III, No. 2 (1950), 53; Louise Wallace Hackney and Yau Chang-foo, *A Study of Chinese Paintings in the Collection of Ada*

Small Moore (London, New York, and Toronto, 1940), 197; and Alexander Coburn Soper, *Kuo Jo-hsü's 'Experiences in Painting'* (*T'u-Hua Chien-Wen-Chih*) (Washington, 1951), 15.

46. T'ang Chih-ch'i, *Hui shih cheng-yen* (Shanghai, 1935), 1.1.

47. Sirèn, 'An Important Treatise', 155, 161.

48. Lu Ch'ien, *Pa-ku wen hsiao-shih* (Short history of the eight-legged essay) (Shanghai, 1937), 44.

49. Friedrich Hirth, *Native Sources for the History of Chinese Pictorial Art* (New York, 1917), 11; Florence Wheelock Ayscough, *Catalogue of Chinese Paintings Ancient and Modern by Famous Masters* (Shanghai, n.d.), 19.

50. 'Shin Sekiden hitsu "*Zō Go Kan gyō*" emaki kai' (Analysis of Shen Shih-t'ien's scroll-painting, 'A gift to Wu K'uan upon his making a journey'), *Kokka*, 545 (April 1936), 113.

51. Goethe, quoted in Nikolaus Pevsner, *Academies of Art* (Cambridge, 1940), 191.

52. Edward Young, 'Conjectures on Original Composition', *Criticism: the Foundations of Modern Literary Judgment*, ed. Mark Schorer, Josephine Miles, and Gordon McKenzie (New York, 1948), 15.

53. Harold A. Small, ed., *Form and Function, remarks on art by Horatio Greenough* (Berkeley and Los Angeles, 1947), 22.

54. Contag, 'Tung Ch'i-ch'ang's', IX (3–4), 96.

55. Yün Shou-p'ing, 'Ou hsiang kuan hua pa' (*chüan* 11–12, *Ou hsiang kuan chi*), *Pieh hsia chai ts'ung-shu*, ed. Chiang Kuang-hsü (Shanghai, 1923), *ts'e* 16.4.

56. T'eng, 80.

57. Yukio Yashiro, 'Connoisseurship in Chinese Painting', *Journal of the Royal Society of Arts*, LXXXIV, No. 4339 (Jan. 17, 1936), 266.

58. Sheng, *ts'e* 3, 2.3b.

59. Tanaka, 81.

60. Serge Elisséev, 'Sur le paysage à l'encre de Chine du Japon', *Revue des Arts Asiatiques*, 2 (June 1925), 31–2.

61. For this distinction, see Michael Oakeshott, *Experience and Its Modes* (Cambridge, 1933), 21–3.

62. Ananda K. Coomeraswamy, 'The Nature of Buddhist Art', *Figures of Speech or Figures of Thought* (London, 1946), 177. Cf. Croce's distinction between intuitive and intellectual activity, as the distinction between apprehending the individuality of a thing by thinking oneself into it, making its life one's own, and analysing or classifying it from an external point of view: 'Do you wish to

understand the true history of a blade of grass? Try to become a blade of grass; and if you cannot do it, satisfy yourself with analysing its parts. . . .' See Collingwood, *The Idea of History* (Oxford, 1946), 199.

63. H. W. Cassirer, *A Commentary on Kant's 'Critique of Judgment'* (London, 1938), 19; and Christopher Gray, *Cubist Aesthetic Theories* (Baltimore, 1953), 47–9. For the iron law of correlation between ideal and intuition, note also the place of *Ion* (in which art is 'the god speaking through one', hence art cannot be taught) among the dialogues of the greatest idealist, Plato; and for the reverse of the coin, the artist's willing acceptance of the discipline of teachable rules and his denial of the necessity of the intuitive oneness of art and contemplation, note Valéry's warning against the 'devil of the line of least resistance' (i.e. audacious 'anti-academic' refusal of set forms) and his corollary teaching, 'Beautiful lines are matured on the day after inspiration'. See Paul Valéry, *Reflections on the World Today* (London, 1951), 60, 145.

64. The literature of art-criticism ran riot in the Ming era, so that no attempt has since been made to collect it all; see Hirth, 25–6.

65. Contag, 'Das Mallehrbuch für Personen-Malerei des Chieh Tzu Yüan', *T'oung Pao*, XXXIII, No. 1 (1937), 18. The critics' division of painters into three classes, according to talent, went back at least to the T'ang dynasty.

66. *Ibid.*, 20.

67. Elisséev, 32. For descriptions of Ming and Ch'ing recorded vocabularies of abstractions—epitomes of typical and permanent features of natural forms and rules of composition to produce them—see, *inter alia*, Victor Rienaecker, 'Chinese Art (Sixth Article), Painting—I', *Apollo*, XL, No. 236 (Oct. 1944), 81–4; Benjamin March, *Some Technical Terms of Chinese Painting* (Baltimore, 1935) xii–xiii; Fang-chuen Wang, *Chinese Freehand Flower Painting* (Peiping, 1936) 98–9; William Cohn, *Chinese Painting* (London and New York, 1948), 18.

68. Laurence Sickman, in *Great Chinese Painters of the Ming and Ch'ing Dynasties* (catalogue of an exhibition, March 11–April 2, 1949, at Wildenstein Galleries, New York); concurred in by Benjamin Rowland, in *Masterpieces of Chinese Bird and Flower Painting* (catalogue of an exhibition, Oct. 30–Dec. 14, 1951, at the Fogg Art Museum, Cambridge), 4.

69. Arnold, 'The Literary Influence of Academies', *Essays in Criticism* (Boston, 1865), 47–51.

70. Naitō Tọrajirō, *Shinchō shoga fu* (Treatise on Ch'ing calligraphy and painting) (Osaka, 1917), 3. Text in Chinese.

71. Contag, *Die Beiden Steine*, 10.

72. *Ming-jen shu hua chi* (Collection of calligraphy and painting of famous practitioners) (Shanghai, 1921), IV, plate 2.

73. Sirèn, *The Chinese on the Art of Painting* (Peiping, 1936), 188.

74. Werner Speiser, 'Ba Da Schan Jen', *Sinica*, VIII, No. 2 (March 10, 1933), 49.

75. Sirèn, 'Shih-t'ao, Painter, Poet and Theoretician', *Bulletin of the Museum of Far Eastern Antiquities*, XXI (Stockholm, 1949), 55.

76. Aoki Masaru, 'Sekitō no ga to garon to' (Shih-t'ao's painting and his views on painting), *Shinagaku*, I, No. 8 (April 1921), 583.

77 Yawata Sekitarō, *Shina gajin kenkyū* (Study of Chinese painters) (Tokyo, 1942), 170.

78. Herbert Franke, 'Zur Biographie des Pa-Ta-Shan-Jen', *Asiatica: Festschrift Friedrich Weller* (Leipzig, 1954), 130.

79. *Chung-kuo jen-ming ta tz'u-tien*, quoted in Speiser, 'Ba Da Schan Jen', 46.

80. Yū Yamanoi, 'Meimatsu Shinchō ni okeru keiji jiyō no gaku' (The 'practical affairs' school of the end of the Ming and the beginning of the Ch'ing), *Tōhō gaku ronshū* (Memoirs of the Institute of Eastern Culture) (Tokyo, 1954), 140–1, 149.

81. Bokuyūsō shujin, *Sekitō to Hachidaisenjin* (Shih-t'ao and Pa-ta-shan-jen) (Kanagawa ken, 1952), 3.

82. Aoki, 586. A conventional acceptance of Shih-t'ao's 'no method' principle of unconventionality is indicated, too, in this early seventeenth-century appraisal of Shen Shih-t'ien: 'He was, as Ch'an followers say, "absorbed in play unfettered by rules".' Shen, of course, was entirely in the main stream of the *wen-jen* southern tradition; see Kojiro Tomita and A. Kaiming Chiu, 'An Album of Landscapes and Poems by Shen Chou (1427–1509)', *Bulletin of the Museum of Fine Arts* (Boston), XLVI, No. 265 (Oct. 1948), 60.

83. Sirèn, 'Shih-t'ao', 41.

84. It should be noted that in the Sung period, an age of both Confucian consolidation and Confucianists' patronage of Ch'an ideals, a process called *Ch'an chiao i-chih*, a syncretism of intuition and learning, was observed in Ch'an as sutra-study pushed its way back in; see Heinrich Dumoulin, *The Development of Chinese Zen after the Sixth Patriarch in the Light of Mumonkan* (New York, 1953), 35.

85. Sirèn, *The Chinese on the Art of Painting*, 164. As an example of the literati's disinterest in originality, the same reference to the 'ten thousand volumes' and the 'ten thousand li' may be found in a contemporary treatise by Mo Shih-lung and in the later work, the *Mustard-seed Garden*; see Yoshizawa, 'Nanga to bunjinga' (part 1), *Kokka*, 622 (Sept. 1942), 260, and Petrucci, 4–5.

Sir Herbert Read, shifting the emphasis, misses the strain in Tung Ch'i-ch'ang which makes him such a revealing figure, when he writes: 'But one of the great artists of the Ming epoch, Tung Ch'i-ch'ang, said with perhaps obvious truth that no one was likely to gain such a state of grace, even if he read ten thousand books and ranged over ten thousand leagues; the artist is born, not made.' See Herbert Read, 'Modern Chinese Painting', *A Coat of Many Colours* (London, 1945), 266.

86. Contag, *Die Beiden Steine*, 10.

87. Yün, *ts'e* 16.8–8b.

88. Hackney and Yao, 56.

89. Yoshizawa, 'Nanga to bunjinga' (part 3), *Kokka*, 624 (Nov. 1942), 346.

90. Hsü Ch'in, 'Ming hua lu' (Records of Ming painting), *Ts'ung-shu chi-ch'eng* (Shanghai, 1926), 27.

91. See 'Ran Ei hitsu: *Hisetsu senzen zu kai*' (Analysis of 'Flying snow and a thousand mountains', by Lan Ying), *Kokka*, 477 (Aug. 1930), 228. For the distinction between the Che school (in the Ma Yüan—Hsia Kuei tradition of the monochrome landscape of the Southern Sung academy), Yüan school (particularly figure-painting and decorative colour landscape, 'blue-green', etc., more meticulous than Che), and Wu school (for whom both the preceding schools were academic)—and for an account of their intermingling, see Hu, 150–1, and P'an, 167–70.

92. For Ming and Ch'ing varying assignments of these painters to schools, see Tajima, *Tōyō bijutsu taikan*, X (Tokyo, 1911), 16; Yawata, 68–9; Ichiuji Giryō, *Tōyō bijutsu shi* (History of Far Eastern art) (Tokyo, 1936), 215; Huang Pin-hung, *Ku hua cheng* (Evidence on old painting) (Shanghai, 1931), 30–2; and Speiser, 'T'ang Yin' (Part 2), OZ, XI, Nos. 3–4 (May–Aug. 1935), 109.

93. Yonezawa Yoshiho, 'Kyū Ei hitsu: hakubyō *Tan ran tei* zu' (The *Chuan lan ting*, a picture in the *pai-miao* method, by Ch'iu Ying), *Kokka*, 708 (March 1951), 122; Lin Feng-mien, *I-shu ts'ung-lun* (Essays on art) (Shanghai, 1937), 121; Arthur Waley, 'A Chinese Picture', *The Burlington Magazine*, XXX, No. 1 (Jan. 1917), 10.

94. Unzansei, 'Kyū Ei no gasatsu ni tsuite' (On a picture book by Ch'iu Ying), *Kokka*, 475 (June 1930), 159–60; Kyū Ei Tōjin shii e kai' (Explanation of Ch'iu Ying's paintings on themes from T'ang poetry), *Kokka*, 481 (Dec. 1930), 344–5.
There is a similar album by Shen Shih-t'ien, one of nine paintings, each after an individual early artist; see Taki, 'Shin Keinan *Kudan nishikie satsu* ni tsuite', 35.

95. Sirén, *Later Chinese Painting*, I, 133–4; Speiser, 'T'ang Yin' (part 1), OZ, XI, 1–2 (Jan.–April 1935), 21. Cf. the note on T'ang by the famous sixteenth-century collector, Wang Shih-chen, which mentions as a matter of course T'ang's derivations (all Wang's notes have an account of derivations at the beginning of his brief biographical sketches). Wang acknowledges a thoroughly eclectic background for T'ang, in which Sung academicians like Li T'ang, Ma Yüan, *et al.*, and Yüan intuitive masters like Huang Kung-wang all figure; see Wang Shih-chen, 'I-yüan chih yen fu lu', *Yen-chou shan jen ssu pu kao*, ed. Shih ching t'ang, n.d., 155, 16b–17.

96. Tajima, *Tōyō bijutsu taikan*, XI, plate 6.

97. See *Kokka*, 481, no. 5 in the illustrated set. Cf. a late Ming account of a Ch'iu Ying painting, which identified the styles (and praised the combinations) of various masters in Ch'iu Ying's stones and mountains, trees, figures, and colouring; see Sirén, *Later Chinese Painting*, I, 146.

98. 'Sei Moyō hitsu: *Sankyo hōmon* zu kai' (Analysis of 'A visitor to a mountain abode', by Sheng Mao-yeh), *Kokka*, 543 (Feb. 1946), 53. Lan Ying, too, was known to render a background of mountains and mists *à la* Mi Fu (southern), while his pines in the foreground were of the Ma-Hsia, northern type; see 'A Summer Landscape, by Lan Yin (sic)', *Kokka*, 232 (Sept. 1909), 95–6 (in English).

99. Wada Mikio, ed., *Tōyō bijutsu taikan*, XII (Tokyo, 1913), plate 6; Contag, 'Tung Ch'i-ch'ang's' (conclusion), OZ, IX, 5, 181–2. The quotation is from the *Kuo ch'ao hua cheng lu* (1739), by Chang Keng.

100. 'Ō Sekikoku hitsu: semmen sansui zu' (Landscape painted on a fan, by Wang Hui), *Kokka*, 614 (Jan. 1942), 24; 'A Landscape, by Wang Hui', *Kokka*, 250 (March 1911), 283 (in English); 'Ō Sekikoku hitsu: kambaku zu' (Looking at a waterfall, by Wang Hui), *Kokka*, 702 (Sept. 1950), 306.

101. Aimi Shigeichi, *Gumpō seigan* (Tokyo, 1914), II, plate 5; Nakamura Sakutarō and Ojika Bukkai, *Shina ega shi* (History of Chinese painting) (Tokyo, 1923), 163; P'an, 167.

102. Tsou I-kuei, cited in Ch'uan Han-sheng, 'Ch'ing-mo fan-tui Hsi-hua ti yen-lun' (Arguments against westernization in the late Ch'ing period), *Lingnan hsüeh-pao*, V, Nos. 3-4 (Dec. 20, 1936), 128. For *hua-chiang* as a connoisseur's term for mere 'professional qualities', see Gustav Ecke, 'Comments on Calligraphies and Paintings', *Monumenta Nipponica*, III (1938), 569.

103. Wang Shih-chen on T'ang Yin; see Wang Shih-chen, 155.17.

Generally, for the Ming-Ch'ing connoisseurs' cult of brush-work—its sensitivity to nuance, feeling for extra-aesthetic suggestiveness in the painter's strokes, elaborate systems of classification, tendency to proliferate detail (the subject of brushwork) in what might have been truly southern empty space, and gradual change of emphasis from typical motives in an intellectually regulated composition to more individualized motives in free arrangement, more suitable to the range of virtuosity—see, successively, A. Bulling and John Ayers, 'Chinese Art of the Ming Period in the British Museum', *Oriental Art*, III, No. 2 (1950), 79; Contag, *Die Sechs Berühmten Maler der Ch'ing-Dynastie* (Leipzig, 1940), 17; Tomita, 'Brush-strokes in Far Eastern Painting', *Eastern Art*, III (Philadelphia, 1931), 29-31; Waley, *An Introduction to the Study of Chinese Painting* (London, 1923), 247; Fang-chuen Wang, 102; Rienaecker, 'Chinese Art (Seventh Article), Painting—II', *Apollo*, XL, No. 237 (Nov. 1944) 109; Tsou, *ts'e* 3, 2.6; Arthur von Rosthorn, 'Malerei und Kunstkritik in China', *Wiener Beiträge zur Kunst- und Kultur-Geschichte*, IV (1930), 22; George Rowley, 'A Chinese Scroll of the Ming Dynasty: Ming Huang and Yang Kuei-fei Listening to Music', *Worcester Art Museum Annual*, II (1936-7), 70-1; Cohn, 92; John C. Ferguson, *Chinese Painting* (Chicago, 1927), 62; Edouard Chavannes and Raphael Petrucci, *La peinture chinoise au Musée Cernuschi, Avril-Juin 1912* (Ars Asiatica I) (Brussels and Paris, 1914), 49-50; Edgar C. Schenck, 'The Hundred Wild Geese', *Honolulu Academy of Arts Annual Bulletin*, I (1939), 6-10.

104. For details on this prescription of Tung Ch'i-ch'ang *et al.* for the painting of synthetic pictures, see Tung, 2.5-8; Alan Houghton Broderick, *An Outline of Chinese Painting* (London, 1949), 32; Waley, *An Introduction*, 246-50; Contag, 'Schriftcharakteristeken', 48, and *Die Sechs*, 20; Sirèn, *The Chinese on the Art of Painting*, 143, and *Later Chinese Painting*, I, 187; Ferguson, 'Wang Ch'uan', OZ, III, No. 1 (April-June 1914), 58-9.

105. Paul L. Grigaut, 'Art of the Ming Dynasty', *Archaeology*, V, No. 1 (March 1952), 12.

106. As an example of the latter, Waley refers to the transfer of the ideals of literary study to art, in this fashion: a certain river having been mentioned in the *Shih-ching* in connection with autumn, it must always be represented by the painter in an autumn scene. See Waley, *An Introduction*, 246. Sirèn speaks of the Ming taste as demanding an inscription on a painting in a literary style appropriate to the motif and calligraphic style corresponding to the manner in which the picture was painted, i.e. *k'ai-shu* (formal style) calligraphy for *kung-pi* (highly finished, meticulous) painting, and *ts'ao-shu* (cursive style) calligraphy for *hsieh-i* (intuitive) painting; see Sirèn, 'Shih T'ao', 35-6.

107. Kenneth Clark, *Landscape into Art* (London, 1949), 30.

108. C. M. Bowra, *The Creative Experiment* (London, 1949), 2.

109. Speiser, 'Eine Landschaft von Wang Hui in Köln', OZ, XVII, Nos. 1-2 (1941), 170.

110. 'Abe Kojirō zō; Un Nanden hitsu kaki satsu' ('Flowers' by Yün Nan-t'ien in the Abe Kojirō Collection), *Bijutsu kenkyū*, XCII (Aug. 1939), 306.

111. 'Hashimoto Shinjirō zō: Un Nanden hitsu kahin seikyō zu' ('Fruits' by Yün Nan-t'ien in the Hashimoto Shinjirō Collection), *ibid.*, VII (July 1932), 237.

112. Tsou, *ts'e* 3, 1.1.

113. For discussions of this process, see Joseph R. Levenson, *Liang Ch'i-ch'ao and the Mind of Modern China* (Cambridge, 1953), *passim*, esp. 109-28; and below, Chapter VII.

114. For a discussion of nineteenth- and early twentieth-century utilitarian criticism, and proposals for modification, of what had come to appear the aestheticism of the examination-system, see Ssu-yü Teng and John K. Fairbank, *China's Response to the West* (Cambridge, 1954), esp. 139, 145, 178, and 205. For a somewhat earlier suggestion of this mentality, from a time when such opinions were but straws in the wind, see Fang Chao-ying's biography of Kung Tzu-chen (1792-1841), in Arthur W. Hummel, ed., *Eminent Chinese of the Ch'ing Period* (Washington, 1943), I, 432-3: Kung, bitter about his disqualification from the *Han-lin yüan* on grounds of poor calligraphy, became contemptuous of such aesthetic tests for government service and ultimately, charging the Ch'ing regime with decadence, advocated the abolition of the civil service examinations as practised in his day.

As Ralph Powell has pointed out in *The Rise of Chinese Military Power, 1895-1912* (Princeton, 1955), 338, specialization in the newly-founded late-Ch'ing military schools for the training of professional officers riddled the theory of the omnicompetence of Chinese officials.

115. Max Weber, *The Religion of China* (Glencoe, 1951), 248.

116. Chung-li Chang, in *The Chinese Gentry: Studies on Their Role in Nineteenth-Century Chinese Society* (Seattle, 1955), 174–6, has shown that in the first half of the Ch'ing period there was more scope for discussion in the examinations. Classically erudite and formally accomplished exposition, however, was always a *sine qua non*. The eight-legged essay, except for a significantly brief discontinuance in 1663, remained throughout the period the heart of the Ming-Ch'ing examination-system (witness the late-Ch'ing reformist memorials aimed specifically at this feature of the system), and the Ch'ing changes in the eight-legged essay were not in the nature of increasing formalism but of altering details of the forms: viz. (*Tz'u-hai*, I, 325), the number of characters in the essay, which had been fixed at 450 in the Hsün-chih reign (1644–61), was changed to 550 in the next reign and later to 600 and over.

Formalism in the late-Ch'ing period, in so far as it was really more intense than before (and not just an endemic quality, freshly noted), should be seen not as a modern aberration but as an always intrinsic potentiality of the examination-system; cf. Waley, *The Life and Times of Po Chü-i, 772–846 A.D.* (New York, 1949), 28, on the 'judgment form' of T'ang examination essay. The modern critical spirit which brought about the abolition of the examinations in 1905 was in the end a spirit to which the whole system was frankly incomprehensible, not one which discriminated between an allegedly earlier examination emphasis on plausible content and a later, correctible emphasis on stylistic frippery.

117. It is in the light of this modern Chinese development that the Chinese communists have used *pa-ku* as a term of opprobrium, and in the 1940's denounced 'party formalism' within their own ranks as a tissue of eight sins (like the hyper-aesthetic, or useless, addiction to 'lengthy phrases and empty words'), one for each leg of the eight-legged essay; see Albert Borowitz, *Fiction in Communist China* (mimeo.), Centre for International Studies, MIT (Cambridge, 1954), 5.

118. *Tz'u-hai*, I, 325.

INTERLUDE

1. Yüan Chieh (723–72), 'Civilization', in Waley, *Chinese Poems* (London, 1946), 118.

CHAPTER III

1. Ku, II, 7.32.

2. 'Ssu-pien lu chi-yao' (Summary of the *Ssu-pien lu*), *Cheng i t'ang ch'üan-shu*, ed. Chang Pai-hsing, suppl. ed., Tso Tsung-t'ang (1866–87), *ts'e* 109, 1.10b–11.

3. For this link between the development of modern science and the rise of the European merchant class, see Needham, 'Thoughts on the Social Relations of Science and Technology in China', *Centaurus*, III (1953), esp. 45–8.

4. *North China Herald*, April 14, 1866.

5. Hsü Shih-ch'ang, *Ch'ing Ju hsüeh-an* (Ch'ing Confucian scholarship) (Tientsin, 1938), 140.9b–11.

6. Tseng Kuo-fan, 'Jih-chi' (Diary), *Tseng Wen-chang kung ch'üan-chi* (Collected works of Tseng Kuo-fan) (Shanghai, 1917), *ts'e* 44, 1.6b.

7. *Ibid.*, 6b.

8. *Ibid.*, 6.

9. Tseng Chi-tse, *Tseng Hou jih-chi* (Marquis Tseng's diary) (Shanghai, 1881), 6b.

10. Tseng, Kuo-fan, 'Sheng-chih hua-hsiang chi' (Portrait record of philosophical masters), *Tseng Wen-chang kung ch'üan-chi*, *ts'e* 27, 2.3; Hsiao I-shan, *Tseng Kuo-fan* (Chungking, 1944), 30.

11. Chiang Chu-ko, *T'ung-ch'eng wen-p'ai p'ing-shu* (A discussion of the T'ung-ch'eng school of writing) (Shanghai, 1930), 68, 74.

12. Though it was the *li* of 'rites' considered in rather a Sung philosophical light, as 'the natural', in Waley's description (*The Analects of Confucius* [London, 1949], 75) 'what one returns to if he can overcome the personal cravings of his human heart and return to the impersonal state that belongs to the heart of Tao'.

13. Hsiao, 31–3. As Hellmut Wilhelm has pointed out, in 'The Background of Tseng Kuo-fan's Ideology', *Asiatische Studien*, Nos. 3–4 (1949), 95–7, Tseng protested that he revered Sung Confucianism but did not wish the Han school to be eliminated, and that he intended with his *li* conception to integrate society and reconcile former opponents.

14. Hsiao, 37, 46.

15. Wilhelm, 97.

16. Teng and Fairbank, 67.

17. As examples of works executed in the same eclectic spirit

by disciples of Tseng Kuo-fan, see Chu Tz'u-ch'i (1808-82), *Ch'ing-ch'ao Ju tsung* (Confucianism during the Ch'ing dynasty), discussed in Hsü Shih-ch'ang, 171.1b, and Ch'en Li (1810-82), *Tung-shu tu-shu chi* (Record of my reading) (Shanghai, 1898). The latter is particularly close to Tseng's eclecticism, attempting to harmonize the Sung Learning and the Han Learning on the grounds that some members of the Han school had made metaphysical researches like those of the Sung school (though the Han Learning generally emphasized textual criticism), while Chu Hsi, the leader of the highly metaphysical Sung school, was the fountainhead of the Han school's textual criticism; see *chüan* 15.

CHAPTER IV

1. This phrase, from the ancient *Mou-kung* (Art of war), by Sun-tzu, was used by Li Hung-chang in a memorial (1863) urging provision for instruction in foreign languages, and used again by Ma Chien-chung in a memorial (1894) recommending the establishment of a translation bureau; see Jen Shih-hsien, *Shina kyoiku shi* (History of Chinese education), Yamazaki Tatsuo, trans. (Tokyo, 1940), II, 95-6. Wilhelm has remarked (in 'The Problem of Within and Without, a Confucian Attempt in Syncretism', *Journal of the History of Ideas*, XII, No. 1 [Jan. 1951], 50) that everyone in this group of innovators conceived of westernization as a matter of defence.

For a translation of statements by representative Confucian westernizers—Lin Tse-hsü, Hsü Chi-yü, Tseng Kuo-fan, Hsüeh Fu-ch'eng, *et al.*—see Teng and Fairbank, *passim*.

2. Chang Chih-tung, *Ch'üan-hsüeh p'ien*, translated (rather, paraphrased) by Samuel I. Woodbridge under the title, *China's Only Hope* (New York, 1900), 63: 'In order to render China powerful, and at the same time preserve our own institutions, it is absolutely necessary that we should utilize western knowledge. But unless Chinese learning is made the basis of education, and a Chinese direction given to thought, the strong will become anarchists, and the weak, slaves.'

Ibid., 137-8: 'To sum up: Chinese learning is moral, Western learning is practical. Chinese learning concerns itself with moral conduct, Western learning, with the affairs of the world. ... If the Chinese heart throbs in unison with the heart of the sages, expressing the truth in irreprovable conduct, in filial piety, brotherly love, honesty, integrity, virtue; if government is loyalty and protection, then let government make use of foreign machinery and the railway from morning to night, and nothing untowards will befall the disciples of Confucius.'

For discussions of the use of this rationalization in nineteenth-century China, see Wilhelm, 'The Problem of Within and Without', 48-60, esp. 59-60; and Teng and Fairbank, 50 and 164.

3. Cf. Whitehead's ruthless emphasis on careerism as a major basis of the predominance of the Greek and Roman classics in western education before the modern emergence of new careers for which other training, especially in science, was necessary. See his sympathetic but unsentimental essay, 'The Place of Classics in Education', *The Aims of Education and Other Essays* (New York, 1949), esp. 69.

4. Ch'uan, 134.

5. Lin Tse-hsü and Wei Yüan (1794-1856) respectively, in 1842, quoted in Teng and Fairbank, 28 and 34.

6. *Ibid.*, 53.

7. Fujiwara Sadame, *Kindai Chūgoku shisō* (Modern Chinese thought) (Tokyo, 1948), 95.

8. Chao Feng-t'ien, *Wan-Ch'ing wu-shih nien ching-chi ssu-hsiang shih* (Economic thought during the last fifty years of the Ch'ing period), *Yenching hsüeh-pao*: Monograph 18 (Peiping, 1939), 88-9.

9. Witness the realization of Ch'i-ying, in his negotiations with the British at Nanking in 1842, that something new was on the horizon. Reporting to the emperor conventionally that the barbarians had been curbed, he went on to observe that the ceremonial forms used for dependent tribes would not restrain them—they would not consent to retire and remain as Annam and Liu-ch'iu. See Teng and Fairbank, 39-40.

10. Oakeshott, 98.

11. *Ibid.*, 41.

12. What industrialization, even just a bit of it, could do to traditional Chinese institutions and values there enshrined has been analysed in Marion J. Levy, Jr., *Family Revolution in Modern China* (Cambridge, 1949).

13. R. W. Meyer, *Leibnitz and the Seventeenth-Century Revolution* (Cambridge, 1952), 51.

14. Whitehead, *Modes of Thought*, 26.

15. Aristotle, *Metaphysics*, 1041b.

16. *Ibid.*, 1071b; Maimonides, *Guide of the Perplexed*, tr. M.

Friedlander (New York, n.d.), 178; Aquinas, *Concerning Being and Essence*, tr. George G. Leckie (New York and London, 1937), 7.

17. W. D. Ross, *Aristotle's Prior and Posterior Analytics* (Oxford, 1949), 284, 660; Aquinas, 44. In connection with notes 14–16, cf. the following passage (XVI, i–ii) in the *Chung-yung* (Doctrine of the Mean), a classical text whose importance was greatly emphasized by Chu Hsi (the translation is that of James Legge, *The Chinese Classics* [Oxford, 1893], I, 397): 'The Master said, "How abundantly do spiritual beings display the powers that belong to them! We look for them, but do not see them; we listen to, but do not hear them; yet they enter into (*t'i*) all things, and there is nothing without them!" ' The meaning of the passage is obscure, but one should note the suggestion of contradiction between *t'i* and objects of sense-perception. Used here in a verbal sense, *t'i* is implicitly identifiable with 'that which makes a thing what it generally *is*'.

18. Aquinas, 5.

19. *Lun-yü*, I, xii; Legge, I, 143: 'In practising the rules of propriety, a natural ease is to be prized.'

20. *Chu-tzu ch'üan-shu* (Complete works of Chu Hsi), ed. Li Kuang-ti (1714), 10.37–8. [Hereafter, CTCS.]

21. *Mencius*, III B, ii, 3; Legge, II (1895), 265.

22. CTCS, 20.76b.

23. Elsewhere (*Mencius*, IV A, xxvii, 2), in a passage which Chu Hsi discussed approvingly more than once, Mencius seems to have defined essentials functionally—a *t'i-yung* interpretation without, however, the use of those terms. The translation of the passage is as follows (Legge, II, 313–14): 'Mencius said, "The richest fruit (*shih*) of benevolence (*jen*) is this—the service of one's parents. The richest fruit of righteousness (*i*) is this—the obeying one's elder brothers. The richest fruit of wisdom (*chih*) is this—the knowing those two things, and not departing from them. The richest fruit of propriety (*li*) is this—the ordering and adorning those two things." ' See CTCS, 10.13b and 21.8. It is doubtful whether, at least for Chu Hsi's interpretation, the translation, 'The richest fruit', gives the full functional force of *shih*: it implies here rather the concept of 'bringing into practical being'.

24. CTCS, 10.13b.

25. See above, Chapter III. The parallel to Chu Hsi is striking: cf. CTCS, 13.2b–3, where *wai-mien*, 'outside', identified as the sphere of *yung*, is juxtaposed with *hsin-chung*, 'within the mind', and

it is maintained that the establishment of outer equilibrium is necessarily correlated with the existence of an inner equilibrium. Chu defines functionally the inner quality, *jen,* as that which perfectly regulates the *t'ien-hsia,* the outer world.

Cf. also a passage from a Classic very important to Sung Confucianism, *Ta-hsüeh,* 1, iv (Legge, I, 357): 'The ancients who wished to illustrate illustrious virtue (*ming-te*) throughout the kingdom first ordered well their own states (*chih ch'i kuo*). . . .' This, the beginning of a famous circular chain of sorites, seems more comprehensible from the point of view of *t'i-yung* logic than from any other: good government is the necessary external manifestation of illustrious virtue, an essence; *ming-te* is that which is evidenced in *chih-kuo.*

26. Legge, I, 150.

27. CTCS, 12.24.

28. CTCS, 22.37–7b. This particular discussion of *t'i-yung* developed from *Mencius,* VI A, xi, 1 (Legge, II, 414): 'Mencius said, "Benevolence is man's mind, and righteousness is man's path." '

29. J. D. Bernal, 'A Scientist in China', *The New Statesman and Nation,* XLIX, No. 1255 (March 26, 1955), 424.

30. Fung Yu-lan, *Hsin shih lun* (Discussions of new issues) (Changsha, 1940), 50–1.

31. Knight Biggerstaff, 'The T'ung Wen Kuan', *Chinese Social and Political Science Review,* XVIII, No. 3 (Oct. 1934), 321.

32. Jen, 107.

33. Ch'uan, 143, 147–8.

34. Swift, selecting Descartes as the villain, did, as a matter of fact, make an occasional 'English' protest against science as a French and Catholic vogue. But the advancement of science was so obviously a common European pursuit, in a web of international collaboration, that this pretext for anti-scientism could have none of the point of Wo-jen's distinction between China and the West.

35. See above, note 12.

36. Ch'en Teng-yüan, 'Hsi-hsüeh lai Hua shih kuo-jen che wu-tuan t'ai-tu' (Arbitrary Chinese attitudes at the time of the coming of western knowledge to China), *Tung-fang tsa-chih,* XXVII, No. 8 (April 1930), 61.

37. Teng and Fairbank, 145.

CHAPTER V

1. I have given a general account of the sources, content, and implications of the *chin-wen* reformist doctrine in *Liang Ch'i-ch'ao and the Mind of Modern China*, esp. 34–51.

2. In the nineteenth century, Protestant missionaries were much more active than Catholic missionaries in the field of secular western education; see Kenneth Scott Latourette, *A History of Christian Missions in China* (New York, 1929), 478.

3. The collaboration of missionaries with reformers is well known—e.g. the Welsh missionary, Timothy Richard, after reading one of K'ang Yu-wei's memorials on the subject of modernization, wrote him a letter which expressed his surprise that K'ang had arrived at Richard's conclusions, remarked that their aims seemed to be the same, and suggested consultations. A meeting of K'ang and Richard took place in Peking, and K'ang's disciple, Liang Ch'i-ch'ao, became Richard's Chinese secretary soon after. See Ch'en Kung-lu, *Chung-kuo chin-tai shih* (History of modern China) (Shanghai, 1935), 439–40.

Reformers and official westernizers met on the common ground of *tzu-ch'iang*, 'self-strengthening'. This phrase, which appears in texts of official recommendations for westernization at least as early as 1863, in Li Hung-chang's memorial recommending the study of foreign languages, was a favourite phrase of the reformers, whose principal organizations, active in Peking and Shanghai in 1895–6, were called the *Ch'iang-hsüeh hui* (Society for the study of strengthening). For this aspect of Li's memorial, see Shu Hsin-ch'eng, *Chin-tai Chung-kuo chiao-yü ssu-hsiang shih* (History of modern Chinese educational thought) (Shanghai, 1929), 25–6.

4. Wu Shih-ch'ang, *Chung-kuo wen-hua yü hsien-tai-hua wen-t'i* (Chinese culture and the question of modernization) (Shanghai, 1948), 55–6.

5. For a summary of the *Ta-t'ung shu*, K'ang's most explicit effort to outline his programme for action and to make Confucius its patron, see Itano Chōhachi, 'Kō Yūi no Daido Shisō' (K'ang Yu-wei's idea of the 'Great Harmony'), *Kindai Chūgoku kenkyū* (Modern Chinese researches), ed. Niida Noboru (Tokyo, 1948), 165–204.

6. Sanetō Keishu, *Shin Chūgoku no Jukyō hihan* (A critique of modern Chinese Confucianism) (Tokyo, 1948), 55, 59.

7. Tanouchi Takatsugi, *Shina kyoikugaku shi* (History of educational theory in China) (Tokyo, 1942), 520.

8. T'an Ssu-t'ung 'Jen hsüeh' (Study of benevolence), *T'an Ssu-t'ung ch'üan-chi* (Collected works of T'an Ssu-t'ung) (Peking, 1954), 69.

9. *Ibid.*, 55.

10. Liang, 'Nan-hai K'ang hsien-sheng chuan' (Biography of K'ang Yu-wei), YPSHC: WC, III, 6.67.

11. For this identification of Luther with freedom of thought, see Liang, 'Lun hsüeh-shu chih shih-li tso-yu shih-chieh' (On the power of learning to control the world), YPSHC: WC, III, 6.111, and elsewhere. Liang wrote of Luther in this fashion after he abandoned the *chin-wen* school's practice of invoking the Classics to justify innovation.

12. A description and analysis of the iconoclasm which succeeded *chin-wen* Confucianism in Liang's writings during the first decade of the twentieth century appears in Levenson, 92–101.

CHAPTER VI

1. See Ch'i Ssu-ho, 'Professor Hung on the Ch'un-ch'iu', *Yenching Journal of Social Studies*, I, No. 1 (June 1938), 49–71, esp. 55–6.

2. See Liang, 'Ch'ing-tai hsüeh-shu kai-lun' (A summary of Ch'ing scholarship), YPSHC: CC, IX, 34.63, where he says that in his thirtieth year he ceased discussion of the 'false classics'.

3. Wei Ying-ch'i, *Chung-kuo shih-hsüeh shih* (History of Chinese historiography) (Shanghai, 1941), 243.

4. E.g. Sun Yat-sen's manifesto at Nanking on Jan. 5, 1912, after he had been named by revolutionaries the first president of the Chinese Republic: '. . . Hitherto irremediable suppression of the individual qualities and the natural aspirations of the people having arrested the intellectual, moral, and material development of China, the aid of revolution was invoked to extirpate the primary cause. . . . Dominated by ignorance and selfishness, the Manchus closed the land to the outer world and plunged the Chinese into a state of benighted mentality calculated to operate inversely to their natural talents. . . .' See Benoy Kumar Sarkar, *The Sociology of Races, Cultures, and Human Progress* (Calcutta, 1939), 177–8.

5. Chan Wing-tsit, *Religious Trends in Modern China* (New York,

1953), 9; Kuo Chan-po, *Chin wu-shih nien Chung-kuo ssu-hsiang shih* (History of Chinese thought in the last fifty years) (Shanghai, 1926), 64–5.

6. Henri Van Boven, *Histoire de la littérature chinoise moderne* (Peiping, 1946), 11.

7. Roswell S. Britton, *The Chinese Periodical Press, 1800–1912* (Shanghai, 1933), 122; Ko Kung-chen, *Chung-kuo pao hsüeh shih* (History of Chinese journalism) (Shanghai, 1927), 140.

8. S. Tretiakov, ed., *A Chinese Testament, the Autobiography of Tan Shih-hua* (New York, 1934), 83.

9. Motoda Shigeyuki, *Ching-hsüeh shih-lun* (On the history of classical scholarship), trans. Chiang Chieh-an (Shanghai, 1934), 365.

10. On this point, see Ch'i, 50–1.

11. Derk Bodde, 'Harmony and Conflict in Chinese Philosophy', *Studies in Chinese Thought*, ed. Arthur J. Wright (Chicago, 1953), 34.

12. Ojima Sukema, 'Rokuhen seru Ryō no gakusetsu (Six stages in the development of Liao P'ing's theories), *Shinagaku*, II, No. 9 (May 1922), 714.

13. Chang Ping-lin, 'Kuo-ku lun-heng' (Discussion of national origins), 2.73b, *Chang-shih ts'ung-shu* (Che-chiang t'u-shu kuan, 1917–19).

14. Wu Ching-hsien, 'Chang T'ai-yen chih min-ts'u chü-i shih-hsüeh' (Chang Ping-lin's nationalist historiography), *Tung-fang tsa-chih*, XLIV, No. 4 (April 1948), 40.

15. Chang Ping-lin, 2.67b.

16. The first words of the *Wen-shih t'ung-i* (General principles of literature and history) of Chang Hsüeh-ch'eng. The same sentiment was expressed and elaborated upon by Chang Hsüeh-ch'eng in many texts, both formal treatises and personal letters. See David Shepherd Nivison, *The Literary and Historical Thought of Chang Hsüeh-ch'eng (1738–1801): a Study of His Life and Writing, with Translations of Six Essays from the 'Wen-shih t'ung-i'*, unpublished Ph.D. thesis, Harvard University (May 1953), 67, 114, 127–30, 190; and Nivison, 'The Problem of "Knowledge" and "Action" in Chinese Thought since Wang Yang-ming', in Wright, 127.

17. Liang, 'Chung-kuo li-shih yen-chiu fa' (Methods of research in Chinese history), YPSHC: CC, XVI, 73.9.

18. Su Hsün, 'Shih-lun shang' (First discourse [of three] on history), *Chia yu chi*, Ssu-pu pei-yao, ed. (Shanghai, n.d.), 8.1b.

19. Nivison, *The Literary and Historical Thought of Chang Hsüeh-ch'eng*, 130.

20. Nivison, *ibid.*, 202, points out Hu Shih's error in representing Chang as a modern critic before his time, seeing the Classics as 'historical material'.

21. Chou Yü-tung, *Ching chin-ku-wen hsüeh* (Study of the *chin-wen, ku-wen* classics issue) (Shanghai, 1926), 32.

22. Wu Ching-hsien, 40–1.

23. Tjan Tjoe Som, *Po Hu T'ung: the Comprehensive Discussions in the White Tiger Hall* (Leiden, 1949), I, 119. The greater part of Ku's researches have been published in *Ku shih pien* (Symposium on ancient history) (Peking and Shanghai, 1926–41), vols. I–VII.

24. See *The Autobiography of a Chinese Historian: Being the Preface to a Symposium on Ancient Chinese History (Ku Shih Pien)*, trans. Arthur W. Hummel (Leiden, 1931), esp. 40–7.

25. Ch'i Ssu-ho, 'Wei Yüan yü wan-Ch'ing hsüeh-fu' (Wei Yüan and late-Ch'ing scholarship), *Yenching hsüeh-pao*, XXXIX (Dec. 1950), 222.

26. Cf. Ku's ultimate reservations about the otherwise highly regarded textual critic, Ts'ui Shu (1740–1816). Ts'ui Shu had done excellent work in the exposure of forgeries, particularly in his discovery of chronological strata of deposits of legend in early literature. Yet, said Ku, Ts'ui Shu probed for forgeries only to establish the really orthodox materials of the ancient sages. He only criticized post-*Chan-kuo* texts for falsifying pre-*Chan-kuo* facts; he did not look at pre-*Chan-kuo* texts (i.e. the Classics) to test their own authenticity. 'He was only a *Ju-che* (Confucianist) making his discriminations in ancient history, not a historian doing so.' And— 'The distinction between "Classics" (*ching-shu*) and "tales" (*ch'uan-chi*) is only one of time.' See Wei, 244.

CHAPTER VII

1. Not, of course, its ultimate cause. I am speaking here in terms of logical sequence, not of social consequence.

2. Fujiwara, 136.

3. At the very beginning of Manchu rule in China there were edicts warning the Manchu princes and highest nobles against adopting Chinese costume and language, lest the Manchus lose their identity and their dynasty collapse; see Schuyler Cammann, *China's Dragon Robes* (New York, 1952), 20.

4. Ichiko Chūzō, 'Giwaken no seikaku' (The characteristics of the *I-ho ch'üan*), in Niida, 252. For a picture of a Boxer banner bearing the slogan, 'Fu Ch'ing Mieh Yang', see Chien Po-tsan *et al.*, ed., *I-ho t'uan* (The Boxer movement) (Shanghai, 1953), I, frontispiece.

5. Chang Ping-lin, for example, edited a compilation of works by the anti-Manchu scholar, Wang Fu-shih (1619–92). Wang did, indeed, denounce the Manchus fiercely, but his emphasis was more cultural than political, anti-barbarian rather than anti-Manchu *per se*. Note the tone of these extracts from his *Ch'un-ch'iu chia shuo* (1646), wherein it is implied (allegorically) that the Manchus are not just foreign nationals but unregenerate aliens to Chinese, civilized culture:

'Any strife with the barbarians the Middle Kingdom should not call a war. . . . For to annihilate them is not cruel, to deceive them is not unfaithful, to occupy their territory and confiscate their property is not unjust. . . .'

'To annihilate them and thereby safeguard our people is called benevolent, to deceive them and thereby do to them what they must dislike is called faithful, to occupy their territory and thereby transform their customs by virtue of our letters and morals as well as to confiscate their property and thereby increase the provisions of our own people is called righteous.'

See *Ch'uan-shan i-shu* (Remaining works of Wang Fu-chih) (Shanghai, 1933), *ts'e* 29, 3.16b–17.

In the text, Wang specifically distinguishes between strife among the various states of the Empire (hence, civilized states) and strife between a Chinese state and barbarians. Thus, there is a cultural, not a political test as to whether strife is pursued under rules of honour or ruthlessly.

6. Onogawa Hidemi, 'Shō Heirin no minzoku shisō' (The nationalism of Chang Ping-lin), part 2, *Tōyōshi kenkyū* (Journal of Oriental Researches), XIV, No. 3 (Nov. 1955), 46; Wu Ching-hsien, 39.

7. For documented accounts of social-Darwinism in early Chinese nationalism, see Levenson, 115–21, and Onogawa, 'Shimmatsu no shisō to shinkaron' (Late Ch'ing political thought and the theory of evolution), *Tōhō gakuhō* (Journal of Oriental Studies), XXI (March 1952), 1–36.

8. Huang Tsung-hsi, 'Ming-i tai-fang lu', *Hsiao-shih shan-fang*

ts'ung-shu, ed. Ku Hsiang (1874), *ts'e* 5, 1b-2b. A translation of part of this passage appears in Teng and Fairbank, 18.

9. Huang, 4.

10. Ku, I, 1.13.

11. *Ibid.,* I, 13.41.

12. *Ibid.,* I, 13.42.

13. *Ibid.,* I, 7.27.

14. *Mencius,* VII, V, xiii; see Legge, II, 483: 'There are instances of individuals without benevolence who have got possession of a (single) state, but there has been no instance of the throne's being got by someone without benevolence.'

15. Ku, I, 12.9.

16. *Ibid.,* I, 2.41.

17. Liang, 'Hsin-min shuo' (Discourses on the new people), YPSHC: CC, III, 4.20.

18. Ts'ai Shang-ssu, *Chung-kuo ch'uan-t'ung ssu-hsiang tsung p'i-p'an* (General criticism of traditional Chinese thought) (Shanghai, 1949), 13-14. Cf. Emile Durkheim, *Sociology and Philosophy* (London, 1953), 59: 'Society . . . is above all a composition of ideas, beliefs and sentiments of all sorts which realize themselves through individuals. Foremost of these ideas is the moral ideal which is its principal *raison d'être.* To love one's society is to love this ideal, and one.loves it so that one would rather see society disappear as a material entity than renounce the ideal which it embodies.'

19. But not meaningless just because it does not apply in actual individual instances. Cf. Ernst Cassirer, 'Einstein's Theory of Relativity Considered from the Epistemological Standpoint', supplement to *Substance and Function* (Chicago, 1923), 419: 'The philosopher . . . is ever again brought to the fact that there are ultimate ideal determinations without which the concrete cannot be considered and made intelligible.'

20. Nakayama Kujirō, 'Gendai Shina no Kōjikyō mondai ni tsuite' (On the question of Confucianism in contemporary China), *Tōa ronsō,* II (Tokyo, 1940), 4.

21. Henri Bernard-Maitre, *Sagesse chinoise et philosophie chrétienne* (Paris, 1935), 260.

22. M. H. Abrams, *The Mirror and the Lamp: Romantic Theory and the Critical Tradition* (New York, 1953), 219. For an excellent discussion of Chiang Kai-shek's nationalistic Confucianism as a romantic deviation from both nationalist anti-traditionalism and the rational and universal qualities of Confucianism as

traditionally conceived, see Mary Wright, 'From Revolution to Restoration: the Transformation of Kuomintang Ideology', *Far Eastern Quarterly*, XIV, No. 4 (Aug. 1955), 515–32, esp. 520–1 and 525.

23. Van Boven, 147.

24. Liang, 'Ta Chung-hua fa-k'an-tz'u' (Foreword to *Ta Chung-hua*), YPSHC: WC, XII, 33.83–4.

CHAPTER VIII

1. Hsiao Kung-ch'uan, *Chung-kuo cheng-shih ssu-hsiang shih* (History of Chinese political thought) (Shanghai, 1946), II, 424.

2. T. K. Chuan, 'Philosophy Chronicle', *T'ien Hsia Monthly*, IV, No. 3 (March 1936), 291.

3. Ts'ai Shang-ssu, *Ts'ai Yüan-p'ei hsüeh-shu ssu-hsiang ch'üan-chi* (An account of the scholarship and thought of Ts'ai Yüan-p'ei) (Shanghai, 1951), 267–8.

4. Robert K. Sakai, 'Ts'ai Yüan-p'ei as a Synthesizer of Western and Chinese Thought', *Papers on China* (mimeo.), III (Harvard University, May 1949), 180.

5. Ts'ai, *Ts'ai*, 104.

6. Sakai, 182–3.

7. Tai Chin-hsieo, *The Life and Work of Ts'ai Yüan-p'ei*, unpublished Ph.D. thesis, Harvard University (1952), 42.

8. Ts'ai, *Ts'ai*, 133–4.

9. For Zao Wou-ki, see 'La peinture chinoise contemporaine', catalogue of an exhibition at the Musée Cernuschi (Paris, 1946); Neste Jacometti, 'Zao Wou-ki', *Art Documents*, VII (1951), 3; and *Lecture par Henri Michaux de huit lithographies de Zao Wou-ki* (Paris, 1951).

10. Feng Yu-lan, 'Chinese Philosophy and Its Possible Contribution to a Universal Philosophy', *East and West*, I, No. 4 (Jan. 1951), 215.

11. Yeh Ch'ing, *Tsen-yang yen-chiu 'San Min Chü-i'* (How study the 'Three People's Principles'?) (Taipei, 1951), 70–7.

12. Kuo, 61. According to Ts'ai Yüan-p'ei (quoted in Onogawa, 'Shimmatsu no shisō to shinkaron', 8), Yen Fu, who had translated Huxley's *Evolution and Ethics* in 1896, had had an eight-character personal motto in those earlier days: 'Revere the people and rebel against the prince; revere the present and rebel against the past.'

13. Ya-tung t'u-shu-kuan (publ.), *K'o-hsüeh yü jen-sheng-kuan* (Science and the philosophy of life—a symposium), 2 vols. (Shanghai, 1923), and Yang Ming-chai, *P'ing Chung Hsi wen-hua kuan* (A critique of views on Chinese and western civilizations) (Peking, 1924), probably provide the best introduction to the vast post-war literature in the anti-materialist, anti-'western progress' vein.

CHAPTER IX

1. Jacques Maritain, *Religion et culture* (Paris, 1930), 56.
2. *L'art chrétien chinois*, special number of *Dossiers de la commission synodale*, V, No. 5 (Peiping, May 1932), 411.
3. Bernard-Maitre, 113.
4. *Ibid.*, 121.
5. A China Missionary, 'First Thoughts on the Debacle of Christian Missions in China', *African Affairs*, LI, No. 202 (Jan. 1952), 33.
6. Liang, 'Pao-chiao fei so-i tsun K'ung lun' (To preserve the Confucian doctrine is not the way to honour Confucius), YPSHC: WC, IV, 9.53.
7. Léon Wieger, *Le flot montant* (*Chine moderne*, II) (Hsien-hsien, 1921), 9–11. *Hsin ch'ing-nien* and *Hsin ch'ao* were periodicals first appearing in 1915 and 1919, respectively. The *Hsin-ch'ao* society which sponsored the periodical of that name was founded in December 1918.
8. Benjamin I. Schwartz, *Chinese Communism and the Rise of Mao* (Cambridge, 1951), 17–18; Wieger, 10.
9. Fukuda Masazō, 'Shakai bunka hen (kyoiku)' (Section on society and culture—education), *Gendai Shina kōza* (Lectures on modern China), ed. Hideshima Tatsuo (Shanghai, 1939), VI, 4.
10. Hsü Mou-yung, *Wen i ssu-ch'ao hsiao-shih* (Short history of the literary and artistic thought-tide) (Changchun, 1949—author's preface, 1936), 100.
11. Chiang, 91–3.
12. Aoki Masaru, 'Go Teki wo chūshin ni uzumaite iru bungaku katsumei' (A literary revolution in China with Hu Shih as its central figure), part 2, *Shinagaku*, I, No. 2 (Oct. 1920), 124–5.
13. William Ayers, 'The Society for Literary Studies, 1921–1930', *Papers on China*, VIII (Feb. 1953), 51–3.
14. Cf. Lu Hsün, 'The Diary of a Madman', *Ah Q and Others*, tr. Wang Chi-chen (New York, 1941), 205–19, a condemnation,

in the form of tragic irony, of the classical tradition as a scourge of society. The tradition's claims to a rarefied philosophical value are denounced as pretence, as a camouflage for vicious social control.

15. Mannheim, 99. See also pp. 136–7: 'The sympathetic grasp of the nature of historic growth which Burke achieved would never have been possible had not certain strata felt that their social position was threatened and that their world might perish.'

16. Chou Ling, *La peinture chinoise contemporaine de style traditionel* (Paris, 1949), 9–10.

17. Ch'in, 188.

18. Lu Feng-tzu, 'Chung-kuo hua t'e-yu ti chi-shu' (Technical principles peculiar to Chinese painting), *Chin-ling hsüeh-pao* (Nanking Journal), II, No. 1 (May 1932), 163.

19. Judith Burling and Arthur Hart, 'Contemporary Chinese Painting', *Magazine of Art*, XLII, No. 6 (Oct. 1949), 218.

20. Edward Sapir, 'Culture, Genuine and Spurious', *Selected Writings of Edward Sapir in Language, Culture, and Personality*, ed. David G. Mandelbaum (Berkeley and Los Angeles, 1949), 321.

21. The definition of eclecticism in Theodore Meyer Greene, *The Arts and the Art of Criticism* (Princeton, 1947), 383, applies: 'Eclecticism in the bad sense may be defined as the arbitrary juxtaposition of antipathetic stylistic factors or, alternatively, as the use in a single work of art of unassimilated aspects of sharply divergent styles.'

22. Kao Wěng, 'The Art of Painting Is Not Lifeless', *An Exhibition of Paintings by Kao Weng and Chang K'un-i*, Metropolitan Museum of Art (New York, 1944). Cf. the Lingnan group, founded in 1919, which attempted to create a new style by portrayal of modern subject matter (ships, aeroplanes, bridges, etc.) in traditional technique; see Michael Sullivan, 'The Traditional Trend in Contemporary Chinese Art', *Oriental Art*, II, No. 3 (Winter 1949–50), 108, and Jen Yu-wen, 'Art Chronicle', *T'ien Hsia Monthly*, VI, No. 2 (Feb. 1938), 145.

23. Burling and Hart, 218. (Wu's gambit leaves him open, of course, to a rather effective counter-ploy—a recommendation of painting the nude.)

24. Whitehead, *Symbolism, Its Meaning and Effect* (New York, 1927), 88.

25. Martin Buber, *Moses* (Oxford and London, 1946), 18. Cf. T. S. Eliot, *What Is A Classic?* (London, 1945), 15: 'The persistence of literary creativeness in any people, accordingly, consists

in the maintenance of an unconscious balance between tradition in the larger sense—the collected personality, so to speak, realized in the literature of the past—and the originality of the living generation.' Cf. also D. H. Lawrence's acute distinction, in 'John Galsworthy', *Selected Essays* (Harmondsworth, 1950), 222: 'They keep up convention, but they cannot carry on a tradition. There is a tremendous difference between the two things. To carry on a tradition, you must add something to the tradition . . .'; and the architect, Walter Gropius, in 'Tradition and the Center', *Harvard Alumni Bulletin*, LIII, No. 2 (Oct. 14, 1950), 69: 'Whenever man imagined he had found "eternal beauty" he fell back into imitation and stagnation. True tradition is the result of constant growth. Its quality must be dynamic, not static, to serve as an inexhaustible stimulus to man.'

26. Sapir, 321.
27. Eliot, 15.

CHAPTER X

1. Robert Payne, *China Awake* (New York, 1947), 378.
2. Schwartz, 'Marx and Lenin in China', *Far Eastern Survey*, XVIII, No. 15 (July 27, 1949), 178.
3. Liu Shao-chi, *On the Party* (Peking, 1950), 31.
4. *Ibid.*, 29.
5. *A Guide to New China*, 1953 (Peking, 1953), 112.
6. See *Postage Stamps of the People's Republic of China, 1949–1954* (Supplement to *China Reconstructs*, IV (April 1955), 31–2, for an account of the stamps devoted to the second quartet of giants; the first had not been publicized in this effective way.
7. Chou Yang, 'The People's New Literature', *The People's New Literature* (Peking, 1950), 105.
8. *Ibid.*, 105–6.
9. *Ibid.*, 115–16.
10. *Ibid.*, 116–17.
11. *Folk Arts of New China* (Peking, 1954), 18.
12. Chou Yang, 103.
13. Chou En-lai, 'The People's Liberation War and Problems in Literature and Art', *The People's New Literature*, 32–4.
14. Communist interest in the Taiping Rebellion has been enormous. There has been a great output of communist literature on the subject, particularly in 1950, the centenary year. A cursory study of modern Chinese intellectual history, but one which gives

the quintessence of communist opinion, describes the Taiping Rebellion as *k'ung-hsiang* (fantasy) socialism; see Fei Min, *Chung-kuo chin-tai ssu-hsiang fa-chan chien-shih* (Brief history of the development of modern Chinese thought) (Shanghai, 1949), 12. For another reference to the sound instincts but historical limitations of these forerunners, see 'Soochow Remembers the Taipings', *China Reconstructs*, I (Jan.–Feb. 1953), 49–51.

15. Hsü Mou-yung, 98–9.

16. Chung Chi-ming, *Hsiang min-chien wen i hsüeh-shu* (Studies towards a people's literature and art) (Shanghai, 1950), 2.

17. Kwei Chen, 'Po Chu-i: People's Poet', *China Reconstructs*, IV (July–Aug. 1953), 31.

18. Feng Hsüeh-feng, 'Lu Hsun, His Life and Thought', *Chinese Literature*, 2 (Spring 1952)—reprinted in *Current Background*, 217 (Oct. 30, 1952) (American Consulate General, Hong Kong), 7.

19. Chung, 18–19.

20. Mao Tse-tung, 'Stalin—Friend of the Chinese People', *People's China*, I, No. 1 (Jan. 1, 1950), 4.

21. *Postage Stamps of the People's Republic of China, 1949–1954*, 29–31.

22. See *The New York Times*, Nov. 14, 1954 (Hong Kong dateline), for an account of a government-sponsored movement to promote Chinese herb medicine, acupuncture, etc., and to integrate what is called 'the old national legacy' with modern medical techniques.

23. Kuo Mo-Jo, 'Culture chinoise et occident', *Democratie nouvelle*, V, No. 2 (Feb. 1951), 69.

24. Kuo Mo-jo, 'The United Front in Literature and Art', *People's China*, I, 1 (Jan. 1, 1950), 29.

25. Ch'ien Tuan-sheng, 'Study [*hsüeh-hsi*] for the Purpose of Self Reform and Better Service to the Fatherland', *Jen-min jih-pao* (Peking, Nov. 6, 1951), Chao Kuo-chün, trans. (Harvard University, 1952: mimeo.), 4.

26. Chou Yang, 104–5. Note that western-trained Chinese doctors who oppose 'the motherland's medical legacy' (i.e. a 'popular' tradition) are said to have been 'poisoned by bourgeois ideology'; see *The New York Times, loc. cit.*

27. Li Ch'ang-chih, *Chung-kuo hua-lun t'i-hsi chi ch'i p'i-p'ing* (Chinese systems of aesthetics and a criticism of them) (Chungking, 1944), 9–13.

28. Wen Chao-t'ung, *Hsin Chung-kuo ti hsin mei-shu* (The new fine arts of the new China) (Shanghai, 1950), 1–3.

29. Mao, *Problems of Art and Literature* (New York, 1950), 32.

30. Wen, 1.

31. *Ibid.*, 11–12.

32. *Ibid.*, 2.

33. Cf. the description of an exhibition of proletarian paintings in Peking, 1949, in Bodde, *Peking Diary* (New York, 1950), 182.

34. Yeh Chien-yu, 'On the Classical Tradition in Chinese Painting', *People's China*, VII (1954), 15, 17. Cf. Chou Yang, *China's New Literature and Art* (Peking, 1954), 38, making the convenient identification of the national heritage with the 'popular', not the 'feudal' past: 'The main lesson to be drawn from our national heritage is its spirit of realism.' Some years earlier, Mao Tun (the naturalistic writer, always close to the communists) had characterized as 'national form' the portrayal of the life of all classes in all its reality and completeness; see Amitendranath Tagore, 'Wartime Literature of China—Its Trends and Tendencies', *The Visva-Bharati Quarterly*, XVI, No. 2 (Aug.–Oct. 1950), 128.

35. Chang Jen-hsia, 'Flower-and-Bird Painting', *China Reconstructs*, III (May–June 1953), 51.

36. For this emphasis, *ibid.*, 51–2.

37. *Postage Stamps of the People's Republic of China, 1949–1954*, 15–16, 27.

38. C. P. Fitzgerald, 'The Renaissance Movement in China', *Meanjin*, IX, No. 2 (Winter 1950), 107.

39. Ai Chung-hsin, 'Hsü Pei-hung—an Outstanding Painter', *People's China*, III (1954), 36.

40. Ch'en Yuan, 'Chinese Culture in Wartime', *Journal of the Royal Society of Arts*, XCIV, No. 4728 (Oct. 11, 1946), 681–2.

41. *Folk Arts of New China*, 45. Cf. Lu Chi on music: 'China's new songs of the masses are, on the one hand, a negation of Chinese feudal music and music of the people of the city, and, on the other hand, a negation of the music of European and American capitalism.' Quoted in Clarence Moy, 'Communist China's Use of the Yang-ko', *Papers on China*, VI (March 1952), 123.

CONCLUSION

1. Needham, *Science and Civilization in China*, I, 4.

2. Kobayashi Taichiro, 'Hokusai and Degas', *Contemporary Japan*, XV, Nos. 9–12 (Sept.–Dec. 1946), 359–68.

3. Nagassé Takashiro, *Le paysage dans l'art de Hokuçai* (Paris, 1937), 13–15, 19, 180.

4. Nien Hsi-yao, superintendent (1726–36) of the imperial porcelain factory, quoted in Soame Jenyns, *Later Chinese Porcelain* (New York, n.d.), 44. For the transmission of European rules of perspective to China in the seventeenth century and their employment, by imperial order, in the preparation of two famous sets of engravings, one on agricultural and the other on military and domestic themes, see Paul Pelliot, *Les influences européennes sur l'art chinois au XVIIe et au XVIIIe siècle* (Paris, 1948), 7–8; Pelliot, 'Les "Conquêtes de l'empereur de la Chine" ', *T'oung pao*, XX (1921), 266–7; and Jean Monval, 'Les conquêtes de la Chine: une commande de l'empereur de Chine en France au XVIIIe siècle', *La revue de l'art ancien et moderne*, II (1905), 150. For Chinese appreciation of the eighteenth-century missionary artist, Castiglione (Lang Shih-ning), who combined western technique with predominantly Chinese conventions, see Pelliot, 'Les "Conquêtes" ', 186–9.

5. This point has been made in another connection in Edwin G. Pulleyblank, *Chinese History and World History* (Cambridge, 1955), 9.

6. See Teng and Fairbank, 12, where a late Ming writer on Ricci is quoted as follows: '. . . I am very much delighted with his ideas, which are close to Confucianism but more earnest in exhorting society not to resemble the Buddhists, who always like to use obscure, incoherent words to fool and frighten the populace. . . .'

7. See Teng and Fairbank, 34, for Wei Yüan's apologetic reference (1842) to K'ang-hsi's use of Dutch ships to reduce Formosa, Jesuit-cast cannon to suppress the rebellion of Wu San-kuei, and European appointments to the Imperial Board of Astronomy; and *ibid.*, 83, for Tso Tsung-t'ang's similar reference (1866), in his argument for steamships, to these seventeenth-century cannon.

8. Ku, II, 29.10.

9. We are speaking here of change in peripheral values, not of anything central like the substitution of Christianity for Confucianism, which simply could not generally happen without general social change.

10. This similarity is noted in Bodde, 'Harmony and Conflict in Chinese Philosophy', 72.

11. For an analysis of the conflict, especially in the Six Dynasties period, between the gentry's social commitment to Confucian

society and intellectual attraction to the Buddhist church, and a suggestion of the issue of this conflict in a Buddhist-influenced Confucianism and a revived imperial bureaucratic state, see Arthur F. Wright, 'Fu I and the Rejection of Buddhism', *Journal of the History of Ideas*, XII, No. 1 (Jan. 1951), 31–47.

12. *Mencius*, III A, iv, 6; Legge, II, 249–50: 'Hence, there is the saying, "Some labour with their minds, and some labour with their strength. Those who labour with their minds govern others; those who labour with their strength are governed by others. Those who are governed by others support them; those who govern others are supported by them." This is a principle universally recognized.'

Bibliography

A. CHINESE AND JAPANESE

'Abe Kojirō zō: Un Nanden hitsu kaki satsu' ('Flowers' by Yün Nan-t'ien in the Abe Kojirō Collection), *Bijutsu kenkyū*, XCII (Aug. 1939), pp. 306–7.

Aimi Shigeichi, *Gumpō seigan* (Tokyo, 1914).

Aoki Masaru, 'Go Teki wo chūshin ni uzumaite iru bungaku katsumei' (A literary revolution in China with Hu Shih as its central figure), *Shinagaku*, I, No. 1 (Sept. 1920), 11–26; No. 2 (Oct. 1920), 112–30; No. 3 (Nov. 1920), 199–219.

'Sekitō no ga to garon to' (Shih-t'ao's painting and his views on painting), *Shinagaku*, I, No. 8 (April 1921), pp. 575–92.

Bokuyūsō shujin, *Sekitō to Hachidaisenjin* (Shih-t'ao and Pa-ta shan-jen) (Kanagawa ken, 1952).

Chang Ping-lin, 'Kuo-ku lun-heng' (Discussion of national origins), *Chang-shih ts'ung-shu* (Che-chiang t'u-shu kuan, 1917–19).

Chao Feng-t'ien, *Wan-Ch'ing wu-shih nien ching-chi ssu-hsiang shih* (Economic thought during the last fifty years of the Ch'ing period), *Yenching hsüeh-pao*: Monograph 18 (Peiping, 1939).

Ch'en Kung-lu, *Chung-kuo chin-tai shih* (History of Modern China) (Shanghai, 1935).

Ch'en Li, *Tung-shu tu-shu chi* (Record of my reading) (Shanghai, 1898).

Ch'en Teng-yüan, 'Hsi-hsüeh lai Hua shih kuo-jen che wu-tuan t'ai-tu' (Arbitrary Chinese attitudes at the time of the coming of western knowledge of China), *Tung-fang tsa-chih*, XXVII, No. 8 (April 1930), pp. 61–76.

Ch'i Ssu-ho, 'Wei Yüan yü wan—Ch'ing hsüeh-fu' (Wei Yüan and late-Ch'ing scholarship), *Yenching hsüeh-pao*, XXXIV (Dec. 1950), pp. 177–226.

Chiang Shu-ko, *T'ung-ch'eng wen-p'ai p'ing shu* (A discussion of the T'ung-ch'eng school of writing) (Shanghai, 1930).

Chien Po-tsan *et al.*, ed., *I-ho t'uan* (The Boxer movement) (Shanghai, 1953).

Ch'ien Mu, *Chung-kuo chin san-pai nien hsüeh-shu shih* (History of Chinese scholarship in the last three hundred years) (Chungking, 1945).

Ch'ing Chung-wen, *Chung-kuo hui-hua hsüeh shih* (History of Chinese painting) (Peiping, 1934).

Chou Yü-tung, *Ching chin-ku-wen hsüeh* (Study of the *chin-wen, ku-wen* classics issue) (Shanghai, 1926).

Ch'üan Han-sheng, 'Ch'ing-mo fan-tui Hsi-hua ti yen-lun' (Arguments against westernization in the late Ch'ing period), *Lingnan hsüeh-pao*, V, Nos. 3–4 (Dec. 20, 1936), pp. 122–66.

Chung Chi-ming, *Hsiang min-chien wen i hsüeh-shu* (Studies towards a people's literature and art) (Shanghai, 1950).

Fei Min, *Chung-kuo chin-tai ssu-hsiang fa-chan chien-shih* (Brief history of the development of modern Chinese thought) (Shanghai, 1949).

Fujiwara Sadame, *Kindai Chūgoku shisō* (Modern Chinese thought) (Tokyo, 1948).

Fukuda Masazō, 'Shakai bunka hen (kyoiku)' (Section on society and culture—education), *Gendai Shina kōza* (Lectures on modern China), ed. Hideshima Tatsuo (Shanghai, 1939), VI, pp. 1–40.

Fung Yu-lan, *Hsin shih lun* (Discussions of new issues) (Changsha, 1940).

'Hashimoto Shinjirō zō: Un Nanden hitsu kahin seikyō zu' ('Fruits' by Yün Nan-t'ien in the Hashimoto Shinjirō Collection), *Bijutsu kenkyū*, VII (July 1932), p. 237.

Hou Wai-lu, *Chin-tai Chung-kuo ssu-hsiang hsüeh-shuo shih* (Intellectual history of modern China) (Shanghai, 1947).

Hsia Wen-yen, *T'u-hui pao-chien*, ed. Chieh-lu ts'ao t'ang.

Hsiao I-shan, *Ch'ing-tai t'ung-shih* (General history of the Ch'ing period) (Shanghai, 1927).

Tseng Kuo-fan (Chungking, 1944).

Hsiao Kung-ch'uan, *Chung-kuo cheng-shih ssu-hsiang shih* (History of Chinese political thought) (Shanghai, 1946).

Hsü Ch'in, 'Ming hua lu' (Records of Ming painting), *Ts'ung-shu chi-ch'eng* (Shanghai, 1926).

Hsü Mou-yung, *Wen i ssu-ch'ao hsiao-shih* (Short history of the literary and artistic thought-tide) (Changchun, 1949).

Hsü Shih-ch'ang, *Ch'ing Ju hsüeh-an* (Ch'ing Confucian Scholarship) (Tientsin, 1938).

Hu Man, *Chung-kuo mei-shu shih* (History of Chinese art) (Shanghai, 1950).

Huang Pin-hung, *Ku hua cheng* (Evidence on old painting) (Shanghai, 1931).

Huang Tsung-hsi, 'Ming-i tai-fang lu', *Hsiao-shih shan-fang ts'ung-shu*, ed. Ku Hsiang (1874).

'I Fukyū hitsu: sansui zu' (Landscape, by I Fu-chiu), *Kokka*, 174 (Nov. 1904), p. 108 and plate V.

Ichiko Chūzō, 'Giwaken no seikaku' (The characteristics of the *I-ho ch'üan*), *Kindai Chūgoku kenkyū* (Modern Chinese researches), ed. Niida Noboru (Tokyo, 1948), pp. 245–67.

Ichiuji Giryō, *Tōyō bijutsu shi* (History of Far Eastern art) (Tokyo, 1936).

Ise Senichirō, 'Bunjinga—nanga yori bunjinga e no suii' (Literati painting—the transition from southern painting to literati painting),
Tōyō bijutsu, III (Sept. 1929), pp. 2–12.

Ji Ko Gaishi shi Kei Kō Shina sansuiga shi (History of Chinese
landscape painting from Ku K'ai-chih to Ching Hao) (Kyoto,
1933).

Itano Chōhachi, 'Kō Yūi no Daido Shisō' (K'ang Yu-wei's idea of the
'Great Harmony'), *Kindai Chūgoku kenkyū* (Modern Chinese researches), ed. Niida Noboru (Tokyo, 1948), pp. 165–204.

Jen Shih-hsien, *Shina kyoiku shi* (History of Chinese education), Yamazaki
Tatsuo, tr. (Tokyo, 1940).

Ko Kung-chen, *Chung-kuo pao-hsüeh shih* (History of Chinese journalism)
(Shanghai, 1927).

Ku-kung shu-hua chi (Palace Museum collection of painting and calligraphy) (Peiping, 1930).

Ku Yen-wu, *Jih-chih lu* (Shanghai, 1933).

Kuo Chan-po, *Chin wu-shih nien Chung-kuo ssu-hsiang shih* (History of
Chinese thought in the last fifty years) (Shanghai, 1926).

'Kyū Ei Tōjin shii e kai' (Explanation of Ch'iu Ying's paintings on
themes from T'ang poetry), *Kokka*, 481 (Dec. 1930), pp. 344–6.

Li Ch'ang-chih, *Chung-kuo hua-lun t'i-hsi chi ch'i p'i-p'ing* (Chinese systems
of aesthetics and a criticism of them) (Chungking, 1944).

Liang Ch'i-ch'ao, *'Ch'ing-tai hsüeh-shu kai-lun'* (A summary of Ch'ing
scholarship), *Yin-ping-shih ho-chi* (Shanghai, 1936), *chuan-chi*, IX.

'Chung-kuo chin san-pai nien hsüeh-shu shih' (History of Chinese
scholarship in the last three hundred years), *Yin-ping-shih ho-chi*,
chuan-chi, XVII.

'Chung-kuo li-shih yen-chin fa' (Methods of research in Chinese history), *Yin-ping-shih ho-chi*, *chuan-chi*, XVI.

'Hsin-min shuo' (Discourses on the new people), *Yin-ping-shih ho-chi*,
III.

'Lun hsüeh-shu chih shih-li tso-yu shih-chien' (On the power of
learning to control the world), *Yin-ping-shih ho-chi*, *wen-chi*, III.

'Nan-hai K'ang hsien-sheng chuan' (Biography of K'ang Yu-wei),
Yin-ping-shih ho-chi, *wen-chi*, III.

'Pao-chiao fei so-i tsun K'ung lun' (To preserve the Confucian doctrine is not the way to honour Confucius), *Yin-ping-ho-chi*, *wen-chi*,
IV.

'Ta Chung-hua fa k'an-tz'u' (Foreword to *Ta Chung-hua*), *Yin-ping-
shih ho-chi*, *wen-chi*, XII.

'Tai Tung-yüan sheng-jih ni-pai nien chi-nien hui yüan-ch'i' (The
origins of the conference to commemorate the two hundredth
anniversary of the birth of Tai Tung-yüan), *Yin-ping-shih ho-chi*,
wen-chi, XIV.

'Yen-Li hsüeh-p'ai yü hsien-tai chiao-yü ssu-ch'ao' (The Yen-Li school
and the contemporary educational thought-tide) *Yin-ping-shih
ho-chi*, *wen-chi*, XIV.

Lin Feng-mien, *I-shu ts'ung-lun* (Essays on art) (Shanghai, 1937).

Liu Ssu-hsün, *Chung-kuo mei-shu fa-ta shih* (History of the development of Chinese art) (Chungking, 1946).

Lu Ch'ien, *Pa-ku wen hsiao-shih* (Short history of the eight-legged essay) (Shanghai, 1937).

Lu Feng-tzu, 'Chung-kuo hua t'e-yu ti chi-shu' (Technical principles peculiar to Chinese painting), *Chin-ling hsüeh-pao* (Nanking Journal), II, No. 1 (May 1932), pp. 161–4.

Ming-jen shu hua chi (Collection of calligraphy and painting of famous practitioners) (Shanghai, 1921).

Motoda Shigeyuki, *Ching-hsüeh shih-lun* (On the history of classical scholarship), tr. Chiang Chieh-an (Shanghai, 1934).

Naitō Konan, 'Tō Kishō Sai Bunki ezō' (Tung Ch'i-ch'ang's portrait of Ts-ai Wen-chi), *Tōyō bijutsu* (Far Eastern Art), I (April 1929), pp. 64–5.

Naitō Torajirō, *Shinchō shoga fu* (Treatise on Ch'ing calligraphy and painting) (Osaka, 1917).

Nakamura Sakutarō and Ojika Bukkai, *Shina ega shi* (History of Chinese painting) (Tokyo, 1923).

Nakayama Kujirō, 'Gendai Shina no Kōjikyō mondai ni tsuite' (On the question of Confucianism in contemporary China), *Tōa ronsō* II (Tokyo, 1940), pp. 1–11.

'Ō Sekikoku hitsu: kambaku zu' (Looking at a waterfall, by Wang Hui), *Kokka*, 702 (Sept. 1950), pp. 305–6.

'Ō Sekikoku hitsu: semmen sansui zu' (Landscape painted on a fan, by Wang Hui), *Kokka*, 614 (Jan. 1942), p. 24.

Ojima Sukema, 'Rokuhen seru Ryō Hei no gakusetsu' (Six stages in the development of Liao P'ing's theories), *Shinagaku*, II, No. 9 (May 1922), pp. 707–14.

Onogawa Hidemi, 'Shimmatsu no shisō to shinkaron' (Late Ch'ing political thought and the theory of evolution), *Tōhō gakuhō* (Journal of Oriental Studies), XXI (March 1952), pp. 1–36.

'Shō Heirin no minzoku shisō' (The nationalism of Chang Ping-lin), *Tōyōshi kenkyū* (Journal of Oriental Researches), XIII, No. 3 (Aug. 1954), pp. 39–58; XIV, No. 3 (Nov. 1955), pp. 45–58.

P'an T'ien-shuo. *Chung-kuo hui-hua shih* (History of Chinese painting) (Shanghai, 1935).

'Ran Ei hitsu: *Hisetsu senzen* zu kai' (Analysis of 'Flying snow and a thousand mountains', by Lan Ying), *Kokka*, 477 (Aug. 1930), p. 228.

Sanetō Keishū, *Shin Chūgoku no Jukyō hihan* (A critique of modern Chinese Confucianism) (Tokyo, 1948.)

'Sei Moyō hitsu: *Sankyo hōmon* zu kai' (Analysis of 'A visitor to a mountain abode', by Shang Mao-yeh), *Kokka*, 543 (Feb. 1946), p. 53.

Sheng Tsung-ch'ien, 'Chieh-chou hsüeh hua pien', *Hua-lun ts'ung-k'an* (Collection of treatises on painting), ed. Yü Hai-yen (Peiping, 1937).

Shih Yai, 'Sung-li Han-lin t'u-hua yüan chi hua-hsüeh shih shih hsi-nien' (A chronology of notable historical data and works of the Hanlin painting academy of the Sung dynasty), *Chung-kuo wen-hua yen-chiu hui-p'an* (Bulletin of Chinese Studies, Chengtu), III (Sept. 1943), pp. 327–60.

'Shin Sekiden hitsu 'Zō Go Kan gyō emaki kai' (Analysis of Shen Shih-t'ien's scroll-painting, 'A gift to Wu K'uan upon his making a journey'), *Kokka*, 545 (April 1936), pp. 113–14.

Shu Hsin-ch'eng, *Chin-tai Chung-kuo chiao-yü ssu-hsiang shih* (History of modern Chinese educational thought) (Shanghai, 1929).

'Ssu-pien lu chi-yao' (Summary of the *Ssu-pien lu*), *Cheng i t'ang ch'üan-shu*, ed. Chang Pai-hsing, suppl. ed., Tso Tsung-t'ang (1866–87).

Su Hsün, 'Shih-lun shang' (First discourse on history), *Chia yu chi*, Ssu-pu pi-yao ed. (Shanghai, n.d.).

Suzuki, Torao, 'Kobun hihō no zenku' (The development of the forms of *pa-ku wen*) *Shinagaku*, IV, No. 1 (July 1926), pp. 27–46.

Tai Chen, 'Meng-tzu tzu-i su-cheng', *An-hui ts'ung-shu*, 6th Ser. (Shanghai, 1936).

'Tung-yüan wen-chi', *An-hui ts'ung-shu*, 6th Ser. (Shanghai, 1936).

Tajima Shiichi, ed., *Tōyō bijutsu taikan* (General view of Far Eastern Art), X (Tokyo, 1911); XI (Tokyo, 1912).

Taki Seiichi, 'Shina e no ni dai chōryū' (The two main currents of Chinese painting), *Kokka*, 438 (Jan. 1929), pp. 3–8.

Taki Seiichirō, 'Shin Keinan *Kudan nishikie satsu* ni tsuite' (On the picture album *Chin-tuan chin-hua-ts'e*, by Shen Ch'i-nan), *Kokka*, 495 (Feb. 1932), pp. 33–40.

T'an P'i-mu, *Ch'ing-tai ssu-hsiang shih-kang* (Historical outline of Ch'ing thought) (Shanghai, 1940).

T'an Ssu-t'ung, 'Jen-hsüeh' (Study of Benevolence), *T'an Ssu-t'ung ch'üan-chi* (Collected works of T'an Ssu-t'ung) (Peking, 1954).

Tanaka Toyozō, *Tōyō bijutsu dansō* (Discussions on Far Eastern Art) (Tokyo, 1949).

T'ang Chih-ch'i, *Hui shih cheng-yen* (Shanghai, 1935).

Tanouchi Takatsugi, *Shina kyoikugaku shi* (History of educational theory in China) (Tokyo, 1942).

Tempō Imazeki, 'Shin Seikiden jiseki' (Biographical note on Shen Shih-t'ien), *Kokka*, 457 (Dec. 1928), pp. 349–54; 458 (Jan. 1929), 15–20.

T'eng Ku, 'Kuan-yü yüan-t'i hua ho wen-jen hua chih shih ti k'ao-ch'a' (An examination of the history of 'academic' and 'literati' painting), *Fu-jen hsüeh-chih*, II, No. 2 (Sept. 1930), pp. 65–86.

Ts'ai Shang-ssu, *Chung-kuo ch'uan-t'ung ssu-hsiang tsung p'i-p'an* (General criticism of traditional Chinese thought) (Shanghai, 1949).

Ts'ai Yüan-p'ei hsüeh-shu ssu-hsiang ch'uan-chi (An account of the scholarship and thought of Ts'ai Yüan-p'ei) (Shanghai, 1951).

Tseng Chi-tse, *Tseng Hou jih-chi* (Marquis Tseng's diary) (Shanghai, 1881).

Tseng Kuo-fan, 'Jih-chi' (Diary), *Tseng Wen-chang kung ch'üan-chi* (Collected works of Tseng Kuo-fan), (Shanghai, 1917).

'Sheng-chih hua-hsiang chi' (Portrait record of philosophical masters), *Tseng Wen-chang kung ch'üan-chi.*

Tsou I-kuei, 'Hsiao-shan hua-p'u', *Ssu t'ung ku chai lun hua chi k'o,* ed. Chang Hsiang-ho (Peking, 1909).

Tung Ch'i-ch'ang, *Hua Ch'an shih sui-pi,* ed. Wang Ju-lu (Peking, 1840).

Tz'u-hai (Shanghai, 1936).

Unzansei, 'Kyū Ei no gasatsu ni tsuite' (On a picture book by Ch'iu Ying), *Kokka,* 475 (June 1930), pp. 159–67.

Wada Mikio, ed., *Tōyō bijutsu taikan* (General view of Far Eastern Art), XII (Tokyo, 1913).

Wang Fu-chih, 'Ch'un-ch'iu chia shuo', *Ch'uan-shan i-shu* (Remaining works of Wang Fu-chih) (Shanghai, 1933).

Wang Shih-chen, 'I-yüan chih yen fu lu', *Yen-chou shan jen ssu pu kao,* ed. Shih ching t'ang.

Wei Ying-ch'i, *Chung-kuo shih-hsüeh shih* (History of Chinese historiography) (Shanghai, 1941).

Wen Chao-t'ung, *Hsin Chung-kuo ti hsin mei-shu* (The new fine arts of the new China) (Shanghai, 1950).

Wu Ching-hsien, 'Chang T'ai-yen chih min-ts'u chü-i shih-hsüeh' (Chang Ping-lin's nationalist historiography), *Tung-fang tsa-chih* XLIV, No. 4 (April 1948), pp. 38–42.

Wu Shih-ch'ang, *Chung-kuo wen-hua yü hsien-tai-hua wen-t'i* (Chinese culture and the question of modernization) (Shanghai, 1948).

Ya-tung t'u-shu-kuan, publ., *K'o hsüeh yü jen-sheng-kuan* (Science and the philosophy of life—a symposium) (Shanghai, 1923).

Yang Ming-chai, *P'ing Chung Hsi wen-hua kuan* (A critique of views on Chinese and western civilizations) (Peking, 1924).

Yawata Sekitarō, *Shina gajin kenkyū* (Study of Chinese painters) (Tokyo, 1942).

Yeh Ch'ing, *Tsen-yang yen-chin 'San Min Chü-i'* (How study the 'Three People's Principles'?) (Taipei, 1951).

Yen Yüan, 'Ts'un hsüeh pien', *Chi-fu ts'ung-shu* (1879).

Yonezawa Yoshiho, 'Kyū Ei hitsui hakubyō *Tan ran tei* zu' (The *Chuan lan ting,* a picture in the *pai-miao* method, by Ch'iu Ying), *Kokka,* 708 (March 1951), pp. 121–5.

Yoshizawa Tadashi, 'Nanga to bunjinga' (Southern painting and literati painting), *Kokka,* 622 (Sept. 1942), pp. 257–62; 624 (Nov. 1942), pp. 345–50; 625 (Dec. 1942), pp. 376–81; 626 (Jan. 1943), 27–32.

Yū Yamanoi, 'Meimatsu Shinchō ni okeru keiji jiyō no gaku' (The 'Practical affairs' school of the end of the Ming and the beginning of the Ch'ing), *Tōhō gaku ronshū* (Memoirs of the Institute of Eastern Culture) (Tokyo, 1954), pp. 136–50.

Yün Shou-p'ing, '*Ou hsiang kuan hua pa* (*chüan* 11–12, *Ou hsiang kuan chi*), *Pieh hsia chai ts'ung-shu,* ed. Chiang Kuang-hsü (Shanghai, 1923).

BIBLIOGRAPHY

B. WESTERN

A China Missionary, 'First Thoughts on the Debacle of Christian Missions in China', *African Affairs*, LI, No. 202 (Jan. 1952), pp. 33–41.

A Guide to New China, 1953 (Peking, 1953).

'A Landscape, by Wang Hui', *Kokka*, 250 (March 1911), pp. 283–4.

'A Summer Landscape, by Lan Yin (sic)', *Kokka*, 232 (Sept. 1909), pp. 95–6.

Aaron, R. I., *The Theory of Universals* (Oxford, 1952).

Abrams, M. H., *The Mirror and the Lamp: Romantic Theory and the Critical Tradition* (New York, 1953).

Ai Chung-hsin, 'Hsü Pei-hung—an Outstanding Painter', *People's China*, III (1954), pp. 36–40.

Annan, Noel Gilroy, *Leslie Stephen: His Thought and Character in Relation to His Time* (Cambridge, 1952).

Aquinas, Thomas, *Concerning Being and Essence*, tr. George G. Leckie (New York and London, 1937).

Aristotle, *Metaphysics*.

Arnold, Matthew, *Culture and Anarchy* (London, 1920).

Essays in Criticism (Boston, 1865).

Ayers, William, 'The Society for Literary Studies, 1921–1930', *Papers on China* (mimeo.), VIII (Harvard University, Feb. 1953), pp. 34–79.

Ayscough, Florence Wheelock, *Catalogue of Chinese Paintings Ancient and Modern by Famous Masters* (Shanghai, n.d.).

Balázs, Etienne, 'Les aspects significatifs de la société chinoise', *Asiatische Studien*, VI (1952), pp. 77–87.

Baldwin, James, *Notes of a Native Son* (Boston, 1955).

Bernal, J. D., 'A Scientist in China', *The New Statesman and Nation*, XLIX, No. 1255 (March 26, 1955), pp. 424–6.

Bernard-Maitre, Henri, *Sagesse chinoise et philosophie chrétienne* (Paris, 1935).

Biggerstaff, Knight, 'The T'ung Wen Kuan', *Chinese Social and Political Science Review*, XVIII, No. 3 (Oct. 1934), pp. 307–40.

Boas, Franz, *The Mind of Primitive Man* (New York, 1938).

Bodde, Derk, 'Harmony and Conflict in Chinese Philosophy', *Studies in Chinese Thought*, ed. Arthur F. Wright (Chicago, 1953), pp. 19–80.

Peking Diary (New York, 1950).

Borowitz, Albert, *Fiction in Communist China*, mimeo., Centre for International Studies, MIT (Cambridge, 1954).

Bowra, C. M., *The Creative Experiment* (London, 1949).

Bradley, Kenneth, 'Personal Portrait: Sir Andrew Cohen', *London Calling*, No. 745 (Feb. 11, 1954), p. 13.

Britton, Roswell S., *The Chinese Periodical Press, 1800–1912* (Shanghai, 1933).

Broderick, Alan Houghton, *An Outline of Chinese Painting* (London, 1949).

BIBLIOGRAPHY

Bronowski, J., *William Blake, 1757–1827* (Harmondsworth, 1954).

Buber, Martin, *Moses* (Oxford and London, 1946).

Bulling, A. and Ayers, John, 'Chinese Art of the Ming Period in the British Museum', *Oriental Art*, III, No. 2 (1950), pp. 79–81.

Burling, Judith and Hart, Arthur, 'Contemporary Chinese Painting', *Magazine of Art*, XLII, No. 6 (Oct. 1949), pp. 218–20.

Cammann, Schuyler, *China's Dragon Robes* (New York, 1952).

Cassirer, Ernst, *Substance and Function* (Chicago, 1923).

The Myth of the State (New Haven, 1946).

The Problem of Knowledge (New Haven, 1950).

Cassirer, H. W., *A Commentary on Kant's 'Critique of Judgment'* (London, 1938).

Chan, Albert, *The Decline and Fall of the Ming Dynasty, a Study of the Internal Factors*, MS. (Harvard University, 1953).

Chan Wing-tsit, *Religious Trends in Modern China* (New York, 1953).

Chang Chung-li, *The Chinese Gentry: Studies on Their Role in Nineteenth Century Chinese Society* (Seattle, 1955).

Chang Jen-hsia, 'Flower-and-Bird Painting', *China Reconstructs*, III (May–June 1953), pp. 50–2.

Chavannes, Edouard and Petrucci, Raphael, *La peinture chinoise au Musée Cernuschi, Avril–Juin 1912* (Ars Asiatica, I) (Brussels and Paris, 1914).

Ch'en Yuan, 'Chinese Culture in Wartime', *Journal of the Royal Society of Arts*, XCIV, No. 4728 (Oct. 11, 1946), pp. 674–83.

Ch'i Ssu-ho, 'Professor Hung on the Ch'un-ch'iu', *Yenching Journal of Social Studies*, I, No. 1 (June 1938), pp. 49–71.

Ch'ien Tuan-sheng, 'Study [*hsüeh-hsi*] for the Purpose of Self Reform and Better Service to the Fatherland', *Jen-min jih-pao* (Peking, Nov. 6, 1951), Chao Kuo-chün, tr. (Harvard University, 1952, mimeo.).

Chou En-lai, 'The People's Liberation War and Problems in Literature and Art', *The People's New Literature* (Peking, 1950), pp. 13–40.

Chou Ling, *La peinture chinoise contemporaine de style traditionel* (Paris, 1949).

Chou Yang, *China's New Literature and Art* (Peking, 1954).

'The People's New Literature', *The People's New Literature* (Peking, 1950), pp. 89–131.

Chuan, T. K., 'Philosophy Chronicle', *T'ien Hsia Monthly*, IV, No. 3 (March 1936), pp. 287–93.

Clark, Kenneth, *Landscape into Art* (London, 1949).

Cohn, William, *Chinese Painting* (London and New York, 1948).

Collingwood, R. G., *An Autobiography* (Harmondsworth, 1944).

An Essay in Philosophical Method (Oxford, 1933).

The Idea of History (Oxford, 1946).

Contag, Victoria, 'Das Mallehrbuch für Personen-Malerei des Chieh Tzu Yüan', *T'oung Pao*, XXXIII, No. 1 (1937), 15–90.

Die Beiden Steine (Braunschweig, 1950).

BIBLIOGRAPHY

Contag, Victoria, *Die Sechs Berühmten Maler der Ch'ing-Dynastie* (Leipzig, 1940).

'Schriftcharakteristeken in der Malerei, dargestellt an Bildern Wang Meng's und Anderer Maler der Südschule', *Ostasiatische Zeitschrift*, XVII, No. 1–2 (1941), 46–61.

'Tung Chi-ch'ang's *Hua Ch'an Shih Sui Pi* und das *Hua Shuo* des Mo Shih-lung', *Ostasiatische Zeitschrift*, IX, Nos. 3–4 (May–Aug., 1933), pp. 83–97; No. 5 (Oct. 1933), pp. 174–87.

Coomeraswamy, Ananda K., *Figures of Speech or Figures of Thought* (London, 1946).

Copland, Aaron, *Music and Imagination* (Cambridge, 1952).

Crombie, A. C., *Augustine to Galileo* (London, 1952).

Dubosc, J. P., 'A New Approach to Chinese Painting', *Oriental Art*, III, No. 2 (1950), pp. 50–7.

Dumoulin, Heinrich, *The Development of Chinese Zen after the Sixth Patriarch in the Light of Mumonkan* (New York, 1953).

Duncan, C. S., 'The Scientist as a Comic Type', *Modern Philology*, XIV, No. 5 (Sept. 1916), pp. 89–99.

Durkheim, Emile, *Sociology and Philosophy* (London, 1953).

Ecke, Gustav, 'Comments on Calligraphies and Paintings', *Monumenta Nipponica*, III (1938), pp. 565–78.

Einstein, Albert, 'Autobiographical Notes', *Albert Einstein: Philosopher-Scientist*, ed. Paul Arthur Schilpp (Evanston, 1949), pp. 1–95.

Eliot, T. S., *What Is A Classic?* (London, 1945).

Elisséev, Serge, 'Sur le paysage à l'encre de Chine du Japon', *Revue des Arts Asiatiques*, 2 (June 1925), pp. 30–8.

Evans, B. Ifor, *Literature and Science* (London, 1954).

Fei Hsiao-tung, *China's Gentry: Essays in Rural-Urban Relations* (Chicago, 1953).

Feng Hsüeh, 'Lu Hsun, His Life and Thought', Chinese Literature, 2 (Spring 1952)—reprinted in *Current Background*, 217 (Oct. 30, 1952) (American Consulate General, Hong Kong), pp. 1–14.

Feng Yu-lan, 'Chinese Philosophy and Its Possible Contribution to a Universal Philosophy', *East and West*, I, No. 4 (Jan. 1951), pp. 212–17.

Ferguson, John C., *Chinese Painting* (Chicago, 1927).

'Wang Ch'uan', *Ostasiatische Zeitschrift*, III, No. 1 (April–June 1914), pp. 51–60.

Fitzgerald, C. P., 'The Renaissance Movement in China', *Meanjin*, IX, No. 2 (Winter 1950), pp. 98–108.

Folk Arts of New China (Peking, 1954).

Forbes, Duncan, 'James Mill and India', *The Cambridge Journal* V, No. 1 (Oct. 1951), pp. 19–33.

Franke, Herbert, 'Zur Biographie des Pa-Ta-Shan-Jen', *Asiatica: Festschrift Freidrich Weller* (Leipzig, 1954), pp. 119–30.

Freeman, Mansfield, 'Yen Hsi Chai, a Seventeenth Century Philosopher', *Journal of the North China Branch of the Royal Asiatic Society*, LVII (1926), pp. 70–91.

BIBLIOGRAPHY

Giles, Herbert A., *An Introduction to the History of Chinese Pictorial Art* (London, 1918).

Glatzer, Nahum, ed., *Franz Rosenzweig, His Life and Thought* (Philadelphia, 1953).

Gray, Christopher, *Cubist Aesthetic Theories* (Baltimore, 1953).

Great Chinese Painters of the Ming and Ch'ing Dynasties (Wildenstein Galleries, New York, 1949).

Greene, Theodore Meyer, *The Arts and the Art of Criticism* (Princeton, 1947).

Grigaut, Paul L., 'Art of the Ming Dynasty', *Archaeology*, V, No. 1 (March 1952), pp. 11–13.

Gropius, Walter, 'Tradition and the Center', *Harvard Alumni Bulletin*, LIII, No. 2 (Oct. 14, 1950), pp. 68–71.

Hackney, Louis Wallace and Yau Chang-foo, *A Study of Chinese Paintings in the Collection of Ada Small Moore* (London, New York, and Toronto, 1940).

Hazard, Paul, *European Thought in the Eighteenth Century, from Montesquieu to Lessing* (New Haven, 1954).

Henderson, Lawrence J., *The Order of Nature* (Cambridge, 1917).

Hippolyte, Jean, *Introduction à l'étude de la philosophie de l'histoire de Hégel* (Paris, 1948).

Hirth, Friedrich, *Native Sources for the History of Chinese Pictorial Art* (New York, 1917).

Houghton, Walter, E., Jr., 'The English Virtuoso in the Seventeenth Century', *Journal of the History of Ideas*, III, No. 1 (Jan. 1942), 51–73; No. 2 (April 1942), 190–219.

Huang Siu-chi, *Lu Hsiang-shan, a Twelfth-Century Chinese Idealist Philosopher* (New Haven, 1944).

Hucker, Charles O., 'The "Eastern Forest" Movement of the Late Ming Period', *Thought and Institutions in China*, ed. John K. Fairbank (Chicago, 1956).

Hummel, Arthur W., ed., *Eminent Chinese of the Ch'ing Period* (Washington, 1943 and 1944).

tr., *The Autobiography of a Chinese Historian: Being the Preface to a Symposium on Ancient Chinese History (Ku Shih Pien)* (Leiden, 1931).

Jacometti, Neste, 'Zao Wou-ki', *Art Documents*, VII (1951), p. 3.

Jaeger, Werner, *Paideia: the Ideals of Greek Culture* (New York, 1943).

Jen Yu-wen, 'Art Chronicle', *T'ien Asia Monthly*, VI, No. 2 (Feb. 1938), pp. 144–47.

Jenyns, Soame, *Later Chinese Porcelain* (New York, n.d.).

Kao Weng, 'The Art of Painting Is not Lifeless', *An Exhibition of Paintings by Kao Weng and Chung K'un-i*, Metropolitan Museum of Art (New York, 1944).

Kobayashi Taichiro, 'Hokusai and Degas', *Contemporary Japan*, XV, Nos. 9–12 (Sept.–Dec. 1946), pp. 359–68.

Kuo Mo Jo, 'Culture chinoise et occident', *Démocratie nouvelle*, V, No. 2 (Feb. 1951), pp. 68–70.

Kuo Mo Jo, 'The United Front in Literature and Art', *People's China*, I (Jan. 1, 1950), pp. 11–12, 29–30.

Kwei Chen, 'Po Chu-i: People's Poet', *China Reconstructs*, IV (July–Aug. 1953), pp. 31–5.

'La peinture chinoise contemporaine', Musée Cernuschi (Paris, 1946).

Langer, Susanne K., *Philosophy in a New Key* (New York, 1948).

L'art chrétien chinois, special number of *Dossiers de la commission synodale*, V, No. 5 (Peiping, May 1932).

Latourette, Kenneth Scott, *A History of Christian Missions in China* (New York, 1929).

Lawrence, D. H., *Selected Essays* (Harmondsworth, 1950).

Lecture par Henri Michaux de huit lithographies de Zao Wou-ki (Paris, 1951).

Lehrs, Ernst, *Man or Matter* (London, 1951).

Legge, James, tr., 'Chung-yung' (Doctrine of the Mean), *The Chinese Classics*, I (Oxford, 1893).

tr., 'Lun-yü' (Confucian Analects), *The Chinese Classics*, I.

tr., 'Mencius', *The Chinese Classics*, II (Oxford, 1895).

tr., 'Ta-hsüeh' (The Great Learning), *The Chinese Classics*, I.

Levenson, Joseph R., *Liang Ch'i-ch'ao and the Mind of Modern China* (Cambridge, 1953).

Levy, Marion J., Jr., *Family Revolution in Modern China* (Cambridge, 1949).

Lewis, W. Arthur, *The Theory of Economic Growth* (London, 1955).

Lippe, Aschwin, 'The Waterfall', *Bulletin of the Metropolitan Museum of Art*, XII (Oct. 1953), pp. 60–7.

Liu Shao-chi, *On the Party* (Peking, 1950).

'Lotus Flowers, by Liu (sic) Chih', *Kokka*, 315 (Aug. 1916), p. 38.

Lu Hsün, *Ah Q and Others*, tr. Wang Chi-chen (New York, 1941).

Luthy, Herbert, 'Montaigne, or the Art of Being Truthful', *Encounter*, I, No. 2 (Nov. 1953), pp. 33–44.

Maimonides, Moses, *Guide of the Perplexed*, tr. M. Friedlander (New York, n.d.).

Mannheim, Karl, *Essays on Sociology and Social Psychology* (New York, 1953).

Mao Tse-tung, *Problems of Art and Literature* (New York, 1950).

'Stalin—Friend of the Chinese People', *People's China*, I, No. 1 (Jan. 1, 1950), p. 4.

March, Benjamin, *Some Technical Terms of Chinese Painting* (Baltimore, 1935).

Maritain, Jacques, *Religion et culture* (Paris, 1930).

Martin, Kingsley, 'Rangoon Reflections', *The New Statesman and Nation*, XLV, No. 1142 (Jan. 24, 1953), pp. 84–5.

Masterpieces of Chinese Bird and Flower Painting (Fogg Art Museum, Cambridge, 1951).

McKeon, Richard, 'Conflicts of Values in a Community of Cultures', *The Journal of Philosophy*, XLVII, No. 8 (April 13, 1950), pp. 197–210.

Meyer, R. W., *Leibnitz and the Seventeenth-Century Revolution* (Cambridge, 1952).

Mills, C. Wright, *White Collar: the American Middle Classes* (New York, 1951).

Monval, Jean, 'Les conquêtes de la Chine; une commande de l'empereur de Chine en France au XVIIIe siècle', *La revue de l'art ancien et moderne*, II (1905), pp. 147-60.

Moy, Clarence, 'Communist China's Use of the Yang-ko', *Papers on China* (mimeo.), VI (Harvard University, March 1952), pp. 112-48.

Nagassé Takashiro, *Le paysage dans l'art de Hokuçai* (Paris, 1937).

Needham, Joseph, *Science and Civilization in China*, I (Cambridge, 1954). 'Thoughts on the Social Relations of Science and Technology in China', *Centaurus*, III (1953), pp. 40-8.

Nef, John U., 'The Genesis of Industrialism and of Modern Science, 1560-1640', *Essays in Honor of Conyers Read*, ed. Norton Downs (Chicago, 1953), pp. 200-69.

New York Times.

Nivison, David Shepherd, *The Literary and Historical Thought of Chang Hsüeh-ch'eng (1738-1801): a Study of His Life and Writing, with Translations of Six Essays from the 'Wen-shih t'ung-i'*, MS. (Harvard University, 1953). 'The Problem of "Knowledge" and "Action" in Chinese Thought since Wang Yang-ming', *Studies in Chinese Thought*, ed. Arthur F. Wright (Chicago, 1953), pp. 112-45.

North China Herald, Shanghai.

Oakeshott, Michael, *Experience and Its Modes* (Cambridge, 1933).

Payne, Robert, *China Awake* (New York, 1947).

Pelliot, Paul, 'Les "Conquêtes de l'empereur de la Chine" ', *T'oung pao*, XX (1921), pp. 183-274. *Les influences européennes sur l'art chinois au XVIIe et au XVIIIe siècle* (Paris, 1948).

Petrucci, Raphael, tr., *Encyclopédie de la peinture chinoise* (Paris, 1918).

Pevsner, Nikolaus, *Academies of Art* (Cambridge, 1940).

Plato, *Ion*.

Postage Stamps of the People's Republic of China, 1949-1954 (Supplement to *China Reconstructs*), IV (April 1955).

Powell, Ralph, *The Rise of Chinese Military Power, 1895-1912* (Princeton, 1955).

Pulleyblank, Edwin G., *Chinese History and World History* (Cambridge, 1955).

Read, Herbert, *A Coat of Many Colours* (London, 1945).

Rienaecker, Victor, 'Chinese Art (Sixth Article), Painting—I', *Apollo*, XL, No. 236 (Oct. 1944), pp. 81-4. 'Chinese Art (Seventh Article), Painting—II', *Apollo*, XL, No. 237 (Nov. 1944), pp. 108-13.

Ross, W. D., *Aristotle's Prior and Posterior Analytics* (Oxford, 1949).

Rowley, George, 'A Chinese Scroll of the Ming Dynasty: Ming Huang and Yang Kuei-fei Listening to Music', *Worcester Art Museum Annual*, II (1936–37), pp. 63–79.

Sakai, Robert K., 'Ts'ai Yüan-p'ei as a Synthesizer of Western and Chinese Thought', *Papers on China* (mimeo.), III (Harvard University, May 1949), pp. 170–92.

Sandor, Paul, *Histoire de la dialectique* (Paris, 1947).

Sapir, Edward, 'Culture, Genuine and Spurious', *Selected Writings of Edward Sapir, in Language, Culture, and Personality*, ed. David G. Mandelbaum (Berkeley and Los Angeles, 1949), pp. 308–31.

Sarkar, Benoy Kumar, *The Sociology of Races, Cultures, and Human Progress* (Calcutta, 1939).

Sarton, George, *Introduction to the History of Science* (Washington, 1931).

Schenck, Edgar C., 'The Hundred Wild Geese', *Honolulu Academy of Arts Annual Bulletin*, I (1939), pp. 3–14.

Schücking, Levin L., *The Sociology of Literary Taste* (New York, 1944).

Schwartz, Benjamin I., *Chinese Communism and the Rise of Mao* (Cambridge, 1951).

'Marx and Lenin in China', *Far Eastern Survey*, XVIII, No. 15 (July 27, 1949), pp. 174–8.

Sirèn, Osvald, *A History of Later Chinese Painting* (London, 1938).

'An Important Treatise on Painting from the Beginning of the Eighteenth Century', *T'oung pao*, XXXIV, No. 3 (1938), pp. 153–164.

Early Chinese Paintings from the A. W. Bahr Collection (London, 1938).

'Shih-t'ao, Painter, Poet, and Theoretician', *Bulletin of the Museum of Far Eastern Antiquities*, XXI (Stockholm, 1949), pp. 31–62.

The Chinese on the Art of Painting (Peiping, 1936).

Small, Harold A., ed., *Form and Function, remarks on art by Horatio Greenough* (Berkeley and Los Angeles, 1947).

'Soochow Remembers the Taipings', *China Reconstructs*, I (Jan.–Feb. 1953), pp. 49–51.

Soper, Alexander Coburn, *Kuo Jo-hsü's 'Experiences in Painting' (T'u-Hua Chien-Wen-Chih)* (Washington, 1951).

Speiser, Werner, 'Ba Dan Schan Jen', *Sinica*, VIII, No. 2 (March 10, 1933), pp. 46–9.

'Eine Landschaft von Wang Hui in Köln', *Ostasiatische Zeitschrift*, XVII, Nos. 1–2 (1941), pp. 169–72.

'T'ang Yin', *Ostasiatische Zeitschrift*, XI, Nos. 1–2 (Jan.–April 1935), pp. 1–21; Nos. 3–4 (May–Aug. 1935), pp. 96–117.

Spengler, Oswald, *The Decline of the West* (New York, 1934).

Starkman, Miriam Kosh, *Swift's Satire on Learning in 'A Tale of a Tub'* (Princeton, 1950).

Sullivan, Michael, 'The Traditional Trend in Contemporary Chinese Art', *Oriental Art*, II, No. 3 (Winter 1949–50), pp. 105–10.

Swift, Jonathan, *An Account of a Battel between the Antient and Modern Books in St. James' Library.*

Gulliver's Travels.

Tagore, Amitendranath, 'Wartime Literature of China—Its Trends and Tendencies', *The Visva-Bharati Quarterly*, XVI, No. 2 (Aug.–Oct. 1950), pp. 120–9.

Tai Chin-hsieo, *The Life and Work of Ts'ai Yüan-p'ei*, MS. (Harvard University, 1952).

Teng Ssu-yü and Fairbank, John K., *China's Response to the West* (Cambridge, 1954).

Thorlby, Anthony, 'The Poetry of *Four Quartets*', *The Cambridge Journal*, V, No. 5 (Feb. 1952), pp. 280–99.

Tjan Tjoe Som, *Po Hu T'ung: the Comprehensive Discussions in the White Tiger Hall* (Leiden, 1949).

Tomita Kojiro, 'Brush-strokes in Far Eastern Painting', *Eastern Art*, III (Philadelphia, 1931), pp. 29–37.

—— and Chiu, A. Kaiming, 'An Album of Landscapes and Poems by Shen Chou (1427–1509)', *Bulletin of the Museum of Fine Arts* (Boston), XLVI, No. 265 (Oct. 1948), pp. 55–64.

Tretiakov, S., ed., *A Chinese Testament, the Autobiography of T'an Shih-hua* (New York, 1934).

Valery, Paul, *Reflections on the World Today* (London, 1951).

Van Boven, Henri, *Histoire de la littérature chinoise moderne* (Peiping, 1946).

von Rosthorn, Arthur, 'Malerei und Kunstkritik in China', *Wiener Beigräge zur Kunst- und Kultur-Geschichte*, IV, (1930), pp. 9–26.

Waley, Arthur, 'A Chinese Picture', *The Burlington Magazine*, XXX, No. 1 (Jan. 1917), pp. 3–10.

—— *An Introduction to the Study of Chinese Painting* (London, 1923).

—— *Chinese Poems* (London, 1946).

—— *The Analects of Confucius* (London, 1949).

—— *The Life and Times of Po Chü-i, 772–846 A.D.* (New York, 1949).

Wang Fang-chuen, *Chinese Freehand Flower Painting* (Peiping, 1936).

Weber, Max, *The Religion of China* (Glencoe, 1951).

Wenley, A. G., 'A Note on the So-called Sung Academy of Painting', *Harvard Journal of Asiatic Studies*, VI, No. 2 (June 1941), pp. 269–72.

Whitehead, Alfred North, *Adventures of Ideas* (New York, 1933).

—— *Modes of Thought* (New York, 1938).

—— *Process and Reality* (New York, 1929).

—— *Science and the Modern World* (New York, 1937).

—— *Symbolism, Its Meaning and Effect* (New York, 1927).

—— *The Aims of Education and other Essays* (New York, 1949).

Wieger, Leon, *Le flot montant (Chine moderne*, II) (Hsien-hsien, 1921).

Wiley, Margaret L., *The Subtle Knot, Creative Scepticism in Seventeenth-Century England* (Cambridge, 1952).

Wilhelm, Hellmut, 'The Background of Tseng Kuo-fan's Ideology', *Asiatische Studien*, Nos. 3–4 (1949), pp. 90–100.

—— 'The Problem of Within and Without, a Confucian Attempt in Syncretism', *Journal of the History of Ideas*, XII, No. 1 (Jan. 1951), pp. 48–60.

BIBLIOGRAPHY

Willey, Basil, *The Seventeenth Century Background* (London, 1950).

Woodbridge, Samuel I., *China's Only Hope* (New York, 1900).

Wright, Arthur F., 'Fu I and the Rejection of Buddhism', *Journal of the History of Ideas*, XII, No. 1 (Jan. 1951), pp. 31–47.

Wright, Mary, 'From Revolution to Restoration: the Transformation of Kuomintang Ideology', *Far Eastern Quarterly*, XIV, No. 4 (Aug. 1955), pp. 515–32.

Yashiro Yukio, 'Connoisseurship in Chinese Painting', *Journal of the Royal Society of Arts*, LXXXIV, No. 4339 (Jan. 17, 1936), pp. 262–72.

Yeh Chien-yu, 'On the Classical Tradition in Chinese Painting', *People's China*, VII (1954), pp. 15–17.

Young, Edward, 'Conjectures on Original Composition', *Criticism: the Foundations of Modern Literary Judgment*, ed. Mark Schorer, Josephine Miles, and Gordon McKenzie (New York, 1948), pp. 12–30.

VOLUME TWO

THE PROBLEM OF MONARCHICAL DECAY

PREFACE FOR VOLUME TWO

'THE Problem of Monarchical Decay' is the second volume of *Confucian China and Its Modern Fate*, which began with 'The Problem of Intellectual Continuity'. The work concludes in a third volume, 'The Problem of Historical Significance'.

It is mainly novelists, I suppose, who have brought out works meant to be integral, with a central core of characters and an over-arching design, though offered in several volumes 'complete in themselves'. I have in mind not so much the *roman fleuve*, which may take a family, for example, down through the years, but the broad panoramas, the novels of shifting context, where the same characters, at the same time, appear in different lights and situations. At least some historical themes, I think, can be treated like that. Some, indeed, demand it. A theme like 'Confucian China and its modern fate', if it is not to seem, under such a title, just a bit of Wagnerian pastiche, windy and portentous, has to be scored more than once.

The present book, then, follows on 'The Problem of Intellectual Continuity', but not in the usual chronological way, like 'The War Years' after 'The Prairie Years'. The contents of the volumes run parallel in time, not consecutively. Each volume should have an internal wholeness, while the set, I hope, will make a total effect itself. Certain themes which in one volume receive only limited treatment, appropriate to the part they play in developing a certain train of thought, are treated extensively elsewhere, as befits another context. Yet, the different contexts for the single theme, while separated for the purpose of exposition, should strike the reader of the whole work as mutually reinforcing.

For example, the anti-Confucian Taiping Rebellion

(1850–64) is touched on rather glancingly in Volume One, mainly as a foil to the Confucian syncretisms of the anti-Taiping Tseng Kuo-fan, and as a factor in the problem of the social implications of Christian proselytism, and as an element in a new tradition set in opposition to The Tradition. But in Volume Two it reappears, in a detailed discussion of the Taiping clash with the Confucian conception of monarchy. And this discussion is part of a general exploration of the tension between monarchy and bureaucracy in Confucian China; the significance of that tension for the very definition of Confucian China; and the reasons for the relaxation of that tension and the reduction of Confucianism to vestigial status.

This is an 'institutional' counterpart of the 'intellectual' explanation in Volume One. In Volume One, I posed the problem of Confucian China's modern fate in intellectual terms: how and why, during so much of Chinese history, have new ideas had to face tests of compatibility with received tradition, while in more recent times tradition has had to face tests of compatibility with independently persuasive new ideas? In Volume Two, I pose the problem—the *same* problem—in institutional terms: how and why have monarchy and bureaucracy been so intimately involved in the Confucian view of culture that abolition of the first, and transformation of the second, have rendered partisans of the third more *traditionalistic* than *traditional*?

'Confucianism' is an amorphous term. I have taken it seriously, and and my 'Confucian China' is not just a carelessly chosen loose equivalent of 'traditional China'. Of course, there was more to China, much more, than Confucianism. In Volume One, I gave some attention to the Buddhist side of things, and, in the present volume, to Legalism—not that these are all. Yet, the aim is not just to present a many-sided picture of China; it is still necessary, I think, to lean to one side. Certainly we should realize that a thoroughly Confucian China is an unhistorical abstraction. But we should retain the Confucian abstraction in our minds, instead of dismissing it under the weight of evidence of Legalist qualification. We have to retain it in our minds just because out there, in history, the abstraction is surely blurred. Then we can ask, what blurs it? If Confucius was revered as the Chinese sage (to put it at its simplest), what interfered with his influence? If a moving body ought to continue to move with its first speed and direction, what forces slow it down and redirect it?

Confucianism, then, was never alone in the Chinese universe. But it did not simply yield room to other bodies of thought and institutions. They interacted, in a system with a history. One way to unravel the history is to check the 'revisionist' ardour, retain the concept 'Confucian China' in spite of the prominence of other strains, and see how the latter bring historical tensions to the otherwise pure (or unhistorical) Confucian ideas and offices.

Confucianism, besides sharing space, in a system, had a place in time, in a history. How large a place may we allot it? There can be just as much a question of the length of its existence as of the breadth. How can a book which purports to be about 'Confucian China' spend many pages on the nineteenth century, when Confucius lived about twenty-five centuries earlier?

This is a constructive question, in that it warns, rightly, against smearing the Chinese eras together. Individualities must be respected and the sense of change never dulled. But the question may be obstructive, too, if it puts a case for nominalism. The very truth which the question vindicates, that China has a history, would be obscured by the suggestion that discrete atoms fill it. There was not just one Confucianism over twenty-five hundred years; but there was not just one Confucianism, a school in the age of the 'Warring States'. There have been, instead, Confucianisms—plural, changing, but still with some real persistence. I have tried in this book to give full weight to process, not stasis, and to show what *happened to* Confucianism. But Confucianism was a feature of many landscapes in time, and I have felt it relevant at many moments to refer to the glimpses in many others.

PREFACE

Indeed, the question of generality does not stop there. Along with lines stretching down between such eras as Han, Sung, Ming, and Ch'ing, the lines go out to France, Germany, Russia, and Japan, among others. Here, too, I have meant not to force identities but to recognize relevancies. These are comparisons, not analogies, and they seem to me to throw light not only on Chinese history but on the purpose of history-writing, on this subject, in this day.

From at least the late nineteenth century, men in all parts of the world have looked, with hope or alarm but with more and more conviction, to an impending unification of the world. This has provided the theme for much profound speculation and many banalities. People everywhere wonder about the cultural implications of a universal science and technology, and various intellectual imperatives have been suggested. Some speak of the need to construct a culture out of selected values from particular histories, so that a cultural esperanto will accord with the new technological universe. Others speak rather of essentially parallel histories, whose cultural destinations will be essentially the same. However, I do not consider that history can ever be made in the first way, as though by cultural selection boards, taking the best from East and West for a nice synthetic balance (see Volume One); and I do not think it has been made in the second way, down some universal paradigm, Marxist or Toynbeean or any other.

As a matter of fact, just such assumptions as these are in the record I wish to study in *Confucian China*. But while I study them as historical subjects that need explaining, not as objectively valid explanations themselves of the course that history takes, I share something of the premise behind them. For something is emerging that really can be called world history, not just the sum of histories of separate civilizations. Historians of China can help to make this history as they write of the past. Far removed from any fact or fancy of cultural 'aggression' or cultural apologetics, an historian, by bringing China into a universal world of discourse, helps to unify the world on more than a technological level. There should be no question of contriving syntheses or of warping

viii

Chinese history to fit some western model. Instead, a world is made when an understanding of Chinese history, without violence to its integrity and individuality, and an understanding of western history reinforce each other. They belong together not because they reproduce each other (which is false), and not because economic expansion or political embroilments or intellectual influences bring them into touch (though this is true), but because minds of observers can transpose the problems (not, transplant the problems) of one into the other.

Chinese bureaucracy is not analogous to Prussian, but it is comparable (see Volume Two). When Burckhardt too hastily believed the rumour of the burning of the Louvre by the Communards, he could have no notion of an Imperial Palace Museum; but one who thinks of this museum in Peking and the fall of Chinese principalities and powers must think of Burckhardt's attitude, for the issue of revolution and culture, 'high' and otherwise, is a universal issue (see Volume Three). And Chinese history, then, should be studied not just for exotic appeal or importance to western strategy. It should be studied because—without making the same designs—it can be seen to make sense in the same world of discourse in which we try to make sense of the West. If we can make this kind of sense, perhaps we help to make this kind of world. The act of writing history is an historic act itself.

Like its predecessor, this volume owes a very great deal to conferences held under the auspices of the Committee for Chinese Thought of the Association for Asian Studies. I am very grateful to Arthur F. Wright, the chairman of the committee and of its conferences on Confucianism, and to all the participants, many of whose names will be found in the text or in the footnotes. Their scholarship and penetrating comments have been indispensable, though they are free of responsibility for my uses and abuses. Some of the material, too, was given a hearing at the 'Conference on Political Power in Traditional China', 1959, under the direction of John K. Fairbank. I am delighted to thank him again, as

PREFACE

I have done, or should have done, so many times for so many things since 1939. Among colleagues and students at the University of California, Franz Schurmann and Pow-key Sohn have been especially generous with their help on this volume. My wife, to whom the first volume was dedicated, has gone over the manuscript with a stabbing blue pencil. She was too kind to sharpen it as fine as she might have liked, but I am grateful to her for clearing out at least some of the faults of style.

A fellowship at the Center for Advanced Study in the Behavioral Sciences at Palo Alto, a Guggenheim fellowship for a year at St. Antony's College and the Oriental Institute, Oxford, and the Center for Chinese Studies at the University of California, Berkeley, have all contributed enormously to the research, discussion, and writing which have gone into this book. It seems rather a mini-mouse from such a mountain of support, but I hope the directors and foundations concerned will accept this expression of deep appreciation.

Parts of the book in different form have been published in *Confucianism in Action*, ed. David S. Nivison and Arthur F. Wright (Stanford, 1959), and in *Comparative Studies in Society and History*. I wish to thank the publishers and editors for permission to use the material here.

J. R. L.

Contents

CONTENTS

xii

CONTENTS

Part Four: The Vestige of Suggestiveness:
Confucianism and Monarchy at the Last (II)

Part One

THE SUGGESTIVENESS OF VESTIGES: CONFUCIANISM AND MONARCHY AT THE LAST (I)

Hommes de l'avenir souvenez-vous de moi
Je vivais à l'époque où finissaient les rois . . .

APOLLINAIRE, *Alcools*

CHAPTER I

The Draining of the
Monarchical Mystique

I. THE HUNG-HSIEN EMPEROR AS A COMIC TYPE

IN 1914 Yüan Shih-k'ai, trying to be the strong man not by
muscle alone, but by mystique, contrived a bit of ceremonial. He still called his state the Min-kuo, the Republic,
and he still called himself a president, not an emperor, but he
meant to be a president with quite remarkable staying powers,
and he looked for some awe to reinforce his political arrangements. Accordingly, he embellished his presidential election
law (which was frankly designed as a guarantee that Yüan
would succeed himself and succeed himself) with a ritualistic
rigmarole to add a touch of suspense—three names, the
president's private and secret choices, put in a gold box kept
in a stone house in the presidential palace enclosure, the
president with the one key to the gold box, the president and
two of his appointees with the three keys to the stone house,
the dramatic disclosure to a safe electoral college of the three
names three days before the election, the thoughtful addition
of the president's name to his roster of tame candidates, etc.[1]
It was a cunning plan.

However, he never used it. His real aim was to invoke a
sanctity, not to create one, and the comical complexity of his
'republican' devices—his mummery for presidents and his
plethora of schemes for treadmill rounds of provisional
parliaments and provisional constitutions—were better made
to mock the Republic than to make it seem legitimate. Total

3

discredit of the Republic was a preamble; then, the body of the tale might be a new dynastic history. Yüan's conversation, it was commonly noted, kept turning to the question of 'the success of the Republic'. He put it to all provincial officials when they came to Peking.[2] The implication was plain: they were free, more than free, to denigrate the Republic. Yüan, though its chief executive, would surely take no offence.

Yet, when Yüan finally inaugurated the Hung-hsien reign on January 1, 1916, the parody of a republic yielded (for just a few months) to only a parody of the empire. And this was perhaps inevitable, the result not of some failure of dignity in Yüan himself, but of a condition of modern Chinese history in the large: the vitiation of old conventions, an invincible staleness which all the futilities of the republican alternative, obvious though they were, could not dispel. Goethe's Faust had seen his emperor's court as a world of masks for emptiness, and court and carnival as one.[3] And the question that needs to be asked about Yüan's imperial masquerade, about all the vestigial monarchism in the Chinese Republican era, is the question that Mann's Faust-as-the-artist put to himself: 'Why does almost everything seem to me like its own parody? Why must I think that almost all, no, all the methods and conventions of art today are good for parody only?'[4]

The imperial office in 1916 could not be taken seriously, because the Republic of 1912, while a failure, was not a mistake. Its failure lay in its social meaninglessness; the revolution seemed to have had no substance. As the great Lu Hsün (1881–1936) mordantly remarked of the trivial changings of the guard at the bureaucrats' yamens: '. . . Those who wore cotton clothing when they came to serve in his office had changed into fur gowns within ten days, although the weather was not yet cold.'[5]

But the Republic, however insubstantial, did have meaning as a symbol: by its mere existence after thousands of years of monarchy, it offered licence to new thought, the solvent of Chinese pieties. Yüan Shih-k'ai, by trying to make himself stick as emperor, asserted in effect that no political revolution had occurred in 1911 and 1912, only, at most, a traditional rebellion between dynastic periods. However, his monarchism, in defiance of this interpretation, was compromised by a revolution which *was* occurring, the intellectual revolution. When the Republic, devoid of social achievement though it may have been, shameless political fake though it may have seemed, nevertheless stood for something— iconoclasm—its rival, monarchy, had to stand for something, too (and something, as we shall see, fatally equivocal): traditionalism.

Much of Yüan's support, even during his imperial episode, was not monarchical in principle. He had his personal followers, playing parts in factional struggle, and many of them said yes to monarchy because Yüan wanted it, not because they did. A few men with their private hopes invested in Yüan, and others even with confidence in him, would have followed him anywhere. But he needed more than these companions in his quest for imperial honours. Not Yüan Shih-k'ai but Chinese Empire had to be the cause, and anti-Republican feeling, in the nature of the times, was tied in with tradition.

At first, the only monarchism visible after the revolution was a faint rally for the fallen house, the Ch'ing. There remains an impression that Yüan was mildly indulgent to this campaign; perhaps it would soften up the public for his own.[6] The latter began, it appears, in 1913, when he set up a bureau for a Ch'ing Dynastic History. This respectable patronage of scholarship did double duty politically. It showed Yüan in the old monarchical vein, and it implied a last quietus on the Ch'ing. (At the high point of his imperial drive, Yüan gave Chao Erh-sun, the principal drafter of the History, a new court title as one of the 'four Friends of Sungshan'.)[7]

In November 1914 Yüan elicited a petition with two agreeable features, a plea for a strict ban on the Ch'ing interest, and a list of flaws in the Republic. A somewhat earlier petition had been just as militant on the flaws, but quixotically urged Yüan to restore the Manchu emperor and be his minister. He answered both with an 'edict of chastisement of the restoration movement'.[8] And on December 23, 1914, when Yüan publicly reinstituted the worship of Heaven, he changed the

5

signature on the prayer-tablet from the Ch'ing's *Tzu-ch'en* ('Your son and subject') to 'Yüan Shih-k'ai representing the citizens of the Chinese Republic'.[9] Correctly republican, no doubt—but reminiscent of an older form. He would rather the rite than the presidency. He was still not ready to perform the ceremony in his own imperial name, but he was ready enough for the ceremony, hoping to ease himself eventually from one traditional role up to another.

Yüan made gentle demurrers at the offer of the throne in early December 1915 ('Our sage-master emerged with destiny . . . the people submit to your virtue, the whole nation is of one mind . . .' pronounced his Council of State, humbly petitioning that he 'graciously indulge the feelings of the people').[10] He discreetly extracted a formal blessing from the Ch'ing ex-emperor ('In accordance with the command of the Ch'ing emperor: with regard to changing the form of state and raising the president to imperial honours, the Ch'ing royal house deeply approves').[11] And in striking these poses he conformed to the pattern of *shan-jang*, cession and seemly initial rejection, which derived from the *Shu-ching* (Book of History) lore of Yao and Shun. When modesty ceased to forbid him, Yüan accepted the offer ('For the empire's rises and falls the very commoner has responsibility; shall my love of country lag behind others?')[12]—in Chinese phrases of classical cadence and in part, at least, in direct echo of the seventeenth century's Ku Yen-wu.[13] The republican bureaucracy's *ch'eng* ('submit' [a document]) gave way to the grand old *tsou* ('memorialize'); the ancient monarchical *ch'en*, for 'official' (the Ch'ing mark of Confucian distinction between the Chinese official and the Manchu *nu*, or 'slave'), supplanted the current *kuan* in the bureaucratic nomenclature.[14] And on the last day of 1915, when the next year was proclaimed as Hung-hsien 1, Yüan gave to the *Yen sheng kung*, the 'Holy Duke', K'ung Ling-i, direct descendant of Confucius, the brevet rank of *chün-wang*, a feudal title of Han devising and long in imperial use.[15] In these and a hundred other ways old legitimacies were solicited for Yüan Shih-k'ai. But when the Emperor Yüan was traditionalistic, as he had to be, he ran through an emperor's lines, he followed the ancient stage directions, but he was not (nor could anyone else then be) an authentic, traditional emperor.

2. LATE CH'ING: CONFUCIANISM REDEFINED AS THE COUNTER TO MODERN THOUGHT

Actually, monarchy was lost when the Manchu dynasty, the Ch'ing, was forced to improvise after the Boxer débâcle of 1900, and traditionalistic monarchy, which was untraditional, was preordained for Yüan Shih-k'ai by his Ch'ing dynastic predecessors. For the Ch'ing were in a hopeless dilemma in their last decade. Immobility was impossible, something had to be done to save the State. The Boxer expedients, magic and xenophobia, could surely never be tried again. Science and social renewal insistently commended themselves. There had to be modernization, or the Ch'ing would never escape the blame for continuing Chinese disasters.

Yet, their sponsorship of modernization, the abandonment of traditional Chinese ways, would end their only claim, as an ethnically foreign people, to legitimacy as Chinese rulers. This legitimacy a pre-nationalistic 'culturalism' had once accorded them, since the Manchus had generally supported the Chinese great tradition. But Chinese nationalism, necessarily spreading as Chinese culture changed (see Volume One), found a foreign conquest, old or new, inadmissible, and the Manchu conquest-dynasty entirely illegitimate. In short, in their last decade the Ch'ing had a discouraging choice. They might go down in a traditional way, out of simple cyclical weakness in a world of outer pressures and inner strains. They might go down as moderns, aspiring, at least, to strengthen China, strengthen their hold, and thereby extend their title to the traditional mandate, but running afoul of the nationalism which modern, foreign strengthening methods entailed. Quite naturally, no clear-cut choice was made. Given a situation in which the best of both worlds was in another light the worst, they tried to be modern enough to defend their traditional status, and traditional enough to take the curse off their modernism.

That is why the 'Manchu Reform Movement' in the early

nineteen-hundreds was undertaken in the *t'i-yung* spirit, seductive but self-defeating (see Volume One): Chinese learning should be for 'essence', western learning for 'utility'. The western learning was supposed to strengthen China materially, thus keeping Ch'ing from the typical end of dynasties when China was enfeebled. The Chinese learning was supposed to reconfirm the Manchus' credentials, by preserving traditional values essentially unimpaired, and still the focus of loyalty, so that Manchus could still be Manchu and yet be identified with China. But if the *t'i*, the essence, could really not be saved, Manchus were endangered, even more than the Chinese *t'i* addicts. Chinese advocates of a *t'i-yung* programme might prove wrong in their expectations, and yet their heirs would go on being Chinese, though with a new intellectual content to their lives. But Manchus, once their Confucian ticket of admission became invalid, could go on being Chinese only by assimilation, ethnic disappearance. At most they would survive rather as museum-pieces, a few visible remnants, aristocratic and anachronistic, exquisitely formed by the high Chinese culture of an age that was not their own.

Thus, there was something ominous about the Ch'ing's new educational policies, beginning in 1901. They led to actions perhaps nationally constructive, but dynastically destructive (just as inaction would have been). In part it was simply a problem of allocation of scarce resources. The new learning was supposed to supplement the old, but right at the start it began to look like substitution instead. Where were the new schools coming from? An edict of September 14, 1901, ordained that provincial *shu-yüan*, Confucian academies, be made into new-style institutions of higher learning.[16] The very physical premises of *t'i*, that is, were being invaded by *yung*. And this reflected an intellectual trend, the shortening of perimeter around the unimpeachable essence. From the hint in the eighteen-forties of a readiness to yield military technology to a world of western practice, more and more of what once was Chinese essence had been peeled off, in efforts to guard a deeper core.

The less that remained of the traditional core, the more its character as substance, eternally underlying mere function, had to be insisted on. No memorial about new schools, study abroad, the cultivation of modern talents could be complete without its mention of the Four Books and the Five Classics, the Histories, the filial and other established virtues, as the indispensable first concerns; *then* one could steep the mind in western learning.[17] And so one finds the anomalies of a 1906 decree about the new educational system—a sharp departure from the examination system (abolished the year before), which was centuries old and of incalculable significance for the traditional social order and cultural values. The new education was to have military spirit, industrial spirit, and public spirit generally among its main objectives—so much for the leanings to modernism—and loyalty to the Emperor and reverence for Confucius as vital bequests from the past. At the same time, as if to reinforce the latter strain, the Ch'ing decreed that sacrifices to Confucius be raised to the grade of *ta-ssu*, 'great sacrifices', the highest grade of three. Hitherto these spring and autumn ceremonies had been mostly left to officials, but now the Emperor himself was to perform them in Peking.[18]

Yet, this Confucian zeal of the Manchus (always apparent in Ch'ing history as a means of their growing into China on some principle other than ethnic, and heightened, if anything, at the last) only intensified Confucianism to the point of exhaustion. For it was obviously being 'worked at' for a social purpose, as something to spoil the potentialities, which were anti-Manchu, of implicitly nationalistic modern thought. Sun Yat-sen's Chinese nationalists saw the logic of this modern Confucian commitment. 'Let Confucius not be an amulet for the Manchu,' Sun's Tokyo organ, *Min-pao*, intoned in 1907. 'The Tartar court, with the revolutionary tide rising in the new thought, thereupon makes the worship of Confucius a supreme sacrificial rite.'[19]

Thus, Confucianism was being deprived of almost its last intellectual substance, and left as mainly a symbol of resistance to revolution. When revolution came, it was clear that change in régime had powerfully furthered a change in mind. Classics and ceremonies fell widely into discard, while old Confucianists tried to rally in private organizations, reactionary in the fullest sense.[20] For Confucianists were only reacting to the tide of strange events; they were no longer the natural actors in a society of their own. When the Republic, justified by Sun Yat-sen as the 'latest thing' in a universal process of political improvement, opened the lid on the latest things in every other sphere, people with vested interests in the old régime, or simple nostalgia, clung fiercely and particularly to Confucianism, which was, after all, an early thing itself, and a glorifier of early things.

3. THE REPUBLIC: CONFUCIANISM AND MONARCHISM NARROWED AND INTERWOVEN

It was an attenuated Confucianism, then, more a sentiment than a teaching, which confronted republican scepticism about the value of the past, and which gravitated unerringly to any monarchical movement that seemed to have a chance. Prominent among the petitioners for monarchy in 1915 were the *K'ung-she*, Confucian societies, of Chihli and Honan.[21] In a broad generalization Yen Fu (1849–1921), dubbed at the time, though perhaps unfairly, one of Yüan's 'six *chün-tzu*' (sardonic analogy with the 'six martyrs' of 1898, Reformers sold by Yüan to the Empress Dowager),[22] revealed the new traditionalism's associations. As a conservative statement for that time and place, it was characteristically untraditional: 'Chinese honour the prince and venerate the ancient; westerners honour the people and venerate the modern.'[23]

What is untraditional here is the identification of Chinese monarchism with intellectual traditionalism pure and simple. This was a change from the live imperial days, when the monarchy, or its centralizing agents, often strained against the conservatism of the bureaucratic intelligentsia; from their very beginnings the traditional Chinese bureaucratic and monarchical institutions had existed in a state of mutual and ambivalent attraction-repulsion (Part Two). What is characteristic here, in the contemporary context of Yen's untraditional assumption, is the air of conscious response to a serious foreign challenge, that of democratic thought and other intellectual novelty. The intellectually subversive revolutionary nationalists had injected the *min*, 'the people', into modern political consciousness, and the *min* (or their self-styled representatives) had not only ousted the old monarchy, but had forced their way into the new monarchical thinking —indeed, had made it new.

Wu T'ing-fan (1844–1922), Sun Yat-sen's representative in conversations with the Ch'ing camp in late 1911, made a statement on December 20 to the effect that the new republican government would be based on *jen-min i-chih*, the people's 'will'.[24] On February 1, 1912, the dynasty itself ordered Yüan, its last agent, to come to terms with the revolutionary *min-chün*, 'people's army': 'The people's will has become clear . . .' And in the first edict of abdication, on February 12, came the sad renunciation: 'By the indications of men's minds the mandate of Heaven is known.'[25] Here was the contradiction of the principle of heavenly selection, to which popular control and ratification were essentially irrelevant.

In the ensuing contradiction of republicanism, 'the people' could not be exorcized from the monarchists' apologies. Sometimes the 'people's will' was retained, in the Bonapartist sense, as in Yüan's amusingly hyper-successful plebiscite for monarchy in the fall of 1915; more often, the Chinese people's 'spirit', not its will, was emphasized as the guarantor of the imperial institution. The famous memorandum along these lines by Professor Goodnow, Yüan's American adviser, was issued to the Press in August 1915. It inspired or released a flood of Chinese writings on *kuo-t'i* and *kuo-ts'ui* and *kuo-ch'ing*, the people's proper form of state, the national 'spirit' or temperament, which implied not that this Chinese republic was puerile but that no Chinese republic was possible, that monarchism was inexpungeable from the Chinese people's spirit.

(a) The 'people's will'

Why must the idea of 'the people' as source of political authority be seen as essentially modern in China, and appropriate enough, therefore, to an untraditional republic, but not to a monarchy needing to trade on authentic traditional lineage? After all, there have been plenty of suggestions in the last half-century or so that western democratic theory was anticipated in ancient China; there, the imperial idea (or so it is alleged) demanded the people's happiness as test of fulfilment of the will of Heaven by the Son of Heaven.[26] But such suggestions confuse the priorities in classical Chinese thought. A modern appeal to 'the people' for validation denies, not derives from, the old imperial sanctions.

To say that *vox populi* is *vox Dei* is not to define the latter but to displace it. Here, in any literal sense, the 'voice of God' has lost its power; rendered metaphorical, it only underscores through historical tone the acknowledgement of a new supreme authority. In imperial China the *T'ien-tzu* held the *T'ien-ming* as long as he expressed the *T'ien-i*.[27] Heaven's son, mandate, and will were unequivocally the classical founts of supremacy, and the people's will, when it was worked at all by Confucian thinkers into political theory, was purely symbolic, not effective, in establishing legitimacy. Heaven's hand could not be forced.[28]

In traditional monarchical theory, that is, popular discontent did not by itself invalidate an emperor's claims—nor, by the same token, did popular approbation legitimize him. Popular discontent was a *portent*, as a flood might be a portent, of the loss of the mandate; it was a sign, perhaps, of the loss of imperial virtue. But a flood was not to be greeted with fatalistic acceptance. While an emperor should read the signs aright, he still should try to check the flood. And just so, the outbreak of a popular rebellion was no guarantee of its success or of its Confucian acceptability (far from it). It might be a portent, but it, too, should be and legitimately might be resisted. For the famous 'right to rebel' was a contradiction in terms. People rebelled not because they had any theoretical legal right, but because actual legal arrangements left little scope to their lives. Until they succeeded, rebels had no right, and the people's will, if they claimed to express it, had to wait on Heaven's choosing.

If he had the name, the 'rectified name', of Son of Heaven, the ruler had the *te* which the Ju (Confucian) school thought intrinsic to him—a *te* which was power on the outside and virtue, the *tao i hsing*, in his inner nature, a *te* which would bring no harm to the people's lives.[29] But popular satisfaction was one thing only in the classical political ideal: a sign of some higher ratification of the Emperor's legitimacy. It was another thing in the modern aura of secular democracy: the legitimizer itself.

And just as vestigial monarchy derived, allegedly, from the people's will, instead of simply according with it while reflecting Heaven's, so vestigial Confucianism took the people's will as its novel justification. 'If our parliamentarians really want to represent the people's will, then they cannot but establish Confucianism as the national religion,' wrote a petitioner in 1917, the year after 'Hung-hsien' and unpropitious for Confucian special pleaders. 'Catholics oppose the idea of a state religion,' he went on, 'but some three million Catholics are not the people's will.'[30] Mass identification with Confucianism, then, established by the evidence of history, was the ground of Confucian authority for this thinker and many others. It was the same sort of ground as Yüan had sought as the basis of his dynasty.

(b) The 'people's spirit'

But post-Ch'ing monarchism and Confucianism were linked more directly than that; it was not just that they both claimed identification with the people's will. The writer of this memorial for Confucianism (*not* a Confucian memorial), coming after Yüan's fiasco, had an embarrassed awareness of general opinion, which held Confucianism implicated in the discredited monarchical effort. It was hard to reconcile Confucianism with the symbolically modern Republic, but he did as well as he could. He admitted the charge of the Yüan affinity, dismissed it as a foible of Confucianists rather than a necessity of Confucianism, and suggested an act of oblivion. Christian churches, too, he pointed out, had launched prayers for Yüan's success. Christians, he alleged, were Yüan's loudest extollers, and took part in his government. Buddhists and Mohammedans repeatedly cheered him on. Yüan, he acknowledged, had fabricated a 'people's will' for his own monarchical purposes. But the genuine people's will was with Confucianism. Therefore, if Confucianism were established as the national religion of the Republic, it would prove itself indispensable for consolidating the State.[31]

In short, reasonably enough under the circumstances, this partisan was trying to free Confucianism from any necessary political tie. Of course, the effort to pry Confucius out of the royal box was already an old story in newly republican China. There was an apologist in 1912, for example (with a curious hint of limitation on the Sage he proclaimed eternal), who explained that Confucius, having been born in an age of monarchy, could have had no choice but to respect the institution.[32] Republics or monarchies were uncertain, but Confucianism was permanent while a Chinese people lived, for it was particularly (historically) a part of the Chinese people, its very spirit or essence. Every country has a form which is natural to it alone. Hence, 'Our country ought to establish Confucianism as the national religion . . . especially to protect the national essence.'[33]

It was this idea of Confucianism, its conception as national essence, that completed the ravages wrought by its Ch'ing defenders. Confucianism as 'essence', *t'i*, hopefully combined with 'utility', *yung*, had been a false solution to the problem of keeping alive the ancient wisdom. But when Confucianism slipped to *kuo-t'i*, *national* essence, this was worse than merely no solution to the problem of preservation—it was dissolution of the *t'i* to be preserved. As *t'i*, Confucianism was the essence of civilization, an absolute. As *kuo-t'i* or one of its synonyms, Confucianism was the essence of Chinese civilization, a complex of values (not absolute Value) in a world of historical relativism. A romantic conception of Confucianism as Chinese essence stripped Confucianism of *its* essence: a rationalistic assumption that the Way was the Way, no matter where or when, not just the particular Chinese way of life.

As early as 1905, soon after the abandonment of the examination system, we find an appeal to revere the Classics so as to preserve the national essence.[34] All the propaganda for Confucianism as a religion made the same particular point. Wherein lies the spirit, the soul of China? In the

THE REPUBLIC

Confucian *tao, hsüeh, chiao*—the Way, the learning, the doctrine or religion.[35] President Yüan Shih-k'ai wrangled over it with Sun's party, the Kuomintang, in the legislative session of 1913. Yüan wishing to establish Confucianism, the Kuomintang opposing it, they compromised. According to the 'Temple of Heaven' draft of a constitution, freedom of religion was not to be abridged, but for the national education the *tao* of Confucius was named as the basis of *hsiu-shen,* the inner cultivation of the person.[36]

Yüan soon slammed the door on the 'Temple of Heaven' draft, and, as his imperial ambitions grew, he made stronger statements on his side of the Confucian issue. Toward the end of 1914, for example, presidential mandates praised *tao* and *te,* the Confucian ethic, as the very root of government. Yüan emphasized that these were indelibly Chinese, confirmed by thousands of years of history, and that China must keep its national character, for every viable nation has its essence, a special spirit that forms it and preserves it.[37]

Where the quality of Confucian faith was less tinged with personal interest, outside Yüan's immediate circle, the religious Confucian movement had the same romantic feeling. That is, the Chinese people was urged to practise its own religion, Confucianism (Chinese, not universal, not proper to the West), on the ground that non-Chinese peoples, if well advised, were practising theirs (foreign, not universal, not proper to China). This committed Confucianists to non-Confucian thinking, a doctrine of separate but equal ultimate values. These men would not adopt a Christian *message* for China; they had to resist displacement of one universal world-view by another. But they could adopt a Christian *model* in a particularistic spirit, and preserve Confucius by seeing the world as a congeries of irreducible loyalties. Christians had cathedrals; then let Confucianists build a cathedral and start out, not on the road to Rome, but nevertheless on the road to a holy city—Ch'ü-fu, in Shantung, the birthplace of Confucius, which ought to be a pilgrimage place like Mecca or Jerusalem.[38] Christians dated by *Anno Domini*; then chih-sheng 2467 (from the birth-date of the Sage) stood for *Min-kuo* 5 or 1916.[39]

15

But why should 'national essence' Confucianism come in religious form? After all, not foreign missionaries now but Chinese secularists were making the really wounding assault on Confucianism. What defence should it be against these foes to stand off Christianity, by matching it? Yet, when Confucianists like K'ang Yu-wei (1858–1927) and his follower, Ch'en Huan-chang, deliberately courted religious comparisons, they were trying to reach the secular iconoclasts. For, as long as the adjective 'Confucian' was simply pinned on to Chinese culture, it was hard to escape the cultural critics in the harsh times of the early twentieth century. But if Confucianism was a church, like Christianity, then the modern progress of western states was no stick for belabouring Confucius. Western example proved that Church and State could coexist, and men could worship while enriching their society. As Christian religious bodies survived with science, just so (and only so), as a religious body, would Confucianism survive.

This was an effort, then, to dissociate Confucianism from Chinese material weakness. Sometimes the earlier Reformist argument, cool but not extinguished, was made again: Confucianism was the source of strength, and the West was strong where it came close to the message of the Analects, the Annals, Mencius—nourish the people, protect the people, teach the people.[40] But more characteristically for the Republican period, even the same writer, same text, would cordon off this wisdom in a church, so as to spare it imputations of failure, rather than claim for it social success. Why should Confucianism be compromised by Chinese weakness? Judaea fell, Christian imperial Rome fell, Catholic Spain and Portugal and Latin America, the Mohammedan countries, all were weak; yet their religions were not ruled out by their national incapacities.[41]

In this apology one sees the significant relativism of the post-Confucian Confucianist, the traditionalistic traditionalist. The faith is not a universal, but a matter of *mutatis mutandis*. Truth, forsooth—you have your religion, I have my religion. And all religions have a claim on life in their proper historical contexts. Confucianism certainly makes its claim in its own environment, China. 'The whole history of China is only the history of *K'ung-chiao*, the Confucian religion. We love China; therefore we love the *K'ung-chiao* . . . *K'ung-Chiao* is an interchangeable term for *Chung-kuo*.'[42] Or, in brief, from the father of them all: 'China's soul is in the *chiao* of Confucius.'[43]

More deeply than any merely strategic connection, K'ang Yu-wei felt this mystical connection between Confucius and China. It is true that he looked to his state religion to improve morality, since he believed that law and philosophy were not enough to restrain the wayward crowd.[44] Still, K'ang's candidate for state religion was specifically Chinese—not Christianity, for example, which might claim as well as Confucianism (or a little better) to endow men with a healthy sense of supernatural power. For it was the soul of China that interested K'ang, not the souls of individuals, irrespective of the cultures they were born to.

Now, the anti-Confucianists were especially exercised by this national essence-spirit-soul equation with Confucianism. One line of attack was to deny that Confucianism was any more 'Chinese' than the other currents of ancient thought.[45] But Ch'en Tu-hsiu (1880–1942), though he made that point, more forcefully simply swept away the idea of national essence. China should have what modern men required, and Confucianism (he wrote in 1916) was a fossil, fatal to vitality in the present.[46] When Confucian religionists tried to dissociate their creed from Chinese secular weakness, it was in answer to such attacks; indeed, they offered the *Church* Confucianism as a saving rock in the sea of material troubles.

Religion, they averred, was strength when all else failed, not the cause of failure itself. China should keep Confucianism, its very life for ages past, so suited to the people's hearts, because the nation, like a rudderless boat, would crack without it.[47] Confucianism was China's special nature; if stripped of it the nation would die, the people would not continue.[48] Jewish history was frequently cited as an inspiration to China, and Mexican history as a cautionary tale: the Jews, by preserving Judaism, had kept themselves alive when they were politically ruined, but the Mexicans, Hispanicized and weaned away from their own religion, were languishing in a travesty of a nation.[49] A nation that scuttled its historic religion prepared the way for its enemies. In a remarkable feat of kaleidoscoping, selection, and not very gallant aspersion on a lady of the theatre, K'ang observed that in the French Revolution the worship of a prostitute ('Goddess of Reason' in a public Deist charade) had been substituted for the worship of Christ; along came the 'hundred days' and the end.[50] When Norway split off from Sweden in 1905 (ran another expression of opinion) many changes were made in the constitution, but Lutheranism, long the state religion, remained so, as the link with the people's past. Moral: 'As the physical body without the spirit must die, so must the nation without a national religion.'[51] 'Other countries, in some numbers, have established national religions. Is there not still more reason for us to do likewise? For Confucianism is our religion by nature.'[52]

And so states may die for the lack of their own religions, and peoples may survive, though states die, if their religions are kept alive. This was another argument to extricate Confucianism from the modern plight of China (not quite the same argument as the one about religion and progress co-existing, so that Confucian *religion* was out of the way when the modernists came to arrest Confucian *culture*). For K'ang Yu-wei and his fellow thinkers, Confucianism was a religion for the ice age in China; for the revolutionary iconoclasts, Confucianism was the very thing congealed, and anti-Confucianism would melt the ice.

The romantic apologia was not the only recourse of Confucianists. Sometimes they still seemed to plead in a rationalistic spirit, stressing the simple rightness of Confucian doctrine. Thus, we find the familiar kind of statement, vintage 1913 (strained), that the excellent Republic had Confucius as its ancestor. Grouping Confucius with Rousseau and Montesquieu (though, of course, 'their forerunner by some thousands of years'), one Hsüeh Cheng-ch'ing claimed *kung-ho* ('republicanism' in contemporary usage) as Confucius's invention. Yet, Hsüeh's message was really particular, not universal. For the truth of Confucius's idea was not enough. The Chinese Republic notwithstanding—be it validated by ever so many foreign exponents of truth—Hsüeh feared for the existence of the Chinese people if its own teaching, Confucianism, declined.[53]

Again, Confucianism was commended over religions of the outside; as a *jen-tao chiao*, a humanistic creed, it was more advanced than the *shen-tao chiao*, theologies, 'superstitions', of the non-Chinese world.[54] Yet, in the context of Republican iconoclasm, such statements of rational conviction might represent romantic particularism in a special form. It was not the particularism which emphasized that foreign bodies would die if grafted on to the Chinese organism (hence, for example, the hopelessness of the Republic, as it seemed to those who would not enlist Confucius as its advocate). It stressed, rather, that the Chinese organism might die of the intrusion, an intrusion which could indeed take place. Consequently, rational argument, depending on appeals to universal criteria, could rather derive from than challenge a feeling for the national essence, so that a special concern for 'our' religion would drive one to establish it as generally 'better'.

'*Our* religion': Chinese, that is, characteristically and exclusively so, as long as any people could be called Chinese. It was an allegation of permanence, an unshakeable attribute of essence, and safer as an approach to the 'people's will' than any electoral soundings. This was the real trump (and the last card) of Confucianists under the Republic. And whatever their ultimate tactical wish to disengage from Yüan, it was monarchy's card, too. The particular spirit of the Chinese people, not the universal reason of the way of Heaven, became an emperor's justification. 'In today's "people's government",' wrote a monarchist and Confucianist in 1916, 'the model is utterly western. Though in name they perversely call it Chinese (literally, "bend it to China"), in fact, down deep, they know it is not.'[55] Once, republicanism had seemed repulsive to Confucianists as a degradation of human nature.[56] Now, it was a violation of the Chinese nature that repelled an anti-republican.

This new strain of romantic determinism, then, in both

Confucianism and monarchism, ruled out free choice of values; while free choice in the here and now, regardless of historical origins, was the premise for detachment from tradition, the corollary of republican revolution. Nothing could be more constraining than K'ang's lampoon of the anti-Confucian spirit—the equivalent, he bitterly charged, of a desperate will to dye the eyes and make them blue, powder faces and make them white, doctor the hair and make it blond.[57] Chinese traditionalism became a relative, not an absolute principle, a charge upon China, not upon man. Compulsion to preserve the gifts of the Chinese past was psychological now, from an emotional sense of threat to special identity; it was not philosophical, as of old, from an intellectual conviction of the general value of Chinese classic experience. Conservatism and monarchy were welded together, but when novelty was repelled on grounds of the limitations of the Chinese genius rather than on grounds of its fullness or universality, this conservatism was novelty itself. Equally paradoxically this monarchy, trading on the symbols of the past, was itself, no less than the Chinese Republic, a symbol of revolution.

For truly traditional, not merely traditionalistic, Chinese monarchy was ideally monarchy for the world, though centred in one intellectually self-sufficient society. Now, republican nationalistic iconoclasts defined the world as larger than China. They saw Chinese society as very far from intellectually self-sufficient. In reaction monarchist traditionalists, finding it simply impossible in modern times to sustain Chinese cultural pretensions to universality (a Lutheran Norway as justification for a Confucian China!), could preserve the ideal of Chinese monarchy only as monarchy for China alone. And they could preserve the ideal of intellectual self-sufficiency, or renewal of Confucian dominance, only as (something new to Confucianism) 'spirit-of-the-people' imperviousness to new ideas.

Culturally, men who still conceived of Confucian China were much more parochial than their Confucian ancestors, though the latter knew less and cared less about anything non-Chinese.[58] Politically, too, the universal faded. Yüan

Shih-k'ai could not be the 'son of Heaven'; he could only, possibly, be king of China. And Yüan at the winter solstice, miming in the Temple of Heaven (and contemplating ploughing in the spring) was a parody—and not just because he pulled up to the Temple in an armoured car.

Part Two

TENSION AND VITALITY

Almost every party understands how it is in the interest of its own self-preservation that the opposition should not lose all strength.

NIETZSCHE, *The Twilight of the Idols*

CHAPTER II

Confucianism and Monarchy: the Basic Confrontation

Yüan ends, then, supported by a Confucianism turned inside out. As Confucianism, that is, it still had a commitment to tradition. Yet, the traditionalism, for the most part, no longer derived philosophically from Confucianism. Instead, the Confucianism derived psychologically from traditionalism: when the people's Chinese identity seemed threatened by Republican westernization, the 'Chineseness' of Confucianism, more than its own traditionalist message, made it an object of traditionalists' reverence and a pillar of the throne. Thus, as suggested already, the cement of the 'national spirit' joined the new monarchism and the new Confucianism in a new sort of partnership, new in its rather simple, uncomplicated character in contrast with the devious, uncertain, *tense* partnership of pre-western days. For the classical imperial system, for which Confucianism became philosophy *par excellence*, was founded by Ch'in (221 B.C.) on anti-Confucian Legalist principles, and this paradox, right from the start, remained at the core of Chinese history; a bureaucratic intelligentsia, while it cherished the social stability attending imperial centralization, yet was recurrently centrifugal, hence dangerous to a dynasty, by reason of its acquisitive tendencies. This ancient imperial paradox, which distinguishes true monarchy of the Confucian age from its parody, deserves to be examined.

25

The loss of this ambivalence, this Confucian-monarchical attraction-repulsion, comprised the Chinese state's attrition. And if in its time that traditional state was a very hardy perennial, perhaps its vitality, in a truly Nietzschean sense, was the measure of its tolerance of tensions: their release was the bureaucratic monarchy's death.

I. NOTES OF STRAIN

Over the long span of imperial Chinese history, there developed a Confucian literatus-type; the figure of the emperor failed to conform to it. In many of his cultural and institutional affinities, he offended literati taste. The literati were eclectic enough philosophically, of course, and for any period from 'Warring States' (403–221 B.C.) on, Confucian texts may be shredded into all sorts of ingredients—Taoist, Buddhist, and what-not—but Chinese history does know intellectual confrontations, not just a happy melange, and relatively pure distillations of non-Confucian ideas had tendencies to seem at least in part imperial. Non-philosophical Taoism, for example, jarred on fundamentally rationalistic Confucianists not only in its form of popular 'enthusiasm' but in its connection with the elixir lore often strongly associated with emperors. Buddhism, too, had not only popular backing (often, from late T'ang on, as an anti-gentry, i.e., anti-Confucian, symbol) but imperial patronage as well, in times when its standing was extremely low or at best equivocal among the literati.[1] What could cause more revulsion in Confucianists, with their code of ethical relationships, than the patricidal or fratricidal episodes that disfigured so many imperial family histories? Eunuchs, whom Confucianists scorned and often hated and coupled with monks as 'bad elements', were characteristic members of imperial retinues. Trade, which Confucianists affected to scorn (while Buddhism gave it impetus),[2] was a matter of imperial interest. It was an interest deriving from a court society's demands for luxury, which were not approved by Confucianists, and it was manifest in such various phenomena as the eunuch Cheng Ho's voyages (1403–33), which Confucian

26

historians buried;[3] eunuchs' prominence, protested by officials, in trading-ship control organs;[4] and the Canton system of trade (1759–1839), in which the superintendent, the 'Hoppo', was a specifically imperial appointee and outside the regular bureaucratic chain of command.[5] And the history of aesthetics in China records the distinction, Sung and later, between the 'officials' style' (*shih-ta-fu hua*) and the style of the court academy (*yüan-hua:* see Volume One). The distinction may have been blurred by artistic eclecticism but it was nonetheless significant, for it spoke of the self-detachment of the literati critic, his sensing of a dissonance of gentry and palace tones.[6]

2. THE RELATION TO FEUDALISM

Now, cultural rifts like these were far from extreme, for, after all, the social roles of bureaucracy and monarchy were only clashing, not incompatible, and were complementary even as they clashed. To put it another way: at least from the reign of Han Wu-ti (140–87 B.C.) monarch and civil official had a common stake in anti-feudalism (and in this their interests were complementary), while at the same time each had leanings (and here they clashed) to just that side of feudalism which was poison to the other. The ambivalence of bureaucracy toward monarchy and of monarchy toward bureaucracy was comprehended in the ambivalence of each toward feudalism: bureaucracy had some, at least, of the dynamics of feudalism without the statics, monarchy had the reverse.

The imperial state was the proper milieu for bureaucracy (emperor and official, that is, were to this extent drawn together) in the following sense. A pre-Ch'in nobility, extending back in time from the third century B.C., exploited land withdrawn from the reach of the public power, the would-be imperial state, which thus became a nullity. But the instability which China's political fragmentation portended reduced the private feudal power itself, and in the post-Ch'in empire the feudal nobility was superseded by a bureaucracy, which exploited the power of an anti-feudal state. The centralized state, as the universal tax-gatherer, ideally inhibiting instability, had a basic though ambiguous value to a power-seeking bureaucracy—it provided something rich and real that could be eaten away in the feeding of private power. And it was eaten away recurrently. The process began anew each time the imperial state was reconstituted, after such attrition had brought it toward an impossible (because self-dissolving) feudal dissolution. Bureaucracy, then, perennially suspicious of imperially-backed strong men, with their infinitely various ideas for checking private aggrandizement in land (the *hsien-t'ien*, or 'limit-the-fields', central government policies), was, though abortively, a 'feudalizing' force.

But it was never feudal. Needing the centralized state as it did, after its fashion, the Confucian corps had very serious anti-feudal commitments. As a type, Confucian intellectuality runs counter to the feudal admiration of martial vigour. War is mainly for the young, and Confucian opposition to a chivalric code of heroes was a turn to the elders, to learning over courage, and to a system of examinations of learning as the ideal road to power and prestige, circumventing those juridical guarantees of status which feudalism accorded to birth. And the examinations stressed a *traditional* learning, not original thought, because age over youth means not only counsellor over warrior but old over new—the rule of precedent, the rule of example. Such reverence for precedent may sound close to feudalism, but feudal spokesmen for the most part dwell extensively on tradition only when feudalism is coming to be obsolete and under fire.[7]

However, this Confucian hostility to the 'static' attributes of feudalism implied tension, too, with monarchy. It was a tension explainable socially by monarchy's resistance to that erosion of public power which bureaucracy furthered dynamically, in its own gesture toward feudalism; and it was explainable intellectually by monarchy's leaning to just those feudal attributes that Confucianism countered. For in a feudal system, after all, monarchy has its familiar place at the pinnacle, and, with the marked exception of the feudal propensity for draining the central power (the Confucian bureaucracy's side of feudalism), many feudal associations were Chinese-imperial as well.

Dynasties were not pacifist like Confucianists but military like feudalists, always trying to keep a grip on the Confucian-suspect military organs. To see the divergence, not just of taste but of interest, one has only to watch a Han emperor detouring around his civil bureaucracy, entrusting the military to utter dependents like his relatives in the female line.[8] The Confucian ideal, embodied in the examination system and model-emperor lore, of non-inheritance of political standing, was inapplicable to hereditary monarchy, as it was to a feudal system in the round. It is probably in this connection that the Confucian sage-emperor lore had some of its greatest significance. The pre-Hsia period of Yao and Shun (the sagest of the sage) was sometimes referred to as the 'Yao Shun *shan-jang* era'; and the *shan-jang* convention for solemnizing an imperial abdication and succession was a convention for transmission of the throne to one of a different surname.[9] What was the *shan-jang* idea (projected into the past by Confucianists) but an expression of Confucian anti-dynastic feeling? It was after Yao and Shun, who chose their successors by the Confucian criterion of virtue, not the feudal criterion of hereditary right, that dynasties began: a falling off.

And monarchs were vaguely compromised in Confucian eyes not only by their quasi-feudal aura but by the simulated feudal systems which dynasties successively created and literati continually condemned. 'Nothing did more harm to the people,' wrote Ch'ing historians of the Ming period, 'than the *kuang-chuang* and *chuang-t'ien* (villas) of the princes and princesses, eunuchs and nobles.'[10] We should note the emphasis on eunuchs and aristocrats, both non-bureaucratic types, and both having corporate existence only as imperial appendages.

It may be assumed that in the full light of imperial history, after classical antiquity, enfeoffment did not represent any genuine monarchical sentiment for feudal fragmentation of the state. Rather, the monarch allowed the existence of what was after all a shadow feudal structure—never with a weight of power to threaten the bureaucracy's—because the state was bureaucratically centralized enough to survive it. And the monarchy willed the existence of this feudal structure because bureaucratic centralization had its inner seed of dissolution. The imperially patronized nominal feudal system —in most dynasties mainly an extended imperial family affair—was of such a character as to be safe for the emperor as long as gentry-literati-officials were with him, while it symbolized his awareness of their potential defection. There is something more to this; I shall recur to it.

From the monarchy's side, too, the priority of family might be deplored. The Confucian *hsiao*, filial piety, was potentially irreconcilable with *chung*, political loyalty, an imperial requirement as well as originally a feudal conception;[11] while on their side Confucianists (especially of the Sung variety), at least in their ideals, tended to moralize *chung* as they had moralized other originally feudal concepts. They accepted loyalty as an obligation, but they meant to impose their definition of loyalty upon the emperor, not to have simply a blind requirement imposed upon themselves. As the neo-Confucianist Ch'eng Hao (1032–85) put it, the emperor must distinguish between those who are loyal and those who are disloyal.[12] This imperative implies a Confucian sense of discrimination. The onus is on the emperor. Loyalty may not be defined as unquestioning obedience to his (perhaps improper) wishes. Rather the advice or example (the same thing) of a true Confucianist demonstrates loyalty, and the emperor should recognize that those who agree with such sage advice are the loyal ones.

3. THE RELATION TO LAW

And when it came to the rule of law (more acceptable in feudal than in Confucian society), Ch'in Shih Huang-ti (246–210 B.C.) was the Legalist and truly the First Emperor, the prototype. For the codes were imperial and their very existence was an implied rebuke to emperors, whose virtue, thought Confucianists, was evidently not enough to make for a flawless (law-less) social order.[13] A Stoic parallel in the

Greek and Roman world (the Stoics, like the Confucianists, stressed harmony rather than action) corroborates the logic of this anti-legalist deprecation of actual monarchical power. Like the Confucianists again, the Stoics were far from admitting the unqualified legitimacy of contemporary absolute monarchy. Only the Sage, they felt, is capable of absolute royal rule, and he rules by calling others to imitation of himself (Cicero, *De Legibus* and *De Republica*). Possessing reason in himself, he can dispense with written laws; he is the living law.[14]

Just so, in the *Analects* (*Lun-yü* VI, 29) Confucius refuses to credit a ruler with *jen* (human-heartedness) if he makes a 'wide conferring on the people' and shows 'ability to aid the multitudes'. Exerting the inner force of sage example: only this, to Confucius, is the technique of *jen*. But in actual history many monarchs had social programmes, or at least made protestations, of 'wide conferring on the people', and many Confucianists deplored them. In ultimate Confucian terms these would be *yung* without *t'i*, action without essence, programmes of compulsion (merely Legalist) without the essential Confucian *jen* to compel them to exist.

This all sounds very high-minded, to be sure, and a sceptic may see only a cover for material interest, gentry resentment of monarchical land-tenure schemes or the like. But this opinion, while too cynically reductive, simply reflects the fact that the Confucianist as a social person and the Confucian intellectual come together; he demonstrates in both these aspects his distance from the monarch (yet also his place in the monarchical system, a solar system of gravitational ties). When the Sung scholar Ch'en Liang (1143–94) professed to discern sage-king patterns not merely in classical high antiquity but in the prosaically historical Han and T'ang dynasties, Chu Hsi (1130–1200), incomparably more influential, denounced him, and with appropriate emphasis stressed *hsiu-chi*, self-cultivation—the 'inner' pole of a famous Confucian dichotomy—over the 'outer' pole, *chih-jen*, ruling men.[15] Morality, the inner test which non-ideal, actual monarchs do not pass, transcends the legally constituted externals.

4. THE FACTOR OF FOREIGN CONQUESTS

The over-all distinction between the necessary partners, Confucian literati and monarchy, and the basic condition of the tension between them, lay in their respective attitudes toward tradition. Here Ch'in Shih Huang-ti again, at the beginning, and the *T'ien-wang* of the Taipings (1850–64) near the end, seem the purest representatives of anti-literati, anti-traditional, undiluted monarchy. They were too pure to survive, too unequivocally unrestricted, without that blurring of the timeless monarchical abstraction which could make them historically viable; dynasties in general had to make the adjustments these disdained with traditionalist Confucianism.

But the adjustments came from practical necessity, not from the genius of the institution of Chinese monarchy itself. One who contemplates the relation of monarchy to bureaucracy from this standpoint may reverse a familiar emphasis: perhaps the real issue is not the degree to which alien dynasties proved acceptable to Chinese literati, but the degree to which native dynasties proved alien to them. In the complex of Chinese political society, foreign dynasties may well have been nothing peculiar, only native dynasties to a higher power, and ethnic distinction no special problem of bureaucratic-dynastic relations, only an exacerbation of the endemic problem of the division of powers. A foreign conquest-people and its chiefs might well in their hearts be culturally out of touch with the ideals of the literati. But so, to some extent, would be any Chinese Court.

What Manchu prerogatives represented to Ch'ing Confucianists, the prerogatives of eunuchs may have represented to their predecessors under the Ming. And eunuchs or no, Manchus or no—as long as monarchs kept a sense of proportion, and never faced the literati with too rich an alien mixture—Ming and Ch'ing were dynasties that Confucianists could live with. The Taipings' anti-Manchu propaganda was symbolic, perhaps, of a nationalistic revulsion from gentry culture, an ethnic displacement of a cultural Chinese identity. But it was a sham as an anti-Ch'ing weapon. For the gentry-literati-Confucianists were ostensibly more likely than any other Chinese to respond to an anti-Manchu call, since they suffered from the unfair proportion of Manchus to Chinese in high governing circles, while nineteenth-century peasants could barely have known Manchus as such. Yet, the Confucianists were loyal. They felt no special ethnic revulsion from the Manchus, but simply an expected strain between monarchical and bureaucratic bodies, a strain far less traumatic than the Taiping break.

Indeed, as the almost immediate dissolution of the Manchu people in twentieth-century Republican China would show, the Manchus were kept afloat by the Ch'ing dynasty, not the dynasty by the Manchus. Thus, ultimately, their foreignness must have been barely more than the permissible (though censurable) foreignness of monarchy itself. The Yüan dynasty (1279–1368), in this respect, had not been like the Ch'ing: as that Mongol dynasty rebuffed and repelled the Chinese literati more than the Manchus were to do, so it preserved its internal integrity with far greater persistence. The Mongols as a people did not vanish with Yüan.

Of course Confucianists were susceptible to anti-foreignism. As we have seen in Volume One, Confucianism held centrally to the amateur ideal, countering specialization, the vocational training of men who were to be merely used as instruments. Confucianists opposed depersonalization, and that is why they emphasized the humanities even in (or especially in) their education for office: they were to be ends, not means, not a monarch's tools. Indeed, for Confucianists, one of the qualities that tainted the monarch's province of law was its air of impersonality and abstraction. (Wherever, it seems, 'experts' are disliked and the amateur ideal encouraged, the instruments of legal transaction tend to be technically weak.)[16]

Now, hostility to foreigners, particularly ethnic minorities, tends to focus on stereotypes, and impersonality and special role are the very stuff of stereotypes. Ethnic assimilation implies the break-up of the 'specialized' image, as the group disperses into the whole variety of human possibilities. In China, in so far as conquest dynasties forbade assimilation, they limited their cohorts in social scope and clapped them into specialized roles. Indisputably their foreignness made for tense relations with Confucian literati; but it was a Chinese ethnic antipathy reducible to Confucian cultural terms. When, as the special tools of their foreign-dynastic leaders, they aroused ethnocentric feeling among the literati, this was not just gross discrimination, native against foreign. They were really offending a finer sensibility—anti-specialist and anti-despotic.

While the Ch'ing's Manchus had their military examinations, the Chinese scholars who sneered at 'the scholarship of a Manchu' were expressing distaste for the specialized garrison type, or stereotype. Impersonal, dehumanized by association with a special function—so the Manchu might appear in Chinese eyes. But it was a cultural appearance and a political one; race was not the crime. Race only made it plausible that a Manchu should seem to be wholly owned and operated. That was the crime. And it was not a mortal one for the Manchus, since Confucianists needed monarchs, and monarchs, native or foreign, had such a penchant for control.

By this token, the familiar statement that pre-nationalistic culturalism legitimized any patrons of Confucianism, whatever their ethnic background, can be stated more precisely as follows: Any dynastic establishment, whatever its ethnic background, had the same need to patronize (failing at its peril) but *also the same need to qualify* Confucianism. It was not that foreign dynasties should meet some minimum of expected cultural conformity; it was rather that foreign dynasties should practise no more non-conformity than a maximum expected of rulers in general and grudgingly allowed them. It is because this was the state of affairs that we find Confucianism, for its part, always needing monarchy and always assuming its existence, but always implying restraints on its innate waywardness.

CHAPTER III

The Evolution of the Confucian Bureaucratic Personality

1. ARISTOCRACY, MONARCHY, BUREAUCRACY: TRIO IN THREE MOVEMENTS

THE 'Doctrine of the Mean' is one of the 'Four Books', familiar to Confucian-trained officials from the Southern Sung period to the end of Ch'ing, from the thirteenth century to the twentieth. The metaphysical aim for dead centre, 'the still point of the turning world', where harmony had its Confucian apotheosis, was politically true. Since the officials' culture favoured the study of history, they were well acquainted with the Chou period of local aristocracies and the subsequent Ch'in period, that famous burst of the utterly despotic. And it was the genius of Confucian bureaucracy (though not always its achievement) to be poised between the poles of local and central power, magnetized to both, and resisting in its values the final claims of either. If one speaks one-sidedly of Confucian (bureaucratic)–monarchical tension as the major motif in imperial Chinese history, this is because aristocracy in the technical sense, with its perquisites and hereditary status, though never dying, generally languished. But the aristocratic ideal, as a rival for Confucianism to banish—in part by resistance and in part by pre-emption—fixed the bureaucracy's location as surely as the royal reality on the other side of the centre.

Consider the perennial question of alienability of land. At least sporadically, both Chou nobility and later monarchs

35

tried to impair it, the former in a spirit of feudal inequality, the latter in pursuit of an anti-feudal despotic egalitarianism.[1] By and large the bureaucracy, public officials with private interests, set itself against this expression of both an ultimate resistance to the public power and its ultimate pretension. In the main, bureaucracy defended the right to alienate (and its corollary, to accumulate by purchase), a right that was just as opposed to a power-inhibiting feudalism's premise, as it was to the most extreme of a power-seeking monarch's desiderata. And on the same intermediate line, Confucianists favoured undivided large-family holdings—social expression of the 'harmony' which Confucianists as philosophers so incessantly commended. This was equidistant from feudal primogeniture, on the one hand, and the centralizers' policy (against the threat of local concentrations) of pressing for fragmentation by exacting dues progressively according to the number of a household's adult males.[2]

When cultural rather than economic values come under review, Confucianist and aristocrat clash just as vividly. Both agree that there is something about a soldier, but not on what it is. The Confucianist, after all, is the eternal civilian. In *The Romance of the Three Kingdoms*, after Ts'ao Ts'ao has some of his stalwarts do wonderful martial feats, he summons a few tame scholars whom he keeps around, 'stuffed with learning', to produce *their* tricks. They snap to attention on the spot with some canned Confucian poesy in praise of their warlike patron. Here, in a form of literature which Confucianists on duty never approved of, in a setting of the decay of the Han, the first of the bureaucratic, centralizing dynasties which 'established' Confucianism, this flash of contempt for the Confucian higher life exposes it appropriately against the counter-value of military prowess.[3]

In feudal Chou China, men were thought of in four categories, in descending order of esteem: *shih, nung, kung, shang*—warrior, farmer, artisan, merchant. By the middle of the first millennium, B.C., with feudalism crumbling, the warrior-class of *shih* was losing power and inferiors were rising.[4] When supremacy finally passed to a bureaucracy of the Confucian persuasion, the four categories were still retained (an example of what Confucianists meant by their 'perpetuation of feudal values', while really they created anew), but *shih*, designating precisely the power group, changed its connotation, from military to literary.

It was characteristically Confucian on the one hand to retain the old term, as a traditional piety, and on the other hand to 'moralize' it (as Confucius did to *chün*, prince, or as Mencius to the *kung* of *kung-t'ien*, which had the sense of 'noble's' field in the *Shih-ching*, the 'Book of Songs', but 'public' field in Mencius' picture of the 'well-field' system). To moralize it was to 'civilize' it, quite literally. *Wen-hua*, the Confucianists' 'civilization', was plainly an enshrinement of *the civil; wen*, letters, and *wu*, arms, always remained in antithesis. Right at the end of Confucian history, in the early twentieth century, a Chinese nationalist and former Confucianist, Liang Ch'i-ch'ao (1873–1929), admired the evolution (as he saw it) in Japan of self-transcending feudal loyalties to national loyalties, and deplored the Confucian extinction of *shih* as devotees of *wu*, the capture of the title, *shih*, by pacific literati. He said that *wu-shih tao*, the 'way of the warrior' (in Japanese the *bushidō* of modern chauvinists and mediaeval aristocrats), had flourished up to the 'Spring and Autumn' period, dwindled to knight-errantry by the beginning of Han (the beginning of Confucian ascendancy), and soon was nothing.[5]

In fact, however, aristocracy as a serious contender with Confucian bureaucracy in its own right—not just as an imperial auxiliary—seems not to have been silenced conclusively until the Sung period (960–1279). The Sung, in this way, too, as in others, was one of the great watersheds in Chinese history. With Sung, both the institutions of bureaucracy and the formulations of Confucianism were highly elaborated, and they were such as to spell effective triumph for *wen* over *wu*. Previously T'ang (618–906) had seen the link forged, with the examination system, between intellectual life and bureaucratic power, and heard the last cry of the *men-t'i*, 'social notables', as they felt themselves cordoned off. Li Te-yü (787–849), for example, hated the *chin-shih*, high degree-holders, the new men rising through the bureaucratic channel. He said defiantly that since his grandfather's time as minister (at the end of the reign of Hsüan-tsung, mid-eighth century, just before the An Lu-shan rebellion), the family had not acquired literature and classics, for these had no relation to skills and practicality. The great officials of the court, he said, ought to be drawn from the *kung-ch'ing*, the aristocratic lineages.[6]

In such a statement, aristocracy's discomfiture is plain to see. The menace of Confucian bureaucracy seems confirmed by the pitch of aristocratic resentment. But more than that, it is the aristocrat's 'bureaucratized' self-image that marks so clearly the lowering of his estate. He offers himself as a superior brand of official, knowing practical statecraft—a monarch's man, that is, no longer someone with the typically fierce aristocratic resistance to an autocrat's infringement on nobility's prerogatives. Indeed, the crown had so nearly triumphed over the classical pretensions of aristocracy that the pattern of three has rearranged itself.

Aristocracy had been an impediment, in Chou times, during most of the first millennium, B.C., to centralized authority. And though aristocracy was blighted by the autocratic Ch'in, it was seriously revived from the third century A.D., in the post-Han period of hollow dynasties and military conquests. Stricken by T'ang, it moved to the side of *monarchy*. *Bureaucracy*, the Ch'in–Han and later the T'ang instrument of anti-feudal monarchy, now confronted the crown directly; after helping to clear the field of the crown's rivals, it held the field itself as the only remaining counter-vailing force. The monarch, served to such good effect by bureaucracy that aristocracy was tamed, repelled bureaucracy in some degree by his now unbalanced power. And Confucianists, who owed their corporate existence to imperial sponsorship in the teeth of aristocracy's hostility, took up the role of resistance when the aristocrats' teeth were blunted. Aristocrats, now the monarch's creatures, sounded more and more like kept men, while Confucian officials strained to get out of the monarchy's keeping. And so while some aristocrats became Confucian enough to see themselves in a bureaucratic context, but approached a monarch's non-Confucian ideal of a bureaucracy of means, Confucianists took on some aristocratic colour, conceived of themselves as ends in themselves, and set out to prise open the imperial clutch.

There are a series of steps in the minuet thus described. I should like to examine them one by one.

2. BUREAUCRACY AS THE MONARCH'S TOOL TO CHECK ARISTOCRACY

It is a commonplace that feudal aristocratic status was based on private possession of essentially public powers, private exercise of public executive functions. The anti-feudal 'public' is the state (a community, as Weber defined it, that successfully claims monopoly of the legitimate use of force within a territory), or the public is the prince who makes the state by expropriating the 'autonomous' and 'private' bearers of executive power.[7] As Montesquieu put it flatly, 'abolish the privileges of the lords, the clergy and cities in a monarchy, and you will soon have a popular state, or else a despotic government'.[8]

Conservative apologists for aristocratic institutions have always made much of this connection between autocracy and a 'public's' obliteration of rank and its privileges. What makes despotism characteristically arbitrary is the despot's ability to raise and lower his subjects at will. The infinite power of such a sovereign depends on basic equality beneath the throne, so that no guaranteed distinctions exist between men to spoil the infinite malleability of the body politic.[9] Orwell speaks of 'an idea almost as old as history', the idea of King and the common people in a sort of alliance against the upper classes.[10] In the Peasants' Revolt in Germany (1525), for example, the readiness to attribute real authority to the Holy Roman Emperor was identical with the passion for destroying aristocracy.[11]

World history yields many plain illustrations of this model issue between sovereign and aristocracy. In the later Roman Empire in the West, the aristocratic Senate saw in such a bureaucratizing emperor as Valentinian I (364–75) only a proletarian's hatred for his betters. For while members of the senatorial party, as incipient feudalists, were building estates by sheltering fugitives from the tax rolls and sequestering their lands, the emperor tried to preserve his central power by bureaucratically undercutting this protection racket of the great lords. The new imperial institution of *defensor plebis* was meant to guarantee the poor peasant a free legal defence. Naturally, with such a policy, Valentinian pushed senators well into the background when he staffed his bureaucracy; he could pit only special aides against the senatorial oligarchy, cohorts who leaned on him alone, because he made them.[12]

If effective monarchy was one that bureaucratically encroached on aristocracy, enfeebled monarchy spoke for the centralizers' failure to impinge on private powers. Thus, reflecting Valentinian's ill success and the fading of the Roman imperium, the imperial post of 'vicar of the city' (fourth–sixth century) failed to remain a counterpoise to the senatorial 'prefect of the city'. And as the supremacy of the great senatorial landholders became more and more unmistakable, subverting the imperial social order, the central government tried to survive by binding subjects to their home places and inherited lots in life—by freezing social mobility.[13] This was the cure that guaranteed demise. This, the exertion of a spurious despotic power, was the sacrifice of the purest power of unharassed autocracy: the power to co-opt whom it pleases and raze the defences of class.

Such was the power claimed naturally by a monarch with truly oecumenical pretensions. The 'lawbook of Melfi' of the dazzling Hohenstaufen Frederick II (1194–1250) has been styled 'the birth certificate of modern bureaucracy'. Flashing briefly to the heights of rulership he drew men to his service not with the *beneficium*, a fief to possess, but with the *officium*, a service to fulfil. Non-transferable and non-hereditary, office was his alone to give, his to repossess, graced with his grace. He made officers from any rank, and no considerations of rank could mitigate the power of his omnipresent hand—his bureaucracy.[14]

Byzantium, which filtered Roman imperial conceptions through to Frederick, did the same for Russian czars. In the sixteenth century Ivan IV ('The Terrible') flouted old

Kievan aristocratic ideas and sapped the position of the noble boyars with a band of faithful servants, the Oprichnina, chosen without regard to class, for Ivan called all his subjects 'slaves'. The boyars recovered sufficiently by the next century to stand off, weakly, the new régime of the Romanovs— social privileges retained, but political power unreplenished.[15] And here we have a suggestion of the 'Sun King's' arrangement in contemporary France, a tactic fateful for the future of French monarchy and provocative to the observer of Chinese.

What Louis XIV did after the various rebellious actions of the Fronde (the nobles' and the *parlements*', 1648–53) was to bring new men to power, but to separate actual power from apparent grandeur. He meant to preserve a politically shorn but socially splendid aristocracy so that its political supplanter, the king's bureaucracy, should be cut off from the social dignity which could make it aristocratic itself, and thus a potential rival, not a tool. The very model of an autocrat speaks in Louis' words: '. . . it was not in my interest to seek men of more eminent station because . . . it was important that the public should know, from the rank of those whom I chose to serve me, that I had no intention of sharing my power with them. (It was also important) that they themselves, conscious of what they were, should conceive no higher aspirations than those which I chose to permit.'[16] Louis' 'intendants', their very title a new creation, took over the government of the countryside from a nobility either soothingly sinecured (the 'sleeping abbots', et al.) or ineffectually rustic or emptily grand at Versailles, where the king and his bourgeois ministers left only something of war and something of diplomacy to the heirs of feudal greatness.[17] Before Richelieu, the centralizing genius behind Louis' achievement, the king demanded fidelity; after (an important nuance) he exacted submission.[18] The Duc de Saint-Simon complained that Louis surrounded himself with nothing but 'vile bourgeois'. Saint-Simon, of course, was in favour of an aristocratic reaction against royal absolutism (and especially against the bureaucratic secretaries of state, whom he described as monsters devouring the *noblesse*). But reluctantly he ascribed the failure of the Regent's aristocratically weighted 'Polysynodie', in the first years after Louis XIV, to the emptiness of a nobility good for nothing but getting itself killed in war.[19] That was the Richelieu effect: the monarchy absolute, nobility dissolute, and its autonomous powers dissolved.[20]

This refers primarily to the *noblesse d'épee*, the old 'nobility of the sword'. The newer *noblesse de robe* was still to be heard from, leading the movement in the eighteenth century for aristocratic revival, and I shall take note of this soon. But the initial attempt (though it proved abortive) to make the king omnipotent remains highly suggestive. The conception of an aristocracy still in being, but sterile and ornamental, has a part in a logic of absolutism. And the logic applies in other lands as well.

In Prussia the French emphases were altered but the triumvirate was there; monarchy, bureaucracy, and aristocracy still confronted each other. Frederick William I, in the first half of the eighteenth century, looked for ministers, he said, who were ordinary persons (or, indeed, 'yapping little dogs'), less intent on their honour than aristocrats, who might refuse him blind obedience. The Hohenzollerns eventually softened their approach and compromised between a Junker aristocratic 'private law state' (a spoils system of patronage appointment) and a dynastic bureaucratized 'public law state' (merit appointment of experts). Still, though the monarch never pushed the bureaucratic attack on the nobles to a logical culmination, the hereditary noble 'officier' and the upstart royal 'commissaire' were distinguishable types, which had their distinctive relations with the monarch. The government of Frederick William I, like that of Louis XIV, had an unmistakably bourgeois impulse in it, and this accorded with the basic character of the *ancien régime*. It was a character formed by the accommodation of aristocracy to absolute monarchy, an accommodation whereby aristocratic social privilege was preserved, while the nobility was politically transformed. These civil relations of aristocracy and monarch reflected a power-shift in military relations—from the feudal nobility's abhorrence of the emerg-

ing monarch's 'public' armed forces, to the monarch's refurbishing of the status-honour of nobles, in their new
personae as the members of his officer corps. As they were *his*,
they were damaged in their aristocratic licence; but as they
were *officers*, they were still aristocratic.[21]

What those aristocratic-bureaucratic-monarchical relations involved (as surely in China as in the western examples)
was tension between a centralizing power and vested interests.
Some of the latter were feudal-aristocratic, impeding a
monarchy's rise or expediting its fall; and some were bureaucratic, new, and of the monarch's own contriving as he
asserted himself against the aristocracy. Resolutions differed
from place to place, but everywhere the tension was an autocrat's concern. When Ch'in united the Chinese Empire
against the feudal hierarchies, which were territorially and
jurisdictionally divisive, and when it determined to stave off
re-feudalization, it had an appropriate motto, an anti-
hierarchical one: 'When fathers and elder brothers possess
the Empire, younger sons and brothers are low common
men.'[22] Han emperors acted decisively on a Confucianist's
advice to dilute the ranks of nobles of the Liu (the imperial)
family, and drain their strength; it was a strength which had
served the Han against nobles 'of different surnames', but
which central authority had to fear when the rivals common
to all the Lius were duly vanquished.[23] An early T'ang
hereditary aristocracy, flourishing in its natural environment
of military conquest, was deliberately subverted by Empress
Wu (684–705), who conjured up a royal, rival class of literati
from an 'open' examination system.[24] And a thousand years
later three Ch'ing emperors, Yung-cheng *et seq.*, showed the
same penchant of autocrats for levelling up, this time from
the bottom: they ordered that various local pariah peoples—
the Shansi *lo-hu*, descendants of families with a criminal
stigma; Chekiang *to-min*, 'fallen people', and *chiu-hsing yü-hu*,
the endogamous 'fishing people of the nine surnames'; Anhui
shih-p'u, 'slaves'—be officially treated without distinction
from others of better standing.[25] This is a standard type of
anti-feudal measure, part of a programme to flatten status
barriers against effective central power (like Meiji dismissal

of the legal disabilities of Japanese pariahs, the *tokushu buraku*, 'special villages' of *eta*).

Yung-cheng, however, and the Ch'ing dynasty were on the far side of the great divide, the Sung. In that earlier period, though 'outside lords' were already effectively extinguished and the weight was shifting definitively toward bureaucracy and autocracy, the emperor could still seem poised (and sometimes paralysed) between his aristocratic near relations and his bureaucratic aides.[26] But by early Ch'ing there could be no question of the emperor in the middle. He was at one of the poles, and though Yung-cheng had an aristocracy around him, he owned it. Confucian bureaucracy, the guarantor of the harmlessness of nobles, had long since been the status group whose solidarity autocrats had to melt. And formal aristocracy, gratifyingly choked off by bureaucracy as a major threat to the monarch, was fanned into life as part of the flame to be turned against its stifler.

3. ARISTOCRACY AS THE MONARCH'S TOOL TO CHECK BUREAUCRACY

The founder of the Ming dynasty in 1368, an autocratic centralizer with the best of them, nevertheless, with his eyes wide open, provided for enfeoffment of imperial princes. He hardly intended to let it get out of hand, and regular bureaucrats were to supervise the princes' troops and communications. Then, presumably safely subject to the centre and incapable of disintegrative mischief, they were supposed to be converted to the centre's support. The main threat in the early Ming was Mongol. But what the monarch cared about was defence against infringement of the imperial power in any case, by invader or official. Enfeoffment, hopefully *controlled*, so that by itself it should breed no rivals to the throne, was a dynastic response to eccentric forces from any rival quarter.[27]

The Ch'ing, too, had an aristocracy of their own as an anchor against the bureaucratic drift. The Manchu conquest meant that villas of the Ming imperial family nobility and much other land lay abandoned, without owners. Part of it was taken over by the Ch'ing imperial house, part was given to deserving officials and the like who had come with the winners from Manchuria. In 1650 the dynasty established a regular system of land allotment to various grades of feudal notables, from *ch'in-wang*, hereditary princes (8 *so*, every *so* being 180 *mou* or about 27 acres) down to *feng-en chiang-chün* (60 *mou*). This scale applied to subsequent ennoblements. The lands were all hereditary and *inalienable*.[28]

This feudal conception, so much at odds with the predominant social practice, was clearly meant to invest the imperial house with an aristocratic bulwark, shored up against the solvent forces of the general Confucian society. Yet, to render the aristocrats themselves harmless, the dynasty used a Confucian technique, an examination system, and controlled them bureaucratically. The rules called for tests in archery and the Manchu language, to be administered four times annually by the 'Court of the Imperial Clan' to not yet enfeoffed or not yet adult sons of nobles; and in the examination in the first month of winter, overseen by a specially appointed imperial high official, not only sons but the lesser nobles, too (with fiefs ranging down from 240 *mou*) were subject to the trial.[29]

How effective, really, could these Ming and Ch'ing aristocracies be as checks on the regular officialdom? They were so hedged in themselves that they were hardly impressive as restraints in the world outside. Rather than putting a positive curb on Confucian bureaucracy, they represented, perhaps, the monarch's attempt to withdraw, for associates of his own, some stores of strength from the field open to official depredations. To cut down actively on the latter and thus preserve his power, the monarch needed private bureaucratic agents more than aristocratic consumers. These agents should form a personal corps, depending on him for honour and place, therefore approaching the despotic ideal in bureaucracy: a set of instruments. This was just the ideal which Confucianists resisted—once the eclipse of aristocracy had made them and *their* honour less dependent on the throne.

Therefore, in the last analysis not 'princes' and 'dukes' but eunuchs and simple Manchus became the centralizer's tools. Indeed, even a millennium and a half before the Manchu era,

Han emperors were feeling pushed to marshal a 'third force', in this instance eunuchs, to weigh against the Confucian element, and the scholars were duly recording disapproval.[30] They disapproved less of the T'ang practice of appointing eunuchs to check on the deviationism of military commanders[31]—the latter were no great favourites either in Confucian circles. Still, the lesson was the same: eunuchs, despised by literati, were used by the emperor personally to guard his central power. However (to make the comparison more immediate), at the Ch'ing courts, even the relatively indulgent Empress Dowager's, eunuchs were markedly fewer and more strictly restrained than under the Ming.[32] This suggests again what we have already suggested, that eunuchs and Manchus, in the Sino-foreign, Ming and Ch'ing dynastic sequence, were functionally equivalent. For by themselves Manchus would play the role of auxiliaries well enough, outsiders thrown back on the monarch who made them— made them both in spite and because of the literati's resentment.

And what was the nature of this resentment? Of all things, it had a certain aristocratic air about it, as befitted a self-regarding group's contempt for mere dependents, the men from nowhere who needed a monarch to guarantee their rise. If this sounds like a Han or T'ang aristocratic resentment of the Confucianists themselves, it is no accident. When the older, vital aristocrats went down as the Chinese imperial power became transcendent, the Confucianists' self-regard became the monarch's concern—for would they be loyal to him?—and the Confucianists' self-regard withered the newer recruits to the monarch's loyal coterie.

4. THE CONFUCIAN BUREAUCRACY'S RESISTANCE

That the literati felt lofty enough to scorn this sort of coterie confirms the fact that a monarch needed to own such objects of scorn. That is, aristocracy was no longer lofty enough itself in social prestige to monopolize it, and so divorce it (like Versailles from Louis XIV's intendants) from the officials' political functions. The officials, accordingly, were not so bound to the crown. Failing any serious competition from a rival elite (feudal aristocracy being so curtailed), feeling no social gaucherie in comparison, Confucian officials could have an aristocratic pride of their own, unvitiated by the self-doubts of the *arriviste*—*theirs* was the circle where climbers yearned to arrive. They themselves, functionaries though they were, set the tone of culture instead of facing the scorn of the functionless, like the late Bourbon politically stripped aristocrats, who dismissed local government as the province of clowns and clerks.[33] Chinese emperors could neither deprive bureaucracy initially of that formidable combination, prestige and executive function, nor dangle before it subsequently, as prizes (and seeds of obligation), titles conveying lustre from a truly noble estate, beyond bureaucracy.

Prussian kings eventually did the latter. Since the Junkers had by no means utterly succumbed to Frederick William I's 'yapping little dogs', the 'von' was still precious enough for the *nouveaux* to covet—while the king was both autocratic enough to give it, and not quite autocratic enough to banish the need or obliterate the glory of the gift. Bureaucratic 'nobles of ascent' began to meet feudal 'nobles of descent', with the latter now constrained to join the bureaucratic endeavour, and ultimately even to mingle with commoners on the basis of *Bildung*, a new cultural bond. *Bildung*, an amorphous but deep feeling for an inner moral and intellectual cultivation, impaired the monarch's ability to impose himself as master and impose on officials the character of tools. Old nobility, to some extent cut down to bureaucratic stature, preserved and spread some aristocratic resistance to the centre; and new bureaucratic nobility, for all its dynastic and anti-aristocratic origins, became set in reaction against royal autocracy and competition in government service. As a Königsberg colleague of Kant remarked in 1799: 'The Prussian state, far from being an unlimited monarchy, is but a thinly veiled aristocracy—this aristocracy rules the country in undisguised form as a bureaucracy.'[34]

Confucianists came to their resistance by a different road. In Prussia there was some degree of devolution of aristocracy to bureaucracy. But the hybrid form at the end of the (pre-

Napoleonic) process—an intellectualized conception of aristocracy—was remarkably like the Chinese amalgam. Seeing the process as evolution towards rather than devolution from aristocracy, we may read the hybrid the other (and even more clumsy) way round, 'aristocratized intellectualism', but the Prussian analogy is surely compelling. The future statesman Wilhelm von Humboldt, writing in 1789 and after about how 'one forms oneself' ('man *bildet* sich'), prized freedom and anti-despotic self-mastery, general culture over useful knowledge. He felt contempt for the philistine who lived to work and worked toward material goals, and he stood for things and states of mind valuable in themselves, for men who were more than things, for ends over means.[35] A Confucian '*Bildung*', infused with the same spirit of anti-vocational, humanistic amateur ideal, had the same implications of tension with autocracy.

What *Bildung* meant, and what Confucian cultivation meant, was the achievement and vindication of a kind of prestige which was not the monarch's to confer. In an unmitigated despotism, the government employee is the most vulnerable of men, totally insecure in his legal status and social standing.[36] But a Confucian official, non-vocationally educated, was no mere 'employee'. He might be summarily retired, even executed, or he might retire in self-abnegation, but his dignity and social status were not destroyed; for regular official position was taken as a sign of a quality (high culture, not simply professional expertise) which existed irrespective of the holding of office. The Confucianist brought it to office, not office (as the monarch's gift) to him. And if a monarch lacks the sole power to confer prestige, he cannot enslave his bureaucracy by threatening to withhold it.

Thus, the submergence of true aristocracy gave Confucian bureaucracy something of the latter's quality. But while officials strained against the monarchy, they needed it, as the guarantor of a central power that had to exist for them to enjoy consuming it. It was an ambiguous position, reflected, perhaps, in the ambiguous status of Mandarin, the *Kuan-hua* or modern 'officials' language' (being the standard speech of the capital, effectively Peking from fairly early Ming to mid-Republic). During imperial days Mandarin was by no means secure in its prestige, since with the more rapid phonetic changes in the north it had lost ancient distinctions which central and southern dialects had preserved. There were grounds for fastidious—one might say aristocratic—reserve towards this linguistic instrument of the centralizing power.[37] Yet, scholarly sophisticates were, after all, bound up in the bureaucratic system, and Mandarin, from being useful as the officials' *lingua franca*, went on to assume an aristocratic tone of its own. It was not exactly a language of the happy few—not with millions of commoners tuned in on its sounds—but it took on the distinction of guild speech (and a proud guild, surely), transcending the provincial associations of common local dialect.

So, in and out of the monarch's service, drawn to it and drawing back, Confucianists might seem to speak out of both sides of their mouths. And the monarch was just as ambiguous. For he needed them to make good his centralization; then, in turn, to protect it, he had to restrain their ominous appetites. Therefore, even in flouting Confucian taste, the emperor might pander to it in his covering explanation. For example, after the Yung-lo emperor usurped the throne in 1403, he had his historians libel his ousted nephew as a patron of Buddhists and eunuchs. As it happened, the really active recruiter of monks and eunuchs had been Yung-lo himself,[38] with the autocrat's feel for the usefulness of a personal force of outsiders, as a check on the orthodox element that he needed to win and needed to keep. Thus, Yung-lo could not just counter Confucianists nakedly with Buddhists and eunuchs; he had to indulge these anti-Confucian coteries, then mask it with a Confucianist's apology.

This was the monarch's side of the line of strain. He might resent the hierarchical tone of Confucianism as he resented aristocracy's, but if he failed to indulge Confucianists in their quasi-aristocratic taste for freedom and status, he risked the ultimate Ch'in fate of bureaucratic and general revulsion. On their side, Confucianists had to acknowledge that if they strained against the centre too successfully, they might deliver themselves as well as the state to a host of brutal

Ts'ao Ts'aos. That is why monarchy could be despotically Legalist, military, and yet the patron of Confucianists; why bureaucracy could be aristocratically Confucian, pacifist, and yet the agent of monarchs; why, inclusively, Confucianism persisted not only in tension with monarchy, but in tension within itself.

CHAPTER IV

Confucianism and Confucianism: the Basic Confrontation

I. INNER AND OUTER

BENJAMIN SCHWARTZ has pointed out an ambivalence in Confucian thinking, a persistent wavering between concern for the 'inner' and concern for the 'outer', though a symbiosis of both concerns was in theory essential. The spheres of *nei* and *wai*, that is, inner and outer, were considered interrelated, so that (in a famous phrase) *hsiu-shen* (or *hsiu-chi*) and *p'ing t'ien-hsia* were joined ideally in one concept. Self-cultivation and world-pacification must imply each other; if there is a true *sage* (sageliness being a quality of inner perfection), he should properly make an outside mark on the world, as the true king.[1] And yet, Confucianists as historians have known that imperfect 'kings' (or men with the unrectified name of 'king') have done most of the ruling, while at least one of the sages, Confucius himself, was notoriously a 'throneless' king. The great founding historian Ssu-ma Ch'ien (145–90? B.C.) made the classical contrast between powerless but memorable Confucius and powerful but forgotten (or ultimately uninfluential) monarchs.[2]

This gives Confucian historical thinking much of its pathos. Knowledge and action (another inner-outer dichotomy) should be one, but the 'times', the mysterious 'times', so often thrust them apart. 'Though Confucius had *te*, virtue,

51

he did not attain *i*, position':[3] those who know, in the Confucian sense, cannot act. Or they *should* not act, as
Confucian officials, under monarchs who are in the supreme
position to act, but who do not *know*. The note is there in a
neo-Confucian poet: 'When one is born in a degenerate and
disorderly age, and there is no one worthy of being called a
ruler, who would want to serve? . . .'[4]

Han Yü (768–824), the first great figure of 'neo-Confucianism', had adumbrated this idea. The T'ang scholar
drew on Mencius' authority to urge Confucian independence
of a court's demands, and Confucian scorn of the merely
time-serving, court-manipulated, unprincipled official.[5] This
leaning to the 'inner' pole became a characteristic of neo-
Confucianism—witness the strictures on monarchy which
Chu Hsi implied when he firmly separated the age of sage-
kings from the ages that came after[6]—but the inner-outer
ambivalence was never banished. On such a question as the
reinstitution of the *ching-t'ien* (well-field) system, there was
conflict among Confucianists and indeed in individual minds
(see Volume Three). For they had a social, outer commitment
to strive for perfect governance, a commitment which coincided with the monarchical interest in curbing private
aggrandizement in land; and they had an inner commitment
to morality, as against the force that would be needed to
wrest the land, in egalitarian spirit, from acquisitive possessors
like the bureaucrats themselves.

2. PRIVATE AND PUBLIC

To say (like Chu Hsi) that *ching-t'ien* could not be revived was
as much as to say that the outer world, the province of kingly
government, was too badly flawed to accept perfect institutions without having them forced on it. And to that side of
Confucianism leaning to inner morality, the outer application
of force (proof that an emperor was falling short of a sage's
emanation of virtue) must compromise the value of the
effort. But to the side of Confucianism leaning to ethical
obligation out in society, such quietist defeatism was uncongenial. So it was to Wang An-shih (1021–86), for example;

though certainly Confucian, he was the very type of centralizing, imperial strong man, and action, necessarily
imperial, was recommended. To the defenders (mostly
officials or the officially well-connected) of the material
interests threatened by such action—precisely the 'private'
interests which the 'public' state intended to curtail—the
moral reproach to the central power was invaluable. For all
the fact that when Han Yü excoriated court sycophants he
was condemning the pursuit of advantage instead of morality,
advantage could quote morality for its purposes. Unimpeachable moral heroes like Han Yü provided a treasury of grace, a
store of the highest-minded anti-despotic feeling, for self-
indulgent materialists to raid. Perhaps that is why, like some
other idiosyncratic individuals, of really questionable orthodoxy, he could finally go down in Confucian history as so
uncannily orthodox.

Thus, the lines are drawn, but they are very blurred and
wavy, with Confucianism on both sides, just as bureaucracy
was on both sides of the issue of central power. Chu Hsi
praised the famous reformer Fan Chung-yen (989–1052), but
praised him for his moral character (the basic subject in
Confucian critiques of emperors), not especially for his
reformist action (which was of a sort that monarchs always
found in their interest, for its strengthening of the central
apparatus).[7]

3. FAMILY AND CLAN

Fan Chung-yen was prominent in another capacity, one that
also fits into the framework of the bureaucracy-monarchy
problem. The system of clan properties and formal organization in China, which Fan was so important in moulding, is
at issue here. There was an imperial influence on clan rules,
appropriately in the Legalist strain;[8] the state had a plausible
interest in furthering clan organization, since aid to the clan
implied transcendence of the family. It was an interest in a
certain kind of collectivity, which might preclude a system of
family atoms, ranged in classes, and therefore likely to
collapse into the wrong kind of social combinations.

Monarchy, with its ultimately levelling propensities (as seen in the centralizers' perennial ideal of land-equalization) sought to enlist the clan idea of vertical solidarity, i.e. class *un*consciousness, as a check against social fissure on a horizontal line.

And yet, if the clan became the family writ large, any high degree of social autonomy for clans might seem an assault on the state toward the ends of private power, and so the clan itself became subject to imperial restriction.[9] The family was supposed to have its proto-feudal possibilities diluted in the classless clan; but the clan should have its own strength, which it collected from its family components, re-divided so that the state might safely rule. In effect, the post-Sung state moved ambivalently to break down potential private power, by checking the clan with family and family with clan. And Confucian sentiments could be marshalled for both these operations.

When clan leaders, impelled by clan loyalties, acted to soften state pressures against their more obscure fellows, the clan, even while it thus resisted the central authority on an *ad hoc* basis, was serving it generally by diffusing the benefit of gentry status throughout the social system. This suited the monarch's anti-aristocratic purposes, his will to keep officials and their affiliates from hardening into a quasi-aristocracy. And in this he had the officials and clan leaders at least as much with him as against him. For one of the alternatives to clan solidarity was a freemasonry of the secret societies, which cut across clan lines in uniting lower-class dissidents against the state; neither Confucian leaders, with their zeal for harmony, nor monarchs, whatever their straining against each other, could countenance this.[10] Indeed, in as much as secret societies implied potential rebellion, and rebellion implied a decisive (hence upsetting) commitment to a cause, ambivalent wills were just what the party of order, in counterpart, should naturally display. For ambivalence, fundamental as it was to Chinese monarchy and bureaucracy, within each one and toward the other (if not toward popular, unambivalent class-violence), is nothing if not the forswearing of decisive single-mindedness.

4. CHARACTER AND SCHOLARSHIP

One of the important functions of the clan organization was to spread more widely the opportunities for education, and thus for socially valuable success in the state examinations. The monarchist central power would naturally be interested in this at two historical removes—first, approvingly, because the examination idea was incompatible with counter-imperial feudal assumptions; and second, warily, because once the examination was well established the monarch had to guard against the development of a potentially divisive, hardened power-class perpetuating itself by simple capture of the examination system. In 962, out of fear of cliques, the founder of the Sung dynasty forbade use of the terms *tso-chu* ('master') and *men-sheng* ('disciple') between successful candidates and examination administrators.[11] The Ch'ing's thoroughly and self-consciously authoritarian Yung-cheng emperor felt particularly queasy about this. In his zeal against factions he wanted no undue solidarity among officials, and he was endlessly suspicious of ties and cover-ups—the fellow-feeling of examinees of the same year, of examinees and their examiners, other such bonds and alignments.[12] Responding nicely to such suspicion, and corroborating its rationale, was an eighteenth-century careerist, calculatingly slavish, wilfully seeking friendlessness (or so it was said) to commend himself directly to the emperor.[13]

For its part, the Confucian bureaucracy, too, held the examination system both dear and suspect. In many ways it expressed what was most characteristic in the Confucianists' existence, and one of the ways was in its challenge to non-literati, precisely imperial types like eunuchs and soldiers. The latter, for instance, in the Ch'ing dynasty, were frequently able as new men to penetrate bureaucracy and to compete with literati in seniority—doing violence to Confucian pride by rising in wartime, *sans* classical study and literary tests.[14] Thus, the civil Confucianists had to keep on insisting that these tests gave a special cachet.

But if the system were operated with a cold, impersonal purity, with no room for 'character' (often, in practice,

55

equated with lineage) to come to the fore, the Confucian sense of hierarchy might thereby be flouted by a levelling monarch. There were early Ming examination laws directed against the older official families, as the emperor, meaning to thwart this taste for hierarchy, tried to hold the ring for new plebeian contestants.[15] What the emperor tried to contain was just the sort of sentiment, a discriminating feeling for status, which tinged Confucianism with aristocratic colour. In the T'ang period, when the examination system was formalized as the Confucian channel of mobility, aristocrats (like Li Te-yü, as we have seen) had protested in defence of 'character'. Men of good family favoured direct recommendation; new men needed impartial examinations.[16] The examination question, an issue between aristocrats and Confucianists in T'ang times, when these groupings still contended, was intra-Confucian thereafter.

David Nivison, dwelling on the examination system, caught the ambivalence of the Confucian position (and, one might think, its not unrelated vitality) in his splendidly circular title, 'Protest against Conventions and Conventions of Protest'.[17] The protest was fundamentally one against the conquest of spontaneity by rote. Now, why should spontaneity be a Confucian value? This problem was treated in Volume One, with its discussion of Chinese literati-painting (significantly opposed, we have seen, to 'court painters' and the imperial 'academy'), and, with something of Mr. Nivison's sense of being driven to paradox, I committed myself to the mouthful, 'academic anti-academicism'.[18] If the intellectual derivation of literati-painting's aesthetic was neo-Confucian,[19] this seems the philosophical corollary of my own rather sociological thesis of the painting-Confucianism affinity—a thesis stressing the *anti-professional* bias of the bureaucrat. As a professional the official would be simply a functionary, an imperial tool. But as an amateur, the official would be a free spirit, not the organizational mandarin whom the centralizing authorities so dearly loved to cultivate, and 'spontaneity' was the Confucian key to this precious non-attachment.

If Greek education was designed to produce gentlemen

amateurs, while 'eastern' education (i.e., Egyptian) was designed to perpetuate a guild of professional scribes,[20] the Confucianists were Greek. And yet they were 'eastern', too, at least a little—ambivalent—for, unlike the Greek paidaeia,˙ Confucian education led to bureaucracy in the end. And yet, again (back over the net): it was not an 'Egyptian' scribal bureaucracy, but a system in which the bureaucrats could dominate society, or at least tense the line between themselves and intrusive monarchs.

The imperial academy of painting, it has been observed, was created in the Northern Sung period for substantially the same purposes and with many of the same characteristics as the Académie Française that glorified Louis XIV.[21] The analogy with Louis points to the monarch's will to make tools of his subordinates; the Confucian critique of the academy points to the Chinese literati's resistance. And the resistance was far from token, since the anti-academic aesthetic became 'official', in both senses of the word: the bureaucracy set the styles, not the monarchy, for the values of the Chinese world.

And yet the anti-academic became academicized, the protests against convention became conventional, because, after all, the very examination system which enshrined a liberal, anti-vocational learning stressing high culture and moral character made that learning *useful* though not utilitarian. Thus, inevitably, men *did* direct their study to an end which was not itself and became subject to condemnation from their own standpoint, as rote-trained, unspontaneous, manipulable placemen, not self-cultivated with an inner independence—*little* men in an imperial apparatus. Small wonder, then, that there was scope for a truly Confucian fear lest moral character be slighted in a quasi-Legalist impersonal machinery of stereotyped tests. For all the fact that the examination system was a distinguishing mark of Confucian civilization, a *sine qua non* for Confucianists' social prominence, it was still a Confucian morality that expressed itself in various modes of circumventing the state examinations.

Original Confucian requirements (anti-feudal in the sense of raising 'character' and 'culture' above lineage and military command) had led, then to an examination system which seemed to violate Confucian requirements in so far as it raised culture above character in the would-be official's concerns. After all, learning was, but morality was not, susceptible of systematic testing. Since the system could be seen as splitting what Confucianism saw ideally as inseparable, good character and high culture, the anti-examination Confucianist, not admitting the possibility of the split, condemned, as stereotyped, the 'culture' fostered by the test. 'Some said, "The learning of the examinations corrupts men's minds. Recently the scholars read only poems and essays to plagiarize and do not take any notice of how important it is to cultivate one's moral standard and govern oneself." '22

One of the tentative detours around the examination system, supposed to have some relevance to 'character', was *yin* privilege, whereby the official distinction of fathers gave easier bureaucratic entree to sons. Here a hereditary factor, quasi-aristocratic but with the 'family' note Confucian, after all, impinged somewhat on the anti-feudal Confucian idea of careers open to talent. *Yin* privilege was particularly associated with conquest dynasties.23 We suggested, in analysing the basic confrontation of Confucianism and monarchy, that native dynasty and conquest dynasty were both aliens in the world of the Confucian ideal. Differences were in degree but not in kind. We may now put it another way: if the domestic was just as alien as the foreign (or a little less so) in its tension with Confucianism, the foreign was just as native as the domestic (or a little more so) in setting up Confucianism for tension within itself.

5. PRECEDENT AND RULES

The Confucian-Legalist (literati-imperial) ambiguity of the examination system was just a version of the ambiguity of 'precedent', which in different lights was a Confucian or Legalist value. True authority (if one may speak tautologically) is ultimately bound by nothing, including precedent. The despotic Ch'in Shih Huang-ti, burning the books and burying the scholars, knew it well. Hence, Confucianists strained against Legalist monarchy in their capacity as traditionalists—like the aristocratic Senators, straining against Valentinian in defence of the traditions of Rome.[24] But the establishment of *rule* (i.e., precedent in the Legalist sense) is the key to an unspontaneous controlled bureaucracy; it was the monarch and his centralizers who stressed *fa*, law, method, rule. Precedent, then, so richly entitled to Confucianists' respect, could be subversive of Confucianism, and to the Confucianists the examination system, with its similar potential, was both suspect and indispensable.

6. FREEDOM AND SURVEILLANCE

And so it was to the monarch. In so far as he and his Confucianists (not his, too) were both on all sides of the examination issue, so he and they, in general bureaucratic dispositions, seemed to give and take with one hand what they took and gave with the other. In the Ch'ing period, for example, we see the emperor forced to choose between two of an autocrat's objectives, political safety and administrative efficiency. One man would be appointed to several offices, several offices to one function (which was rarely defined precisely).[25] This certainly, and gratifyingly for the monarch, made it difficult for officials to dig themselves in. But it could not add up to a 'modern' bureaucracy, the rationalized corps of experts which a central power ideally would command. It rather conformed to the literati ideal of amateur omnicompetence. Yet, it was in his own interest that the monarch made his bureaucracy thus. What was that interest, but to check the bureaucracy's pull against him? And how was the pull exerted, if not by the very character-type, that of the amateur-independent, which his rulings contrived to restrain so well, yet also contrived to harden?

CHAPTER V

Confucianism and Monarchy: the Limits of Despotic Control

1. MORALISM

IF the examination culture tended to stereotype and stale-ness, Confucianists developed both a commitment to the routine and misgivings about it. The imperial attitude was ambivalent, too. The monarch was a centralizer who might deplore stereotypes, as obstructing his officials' effectiveness. But as a centralizer he was also seeking his officials' docility, and to that end he was well served by the pressure of stereotype against 'inner' spontaneity, the sign of an 'inner' moralism which could serve as a restraint on him.

We have already met the theme of Confucian moral strictures against force, which was a prerogative that mon-archs naturally assumed for themselves, and morality in-deed was the Confucian approach to monarchical restraint. The nature of dynastic succession (as distinct from bureau-cratic appointment) being what it is, royal legitimacy in China could not possibly be subject to any formal examina-tion of cultural attainment, and the morality which had to be left out of the bureaucrats' tests had to be left in the Confucian assessment of monarchs. The early stereotype of the dynasty's 'bad last emperor' showed how the very Confucian respect for the monarch, as holder of the *T'ien-ming* or 'mandate of Heaven', and thus first in a moral hierarchy, furnished the grounds for censure[1]—and for Confucian preservation, since

60

the moral fire on dynasties protectively screened the officials' material system.

We have observed that a genuinely Confucian concern about satisfying the *min*, the people, carried no implications of 'democracy', Caesarist or otherwise. On the contrary, it was essentially Confucian to reject majority rule, with all its air of impersonal, mathematical abstraction. But if the strongest in numbers were not to rule, the strongest in power would, and brute power was no more congenial to Confucianists than impersonal number. Still, individuals, unlike faceless masses, have moral possibilities, so Confucianists had attached themselves to emperors. While a dynasty worked, they covered its monarchs with a veneer of morality; this would gloss over (to their emotional and the monarch's political advantage) the actual basis of rule, sheer power. When Confucianists hypocritically, even slavishly, ascribed morality to an emperor, they seemed indeed his creatures. But this very morality, or the assumption that he required it and that they could judge it, was the mark of their independence—co-dependence, to put it a little lower.

2. LOYALTY

Yet, we face the problem of the shift away from 'bad last emperor' judgments in later Chinese history. Certainly from Sung, there was strong Confucian insistence on loyalty to an emperor one had served, a loyalty which committed an old official not to serve a new dynasty.[2] This seems hard to reconcile with the 'mandate' response, moralistic revulsion from a last emperor, and recognition of the line which effectively succeeded. Should we conclude that the emperor now was truly irreproachable, and officials at last were really only tools? But Confucianists never completely yielded to monarchs what the latter always sought, the right to define *chung*, 'loyalty'. A whole sea of Confucian feeling against the simple equation of loyalty with obedience was distilled in an episode of the *Tung Chou lieh-kuo chih*, in its last revisions a late Ming novel. A minister kills himself—as an expression of the higher loyalty *to his ruler*—when he fails to persuade the latter, with the following proposition, that he should spare the life of a friend: 'When the ruler is right and the friend is wrong, one should oppose his friend and obey the ruler; when the friend is right and the ruler is wrong, he should disobey the ruler and follow the friend.'[3]

Confucian disapproval of the transfer of loyalty from a deposed dynasty to its successor was a way of refurbishing, not destroying, the official's self-image as end, not means—not vocationally educated, hence not professional, hence not bound. The *ch'en-chün* relationship, minister to monarch, was one of the *personal* relationships so prominent in Confucianism, and a minister's loyalty, then, was no sign that an imperial owner disposed of him completely, but rather a sign that the minister *was* a person, not a thing—not a cog in a bureaucratic wheel that kept on turning, whatever the Legalist dynasty that generated the power. Confucian refusal to serve (unlike Taoist withdrawal) was an affirmation that public service was a high ideal, so high that it must not be compromised by dishonourable conditions. Honour counted, more than the deprived sovereign's (and the deceased sovereign's) pressure.

Chao Meng-fu, the famous painter, calligrapher, and relative of Sung emperors, became an official under the Yüan. Confucianists, who condemned him for disloyalty, were certainly not acknowledging a despotic right (the Yüan emperors') to command him into service. The seventeenth-century Ch'ing *i-lao*, 'Ming remnants', who refused to serve the Ch'ing—and were not dragooned or markedly harassed—were not chained to a dead emperor; they were keeping free of a living one. The authority was classical (Book of History, Analects, Mencius): the example of Po I, who starved himself to death rather than shift his loyalty from Shang to Chou. It was a counsel of moral freedom, not surrender.

3. TERROR

Especially in the Ming period (and especially near the beginning and the end), we find officials being assisted to death in great numbers and in terrifying ways. This was sometimes accompanied by self-abasement, the subject's protestation, even in his last anguish, of his loyalty to the ruler-torturer: '. . . my body belongs to my ruler-father. . . .'⁴ Was this surrender, the achievement of absolute despotism, the snapping of tension with the snapping of Confucianists' fibre?

It is hard to say whether this is social or psychological evidence. Observations under desperate modern conditions, in the concentration camps of Europe, have disclosed the possibility of morbid attachments between victims and tormenters. Still, even if the spectacle of submissive contrition, not defiance, is given a thoroughly social significance, it is not a conclusive sign of uncontested power. For one thing, 'ruler-father' was more than a pitiful lapse into childishness under pressure of the extreme exertion of unrestrained authority. It is generally agreed that monarchical absolutism did increase from Sung through Ming, but this filial language existed quite apart from that development. It was already there in T'ang, perhaps expressing the new elite's affinity with monarchs, during the crucial stage of the conflict with aristocracy: 'In that time (eighth century) ministers called their *chün-fu*, their ruler-father, "sage".'⁵

But more important: a father and son have a *personal* connection. It is a *relationship*—implying, it is true, subordination (even the material body may be offered up). But tools have no human relationship, they are used; things are not subordinate, they are owned; while the Confucian official *in extremis*, whatever his inner quality or his practical helplessness, still speaks in the language of humanistic culture. Though his sovereign disown him and abuse him, he will not in his total person be a thing or a tool; he will acknowledge a father, yet not an owner-despot. He has no price, and when he serves and dies he has not been bought and squandered. He has value. Though the monarch put an end to his life, he cannot end the Confucian self-image of the princely man (though lower than his prince) as an end in himself.

4. THE PIE OF POWER

Still, fine words pickle no bean-cakes. Officials were often humiliated at the Ming court, to say the least of it, and there were other unmistakable signs that Sung had bequeathed its successors an enhanced imperial power. But there is more to the Ming imperial situation than meets the eye. If Ming was an age of heightened despotism, a monarchical prerogative, it was also an age of heightened traditionalism, the special care of the culturally conservative Confucianists. And traditionalism, we noted, is not the prescription for un-trammelled imperial power. Traditionalism, rather, is one kind of intellectual demand which despotism, in the pursuit of its absolute, always needs to check.

There seems, then, to be a confrontation here, even an incompatibility. But there is nothing incompatible about the enhancement of monarchy and the enhancement of Confucian bureaucracy at the same time. We need not think in terms of just one set of mutually exclusive alternatives, as though one should sum up the later dynastic world in the emperor as the One in the state, the bureaucrats as nothing. Such an assumption is not entirely misleading, for it indicates quite rightly that in the end, before the western intrusion, bureaucracy and monarchy were the only real contestants—not aristo-cracy, long since worn away, and not capitalists, who never got away. Aristocrats dropped back in Sung, merchants came forward, but in bureaucratic reins. These are groups which certainly did lack power. But if we ask who took it from them, who inhibited their growth, we find bureaucracy the inhibitor, quite as much as monarchy. Learning and captur-ing hauteur from aristocrats, Confucian officials sustained it against merchants, and in Sung and Ming, at any rate, they grew as much as the monarchs in self-esteem and substance.

In short, with Sung, monarch and bureaucracy got wider slices of the pie of power, until other consumers were pushed from the table, to feed on crumbs. Undoubtedly, the crown had fed its despotism. Yet, even though officials felt the weight of it, they were buoyed up by added weight of their own. Sung centralizers (and after them Yüan, Ming and early Ch'ing) made the capital city the true centre of politics; they reduced the regional powers, especially the military. After Northern Sung itself, no other dynasty was founded by the *chieh-tu-shih* type, the restless independent regional warlord. This was good for the imperial interest, and it left its mark on officials, whose individual standing was rendered more precarious. But it was good for their interest, too, to see a check on the armed usurpers of their own civilian influence. If the individual official was lowered in his standing, yet he rose with his estate.

That is why Northern Sung Confucianists, writing with a seemingly Legalist concern for enriching and strengthening the state, were not so inconsistent. They were not necessarily puppets, doing all for the imperial master and nothing for the old Confucian tradition of the minister's integrity. For now, when Confucian bureaucracy (like monarchy) had increased its power within the state, a more powerful state meant a goodlier portion for the whole man.

5. THE 'SUPREME ULTIMATE'

Along these lines, another paradox can be riddled out. Certain Sung Confucianists, especially the great historian Ssu-ma Kuang (1019–86), undeniably magnified the emperor more than earlier Confucianists had. Yet, he was one of the opponents of Wang An-shih, that centralizing activist with strong imperial support. Our question is not why Wang had enemies (the reasons are many and complex), but how the hostility fitted in with the will to exalt the emperor. Perhaps the answer is this. First, when Confucianists came into their own it was with, not against, the raising of the monarch: they both enjoyed reducing the same rivals. But second, 'coming into their own' implied awareness of a need to defend themselves, to resist Wang, to resist anything that might appear as an autocratic raid on their position. They owed the prize to the autocrat, and repaid him with awe. But just because they prized it they cherished it against all comers, including the prize-giver.

If on its political side neo-Confucianism was far from slavishly imperial, metaphysically, too, it was by no means categorically pro-despotic. What connection may we establish between *t'ai-chi*, Sung philosophy's 'supreme ultimate', and the supreme ruler in the Sung political conception? *T'ai-chi* is the norm of norms, the form of forms; it is immanent, impersonal, and passive, having logical priority but nothing of the creative priority, the active power, of transcendental monarchy. As we shall see, when the nineteenth-century Taipings assailed Confucianism and raised up a monarchy of truly transcendent, absolute pretensions, their 'supreme ultimate' (*Shang-ti*, not *t'ai-chi*) was neither impersonal, passive, nor immanent, but their own version of the Lord of Hosts. On the level of casual mental association, to be sure, the Sung hierarchy of concepts—with room for just one at the top—might carry over to reinforce a hierarchy of men. Yet, psychology aside, if there is any systematic relation between *t'ai-chi* and the scope of imperial power, that relation is to the quietist strain in Confucian political thought, the immanentist, anti-power emphasis on the Son of Heaven's necessary virtue.

Perhaps, then, imperial confirmation of the neo-Confucian *li-hsüeh*, this Sung rationalism, as orthodox and mandatory has sometimes been over-interpreted. It need not be taken to prove that monarchs at last had a perfect Confucian rationalization for their purposes, nor that the Confucian establishment had finally become a wholly-owned subsidiary. The imperially sanctioned neo-Confucian monopoly came about not because, in itself, the philosophy flattered the monarch, but because in itself (i.e., in intellectual terms, not political) it was impressive enough to be an orthodoxy: it was intellectually possible to name and accept it as such. We ought not to be super-political here, implying that it was imperial fiat alone that made it orthodox. It is enough that monarchy appreciated the *li-hsüeh*, as a politically useful gift from intellectually powerful thinkers—useful, because intellectual orthodoxy would foster intellectual docility, with political docility as a by-product. Useful, too, because the monarch's seal on the orthodox learning would give the scholars a *quid pro quo*, subsidy in return for loyal support. And if the scholar had support to offer, some power to sell for his *quid*, the monarch still fell somewhere short of monopoly. There was more than One in the state.

In sum: the development of despotism at the centre, in early modern Chinese history (from Sung into Ch'ing), did not preclude (nor should its description overshadow) the development of a stronger position for bureaucratic Confucianists. They had a feast of agreement with monarchs on the spoils of aristocracy. And, just as much as monarchs, or rather more, they skimmed off or squeezed from the increasing product of mercantile activity, and grew with the companies. They were not abject; they were still in a position to strain against the power that might make them so. The picture of Ming imperial horrors perpetrated against hapless officials and gentry needs a balancing picture, perhaps one of the 'Wu culture' of confident gentleman-amateurs,[6] at a humanistic summit of refinement, unshrivelled by terror—and just as quintessentially 'Ming'.

6. UNIVERSAL DOMINION

Just as the seemingly absolute dynastic claim on loyalty may well have been ambiguous, so even the famous ceremony of prostration before the emperor, the *k'ou-t'ou* (kow-tow) cannot be viewed simply as 'the great symbol of total submission' of the Confucian bureaucracy.[7] The gesture dramatized a *Confucian* conception of imperial power, a conception that went so far beyond Legalist monarchy's own requirements that it hints, paradoxically, at a submission far from total. This act of abject deference identified a monarch infinitely high because his mandate of Heaven, his *T'ien-ming*, made him Vicar of Heaven on earth. The earth was all that was *T'ien-hsia*, all 'under-Heaven'—and Confucianists at an early date used this formulation in support of their own authority, when Buddhism threatened its political basis, challenged its universality. Originally, eloquent Chinese monks claimed to be in the world but not of it. For Confucianists, anyone who was in the world was in the Empire (*T'ien-hsia*, too), hence subject to (the officials of) the holder of *T'ien-ming*.[8]

Now, it is not for nothing that scholars sometimes render

fa-chia, the 'Legalist' party of the Ch'in founders of the imperial dynastic system, as 'Realists'. As the winners and holders of power by force (the 'virtue' gloss was Confucian, something ideologically useful to emperors, and suspect: another inner tension), dynasts were ready, being practical men, to define their world not as *the* world, but as the area where their writ could possibly run. This might impel them to conquest, out to Tibet or Turkestan or the like. But at least such regions were militarily accessible. Beyond that, monarchs could leave the merely metaphysical power claims to Confucian spokesmen.

Perhaps that is why, after Chinese envoys to Moscow in 1731 performed the kowtow before the Russian Czarina, the record of this interesting act was preserved only in a Russian source, and not in any Chinese.[9] Did Confucian recorders suppress it because such a gesture to a sovereign outside their system clashed with their idea (not necessarily their monarch's) of universal kingship? Why should the redoubtable Yung-cheng emperor, whose claims to absolute power in China were not modest, seem to give more licence to envoys in a matter touching his dignity than Confucian archivists were willing to give? Was it because a Confucianist could not, and a Chinese monarch could, sanction a Chinese kowtow in Russia which would make uncertain the *Confucian* implication of a Russian kowtow (or any other) in China? This Confucian implication included, first, in its identification of the Confucianists' monarch with the world's monarch, recognition of the universal supreme value of Chinese culture (a characteristically Confucian, not a monarchical tenet). And it included, second, in the very 'mandate' conception which justified monopoly of power and the appropriate gesture of abasement, a reminder of the monarch's moral responsibility. The allegiance of 'tributary states' to Chinese emperors enhanced the imperial prestige—but in a cautionary Confucian manner. For such acceptance of Chinese suzerainty, for the very reason that it often went unenforced by military strength, could be understood as a dramatization of 'dominion through virtue', which Confucianism conferred on no dynastic line as an inalienable right.

Yung-cheng might exact the kowtow in China and appreciate it there, as a flattering recognition of the power he exerted where, realistically, he could expect to exert it. But when he sent a mission abroad he was free, consistent with his own understanding of power, to step out of the character, the universal role, ascribed to him by Confucianists, whose conception of kowtow made it not only flattering but potentially inhibiting. Doubtless, on his own home ground, Yung-cheng was pleased to receive kowtow as a symbol of total submission. But the ceremony suited not only dynastic but bureaucratic preferences, for Confucianists attached a rider to the monarch's interpretation, endowed him philosophically (not materially) with an authority over far more than home ground, and in their very hyper-inflation of his power proclaimed their own integrity, as its judges. Nietzsche suggests that to serve, not curb, their will to power, men may impose their own chains[10]—or their own kowtow?

7. FACTION

Yung-cheng knew well enough that no symbolic procedure like kowtow assured him of perfect peace with a docile bureaucracy. He acknowledged this by bringing the relationship's contradiction into the open. We have already seen that he meant to guard the examination system from what he construed as factional abuse. What he feared was possible combination, the banding of quasi-aristocrats against his authority, and he singled out a famous Sung official for posthumous chastisement. 'Yü-cheng p'eng-tang lun' ('Imperially corrected "on cliques and factions"'), 1724, was his answer to Ou-yang Hsiu's essay of 1004, which had argued a case for beneficial factions: even filial obligation, said the emperor, must give way to the demands of office.[11] He was not nominating himself as 'ruler-father', metaphor that was still within the Confucian realm of discourse. He was not building a bridge of connotation, but disconnecting, with painful literalness, a Confucian filial obligation from an imperial demand.

Yung-cheng's ideal was an autocracy in which officials

fanned out from a single point of concentration, the emperor, with no individual connections between official and official. There were to be no groupings which would make so bold as to voice a literati 'public opinion'. When an edict was handed down, he proclaimed in 1726, his only consideration was its conformity to reason, to the needs of the situation, not in the slightest to any group's preferences. As part of his argument against bureaucratic faction, he dismissed 'public opinion' as a matter of 'small men trying to cover up their own deficiencies by making warped judgments on the empire'. And in all this he made the supremely autocratic assumption that he was acting on the basis of a famous principle of the *Lun-yü*, the 'Confucian Analects' (VIII, ix): 'The Master said, "The people may be made to follow a path of action, but they may not be made to understand it." '[12] One could hardly be more insulting to officialdom. For it was one thing when the Confucianists, hierarchically minded, spoke of the *min*, 'the people', in this fashion; it was another thing, a levelling act of monarchy, when the emperor implied that officials were *min* themselves.

It is no wonder, then, that Yung-cheng earned the reputation of relying more on law than on moral influence. His fetish was efficiency, a ruler's word and an engineer's word; in neither association, in one no more than the other, did it chime sweetly with the Confucian tone. As with the tone, so with the tactics. Yung-cheng got some efficiency (probably more than any other Manchu ruler) largely because of his checks against corruption, his vigilant surveillance.[13]

Yung-cheng tried to impress local officials with his burdens. In a touchingly confiding edict he told them of a tablet at the entrance to his chambers, with three characters on it, *wei chün nan*, 'It is hard to be the ruler.' On two sides of a pillar there were hanging scrolls with antithetical messages, 'It is the responsibility of one man to govern the empire', and 'It is not the responsibility of the empire to serve one man.'[14] The sentiment seems Confucian, but, for all the self-immolating devotion to duty, emphasis is on the one man. He knew his supreme and solitary place.

8. VIRTUE, POWER, AND IMPOTENCE

And yet he knew, too, what a strain it was to get there, a strain against Confucian bureaucracy. Even he, even his grandly self-assertive son, the Ch'ien-lung emperor (1736–96), with the balance of power tipped sharply toward the throne and away from bureaucracy, still spoke Confucian political language. Ch'ien-lung scoffed at the idea of a sovereign dwelling 'in lofty seclusion, cultivating his virtue'.[15] He had the power to scoff; but still, he had to exert that power against a moralistic conception of monarchy.

Maybe he, too, found restraint something he needed for his own good. The officials had it in kowtow, self-aggrandizement through self-abasement, as they quietly reserved, the harder they knocked, their Confucian right to judge. Just so, when the monarch acknowledged their right, with its implied impairment of the fullness of his power, he fulfilled a vital condition for holding the ample power he retained. The fetters of a master: was his burden of virtue a chain that *he* imposed, as well as his colleague-rivals? For a monarch whose virtue is unassailable may be unrestrainable. But also, he may be nothing more than a symbol, always Good King George while his ministers make the record—maybe blameworthy folly, but *they* make it.

In China, the very insistence by Confucianists, however muted, that imperial virtue had something to do with what happened in history, and could be impugned by it, kept the emperor inside the arena of power (while it gave the arena walls). He was not elevated to impotence, to that empyrean height where only officials had real responsibility—in both senses, executive and moral.

9. THE STATE AND THE IMPERIAL HOUSE

Thus, Ch'ien-lung clung to power. He did it, paradoxically, by accepting a world in which Confucian censure was always latently possible. And he did it, in further paradox, by grandly refusing to entertain any hint of Confucian censure. Representing power, precisely what Confucianists were striving to restrain, he made in all consistency an imperial variation on a characteristic Confucian judgment. As we have seen, those literati who opposed the revival of *ching-t'ien* (the stylized classical 'well-field' system of co-operative land-tenure, with its air of public-spiritedness) gave up on that institution—perfect though they acknowledged it—because the virtue of emperors had fallen off after the sage-kings' era. And therefore, these critics felt, only the force of inadmissible power could bring the *ching-t'ien* back, not the solely per-missible, yet impossible force of morality.[16] Ch'ien-lung, however, complacently gave other grounds for his own scepticism about *ching-t'ien*: it was the nature of modern *man* (no mention of monarchs, and certainly no suggestion of self-indictment) which had grown meaner—'Who is willing to put public ahead of private interest?'[17]

And who was willing to call his own interest private, while others presumably protected the public? Yung-cheng took pains to impute private, anti-state interests to officials: 'The phrase *ta-kung wu-ssu*, public, not private, sums up what We expect of officials.'[18] It was a clear case of state versus estates, as the centralizing monarch, in the universal pattern of counter-feudalism, identified his own conquest of power with the emergence of the public interest. But although Chinese dynasties ended feudalism, they did not create the modern state—which is only to say that Confucian bureaucracy was never the professional bureaucracy of experts which joined the European princes on their modern rise to power. The Confucianists remained independent enough and became aristocratic enough to call the monarch's encroachment not public but private itself. It was the prince, charged the most extreme of the Confucian critics (like the seventeenth-century scholar, Huang Tsung-hsi), who treated the empire as *his* estate, who made *ssu* where there should be *kung*.[19] Huang's contemporary, T'ang Chen, put it most bitterly: 'From the Ch'in, monarchs have been bandits...The prince became aggrandized, the people became his sheep and pigs.'[20]

However one interpreted the fusing of the 'public' interest with the private imperial interest—whether as the emperor's plunder or the state's restraint on private plunderers—

certain dynasties, the Ch'ing among them, made the ultimate claim that, technically, all land was imperial land. The standing principle of the Ch'ing dynasty was, 'Court and government are one essence.' But this was merely a verbal formulation; it did no more than formally ascribe full power to the imperial house. Actually, as the early nineteenth-century *Chia-ching hui-tien* indicates, a distinction between government land and imperial land was preserved. The categories of *t'un-t'ien* (military fields), *mu-t'i* (pastoral land), *hsüeh-t'ien* (study fields), etc., were government. Imperial property, the monarchical interest as 'private', had its own designation, *chuang-t'ien* (villas).[21] Just as land in the Ch'ing period generally was alienable, hence not really the emperor's or 'nationalized' (depending on one's interpretation of the intrusive role of the monarch), so this distinction between government and imperial lands shows the reality of private property. Neither monarchs nor Confucianists could convincingly maintain that their opposite numbers imposed the selfishness of *ssu* on the Chinese world, or establish that they themselves stood unequivocally for *kung*.

This was the tension between companions, Chinese monarch and Chinese bureaucracy, which only the Taiping Rebellion (1850–64) finally began to resolve. Until that beginning of the post-traditional era, the monarchy, standing for central power, worked against the bureaucracy's private aggrandizement, while Confucian bureaucracy, resisting such pressures, interpreted them as the monarch's moves to make the *t'ien-hsia* private, and thus to fail in moral concern for the public well-being.

Part Three

THE BREAK IN THE LINE OF TENSION

CHAPTER VI

Bureaucracy's Long Imperviousness to Social Revolution: the Role of Confucianism

I. MONARCH AND PEOPLE

THE tension between emperor and bureaucracy was not the old order's weakness but its strength. When it ended, when Confucianism ceased to imply conflict as well as confederacy with monarchy, this was the decline of Confucianism as the specific intelligence of the Chinese world. With that decline, the bureaucracy slid all the way (or seemed so, to a fatally large mass of the people), for the first time, to utter parasitism. And a ruling class of parasites incites to revolution.

Conventional Chinese monarchy could reap no gains from this. Whatever its old interest in breaking the independence of bureaucracy, its involvement with bureaucracy was too close to give it the pleasures without the pains of the latter's devastation. The monarch tried recurrently to level away the aristocratic potential in bureaucracy, his agent against the feudal aristocracies, but he never came to identity of interest with rebels against bureaucracy from below. In their traditional attitudes toward Taoism, for example, monarchs showed, on the one hand, affinity with the public beneath bureaucracy, and yet, on the other hand, acknowledgment of the common lot of Confucianism and monarchy.

It is well known that Taoism in its religious form, which

77

jarred on sophisticated Confucian officials, was widely popular, and never so much as when social order (a precious state to Confucianists in particular) was menaced. Monarchs, too, had frequently shown some interest in formal, creedal Taoism (beyond its general implications for aesthetics) which Confucianists disliked—indeed, this was one of the many marks of Confucian-monarchical tension. In T'ang times, for example, an eighth-century emperor established temples to Lao-tzu and a school of Taoist studies; and the school's curriculum, with Taoist texts as its 'Five Classics', matched and rivalled the Confucianists'.[1] For in a way, Taoism was as appropriate as Legalism to the emperor's counter-Confucian interest. Just as a Legalist approach implied restraints on Confucian officialdom, so Taoism (with its doctrine of following nature, a welcome corrective to the Confucian system of fixed forms imposed on natural behaviour) appealed to emperors who longed to escape Confucian restraints. After all, even when monarchy rode hardest on Confucian officials, Confucianism almost smothered the monarch in expectations of ritual and routine.

But if the intrusion of Taoist 'Classics' on the Confucian examination syllabus was possible for monarchs, the enjoyment of Taoist rebellious effervescence was not. They were curbed by the Confucian blackmail of the 'mandate of Heaven', which made rebellions a sign, not of a popular-royal front against the literati, but of the failure of royal virtue—while the literati as a type, if not always as individuals, rode out the storm. Accordingly, the Ch'ing dynasty, for one, took great pains to bring religious sects, Taoist and others, under government supervision. Some of the discipline may have been primarily just accommodation to Confucian bias—an edict of 1740, for example, forbidding an only son to become a priest, or a provision in the Ch'ing code, the *Ta Ch'ing lü-li*, insisting that priests perform ancestor ceremonial.[2] But the imperial government was doubtless disparaging in its own right when it took note in 1754 of the likely link of Taoism (and Buddhism) with low fellows, lawless *fei* or vagabonds, when it referred to priests deluding the people and improperly fostering mingling of the sexes, when it set up controls for priests' and temples' finances and the temples' numbers and acquisitions of land. Such departments as the Ming and Ch'ing *Tao-lu ssu*, office for records of Taoist priests, were for control of the Taoists, not imperial encouragement and expression of fellow-feeling.[3]

In short, post-feudal, pre-Taiping Chinese monarchs were never so closely identified with popular causes that they could take popular violence with equanimity, as tending to curb their literati rivals; rather, what made the literati rivals, in the last analysis, was their propensity for embroiling a ruling house by goading the people to violence. (When the ruling house did its own goading, like Ch'in and Sui, the bureaucracies were least the monarch's rivals, most his tools.) In Confucian eras, the Chinese masses and monarchs lacked that intimacy which one could see in pre-revolutionary Europe. There, for example, John Ball's rising in 1381 was impelled by faith in the benevolence and omnipotence of the English King.[4] When the Paris crowd turned against the royalists in 1789, it was a novel, revolutionary departure from centuries of urban popular riots in favour of 'Church and king'.[5]

2. THE 'PARASITE' EFFECT

What finally doomed the French king was the fading of the old popular impression of him as one fulfilling the *thèse royale*, encroaching on aristocracy and straining feudal bonds. Instead, the conviction spread that the king's interests and the aristocrats' were no longer distinguishable, so that he was a target in a revolution against them, as one parasite among many. When Mirabeau wrote to Louis XVI, in 1790, to the effect that he should relax and enjoy the Revolution, he referred to the old objectives of the centralizers ('Is it not something to be done with *parlements*, with *pays d'états*, with an all-powerful priesthood, with privilege and the nobility? The modern idea of a single class of citizens on an equal footing would certainly have pleased Richelieu, since surface equality of this kind facilitates the exercise of power').[6] Alas, poor Louis—the abstract cogency of this analysis, which should have put the king quite happily on the anti-aristocratic, centralizing side, broke down historically. The very fact that the Revolution had so much to do (Mirabeau: 'Absolute government during several successive reigns could not have done as much as this one year of revolution to make good the king's authority')[7] showed that monarchy had long since lost the power to press its case, but had made an accommodation with the nobles, one which delivered the king with them to revolution. The defenders of Louis before the Convention were not statist bourgeois, but aristocrats who in earlier days had stood for their estate against the crown.[8]

In the eighteenth century, the aristocrats had come back a good way from the days of their discomfiture at the hands of Louis XIV: but to recover their potency at the cost of making Louis XVI impotent only led to their languishing again. They had a 'victory' in the 'aristocratic revolution', beginning in 1787, culminating two years later, when the Estates General, preponderantly aristocratic, had to be convened. It espoused the *thèse nobiliaire*, calling for liberty in the sense of Montesquieu—that is, the weakening of the royal power. But now it was far too late to realize the hopes of the old Fronde, which the greater Louis had crushed so long before. On the eve of the real French Revolution, aristocracy, by draining the royal power, was drying up the channel of its own privilege.[9] Louis XIV had certainly not ruined the nobles for good in his own day; but he had taken so much, made them so much a part of him, that when they took from his royal descendants they were plundering themselves.

The fatal thing about the French monarchy's accommodation to aristocracy was that it was originally achieved, first, by taking the peerage's power, and second, by leaving it with its grandiose pretensions, so that no force might unite the two and seriously compete with the king. The lure of Versailles and the dangers of staying away, together with the power of the king's ministers and *intendants*, drastically diluted the aristocratic leadership in the country. Thus the king, though starting on the revolutionary road by stripping the aristocracy of its traditional place in local life and government, failed to wipe out the aristocracy (revolution's objective); rather, he himself seemed responsible for keeping it going, binding it to himself for his own purposes, and rendering it useless, merely consumptive, hence far more inflammatory than ever.[10] By denaturing, then sponsoring the nobles, he made himself, not the patron of the public, but the grandest and most private seigneur of them all. Once they had been assimilated to his interest, he was assimilated to theirs, and to their reputation.

When the aristocrats rose from their Louis XIV nadir, the political functions they recovered (even invading the intendancies) were made for the most part into functions of patronage, not service. To the extent that nobles (that is, the court nobles, not the provincial backwoodsmen) were ready to marry rich bourgeoises, the will to consume had eaten into the old noble pride in separation, the pride of men with a fair claim to fancy themselves the conspicuous actors, not just the conspicuous eaters, in society. And at the last, their will to consume had prevented the monarch from taxing nobles to strengthen the state. Easy, automatic manorial dues were jealously defended.[11]

De Tocqueville and Taine, historians of the Old Régime, went too far in dramatizing a royal assault on aristocratic power. Adopting the *thèse nobiliaire* themselves, they wrote almost as though nothing had happened after Louis XIV to bring the nobles back, as though a despotic, royal-bureaucratic assault on freedom had reduced the nobles to permanent subservience.[12] But, though their view was distorted, and by and large the aristocracy was not weak in eighteenth-century France, its strength was strength to obstruct, to sap any central authority, but not to reinvigorate regional life, or to act constructively from Paris and Versailles, where most preferred to live. Their reputation as gentlemen—and the king's too, as the first gentleman—became the reputation of parasites. When Sieyès, in his famous revolutionary pamphlet, *What Is The Third Estate?*, called the privileged orders *useless*,[13] he confirmed at least the subjective impression of the nobles' emasculation.

3. THE IMPORTANCE OF INTELLECTUAL WORK

What was the difference between the revolutionary French situation and the pre-revolutionary Chinese? Alignments of forces in the two countries seem analogous: a monarch so situated vis-à-vis the aristocracy (or what in certain respects could pass for one) that revolts against this privileged class had to implicate him. By the respective fruits of these revolts we know that a difference existed somewhere—that is, French monarchy and aristocracy were never the same again after 1789, while Chinese monarchy and bureaucracy kept on recovering their institutional places. And this was so because one crucial factor distinguished the French and Chinese situations, making the one ultimately revolutionary, and the other perennially rebellious: Chinese nobility was so overshadowed by Confucian bureaucracy that the nobility, however useless, could not compare with the French nobility as a focal point of hostility—and Confucian bureaucrats, more nearly equivalent to the French peers as the *visible* aristocracy, had never been spoiled by the crown, never been made (at least as a public, *à la française*, might see them) into popinjays. Never, even when economically and politically they seemed most purely exploiters and least contributors, had they abdicated that last responsibility which ties potential parasites to the world of function, the responsibility of thought.

A Chinese peasantry might groan under the burden of Mencius' famous dictum (III A, iv, 6): 'Some labour with their minds, and some labour with their strength. Those who labour with their minds govern others, those who labour with their strength are governed by others. Those who are governed by others support them: those who govern others are supported by them.' But as long as the governors did indeed 'labour with their minds', as long as they maintained their occupational badge, their Confucian intelligence, as *the* intelligence of the society, they were never, as a ruling class, parasites in the full sense of the term. Chinese peasants might rebel against them, but in France, where 'parasite' was rather more appropriate, revolution came. For French aristocrats were not only economically exploitative and politically un-productive; they showed every sign of defecting intellectually to the *new* intelligence of the bourgeois *philosophes*. French aristocrats, but not Chinese, began to bear the unmistakable stigmata of parasites, the marks of intellectual abdication. Both the labour with strength and the labour with mind were being done by others in France. How could a coterie which was reduced to talk resist the charm of another which talked so well?

In 1635 this intellectual eclipse of the French aristocracy had been foreshadowed, even fostered, by the founding of the Académie Française. This was the work of Richelieu, the centralizer whose grand design, as Mirabeau assumed, the Revolution furthered. Richelieu's essential principle for the Academy was equality. No privilege whatever should accrue to rank, and under Richelieu no great lords were members. Richelieu himself did not take part, but made himself the protector of academicians, not their confrere.[14] For pride of place in the Academy, Latin was displaced by French—the vulgar language and the national language, anti-feudal on both these counts. It was national, too, in its dedication to the intellectual and religious unity of France; Richelieu approved as initial members a number of Cartesians and Protestants.[15] Voltaire, who was a great partisan of the *thèse royale*, opposed to infringements on the royal prerogative, had no doubt how to relate the *parlements*, the voices of aristocracy, to this intellectual body. They had persistently opposed all healthy innovations, he said, from the Academy on.[16]

This was the Academy (an appropriate instrument for the assailant of aristocratic power) which glorified Louis XIV. Here, as in China, we see dignity accorded to intellectual achievement. But in France this finally gave aristocrats the look of utter parasites, who not only dropped out of active service but even relinquished the function of intellect to outsiders.[17] In China, the insiders remained the intellectuals. What preserved the quasi-aristocratic Chinese bureaucracy from parasitism was, quite simply, the fact that unlike the genuine aristocracy of France it had not been broken, then preserved. Instead it kept its distance from (its tension with) the royal power, *served* as bureaucracy, *thought* as Confucianists, never merely tripped and strutted, in the world of affairs and the world of mind, in florid impotence. Even for France, the parasite picture is overdrawn; yet, caricature though it may have been, it was spread around. It could seem believable—and this was fact—even if its patches of fiction make it unworthy of full belief.

The intellectual histories of both China and France in the eighteenth century were distinguished by great encyclopaedic efforts. One has only to quote the *philosophe*, Diderot, on (and in) the French *Encyclopédie* ('Today . . . we are beginning to shake off the yoke of authority and tradition in order to hold fast to the laws of reason . . . we dare to raise doubts about the infallibility of Aristotle and Plato. . . . The world has long awaited a reasoning age, an age when the rules would be sought no longer in the classical authors but in nature'[18]) to see how far he was from the world of the *T'u-shu chi-ch'eng*, or 'Ch'ing Encyclopaedia', and the *Ssu-ku ch'üan-shu*, the 'Four Treasuries'. The tone of the Chinese works was traditional, not rationalistically 'modern': and these greatest of eighteenth-century Chinese intellectual achievements were unimpeachably official, products of the 'establishment'. No rival, seductive party in China, in their thought and by *their* thinking it, had yet confirmed the established ones as parasites.

There were some Confucian literati who saw the spectre of parasitism in these eighteenth-century literary projects. *K'ao-cheng*, close textual study, was the vogue associated with such labours, and *k'ao-cheng* was as apolitical in its own way as Sung-school metaphysics, which the early Ch'ing scholars of the *Han-hsüeh*, the 'Han Learning', had criticized severely. The masses were said to have been drained dry in Ming times, and the dynasty's strength sapped before the Manchus, by economic exploitation which neo-Confucian quietists had done nothing to correct. Practical statesmanship, *ching-shih chih-yung*, had been the recommendation of the *Han-hsüeh* (or later, the *Kung-yang* school, after a relatively neglected, suggestive text which the *Han-hsüeh* rehabilitated). The recommendation was made in order to keep the bureaucracy functional. But textual criticism, though non-metaphysical itself, had cancelled the corrective of the excessive metaphysics.[19]

Still, however necessary such a corrective was deemed to be, the corrective was sought, by those who did seek one, within the Confucian tradition. As long as Confucian near-parasites were condemned by standards of Confucian reformism, they were not the pure parasites, utterly divorced from the sources of contemporary intellectual vitality, whom revolutionaries identified. The *Kung-yang* reformist, Wei Yüan (1794–1856), wrote, 'The princely man takes the *tao* as pleasant and sees the bitterness of desire; the small man takes desire as pleasant and sees the bitterness of tao.'[20] There is no doubt that Wei Yüan saw most of his contemporary fellow-literati as small men, *hsiao-jen*. But he still held up before them the time-honoured Confucian ideal of the princely man, the *chün-tzu*, and tried to renew the traditional intelligence. The Taipings, however, who made their bid before Wei died, threw out the old criteria, and proclaimed by their anti-Confucian, non-reformist challenge, not that there were *hsiao-jen* where *chün-tzu* ought to be, but that the title of *chün-tzu* had no honour left.

True princes, such as the noble members of the Ming imperial family, could be deemed parasites by Confucian standards and out of Confucian motives, but when 'princely men' were despised, as the Taipings were ready to do, the Confucianists themselves were sent to the wall. Taipings ceased to acknowledge that what was in the mind of those who 'laboured with their minds' was compelling enough to endow the latter with the dignity of labour. Without that grant of dignity there was nothing left but the sense of exploitation.

The Taiping indictment was not in itself sufficient to stamp the literati as parasites. They rejected the imputation, and Confucianism was still around for a final phase as the society's intelligence, a *Kung-yang* reform movement at the end of the nineteenth century. Wei Yüan's hope for the redemption of Confucianists survived, for a while, the Taipings' rejection of Confucianists *en masse*, the princely with the small. Yet, the damage was done. Though Taipings did not establish in their own day that Confucianism was finished as the intelligence of the society (and Confucian officials thus reduced to parasites), they drove Confucianism to end its tension with conventional Chinese monarchy, to lose what gave it its character, its vitality—and, in its new fatal pallor, to condemn its official exponents to the parasitical state. Proto-revolutionary Taiping rebels took the Confucian-imperial order out of the path of rebellions, and set it up for the unmistakable revolutionaries who were still to come.

CHAPTER VII

Bureaucracy's Vulnerability: the Intellectual Point of attack

I. THE NOVELTY OF THE TAIPING ASSAULT ON CONFUCIANISTS IN POWER

W HY was this rebellion different from all other rebellions? In all other rebellions such non-Confucian doctrine as the rebels held, Taoist or Buddhist in overtones, was not really a positive challenge to Confucianism as the intelligence of society; but the pseudo-Christianity of the Taipings was just such a challenge. In Taoist or Buddhist rebellions the doctrine, for the time of violence, was chiliastic —i.e., anti-social, anti-historical in the messianic sense of a vision of the 'end of days', with Confucianism left undisturbed as the dominant thought for prosaic social history. And when society struggled through the welter of violence, the Confucian arrangement with monarchy continued to govern history, while Taoism and Buddhism, losing their transitory associations with what Han 'Yellow Turbans' or Ch'ing 'White Lotus' felt almost as the 'pangs of the Messiah', resumed their low-temperature state in a continuing dynastic history. True, Taiping Christianity shared with earlier non-Confucianist movements a symbolic character, as a challenge to Confucian social superiors, a secession from the latter's intellectual world when its social cleavage seemed hopelessly sharp. Yet, for all this common character, Taiping Christianity was a new departure.

For one thing, Christianity was a really drastic break with

Confucianism, and Buddhism and Taoism were not, because Buddhism and Taoism were more broadly significant than Christianity in the 'normal' China. That is, Buddhism and Taoism had a wide, *extra-rebellious* existence in China. However they came to be invoked in times of stress, they had more than a pathological existence. But Christianity of the Taiping stamp was purely rebellion-bred, rebellion-nourished, with no social existence in China except as a cultural concomitant of violence. Its newness as a colouring for rebellion in China was not just a matter of chronology, of the fact that the Christian alternative to Confucianism came to China later than the others; it was a matter of kind. Taiping rebels as 'Christians' were specifically refusing to take what lay at hand, actually existing in times of peace, and only potentially convertible into rebellious energy: Taoism or Buddhism. Instead, the Taipings took something whose only life in China was lived not in peace but in paroxysm. The fate of Taiping Christianity after the fall of the Taiping state in 1864 bears this out. If this religion had any true independence of the political and social régime with which it was associated (as Taoism and Buddhism always had), we would expect to find its traces in Chinese history of the post-Taiping century. Yet, whatever the inroads Christianity made in China in these recent times, Taiping religion seems to have laid none of the groundwork. It vanished. And as the histories of Judaism and Orthodox Christianity show, this need not be the case when a religion associated with a political order sees that order destroyed.

If the Buddhist and Taoist religious challenges to Confucianism were softened both by their sufferance in normal times and their chiliastic character in times of rebellion, the Taiping deviation was consistent: just as the Taiping religion had no existence in normal times, so its character in rebellion was an equally novel feature. Taiping doctrine did not abandon history to Confucianism by imbuing itself with chiliastic fervour for the end of history. Instead it attacked Confucianism directly by proposing to make history itself. It did this by setting up a monarchy perfectly non-Confucian in its premises, a monarchy, that is, based on a transcendental

88

religious conception, diametrically opposed to the Confucian insistence on immanence. Immanent virtue, not trans-cendental power, was the Confucian ideal for monarchy. And so the Taiping denial of immanence (which was also the Taiping rejection of the bureaucratic intelligence) was denial of Confucianism at just the point where the latter strained against monarchical pretensions.

Thus, the very Taiping religion which was a more vivid symbol of disaffection with Confucianism than the Buddhist or Taoist religions had a more truly incompatible substance. Confucianists of that day were profoundly convinced of it; no rebellion was ever more rebelled against. The great Ch'ing loyalist and Confucianist, Tseng Kuo-fan (1811-72), saw the hitherto despised late-Ming rebels, Li Tzu-ch'eng (1605?-45) and Chang Hsien-chung (1605-47), as rela-tively blameless and orthodox, compared to the Taipings, and arraigned the Taipings for their assaults on Taoists and Buddhists—who ordinarily would be suspect them-selves.[1]

When Li claimed the empire in 1642, he took the three characters for 'eighteen sons' (in a prophecy that eighteen sons would conquer the throne) and re-arranged them to make the single character *li*, his name.[2] This was a typical bit of Chinese magic word-play. But when the Taiping claimant, Hung Hsiu-ch'üan (1813-64), declared himself the 'Heavenly Younger Brother' (to Jesus) in a new Trinity, and 'Heavenly King' because of that, his mystic chosenness came from a world of foreign imagery. Yet, the foreignness of the root conception, in Confucian eyes, lay in more than the fact that it came from over the borders. Just as, by the touchstone of the fullest Confucian ideal, native Chinese dynasties had something metaphorically alien about them, so the ideas of native Chinese Taiping rebels were alien, too, and not only in origin.

The core of the ideology which so disturbed literati-officials like Tseng was a blasphemy against Confucian monarchical premises. Nothing betrays so well the central importance of those premises, with the tension they implied, to Confucian vitality.

2. THE CRUCIAL QUALITY OF THE CONFUCIAN DOCTRINE
OF IMMANENCE

To Confucianism, what monarch could be justified in his pride of place when Confucius, the sage, had not been king? Kingship was not despised by Confucianists, but what the world saw as the king's 'position', the outer trappings (and that meant kings in history, not the ideal conception), was hardly precious when the true king in his own day was the uncrowned Confucius, a *su-wang*, a 'monarch unadorned'.[3] 'Su-wang' implied a possible separation between *wang-tao*, the Confucian ideal of the hidden royal 'way', and *wang-wei*, the monarchy's statement of visible royal rank. It was the impulse to restrain this natural tendency of monarchy to be *visible* that gave point to some of Confucianism's most vital conceptions.

Inescapably, everywhere, splendour and spectacle attach themselves to monarchy. As the ultimate leader of society, and as one not to be scrutinized for human frailties (for in that case, he might not pass), a monarch requires acceptance as something more than man, something related to divinity; majesty is the visible reflection in society of a divine splendour.

But it is a special conception of divinity—the transcendental—which spectacle connotes. Just as it sets the monarch apart, so it speaks of a divine power that is truly 'other', and truly power, the combination that spells Creator. In one mediaeval Christian theory, the king was in a sense deified (just as the Roman emperor's *consecratio* was his *apotheosis*)— the inherent distinction between God and the king (God's transcendence 'by nature' over the one He makes god 'by grace') being blurred in just the crucial category, *power*: the power of the king was the power of God.[4] And glory belonged with kingdom and power, in the earthly realm as beyond it; common forms of spectacular acclamation, eulogizing militance, successively served Roman emperors and Christian godhead and Christian monarchs.[5] The injunction to 'render unto God . . .' and 'render unto Caesar . . .' did more than distinguish the spiritual realm from the temporal; it suggested analogy as much as distinction, in that *both* God and Caesar must be 'rendered unto'—surrendered to. And so the royal power reflected the Highest Power. 'In his earthly being the Caesar is like every man, but in his power he has the rank of God. . . .'[6]

A creator, however (like martial values), was alien to Confucian thought, as the literati came to profess it. However much a transcendental sentiment may be recognized in popular Chinese religion or suspected in the Classics, in a perhaps irrecoverable stratum of meaning, buried far beneath the commentaries, the literati's Confucianism—certainly by Sung, the civil bureaucracy's time of fulfilment—was committed unequivocally to immanence. It was left to nineteenth-century Christians, Western and Taiping, to dwell on the shadowy classical concept of *Shang-ti* as a transcendental supreme power. The traditional Confucian sancta were all bound up in *T'ien*, Heaven, whose 'mandate' (*ming*) made rulers legitimate and committed them to virtue (not power), to the end of harmony (not creative change). *T'ien* and *Shang-ti* had different origins. *Shang-ti* was a Shang conception (though the 'Shangs' were different characters); *T'ien* came in with the conquering Chou, who spread the doctrine of the 'mandate of Heaven' to sanctify their succession.[7] And one must not be betrayed by foreign verbal associations into the equation of the Confucian concept of 'Heaven', *T'ien*, with a transcendent God, just because in Judaism, for example, Heaven (*hashamayim*, etc.) frequently occurs as a metonym for Deity seen in that transcendental light.[8] It is not some hypothetically definitive connotation of 'Heaven' which characterizes a religion, but the character of the religion which imparts the connotation.

Scholars have recently suggested that in the period of the Warring States, in the time and region of Confucianism's first emergence, the *huang* of *Huang t'ien shang ti* (sovereign heavenly emperor) had passed over into its homonym, in *Huang-ti*, the 'Yellow Emperor'.[9] What had been heavenly became a supposedly historical monarch, and the first one, thereafter, in the Confucian list of the five model sage-kings. This would represent etymologically the Confucian transfer of emphasis from the celestial to the earthly-political sphere—

a shift from a vision of transcendental power to one of the monarch as exemplar. It is significant that the implacably anti-Confucian Ch'in Shih Huang-ti, the most challenging power-monarch of them all, claimed (as an anti-traditionalist might) to surpass the ancient 'Three Huang' and 'Five Ti', and called himself Huang-ti:[10] the pre-Confucian term, with its transcendental overtones.

Philosophically, no Creator meant no 'in the beginning', hence no progressive conception of time to threaten Confucian equilibrium, or to shatter the absolute quality of the historical thought (leaning more to paradigm and example than to process and relativity) that went with it. The corollary in political theory was a Confucian ideal of an emperor radiating virtue, analogically reflecting harmony to society, not logically interfering with it to move it; he should be sympathetically stabilizing an eternal cosmos, which had never been once created, and should never be freshly tampered with by some mock-transcendental earthly ruler, acting, creating anew. Thus Han Confucianism, with its 'Five Element' theory, gave a cyclic role to emperors in a universe of cosmic interaction, where the course of nature and human events were locked together.[11] How different this was—consistently—from a transcendentalist system. Judaism, for example, which posits a Creator who never rose and never dies, developed therefore in permanent contrast to natural, cyclical cosmologies; and the cultic function of the Davidic king (on the pattern of ritual drama, the dying and rising god of nature) was severely repressed.[12]

In the *Shuo-wen*, where the *Tso-chuan* is given as *locus classicus* (cheng i cheng min), cheng[a], 'to govern', is a cognate of cheng[b], 'to adjust'. The emperor's role is government, its definition 'adjustment' of the people's transgressions and errors.[13] The assumption here is of an eternal pattern: cheng[b] is the process of restoring conformity to it. The Sung neo-Confucianist Ch'eng Hao, memorializing his emperor, saw the 'way' of Yao and Shun as the perfecting of the five social relationships, achieving adjustment to heavenly reason.[14] This is essentially the task of a silent one, a sage in concealment (the immanent is always hidden, never spectacular).

The very idea of it clashed with a real emperor's natural place as a focal point for spectacle: note, for example, Ch'ien-lung's Confucian statement of modest expectations for his receptions on tour in 1751, and his actual prompting to flamboyant extravagance.[15] And the idea of silence and concealment clashed, too, with an emperor's natural penchant for wielding power to change the world, not for emanating perpetuation of a changeless pattern.

Where God is transcendent, man tends to be seen as intrinsically morally limited, and kings as necessarily coercive (as in patristic Christian thought, where the Fall brings sin and social disorder and the need for a power-authority;[16] and as in Maimonides' philosophy, where man's distance from transcendent God is measured by the redemptive bridge of the Law that God revealed, and where kings are those who accept the dictates of lawgivers and have the power to enforce them, compelling the people to obey).[17] But the seminal Han Confucianist Tung Chung-shu (second-century B.C.), reasoning from a premise of unfallen man, man with a good nature, sees the need of a *moral* authority—an exemplar, not a coercer—whose Heavenly Mandate is not a licence to God-like power but a certification of charm. People are good and thus can be, as it were, magicked (by *li* and *yüeh*, ritual and music) into the harmony that Heaven implies; the Son of Heaven, by his being, not his doing—as a sage, not a potentate—is the one to work or waft the magic, to bend the grass (the masses) into the immanent order of Heaven. That is what he exists to do. Man's nature is perfectible but, left to itself, not perfect—'therefore Heaven sets up the king to perfect it. . . . If the (masses'?) natures were already perfect, then to what end would the king receive the mandate?'[18]

What Confucianists, then, made of monarchy was something particularly Chinese. But we can hardly understand what they made of it unless we recognize in monarchy what is potentially universal. Just what are the Confucianists doing? They are straining against the implications of uninhibited monarchy, and to know what *those* are (and thus to know the character of Chinese history) one should look to other histories as well as to Chinese. If comparable histories yield a consistency of relations between religions and kings and bureaucracies, then in a single history (Chinese) these relations may be significant, not casual and empty.

In mediaeval European political theology, as literature and iconography show, there developed an interesting difference between Christ-centred and God-centred monarchy. Ninth-century Carolingian throne images reflect a direct relationship of God to the king as God's vice-regent; Christ is absent. But a subsequent concept of kingship, affected by a century or more of Christ-centred monastic piety, was 'liturgical' (exemplary), centred in the God-man rather than in God the Father—centred, that is, in a Christ of the Gothic age, an intimately human figure, not the regal and imperious Christ, almost *in loco Patris*, of Constantinian origins. And after that, when the christocratic-liturgical concept of kingship gave way, the theory succeeding it was theocratic again, and juristical.[19] Once more we see, as in China (and as we shall see in Byzantium), the non-Confucian, power-imperial identification with law. 'The omnipotent God is known to have set over men a king . . . that he may coerce the people subject to him by his terror, and that he may subdue them with laws for right living,' wrote a twelfth-century partisan of Emperor over Pope, setting God above Christ ('just as the head rules the body'), seeing the king in the likeness of God, and quoting St. Paul (Romans, XIII, i) with crushing imperial finality: 'Let every soul be subject to the higher powers. For there is no power but of God: the powers that be are ordained of God.'[20] This was the pretension, this drive for an unrivalled royal power, that put a divine nimbus around the heads of kings, and made the king's touch for the 'king's evil'—that derivation from God's power as the fountainhead of healing—so potentially 'Gallican' in France, so imperiously challenging and antipathetic to popes.[21]

What is the political implication of these different religious associations? It seems to be this: Whatever may have been the compulsion on Constantine, as a convert, to take his new Christ-image (not God the Father) as the heavenly antitype of the emperor on earth, Charlemagne, without the need to insist on the already accepted idea of Christ's divinity, could

CONFUCIAN DOCTRINE OF IMMANENCE

reach above him to the proper seat of power. Charlemagne, the centralizer, the mighty wielder of real (though transitory) power through a bureaucracy (though ephemeral) of regimented king's-men, was seen in the image of the *active* God, God the Creator, not Christ—agent, not patient. 'Sub Pontio Pilato *passus*,' the Mass declares of Christ: Christ suffered. To suffer is to be acted upon; it is God alone who acts. Truly, not king-as-Christ (ultimately a monastic, i.e., a contemplative, not an activist conception) but king-as-God (or rather, His analogue) was the appropriate image for Charlemagne, who was an ideal monarch in actively trying to break all earthly trammels. Suffering, in the deepest sense of the word, attends upon immanence. But power reflects transcendence.

This is not to say that belief in a transcendental, creative God demands the royalist analogy. John Milton, after all, believing in God, believed in the people, not the king, as the source of authority. It is interesting, though, that Milton, in visualizing King Charles I as a subject under indictment, not as a ruler enforcing law, spoke, in a way, in the Confucian vein. The fact that Charles had been defeated, imprisoned, and brought to trial was a portent to Milton, a sign of God's will that Charles be done away with[22]—a Confucianist would say, the loss of Heaven's mandate. Still, no Confucianist, before the modern rout, would have wished his monarch succeeded by a sovereign people. Milton was not so Confucian, after all, and as he worshipped a different Heaven, so he accepted a different sovereign.

God, then, need not validate king, nor the idea of God make the acceptance of kingship follow. But the logic still works the other way round: kings need God, and as kings seek power, the power of God (where divine worship is at all current) is a main on which they draw.

In the most completely austere of transcendentalisms, with idolatry under an absolute ban, the monarchical idea is basically discouraged: if God is King, there ought to be no king to play at God (see I Samuel 8: 4–7, before the enthronement of Saul in Israel). For that is surely what kingship carries with it—Deuteronomy 17: 16–20 has Moses,

95

out of respect for God's uniqueness, vigilantly legislating modesty for kings,[23] and Mme. de Sévigné referred to Louis XIV, that lover and embodiment of spectacle, as a being compared to God in such a manner that God, not the king, was the copy.[24] Philo Judaeus of Alexandria (nothing sardonic here), accepting monarchy as Samuel had had to accept it, had seen the king as a divine simulacrum ('for there is nothing on earth that is higher than he'), administering the Law, in a world in which God is eternal king and model for human monarchs.[25] Idealistic, impersonal coinage-portraiture of Augustus expressed the idea of the *genius* or *numen*—Augustus' more than normal will, his universal and superhuman efficacy—in Greek, *daimon*, that is, *theos* viewed as an efficient agent in daily life: the impersonality of the ruler's image reflects the early Imperial Graeco-Roman religious emphasis on divine power (rather than on divine personalities).[26] In mediaeval Islam, the ruler was 'the shadow of God on earth'; the caliph or imam was 'the khalifa of Allah and the shadow of Allah who imitates the lawgiver in order to make his government perfect'.[27] The monarch in early modern Europe, unimpeded by the claims of merit, gives grace: like God (the version of Jean Calvin).[28] To the fourth century Byzantine philosopher Themistus, the ruler's primary attribute, the divine *philanthropia* (love of man), made the emperor God-like, with God's prerogative of mercy being the emperor's prerogative, too, marking for both transcendence over what they give the world—the legal codes of justice.[29] For dominant Christianity in the Byzantine Empire, this was the ground for submission to imperial authority; for dominant but very different Confucianism in China, this imperial link with formulated law, with its transcendental implications, was, we saw, a ground of conflict.

From the standpoint of Samuel's terrible warning of what a king would really mean in exercise of power (I Samuel 8: 11–18), the Byzantine's active *philanthropia* was a myth to gloss over the true potential of monarchy. From the same standpoint, the Confucian ideal of sage-like non-activity was a myth, too: the king does not stay hidden. The difference between the myths is that the Byzantine coincided with an emperor's naturally transcendental pretensions, and strengthened his hold; while the Confucian was at odds with the character of the throne, and stood as a reproach. Byzantines conceived of imperial government as a terrestrial copy of the rule of God in Heaven.[30] Confucianists had no God in Heaven, no autonomous Voice that spoke from above. In so far as monarchy inevitably approached that transcendental model, the Confucianists strained against it. They would not condemn it in the Deuteronomic, pre-Philonic Hebraic fashion, out of an utter transcendentalism unvitiated by the Greek idea of incarnation, but would correct it, as far as they could, towards silence.

Perhaps the nearest approach a Chinese emperor made to the crypto-Taoist non-activity[31] which Confucianists commended to the throne was in the imperial ineffectualness which often accompanied social breakdown. But in that case, one may be assured, there was no Confucian approval. Instead, the emperor's virtue was disparaged (usually from the safe vantage point of a later dynasty), since he had evidently not fulfilled his symbolic responsibilities as holder of Heaven's mandate. And the disparagement might be framed precisely as a charge of inactivity—*openly* labelled 'Taoist', and thus a proper object of Confucian censure.[32] Clearly, the Chinese emperor was subject to checks, material non-cooperation in his own day and at least posthumous moral reproach.

I have already suggested (in discussing 'the people's will') that these moral reproaches, for whatever they were worth, were no testimony to 'the innate democracy of Chinese political thinking'. But what still needs to be emphasized is that the immanentist *T'ien-ming* (mandate) doctrine really was an expression of conflict with the emperor (Byzantine Christian officials, much more than Chinese Confucianists, were a despot's faceless men), though a bureaucratic, not a democratic expression. (Just so, in the mediaeval European papal-royal tension, the moral challenge to monarchy—glossing over St. Paul's blanket endorsement of the 'powers that be', which was the textual underpinning of monarchical apologies—was an ecclesiastic, not a democratic challenge.)[33]

Bureaucratic historians, in their Confucian moralism, charged up to the emperor symptoms of social decay which were actually effects of the normal functioning of the bureaucracy itself.

Confucianists had to have an emperor as a reflector of morality (in social terms: officials needed a state), but by the system of morality he crowned, the emperor could be indicted to cover the part which officials played in wasting the state they needed. 'Mandate' theory was no defence of the people, mitigating absolutism, but it was a defence of gentry-literati in their conflict-collaboration with the emperor in manipulating the state.

I have no wish to imply here any organized cynicism, or conscious cabals to fool the people and bind the emperor. This is a statement of the logic of a world, not an assumption of cool detachment and logical calculation on the part of the world's leaders. What we see in the Confucian political order is an inner consistency—something not depending on the exercise of rational cunning or on any other melodrama—a consistency of intellectual theory and the intellectuals' social concerns. A conservative social group, opposed above all else to revolution while it contributes provocation to that end, favours an almost exquisitely appropriate doctrine: by making an explanation of the workings of the social system moral inner, rather than social outer, it makes the system sacrosanct and intellectually untouchable. Dynasties, the Confucianists' lightning rods to draw off the fury of social storms, go through *ko-ming*, exchanges of the mandate, but bureaucracy goes on and on, not subject to revolution.

It was subject, however, to rebellion. And Chinese bureaucracy in its characteristically Confucian form finally met its last rebellion—last, because the seeds of revolution were in it at last—with the irruption of the Taipings in 1850. All that had summed up the Confucian strain with monarchy, all the clashes in interest and taste, were intellectually gathered in the Confucian conception of Heaven, which defined (in every sense of the word) the Son of Heaven. To deny the Confucianists there was to add intellectual rejection to social hostility, and thus fill out the fatal conception of parasitism. 'French' revolution became a Chinese possibility.

Certainly, the Taipings did not rise in order to revise a definition. Their agony was social, and we may take the ideological form of the rebellion as an index of what was happening—shattering, qualitative change—not as a first cause of the change. Yet, it was some kind of a cause, too; while corollaries coincided, consequences flowed. High as they were, the clash of Heavens, immanent versus transcendent, was not just a pseudo-event in an airy 'superstructure'. The ground of Chinese history was shifting. Confucianism and monarchy would change their role in China and their posture toward each other. And the change in posture, from a bout to an embrace, decided the change in role. Confucianism and monarchy passed from expressing general reason, alive with a tense vitality, to making claims on a special Chinese emotion, but one with a dying fall.

CHAPTER VIII

Taipings Storm the Confucian Heaven

A SIXTEENTH-CENTURY German, dilating on the absolute authority of the Russian Czar, reported that the Russians conceived of their abject obedience to the will of the prince as obedience to the will of God.[1] When Hung Hsiu-ch'üan, *T'ien-wang* of the *T'ai-p'ing T'ien-kuo*, was the prince in question, he, too, took obedience to the prince as obedience to the will of God, and he was just as alien to the crucial rationalistic Confucian doctrine of 'Heaven' as any foreign divinely-mantled autocrat. When he rejected ties with certain contemporary fellow-rebels against the Ch'ing dynasty, he did so not merely because he, an aspiring monarch in his own right, could hardly share their zeal for a Ming restoration.[2] The Taiping ideal of monarchy was simply far removed from the conventional ideas of the traditional sort of rebels.

1. 'TRADITIONAL' REBELS: DIVERGENCE FROM TAIPING IDEAS

For a time in the 1850s, the shadowy figure of an Emperor T'ien-te ('Heavenly Virtue') came, in rumour, to the attention of fascinated foreign observers of a torn China. Some confused him with Hung Hsiu-ch'üan, but in fact the 'T'ien-te' manifestoes came from the circles of the *T'ien-ti hui*, 'Society of Heaven and Earth', which was also known as the Triads, and by other names as well;[3] and Hung, very early, lost any sense of common cause with them. For the Triads' assault on the Ch'ing system was such as to confirm Confucianism as the intelligence of Chinese society, while the Taipings thrust it off. The Taipings, for example, made little of filial piety. They could hardly take this Triad appeal as an acceptable piece of anti-Manchu rhetoric: 'To help an enemy to attack one's homeland is the same as leading children to attack their parents.'[4]

The secret societies reviled the Manchus, repeatedly, for 'selling office, vending noble rank' ('like Shang Yang oppressing the people'), and thus bypassing the legitimate claims of Confucian learning.[5] That is, the Manchus were equated with a Confucianist's villain (the ancient 'Legalist', Shang Yang), and Confucianists were included among the victims of parasites. But the Taipings named the Confucianists themselves in the charge against parasites, and made that charge more sweeping, because so much more inclusive. When the learned Confucianists were not the injured ones but the worthless injurers, not just the dynasty but the whole legitimate system was arraigned. And not just this dynasty but the Ming or any like it was rejected when the Confucian learning, in its application to monarchy, was explicitly supplanted, as worthless. For the 'T'ien' of *T'ien-te* was the impersonal cosmic harmony of the neo-Confucianists: 'Ta Ming T'ien-te Huang-ti *t'i T'ien hsing jen*,' a proclamation ran, 'The T'ien-te Emperor of the Great Ming *has Heaven as his essence and benevolence as his function*' (hsing = yung in the famous neo-Confucian *t'i-yung* dichotomy).[6] 'T'ien' as his essence—this 'inner' conception of the relation of monarch to the harmony of the cosmos was never the Taiping 'T'ien', which pertained to a transcendent God, whose *T'ien-ming* was personal commandment from on high, not the Confucian impersonal mark of election. Hung as *T'ien-wang* was not 'King of Heaven' (in the fashion of a Ming pretender, hopefully *T'ien-tzu*, 'Son of Heaven')—he was 'Heavenly King', a ruler receiving orders from God in Heaven, set apart, not one with Heaven 'in essence'.

The term *T'ien-wang* was not new with the Taipings. Ku Yen-wu (1613–82) discussed it as a classical term of Chou.

But only with the Taipings was *T'ien-wang* set against *T'ien-tzu* as the term for the claimant to oecumenical rule.[7]

2. TAIPING 'T'IEN' AND THE TRANSCENDENTAL AURA OF POWER

Hung Hsiu-ch'üan never maintained that the Ch'ing dynasty had lost the Mandate of Heaven. He never made this conventional rebel claim because he never thought of his own position as legitimized by the Mandate. Not 'Heaven' but 'God in Heaven' was the source of his authority, and when *T'ien-ming* appears in Taiping documents *T'ien* is, metonymously, 'God', and *ming* is 'order' in its Biblical sense of commandment, not in its Confucian sense of timeless pattern.

For the metonymy, it is sufficient to note that when Hung Jen-kan (the 'Shield King' of the Taipings) enjoined, *Ching T'ien ai jen* ('Revere Heaven and love men') he meant explicitly to quote words of Jesus,[8] whose object of reverence was what the Taipings, too, repeatedly called their 'Heavenly Father'. 'Wo T'ien-wang feng *T'ien-fu* Shang-ti chih *ming*,' declared the Taipings, 'Our Heavenly King receives the commandments of God (*Shang-ti*), the Heavenly Father (*T'ien-fu*).'[9] Clearly, on this showing, the Taiping *T'ien-ming* compound is an ellipsis: between 'T'ien' and 'ming' falls the Father-God.

It is clear, too, that just as 'Tien' signifies God for the Taipings, God who as creator brings time into the timeless, so *ming* is a different 'order' from the Confucian timeless one. How does the 'T'ien-wang' receive 'T'ien-fu Shang-ti chih ming?' *Feng* is the verb, signifying receipt from a superior, while an emperor in Confucian texts almost never receives his *T'ien-ming* thus, but with *ch'eng* or (usually) *shou*. The great Han Confucianist, Tung Chung-shu, had laid it down, 'only the Son of Heaven receives (*shou*) the *ming* from Heaven; the Empire receives the *ming* from the Son of Heaven.'[10] The *ming* so received and transmitted was an imprint of order (we have seen Tung Chung-shu allotting the monarch the role of ordering men's hearts by an example that only he can radiate). But Hung Hsiu-ch'üan 'feng T'ien-ming hsia-fan', receives the heavenly order *to come down* to earth (while Confucian *T'ien-ming* is not an order *to do* anything, and the holder, of course, is on earth already); 'feng T'ien-ming', here, has the same significance as in the subsequent phrase, '*feng Shang-ti chih ming* (receives God's order) to exterminate the goblin people . . .'[11] When the Taiping 'Heavenly Father' demands acceptance of himself, Jesus (*T'ien-hsiung*, Heavenly Elder Brother), and Hung Hsiu-ch'üan (the Heavenly King and Heavenly Younger Brother), he endorses the latter's political supremacy in this quite different fashion: 'When he utters a word it is *T'ien-ming*; you are to obey it.'[12]

This is God's injunction to men to obey the *T'ien-wang* and obey the *T'ien-ming* because God speaks the latter, His orders, through the former, His younger son. The *ming* of Confucian *T'ien-ming* could never be governed as it is here, by *tsun*, 'obey', just as the *T'ien* who 'speaks' it here could only, really, be the Taiping *T'ien-fu*, the Heavenly Father: when Confucius asked, rhetorically, 'Does Heaven speak?' he went on to identify it with the timeless cosmic pattern.[13] And so the Confucian *ming* of Heaven perennially exists, with only the qualified holders changing. But the Taiping *ming* is given in time, spoken from above, to be obeyed from below. The books of the 'true Tao' of the Taipings are given as three, Old Testament, New Testament, and *Chen T'ien-ming chao shu* (Book of the true heavenly decrees and edicts); Confucian books are daemonic, noxious, and ought to be burned.[14] Or, in sum, the 'true *T'ien-ming*' of the Taipings must be far removed from the Confucian understanding— Hung does not receive the 'mandate' because the Ch'ing have 'lost' it—for, if that were the Taipings' contention, they would appeal to the sanction of Confucian books instead of advancing a canon to supplant them. The anti-Confucian *régime* may be referred to as 'true *T'ien-ming*',[15] but the monarch, unlike a Confucian monarch, never assumes that mandate.

It was a new canon, then, enshrining the record of God who speaks. If Confucius preferred not to speak because Heaven did not speak, Hung Hsiu-ch'üan arrogated to himself an earthly version of the speech, the power, of a Heaven personified. 'Do you know that the Heavenly Father is omnipotent, omnipresent, omniscient? I know . . .'[16] ran a Taiping catechism. Over and over again the changes were rung on Shang-ti as God of power, unlimited, inexhaustible power, and sovereigns are *neng-tzu*, those of his children whom he clothes with power.[17] There is no *neng-tzu* in the Confucian vocabulary, in which *te*, virtue, the very antithesis of outer physical force, was the ideal 'power' of monarchs. Not virtue but power is what the *T'ien-wang* gets from Heaven. God is greater than his sons—God alone is *shang*, God alone is *ti* (cf. the regular dynastic emperors, all *ti* themselves), God and Jesus alone are *sheng* or 'holy', Hung Hsiu-ch'üan is only *chu*, the people's lord.[18] God, thus transcendent, routes his authority down through the Heavenly King. Obedience to him is service to God and Jesus.[19] Hung's cousin and aide, Hung Jen-kan, distinguishing between classical titles of nobility (*kung, hou, po, tzu, nan*) and the Taiping designations, calls the latter far superior. For the classical ranks, he says, were taken from the nomenclature of the family system (indeed, they are kinship terms as well as political ones), and this arrangement was confused and inelegant. But the Taiping terms are all prefixed with 'T'ien'—the capital is *T'ien-ching*, soldiers are *T'ien-ping*, officials are *T'ien-kuan*— for the *T'ien-wang*'s authority derives from the *T'ien-fu*.[20]

3. SIGNIFICANCE OF THE BIBLE AS SUCCESSOR TO THE CLASSICS

These *T'ien-kuan* were supposed to be chosen for the Taiping service by an examination system, and for this traditional procedure the Taipings modified their strictures on the traditional literature. God was said to have acknowledged that Confucius and Mencius had many good points in common with divine sentiment and reason, and that the Four Books and Five Classics, *imperially revised*, their falsehoods noted, could be studied again as supplementary texts for examination candidates. But the fundamental texts were the *Chiu-yüeh*, *Ch'ien-yüeh* and *Chen-yüeh*—the Old Testament,

New Testament, and 'true testament' of Taiping decrees and edicts.[21]

A Ch'ing intelligence report on this examination system noted that the essay retained the 'eight-leg' (*pa-ku*) form, and the poem the regular Ch'ing form (*shih-t'ieh*; eight five-character lines). However, the subjects were all drawn from false books. For example, a Hupei essay was set on the theme, 'The true God (*chen-shen*) is the sole Lord (*Huang-shang-ti*)', with the next phrase, '*Huang-shang-ti* is the true emperor (*Huang-ti*)'. The poem dealt with the Incarnation and the Passion.[22] (The 'false books' are *wei-shu*. One may note in passing that wherever the Taiping documents prefix *T'ien*, this Ch'ing account prefixes *wei*, 'spurious'—*wei-ching*, *wei-ping*, *wei-kuan*, etc.—with much the same regularity and ritualistic impact as the sanguinary or conjunctive expletives of the British or American military argot.)

Does the retention of traditional forms—the examination system itself, and the form of questions—make a nullity of the shift in content? To say so would be to deny the significance of Confucian content throughout previous Chinese history, to make any intellectual content inconsequential in itself, as though it served only as a symbol of the importance of intellect in the abstract, not as serious intellectual substance. But something really significant did happen with the Taiping change from Confucian to Biblical subject matter; it was no change in 'mere form'. For just as Taiping *T'ien-ming* cut through the restraints in the Confucian conception of monarchy, Taiping examinations demanded officials' adherence to the monarch's ideology, to the books which made him legitimate. But Confucian examinations enshrined the books which made *officials* legitimate in their high places (and a monarch legitimate *in their way*), and which confirmed their grandeur, their freedom from a royal proprietor, by commanding his adherence as well, the monarch's adherence to the officials' ideology.

The T'ang monarch who in the eighth century A.D. put the Taoist 'Five Classics' on the scholars' curriculum was doubtless showing some independence of Confucian authority in the examination sphere. But the very devising of a Taoist canon of 'Five Classics' was clearly a tribute to the Confucian Classics' prestige, and the Taoist canon, tentatively put forward as rival to the Confucian, was never supposed to supersede it. Just that, however, was what the Taipings' triple testament was meant to do. The Taiping examination, far from confirming a continuity of Confucianists and Taipings, marked a rupture with the past, the displacement of the Confucian intelligence.

4. THE TAIPING RELATION TO CONFUCIANISM

In the harshest of Taiping anti-Confucian writings, Confucius is questioned and whipped before God for his deception of mankind. His books are invidiously compared with the Taiping canon, which God is said to have handed down, free of error.[23] Such a purely anti-Confucian note was not sustained. But selective borrowings from Confucian materials commonly served only to enrich iconoclastic statements. 'T'ien-hsia (the empire, the world) is one family', 'Within the four seas all men are brothers' were statements whose antiquity the Taipings acknowledged while avowing them as their own. Yet these phrases, Confucian enough (though rather special), were adduced to support their Christian heresy: 'Your flesh is all flesh begotten by fathers and mothers, but your souls are begotten of God.'[24] Here, with this matter-spirit insinuation, we see (as in Hung Jen-kan's distinction between Taiping and classical hierarchies) a deprecation of the family.

Statements of Confucian universalism, then, were wrenched into the service of a very different, a Christian universalism (the preceding classical phrases were used in a proclamation entitled, 'Saving all God's Heaven-begotten, Heaven-nurtured children'). After declaring that God's love and his summons to bliss in heaven are available to all, all can become his sons and daughters through following his commandments, a Taiping prophet declares: 'In all the world under Heaven there shall be neither China nor barbarian (foreign) nation (*pu lun Chung-kuo fan-kuo*), neither male, nor female . . .'[25] This is 'neither Jew nor Greek' theology, and Confucianists, with their strong sense of history and culture—their own universalism bound up in the oecumenical pretensions of Chinese culture—could hardly accept this anti-historical Pauline version of universalism, with its disparagement of cultural significance.

There are words here which are words of Confucianists— *T'ien-hsia* (under Heaven), *fan-kuo* (barbarian country)—but the language is new. For while the Taipings might conclude that 'when *T'ien-hsia* is one family, *Chung-kuo* is one person',[26] Confucianists must deny this species of all-under-God equality, and take *fan-kuo* literally, as barbarian nations truly inferior to *Chung-kuo*. But the Taipings made *fan* a metaphor, with the neutral connotations of 'foreign' succeeding the primary sense of 'barbarian', inferior to China. '*Huang-shang-ti* in six days created heaven and earth and mountains and seas and men and things. *Chung-kuo* and *fan-kuo* were all together proceeding on this great road. However, each *fan-kuo* of the West has proceeded on this great road to the bottom, but *Chung-kuo*, after proceeding on this great road, then strayed on to the devil's road in the last one or two thousand years and was taken into the clutch of the daemon king of Hell.'[27] Here it is *China* which has fallen away from the highest value, while *fan* can have no offensive significance, since the *fan-kuo* have been loyal.

It has been noted[28] that the compound, *T'ai-p'ing*, comes from a text much studied in Hung Hsiu-ch'üan's home region, the *Kung-yang chuan*, key document of that Confucian reform movement which ran through scholars like Wei Yüan to its final phase in the school of K'ang Yu-wei. Just as *Kung-yang* reformers contended that China had abandoned its genuine ancient wisdom, so the Taipings insisted that in high antiquity there was only the 'true way', when the whole people worshipped God, *Huang-shang-ti*, and they culled Shang-ti references from the Classics.[29] But only the *Kung-yang* school, not the Taipings, were conceivably perpetuating the Confucian intelligence. The reformers were still Confucian enough to have their universalism begin with China; the world was held to be following a pattern of history discerned only by the prophetic Confucius. The Taipings, on the contrary, saw it as a universally shared revelation. To K'ang Yu-wei, China had fallen away from a truth, an idea of progress through history, which the Chinese sage propounded and which the West had only exemplified. To the Taipings, China had fallen away from a truth which the West had both *known* and accepted. Taipings averred, not China's particular reception of universal truth, but China's defection from the universal. And when they offered China a recovered sense of primacy, it was by exalting China as the setting of the newest revelation, elevating a contemporary Chinese to a new universal trinity.[30] Confucius, the master of the old, was not their sage, and Confucianism not the intelligence of the China they foresaw.

5. TAIPING EGALITARIANISM

Thus, though the influence of the *Kung-yang* school may have turned Taiping attention to the *Li-yün* section of the *Li-chi* (another favourite classical text of the school), the effect was not Confucian but despotically levelling in the Taipings' purest monarchical manner. A Taiping document calling all men brothers and all women sisters continued directly with, *Ta tao chih hsing yeh, T'ien-hsia wei kung*—in Legge's translation from the *Li-chi*, 'When the Grand Course was pursued, a public and common spirit ruled all under the sky.'[31] This same Taiping document which dwells on the *kung*, the public, explains the equality as deriving from the (strictly non-Confucian) universal fatherhood of God,[32] and another document, declaring that the Heavenly Father wants no inequalities, goes on to say: 'The *T'ien-hsia* is all God's one great family, the *T'ien-hsia*'s population does not receive private property.'[33] It has been remarked clearly that this levelling sentiment ran counter to the traditional vertical 'five relationships' and the 'five constant virtues'.[34]

An intelligence report on the Taipings to Tseng Kuo-fan noted the long background in Chinese history of heterodox *chiao*, religions, and their relations to class disturbances. Most recently the *T'ien-chu chiao* (Lord of Heaven religion, Christianity), repressed by officials, changed names from *chiao* to *hui*. After the English barbarians were soothed, the disobedient people of the southeast coast became more and more violent. Hung Hsiu-ch'üan and others consolidated some of the bandit *hui*, beginning as the *Shang-ti hui*, then changing the name to *T'ien-ti hui* (in either of two homophonous compounds, meaning, respectively, 'Emperor of Heaven Society' and 'Increase Younger Brothers Society'; the *T'ien-ti* of the 'Heaven and Earth Society', that *alter ego* of the Triads, does not appear in this account, but it is certainly suggestive concerning the Taipings' entanglement with the secret societies). Initiates paid no heed to seniority, and for this reason they were all 'younger brothers' thereafter.[35]

Here, in this Aesopian language of interchangeable parts, is the Taiping identification of an anti-Confucian acceptance of a transcendental God with an anti-hierarchical (hence anti-Confucian) social system. And it is linked with a feeling for monarchical supremacy which recalls the conventional straining of monarchy against hierarchical, immanentist Confucianism. 'Men should know', ran a Taiping hymn, 'that *ching-t'ien*, the reverence due to Heaven, is superior to *hsiao-ch'in*, filial obligations to parents.'[36] We can almost hear the Yung-cheng emperor here, *contra* the Sung Confucianist, Ou-yang Hsiu, insisting that an official 'gives himself to his prince, and can no longer consider himself as belonging to his father and mother'.[37] We hear him again in the voice of Hung Jen-kan, attacking 'faction', Yung-cheng's particular target. The Taiping, like the Ch'ing, rules that *p'eng-tang*, factions, cannot exist, for the *kuan* are attached to the court, as officials committed to serving the public interest, not a private one, and they must not make alliances among themselves. For a sovereign is to his ministers as a general to his subordinates: if the underlings combined, they would impair the sovereign's power.[38]

Taipings, however, were not the men to admit that a Ch'ing emperor united power with the public interest. A Taiping document proclaiming God's universal ownership excoriated the Manchus: 'The *T'ien-hsia* is *Shang-ti*'s, not the *Hu-lu*'s, the despicable northerners'.[39] Taipings saw the

Ch'ing dynasty—and any dynasty so Confucianized that it could not acknowledge, 'The earth is the Lord's' . . . as *ssu*, not *kung*, private, not public. The Taipings were no more just simple monarchists straining against a Confucian bureaucracy which nevertheless influenced them, than they were simple Confucianists, straining against a monarchy which nevertheless patronized them. This rising against Confucianists as parasites was a rising, too, against the imperial system, that traditional monarchy which, whatever its own public-private tensions with the same Confucianists, could never break them in the Taiping spirit, as the purely private purveyors of a dead intelligence—*purely* private just because the intelligence was dead.

6. PSYCHOLOGICAL REPERCUSSIONS OF THE PECULIAR TAIPING ASSAULT

Faced with a common foe, Confucianism and monarchy kept their relationship but lost their tension; the attack on both together fused their interests and thereby changed their character. The new character was one in which, ultimately, the *Chinese* associations of both Confucianism and the imperial system were stressed—Chinese, as distinct from the alien creeds and systems whose mounting influence in modern China was prefigured in the Taipings. 'Internal barbarians', the culturally heretical Taipings, had to be put down in the name of Confucian culture for *all* Chinese; Confucianism could not be acknowledged as just the weapon of a class. And external barbarians, the culturally alien westerners, had to be resisted in the name of Confucian culture for all *Chinese*. It could no longer be really conceived of as culture for the world—*T'ien-hsia*, the world as well as 'the Empire'.

For the fact that, within, Taipings had to be reckoned with meant that, without, western nations were not really barbarian any more (which is just what the Taipings implied, when they metaphorized *fan*, 'barbarian', to the morally neutral 'foreign'). Westerners, that is, could no longer be deemed barbarians in the old sense, men, perhaps recalcitrant, who yet conceivably aspired to Confucian culture, men who were potentially Chinese though handicapped by distance from the centre of the world. Instead, they were genuine rivals, able, obviously, to pose cultural alternatives even to Chinese; for they had made the Taipings, *and hence the Confucianists*, culturally equivocal. And so the demands of Chinese identity, not the claim of universality, came to dominate the world of Chinese thought and institutions. All tension spent, a twentieth-century Confucianism, entangled with monarchy in a 'national spirit' traditionalism, departed from the original, the tension-ridden tradition, to which it yearned back.

It must be said again: Confucianism ceased to tense against monarchy because the Taipings stabbed it at the point ('Heaven') where the tension expressed itself. It was this that made the Taipings irredeemable foes. Taiping religion, in its transcendentalist attack on Confucian 'T'ien-ming' immanence, denied Confucianism just where it declared its peculiar freedom, where the Confucian official refused to concede the monarch's right to make him a tool; Confucian 'Heaven' belonged in a culture which elevated the amateur. But Taiping 'Heaven' blotted out the amateur ideal, and in two ways. For Taiping Christianity was a harbinger of science, which menaced Confucian amateurs culturally, just as Taiping Christianity (with its *Shang-ti* versus *T'ien*) menaced Confucian amateurs politically. The values of science (see Volume One) were specialist, impersonal, anti-traditionalist—everything incompatible with the purport of Confucianism. And so, in relation not only to power but to cultural tone, Taiping religion beat against Confucianism. The religion was shattered, but it made its impression.

In the twentieth century, anti-Confucian advocates of science have often been anti-Christian as well. Christianity, taken as the adversary of science, seemed to them a kind of ballast to throw out, to right the national balance when Confucianism, as the victim of science, had also been dismissed. But, for the Taipings, anti-Confucian without tears, Christianity seemed the ally of science against Confucian culture, not the fellow-victim of science, paired with

Confucianism. Hung Jen-kan denounced idolatry and related superstitions, and he offered Christianity as the antidote. He rejected the worship of wood and stone on the grounds of its connection with wrong-headed judgments like this: 'When there is sickness they do not call it disequilibrium of blood and "ch'i", but call it a calamity made by daemons.'[40] The medical doctrine was quaint, but the premise was naturalistic. Thus, because idolatrous superstition seemed a foe they shared ('my enemy's enemy . . .') transcendentalist religion commended science (of a sort) to the Taipings. And science, under Christian auspices or any other, was out of harmony with Confucianism—like the Taiping brand of monarchy under (a sort of) Christianity.

A taste for science meant a taste for western technology. This meant, in turn, that Taiping approval of western techniques (along with religious motifs) might implant a successor to Confucian values, not just a material supplement. And this accounts for the heavy late-Confucian investment in the *Chineseness* of Confucianism, eternal and inexpungeable and admitting of no successor, even when—naturally when— Confucian 'self-strengtheners' themselves were selling some of the pass to the West. It was not the West solely in itself that wrought a change in the essence of Confucianism; it was the West at one remove, seen through the dark glass of Taiping ideology. For that showed the threat of apostasy within the Chinese world, and heightened the passion (while warping the credo) of the true Confucian believer.

In short, when the Taipings attacked Confucian bureaucracy as intellectually hollow, more than just socially corrupt, the attack proceeded from a self-confirming premise. For the Taipings defected from Ch'ing (an action which, by itself, Confucianists could contemplate) in a spirit that flouted Confucianists as well. And because the Taipings were, not foreign assailants, but Chinese, Confucianism became *just* Chinese, like the monarchy—too much alike for the two to sustain each other, in a Chinese world narrower now than Confucianism assumed.

If Confucianism was forced into this condition, in which it lost its standing as the creative intelligence of Chinese society, and yet remained on high with the gentry-officials—what was it? Whatever it had been before, the Taipings' vision made it what they saw, ideology, its character as general idea yielding to the idea of its class character. Confucianism was compromised by the rebellion, which made it seem the cultural cloak of gentry domination, interposed against iconoclastic, nationalistic levellers. Class analysis of Confucianism was a communist inheritance from the Taipings.

The Taipings' chances for victory in their own day, as traditional rebels, were spoiled by their proto-revolutionary novelty; Confucianists were still vital enough to make their alienation from the Taiping cause fatal to it. But because of what the alienation exacted of Confucianism, Confucian vitality was drained at last, and revolution came. It took time, almost a century, for this to happen conclusively. The 1860s 'T'ung-chih Restoration' of hopeful monarchy and Confucian bureaucracy was still 'traditional'. It was not yet traditionalistic and abortive, like the mediaevalist Restoration of the 'Ultras' in France after Napoleon's fall (and Louis XVIII's death)—or the restorations in the Chinese Republican era.[41] The very violence of the Rebellion, the terrible wounds it dealt society, obscured, at first, the Confucian fate. Just because the Taipings had so ruthlessly challenged Confucianism, the latter could still be taken as an antidote, the age-old concentrate of civilization, to be swallowed again after the sickening years of anarchy. For a while, it was helpful to Confucianism to be *not* something— Taiping and outlandish. For another while, it was mildly helpful to be something—familiarly Chinese, not western.

But a body of thought, finally, has to command intellectual assent. Confucianism had to have meaningful applications, not just pleasant associations. Already thin, it has been blown over by the communist revolutionaries, who followed the Taipings in relegating Confucianism historically to a class, thus stripping it intellectually of general authority. It was not doctrine that the communists owed to the Taipings; that came straight from Marxist sources. But the doctrine reflected the Taipings'. And it was able to reflect it because the Taipings did enough damage to make the analysis plausible. As the new society measured work, Confucianists were failing to labour even with their minds. The Taiping indictment had conjured up the basis for their charge.

7. THE DIVORCE BETWEEN CONFUCIANISM AND BUREAU-CRATIC ACTION

From the 1860s on, Confucian-western syncretisms began to fill intellectual life. Though these were in the province of reformers, not anti-Confucian revolutionaries, they drastically diluted Confucianism's authority—in spite of, and because of, the syncretists' insistence that Confucian learning was the core of Chinese being. The old *nei-wai* tension, inner and outer, vanished from within Confucianism when Confucianism *en bloc* became *nei* and *t'i*, inner essence, the Chinese learning which 'western' learning should 'supplement'.[42]

And this very transformation that made Confucianism intellectually banal, all inner instead of inner-outer, made it socially ineffective. It became more and more a fetish for sentimentalists, something removed from the field of bureaucratic action—and thus not only lacking the intra-Confucian tension, but lacking, too, in consequence, external tension with monarchy. Confucianism's relation with officialdom (while imperial China lasted, and any relation lasted) came to consist of officials' concern to defend Confucianism, from the outside, as it were. This was vastly different from the authentic relation, where bureaucratic action was presumed to be inferred from Confucianism itself.

Along with the dilution of Confucian authority in the wider world, there went an inflation of Confucius' authority within Confucianism. This was no less enfeebling. The *Kung-yang* school, last of the Confucian schools, tried to provide reformist Confucian social correctives where the Taipings were revolutionary and heretical. It ended up with a Confucius so mystically prophetic, so little the guide to practical statecraft, that its proponents, appropriately, lost their bureaucratic tie and finished as politically impoverished fantasts, lacking the old institutional basis for Confucian-monarchical tension. Liao P'ing (1852–1932), envisaging his

T'ai-p'ing age, in the *Kung-yang* prophetic vein, as the time when men might levitate,[43] brought a fitting, futile denouement to the classically earthbound, socially 'engaged', politically embroiled Confucian tradition. Bureaucracy continued—though sputtering—in the late Ch'ing and Republic, but with less and less connection with Confucianism.

When the examination system was abolished in 1905, Confucian learning became pure indeed, no longer useful in a regular way for official qualifications. But Confucianism needed the dross of involvement, the examination tie, in spite of the risk of formula and rote. Of course, the idea of the non-government scholar was an old one. But voluntary retirement, in earlier times, was often still conceivably a political act. In the healthy, Han Yü type of Confucian tradition, the point of retirement was to criticize government by abstention and so improve it. But in the twentieth century, even before the monarchy fell (and a sure sign that it would stay fallen), the Confucianist out of office took his learning with him, while the Confucianist still in office did his learning on his own time. This was more than non-participation—it was the end of the Confucian tie between knowledge and action, Confucian knowledge (*t'i*) and official action (*yung*). The old order was not being renewed. Deprived of the outlet in action, the knowledge itself was not the same.

The post-Confucian communist autocracy has a bureaucratic instrument; but when Confucianism was a live intelligence, the Confucian bureaucracy was never a dead tool. The communist cadre is only a worker, replaceable at any moment (Lenin: *The State and Revolution*),[44] instead of being the superior man, who is 'not a utensil' (Confucius: *Lun-yü*, 'The Analects'). True, both these pretensions sound a little hollow, given the facts. Confucian bureaucrats, after all, were often made utensils and were easily replaced; communist bureaucrats have to strain to keep their humilities from slipping. But these are not the only facts. Official pretensions are facts, too, and they will not permit distinctions to be blurred. Confucianists and communists do not come out identical. Taipings (and other moderns) did not fail to leave their marks.

Today, Chinese bureaucracy cannot be self-centred in the old ambiguous Confucian way. In the Han dynasty, Confucianism was 'established' by the state. Now Marxism is established—but not in the spirit of *concession*. For the state now has what would-be Legalist monarchs in the old days lacked, technological means for concentrating power. And this same modern technology that builds up politically the Legalist element of the old amalgam, breaks down culturally the Confucian element.

In the contemporary scene, with the new technology at the government's disposal, no private power, like aristocracy, can parallel the sovereign as a frame for a vital centre, a privileged and trammelled bureaucracy, which radiates to both. And the new bureaucracy, unlike the old—the professional scientism of the new diverging sharply from the non-specialized humanism of the old—can hardly dwell on itself as the end and joy of man's desiring.

Part Four

THE VESTIGE
OF SUGGESTIVENESS:
CONFUCIANISM AND
MONARCHY AT THE
LAST (II)

CHAPTER IX

The Making of an Anachronism

I. THE NAME AND NATURE OF REVOLUTION

BUREAUCRACY without Confucianism—Confucianism without bureaucracy—Confucianism's intellectual content had profoundly altered. When a school of thought persists outside its familiar matrix, does this prove its vitality or its emptiness? Burckhardt, referring to Orthodox Christianity after the fall of the Byzantine Empire, which had been so intimately bound up with it, left this question open.[1] With Confucianism, it seems, the issue is less in doubt. For revolution had at last intervened in modern Chinese history, putting an end to bureaucracy's long imperviousness to the *ko-ming*, mandate-changing, of the old monarchical system. And the literal meaning of Confucian language was shaken.

When revolution came in 1911 and 1912, establishing the Republic, its participants called it *ko-ming*. But was it the same old term? It seems rather a translation back into Chinese, as it were, of the modern Japanese *kakumei* (the Japanese reading of the *ko-ming* characters) which had used the 'mandate' characters metaphorically to convey the idea of revolution. It could have been nothing but metaphor in Japan, where a monarchist theory stressing descent, not heavenly election, genealogical qualifications, not moral ones, had never been Confucian.

For the primordial heroes in Confucian myth are men, not gods or descendants of gods; but the Japanese myth begins with the sun-goddess and her Japanese warrior-offspring. Thus a Chinese monarch is legitimate when he repeats the example of sage-kings of independent lineage, while a Japanese monarch is legitimate when he descends from divinity, which bequeaths his line eternity; *his* mandate is irrevocable. Only for China was Tung Chung-shu, the great Han Confucianist, really comprehensible: 'Therefore, with royalty, there is the *name* of changing régimes, there is not the *fact* of revising the Tao.'[2] The really eternal Way, that is, underlies kingship, not any particular line of kings.

Joseph de Maistre, the French Restoration royalist and ultramontane, had a quite non-Confucian transcendental religious standpoint: kings were related to God through Popes, who were entrusted by God with the education of sovereigns. And de Maistre had the Japanese, non-Chinese, reliance on genealogy. He held the Confucian-sounding opinion that in order to reign it is necessary to be already royal. Yet, de Maistre had in mind no Confucian rectification of names, no Chinese sort of suggestion that a merely *politically* legitimate king might be morally illegitimate. Like the Japanese, he made political legitimacy central, and believed that royal qualities depended on royal birth:[3] Any force that supplanted in power a genealogically qualified monarch was the force of revolution, with no legitimate 'change of mandate' about it. Thus, change of mandate, which a Chinese Confucianist could contemplate with equanimity, as a perpetuation of legitimacy, could not be reconciled with monarchical systems like European or Japanese, where the moralism of an immanent Heaven-concept paled before the inherited right of the transcendentally graced. One of the most highly esteemed of Ming writings published in Japan (Hsieh Chao-chi [chin-shih 1593], *Wu tsa tsu* ['The Five Assorted Vessels', there being five sections, on heaven, earth, man, objects, and events]) had its passages from Mencius deleted; as a modern scholar explains it, the *ko-ming* conception was thought inappropriate to the Japanese form of state.[4] (It is noteworthy that in China, too, in Ming times, Mencius was expurgated—by the founding monarch, Hung-wu, who also felt a dynast's revulsion from moralistic restraints.)[5]

Ko-ming, then, had no natural place in the Japanese

vocabulary as long as its literal Confucian sense, which was nonsense in Japan, was the only sense it had. But when modern Japan, in her foreign borrowings, moved from Chinese to western influences, and enlarged her vocabulary to encompass western ideas, the *ko-ming* compound had enough flavour of sharp political break to be assigned the meaning of revolution. Modern Chinese enlarged their vocabulary in their turn, and found in the modern Japanese language a repository of modern terms in characters. When they reached for 'revolution', they took *ko-ming*, and made the same transformation, from literal to figurative. Sun Yat-sen accepted himself as leader of a *ko-ming tang* only when (1895) in a flash of revelation of new meaning in the old term, he read in a Kobe newspaper that that was what he was: 'We saw the characters "Chung-kuo ko-ming tang Sun Yat-sen". . . . Hitherto our cast of mind had been such as to consider *ko-ming* something applying to the will to act as emperor, with our movement only to be considered as rebelling against this. From the time we saw this newspaper, we had the picture of the three characters *ko-ming tang* imprinted on our minds.'[6]

And not just Sun, who favoured revolution, but avowed traditionalists acknowledged by their usage that *ko-ming* had been captured by the moderns. In 1913, after the republican deluge, a follower of K'ang Yu-wei related *ko-ming* to Cromwell, the French Revolution, Belgian, Italian, and Swiss risings, and noted with Confucian disgust that in those *ko-ming* sons attacked their brothers and parents.[7] K'ang himself, in the same year, made an even more interesting acknowledgement of a metaphorical turning. He wrote that a '*T'ang Wu ko-ming*' (i.e., change of mandate in the Hsia-to-Shang and Shang-to-Chou fashion) was an ordinary thing in China. This was to change a dynasty's mandate, to *ko* a dynasty's *ming*. How different it was from *ko*-ing the age-old *ming* of China! Now, with the founding of the Republic, there was cultural *ko-ming*, the overthrow of historical political principles, laws, customs, morality, and the national soul: a great disaster.[8] And K'ang might have added, on his own showing, the overthrow of traditional meanings. For he accepted *ko-ming* as applying now, with an air of sad finality, to something apart from a dynasty's virtue—to the nation's very 'essence'.

It was not only the *ko-ming* which had changed its connotation. When Sun accepted the *tang*, too (as in *Ko-ming tang*, or 'Revolutionary Party'), he was talking revolution figuratively as well as literally. For the connotations of *tang* were really anti-ideological in the old monarchical world. The associations of *p'eng-tang*, 'friends' ' *tang*, personal clique or faction, were hard to shake. But *tang* now, as 'party', a modern political vehicle (or so it was hoped) for men who intended to break an old consensus, was a transformed concept—like its fellow, *ko-ming*, whose transformation had made it into nothing less than the call for transformation.

The phrase was not stripped of its old associations, its historical depth was recognized. But this very recognition reduced an ancient Confucian concept to something quaint and 'period'. For a modern, to say that Hsüan-t'ung 'lost the mandate' in 1911 was to strive with conscious anachronism for allusive effect. Once-serious Confucian content was turned into rhetoric.

The plain fact was that when *ko-ming* finished the Ch'ing it was Chinese ousting Manchus, not dynasty ousting dynasty— hence, it was Republic ousting Empire, in revolution, not in 'mandate' continuity. What could be more republican, more revolutionary, than the nationalists' slogan in late imperial times, 'fan Ch'ing fu Han', 'oppose the Ch'ing, restore the Chinese'[9]—not 'fan *Man* (Manchu) fu Han', which would have been a consistent ethnic confrontation in a more traditional age, or 'fan Ch'ing fu *Ming*', for a similar balance of dynasties. Instead of these, 'Ch'ing' (a dynasty) stood for 'Man' (a people), and the Chinese monarchical name, though culturally earned, was no protection against the ethno-national emphasis of Chinese anti-monarchists.

The violently anti-Manchu Chang Ping-lin (1868–1936), for all his cultural conservatism (see Volume One), was a republican opponent of the Ch'ing. 'Sweeping out the Manchus,' he wrote in Sun's organ, *Min-pao* (#16), 'is sweeping out the aggressor race; sweeping out Ch'ing rule is sweeping out the royal sway.'[10] There was no help for monarchy; its mystique was waning with its feeble last exponents.

Yang Tu, the foremost among Yüan Shih-k'ai's 'six martyrs', had once, without turning republican, turned away from the pro-Ch'ing *Pao-huang hui* (Protect-the-emperor society) of K'ang Yu-wei. Yang Tu sought a 'chen-ming T'ien-tzu', a son of Heaven with the true mandate.[11] But it was too late for that. He found, incredibly, Yüan Shih-k'ai. And Yüan, the Hung-hsien Emperor, buckling on his virtue where the Ch'ing had dropped it, denying the anti-traditional purport of the republicans' *ko-ming*, was an anachronism, a farceur, a period piece come to life. There was travesty, not just mis-statement, in this paean to his glory: '. . . Now the hundred names in swelling chorus sing the virtue of the (raised characters) monarch. His ministers (legs and arms) are upright and good. The general state of affairs is tranquillity and peace.'[12]

It was a starved life and it had to be. The royal latecomer was forced to look back to a sacred past, in which his brand of traditionalism and his Confucian supporters', unfortunately, was not prefigured, and in which Confucian support for monarchy, anyway, was not so straightforward. How could 'the spirit of the people', the basis of traditionalism for modern monarchists and modern Confucianists, have any place in the earlier Chinese complex, in which a foreign dynasty, patently unassimilable to the 'spirit' of the Chinese people, was always, nevertheless, an orthodox possibility? And where was the old tension between literati-Confucian traditionalism and essentially Legalist, anti-traditionalist dynastic monarchy, whether Chinese or foreign? In the great imperial ages some Confucian ideals, sacrificed in practice to the need for accommodation with the throne, had remained in force implicitly as restraints on imperial power, while *mutatis mutandis*, the same may be said on the other side. But now, revolutionaries were occasionally helping themselves to some of the old Confucian specifics against the pretensions of the throne; Yao and Shun, for example, once Confucian exhibits of virtue *versus* mere imperial descent, could now be the pride of democrats, as anti-dynastic.[13] And therefore such moral checks, after such a revolutionary take-over, had to be relinquished by surviving Confucian monarchists (though not by Confucianists who were defeatist about monarchy and tried to make a place in the Republic).[14] Now the old tension was released. Yet it was a release that brought only the rest of death, as a wraith-like monarchy and a wraith-like Confucianism faded into a final association, untroubled at last by each other, but untroubled, also, by very much of life.

2. FORM AND CONTENT

Thus, the apparent emptiness of the Chinese Republic did nothing for monarchy. The monarchical symbols were just as thoroughly drained, and this in itself reminds us that the new form of republican China was not only form but content. The Republic was really new, and *sui generis* in Chinese history—no matter what may be said, sceptically, about a carry-over of the Ch'ing system, with only the titles changed.[15]

A Confucianist in 1918, trying to make a home for Confucius in the Republic, depended on such an assertion that only names were changing. The *chün-ch'en* (prince-minister) relation, he soothingly observed, was simply a general formula to give the state a head. *Ta huang-ti* (Emperor) or *Ta tsung-t'ung* (President), what did it matter? There was still, under the Republic, a valid field for eternal Confucian relationships.[16] But the reasoning is circular: the form of state is inessential, Republic equals Empire, because the sole essential is Confucian content, which underlies inconsequential form. Or—Confucianism is central because it is central; if Confucianism were known to be lost, Confucianists could hardly maintain that 'only form' had changed.

The institution of monarchy was of just as much consequence as the philosophy (or religion) of Confucianism. When monarchy was literally lost, it was not figuratively regained. The early republican period should not be viewed as just one more warlord pendant to an imperial era, with the Nanking government of Chiang Kai-shek as the Ch'in or Sui, type of abortive régime, uniting the Empire and preparing the way for a more lasting dynasty.[17] If, by traditional standards, the Hung-hsien movement was monarchical in form only (because its justifications and associations had to be new), the Republic could not be monarchical 'in all but form'.

The swift descent from revolution to a politics of faction made the Republic seem meaningless. But the expectation of meaning, even though disappointed, supplied meaning. It signified that the world of cliques, the accepted, familiar world of Confucian politics, was at last unacceptable—no longer just to emperors, but to new men from below. For new culture, with the Republic its symbol, was dissolving the familiar Confucianism; and there was a new political order, even if honoured solely in the breach.

Radical depreciation of the significance of 'form' in comparison with 'content' (a depreciation involved in suggestions that things are 'really' the same as ever in what is merely formally the Republican era in Chinese history) is both trite and misleading. If form has any 'mereness', it is not in its unimportance when it changes; it is in its failure to hold a specific content when it, form, remains the same. The forces which revised the content of monarchy likewise made the Republic more than superficially new. *Plus c'est la même chose, plus ça change:* if Yüan Shih-k'ai was a parodist as Emperor, he was not 'in essence' Emperor as President.

What was really involved in Yüan's effort to reinstate *ch'en* as the word for 'official' in his reign? There was the simple fact of its monarchical affinities, of course: there were the classic pairs of *chün* and *ch'en*, prince and minister, a relationship found in such famous catalogues as the *Tso-chuan*'s 'six *shun*' and 'ten *li*', the *Li-chi*'s 'ten *i*' and 'seven *chiao*';[18] and *wang* and *ch'en*, monarch and minister, bound together as firmly as the *Ch'un-ch'iu* and *Tso-chuan*, for of the two reputed authors, when Confucius was called a *su-wang*, Tso Ch'iu-ming was a *su-ch'en*.[19] But there was something more deeply significant about *ch'en* than any merely verbal associations. It was something relating not just to monarchy but to the cultural air of Confucian, imperial China, so that its banishment from the Republic (and consequently, Yüan's effort to restore it) symbolized a genuine change of social and intellectual climate.

Kuan, the Republic's term for official which Yüan wished to displace, was a very old one, too, but in the pre-Republican Confucian bureaucratic world it had a sense quite distinguishable from *ch'en*. *Kuan* denoted the bureaucrat in his technical, functional, impersonal capacity. It had no connection with personal cultural dignity and individuality. For example, *kuan-t'ien*, set apart from *min-t'ien* in the Ming tax system,[20] was not 'officials' land', the land of officials as persons; it was 'official land', i.e., public land as opposed to private. *Kuan* suggests the state apparatus and *min*, here, the private sector. If 'people' and 'official' were being counterposed as human types, 'official' would be *ch'en*.

For the outstanding attribute of *ch'en* (and this made it a 'grander' word) was personal status, free of technical, professional connotations. Not the task but the personal tie defined him: 'The loyal *ch'en* does not serve two princes.'[21] An official was *kuan* in his job, something akin to being a tool, a means—and *ch'en* in his position, an end.

One of the outstanding, all-pervasive values of Confucian culture, as we have seen, was its anti-professionalism. The Confucian ideal of personal cultivation was a humanistic amateurism, and Confucian education, perhaps supreme in the world for anti-vocational classicism, produced an imperial bureaucracy, accordingly, in which human relations counted for more than the network of abstract assignments (just as in Confucian society generally, human relations counted for more than legal relations). In these respects—not by accident—it differed from bureaucracies of the modern industrial West and, at least in conception, from that of the Chinese Republic. A comparison of the Ch'ing dynasty's *mu-liao* or *mu-yu* and the Republic's *k'o-chang mi-shu* may be illustrative. All these designations, on both sides of the great divide, applied to the private secretary-advisers of administrative heads. There was nothing fundamentally dissimilar in their roles, but there was a great difference in their relationships with their respective seniors and in their legal positions: the Republic's secretary-adviser was formally an official (*kuan-li*); his Ch'ing counter-part was the official's friend and technically not attached to the *pu*, the office, or paid from the public granaries.[22] As Chang Chien, a modern-minded industrialist (and later one of Yüan's supporters, though with misgivings and out of old friendship, not out of archaism) caustically observed, all Ch'ing officials, provincial and local, could appoint their own assistants, as in the Han and T'ang *mu-chih*, government by staffs of intimates.[23]

The Republican emphasis on *kuan*, then, to the exclusion of *ch'en*, was the mark of a specifically modern commitment, to a professionalized, anti-literati world in which science, industry, and the idea of progress (all of them having impersonal, hence un-Confucian, implications) claimed first attention. This was not just the preference of a faction. It was really the world which for some time had been making over and taking over China, not only manufacturing icono-clasts but transforming traditionalists. The *ch'en*, the non-specialized free man of high culture as the master-creation of civilization, who relegated to the *kuan* category the 'jobs', the 'business' of government (necessary even in the old régime, of course, but faintly unsavoury, more the price paid than the prize won with prestige), was a figure of the irredeemable past. The Republic of *kuan* meant a genuine change from the Empire of *kuan* and *ch'en*.

The Empire dissolved in *ko-ming*. *Ko-ming*, itself drained of its traditional literal meaning and metaphorized into modern 'revolution', freed men's minds and made them aware of the changing content of Chinese civilization. Chinese imperial forms became anachronisms. And *ch'en*, one of them, had its meaning changed like the *ko-ming* that had destroyed its proper world.

For *ch'en*, as was earlier suggested, had been paired not only with *kuan*, but in the Ch'ing dynasty with *nu*, 'slave'. *Nu* was the term for Manchu officials, relating them to the Ch'ing as Manchu monarchs, while the Ch'ing as Chinese emperors left Chinese officials the Confucian status of *ch'en*, in the classically noble relationship of minister to throne. Revolutionary republicanism, however, extended the application of the term 'slave', and in this way, too, marked the obliteration of the world of *ch'en*. By doctrinaire republicans, 'slave' was stripped of its literal, technical significance (which it had had for the Manchu officials, who were *nu* in a juridical sense, for all that their use of the term may seem to be simple etiquette) and made expressive, metaphorically, of all subjects of supreme monarchs. As the republican minister, Wu T'ing-fang, put it in 1912, in a placatory cable to Mongol princes, all had suffered the bitterness of slaves under the Ch'ing crown—Chinese, Manchus, Mongols, Moslems, Tibetans—and all would be brothers in the one great republic.[24] From the republican standpoint, then, to have been *ch'en* was not to have distinguished oneself from slaves but to have been a slave. For there was no *ch'en* without his *wang* or *chün*, no Confucian gentleman outside a realm—at least an ideal one, however much the real one may have strained against Confucianism. (Confucianists *had* required the Empire, even if they execrated Ch'in Shih Huang-ti.) *Ko-ming* as change of mandate would have struck off *nu* (Manchu officials) and left *ch'en* (Chinese officials) in a continuing imperial bureaucracy. But the *ko-ming* revolution, anti-imperial in more than form, retroactively confounded *ch'en* and *nu*, struck them off together, and in this alone set a seal on the end of the Empire.

Nevertheless, just as for Mao Tse-tung and his régime today, so for Yüan Shih-k'ai in his lifetime (and the same issue is at stake: changing content behind changing form, or not?), some contemporaries saw analogies with the old monarchical past. A Japanese observer in 1914, Sakamaki Teiichirō, fixed Yüan as the Wang Mang in a late version of the fall of the Former Han. Yüan, as rumour had it, was implicated in the death of the Emperor Kuang-hsü (1908), just as Wang Mang was involved in the murder of the Emperor P'ing. Subsequently, Yüan's manoeuvre to transfer power from the young successor of Kuang-hsü to himself was exactly the story of Wang Mang and the Emperor P'ing's successor. Yüan's *Chung hua min-kuo*, to sum up, stood in the same relation to regular dynastic history as the *Hsin-kuo* of Wang Mang.[25]

That was what Ch'ing loyalists thought, too—Yüan was a Wang Mang or a Ts'ao Ts'ao, depending on whether one cursed him with a Former Han or a Latter Han analogy. Yüan himself was conscious of the sinister parallel which the public was tempted to draw. In late 1911, with an open acknowledgement of the Han reference sure to be in the mind of any Chinese with a spot of malice in his historical sensitivity, Yüan had pledged himself to protect 'the infant and the widow' (P'u-i and his Empress-dowager mother): the popular designation of the last unfortunates of the Former Han. He later maintained (while trying to quash premature rumours of his ultimate ambition) that the Ch'ing had offered to yield in his favour when the revolution began, but that he was not the sort of man to violate the canons of *jen* and *i*.[26]

Two of Yüan's puppets (one of them his 'sworn brother' Hsü Shih-ch'ang, who had been brought up by Yüan's great-uncle, Yüan Chia-san) became 'Grand Guardians of the Emperor' in November, 1911, after the Prince Regent retired.[27] Suspicion grew that Yüan, in imperial fashion, was easing out the Ch'ing. There is a note of innuendo in some of Sun Yat-sen's expressions in late January, 1912, when Yüan was proceeding, in sweet independence of the Nanking Kuomintang, to set up a government in Peking, a city Sun feared for its imperial associations.[28] 'No one knows whether this provisional government is to be monarchical or republican,' said Sun on January 20. 'Yüan not only specifically injures the Republic, but is in fact an enemy of the Ch'ing emperor,' said Wu T'ing-fang, at Sun's direction, on January 28.[29] By 1913, though Yüan had crowned the occasion of the Ch'ing abdication in February 1912 with a statement that monarchy would never again function in China[30] (and Sun himself, whistling past the graveyard, had echoed this assurance as he yielded the president's office to Yüan),[31] Sun was sure that Yüan was imperial as well as imperious. The very term 'Second Revolution' for the Kiangsi rising in the summer of that year had anti-monarchical overtones, and Sun's provocative public cable to a number of addressees, on July 18, read Yüan out of the Republic, right back to the ranks of Chinese absolute monarchs. Public servants, said Sun, should be subject to the people's approval. This was the case even in constitutional monarchies—how much more should it be so in a republic.[32]

3. VESTIGIAL MONARCHIES AND THE MEANING OF JAPANESE SPONSORSHIP

Yet, despite the pedantic or polemical impulses of the moment which moved men to interpret Yüan's republic as a monarchical régime, Yüan himself knew that his republic was not his empire—knew it emotionally, at the level of desire for an emperor's baubles and trappings, and knew it intellectually, at the level of tactics, in his grasp of the need to shift his base of support. Nationalism, with its iconoclastic implications, was the Republic's grain of novelty. As at least the ostensible exponent of the nation's cause against Japan in the 1915 crisis of the 'Twenty-one Demands', Yüan, the president, had the most solid public support of his life. But immediately thereafter Yüan was a would-be emperor, and he tried to feel his way to Japanese support. It was a logical effort. He was searching for something to replace the nationalists' backing. For this had been available to him as a nationalistic president, but it would necessarily be withdrawn from a traditionalistic emperor.

Yüan failed to get useful Japanese help. He had first come to Japanese attention, after all, as the main defender of the Chinese interest in Korea in the 1880s and early 1890s, and subsequently he was assumed to be playing off Westerners (or playing their game) against Japan. He was thus too old a foe of Japanese diplomacy to be rehabilitated in that quarter overnight, and his imperial chances, it was soon apparent, were too dim to convert him at the last into a likely protégé. Given the Japanese aims in China, and Yüan's reputation and self-advertisement, for so many years, as China's strong man, Japanese leaders naturally found their habit of hostility to Yüan hard to break. Certainly, to the extent that Chinese opposition to Yüan might lead to anti-national regionalist fragmentation, the care and feeding of his opponents was at least plausible for Japan.[33]

It was not surprising, then, that Japanese 'volunteers', including officers who had 'resigned their commissions', should have made contact with the anti-Yüan southern forces at the time of the 'Second Revolution', in 1913,[34] and that a Japanese newspaper in Peking, under the protection of extraterritoriality, should openly oppose Yüan's imperial adventure.[35] Officially, several times in late 1915 and early 1916 the Japanese government, in concert with other powers and by itself, advised at least postponement. Chauvinist elements, like the *Kokuryūkai* (Amur River ['Black Dragon'] Society), resented especially what they saw as Yüan's obstructionism in the affair of the 'Twenty-one Demands', his false propaganda to curry domestic favour, his swollen 'hate Japan, love America' feeling. And spokesmen for 'East Asian principles' did not fail to indict Yüan for his breach of Confucian ethics in stabbing the Ch'ing, dishonouring his commitment, throwing in his lot with revolutionaries.[36] Such men were not disposed to let him ride with tradition. To Japanese idealists of a certain type, Yüan as strong man seemed immoral. In more matter-of-fact appraisals, he seemed inconvenient.

Yet Yüan as emperor, by his forfeiture of the support of modern-minded nationalists, actually had potentialities as China's weak man. He might have been exploitable by expansionist Japan, since he needed aid to make himself strong enough to survive, and, once surviving, to recognize his debt. Japanese support of Chinese monarchy would bring Japan at least a minority backing, minor enough to need Japan to protect its cause in China, not major enough to threaten Japan with Chinese independence. Japanese who looked on China as empty of vitality and devoid of national feeling (as many did in 1916, more than were able to later) might think this solicitude for Chinese monarchism unnecessary, and resent Yüan as an ambitious flouter of these anti-nationalist Chinese virtues.[37] But when Chinese nationalism was invoked against Yüan as emperor, invoked in its aspect of anti-traditionalism, its sanction for the free thought and open prospects which the historicism of the monarchists denied, some few Japanese discerned at last the impending maturity of Chinese nationalism. They recognized that it must work against Japan, though Japan had helped so much to bring it to birth. And they turned pro-Yüan in the end.

The famous military leader and *genro*, Yamagata, had considered the Chinese Republic, right at the start, a threat to the Japanese programme, and he fixed on Yüan as candidate for Japan's man and foe of the Republic. For Yamagata saw nationalism, bad news for Japan, in the revolution against Chinese monarchy, and anti-nationalist possibilities in Yüan's attempt to restore it. Racial solidarity, a bond between an anti-nationalist China (Emperor Yüan's?) and Japanese supporters, would define the great issues of world politics as they really were: issues of white-coloured rivalry, not of national tensions within the Asian races.[38]

The balance, nevertheless, was still against Yüan, in Japan as in China. Yet, the Hung-hsien movement was the turning point for Japan in China and Japanese influence on Chinese culture. From being the school of Chinese radicals and nationalists, Japan became the temple of the deepest Chinese traditionalism.

The Japanese 'great power' example had for a long time encouraged the Chinese new-thinkers; intellectually, Japanese had anticipated by decades the Chinese denouncers of the numbing effect of Confucian authority. In 1884, for instance, Hidaka Sanenori gave thanks that Confucianism, the binder of scholars' thoughts, had at least been confined to the East, so that science had not been stifled in the West as well. The harm brought to the world by Confucianism, he said, was much greater than the help. If only Confucianism had not been tended and developed, Eastern culture might have grown beyond the West's.[39] Even Chinese thinkers who could not go so far (like the younger K'ang Yu-wei, who would scorn most of the successors but praise Confucius himself) had looked to Japan progressive, not Japan traditionalist, as a model for China.

Yet, just when Japan, by its exertions in China, became a

target of the nationalists whom it had fostered by its example, Chinese monarchists and Confucianists, fused together by the traditionalistic spirit, turned now in their turn to a meeting with Japan, and the 'Asian' Japan, not the newly-Western, turned to seek them out. The later K'ang admired Japan as a place where men learned the *Analects* by heart in their homes, where Confucian learning was nationally respected.[40] When Yüan encouraged Confucian societies, *K'ung-chiao hui* and *Ts'un-K'ung hui*, branches appeared in Japan.[41] Under Japanese auspices, a Chinese published (in 1928!) doggedly anti-Republican references to 'the Confucian scholarship of the present dynasty'; to the 'Ju-chiao' (Confucianism) as 'the eternal standard, the indestructible principle for governing the *T'ien-hsia*'; to the state of the doubting moderns, lacking *chün* and *ch'en*, as the situation of savages.[42]

This writer went on to more of the same in 'Manchukuo' (Manchuria) during the nineteen-thirties. There the Japanese sponsored a Ch'ing revival, which drew numbers of anti-nationalists to monarchy and Confucianism. Many entered government service in the old-new dynastic state, which had *wang-tao*, the 'kingly way', as its grand Confucian pro-gramme.[43] *Wang-tao* was offered explicitly in opposition to *San min chu-i*, the Sun Yat-sen and Kuomintang 'Three People's Principles', which the Japanese and the Manchukuo men stigmatized as western.[44]

But the situation of these Chinese officials impaired the traditional wholeness of the Confucian personality. For their traditionalistic personality made them puppets, worked by the Japanese, not self-serving (in the double sense, like the old Confucian bureaucracy) in living tension with monarchy. And something else made the Confucianism of Manchukuo untraditional. What could it be but a symbol of old China, culturally 'authentic' and politically 'safe', when the sub-stance of Japanese policy there was industrial moderniza-tion?[45] Manchukuo was to feed the power of nationalist Japan with modern industry; and to sap the power of Nationalist China with an appeal to anti-modernism.

Here, then, Chinese sentiment divided, the anti-Japanese nationalist going to one of the poles and the philo-Japanese traditionalist to the other; the vestiges of monarchism were nothing more than a version of the latter. The same historical circumstances had favoured them both. Modernistic nationalism was a reaction to blows against Confucian culture, which had suffered in its central claim of universal value. And traditionalistic conservatism accepted this condition, by redefining Confucian culture as essentially Chinese, a non-universal Chinese essence. It was a dialogue of true contemporaries, no matter how premature, or how outworn, one of these Chinese parties seemed to the other.

Japan was the point of reference to which both parties turned. It was Japan, an eastern recruit to the ranks of 'western' rivals—not England, the United States or the rest—that brought home to China the contraction to China of Chinese civilization. Japan had inspired modernists in China, showing a path of resistance to the West. But when Japan itself was the sharpest spear in the Western armoury, sharper than a serpent's tooth, Chinese culture was not just hit from the outside; it was suffering defection, a significant cultural roll-back.

For the early influence of Chinese culture on Japan, where politically the Chinese nation had never really encroached, had made Chinese culture supra-national—properly, according to traditional lights. But now 'modern' Japan, no longer a vessel for Chinese influence but a vehicle for western, was only using, not living much of a Chinese traditional culture. And when in Japanese hands the culture was just a tool for a 'western' aggression, in Chinese eyes it could hardly be anything more than national. To those Chinese who compensated with nationalism for the blight on their more than national Confucian heritage, the anti-nationalist sponsorship of Confucianism only gave it a final curse. To those Chinese who felt, on the other hand, that anti-Confucianism was the curse, the national enemy was cultural friend. Paradoxically, the new Japan, which had cut Confucianism down to the organic plant that the neo-traditionalists nurtured, was the sole recourse for propping it up; though Japan, in propping it up, was taking another cut.

Thus, late monarchy, the Chinese twin of Confucianism,

was ultimately confided to foreign sponsorship. This had been foreshadowed in the ambiguous Japanese attitude toward Yüan in 1915, and it culminated in the Japanese revival of the Ch'ing dynasty in Manchuria. When nationalism implied both iconoclasm culturally and anti-Japanese feeling politically, the cause of Chinese monarchy quite plausibly qualified for Japanese backing; for with its imprisonment in cultural traditionalism, latter-day Chinese monarchy committed itself to anti-nationalism, and to a political ambiance, accordingly, at least passively pro-Japanese.

Conclusion: The Japanese and Chinese Monarchical Mystiques

IRONICALLY enough, Chinese monarchism not only ended as bankrupt with Japanese receivers, but had marked its panic long before with a desperate reaching out for Japanese procedures. The Ch'ing and their supporters, back in the days of the post-Boxer 'Manchu Reform Movement' and right down to 1911, had taken to insisting on Ch'ing eternity in the midst of the myriad changes that the Ch'ing were forced to bless, and they did it by repeating '*Wan-shih i-hsi*', the *Bansei ikkei*, 'One line throughout ten thousand ages', that celebrated Japan's imperial house.[1] It hardly belonged in China, with the latter's long centuries of non-feudal imperium, in which the mandate was not necessarily inheritable.

It is this difference between the premodern societies, Chinese bureaucratic and Japanese feudal, that accounts for the different fates of the Chinese and Japanese monarchies. In modern Japan, monarchy has been no parody, the mystique of the throne has been strengthened, not dispelled (the repercussions of the Second World War are not considered here). For in Japan, unlike China, a postfeudal régime could cite prefeudal precedents against the feudal intermission. The nineteenth-century Japanese revolution, that is, could strike against the *de facto* Tokugawa feudal shogunate (est. seventeenth century) in the name of Nara (eighth century), and Meiji (nineteenth century), *de jure* imperial control: modernization could be combined with myth-making about antiquity. But in China, the modern breach with things as they were was a breach precisely with a *de jure* situation, a dynastic and bureaucratic régime which was, in general terms, as tradition had dictated it, and modernization required myth-breaking. Compare only the early modern contemporaries, the Chinese 'Han Learning', with its probing for forgeries and its ultimately revolutionary and republican implications, and the Japanese 'Pure Shintō', with its writing of forgeries and its ultimately revolutionary but monarchist implications. The Japanese could combine a prefeudal form with postfeudal content; the strengthening of Japanese monarchy was compatible with modernization. But the strengthening—or the mere re-establishing—of Chinese monarchy was incompatible with modernization. Indeed, as we have seen, Yüan Shih-k'ai's effort to re-establish monarchy was undertaken deliberately as an anti-modernist counterthrust.

Kokutai, or 'national form', intimately individual polity, was ancient Japanese term with tremendous modern and nationalist-monarchist currency. But its Chinese counterpart, with the same characters, *kuo-t'i*, was just another of those terms proper to Japan, exotic in China, which were rushed to the aid of a Chinese monarchism having none of the circumstances favouring monarchy in the modern age in Japan. It was as foreign as *tsung-chiao* (religion), for example. Like the traditionalistic monarchists choosing *kokutai/kuo-t'i*, a traditionalistic Confucianist, speaking for *K'ung-chiao*, Confucianism as a religion, chose the originally Japanese compound *shūkyō* (*tsung-chiao*) to define it; indeed, he drew attention to the fact that in standard Chinese *chiao*, in such a context, stood alone.[2] As to *kuo-t'i* itself, there was no doubt about who felt most at home with it. If Chinese neo-traditionalists came to prize it, and to press it against the nationalist republicans, so did the anti-(Chinese) nationalists of Japan, following the logic of the Chinese monarchist—Japanese imperialist affinity. The well-known Japanese expansionist thinker, Kita Ikki (1882–1937), was most contemptuous of Sun Yat-sen's original American presidential model. It was bad for China, he said, because China's *kokutai* was totally different from that of the United States.[3] *Kokutai* was obviously something 'given', not a subject for experiment.

Liang Ch'i-ch'ao (1873–1929) saw the difference and the significance at the time of the Hung-hsien movement. In 1915 he rebuffed the *kuo-t'i* monarchical blandishments of Yüan's son, with their invitation to see the *kuo-ch'ing* or 'national spirit' in just this form of state. Liang preferred to speak, he said, of *cheng-t'i*, of the practical question of the workings of government rather than the more metaphysical, 'essential' question of the location of national authority[4]— this distinction having first been made as a Japanese distinction, between *kokutai* and *seitai*, in the *Kokutai Shinron* of Katō Hirayuki in 1874.[5] *Kokutai* was a living word, *kuo-t'i* was a contrivance.[6] To speak a living language, one must say that the Hung-hsien reign was supposed to be a revival of Chinese *kokutai*. But how could a Chinese *revive* in China a new and foreign importation? What was this traditional 'national form' which tradition had never named and nationalists could hardly accept? It was paradox which made of Yüan a parodist.

Yüan had hopes of Liang's support because Liang, after all, right down to 1911, had opposed the republicanism of Sun Yat-sen. Why should Liang not welcome the resumption of monarchy, and not necessarily through a Ch'ing restoration but in the time-honoured way of acknowledging change of mandate? Certainly, his defence of the Ch'ing before 1911 was more defence of monarchy (ideally, constitutional monarchy) than defence of the Manchu incumbents. He was only an anti-anti-Manchu.

And yet, confounding Yüan's hopes (both the minor one about Liang and the major one about monarchy) was the very fact, the supposedly promising fact, that Liang's support of the Ch'ing lacked any grain of positive commitment— certainly after the death in 1908 of the Kuang-hsü emperor, so sadly related to the old Reformers' cause. When Liang supported the dynasty in spite of this lack, it suggested that no dynastic succession was conceivable. And this was because the monarchical mystique was dead. If, to ward off republic and anarchy, a monarchy seemed essential, the going dynasty had to be kept going. The inertia of establishment was monarchy's only resource; if the mandate were dropped by the Ch'ing house, no Manchu, Mongol, Turk, or Chinese, whatever their fortunes in the Chinese past, would ever pick it up.

Yen Fu, more monarchist than Liang under the Republic, and in many ways a Yüan Shih-k'ai man, felt nevertheless in 1915 that Yüan was not the man of the hour, the emperor for the age. In 1917, Yen unequivocally supported the abortive restoration of the Ch'ing, all two weeks of it. He wished, though, that the circumstances of 1915 and 1917 could have been combined: Hsüan-t'ung, the last of the Ch'ing, as emperor, Yüan as prime minister.[7] What was he saying? That Yüan's talents were fine enough to make him deserve to rule. That his *mana*, his aura, was wrong. That no new claimant, however talented, could rule any longer as emperor. That only an old emperor (though in this case young in years) might conceivably sustain a precarious mass conformity, and string out the monarchical idea.

For the kings were truly finished—*wang* and *su-wang* both, the merely royal and the Confucian sage-ideal. Monarchism and Confucianism, which had belonged together in their own way and run dry together, were garbled together in a new way now that failed to elicit the old responses. When republican 'men of the future' set the pace, they not only abandoned traditionalism on their own account, but transformed the traditionalism of those who never joined them, turning it into nostalgia—which is thirst for the past, not a life-giving fluid itself.

Notes

CHAPTER I

1. *North China Herald*, CXIV, No. 2474 (Jan. 9, 1915), 87.
2. T'ao Chü-yin, *Chin-tai i-wen* (Items about the modern era) (Shanghai, 1940), 1.
3. *Faust*, Part II, Act 1, Scene 3.
4. Thomas Mann, *Doctor Faustus* (New York, 1948), 134.
5. Lu Hsün, 'Morning Flowers Gathered in the Evening', cited in Huang Sung-k'ang, *Lu Hsün and the New Culture Movement of Modern China* (Amsterdam, 1957), 40.
6. Kuzuu Yoshihisa, *Nisshi kōshō gaishi* (An unofficial history of Sino-Japanese relations) (Tokyo, 1939), 119.
7. Thurston Griggs, 'The *Ch'ing Shih Kao*: a Bibliographical Summary', *Harvard Journal of Asiatic Studies*, XVIII, Nos. 1–2 (June 1955), 115; Franklin W. Houn, *Central Government in China, 1912–1928; an Institutional Study* (Madison, 1957), 113.
8. Kao Lao, *Ti-chih yün-tung shih-mo chi* (An account of the monarchical movement) (Shanghai, 1923), 2; Yang Yu-chiung (Moriyama Takashi, tr.), *Shina Seitō shi* (History of Chinese political parties) (Tokyo, 1940), 70.
9. T'ao Chü-yin, *Pei-yang chün-fa t'ung-chih shih-ch'i shih-hua* (Historical discourses on the era of the *Pei-yang* military clique's dominion) (Peking, 1957–8), II, 28. (Hereafter, *Pei-yang chün-fa*.)
10. Kao, 17.
11. *Ibid.*, 19.
12. *Ibid.*, 18.
13. Ku Yen-wu, *Jih-chih lu* (Record of knowledge day by day), ed. Huang Ju-ch'eng (1834), 13. 5b–6a.
14. Kao, 20–21.
15. *Ibid.*, 22.
16. Chu Shou-p'eng, ed., *Kuang-hsü Tung-hua hsü-lu* (Kuang-hsü supplement to the archival records: hereafter, THL), 169, 1a.
17. e.g. THL 171. 16a; THL 184. 10a.

18. THL 199. 12b for memorialists' reference to these objectives, THL 203. 16b for edict; Imazeki Hisamaro, *Sung Yüan Ming Ch'ing Ju-chia hsüeh nien-piao* (Chronological tables of Sung, Yüan, Ming, and Ch'ing Confucianism) (Tokyo, 1920), 216 (in Chinese); Hattori Unokichi, *Kōshi oyobi Kōshikyō* (Confucius and the Confucian religion) (Tokyo, 1926), 119, 371.

19. Wu Li, 'K'ung-tzu fei Man-chou chih hu-fu' (Let Confucius not be an amulet for the Manchu), *Min-pao*, No. 11 (Jan. 30, 1907), 81.

20. Cf. Li T'ien-huai, 'Tsun K'ung shuo' (On reverence for Confucius), *Chung-kuo hsüeh-pao*, No. 7 (May 1913), 27. (Hereafter, CKHP.)

21. Kao, 7.

22. T'ao Chü-yin, *Liu chün-tzu chuan* (Biographies of the 'Six Martyrs') (Shanghai, 1946), 2. Yen's name was attached to the manifesto of the monarchist *Ch'ou-an hui* in the summer of 1915. He later maintained that this was done without his permission; though he did not disclaim it at the time (perhaps feeling this imprudent), he claimed illness as an excuse to keep out of the society's deliberations. Nevertheless, Yen was subsequently tarred with this association, which was felt to be plausible, since he had praised Yüan Shih-k'ai in 1909, when the Manchus dismissed him, and had been close to Yüan ever since the latter assumed the presidency of the Republic, offered Yen the presidency of the university in Peking, and brought him into various government offices and commissions. Cf. Yang Yin-shen, *Chung-kuo wen-hsüeh-chia lieh-chuan* (Biographies of Chinese literary figures) (Shanghai, 1939), 488–9, and Tso Shun-sheng, *Wan-chu lou sui-pi* (Sketches from the Wan-chu chamber) (Hong Kong, 1953), 36–38. Ch'en Tu-hsiu, later the first chairman of the Chinese Communist Party, flatly maintained that Yen Fu approved of Yüan's worshipping Heaven, then approved of Yüan's naming himself emperor; cf. Fukui Kōjun, *Gendai Chūgoku shisō* (Recent Chinese thought) (Tokyo, 1955), 67, 106–7. But Jerome Ch'en, *Yuan Shih-k'ai: Brutus assumes the Purple* (London, 1961), 205–6, reports that Yen Fu, hesitant, was forced to lend his name to the *Ch'ou-an hui* by pressure from Yüan, transmitted through Yang Tu, the founder of the society.

23. Chou Chen-fu, 'Yen Fu ssu-hsiang chuan pien chih p'ou-hsi' (A close analysis of the changes in Yen Fu's thought), *Hsüeh-lin*, No. 3 (Jan. 1941), 117.

24. Sakamaki Teiichirō, *Shina bunkatsu ron: tsuki, 'Gen Seikai'*

(The decomposition of China: supplement, 'Yüan Shih-k'ai') (Tokyo, 1914), 183.

25. *Ibid.*, 228, 229.

26. e.g. Rinji Taiwan kyūkan chōsakai dai-ichi-bu hōkoku (Temporary commission of the Taiwan Government-general for the study of old Chinese customs, report of the First Section), *Shinkoku gyōseihō* (Administrative laws of the Ch'ing dynasty), kan 1, revised (Tokyo, 1914), I, 46.

27. Cf. Tung Chung-shu, *Ch'un-ch'iu fan-lu* (Luxuriant dew from the Spring and Autumn Annals) (Shanghai, 1929), 10. 1b: 'The monarch who has received the mandate is given the mandate by the will of Heaven; therefore he is called the son of Heaven . . .' (This passage is also cited in Vincent Shih, *The Ideology of the T'ai-p'ing T'ien-kuo*, ms.)

28. A proper corrective to the authority cited in note 16 is Hara Tomio, *Chūka shisō no kontai to jugaku no yūi* (The roots of Chinese thought and the pre-eminence of Confucianism) (Tokyo, 1947), 183, which emphasizes that in classical Chinese thought *t'ien-i*, the will of Heaven, was independent and self-existent. That is, it was not derived from the *min-i*, the people's will, and was certainly not reduced, in the modern metaphorical fashion, to being simply a rhetorical equivalent of the latter term.

29. Sagara Yoshiaki, 'Toku no gon no igi to sono hensen' (The meaning of the word *te* and its evolution), in Tsuda Sokichi, *Tōyō shisō kenkyū* (Studies in Far Eastern thought), No. 1 (Tokyo, 1937), 290–1.

30. Wang Hsieh-chia, 'Chung-hua min-kuo hsien-fa hsüan ch'uan chang ting K'ung-chiao wei kuo-chiao ping hsü jen-min hsiu chiao tzu-yu hsiu-cheng an' (Proposal that the constitution of the Republic of China promulgate a special clause establishing Confucianism as the state religion and permitting modification of the freedom of religion), 1, 4–5, *K'ung-chiao wen-t'i* (Problems of Confucianism), No. 18, supplement (Taiyuan, 1917). (Hereafter, KCWT.)

31. *Ibid.*, 1–3.

32. Ch'ang-t'ing, 'K'ung-hsüeh fa-wei' (The inner meaning of the Confucian learning revealed), CKHP, No. 1 (Nov. 1912), 4.

33. Wang Hsieh-chia, 10.

34. THL 197. 1b.

35. Sung Yü-jen, 'K'ung-hsüeh tsung-ho cheng chiao ku chin t'ung-hsi liu-pieh lun' (On Confucianism as uniter of political and intellectual, ancient and modern systems and classes), CKHP,

No. 9 (July 1913), 2; K'ang Yu-wei, 'Chung-kuo hsüeh-pao t'i-tz'u' (The thesis of the *Chung-kuo hsüeh-pao*), CKHP, No. 6 (Feb. 1913), 7, and 'Chung-kuo hsüeh-hui pao t'i-tz'u' (The thesis of the journal of the Society for Chinese Learning), *Pu-jen*, II (March 1913), *chiao-shuo*, 2.

36. Sanetō Keishū, *Nihon bunka no Shina e no eikyō* (The influence of Japanese culture on China) (Tokyo, 1940), 228; Fukui, 96.

37. 'Ta-tsung-tung kao-ling' (Presidential mandate), Sept. 25, 1914, *Chiao-yü kung-pao* (Educational record), V (June 20, 1915), *Ming-ling* 1; Nov. 3, 1914, *Chiao-yü kung-pao*, VII (Aug. 1915), *Ming-ling*, 1.

38. Henri Bernard-Maitre, *Sagesse chinoise et philosophie chrétienne* (Paris, 1935), 211; Fukui, 101–2.

39. Cf., for example, *Tsung-sheng hsüeh-pao*, the principal organ of the Confucian religionists.

40. Ch'en Huan-chang, *K'ung-chiao lun chieh-lu* (Chapters on the Confucian religion) (Taiyuan, 1918), 1b (also 7b, in the *Kung-yang*, *chin-wen* vein, for Confucius as a democrat, with the author's exculpation of Confucius's *seeming* monarchism). Ch'en, a very important editor and writer for the cause of Confucian religion, had supplemented his Chinese education with study at Columbia University and the University of Chicago. In 1912 he was one of the principal founding members of the *K'ung-chiao hui* (Confucian religious society); cf. Imazeki, 217–18.

41. Ch'en Huan-chang, 1a.

42. *Ibid.*, 2a.

43. K'ang, 'Chung-kuo hsüeh-pao t'i-tz'u', 5.

44. Tse-tsung Chow, 'The Anti-Confucian Movement in Early Republican China', *The Confucian Persuasion*, ed. Arthur F. Wright (Stanford, 1960), 297.

45. Ch'en Tu-hsiu, 'Hsien-fa yü K'ung-chiao' (The constitution and the Confucian religion), *Tu-hsiu wen-ts'un* (Collected essays of Ch'en Tu-hsiu) (Shanghai, 1937), 104–5.

46. *Ibid.*, 103.

47. Hsia Te-wo, 'Hu-nan An-hua chiao-yü-chieh ch'üan-t'i ch'ing-ting K'ung-chiao kuo-chiao shu' (Letter from the entire educational circle of An-hua, Hunan, requesting that Confucianism be established as the state religion of China), 4, KCWT, No. 17, supplement (Taiyuan, 1916).

48. Ch'en Huan-chang, 16b.

49. *Ibid.*, 16b; K'ang Yu-wei, 'K'ung-chiao hui hsü' (Preface

to the Confucian Society), *Pu-jen*, I (March 1913), *chiao-shuo* 5; K'ang Yu-wei, 'Fu Chiao-yü pu shu' (Reply to the Ministry of Education), *Pu-jen*, IV (May 1913), *chiao-shuo*, 5–6; K'ang, 'Chung-kuo hsüeh-pao t'i-tz'u', 3–4.

50. K'ang Yu-wei, 'K'ang Nan-hai chih Tsung-t'ung Tsung-li shu' (Letter from K'ang Yu-wei to the President and Premier), 2, KCWT, No. 17, supplement.

51. 'Hu-pei kung-min Liu Ta-chün shang ts'an chung liang yüan ching ting kuo-chiao shu' (Letter from Liu Ta-chün of Hupei to the parliament requesting establishment of a state religion), 4–5, KCWT, No. 18, supplement.

52. Wang Hsieh-chia, 1.

53. Hsüeh Cheng-ch'ing, 'K'ung-tzu kung-ho hsüeh-shuo' (The republican theory of Confucius), CKHP, No. 7 (May 1913) 11–12, 20, 23.

54. Li Wen-chih, 'Ching ting K'ung-chiao wei kuo-chiao ti erh-tz'u i-chien shu' (Second communication of views favouring establishment of Confucianism as the state religion), 2–3, KCWT, No. 18, supplement.

55. Liu Shih-p'ei, 'Chün-cheng fu-ku lun (chung)' (On the monarchical revival, part two), CKHP, No. 2 (Feb. 1916), 3.

56. Fukui, 1, for this response, in the seventeenth century, to Jesuit reports of the founding of the Dutch Republic.

57. K'ang, 'Chung-kuo hsüeh-pao t'i-tz'u', 13.

58. Cf. D. W. Brogan, 'The "Nouvelle Revue Française" ', *Encounter* (March 1959), 66: ' . . . this is a French inspection of the French mind almost as introverted as if it had been produced around 1680. . . . But France in 1680, in most realms of thought and action, was dominant in Europe. France in the heyday of the NRF was not. Necessarily, a nation-centred culture in a nation that is no longer the centre of a super-national culture must be parochial. . . .'

CHAPTER II

1. For example, cf. Jacques Gernet, *Les aspects économiques du Bouddhisme dans la société chinoise du Ve au Xe siècle* (Saigon, 1956), 293–4 et seq., for the exploitation of Buddhism to support the imperial power. To cite a later period: Ming imperial indulgence toward Buddhism was marked. Even while Confucian scholars biased in favour of their master, the Yung-lo emperor (reigned 1403–24), taxed his predecessor (whose throne he had usurped)

with favour to Buddhists, Yung-lo himself retained his ties with the monks who had helped him to power; see Chapter III.

2. For the Buddhist contribution to trade and capital formation, see Gernet, esp. 138–90.

3. J. J. L. Duyvendak, *China's Discovery of Africa* (London, 1949), 27–28.

4. For Ming, see Charles Whitman MacSherry, 'Impairment of the Ming Tributary System as Exhibited in Trade Involving Fukien', unpublished Ph.D. dissertation, University of California, 1957.

5. For the Hoppo's appointment by the 'inner court' (imperial) rather than the 'outer court' (general bureaucratic), see William Frederick Mayers, *The Chinese Government* (Shanghai, 1886), 40; and for his practice of sending memorials directly to the emperor, not through normal channels, see *Shinkoku gyōseihō*, kan 5 (Tokyo, 1911), 311–12.

6. See the chapter, 'The Amateur Ideal in Ming and Early Ch'ing Society: Evidence from Painting', in Volume One of this work, 15–43. It is interesting to note that a Chinese Communist critic, in the interests of isolating the literati tradition as 'the enemy', has set the 'academic' style apart (the Sung Emperor Hui-tsung is specifically praised) as the anti-Confucian precedent for the Communist-sponsored 'realism' in art; see Chang Jen-hsia, 'Flower-and-Bird Painting', *China Reconstructs*, III (May–June 1953), 51.

7. Cf. Joseph R. Strayer, 'Feudalism in Western Europe', *Feudalism in History*, ed. Rushton Coulborn (Princeton, 1956), 23.

8. Pan Ku, *The History of the Former Han Dynasty*, tr. Homer H. Dubs, Vol. Two (Baltimore, 1944), 292. As Pow-key Sohn has pointed out in 'The Theory and Practice of Land-systems in Korea in Comparison with China' (ms. University of California, 1956), the Koryö victory of military over civil interests played a large part in defeating the trend in Korea toward a private-property system; it encouraged, rather, a return to a strict system of state ownership and state allocation—a system, be it noted, which T'ang and other rulers in China favoured at times, but which civil-official recalcitrance broke down.

9. Tezuka Ryōdō, *Jukyō dōtoku ni okeru kunshin shisō* (The sovereign-minister idea in Confucian ethics) (Tokyo, 1925), 112; Miyakawa Hisayuki, 'Zenjō ni yoru ōchō kakumei no tokushitsu' (The special quality of dynastic overturns depending on '*shan-jang*'), *Tōhōgaku*, No. 11 (Oct. 1955), 50.

10. *Ming-shih,* Shih-huo chih, ch. 77, 11a–11b, cited in Shih ms.

11. As Shih points out, the Taiping state stressed the motto, *i hsiao tso chung,* 'transform filial piety into loyalty'. The Taipings seem to me to represent in Chinese history (among other things) the assertion of a pure monarchical spirit, i.e. a spirit of unqualified autocracy, a refusal to compromise with bureaucratic ideals. A régime which understandably alienated the Confucian literati unequivocally, the Taiping state was trying to rule out the possibility of the traditional intra-bureaucratic conflict between private and public impulses.

12. Carsun Chang, *The Development of Neo-Confucian Thought* (New York, 1957), 203.

13. See R. H. van Gulik, tr., *T'ang-Yun-Pi-Shih,* '*Parallel Cases from under the Pear-Tree*' (Leiden, 1956), vii, for the oft-quoted statement applying to the scholar-official, 'One does not read the Code', and its bearing on theories of the ideal state and ideal ruler.

14. Louis Delatte, *Les traités de la royauté d'Ecphante, Diotegène, et Sthénidas* (Liege and Paris, 1942), 140–2.

15. Shōji Sōichi, 'Chin Ryō no gaku' (The thought of Ch'en Liang), *Tōyō no bunka to shakai,* IV (1954), 98–100.

16. Cf. J. Walter Jones, *The Law and Legal Theory of the Greeks* (Oxford, 1956), 292–3.

CHAPTER III

1. For the monarchical interest in 'field-limitation' or 'field-equalization' (*hsien-t'ien, chün-t'ien*), see Joseph R. Levenson, 'Ill Wind in the Well-field: the Erosion of the Confucian Ground of Controversy', *The Confucian Persuasion,* ed. Arthur F. Wright (Stanford, 1960), 268–87; and Volume Three.

2. Niida Noboru, *Chūgoku no nōson kazoku* (The Chinese peasant family) (Tokyo, 1952), 105–6.

3. C. H. Brewitt-Taylor, tr., *The Romance of the Three Kingdoms* (Shanghai, 1925), I, 581–2.

4. Shimizu Morimitsu, 'Kyū Shina ni okeru sensei kenryoku no kiso' (The basis of autocratic power in pre-revolutionary China), *Mantetsu chōsa geppō* (Bulletin of the research bureau of the South Manchuria Railway), XVII, No. 2 (Feb. 1937), 9.

5. Liang Ch'i-ch'ao, 'Chung-kuo chih wu-shih-tao' (China's *bushidō*), *Yin-ping-shih ho-chi* (Shanghai, 1936), *ch'uan-chi* 6: 24. 60–61.

6. Ch'ien Mu, *Kuo-shih ta-kang* (Outline of Chinese history) (Shanghai, 1940), I, 354. For a summary of literature on the examination system, matured by Sung, as an enhancer of monarchical absolutism over aristocratic privilege, see Wolfgang Franke, *The Reform and Abolition of the Traditional Chinese Examination System* (Cambridge, Mass., 1960), 2–7.

7. Max Weber, 'Politics as a Vocation', *From Max Weber: Essays in Sociology*, ed. H. H. Gerth and C. Wright Mills (New York, 1946), 78, 82.

8. Montesquieu, *The Spirit of the Laws*, tr. Thomas Nugent (New York, 1949), I, 16.

9. For a similar analysis and an application of it, see L. A. Fallers, 'Despotism, Status Culture and Social Mobility in an African Kingdom', *Comparative Studies in Society and History*, II, No. 1 (Oct. 1959), 11–32.

10. George Orwell, *The English People* (London, 1947), 25.

11. Leonard Krieger, *The German Idea of Freedom: History of a Political Tradition* (Boston, 1957), 16–17.

12. Andrew Alföldi, *A Conflict of Ideas in the Late Roman Empire: the Clash between the Senate and Valentinian I* (Oxford, 1952), 51–57.

13. William G. Sinnigen, 'The Vicarius Urbis Romae and the Urban Prefecture', *Historia*, VIII, No. 1 (Jan. 1959), 112; William Gurnee Sinnigen, *The Officium of the Urban Prefecture During the Later Roman Empire* (Rome, 1957), 5.

14. Ernst Kantorowicz, *Frederick the Second (1194–1250)* (London, 1931), 227–38, 519.

15. Robert Lee Wolff, 'The Three Romes: the Migration of an Ideology and the Making of an Autocrat', *Daedalus* (Spring 1959), 302–3; George Vernadsky, *A History of Russia* (New Haven, 1951), 66–68, 78.

16. G. d'Avenel, *La noblesse française sous Richelieu* (Paris, 1901), 342; Franklin T. Ford, *Robe and Sword: the Regrouping of the French Aristocracy after Louis XIV* (Cambridge, Mass., 1953), 6–7.

17. Alexis de Tocqueville, *The Old Régime and the French Revolution* (New York, 1955), 26–28, 58; Hippolyte Adolphe Taine, *The Ancient Régime* (New York, 1931), I, 36–37, 43–44; Elinor G. Barber, *The Bourgeoisie in 18th Century France* (Princeton, 1955), 128. Lucy Norton, tr., *Saint-Simon at Versailles* (New York, 1958).

18. d'Avenel, 11.

19. Georges Lefebvre, *The Coming of the French Revolution, 1789* (Princeton, 1947), 16; Alfred Cobban, *A History of Modern France:*

I, Old Régime and Revolution, 1715–1799 (Harmondsworth, 1957), 20–21.

20. Franz Neumann, 'Montesquieu', *The Democratic and Authoritarian State: Essays in Political and Legal Theory* (Glencoe, 1957), 106; Peter Gay, *Voltaire's Politics: the Poet as Realist* (Princeton, 1959), 90–91.

21. Wolfgang H. Kraus, 'Authority, Progress, and Colonialism', *Nomos I: Authority*, ed. Carl J. Friedrich (Cambridge, 1958), 148; Hans Rosenberg, *Bureaucracy, Aristocracy, and Autocracy: the Prussian Experience, 1660–1815* (Cambridge, 1958), 43–75; Otto Hintze, 'Staatsverfassung und Heeresverfassung', *Staat und Verfassung: Gesammelte Abhandlungen zur Allgemeinen Verfassungsgeschichte* (Leipzig, 1941), 61–62.

22. Lü Ssu-mien, *Chung-kuo t'ung-shih* (General History of China) (n.p., 1941), II, 390.

23. *Ibid.*, II, 397.

24. Edwin G. Pulleyblank, *The Background of the Rebellion of An Lu-shan* (London, New York, and Toronto, 1955), 47–48.

25. Miyazaki Ichisada, *Yō-sei-tei, Chugoku no dokusai kunshu* (The Yung-cheng Emperor—China's autocratic ruler) (Tokyo, 1950), 24. Miyazaki ascribes all four cases (instead of only the first two, plus two more that he does not mention) to Yung-cheng.

26. Cf. Jacques Gernet, *Daily Life in China on the Eve of the Mongol Invasion, 1250–1276* (New York, 1962), 75.

27. David B. Chan, 'The Problem of the Princes As Faced by the Ming Emperor Hui (1399–1402)', *Oriens*, XI, No. 1–2 (1958), 184–5; C. T. Hu, 'The Ning Wang Revolt: Sociology of a Ming Rebellion', ms. read at annual meeting of Association for Asian Studies, 1959.

28. *Shinkoku gyōseihō*, kan 1, I, 119.

29. *Ibid.*, I, 122.

30. Cf. reference to the Hsiang K'ai memorial of A.D. 166 in E. Zürcher, *The Buddhist Conquest of China: the Spread and Adaptation of Buddhism in Early Medieval China* (Leiden, 1959), I, 37.

31. Howard S. Levy, *Biography of Huang Ch'ao* (Berkeley and Los Angeles, 1955), 54.

32. Naitō Torajiro, *Shinchō shi tsūron* (Outline of Ch'ing history) (Tokyo, 1944), 31–32.

33. Taine, I, 37, 43–44.

34. Rosenberg, 139, 151–2, 186–8, 201.

35. W. H. Bruford, 'The Idea of "Bildung" in Wilhelm von Humboldt's Letters', *The Era of Goethe: Essays Presented to James Boyd* (Oxford, 1959), 21, 32, 34, 38, 45.

36. Cf. Fritz Morstein Marx, *The Administrative State: an Introduction to Bureaucracy* (Chicago, 1957), 164.

37. Chao Yuen Ren, 'What is Correct Chinese?', *Journal of the American Oriental Society*, LXXXI, No. 3 (Aug.–Sept. 1961), 171–2.

38. David B. Chan, 'The Role of the Monk Tao-Yen in the Usurpation of the Prince of Yen (1398–1402)', *Sinologica*, VI, No. 2 (1959), 95–96.

CHAPTER IV

1. Benjamin Schwartz, 'Some Polarities in Confucian Thought', *Confucianism in Action*, ed. David S. Nivison and Arthur F. Wright (Stanford, 1959), 50–63.

2. Burton Watson, *Ssu-ma Ch'ien. Grand Historian of China* (New York, 1958), 173–4.

3. Chang Hsüeh-ch'eng (1738–1801), recognizing the vagaries of *shih*, the times, for the realization of sage-wisdom in action; quoted in Nomura Kōichi, 'Seimatsu Kōyō gakuha no keisei to Kō Yūi gaku no rekishiteki igi' (The formation of the late-Ch'ing *kung-yang* school, and the historical meaning of K'ang Yu-wei's doctrine), Part I, *Kokka gakkai zasshi*, LXXI, No. 7 (1958), 22.

4. Frederick Mote, 'Confucian Eremitism in the Yuan Period', *The Confucian Persuasion*, 225.

5. W. Theodore de Bary, 'A Reappraisal of Neo-Confucianism', *Studies in Chinese Thought*, ed. Arthur F. Wright (Chicago, 1953), 86–87.

6. See above, Chapter II, for Chu Hsi vs. Ch'en Liang, with another version of the *hsiu-shen p'ing t'ien-hsia* polarity.

7. For Chu Hsi on Fan Chung-yen, see James T. C. Liu, 'Some Classifications of Bureaucrats in Chinese Historiography', *Confucianism in Action*, 173. For Fan on clan properties, as discussed below, see Denis Twitchett, 'The Fan Clan's Charitable Estates, 1050–1710', *ibid.*, 100–8.

8. See Hui-chen Wang Liu, 'An Analysis of Chinese Clan Rules: Confucian Theories in Action', *ibid.*, 72–77.

9. For the State's ambivalent indulgence and restraint of clans, see *ibid.*, 75–76, for eighteenth-century examples; and Maurice Freedman, 'The Family in China, Past and Present', *Pacific Affairs*, XXXIV, No. 4 (Winter 1961–2), 325.

10. For the ambiguity of the gentry's position between clan and state, and the clan and secret society as rival alignments based

on different conceptions of kinship, see Maurice Freedman, *Lineage Organization in Southeastern China* (London, 1958), 123–5.

11. Araki Toshikazu, 'Sō-dai okeru denshi seiritsu no jijō' (Circumstances leading to the establishment of the palace examinations), *Tō-A jimbun gakuhō*, III, No. 2 (Oct. 1943), 223–4.

12. Miyazaki, 96–97.

13. Arthur Waley, *Yuan Mei, Eighteenth Century Chinese Poet* (New York, 1956), 57; and (following Waley) Robert M. Marsh, 'Bureaucratic Constraints on Nepotism in the Ch'ing Period', *Journal of Asian Studies*, XIX, No. 2 (Feb. 1960), 121.

14. Marsh, 126.

15. Ping-ti Ho, 'Aspects of Social Mobility in China, 1368–1911', *Comparative Studies in Society and History*, I, No. 4 (June 1959), 345.

16. See E. G. Pulleyblank, 'Neo-Confucianism and Neo-Legalism in T'ang Intellectual Life, 755–805', *The Confucian Persuasion*, 93.

17. In *The Confucian Persuasion*.

18. 'The Amateur Ideal in Ming and Early Ch'ing China: Evidence from Painting', *Chinese Thought and Institutions*, ed. John K. Fairbank (Chicago, 1957), 325–34; and *Confucian China and its Modern Fate*, I, 22–34.

19. Cf. James F. Cahill, 'Confucian Elements in the Theory of Painting', *The Confucian Persuasion*, 115–40.

20. Moses Hadas, *Hellenistic Culture: Fusion and Diffusion* (New York, 1959), 68.

21. Alexander Soper, 'Standards of Quality in Northern Sung Painting', *Archives of the Chinese Art Society of America*, XI (1957), 9.

22. A seventeenth-century quotation from an earlier work; cited in Franke, 22.

23. Karl A. Wittfogel and Feng Chia-sheng, *History of Chinese Society: Liao (907–1125)* (Philadelphia, 1949), 456–63.

24. Alföldi, 51.

25. Kung-chuan Hsiao, *Rural China: Imperial Control in the Nineteenth Century* (Seattle, 1960), 4, 8.

CHAPTER V

1. See Arthur F. Wright, 'Sui Yang-ti: Personality and Stereotype', *The Confucian Persuasion*, 47–49, 59–65.

2. See Mote, 208, 220, 229–40.

3. Joshua Liao, 'The Empire Breaker', *The Orient*, 10 (May 1951), 27.

4. Charles O. Hucker, 'Confucianism and the Chinese Censorial System', *Confucianism in Action*, 208.

5. Ch'en Yin-k'o, *T'ang-tai cheng-shih shih shu-lun kao* (Draft account of T'ang political history) (Shanghai, 1947), 26—quoting a thirteenth-century commentary on the *Tzu-chih t'ung-chien* of Ssu-ma Kuang.

6. See Volume One, Chapter II.

7. So defined in Karl A. Wittfogel, *Oriental Despotism: A Comparative Study of Total Power* (New Haven, 1957), 153.

8. Leon Hurvitz, ' "Render unto Caesar" in Early Chinese Buddhism', *Sino-Indian Studies: Liebenthal Festschrift*, ed. Kshitis Roy (Visvabharati, 1957), 81.

9. Mark Mancall, 'China's First Missions to Russia, 1729–1731', *Papers on China*, IX (Harvard University, August 1955), 87, 99, Mancall, 102, makes several conjectures as to why a Chinese record of the episode is not extant. Any one of these is plausible, but they do not extend to the possibility of different Confucian and imperial conceptions of kingship.

10. *The Dawn*, cited in Walter Kaufmann, *Nietzsche* (New York, 1956), 164.

11. David S. Nivison, 'Ho-shen and His Accusers: Ideology and Political Behavior in the Eighteenth Century', *Confucianism in Action*, 227. See also Marsh, 131–2, for the imperially sponsored central-bureaucratic demand that Ch'ing officials' obligations to the throne take precedence over the Confucian-prescribed bonds of family and friendship.

12. Miyazaki, 76–80.

13. Ping-ti Ho, *Studies on the Population of China, 1368–1953* (Cambridge, Mass., 1959), 215.

14. Miyazaki, 92.

15. Nivison, 'Ho Shen and His Accusers', 231.

16. Levenson, 'Ill Wind in the Well-field', 270–1, see also Vol. III.

17. Ch'en Po-ying, *Chung-kuo t'ien-chih ts'ung-k'ao* (General survey of Chinese land systems) (Shanghai, 1935), 240.

18. Miyazaki, 97.

19. W. T. de Bary, 'Chinese Despotism and the Confucian Ideal: a Seventeenth-Century View', *Chinese Thought and Institutions*, 171; Joseph R. Levenson, *Confucian China and Its Modern Fate*, I, 100–1.

20. Shimizu, 13.
21. *Shinkoku gyōseihō*, kan 1, I, 48, 139–41. Lien-sheng Yang, 'Notes on Dr. Swann's "Food and Money in Ancient China" ', *Studies in Chinese Institutional History* (Cambridge, Mass., 1961), 89–90, discusses the at least nominal distinction under most of the major dynasties, dating back to Han, between the emperor's purse and the empire's purse. Nineteenth-century Ch'ing officials, among others, remonstrated against the imperial penchant for confounding the two.

CHAPTER VI

1. Robert des Rotours, *La traité des examens, traduit de la Nouvelle Histoire des T'ang* (Paris, 1932), 172–3.
2. *Shinkoku gyōseihō*, kan 4 (Tokyo, 1911) 82, 89.
3. *Ibid.*, 93–106.
4. Norman Cohn, *The Pursuit of the Millennium* (London, 1957), 216.
5. George Rude, *The Crowd in the French Revolution* (Oxford, 1959), 227.
6. de Tocqueville, 8.
7. *Ibid.*, 8.
8. E.g. Tocqueville's ancestor Lamoignon de Malesherbes; cf. Richard Herr, *Tocqueville and the Old Régime* (Princeton, 1962), 88.
9. Georges Lefebvre, *Etudes sur la Revolution française* (Paris, 1954), 322–3; Lefebvre, *The Coming of the French Revolution, 1789*, 3.
10. For the growing hatred of aristocrats as anachronisms, beneficiaries bereft of the functions which once had been their justification, and for the king's involvement, see de Tocqueville, 30; Taine, I, 26, 36, 40, 43–44, 77–80, 85; Cobban, 108, 253; and Joseph Schumpeter, 'The Sociology of Imperialism', *'Imperialism' and 'Social Classes'* (New York, 1955), 57–58. Ford, 201, 251, points out that the 'robe' nobility of the *parlements*, the nearest thing left, after Louis XIV's domination of the aristocracy, to an aristocracy of function (and accordingly subject to seventeenth-century 'sword' contempt as upstarts from beyond the ranks of the nobility of 'courage'), became more and more functionless, and leaders in the common defence of privilege.
11. Lefebvre, *The Coming of the French Revolution, 1789*, 17; Barber, 102; R. R. Palmer, 'Georges Lefebvre: The Peasants and

the French Revolution', *Journal of Modern History*, XXXI, No. 4 (Dec. 1959), 339.

12. Herr, 120; Gay, 8; Douglas Dakin, *Turgot and the Ancient Régime in France* (London, 1939), 27–31.

13. Lefebvre, *The Coming of the French Revolution, 1789*, 61.

14. Barber, 136; d'Avenel, 286–7.

15. Gabriel Hanotaux and Le Duc de la Force, *Histoire du Cardinal de Richelieu* (Paris, 1899), VI, 306, 322.

16. Gay, 318.

17. See d'Avenel, 282–6, for a description of the ignorance to be found among aristocrats in Richelieu's day, while the intellectual world was attracting *bourgeois*.

18. Denis Diderot, 'The Encyclopaedia', *'Rameau's Nephew'*, *and other Works*, tr. Jacques Barzun and Ralph H. Bowen (New York, 1956), 301–2.

19. Nomura, 9–13.

20. Wei Yüan, *Ku-wei t'ang chi*, 1878 (Huai-nan shu-chü ed.), ch. 2. 22b–23a.

CHAPTER VII

1. Eugene Powers Boardman, *Christian Influence Upon the Ideology of the Taiping Rebellion, 1851–1864* (Madison, 1952), 124–5.

2. Henri Maspéro, *Etudes historiques* (Paris, 1950), 214–15.

3. According to Tung Chung-shu (second century B.C.), Confucius received the 'Imperial Mandate' in principle; see Fung Yu-lan, *A History of Chinese Philosophy*, Vol. II (Princeton, 1953), 63, 71, 129. For Confucius as *su-wang* see Tu Yü (222–84), *Ch'un-ch'iu Tso-chuan hsü* (Preface to *Ch'un-ch'iu*, with *Tso-chuan*): cf. *Tz'u-hai*, II, 61.

4. The 'Norman Anonymous' of York (*c.* 1100), in Ernst H. Kantorowicz, *The King's Two Bodies: a Study in Mediaeval Political Theology* (Princeton, 1957), 47–48, 63.

5. Ernst H. Kantorowicz, *Laudes Regiae: a Study in Liturgical Acclamations and Mediaeval Ruler Worship* (Berkeley and Los Angeles, 1946), 13–31.

6. Medieval Russian chronicle, continuing a Byzantine tradition of the sanctity of power, quoted in Michael Cherniavsky, *Tsar and People: Studies in Russian Myths* (New Haven and London, 1961), 12.

7. Tu Ehr-wei, *Chung-kuo ku-tai tsung-chiao yen-chiu* (Studies on the ancient religions of China) (Taipei, 1959), 84–88, 106–10.

8. A. Marmorstein, *The Old Rabbinic Doctrine of God* (London, 1927), I, 105–7.

9. Toda Toyosaburō, 'Gogyō setsu seiritsu no ichi kōsatsu' (Reflection on the formation of five-element theory), *Shinagaku kenkyū*, XII (1956), 44.

10. Hattori, 231.

11. Fung Yu-lan, *A History of Chinese Philosophy*, Vol. I (Peiping, 1937), 162–3.

12. Salo Wittmayer Baron, *A Social and Religious History of the Jews* (New York, 1952), I, Chapter One (esp. 4–8); E. I. J. Rosenthal, 'Some Aspects of the Hebrew Monarchy', *The Journal of Jewish Studies*, IX, Nos. 1 and 2 (1958), 18.

13. Hara, 233.

14. Ch'eng Hao, 'Lun wang pa cha-tzu' (Memorial on *wang* and *pa*), *Erh Ch'eng wen-chi* (Collection of writings of the two Ch'engs) (Changsha, 1941), 4.

15. Waley, 54–55.

16. Ewart Lewis, *Medieval Political Ideas* (New York, 1954), I, 142–3.

17. Moses Maimonides, *Guide of the Perplexed*, tr. M. Friedländer (New York, n.d.), II, 190.

18. Yang Yu-chiung, *Chung-kuo cheng-chih ssu-hsiang shih* (History of Chinese Political Thought) (Shanghai, 1937), 181–3; Tung Chung-shu, 19b.

19. Kantorowicz, *The King's Two Bodies*, 61–78, 87–93 et passim; *Laudes Regiae*, 145–6.

20. Hugh of Fleury, 'Tractatus de Regia Potestate et Sacerdotali', (*c.* 1102), quoted in Lewis, I, 166–8.

21. Marc Bloch, *Les rois thaumaturges* (Strasbourg, 1924), 20, 140–4, 215.

22. J. W. N. Watkins, 'Milton's Vision of a Reformed England', *The Listener*, LXI, No. 1556 (Jan. 22, 1959), 169.

23. Guglielmo Ferrero, *The Principles of Power* (New York, 1942), 150, observes that when Moses here prescribed that the king 'shall not multiply horses to himself', and that 'neither shall he greatly multiply to himself silver and gold', he condemned monarchy as the West has conceived it since the Middle Ages.

24. Ford, 9. This is precisely the materialist interpretation of the origins of Biblical monotheism in M. J. Shakhnovich, *Reaktsionnaia sushchnost' Iudaizma: Kratkii ocherk proiokhozhdeniia i*

klas-sovoi sushchnosti iudeskoi religii (The reactionary essence of Judaism: a short sketch of the derivation and class nature of the Jewish religion) (Moscow, Leningrad, 1960). See review in *Judaism*, XI, No. 1 (Winter 1962), 74.

25. Harry Austryn Wolfson, *Philo: Foundations of Religious Philosophy in Judaism, Christianity and Islam* (Cambridge, Mass., 1947), II, 331, 334–7, 381–2.

26. Michael Grant, *From Imperium to Auctoritas: a Historical Study of Aes Coinage in the Roman Empire, 49 B.C.–A.D. 14* (Cambridge, 1946), 356–9.

27. Erwin I. J. Rosenthal, *Political Thought in Mediaeval Islam: an Introductory Outline* (Cambridge, 1958), 43, 219.

28. Zevedei Barbu, *Problems of Historical Psychology* (New York, 1960), 68; Lucien Febvre, *Au coeur religieux du XVIᵉ siècle* (Paris, 1957), 264–5.

29. Norman H. Baynes, *Byzantine Studies and Other Essays* (London, 1955), 55–57.

30. *Ibid.*, 168.

31. The *su-wang*, as the true sage and an implied rebuke to the politically visible royal incumbent, figures in the Taoist *Chuang-tzu* (T'ien-tao section); see Tz'u-hai, II, 61; also Inoue Gengo, 'Juka to Haku I Tō Seki setsuwa' (Confucianism and the tales of Po I and Tao Chih), *Shinagaku kenkyū*, No. 13 (Sept. 1955), 21, where *Kung-yang* Confucian influence on Chuang-tzu is seen in the *su-wang* concept. In so far as we speak of Taoism as politically anarchistic, we identify it with an *essential* Confucianism which affects Confucianism-in-action, but is not coterminous with it. The Confucianism which is implemented, visible in history, is the credo of officials, who are naturally no anarchists. But the Taoist boycott of the world of affairs (as by hermits, who flout the values of Confucian-in-action, i.e. Confucianism-cum-Legalism, but confirm them, too, by abandoning the world to Confucianists—and dynasts—alone) dramatizes the theoretical principle which Confucianists invoke, as Confucianism-cum-Taoism, to rebuke emperors.

32. Cf. Howard S. Levy, tr., *Biography of An Lu-shan* (Berkeley and Los Angeles, 1960), 19, for a *Chiu T'ang-shu* indictment of the rebellion-cursed eighth-century Emperor Hsüan-tsung as a believer in the Taoist doctrine of *wu-wei*, inactivity.

33. Cf. Manegold of Lautenbach (a partisan of the greatest anti-imperial pope, Gregory VII), 'Ad Gebehardum Liber' (*c.* 1085), quoted in Lewis, I, 165: 'Therefore it is necessary that

he who is to bear the charge of all and govern all should shine above others in greatest grace of the virtues. . . . Yet when he who has been chosen for the coercion of the wicked and the defence of the upright has begun to foster evil against them . . . is it not clear that he deservedly falls from the dignity entrusted to him and that the people stand free of his lordship and subjection . . .?'

CHAPTER VIII

1. Wolff, 304.

2. A rebel proclamation addressed to the Ch'ing emperor in 1853 assailed the latter's ancestors for betrayal of the 'good government of the Ming' in 1644, and referred to the rebel claimant as the seventh descendant of the Ming Emperor Kuang-tsung (1620–1). See 'T'ien-ti hui chao-shu' (Decree of the *T'ien-ti hui*), *T'ai-p'ing T'ien-kuo shih-liao* (Historical materials on the *T'ai-p'ing T'ien-kuo*), ed. Chin Yü-fu et al. (Peking, 1955) (hereafter TPTKSL), 256; 'Passing Events in China (from Dr. D. J. MacGowan's Note Book)', *North China Herald* (hereafter NCH), No. 159 (Aug. 13, 1853), 7.

3. See *T'ai-ping T'ien-kuo* (The Heavenly Kingdom of Great Peace), ed. Hsiang Ta et al (Shanghai, 1952) (hereafter TPTK), I, frontispiece and caption. *The North China Herald* originally gave the impression that T'ien-te and Hung were the same person: e.g. in 'Proclamation of One of the Insurgent Chiefs', NCH No. 137 (March 12, 1853), 126. But later in the year a correspondent noted that, after the recent fall of Nanking to the Taipings, no more T'ien-te proclamations had been issued, and the Taipings were said to deny his existence. The correspondent conjectured the existence of two parties, one of Ming legitimists, who spoke in the name of T'ien-te or Huang-ti, and the other of Taiping rebels, who considered the use of *ti* in a sovereign's designation as blasphemous, since they reserved it for God. See 'Passing Events in China', 7.

The personal name of T'ien-te was Hung Ta-ch'üan. In Ch'ing official sources, he was identified as T'ien-te and taken to be Taiping co-sovereign with Hung Hsiu-ch'üan; see Teng Ssu-yü, 'Hung Hsiu-ch'üan', in Arthur W. Hummel, ed. *Eminent Chinese of the Ch'ing Period* (Washington, 1943), I, 363. For Hung Ta-ch'üan correctly identified as T'ien-te Wang in the ranks of the *T'ien-ti hui*, see Kuo Ting-yee, *T'ai-p'ing T'ien-kuo shih jih-chih*

(Daily record of *T'ai-p'ing T'ien-kuo* historical events) (Shanghai, 1946), II, Appendix, 37.

4. 'Hsü Chien-chieh kao-shih' (Proclamation by Hsü Chien-chieh), TPTK, II, 893.

5. 'Hsün-t'ien Huang-ti chao' (Proclamation of the Hsün-t'ien Emperor), TPTKSL, 255; 'T'ien-te Wang t'ieh Liu-chou kao-shih' (Proclamation of T'ien-te Wang affixed at Liu-chou), TPTK, II, 891; 'T'ien-ti hui chao-shu', 256, and 'Passing Events in China', 7; 'Proclamation of One of the Insurgent Chiefs', 126.

6. 'Huang Wei kao-shih' (Proclamation by Huang Wei), TPTK, II, 898.

7. Ku Yen-wu, *Jih-chih lu* (Record of knowledge day by day) (Jui-ch'u t'ang ed., 1695), ch. 4.8a.

8. 'Ch'in-ting shih-chiai t'iao-li' (By imperial order: regulations for official ranks), TPTK, II, 551.

9. 'Pien yao-hsüeh wei tsui-li lun' (Despising the pit of fiends as durance vile), TPTK, I, 293.

10. Yang Yu-ch'iung, 181.

11. 'Chien T'ien-ching yü Chin-liang lun' (On building the Heavenly Capital in Nanking), TPTK, I, 267, 269.

12. 'T'ien-ming chao-chih-shu' (Book of heavenly decrees and imperial edicts), TPTK, I, 59–61; 'The Book of Celestial Decrees and Declarations of the Imperial Will', NCH, No. 148 (May 28, 1853), 172.

13. See *Lun-yü*, 'The Analects', XVII, 2–3: 'The Master said, "I would prefer not speaking." Tsze-kung said, "If you, Master, do not speak, what shall we, your disciples, have to record?" The Master said, "Does Heaven speak? The four seasons pursue their courses and all things are *continually* being produced, *but* does Heaven say anything?" ' Cf. 'T'ien-fu hsia-fan chao-shu' (Book of declarations of the divine will made during the Heavenly Father's descent upon earth), TPTK, I, 9 (NCH, No. 149 (June 4, 1853), 175), where *T'ien-fu* speaks to *T'ien-wang*.

14. 'Chao-shu kai-nien pan-hsing lun' (On the promulgation of imperial proclamations under fixed seal), TPTK, I, 313.

15. Cf. 'Chen T'ien-ming T'ai-p'ing T'ien-kuo . . .' in Yang Hsiu-ch'ing Hsiao Ch'ao-kuei hui-hsien kao-yü (Joint proclamation of Yang Hsiu-ch'ing and Hsiao Ch'ao-kuei), TPTK, II, 691; NCH, No. 151 (June 18, 1853), 182.

16. 'T'ien-fu hsia-fan chao-shu', 10; NCH, No. 149, 175.

17. 'T'ien-lu yao-lun' (On the essentials of the principles of Heaven), TPTK, I, 345–8 et passim; 'T'ien-t'iao shu' (Book of the

laws of Heaven), TPTK, I, 73 ('The Book of Religious Precepts of the T'hae-ping Dynasty', NCH, No. 146 [May 14, 1853], 163). The NCH article corresponds to 'T'ien-t'iao shu' only in certain passages.

18. 'T'ien-ming chao-chih-shu', 67; NCH, No. 148, 172.

19. 'T'ai-p'ing chiu-shih-ko' (Taiping songs on salvation), TPTK, I, 242–3; NCH, No. 178 (Dec. 24, 1853), 83.

20. 'Ch'in-ting ying-chieh kuei-chen' (By imperial order: a hero returning to truth), TPTK, II, 574–5.

21. 'Ch'in-ting shih-chiai t'iao-li' (By imperial order: regulations for official ranks), TPTK, II, 546, 552, 561.

22. 'Tsei-ch'ing hui-tsuan' (Collected materials on the circumstances of the thieves), TPTK, III, 112.

23. 'T'ai-p'ing T'ien-jih' (Taiping days), TPTK, II, 635–6.

24. 'Pan-hsing chao-shu' (Proclamations published by imperial authority), TPTK, I, 164.

25. 'T'ien-t'iao shu', 74.

26. 'Chien T'ien-ching yü Chin-ling lun', 261.

27. 'T'ien-t'iao shu', 73. See NCH, No. 146 (May 14, 1853), 163, for a translation of another version of this sentiment.

28. Boardman, 116, following Chien Yu-wen.

29. 'T'ien-ch'ing tao-li shu' (Book of the divine nature and principles), TPTK, I, 360.

30. See Boardman, 4, for the Western denunciation of this claim as blasphemy.

31. 'T'ai-p'ing chao-shu' (Taiping imperial proclamations), TPTK, I, 92; NCH, No. 150 (June 11, 1853), 180; James Legge, *the Li Ki*, Books I–X, *Sacred Books of the East*, ed. F. Max Müller (Oxford, 1885), 364.

32. 'T'ai-p'ing chao-shu', 88; NCH, Nos. 150–80. It should be noted in this connection that the Taipings held that God could be worshipped by all the people, not just by sovereign princes, in marked contradistinction to the standard Confucian reservation to the Emperor alone of the sacrifices to *T'ien*. See 'T'ien-t'iao shu', 73; NCH, No. 146, 163.

33. 'T'ien-ch'ao t'ien-mu chih-tu' (The land system of the Heavenly Court), TPTK, I, 321.

34. Nomura, Part II, *Kokka gakkai zasshi*, LXXII, No. 1, 321.

35. 'Tsei-ch'ing hui-tsuan', 249.

36. 'T'ai-p'ing chiu-shih-ko', 244; NCH, No. 181 (Jan. 14, 1854), 95.

37. See Chapter V, note 11.

38. Hung Jen-kan, 'Tzu-cheng hsin-p'ien' (New essay to aid in government), TPTK, II, 524.

39. 'Pan-hsing chao-shu', 161; NCH, No. 152 (June 25, 1853), 187, translates this portion of the text, but says, 'the Empire belongs to the *Chinese* [i.e. unaccountably and confusingly substitutes 'Chinese' for 'Shang-ti's'], not to the Tartars . . .'

40. 'Ch'in-ting ying-chieh kuei-chen', 592.

41. For the prospects of French monarchy after the Revolutionary era (with implications for the parody of Chinese kingship in a comparable emotional atmosphere), see the famous set of reflections on the romantic Restoration state of mind, Alfred de Musset, *La confession d'un enfant du siècle* (Paris, 1862), 10: 'Napoleon . . . destroyed and parodied the kings. . . . And after him a great noise was heard. It was the stone of St. Helena which had just fallen on the ancient world.'

42. See Fukui, 58–59, for *Chung-hsüeh* as *nei-hsüeh* in the thought of Chang Chih-t'ung, and for *nei-hsüeh* as the equivalent of *t'i* in the *t'i-yung* dichotomy.

43. Fung, II, 716; and Vol. III of the present work.

44. Cited approvingly for its Chinese application, with manual labour for cadres ensuring the (strictly non-Confucian) equality or integration of manual and intellectual work, in Li Fang, 'Cadres et Intellectuals "XIAFANG" ', *Démocratie Nouvelle* (May 1959), 43 (from editorial in *Hung-chi*, March 16, 1959).

CHAPTER IX

1. Jacob Burckhardt, *Force and Freedom* (*Weltgeschichtliche Betrachtnngen*) (New York, 1955), 181.

2. Tung Chung-shu, 1. 5a.

3. Joseph de Maistre, *Du Pape* (Paris, n.d.), 315.

4. Ojima Sukema, 'Shina shisō: shakai keizai shisō' (Chinese thought: social and economic thought), *Tōyō shichō* (Far Eastern thought-tides) (Tokyo, 1936), 23–24.

5. Hucker, 199.

6. Ch'en Shao-pai, 'Hsing Chung Hui ko-ming shih yao' (Essentials of the Hsing Chung Hui's revolutionary history), *Hsin-hai ko-ming* (Documents on the 1911 revolution) (Shanghai, 1957), I, 32.

7. Hsüeh, 19.

8. K'ang, 'Chung-kuo hsüeh-pao t'i-tz'u', 4.

9. Feng Tzu-yu, *She-hui chi-i yü Chung-kuo* (Socialism and China) (Hong Kong, 1920), 50.

10. Hu Shen-wu and Chin Ch'ung-chi, 'Hsin-hai ko-ming shih-ch'i Chang Ping-lin ti cheng-chih ssu-hsiang' (The political ideas of Chang Ping-lin at the time of the 1911 revolution), *Li-shih yen-chiu*, No. 4 (1961), 5.

11. T'ao, *Pei-yang chün-fa*, II, 112.

12. Liu Shih-p'ei, part one, CKHP, No. 1 (Jan. 1916), 3a.

13. E.g. Sun Yat-sen on Yao and Shun ('The name was monarchy, the fact was the rule of democracy'), and on Confucius and Mencius as 'pro-people's rights' on the strength of their praises of Yao and Shun; cf. Kuo Chan-po (Kōya Masao, tr.), *Gendai Shina shisō shi* (History of modern Chinese thought) (Tokyo, 1940), 108.

14. E.g. Wang Hsieh-chia, 'Chung-hua min-kuo', 2, KCWT, No. 18, for the admission that Confucianism uses heavily monarchical language—but—'What was the origin of *ko-ming*?' A 'people's rights' version of Confucianism had, of course, been worked up by K'ang Yu-wei and his Reform group, and was frequently refurbished by men like Wang, here adapting himself to the republican environment and quoting, without referring to K'ang, some of the latter's old proof-texts in the *Li-yün* section of *Li-chi*. Liu Ta-chün (see note 51, Chapter I above) does the same (KCWT, 1–2). The thinness of Confucianism in this 'republican' version is apparent, not only from its highly special selectivity but from the fact that authority has clearly been stripped from it; Confucianism, instead of dictating the polity, must be interpreted by its defenders so that it conforms to a polity established on other authority. The rhetorical question 'What is the origin of *ko-ming*?' suggests, at bottom, not that the Republic is Confucian, but that western standards have invaded even Confucianism: *Ko-ming* as revolution was from the western political vocabulary, out of Japan.

15. Cf. T'ao, *Pei-yang chün-fa*, II, 26–27, for correspondence between Ch'ing and initial Republican nomenclature. Cf. also the opinion of a dedicated republican, Liu Pai-ming, 'Kung-ho kuo-min chih ching-shen' (The spirit of a republican citizenry), *Hsüeh-heng* ('The Critical Review'), No. 10 (October 1922), 1; acknowledging disappointments, he noted that the Republic had had only ten years' trial, one three-hundredth of 'despotism's duration'. Democracy, he said, was not just a form of government, but an expression of the spirit.

16. Ch'en Huan-chang, 7a.

17. Cf. Nagano Akira, *Shina wa doku e yuku?* (Where is China going?) (Tokyo, 1927), 141-3, for a suggestion that the Chihli and Fengtien northern factions were locked in monarchical competition.

18. Tezuka, 17-19.

19. Tu Yü: see note 3, Chapter VII, above.

20. *Ming shih*, ch. 77, 4a, cited in Sohn ms.

21. Tezuka, 130. Note that the connection between *chün* and *ch'en* (and *ch'en* is located only in this or an equivalent connection) is always denoted by *lun*, human relationship; see *Li-chi*, Mencius, etc., *passim*.

22. Chang Ch'un-ming, 'Ch'ing-tai ti mu-chih' (The private-secretary system of the Ch'ing dynasty), *Lingnan hsüeh-pao*, IX, No. 2 (1950), 33-37.

23. *Ibid.* 47.

24. Sakamaki, 210.

25. *Ibid.*, 54-55.

26. T'ao, *Pei-yang chün-fa*, II, 90, 97; Jerome Ch'en, 117.

27. Sakamaki, 139.

28. Kuo Pin-chia, 'Min-kuo erh-tz'u ko-ming shih' (History of the Republic's 'Second Revolution'), part 2, *Wuhan Quarterly*, IV, No. 4 (1935), 843.

29. Sakamaki, 214-15. Sun's friend Huang Hsing, trying to win over the Ch'ing loyalist, Gen. Chang Hsün, to the anti-Yüan cause in summer, 1913, declared: 'Yüan Shih-k'ai is not only abhorrent to the Republic, he was a robber of the Ch'ing house'; cf. Kuo, part 1, *Wuhan Quarterly*, IV, No. 3, 650.

30. Li Ting-shen, *Chung-kuo chin-tai shih* (Recent history of China) (Shanghai, 1933), 312.

31. Sakamaki, 235.

32. Kuo Pin-chia, part 2, 842.

33. However, some Japanese from the most aggressive circles, ready to contemplate a take-over bid in China, not just encroachment through local action and the manipulation of blocs, opposed Yüan as emperor precisely because domestic resistance, internal disorder, seemed certain; cf. Kuzuu, 123. Perhaps it was felt that this would waste the resources which Japan might hope to attain. But this readiness for uncomplicated direct conquest was premature.

34. Kuo Pin-chia, part 1, *Wuhan Quarterly*, IV, No. 3 (1935), 637.

35. Lin Yutang, *A History of the Press and Public Opinion in China* (Chicago, 1936), 117.
36. Kuzuu, 119, 123–4, 127–30.
37. E.g. for an anti-Yüan Japanese observer's extreme scepticism about Chinese national feeling, see Sakamaki (Part 1), 277–83.
38. Tokutomi Iichirō, *Kōshaku Yamagata Aritomo den* (Biography of Prince Yamagata Aritomo) (Tokyo, 1933), III, 779, 923, 924.
39. Sanetō, 237–8.
40. K'ang, 'Chung-kuo hsüeh-pao t'i-tz'u', 6.
41. Fukui, 98.
42. Lo Chen-yü, 'Pen-chao hsüeh-shu yüan-liu kai-lueh' (General outline of the course of scholarship in the present dynasty), *Liao chü tsa-cho*, series 2, chüan 3 (Liao-tung, 1933), 1a, 2a–2b, 5b, 45a–46a.
43. For Tao, T'ien, Yao, Shun, the whole package of *wang-tao*, see Mo Shen, *Japan in Manchuria: an Analytical Study of Treaties and Documents* (Manila, 1960), 402–3; Nakayama Masaru, *Taishi seisaku no honryū (Nihon, Tōyō oyobi konnichi no seiki)* (The main course of policy towards China: Japan, East Asia, and the contemporary age) (Tokyo, 1937), 139–40.
44. Takata Shinji, *Shina shisō to gendai* (Chinese thought and the modern era) (Tokyo, 1940), 52, 88.
45. For education in Manchukuo as, variously, traditional and modern, see Warren W. Smith, jr., *Confucianism in Modern Japan: a Study of Conservatism in Japanese Intellectual History* (Tokyo, 1959), 187–90; F. C. Jones, *Manchuria Since 1931* (London, 1949), 46; K. K. Kawakami, *Manchukuo, Child of Conflict* (New York, 1933), 116–17.

CONCLUSION

1. Included in the draft constitution of 1908, *Hsien-fa ta-kang* (General principles of the Constitution). This was reiterated in late 1911, after the Wuchang uprising, in article one of the reform proposals of Chang Shao-tseng, the indecisive commander of the imperial Ch'ing Twentieth Division, based on Mukden; see Sakamaki, 132–3 (where the last character of the name is misprinted as 'ts'ao').
2. Ch'en Huan-chang, *K'ung-chiao lun* (On the Confucian religion) (Shanghai, 1912), 1.

3. Kita Ikki, *Shina kakumei gaishi* (Outsider's history of the Chinese revolution) (Tokyo, 1941), 22, 312–13.

4. T'ao, *Chin-tai i-wen* (Shanghai, 1930), 2; *Pei-yang chün-fa*, II, 97.

5. Heibonsha: *Seijigaku jiten* (Dictionary of political science) (Tokyo, 1957), 449.

6. *Kuo-t'i* had some vague ancient usage, as in the *Ku-liang chuan*, irrelevant to modern monarchists, and a colourless existence in occasional documents thereafter. The monarchists' *kuo-t'i* had as much novelty infused in it from Japan as the republicans' *ko-ming*.

7. Wang Shih, *Yen Fu chuan* (Biography of Yen Fu) (Shanghai, 1957), 93–94.

Bibliography

A. CHINESE AND JAPANESE

Araki Toshikazu, 'Sō-dai ni okeru denshi seiritsu no jijō' (Circumstances leading to the establishment of the palace examinations), *Tō-A jimbun gakuhō*, III, No. 2 (Oct. 1943), pp. 214–38.

Chang Ch'un-ming, 'Ch'ing-tai ti mu-chih' (The private-secretary system of the Ch'ing dynasty), *Lingnan hsüeh-pao*, IX, No. 2 (1950).

Ch'ang-t'ing, 'K'ung-hsüeh fa-wei' (The inner meaning of the Confucian learning revealed), *Chung-kuo hsüeh-pao*, No. 1 (Nov. 1912).

'Chao-shu kai-nien pan-hsing lun' (On the promulgation of imperial proclamations under fixed seal), *T'ai-p'ing T'ien-kuo* (The Heavenly Kingdom of the Great Peace), ed. Hsiang Ta et al. (Shanghai, 1952), I, pp. 301–17.

Ch'en Huan-chang, *K'ung-chiao lun* (On the Confucian religion) (Shanghai, 1912).

Ch'en Huan-chang, *K'ung-chiao lun chieh-lu* (Chapters on the Confucian religion) (Taiyuan, 1918).

Ch'en Po-ying, *Chung-kuo t'ien-chih ts'ung-k'ao* (General survey of Chinese land systems) (Shanghai, 1935).

Ch'en Shao-pai, 'Hsing Chung Hui ko-ming shih yao' (Essentials of the Hsing Chung Hui's revolutionary history), *Hsin-hai ko-ming* (Documents on the 1911 revolution) (Shanghai, 1957), I.

Ch'en Tu-hsiu, 'Hsien-fa yü K'ung-chiao' (The constitution and the Confucian religion), *Tu-hsiu wen-ts'un* (Collected essays of Ch'en Tu-hsiu) (Shanghai, 1937), pp. 103–12.

Ch'en Yin-k'o, *T'ang-tai cheng-shih shih shu-lun kao* (Draft account of T'ang political history) (Shanghai, 1947).

Ch'eng Hao, 'Lun wang pa cha-tzu' (Memorial on *wang* and *pa*), *Erh Ch'eng wen-chi* (Collection of writings of the two Ch'engs) (Changsha, 1941).

'Chien T'ien-ching yü Chin-ling lun' (On building the Heavenly Capital in Nanking), *T'ai-p'ing T'ien-kuo* (The Heavenly Kingdom of Great Peace), ed. Hsiang Ta et al. (Shanghai, 1952), I, pp. 249–80.

Ch'ien Mu, *Kuo-shih ta-kang* (Outline of Chinese history) (Shanghai, 1940).

'Ch'in-ting shih-chiai t'iao-li' (By imperial order: regulations for official ranks), *T'ai-p'ing T'ien-kuo* (The Heavenly Kingdom of Great Peace), ed. Hsiang Ta et al. (Shanghai, 1952), II, pp. 543–62.

'Ch'in-ting ying-chieh kuei-chen' (By imperial order: a hero returning to truth), *T'ai-p'ing T'ien-kuo* (The Heavenly Kingdom of The Great Peace), ed. Hsiang Ta et al. (Shanghai, 1952), II, pp. 563–94.

Chou Chen-fu, 'Yen Fu ssu-hsiang chuan-pien chih p'ou-hsi' (A close analysis of the changes in Yen Fu's thought), *Hsüeh-lin*, No. 3 (Jan. 1941).

Chu Shou-p'eng, ed., *Kuang-hsü Tung-hua hsü-lu* (Kuang-hsü supplement to the archival records) (Shanghai, 1908).

Feng Tzu-yu, *She-hui chu-i yü Chung-kuo* (Socialism and China) (Hong Kong, 1920).

Fukui Kōjun, *Gendai Chūgoku shisō* (Recent Chinese thought) (Tokyo, 1955).

Hara Tomio, *Chūka shisō no kontai to jugaku no yūi* (The roots of Chinese thought and the pre-eminence of Confucianism) (Tokyo, 1947).

Hattori Unokichi, *Kōshi oyobi Kōshikyō* (Confucius and the Confucian Religion) (Tokyo, 1926).

Hsia Te-wo, 'Hu-nan An-hua chiao-yü-chieh ch'üan-t'i ch'ing-ting K'ung-chiao kuo-chiao shu' (Letter from the entire educational circle of An-hua, Hunan, requesting that Confucianism be established as the state religion of China), *K'ung-chiao wen-t'i* (Problems of Confucianism), No. 17, supplement (Taiyuan, 1916).

'Hsü Chien-chieh kao-shih' (Proclamation by Hsü Chien-chieh), *T'ai-p'ing T'ien-kuo* (The Heavenly Kingdom of Great Peace), ed. Hsiang Ta et al. (Shanghai, 1952), II, pp. 892–3.

Hsüeh Cheng-ch'ing, 'K'ung-tzu kung-ho hsüeh-shuo' (The republican theory of Confucius), *Chung-kuo hsüeh-pao*, No. 7 (May, 1913).

'Hsün-t'ien Huang-ti chao' (Proclamation of the Hsün-t'ien Emperor), *T'ai-p'ing T'ien-kuo shih-liao* (Historical materials on the *T'ai-p'ing T'ien-kuo*), ed. Chin Yü-fu et al. (Peking, 1955), pp. 255–6.

Hu Shen-wu and Chin Ch'ung-chi, 'Hsin-hai ko-ming shih-ch'i Chang Ping-lin ti cheng-chih ssu-hsiang' (The political ideas of Chang Ping-lin at the time of the 1911 revolution), *Li-shih yen-chiu*, No. 4 (1961), pp. 1–20.

'Huang Wei kao-shih' (Proclamation by Huang Wei), *T'ai-p'ing T'ien-kuo* (The Heavenly Kingdom of Great Peace), ed. Hsiang Ta et al. (Shanghai, 1952), II, pp. 897–8.

Hung Jen-kan, 'Tzu-cheng hsin-p'ien' (New essay to aid in government), *T'ai-p'ing T'ien-kuo* (The Heavenly Kingdom of Great Peace), ed. Hsiang Ta et al. (Shanghai, 1952), II, pp. 522–41.

'Hu-pei kung-min Liu Ta-chün shang ts'an chung liang yüan ching ting kuo-chiao shu' (Letter from Liu Ta-chün of Hupei to the parliament requesting establishment of a state religion) *K'ung-chiao wen-t'i* (Problems of Confucianism), No. 18, supplement (Taiyuan, 1917).

Imazeki Hisamaro, *Sung Yüan Ming Ch'ing Ju-chia hsüeh mien-piao* (Chronological tables of Sung, Yüan, Ming, and Ch'ing Confucianism) (Tokyo, 1920) (In Chinese).

Inoue Gengo, 'Juka to Haku I Tō setsuwa' (Confucianism and the tales of Po I and Tao Chih), *Shinagaku kenkyū*, No. 13 (Sept. 1955), pp. 13–22.

K'ang Yu-wei, 'Chung-kuo hsueh-hui pao t'i-tz'u' (The thesis of the journal of the Society for Chinese Learning), *Pu-jen*, II (March 1913), *chiao-shuo*, pp. 1–8.

K'ang Yu-wei, 'Chung-kuo hsüeh-pao t'i-tz'u' (The thesis of the *Chung-kuo hsüeh-pao*, No. 6 (Feb. 1913).

K'ang Yu-wei, 'Fu Chiao-yü pu shu' (Reply to the Ministry of Education), *Pu-jen*, IV (May 1913), *chiao-shuo*, pp. 1–9.

K'ang Yu-wei, 'K'ang Nan-hai chih Tsung-t'ung Tsung-li shu' (Letter from K'ang Yu-wei to the President and Premier), *K'ung-chiao wen-t'i* (Problems of Confucianism), No. 17, supplement (Taiyuan, 1916).

K'ang Yu-wei, 'K'ung-chiao hui hsü' (Preface to the Confucian Society), *Pu-jen*, I (March 1913), *Chiao-shuo*, pp. 1–10.

Kao Lao, *Ti-chih yün-tung shih-mo chi* (An account of the monarchical movement) (Shanghai, 1923).

Kita Ikki, *Shina kakumei gaishi* (Outsider's history of the Chinese Revolution) (Tokyo, 1941).

Ku Yen-wu, *Jih-chih lu* (Record of knowledge day by day) (Jui-ch'u t'ang ed., 1695).

Ku Yen-wu, *Jih-chih lu* (Record of knowledge day by day), ed. Huang Ju-ch'eng (1834).

Kuo Chan-po (Kōya Masao, tr.), *Gendai Shina shisō shi* (History of modern Chinese thought) (Tokyo, 1940).

Kuo Pin-chia, 'Min-kuo erh-tz'u ko-ming shih' (History of the Republic's 'Second Revolution'), parts one and two, *Wuhan Quarterly*, IV, Nos. 3–4 (1935).

Kuo Ting-yee, *T'ai-p'ing T'ien-kuo shih jih-chih* (Daily record of T'ai-p'ing T'ien-kuo historical events) (Shanghai, 1946).

Kuzuu Yoshihisa, *Nisshi kōshō gaishi* (An unofficial history of Sino-Japanese relations) (Tokyo, 1939).

Li T'ien-huai, 'Tsun K'ung shuo' (On reverence for Confucius), *Chung-kuo hsüeh-pao*, No. 7 (May 1913).

Li Ting-shen, *Chung-kuo chin-tai shih* (Recent history of China) (Shanghai, 1933).

Li Wen-chih, 'Ching ting K'ung-chiao wei kuo-chiao ti erh-tz'u i-chien shu' (Second communication of views favouring establishment of Confucianism as the state religion), *K'ung-chiao wen-t'i* (Problems of Confucianism), No. 18, supplement (Taiyuan, 1917).

Liang Ch'i-ch'ao, 'Chung-kuo chih wu-shih-tao' (China's *bushidō*), *Yin-ping-shih ho-chi* (Shanghai, 1936), ch'uan-chi 6:24, pp. 1–61.

Liu Pai-ming, 'Kung-huo kuo-min chih ching-shen' (The spirit of a republican citizenry), *Hsüeh-heng* ('The Critical Review'), No. 10 (Oct. 1922), pp. 1–6.

Liu Shih-p'ei, 'Chün-cheng fu-ku lun' (On the monarchical revival), parts one and two, *Chung-kuo hsüeh-pao*, No. 1 (Jan. 1916), No. 2 (Feb. 1916).

Lo Chen-yü, 'Pen-chao hsüeh-shu yüan-liu kai-lueh' (General outline of the course of scholarship in the present dynasty), in *Liao chü tsa-cho*, series 2, chüan 3 (Liao-tung, 1933).

Lü Ssu-mien, *Chung-kuo t'ung-shih* (General history of China) (n.p., 1941).

Miyakawa Hisayuki, 'Zenjō ni yoru ōchō kakumei no tokushitsu' (The special quality of dynastic overturns depending on 'shan-jang'), *Tōhōgaku*, No. 11 (Oct. 1955).

Miyazaki Ichisada, *Yō-sei-tei, Chūgoku no dokusai kunshu* (The Yung-cheng Emperor—China's autocratic ruler) (Tokyo, 1950).

Nagano Akira, *Shina wa doku e yuku?* (Where is China going?) (Tokyo, 1927).

Naitō Torajirō, *Shinchō shi tsūron* (Outline of Ch'ing history) (Tokyo, 1944).

Nakayama Masaru, *Taishi seisaku no honryū* (*Nihon, Tōyō oyobi konnichi no seiki*) (The main course of policy towards China: Japan, East Asia, and the contemporary age) (Tokyo, 1937).

Niida Noboru, *Chūgoku no nōson kazoku* (The Chinese peasant family) (Tokyo, 1952).

Nomura Kōichi, 'Seimatsu kōyō gakuha no keisei to Kō Yūi gaku no rekishiteki igi' (The formation of the late-Ch'ing *kung-yang* school and the historical meaning of K'ang Yu-wei's doctrine), Part One, *Kokka gakkai zasshi*, LXXI, No. 7 (1958), pp. 1–61; Part Two, *Kokka gakkai zasshi*, LXXII, No. 1, pp. 33–64.

Ojima Sukema, 'Shina shisō: shakai keizai shisō' (Chinese thought: social and economic thought), *Tōyō shichō* (Far Eastern thought-tides) (Tokyo, 1936).

'Pan-hsing chao-shu' (Proclamations published by imperial authority) *T'ai-p'ing T'ien-kuo* (The Heavenly Kingdom of Great Peace), ed. Hsiang Ta et al. (Shanghai, 1952), I, pp. 157–67.

'Pien yao-hsüeh wei tsui-li lun' (Despising the pit of fiends as durance vile), *T'ai-p'ing T'ien-kuo* (The Heavenly Kingdom of Great Peace), ed. Hsiang Ta et al. (Shanghai, 1952), I, pp. 281–99.

Rinji Taiwan kyūkan chōsakai dai-ichi-bu hōkoku (Temporary commission of the Taiwan Government-general for the study of old Chinese customs, report of the First Section), *Shinkoku gyōseihō* (Administrative laws of the Ch'ing dynasty), kan 1 (Tokyo, 1914); kan 4 (Tokyo, 1911), kan 5 (Tokyo, 1911).

Sagara Yoshiaki, 'Toku no gon no igi to sono hensen' (The meaning of the word *te* and its evolution), *Tōyō shisō kenkyū* (Studies in Far Eastern thought), No. 1, ed. Tsuda Sokichi (Tokyo, 1937).

Sakamaki Teiichirō, *Shina bunkatsu ron: tsuki, 'Gen Seikai'* (The decomposition of China: supplement, 'Yüan Shih-k'ai') (Tokyo, 1914).

BIBLIOGRAPHY

Sanetō Keishū, *Nihon bunka no Shina e no eikyō* (The influence of Japanese culture on China) (Tokyo, 1940).

Shimizu Morimitsu, 'Kyū Shina ni okeru sensei kenryoku no kiso' (The basis of autocratic power in prerevolutionary China), *Mantetsu chōsa geppō* (Bulletin of the research bureau of the South Manchuria Railway), XVII, No. 2 (Feb. 1937), pp. 1–60.

Shōji Sōichi, 'China Ryō no gaku' (The thought of Ch'en Liang), *Tōyō no bunka to shakai*, IV (1954), pp. 82–100.

Sung Yü-jen, 'K'ung-hsüeh tsung-ho cheng chiao ku chin t'ung-hsi lui pieh-lun' (On Confucianism as uniter of political and intellectual, ancient and modern systems and classes). *Chung-kuo hsüeh-pao*, No. 9 (July 1913).

Takata Shinji, *Shina shisō to gendai* (Chinese thought and the modern era) (Tokyo, 1940).

'Ta-tsung-tung kao-ling' (Presidential mandate), Sept. 25, 1914, *Chiao-yü kung-pao* (Educational record), V (June 20, 1915), *Ming-ling*, pp. 1–2.

'Ta-tsung-tung kao-ling' (Presidential mandate), Nov. 3, 1914, *Chiao-yü kung-pao* (Educational record), VII (Aug. 1915), *Ming-ling*, pp. 1–2.

'T'ai-p'ing chao-shu' (Taiping imperial proclamations), *T'ai-p'ing T'ien-kuo* (The Heavenly Kingdom of Great Peace), ed. Hsiang Ta et al. (Shanghai, 1952), I, pp. 85–99.

'T'ai-p'ing chiu-shih-ko' (Taiping songs on salvation), *T'ai-p'ing T'ien-kuo* (The Heavenly Kingdom of the Great Peace), ed. Hsiang Ta et al. (Shanghai, 1952), I, pp. 237–47.

'T'ai-p'ing t'ien-jih' (Taiping days), *T'ai-p'ing T'ien-kuo* (The Heavenly Kingdom of Great Peace), ed. Hsiang Ta et al. (Shanghai, 1952), II, pp. 629–50.

T'ao Chü-yin, *Chin-tai i-wen* (Items about the modern era) (Shanghai, 1940).

T'ao Chü-yin, *Liu chün-tzu chuan* (Biographies of the 'Six Martyrs') (Shanghai, 1946).

T'ao Chü-yin, *Pei-yang chün-fa t'ung-chih shih-ch'i shih-hua* (Historical discourses on the era of the Pei-yang military clique's dominion), Vols. 1–4 (Peking, 1957); Vol. 5 (Peking, 1958).

Tezuka Ryōdō, *Jukyō dōtoku ni okeru kunshin shisō* (The sovereign-minister idea in Confucian ethics) (Tokyo, 1925).

'T'ien-ch'ao t'ien-mu chih-tu' (The land system of the Heavenly Court), *T'ai-p'ing T'ien-kuo* (The Heavenly Kingdom of the Great Peace), ed. Hsiang Ta et al. (Shanghai, 1952), I, pp. 319–26.

'T'ien-ch'ing tao-li shu' (Book of the divine nature and principles), *T'ai-p'ing T'ien-kuo* (The Heavenly Kingdom of the Great Peace), ed. Hsiang Ta et al. (Shanghai, 1952), I, pp. 353–406.

'T'ien-fu hsia-fan chao-shu' (Book of declarations of the divine will made during the Heavenly Father's descent upon earth), *T'ai-p'ing t'ien-kuo* (The Heavenly Kingdom of the Great Peace), ed. Hsiang Ta et al. (Shanghai, 1952), I, pp. 7–20.

'T'ien-lu yao-lun' (On the essentials of the principles of heaven), *T'ai-p'ing T'ien-kuo* (The Heavenly Kingdom of the Great Peace), ed. Hsiang Ta et al. (Shanghai, 1952), I, pp. 327–52.

'T'ien-ming chao-chih-shu' (Book of heavenly decrees and imperial edicts), *T'ai-p'ing T'ien-kuo* (The Heavenly Kingdom of Great Peace), ed. Hsiang Ta et al. (Shanghai, 1952), pp. 5–70.

'T'ien-te Wang t'ieh Liu-chou kao-shih' (Proclamation of T'ien-te Wang affixed at Liu-chou) (The Heavenly Kingdom of the Great Peace), ed. Hsiang Ta et al. (Shanghai, 1952), II, pp. 891–2.

'T'ien-ti hui chao-shu' (Decree of the *T'ien-ti hui*), *T'ai-p'ing T'ien-kuo shih-liao* (Historical materials on the *T'ai-p'ing T'ien-kuo*), ed. Chin Yü-fu et al. (Peking, 1955), pp. 256–7.

'T'ien-t'iao shu' (Book of the laws of Heaven), *T'ai-p'ing T'ien-kuo* (The Heavenly Kingdom of the Great Peace), ed. Hsiang Ta et al. (Shanghai, 1952), I, pp. 71–83.

Toda Toyosaburō, 'Gogyō setsu seiritsu no ichi kōsatsu' (Reflection on the formation of five-element theory), *Shinagaku kenkyū*, XII (1956), pp. 38–45.

Tokutomi Iichirō, *Kōshaku Yamagata Aritomo den* (Biography of Prince Yamagata Aritomo), Vol. III (Tokyo, 1933).

'Tsei-ch'ing hui-tsuan' (Collected materials on the circumstances of the thieves) *T'ai-p'ing T'ien-kuo* (The Heavenly Kingdom of the Great Peace), ed. Hsiang Ta et al. (Shanghai, 1952), III, pp. 23–348.

Tso Shun-sheng, *Wan-chu lou sui-pi* (Sketches from the Wan-chü chamber) (Hong Kong, 1953).

Tu Erh-wei, *Chung-kuo ku-tai tsung-chiao yen-chiu* (Studies on the ancient religions of China) (Taipei, 1959).

Tung Chung-shu, *Ch'un-ch'iu fan-lu* (Luxuriant dew from the *Spring and Autumn Annals*) (Shanghai, 1929).

Wang Hsieh-chia, 'Chung-hua min-kuo hsien-fa hsüan ch'uan chang ting K'ung-chiao wei kuo-chiao ping hsü jen-min hsiu chiao tzu-yu hsiu-cheng an' (Proposal that the constitution of the Republic of China promulgate a special clause establishing Confucianism as the state religion and permitting modification of the freedom of religion), *K'ung-chiao wen-t'i* (Problems of Confucianism), No. 18, supplement (Taiyuan, 1917).

Wang Shih, *Yen Fu chuan* (Biography of Yen Fu) (Shanghai, 1957).

Wei Yüan, *Ku-wei t'ang chi*, 1878 (Huai-nan shu-chü ed.).

Wu Li, 'K'ung-tzu fei Man-chou chih fu-hu' (Let Confucius not be an amulet for the Manchu), *Min-pao*, No. 11 (Jan. 30, 1907).

'Yang Hsiu-ch'ing Hsiao Ch'ao-kuei hui-hsien kao-yü' (Joint proclamation of Yang Hsiu-ch'ing and Hsiao Ch'ao-kuei), *T'ai-p'ing T'ien-kuo* (The Heavenly Kingdom of the Great Peace), ed. Hsiang Ta et al. (Shanghai, 1952), II, pp. 691–2.

Yang Yin-shen, *Chung-kuo wen-hsüeh-chia lieh-chuan* (Biographies of Chinese literary figures) (Shanghai, 1939).

Yang Yu-ch'iung, *Chung-kuo cheng-chih ssu-shiang shih* (History of Chinese political thought) (Shanghai, 1937).
Yang Yu-ch'iung (Moriyama Takashi, tr.), *Shina seitō shi* (History of Chinese political parties) (Tokyo, 1940).

B. WESTERN

Alföldi, Andrew, *A Conflict of Ideas in the Late Roman Empire: the Clash between the Senate and Valentinian I* (Oxford, 1952).
Barber, Elinor G., *The Bourgeoisie in 18th century France* (Princeton, 1955).
Barbu, Zevedei, *Problems of Historical Psychology* (New York, 1960).
Baron, Salo Wittmayer, *A Social and Religious History of the Jews*, Volume One (New York, 1952).
Baynes, Norman H., *Byzantine Studies and Other Essays* (London, 1955).
Bernard-Maitre, Henri, *Sagesse chinoise et philosophie chrétienne* (Paris, 1935).
Bloch, Marc, *Les rois thaumaturges* (Strasbourg, 1924).
Boardman, Eugene Powers, *Christian Influence Upon the Ideology of the Taiping Rebellion, 1851–1864* (Madison, 1952).
Brewitt-Taylor, C. H., tr., *The Romance of the Three Kingdoms* (Shanghai, 1925).
Brogan, D. W., 'The "Nouvelle Revue Française" ', *Encounter* (March 1959), pp. 66–68.
Bruford, W. H., 'The Idea of "Bildung" in Wilhelm von Humboldt's Letters', *The Era of Goethe: Essays Presented to James Boyd* (Oxford, 1959), pp. 17–46.
Burckhardt, Jacob, *Force and Freedom* (*Weltgeschichtliche Betrachtungen*) (New York, 1955).
Cahill, James F., 'Confucian Elements in the Theory of Painting', *The Confucian Persuasion*, ed. Arthur F. Wright (Stanford, 1960), pp. 115–40.
Chan, David, 'The Problem of the Princes As Faced by the Ming Emperor Hui (1399–1402)', *Oriens*, XI, Nos. 1–2 (1958), pp. 183–93.
Chan, David B., 'The Role of the Monk Tao-Yen in the Usurpation of the Prince of Yen (1398–1402)', *Sinologica*, VI, No. 2 (1959), pp. 83–100.
Chang, Carsun, *The Development of Neo-Confucian Thought* (New York, 1957).
Chang Jen-hsia, 'Flower-and-Bird Painting', *China Reconstructs*, III (May–June 1953).
Chao Yuen Ren, 'What is Correct Chinese?' *Journal of the American Oriental Society*, LXXXI, No. 3 (Aug.–Sept. 1961), pp. 171–7.
Ch'en, Jerome, *Yuan Shih-k'ai (1859–1916): Brutus assumes the Purple* (London, 1961).
Cherniavsky, Michael, *Tsar and People: Studies in Russian Myths* (New Haven and London, 1961).

Chow Tse-tsung, 'The Anti-Confucian Movement in Early Republican China', *The Confucian Persuasion*, ed. Arthur F. Wright (Stanford, 1960).

Cobban, Alfred, *A History of Modern France: Volume One, Old Régime and Revolution, 1715–1799* (Harmondsworth, 1957).

Cohn, Norman, *The Pursuit of the Millennium* (London, 1957).

Dakin, Douglas, *Turgot and the Ancien Régime in France* (London, 1939).

d'Avenel, G., *La noblesse française sous Richelieu* (Paris, 1901).

de Bary, W. Theodore, 'A Reappraisal of Neo-Confucianism', *Studies in Chinese Thought*, ed. Arthur F. Wright (Chicago, 1953), pp. 81–111.

de Bary, W. T., 'Chinese Despotism and the Confucian Ideal: A Seventeenth-Century View', *Chinese Thought and Institutions*, ed. John K. Fairbank (Chicago, 1957), pp. 163–203.

Delatte, Louis, *Les traités de la royauté d'Ecphante, Diotegène, et Sthénidas* (Liege and Paris, 1942).

de Maistre, Joseph, *Du Pape* (Paris, n.d.).

De Musset, Alfred, *La confession d'un enfant du siècle* (Paris, 1862).

des Rotours, Robert, *Le traité des examens, traduit de la Nouvelle histoire des T'ang* (Paris, 1932).

de Tocqueville, Alexis, *The Old Régime and the French Revolution* (New York, 1955).

Diderot, Denis, 'The Encyclopaedia', *'Rameau's Nephew' and Other Works*, tr. Jacques Barzun and Ralph H. Bowen (New York, 1956), pp. 291–323.

Duyvendak, J. J. L., *China's Discovery of Africa* (London, 1949).

Fallers, L. A., 'Despotism, Status Culture and Social Mobility in an African Kingdom', *Comparative Studies in Society and History*, II, No. 1 (Oct. 1959), pp. 11–32.

Febvre, Lucien, *Au coeur religieux du XVIᵉ siècle* (Paris, 1957).

Ferrero, Guglielmo, *The Principles of Power* (New York, 1942).

Ford, Franklin L., *Robe and Sword: the Regrouping of the French Aristocracy after Louis XIV* (Cambridge, Mass., 1953).

Franke, Wolfgang, *The Reform and Abolition of the Traditional Chinese Examination System* (Cambridge, Mass., 1960).

Freedman, Maurice, *Lineage Organization in Southeastern China* (London, 1958).

Freedman, Maurice, 'The Family in China, Past and Present', *Pacific Affairs*, XXXIV, No. 4 (Winter 1961–2), pp. 323–36.

Fung Yu-lan, *A History of Chinese Philosophy: the Period of the Philosophers* (from the Beginnings to *circa* 100 B.C.), tr. Derk Bodde (Peiping, 1937).

Fung Yu-lan, *A History of Chinese Philosophy: Volume Two, The Period of Classical Learning*, tr. Derk Bodde (Princeton, 1953).

Gay, Peter, *Voltaire's Politics: the Poet as Realist* (Princeton, 1959).

Gernet, Jacques, *Daily Life in China on the Eve of the Mongol Invasion 1250–1276* (New York, 1962).

BIBLIOGRAPHY

Gernet, Jacques, *Les aspects économiques du Bouddhisme dans la société chinoise du Ve au Xe siècle* (Saigon, 1956).

Grant, Michael, *From Imperium to Auctoritas: a Historical Study of Aes Coinage in the Roman Empire, 49 B.C.–A.D. 14* (Cambridge, 1946).

Griggs, Thurston, 'The *Ch'ing Shih Kao*: a Bibliographical Summary', *Harvard Journal of Asiatic Studies*, XVIII, Nos. 1–2 (June 1955), pp. 105–23.

Hadas, Moses, *Hellenistic Culture: Fusion and Diffusion* (New York, 1959).

Hanotaux, Gabriel, and Le Duc de la Force, *Histoire du Cardinal de Richelieu* (Paris, 1899).

Heibonsha: *Seijigaku jiten* (Dictionary of political science) (Tokyo, 1957).

Herr, Richard, *Tocqueville and the Old Régime* (Princeton, 1962).

Hintze, Otto, *Staat und Verfassung* (Leipzig, 1941).

Ho Ping-ti, 'Aspects of Social Mobility in China, 1368–1911', *Comparative Studies in Society and History*, I, 4 (June 1959), pp. 330–59.

Ho Ping-ti, *Studies on the Population of China, 1368–1953* (Cambridge, Mass., 1959).

Houn, Franklin W., *Central Government in China: an Institutional Study* (Madison, 1957).

Hsiao Kung-chuan, *Rural China: Imperial Control in the Nineteenth Century* (Seattle, 1960).

Hu, C. T., 'The Ning Wang Revolt: Sociology of a Ming Rebellion' (Association for Asian Studies, ms., 1959).

Huang Sung-K'ang, *Lu Hsün and the New Culture Movement of Modern China* (Amsterdam, 1957).

Hucker, Charles O., 'Confucianism and the Chinese Censorial System', *Confucianism in Action*, ed. David S. Nivison and Arthur F. Wright (Stanford, 1959), pp. 182–208.

Hurvitz, Leon, ' "Render unto Caesar" in Early Chinese Buddhism', *Sino-Indian Studies: Liebenthal Festschrift*, ed. Kshitis Roy (Visvabharati, 1957), pp. 80–114.

Jones, F. C., *Manchuria Since 1931* (London, 1949).

Jones, J. Walter, *The Law and Legal Theory of the Greeks* (Oxford, 1956).

Kantorowicz, Ernst, *Frederick the Second, 1194–1250* (London, 1931).

Kantorowicz, Ernst H., *Laudes Regiae: A Study in Liturgical Acclamations and Mediaeval Ruler Worship* (Berkeley and Los Angeles, 1946).

Kantorowicz, Ernst H., *The King's Two Bodies: a study in Mediaeval Political Theology* (Princeton, 1957).

Kaufmann, Walter, *Nietzsche* (New York, 1956).

Kawakami, K. K., *Manchukuo, Child of Conflict* (New York, 1933).

Kraus, Wolfgang H., 'Authority, Progress, and Colonialism', *Nomos I: Authority*, ed. Carl J. Friedrich (Cambridge, 1958), pp. 145–56.

Krieger, Leonard, *The German Idea of Freedom: History of a Political Tradition* (Boston, 1957).

Lefebvre, Georges, *Etudes sur la Revolution française* (Paris, 1954).

Lefebvre, Georges, *The Coming of the French Revolution, 1789* (Princeton, 1947).

Legge, James, tr., *The Li Ki*, Books I–X, *Sacred Books of the East*, ed. F. Max Muller (Oxford, 1885).

Levenson, Joseph R., 'Ill Wind in the Well-Field: The Erosion of the Confucian Ground of Controversy', *The Confucian Persuasion*, ed. Arthur F. Wright (Stanford, 1960), pp. 268–87.

Levy, Howard S., *Biography of An Lu-shan* (Berkeley and Los Angeles, 1960).

Levy, Howard S., *Biography of Huang Ch'ao* (Berkeley and Los Angeles, 1955).

Lewis, Ewart, *Medieval Political Ideas* (New York, 1954).

Li Fang, 'Cadres et Intellectuels "XIAFANG"', *Démocratie Nouvelle* (May 1959), pp. 43–44.

Liao, Joshua, 'The Empire Breaker', *The Orient*, 10 (May 1951).

Lin Yutang, *A History of the Press and Public Opinion in China* (Chicago, 1936).

Liu, Hui-chen Wang, 'An Analysis of Chinese Clan Rules: Confucian Theories in Action', *Confucianism in Action*, ed. David S. Nivison and Arthur F. Wright (Stanford, 1959), pp. 63–96.

Liu, James T. C., 'Some Classifications of Bureaucrats in Chinese Historiography', *Confucianism in Action*, ed. David S. Nivison and Arthur F. Wright (Stanford, 1959), pp. 165–81.

MacSherry, Charles Whitman, *Impairment of the Ming Tributary System as Exhibited in Trade Involving Fukien* (dissertation, University of California, 1957).

Maimonides, Moses, *Guide of the Perplexed*, tr. M. Friedländer (New York, n.d.).

Mancall, Mark, 'China's First Missions to Russia, 1729–1731', *Papers on China*, IX (Harvard University, August 1955), pp. 75–110.

Mann, Thomas, *Doctor Faustus* (New York, 1948).

Marmorstein, A., *The Old Rabbinic Doctrine of God* (London, 1927).

Marsh, Robert M., 'Bureaucratic Constraints on Nepotism in the Ch'ing Period', *Journal of Asian Studies*, XIX, No. 2 (Feb. 1960), pp. 117–33.

Marx, Fritz Morstein, *The Administrative State: an Introduction to Bureaucracy* (Chicago, 1957).

Maspéro, Henri, 'Comment tombe une dynastie chinoise: la chute des Ming', *Etudes historiques* (Paris, 1950).

Mayers, William Frederick, *The Chinese Government* (Shanghai, 1886).

Mo Shen, *Japan in Manchuria: an Analytical Study of Treaties and Documents* (Manila, 1960).

Montesquieu, *The Spirit of the Laws*, tr. Thomas Nugent (New York, 1949).

Mote, Frederick W., 'Confucian Eremitism in the Yüan Period', *The Confucian Persuasion*, ed. Arthur F. Wright (Stanford, 1960), pp. 202–40.

Neumann, Franz, 'Montesquieu', *The Democratic and the Authoritarian State: Essays in Political and Legal Theory* (Glencoe, III, 1957), pp. 96–148.

Nivison, David S., 'Ho-shen and His Accusers: Ideology and Political Behavior in the Eighteenth Century', *Confucianism in Action*, ed. David S. Nivison and Arthur F. Wright (Stanford, 1959), pp. 209–43.

North China Herald, Shanghai.

Norton, Lucy, tr. *Saint-Simon at Versailles* (New York, 1958).

Orwell, George, *The English People* (London, 1947).

Palmer, R. R., 'Georges Lefebvre: the Peasants and the French Revolution', *Journal of Modern History*, XXXI, No. 4 (Dec. 1959), pp. 329–42.

Pan Ku, *The History of the Former Han Dynasty*, Vol. II, tr. Homer H. Dubs (Baltimore, 1944).

'Passing Events in China (from Dr. D. J. Macgowan's Note Book)', *North-China Herald*, No. 159 (Aug. 13, 1853), p. 7.

'Proclamation of One of the Insurgent Chiefs', *North-China Herald*, No. 137 (March 12, 1853), pp. 126–7.

Pulleyblank, Edwin G., 'Neo-Confucianism and Neo-Legalism in T'ang Intellectual Life, 755–805', *The Confucian Persuasion*, ed. Arthur F. Wright (Stanford, 1960), pp. 77–114.

Pulleyblank, Edwin G., *The Background of the Rebellion of An Lu-shan* (London, New York, and Toronto, 1955).

Rosenberg, Hans, *Bureaucracy, Aristocracy, and Autocracy: the Prussian Experience, 1660–1815* (Cambridge, Mass., 1958).

Rosenthal, Erwin I. J., *Political Thought in Medieval Islam: an Introductory Outline* (Cambridge, 1958).

Rosenthal, E. I. J., 'Some Aspects of the Hebrew Monarchy', *The Journal of Jewish Studies*, IX, Nos. 1 and 2 (1958), pp. 1–18.

Rude, George, *The Crowd in the French Revolution* (Oxford, 1959).

Schumpeter, Joseph, 'The Sociology of Imperialism', *'Imperialism' and 'Social Classes'* (New York, 1955), pp. 1–98.

Schwartz, Benjamin, 'Some Polarities in Confucian Thought', *Confucianism in Action*, ed. David S. Nivison and Arthur F. Wright (Stanford, 1959), pp. 50–63.

Shih, Vincent, *The Ideology of the T'ai-p'ing T'ien-kuo* (University of Washington, ms.).

Sinnigen, William Gurnee, *The Officium of the Urban Prefecture During the Later Roman Empire* (Rome, 1957).

Sinnigen, William G., 'The Vicarius Urbis Romae and the Urban Prefecture', *Historia*, VIII, No. 1 (Jan. 1959), pp. 97–112.

Smith, Warren W., jr., *Confucianism in Modern Japan: A Study of Conservatism in Japanese Intellectual History* (Tokyo, 1959).

Sohn, Pow-key, 'The Theory and Practice of Land-systems in Korea in Comparison with China' (University of California, ms., 1956).

Soper, Alexander, 'Standards of Quality in Northern Sung Painting', *Archives of the Chinese Art Society of America*, XI (1957), pp. 8–15.

Strayer, Joseph R., 'Feudalism in Western Europe', *Feudalism in History*, ed. Rushton Coulborn (Princeton, 1956), pp. 15–25.

Taine, Hippolyte Adolphe, *The Ancient Régime* (New York, 1931).

Teng Ssu-yü, 'Hung Hsiu-ch'üan', *Eminent Chinese of the Ch'ing Period*, ed. Arthur W. Hummel (Washington, 1943), I, pp. 361–7.

'The Book of Celestial Decrees and Declarations of the Imperial Will', *North-China Herald*, No. 148 (May 28, 1853), p. 172.

'The Book of Religious Precepts of the T'hae-ping Dynasty', *North-China Herald*, No. 146 (May 14, 1853), p. 163.

Twitchett, Denis, 'The Fan Clan's Charitable Estate, 1050–1760', *Confucianism in Action*, ed. David S. Nivison and Arthur F. Wright (Stanford, 1959), pp. 97–133.

van Gulik, R. H., tr., *T'ang-Yun-Pi-Shih*, '*Parallel Cases from under the Pear-Tree*' (Leiden, 1956).

Vernadsky, George, *A History of Russia* (New Haven, 1951).

Waley, Arthur, *Yuan Mei, Eighteenth Century Chinese Poet* (New York, 1956).

Watkins, J. W. N., 'Milton's Vision of a Reformed England', *The Listener*, LXI, No. 1556 (Jan. 22, 1959), pp. 168–9, 172.

Watson, Burton, *Ssu-ma Ch'ien, Grand Historian of China* (New York, 1958).

Weber, Max, 'Politics As a Vocation', *From Max Weber: Essays in Sociology*, ed. H. H. Gerth and C. Wright Mills (New York, 1946), pp. 77–128.

Wittfogel, Karl A., *Oriental Despotism: A Comparative Study of Total Power* (New Haven, 1957).

Wittfogel, Karl A., and Feng Chia-sheng, *History of Chinese Society: Liao* (907–1125) (Philadelphia, 1949).

Wolff, Robert Lee, 'The Three Romes: the Migration of an Ideology and the Making of an Autocrat', *Daedalus* (Spring 1959), pp. 291–311.

Wolfson, Harry Austryn, *Philo: Foundations of Religious Philosophy in Judaism, Christianity and Islam* (Cambridge, Mass., 1947).

Wright, Arthur F., 'Sui Yang-ti: Personality and Stereotype', *The Confucian Persuasion*, pp. 47–76.

Yang Lien-sheng, 'Notes on Dr. Swann's "Food and Money in Ancient China" ', *Studies in Chinese Institutional History* (Cambridge, Mass., 1961), pp. 85–118.

Zürcher, E., *The Buddhist Conquest of China: the Spread and Adaptation of Buddhism in Early Medieval China* (Leiden, 1959).

VOLUME THREE

THE PROBLEM OF HISTORICAL SIGNIFICANCE

To

MY FATHER AND MOTHER

PREFACE FOR VOLUME THREE

WITH 'The Problem of Historical Significance', the successor to 'The Problem of Intellectual Continuity' and 'The Problem of Monarchical Decay', *Confucian China and Its Modern Fate* is concluded. In this work I do not maintain that China's connection with its past is concluded. The past certainly has historical significance for the latest China. But that term, historical significance, is significantly ambiguous. Volume Three, which gathers up themes from its predecessors, is about the ambiguity.

Much devoted attention is given to aspects of the Chinese past in China today; the intellectual tone seems quite different from an earlier generation's 'May Fourth' iconoclasm. But it would be perfunctory to conclude, simply, that the Chinese had returned to 'Chinese' affirmations after an aberration of cultural defeatism. One has to ask why the generations differ in tone. I believe this difference indicates, not that the Chinese past exerts a consistent, unvarying claim to devotion, but that men at different times face different pressures, and have different scope for expressing their devotion.

Two interpretations seem extreme, and inadequate to deal with the issues in modern Chinese history. One is the 'Oriental despotism' notion which implies that China was impervious to process. The other is a contention that the western intrusion had little or no part in locating the end to which Chinese process was tending.

Men have restored what they cease to resent. But they cease to resent what seems safely lodged in history; so that what they restore is not the past, but what now is in the past. And when they came to resentment in the first place, they did not come unassisted, moved solely by Chinese influences.

In Volume Two I tried to give the institutional context in Chinese history for the central significance of Confucianism, in both its predominance and its attrition. In Volume One I concluded with the metaphor of 'language and vocabulary', to capture the sense of attrition: change in the language of Chinese culture, not just enrichment of its traditional vocabulary. Volume Three suggests a connection between this and another metaphor, that of 'the museum'. 'Language and vocabulary' applies to innovation; 'the museum' applies to preservation. Innovation and preservation make a recipe for tension—perhaps as vital a tension now, for as vital a Chinese culture, as that other tension (see Volume Two) in that world of another language, the Confucian language of an earlier long day.

Again I must thank the Committee for Chinese Thought and the Center for Advanced Studies in the Behavioral Sciences for providing occasions for discussing much of the material in this volume. I am grateful, too, for a Guggenheim fellowship and the hospitality of St. Antony's College and the Oriental Institute, Oxford, which I enjoyed during my final year of work on the manuscript. In laying the bibliographical foundation for research, I was very greatly assisted by Joseph Chen, Robert Krompart, Pow-key Sohn, and George Yu. My wife has gone through the text exploding mines; she qualifies for the Confucian Medal of Honour.

The book is a publication of the Institute of International Studies, University of California, Berkeley, through its Center for Chinese Studies. I appreciate tremendously the material and intellectual support which, at all stages of the preparation of these volumes, I have received from the Institute and Center.

Parts of Volume Three in different form have appeared in *The Confucian Persuasion*, ed. Arthur F. Wright (Stanford, 1960), *Confucian Personalities*, ed. Arthur F. Wright and Denis Twitchett (Stanford, 1962), *Diogenes, Survey, The China Quarterly*, and *Journal of Asian Studies*. I wish to thank the publishers and editors for permission to use the materials here.

J. R. L.

Contents

CONTENTS

Part Three: Historical Significance

viii

CONTENTS

ix

Part One

OUT OF HISTORY

CHAPTER I

A Little Life: Liao P'ing and the Confucian Departure from History

'BUREAUCRACY without Confucianism—Confucianism without bureaucracy—Confucianism's intellectual content had profoundly altered. . . .' For monarchy offered the proper setting for Confucian bureaucracy, and monarchy, stricken in the nineteenth century, felled in 1912, became a vestigial idea. Confucianism under the Republic was a vestige, too. Monarchy and Confucianism, tied in companionship and suspicion for so many centuries, so many dynasties, had dragged each other down. And when Confucianism lost its institutional context, intellectual continuity was gravely imperilled. The great tradition, sinking, was ready to depart.

To depart from history was to enter it. Confucianism, yielding the future, became a thing of the past. It was remembered, loved by many, but lived only in fragments. It was historically significant.

Anyone writing the history of Confucian China, before it suffered its modern fate, might tell a great part of the story in great Confucian lives. In recent history, however, the conditions of greatness were lost to Confucianists—at least greatness in the open, where achievement may be measured. Liao P'ing (1852–1932), for example, was really unimportant.

Yet, a brief life of a small Confucianist can tell, or introduce, a great part of the modern story. Liao P'ing had an empty career, and his works were full of that old Confucian abomination, 'empty words'. Why was he so unimportant?

3

Not by denying the justice of the question, but by answering it, one can restore Liao to importance. For Liao, too, like the Confucian tradition he lived in and exhausted, gained historical significance in stepping out of history. If Liao was an unpersuasive Confucianist, largely out of action, out of touch with the real issues of the greater part of his time, a real issue comes to light in Liao's very obscurity.

What made his intellectual system fantastic, by any orthodox Confucian standard, was its irrelevance to any conceivable action, and his thought had just the counterpart it deserved, his uneventful life. Confucian thought, before his, had long preserved vitality through a bureaucratic tie, an intimate relationship with politics, the Confucian life—that is, with the Confucian kind of history, the kind Confucianists made and wrote. A close interaction of action and thought was intrinsic to Confucianism. But by the time Liao died in 1932, the Confucian life was available to no one. There was nothing Confucian about politics now (though Confucianism could be a political issue). The sterile public career of Liao, the last thinker of the last Confucian school, attested to the banishment of Confucianism from history. And that was what he echoed in his thought, with the banishment of history from his Confucian intellectual concerns.

I. THE LIFE

Instead of history, Liao made prophecy the stuff of Confucianism: Confucius was a prophet, and Liao as well. Confucius, of course, had to be seen as a mighty force, if a quiet one, in his own day, but in Liao, at the end of the Confucian line, we have the seer without the doer. Certainly he was a prophet without excessive honour in his own county: the gazetteer for his birthplace (Ching-yen, in Szechwan), published in 1900 when Liao was in full maturity, records under the Liao surname simply: 'P'ing of the present dynasty is a *chin-shih* (graduate of the third degree) and a teacher.'[1]

This pale schoolmasterly image is most of the visible Liao. Born in 1852 in a relatively poor family (with a mildly prominent bureaucratic lineage on his mother's side), he

4

devoted himself to study, though his father was a small dealer in medicines and his brothers followed the lead into business. Later, Liao adopted the studio style, 'San-yü t'ang' (Three Fish Hall), to commemorate his scholarly beginnings: one day, as a little boy, he offered his modest catch to the teacher in the village school, and won admittance. And an excellent little boy he sounds.

In any case, we hear no more of lazy times by the ponds and rivers. Books possessed him, and he graduated to teachers of a considerably higher fish-power, like Wang K'ai-yün (1833–1916), a *Kung-yang* classical scholar who taught Liao in the *Tsun-ching* (Revere the Classics) *shu-yüan* in Chengtu (Liao later taught there, too), but who never cared to claim discipleship. Indeed, Yeh Te-hui (1864–1927), a conservative scholar impatient with speculative soaring, recorded a snide bit of hearsay in this connection: Wang had allegedly labelled Liao a 'deep thinker, not fond of study'.

In the 1880s, while Liao was moving through the conventional series of civil-service examinations, Chang Chih-tung (1837–1909), then the Canton Governor-General, made him one of his secretaries, treating him with great informality, and inviting him to teach in a branch of the academy Chang founded in 1887, the *Kuang-ya shu-yüan*. It was in this period that he met K'ang Yu-wei (1858–1927) and influenced him (or was plagiarized by him) in the preparation of the *Hsin-hsüeh wei-ching k'ao* (On the false Classics of the Hsin learning), one of the seminal documents of the Reform Movement of 1898 (see Volume One).

After becoming a *chin-shih*, Liao was appointed an archivist, but he soon requested and received a transfer to teaching duties. In 1898 he was an instructor at Sui-ting-fu in his home province of Szechwan, totally out of active politics, when the Reform Movement, which had such ties with his Confucian scholarship, flourished briefly and was suppressed. The official supervisor of studies in Szechwan, knowing that K'ang Yu-wei, object of the Empress Dowager's most ferocious hostility, had taken his lead in Confucian matters from Liao, impeached the latter for outrageous opinions on the Classics, cashiered him, and committed him to surveillance by local officials. But Liao was so obviously harmless that the new Governor of Chekiang, who admired his talents, was willing to appoint him a master in a school under his jurisdiction.

After the revolution of 1911–12, Liao for several years directed the *Kuo-hsüeh yüan*, a school in Chengtu. His growing reputation as a recluse led the eminent Japanese historian, Naitō, lecturing at Kyōtō University in 1915, to observe that Liao was in the mountains of Szechwan and did not want to come out. There had been an exception—Liao's trip in 1913 to speak to Confucian societies in Peking—but the commitment to withdraw was confirmed in 1919, when he suffered a stroke. His right side was paralysed. Liao continued to write with his left hand, depending on his eldest daughter to reduce the drafts to order. On October 6, 1932, he died during an outing in the country.[2]

2. THE QUESTION OF ORIGINALITY

Is there anything to chew on in this thin gruel? The Liao-K'ang relationship has some substance in it.

K'ang (claiming 'coincidence') never faced up to the accusation, but Liao brought in the indictment; K'ang's sometimes dissident but always respectful disciple, Liang Ch'i-ch'ao (1873–1929), admitted the grounds; and Chinese and Japanese scholars have concurred in the verdict: K'ang's *Hsin-hsüeh wei-ching k'ao* (On the false classics of the Hsin learning, 1891), his first great *succés d'estime* and *de scandale*, was lifted consciously and in considerable detail from the *P'i Liu p'ien* (Treatise refuting Liu Hsin), and K'ang's *K'ung-tzu kai-chih k'ao* (On Confucius as a reformer, 1897) stole thesis and thunder from the *Chih-sheng p'ien* (Treatise on knowing the Sage). Together these treatises made up Liao's manuscript of 1886, *Chin ku hsüeh-k'ao* (On the 'Modern Text' and 'Ancient Text' learning). According to the charge, K'ang saw Liao's work at the home of one Shen Tseng-chih (1853–1922) and sought an introduction in Canton. Seemingly unimpressed by Liao's esoterica, K'ang warned him against publishing these conclusions which would stain him

6

with guilt as a teacher of unlawful doctrine. The next year, K'ang published his *Wei-ching k'ao*—'dashing it off (literally, "leaning on a horse")', said Liao, 'writing his book, truly breaking the tie of ethics'.[3]

This lament, from a Confucianist, about the rape of his originality has a dying fall. Originality *per se* had never been a Confucian virtue, and a touchy insistence that you yourself, not your opponent, had made the startling new departure was the reverse of the rule of old Confucian controversy. Liao was consistent in his jealous claim to priority; his own intellectual history, with its carefully plotted 'six stages', recapitulated his credo of movement and freshness. Anyone who studies, he laid down, should make a 'great change' in his theories every ten years, and a 'small change' every three. One who fails of the small change may be termed a 'mediocre talent', while one who misses the large change is an 'abdicated talent'.[4]

This call to make it new and this claim that K'ang had pilfered the prestige Liao deserved for making a new pronouncement were merely words. It was K'ang, plagiarist or not, who chose to face the music by making history. K'ang took these claims for Confucius as a reformer and made them relate to an actual modern reform, clothing them in action and reeling out for modern China the last thread of authentic Confucian commitment. But Liao, the verbalizer about originality, was just a conventional examination-passer, circumspect enough to move smoothly through the old channels and to earn in 1889 easy traditional accolades from unreconstructed, and obviously untroubled, official examiners: 'He creates splendid phrases . . . cites many Classics . . . is penetrating and clear in ancient teachings . . . selects refined vocabulary . . . is familiar with others' discussions and is not one of those who restrict themselves to their own confirmations or destructive critiques.'[5] K'ang nearly died in 1898 for what he made of Liao's hypotheses. But Liao in 1898 (earning Liang Ch'i-ch'ao's contempt even while Liang acknowledged him as intellectually the first comer) still shrank from implication, declaring that it was no intention of his to expound a battle-position.[6]

7

Once Liao had proclaimed himself above the battle, there was nothing to keep him from soaring higher and higher, borne away from the ground of action and history, where Confucius belonged, on words lighter than even the hottest air. Liao in 1916 was in his self-styled fourth phase, dealing with 'Heaven' and 'man'. He ascribed light and purity to Heaven, heaviness and dross to earth.[7] Heaven was his destination. In the early days of the K'ang coincidence, the issue had still been posed in relatively mundane historical terms: the Confucius of the *chin-wen* (modern text) tradition, espoused by Liao and K'ang, was taken to be the original fountain of wisdom, as against the Duke of Chou in the *ku-wen* (ancient text) tradition. But finally, shuffling off the dross and the heaviness, Liao had come to a fantasy of levitation. At the end of days all men would fly, when the earthy needs of food and clothing would have dropped away.[8]

The millenarian quality of Liao's thoughts could hardly be clearer. And its distance from basic Confucianism was clear, too, For Confucianism, committed above all to civilized order and history, could not be chiliastic and still be one of its many possible selves. It stood for just the reverse of the millenarian yearning for the end of days and the upsetting of institutions.

Not surprisingly, possible disciples kept falling off Liao's ladder to the stars. As Liao moved from 'revering Confucius' to 'worshipping Confucius',[9] his questioning followers turned increasingly to anti-religious anti-Confucianists—Wu Yü (1871–1949), for example, Liao's student in Szechwan, who turned to Ch'en Tu-hsiu (1879–1942) at Peking University[10] —and Liao's little clan rapidly dwindled.

3. FROM PARADIGM TO PROPHECY

When Confucius was revered he was a political man, a figure in history, who invited men (the State's ministers of the Confucian ideal type) to learn from him how history should be made—what principles should apply and what judgements be levelled, in the farthest tomorrow as in classical yesterday. The Classics (*transmitted* by the Confucius who was revered) exposed the paradigms of history, the eternal patterns of action. 'The *Spring and Autumn* records the successes and failures of the World', said the Han Confucianist, Tung Chung-shu, flatly.[11] Process was unimportant, no passage of time could relativize the truth. But when Confucius was worshipped he was a saint and an oracle, a transcendent, supra-historical figure, who foretold to men the end to which time was passing. The Confucius of the Liao P'ing image put all things yet to come into the *I-ching* (Book of Changes), and all rules for posterity into the *Shih-ching* (Book of Poetry), where the religion he founded was set forth in detail.[12] The Classics (*created* by the Confucius who was worshipped), enshrined the prophecies of history, intimations of actions yet unseen. The Classics were *new* with Confucius and, as Liao put it in 1894, new Classics were not old history.[13] Paradigmatic Classics—the classics of *ku-wen* traditionalists, for whom knowledge and action were one— were history, accounts of visible events which made essentials manifest. But prophetic Classics of *chin-wen* provenance were the keys to history, not history themselves.

Liao's early attack on the accepted *ku-wen* Classics had committed him unequivocally to a religious rather than an historical view of Confucius. Liao meant to expose the 'false classics of the Hsin learning'—to borrow K'ang's version of Liao's indictment—to the end of establishing the 'true' Classics (the *chin-wen* Classics) as creations of Confucius. But this amounted to admitting that the *chin-wen* Classics were forgeries by Confucius; that is, Confucius himself might seem like Liu Hsin (d. A.D. 23), the alleged forger of the *ku-wen*, writing texts and pretending they were old. Of course, Liao had no intention of making this equation, and Confucius, therefore, had to be truly superhuman; if he were only human, he would be only an ideologue like Liu Hsin, who was bought and paid for, in Liao's opinion, by the usurper, Wang Mang, the founder of the so-called 'Hsin Dynasty' (A.D. 9–23). How could one 'forger', one concealer of his own authorship, be distinguished from the other unless Liu Hsin and Confucius were simply incommensurable, the first a dishonest historian, the second a pure and divinely

9

inspired prophet? If the Six Classics were not history, it was because in the *ku-wen* version they were fiction, and in the *chin-wen* version a miraculous rending of the veil of future time.

The Classics' passage from paradigm to prophecy can be seen in the space of one generation, from the usages of the practising official, Hsüeh Fu-ch'eng (1838–94), for example, to the fancies of the non-practising Liao P'ing. Hsüeh, in a memorial of 1875, cited an ancient model as a lesson for contemporaries, in the approved traditional fashion of a Confucianist on duty, engaged in political action. 'In ancient times,' he wrote, 'when Yüeh I attacked Ch'i, his first essential was alliance with Chao, and when Chu-ko Liang defended Shu, he first proceeded to unite with Wu. In general, preparedness demands the possession of allies. This is the way things are.' (History, that is, is the record of reality, not process.) And the conclusion: 'The overseas people have come to our China. Our sole recourse is diplomatic combination' (*ho-tsung lien-heng*, a phrase drawn from the pre-Ch'in *Chan-kuo ts'e*, referring to conflicting 'Warring States' diplomatic plans in face of the Ch'in menace). And Hsüeh continued with a discussion of the 'five strongest treaty nations: England—the implacable foe—France, Russia, the United States, and Germany'. He saw the United States in particular as a possible ally, since America, he said, wanted a counterweight to European powers, and China's weakness added to Europe's strength.[14]

Again, in 1879, Hsüeh called attention to Japan's accession to power through her adoption of western material techniques. He commended the same to China as a warning to Japan. 'When Japan hears that China is becoming prepared, she must know the difficulties and retire. Who knows but that she will yield even while China is not yet equipped? This would be the subtle practice of the ancients, *hsien sheng hou shih*' ('first, voice; later, fact'—to begin with deceptive propaganda claims of power so as ultimately to achieve one's objectives).[15] The phrase, considered here so applicable to contemporary circumstances, is a *Ch'ien Han shu* variant (biography of Han Hsin), via *Shih-chi* (his biography as

Marquis of Huai-yin), of a *Tso-chuan* (Chao Kung, twenty-first year) classical original.

Hsüeh, then, proceeding rationalistically, searched the ancient texts for parallels. Liao, on the other hand, mystically found metaphor in his researches. There is all the difference in the world (the difference between fullness of significance for practical action, and emptiness) between formulating a suggestion historically, e.g. 'The situation of ancient Cheng in the Empire was *like* that of modern China in the larger world', and suggesting, with implications of pre-cognition, 'The situation of ancient Cheng *was* that of modern China.'[16] A responsible Confucianist, even such a late and flexible one as Hsüeh Fu-ch'eng, had his antiquity for use. A dreaming Confucianist like Liao P'ing—intellectually irresponsible, and not responsible for the political action which a sound Confucianism entailed—had his antiquity for oracular conviction. Future events *must* come, for the classical sources provided, not prescriptions for freely chosen action, but a deterministic revelation of what actions must amount to.

Thus, Liao saw China's modern plight in the international jungle *prefigured* in Confucius' (alleged) *po-luan* words about the 'age of chaos' in the *Kung-yang chuan*.[17] Confucius saw it coming and conveyed his vision esoterically. For Confucius' *Ch'un-ch'iu* (Spring and Autumn Annals), to which the *Kung-yang* was key, itself unlocked the future, when the ancient vision of the Great Harmony (*ta-t'ung*) would be realized, and the great course would be finally run from dissimilarity (*pu-t'ung*) to sameness—all men the same as one another, then men the same as the *kuei* and *shen*, or spirits.[18] In order to see world prophecies in Classics which orthodox Confucianists deemed Chou-period histories, Liao brought the *Chou-li* (Rites of Chou) back to his canon (from which he had earlier banished it: see note 8). But he now took the character 'chou', the same character, not to suggest the specific dynasty 'Chou', but to signify 'comprehensive', one of its other possible meanings.[19] It was yet another diffusion of the historical particular into a prophetic and universal haze.

4. FROM PROPHECY TO FINIS

Hsüeh Fu-ch'eng, like any Confucianist with a public life, asked of the Classics, 'What are we to do?' Liao P'ing, a Confucianist expelled from the world of doers, chopped the question down, in effect, to 'What (or where) are we?' That which the older order of Confucianists had always meant as a stigma—'empty words' (*k'ung-yen*), the antithesis of action or the basic stuff of history—Liao explicitly, admiringly attributed to Confucius.

Liao's Confucius, in his stories about his idol, Wen Wang, for example, had an esoteric message to convey, wrapped within the spurious, metaphorical, outside 'historical' surface. For Confucius, as a *su-wang* ('throneless king'), was confined to the inner realm of knowledge, barred from the outer realm of executive action, and he expressed his knowledge in specifically 'empty words', words, that is, which did not record what they seemed to record—past and open politics— but future, hidden prospects. The *su-wang* idea, for Liao, was the informing idea of the Six Classics.[20]

Liao, with his claim to originality, boasted to K'ang Yu-wei that in his own work 'there was not a single expression which was not new' (i.e. Liao was the first to reveal the hidden meaning), but, by the same token, 'there was not a single meaning which was not old'.[21] Thus Liao, in effect, paradoxically modelled himself on the *transmitting* Confucius of the orthodox conception. But in transmitting, proudly, the 'empty words' of his 'creative' Confucius, Liao carried the curse of the orthodox meaning of 'empty words' into his own day. He himself was the speaker of empty words, empty of any relevance to the history of his times. Liao was transmitting to no one.

One might say (Liao certainly did) that he seemed to have transmitted to K'ang Yu-wei. And K'ang, to be sure, had not intended to be out of action; he led the Reform Movement of 1898. Was this not, after all, an example of Liao's Confucianism in action? Was Confucian departure from history, from influence on the course of events, necessarily implied in a Confucian departure from history as the locus of wisdom? Or, to put it another way, was Liao's empty life really a counterpart of his empty words, not simply a coincidence?

To place Liao in Chinese history, it is important to see what happened to 'prophetic' Confucianism in K'ang's hands. Liao was out of public affairs, and it was only with this inward bent that he could make more and more fanciful departures from the *chin-wen* or *Kung-yang* Confucianism he once had shared with K'ang and Liang Ch'i-ch'ao. These three went three ways.

Liang went beyond the *chin-wen* to post-Confucian (non-Confucian) considerations.[22] K'ang, however, retained his affirmations, but he ceased to develop them internally—that is, having failed to 'Confucianize' politics (according to his lights), he avoided the Liao alternative of finer and fancier thought-webs and chose to keep a political commitment. But it was a commitment now to 'politicalize' Confucianism, to make the preservation of Confucianism a political issue, in tacit recognition of the fact that Confucianism no longer governed political issues. It was no longer the inspiration of politics, but a bone of contention in politics, a politics conducted on all sides with non-Confucian, truly modern objectives. K'ang had been a radical in a Confucian Chinese world. He became an anti-radical in the post-Confucian nation, the Chinese part of the world, where Confucianism's chances lay with the Chinese 'national essence' (see Volume Two). And K'ang, who had failed in 1898 to establish a Confucian case for radicalism against the traditional Confucian arguments for conservatism, finally, when the Republic came, with its iconoclastic aura, turned to making conservative arguments for Confucianism. Significantly, where once he had deemed it the most important thing in the world to separate 'false' Classics from 'true', now he defended the Classics indiscriminately.

K'ang, in his early phase, when he went part of the way with Liao P'ing, had tried to make novelty Chinese, by claiming for it the authority of Confucius. Confucius was someone to obey, to make history and change the nation. But when the monarchy fell, the new was nakedly foreign;

its sponsors dismissed Confucius instead of invoking his authority. Then K'ang joined those who adhered to the old in a new way. Now Confucius was someone to save, because he was in and of the national history. Chinese mountains, rivers, trees, the very insects were all embodied in Confucius' teaching.[23] What once could be seen as 'Confucian progress' was only soulless imitation of the West. And so K'ang advanced romantic, relativistic arguments from 'national essence', *modern* arguments, rather than rationalistic Confucian arguments from universal validity. If Confucius was not to be the guarantor of Chinese continuity, the presiding genius of change, but a victim of it, then Confucius must be defended against it.

Other arguments for other causes have deafened the twentieth century. Confucius, from being the director, came down with K'ang to a walk-on part on the historical stage—not much more impressive than his walk-off part with Liao. In either case, the brand of Confucianism and the biography of the Confucianist corresponded. The more politically impoverished, the more intellectually extravagant: Liao's 'levitating' utopian creed was beautifully appropriate to a seceder from history and an expeller of history, living into a time when bureaucracy and Confucianism no longer went together. The speculative Liao did not 'cause' the draining of Confucianism; he reacted to it in one way, a way that exemplified it. One might say, as Chu Hsi (1130–1200) had said about Buddhist speculation, that such a Confucianism, *any* modern Confucianism, was *t'i* without *yung*, the essence without the operation, the work. And when, as was the case with modern problems, Confucian solutions ceased to work and Confucian wisdom ceased to compel, dedicated Confucianists were not the operators who made their way in public life.

So much for Liao—and K'ang, after his reformist failure to give his ideas political life, passed into a political limbo himself. The Confucianism he cherished to the last was not strained to Liao's pitch of action-denying fantasy—K'ang never became as politically invisible as Liao—but it was a passive, no longer an action-enhancing Confucianism, a candidate for protection as a sort of historical monument, not a dominant moulder of history in the making.

Liao, surpassing K'ang in utopianism, writing after him as he had written before him, was the last one to work on Confucianism as the primary matter of his mind. In so doing, he contrived cipher-biography and aery Confucianism in their purest form. Out of the main line of history himself, he deprived history of its old Confucian significance. And there lay his life's representative character, as a mirror-image of the times.

For in Liao's day Confucianism was being reduced to historical significance, which had never been its attribute when history was inside it. Liao made it an article of faith that 'the Six Classics were not history'—by which he assisted in making the Classics history, though history in a non-Confucian, relativistic sense. Now the Classics were so clearly 'history' that his warm, living appeal to them made Liao quaint, an historical relic in his own lifetime. One who had long ago claimed title to originality was finally acknowledged an undoubted original: an eccentric, an anachronism. History had passed him by, consigning the Classics, his mind's treasure, to the burial-ground of the past he had scorned to use.

CHAPTER II

Ill Wind in the Well-field: the Erosion of the Confucian Ground of Controversy

Don't chop that pear tree,
Don't spoil that shade;
Thaar's where old Marse Shao used to sit,
Lord, how I wish he was judgin' yet.
From the *Shih-ching*, version of Ezra Pound[1]

A square li covers nine squares of land, which nine
squares contain nine hundred *mau*. The central square
is the public field, and eight families, each having its
private hundred *mau*, cultivate in common the public
field.

Mencius, IIIA, iii, 19[2]

WHEN Liao and the younger K'ang used the Classics
to prophesy, they took them out of the future which
the Classics were supposed to foretell. Their own way
of reading them was finished. They had read them as binding
authorities. And, however much they scandalized the orthodox Confucianists, who read a different message in a somewhat different canon, this appeal to the Classics' authority
was traditional enough. 'Modern text' or 'ancient text', the
last internal Confucian conflict, was irrelevant to anti-
traditionalists, who looked outside Confucianism for a way
out for China.

These men had other ways of reading the Classics. Liao
looked for the keys to ultimate wisdom; K'ang looked for
wisdom, too, and then for 'national essence'. They seemed

dead before they died. Post-Confucianists came to the fore, with theories of history that gave the Classics a place, as historical documentation, instead of taking the Classics seriously as the bar of historical judgement. For these new men looked to the ancient texts not for wisdom, not for essence, but for the raw material of 'scientific study'.[3] It was a non-Confucian idea of history, and it made the Confucian Classics new texts from a newly envisaged past.

Thus, the Confucian departure from history was not just a matter of Confucianists resigning from history, and history (in the Confucian sense) receding from their thoughts. Old Confucian topics, like the theory of the 'well-field', continued to be broached—but all changed, changed utterly, in historical significance.

I. FROM LITERALNESS TO METAPHOR

In 1919, a classic year for Chinese free-thinkers, whose 'May Fourth Movement' laid the whole range of old verities under fire, 'Mencius' was brought into controversy. Hu Han-min (1879–1936), in a journal article, accepted the ancient existence of *ching-t'ien* ('well-field'), a system of landholding originally described and recommended by Mencius in the fourth century B.C. Early in 1920, Hu Shih (1891–1962) responded in the same journal with a denial that ching-t'ien had ever been. Liao Chung-k'ai (1877–1925), Hu Han-min again, and others made rebuttals, and in fact the sceptics did not win out: ching-t'ien lived to turn up regularly in the writings of Chinese communist historians, not as a fable, but as something there in history. This hardly meant, however, that Marxists were back on the grand old road, that Confucianism had somehow withstood the modern temper. Instead, that temper's very emergence can be divined in the persistence of the ching-t'ien idea. For the latter, after centuries of having a literal Confucian significance, as simply a social system which Mencius described, recommended, and challenged his heirs to deal with, turned into metaphor. It *stood for* things, values or social theories which were not Confucian at all. This transformation of ching-t'ien in the twentieth century was effected by all men who in any way—as traditionalists, radical idealists, or materialists—defended its historicity.

The account of the ching-t'ien system in Mencius, with its refinement in the *Chou-li* (the latter ostensibly pre-Mencius, but actually late and derivative), makes up the most symmetrical story ever told. Mencius' *'ching'* unit of land was so-called because it was laid out regularly like the character *ching* 井, or 'well', for his eight families' fields and a ninth, their common field. In the *Chou-li* nine *fu* ('cultivators', here units of cultivation), comprised a *ching*, and *kou* ('drains') four feet wide and deep marked off one *ching* from another; a square of ten *ching* by ten was a *cheng*, and between *cheng* there were *hsü* ('ditches') eight feet wide and deep. This pattern was built up with strict regularity to larger and larger blocks of space and wider and deeper waterworks.[4] Nothing could be more precise and tidy, more literal a statement of design. And nothing, accordingly, could be more vulnerable to Hu Shih's sort of dismissal, as a transparently contrived Confucian ideal of harmony, with nothing of the odour of historical social reality. It was simply, he said, a case of *to-ku kai-chih*, an appeal to (imagined) antiquity as a sanction for change.[5] As a like-minded scholar observed later, ching-t'ien had no history: it was only a species of social thought, an aspiration, an ideal.[6]

Yet, the ching-t'ien theory's weakness to Hu Shih was its strength to his opponents—which is only to say that all of them were modern men together. For, really, the literal ching-t'ien was scrapped by almost everybody, and Hu's denial of ching-t'ien's literal, material existence was countered by a triumphant assertion of its ideal character; there was a subtle difference, however, in the nature of the idealism, a displacement of emphasis from ideals ('what would be best') to ideas ('what really *is*, beneath diverse appearances'). The anti-Hu Shih factions, that is, extricated the ching-t'ien system from its old particular spot in a single national history and made it a universal. The ching-t'ien system, in the eyes of its defenders, became a type.

For some, the more sentimental radicals and some traditionalists, too, it became a sort of divine ground of socialism. For others, mostly more developmental thinkers, it became a form whose content was a stage in a supranational universal history. In either case, ching-t'ien ended up not as its literal self, pinned to time and place in history, but as a free-floating metaphor alluding to something not explicitly stated. When ching-t'ien was read as the 'socialist goal of man', or as 'primitive communism' or 'feudalism', this was a modern *translation* of an ancient text, translation in just the spirit of Ezra Pound assigning an Uncle Remus vernacular to a Chinese poem of some millennia past. A time, a place, an idiom—individual historical bearings—these are only phenomena, Pound intimates, concealing noumenal eternity from men of other times and places. And the literal idiom of Mencius, too, is spirited out of history, metaphorized into a formal suggestion of one or another implicit ideal content.

2. CHING-T'IEN AND CONFUCIAN REFORMISM

When Hu Shih took the ching-t'ien system as nothing more than fantasy, men who rejected his scepticism charged him, in effect, with being too literal-minded. The argument had an interesting dialectic, in that Hu's opponents, defending a Classic, were clearly far from the traditional view of the Classics which Hu attacked. They preserved ching-t'ien for history in their way by deploring literal-mindedness; but pre-modern Confucianists had taken Mencius at face value and his ching-t'ien description literally.

For some two thousand years, from the Han dynasty down to Ch'ing, there were officials and scholars who recommended a return to the ching-t'ien system or who denied the possibility of return. Yet, no professedly orthodox Confucianist, whatever he thought of the prospects of ching-t'ien in a later age, denied that here as elsewhere the Classics were history. Han Ying (*fl.* 150 B.C.) took over the full Mencian idyll of mutual aid on the *ching* (not only on the eight families' common land, but in all their social relationships), and used it as Confucianists always used classical-sage history, as a bar of judgement for a lesser posterity.[7] The literal ching-t'ien, in such a fashion, became a standing reproach to less deserving ages; though to some Confucianists it was a ground for moral pessimism, to others a challenge to moral fervour for a noble climb backward and upward.

In comparing these implications, we would probably do well to avoid psychological conjecture. Doubtless Chinese thinkers have had a random variety of temperaments, some more sanguine than others. But these would be hard to penetrate and would only provide a diversion. Throughout Confucian dynastic history there was a more accessible, pertinent set of alternatives. It was framed in philosophical and political terms—inner and outer (*nei* and *wai*), bureaucracy and monarchy (Volume Two)—and angles of approach to ching-t'ien may be fairly sighted from these poles.

In so far as the 'inner' strain predominated, political action to force ching-t'ien (for land redistribution would have to be forced) was utterly unacceptable. Force was denial of virtue, and the régime that wielded force, the monarchical régime which was supposed to be founded on virtue, would be shamed by the action. But in so far as the 'outer' strain took precedence, Confucianists were committed to strive for social harmony. They had to heed the message of Mencius and the *Chou-li* (The Rites of Chou), and urge (in line with the monarch's interest in levelling those beneath him) some approximation literally to egalitarian ching-t'ien. Either the outer world—the monarch's world—was too corrupt to sustain a flawless institution, unless perhaps, corruptly, it was forced to; hence, ching-t'ien must be left to history. Or (an equally Confucian belief) the sages' ching-t'ien must be realized, the Classics still be made into history, and action, necessarily imperial, had to be recommended. All these Confucianists together took the letter of the Classics seriously.[8]

Su Hsün (1009–66), unmetaphorically mindful of the letter of the Classics, felt that *kou-hsü*, 'drains and ditches' complexity would be one of the factors aborting a ching-t'ien revival.[9] Chu Hsi (1130–1200) denounced an opinion that at least some post-classical monarchs had governed like the sage-kings.[10] Ma Tuan-lin (thirteenth century) lamented the '*san-tai*', the heroic ages of ching-t'ien, the classical ages of

Hsia, Shang, and Chou, 'when there were no very rich or very poor'.[11] These were some of the major figures who believed the ching-t'ien irredeemably past. But Wang Mang (d. 23) and Wang An-shih (1021–86), a would-be emperor and an imperial protégé, were active ching-t'ien enthusiasts, and much more noted for their outer actions than their inner metaphysics. In A.D. 9, Wang Mang, damning the Ch'in dynasty for 'destroying the institutions of the sages and abolishing the ching-t'ien', proclaimed the latter's restoration, with land made public (royal) and inalienable by sale or bequest. Families of fewer than eight males were restricted to one *ching* of holdings. He threatened, and to some extent carried out, deportations of opponents of his ching-t'ien system.[12] Wang An-shih poetically saw ching-t'ien as a possible cure for maladministration: '. . . Even ministers buy their posts / This is more than loyal hearts can stand / For the nine-plot system I long.'[13] The two Wangs were prime targets of the pessimists' recriminations.

Wang An-Shih referred to the *Chou-li* as a model for political reform; ching-t'ien came in with the rest as sacrosanct.[14] The self-identification of Wang, whom they hated, with the *Chou-li* made some literati doubt its authenticity, until Chu Hsi reaffirmed it.[15] The doubters, of course, were right, but for what Hu Shih and the moderns would consider the wrong reasons.

Rather than being critical primarily of a text, they were critical of centralization, though ambiguously so; for as Confucian literati they, too, had an 'outer' strain, and as Confucian officials they, too, needed a State while resisting the State's pretensions to interfere with private accumulation. In this condition of tension, there were naturally Confucianists who tried to make things easier by dismissing the *Chou-li* from the canon, and thus dismissing, too, the menace of a Classic which could lend itself to the exegesis of an actionist like Wang. (In the nineteenth century, significantly, one of the most radical and central-authoritarian Taiping leaders, Hung Jen-kan, held the *Chou-li* in esteem.)[16] Chu Hsi scorned this expedient of discrediting the book, lived with *Chou-li* in its troublesome place of authority, and simply, frankly emphasized the inner over the outer, morality and metaphysics over political activism. This was consistent with a point of view for which not just the *Chou-li* but *Mencius*, especially *Mencius*, was a true and commanding text. It was necessarily a view, then, which included the ching-t'ien ideal, but sadly renounced it for these latter days on grounds of social degeneration from the age of sages; to bring back ching-t'ien would require force, the inadmissible.

There were seventeenth-century scholars who felt that Chu Hsi's *li-hsüeh* philosophy, with its non-empirical metaphysic of reason, was far too much concerned with 'inner' ideas and too little with tangible things. Quite appropriately, they parted from Chu on the ching-t'ien issue. Huang Tsung-hsi (1610–95) believed firmly that ching-t'ien could be revived.[17] For Chu, ching-t'ien was unattainable where rulers were not perfectly virtuous, but Ku Yen-wu (1613–82) commended the system with a less austere counsel of perfection. Citing, as Mencius had, the *Shih-ching* poem asking for 'rain on our public field and then on our private fields', he saw this as a symbol of the relation of *T'ien-hsia*, the Empire, to the family; the sage-kings, said Ku, knowing the primacy of *T'ien-hsia*, yet knew, too, that man's original nature had a private impulse. Far from ruling this out, they sympathized with it, conferred lands in the ching-t'ien system, and so joined communal and private in the *T'ien-hsia*.[18]

Yen Yüan (1635–1704), another Confucianist who preferred activism to speculative philosophy, felt an attendant obligation to press for a modern ching-t'ien. He offered detailed plans, with all manner of measurements, for a literal restoration of the system. For he thought it the key to *wang-tao*, the kingly way. Propriety was violated, he felt, if human feelings were sacrificed to the spirit of wealth, whereby the product of the labour of masses of men leaves one man unsatisfied. 'To have one man with some thousands of *ch'ing* (each a hundred *mou*, or about fifteen acres) and some thousands of men with not one *ch'ing* is like a parent's having one son be rich and the others poor.'[19] He agreed with Chu Hsi that the classical *san-tai*, the 'three eras', whose crowning excellence was ching-t'ien, had set a standard of sageliness which no subsequent dynasty had ever approached. For Yen Yüan, however, the destruction of ching-t'ien caused or comprised the falling off, and this could be reversed, the ching-t'ien re-established. For Chu Hsi, on the other hand, the end of ching-t'ien was a sign of decay, not the fact of decay, a remediable fact, itself.[20] Yen Yüan could enter completely into Su Hsün's sorrow at a world without ching-t'ien. 'The poor cultivate, but cannot escape starvation; the rich sit at their ease and are sated with enjoyment.'[21] But Su, like Chu, took the classical past as past (and for Chu, anyway, the ching-t'ien's aims had not been social equality, but proper discrimination).[22]

Actually, of course, the pessimists were right. As long as thinkers were unequivocally Confucian and took ching-t'ien literally (not metaphorically, as the spirit of something or other), the system could not be legislated. Either it was an immediate fiasco for one who tried to make it general, like Wang Mang, or it was a toy set up in a small corner of a society which ignored it. Such was the short-lived 'eight-banner ching-t'ien', established in 1724 in two counties of Chihli, the metropolitan province, as a tentative effort to solve the problem of livelihood for the Ch'ing's growing number of parasitical banner-men. Some 2,000 *mou* from lands attached to the Board of Revenue and the Imperial Household were allotted to fifty Manchu, ten Mongol, and forty Chinese families. There were private fields, with eight families working a public field; the *Hui-tien* says that the *Chou-li* was supposed to be followed. In 1729 lands in two more counties were brought into the system, but the public-field idea was a failure, and in 1736 Ch'ien-lung abolished the baby ching-t'ien.[23]

What, then, could be the recourse of men who acknowledged both the primacy and the hopelessness of ching-t'ien? Chu Hsi was more gloomy or more high-minded than most, and felt that even an approximation of ching-t'ien was unattainable after the sages' era.[24] Ma Tuan-lin and Su Hsün, however, who shared his views on ching-t'ien, were prepared to try something as near to it as possible. If in ching-t'ien times there were no very rich or very poor, the Emperor and his officials should still see to it that these extremes were banished.[25] *Hsien-t'ien* ('limiting the fields') should be put into practice, to share out the land and check aggrandizement, 'to get the benefit of ching-t'ien without using the ching-t'ien system'.[26]

The sponsors of *hsien-t'ien* in Chinese history (or *chün-t'ien*, field equalization, as it was often called, since limitation was meant to prevent imbalance) always saw their efforts as at least a pale reflection of ching-t'ien. Actual ching-t'ien advocates like Chang Tsai (1020–77) and Wang An-shih identified *chün-p'ing*, equalization, as the essence of ching-t'ien,[27] and statesmen with somewhat lower sights could still call for *chün* as a compensation, a derivative of *ching*.[28] Where authorities who took ching-t'ien seriously as a practical matter were liable to be stigmatized as ruthless (and pure scholars of a like persuasion apt to be thought extravagant), *chün-t'ien* could sometimes satisfy a Confucianist's 'outer' and 'inner' predilections, his concern for the Empire and at the same time his implicit rebuke to emperors.

The rebuke lay in the belief that *chün-t'ien* was second to ching-t'ien, which was not viable because of the Emperor's imperfect virtue. Yet, the rebuke was surely muted, and *chün-t'ien* was largely an interest of the Emperor, not the bureaucracy. It was the Emperor, that is, his dynasty depending on effective centralization, who was most concerned with curbing landed power; for that might eventually drain the State and goad a slipping peasantry to riot. The *chün-t'ien* effort with the ching-t'ien inspiration was a natural expedient for monarchs. Why, then, should we find the arch-monarchical Ch'in State always charged with destroying the ching-t'ien system, and outraging thus, as in other ways, the Confucian sense of what was right?[29]

The facts appear to be these. The pre-Ch'in period, a time to which Confucianists later consigned ching-t'ien, was a feudal period, with political fragmentation and restrictions on the alienability of land. Establishing the free right of buying and selling land (which indeed would be subversive of any ching-t'ien system of regular, fixed allotments), Ch'in

THE SOCIALISM—CHING-T'IEN CLICHÉ

spread its vital power to tax throughout its domain, and bequeathed this ideal of the ubiquitous tax to subsequent dynasties. But to preserve that power, so hard won from a previous feudal age, dynasties every now and then resorted to measures of land equalization; they were trying to infringe on rights of property so as to save the imperial system which secured them in the first place. Thus, *chün-t'ien* programmes with their ching-t'ien aura were attempts to prevent a reversion, via private aggrandizement, to ching-t'ien conditions (i.e. pre-Ch'in conditions) of land not bought and sold under State aegis, and accordingly not in the State's power to tax.[30]

What dynasties needed was the poetry of ching-t'ien, its aura of social equity. It beautified their *chün-t'ien* efforts to stop recurrence of the truth that had passed as ching-t'ien, the feudal deprivation of the public power. And Confucian landowners, hurt by *chün-t'ien* pressures, decried the latter as quasi-Ch'in or Legalist, recalling the infamous liquidators of the ching-t'ien system. Either way, whether as the State's excuse or the gentry's shaming of the State's force, ching-t'ien came down as the highest ideal of polity. The 'Ming History' records a scholar's unequivocal statement that, for ultimate peace in the Empire, ching-t'ien had to be put into practice. *Hsien-t'ien*, field limitation, would not do; *chün-shui*, tax equalization, would not do.[31] And at the end of Ch'ing, when foreign ideals insistently claimed attention, it was for the most part ching-t'ien, with merely its faint classical intimations, not the amply documented *chün-t'ien*, which Chinese thinkers identified with Western egalitarianisms. It may have been precisely the elusive historical status of ching-t'ien which made it so adaptable. It was so much better a metaphor—the distillation of 'socialism', for example—when historically, prosaically, it could not be simply itself.

3. THE SOCIALISM—CHING-T'IEN CLICHÉ

The weakening of ching-t'ien as a denotative term began with K'ang Yu-wei's 'modern text' Confucianism around the turn of the twentieth century. K'ang and his followers made specific statements about ancient ching-t'ien. K'ang, for instance, in one of his typically profuse tributes to Confucius (whose achievements he inflated beyond the traditional estimate), maintained that Confucius had devised the ching-t'ien system, which gave land to every man, and therefore banished slavery from any real place in ancient China.[32] But, however modern thinkers like K'ang stated their premises, they were involved in a totally new sort of Confucian interpretation, an effort to keep Confucius important. To restless Chinese intellectuals the appeal of western ideas and values had become compelling, and Confucius faced oblivion unless Confucianists could put him in tune with western authority. For Chu Hsi and Yen Yüan indiscriminately—opposites though they were on the ching-t'ien issue in its older context—ching-t'ien's value had been self-evident and *sui generis*. Yet, now it was forced to be something shared and identified with an eminent foreign value. 'China's ancient ching-t'ien system stands on the same plane as modern socialism,' said Liang Ch'i-ch'ao in 1899,[33] and even the martyred T'an Ssu-t'ung (1865–98), with his deep though eclectic Confucian faith, may be seen to have taken ching-t'ien as a pass key to the modern world as much as for itself. 'With the ching-t'ien system the governments of the world can be made one'—'ching-t'ien makes the rich and the poor equals'— and then, touchingly, 'Westerners deeply approve of China's ching-t'ien system'.[34]

Here, inspiration still flows from a Chinese institution. An air of prophecy shrouds it, in a good 'modern-text' way, as though the real meaning, esoteric but always there, were unmistakable now. ('Modern text' thinkers in early Han as in late Ch'ing, near the beginning as at the end of the long dynastic sequence, had taken a more allusive approach to the Classics than the literalists of the ultimately orthodox 'ancient-text' school.) Still, its meaning rises not from the exuberant native vision alone, but from a foreign vision: ching-t'ien is its poetic image. 'Westerners deeply approve . . .'—in a 'modern-text' Confucianist, is this a sign of nothing more than passionate universality? It seems to concede that Europe decides what enters the universal.

As recently as the T'ung-chih period (1862–74) a scholar

had wondered, with dogged literalness, how one could count on the *ching's* eight families to have but one son of the house, so that the system might not be fatally committed to infinite expansion.[35] Yet, in the space of a generation the classic conception of the ching-t'ien system, in its literal details, had ceased to compel attention. Connotations were what was wanted, relating to problems not of Confucian implementation but of adjustment to the West.

On the whole, the 'modern-text' school of K'ang Yu-wei was the end of the line in Confucian history, showing the last shreds of authentic dependence on Confucian sources. T'an Ssu-t'ung was killed by reactionaries in 1898, when K'ang had his 'hundred days' of political influence, then *coup d'état*, overthrow, and exile. Confucian reformism was killed, too, and from then on until Mao Tse-tung the main authorities in Chinese thought were from the outside. Accordingly, ching-t'ien ceased to inspire political views, but only gave a familiar gloss to something new and seemingly important. Socialism might be vaguely thrilling, as it sometimes was for Sun Yat-sen (1866–1925) and some of his followers, or it might be unappealing, but in either case, in rashes of statements from 1900 on, it invaded Mencius, dissolved his literal meaning, and made a sentimental metaphor of ching-t'ien. Banality proved a spur to repetition. Socialism, over and over again, was claimed for China (with priority over the West) in triumphant allusions to ching-t'ien.

4. PARADISE LOST AND REGAINED: FROM CLASSICAL UNIQUENESS TO THE COMMON LOT IN HISTORY

A concentrated dose of these socialism-ching-t'ien commonplaces has an altogether soporific effect now. (I have rolled a few pills for the notes.)[36] But for Hu Shih in 1920, exposed to writings in this vein which were not a part of the historical record but presumably living thoughts, the effect was irritating. For one thing, he felt that scientific moderns (and to be modern was to be scientific: Hu had his own clichés) should not be disposed to coddle Mencius, but should question him severely. One should not start reverently with a

Classic and simply assume that the historical facts must fit; rather one should look at the text coolly and try to find out whether it fits the facts or distorts them for ideological reasons.[37] And for another thing, out of this same scientific commitment, Hu suspected the ching-t'ien verbiage which clogged discussion of socialism; it suggested a lingering slavishness to classical authority. Science demanded two things; correction of authority and release from authority. Hu did not believe that the ching-t'ien system had ever existed; and he believed that even if it had, it should not affect decisions on socialism one way or the other.[38]

Hu deals at the end of his basic ching-t'ien essay (actually a composite of published exchanges) with an interesting part of the argument, the suggestion that ching-t'ien is communist in the sense that 'primitive society' is communist. He declines to acknowledge that a politically organized people could have a whole long span of history down to the alleged Ch'in destruction of ching-t'ien, and still be in 'primitive society'.[39] This makes a nice debating point, and others take it up,[40] but Hu drops the argument just where the ching-t'ien question really comes to life as an issue for the post-Confucian temper.

Hu, that is, never analyzed the controversy. He kept essentially to his brief—as someone described it fifteen years later, he denied only the ching-t'ien of the *Ju*, the old Confucianists. 'Hu engages only in *k'ao-cheng*, criticism of ancient texts, but he does not study history. . . . He has only negative doubts, not positive explanations.'[41] Hu, in short, satisfied himself that no one could prove a literal ching-t'ien from Mencius and his successors. But most of the other controversialists were busy establishing a metaphorical ching-t'ien from materials of comparative history, and shifting the base of the argument right under his feet. When Hu looked backward and argued the case for modern assumptions, he was lecturing into an almost empty hall. His real opponents were out in the modern world themselves, and confounding Hu with ching-t'ien systems almost untouched by all his blows at the Classics.

The most straightforward opposition came from the Hu Han-min materialist wing. Hu Han-min had long since given up the easy equation of ching-t'ien and a socialist ideal. As a matter of fact, as a seriously anti-communist Kuomintang ideologue he had no desire to glorify socialism; men who paired off ching-t'ien and socialism usually did it with such an intention.[42]

'Modern socialism stems preponderantly from the industrial revolution,' he said unequivocally. Of course, he went on, 'socialism' has a general aura of freedom and equality; such aspirations are familiar enough in history, and so people have invoked the Greek polis, or Christianity, or Chinese antiquity for the origins of socialism. But ancient methods cannot apply to the present, nor can modern European socialist prescriptions apply to China. All that Hu Han-min will say is that vaguely humanitarian ideas and objectives are common to Chinese and foreign and ancient and modern.[43]

The later Hu Han-min, then, never injected ching-t'ien into policy statements for the future, even when dealing with subjects, like Sun Yat-sen's 'equalization of landed power', which invited the cliché treatment (as Sun himself was dispensing it just then).[44] And in statements about the past he kept his ching-t'ien firmly fixed in the past. His historical materialism demanded it. Hu Han-min insisted on relating ideas to historical context; he would not agree that the only intellectual issue was timeless truth or error. Therefore, in his eyes, it was anti-historical, utopian, to imagine ching-t'ien as the equivalent of modern socialism or communism. Hu Han-min admired Marx for his conclusion, contrary to Plato and all the utopians through Owen and Saint-Simon, that communist society must come from the womb of capitalism.[45] The discovery of socialism was Marx's, not Mencius'.

But the rediscovery of ching-t'ien was a little bit Marx's, too. Hu Han-min took what Marxists might criticize as rather too Malthusian a line on the breakdown of ching-t'ien.[46] Still, his discussion of ching-t'ien in its prime was socially evolutionary, of a sort not originated by Marx or restricted to Marxists, but owing much of its current persuasiveness to Marx's powerful influence. For ching-t'ien Hu Han-min read 'society of primitive communism',[47] a term with more than classical, more than Chinese, significance. And into the breach poured a host of scholars, ready to hang the ching-t'ien label on one world-historical phase or another.

Not all of them were 'primitive communist' partisans. Mencius (III A, iii, 9) had quoted the *Shih-ching*, the 'Book of Poetry': 'May the rain come down on our *kung-t'ien* / And then upon our *ssu* (*t'ien*).' *Ssu* was clearly 'private'. But was *kung-t'ien*, which had such priority, 'public field'? Was *kung-t'ien* 'lord's field'? Was the age of the ching-t'ien system, then, 'primitive communist' or 'feudal'? Yet, whatever answer they chose, these periodizers in the wake of Hu Han-min were beyond the reach of classical authority. Though opposed to Hu Shih, they would have brought no joy to Mencius. To them, as to Hu Han-min, ching-t'ien was not an ideal in the sense of something to aspire to. Mencius was not a sage, but Mencius' favourite institution could be soberly referred to, as a Chinese translation, one might say, of something universal. Ching-t'ien had to be retained; it made it seem possible to document a general phase of history from famous Chinese sources. Sage-kings depart but ching-t'ien remains, shining through other lineaments.[48]

Christianity has had its vicissitudes, too, in modern culture (though suffering nothing like the attenuation of Confucianism); a Christian comparison may indicate just what it was that Hu Han-min portended for Confucianism. For many centuries particular revelation had been at the heart of the Christian claim to supreme religious value. But in recent times comparative anthropology of the Frazer 'Golden Bough' variety came to insist on the universality of myth and ritual patterns (the ubiquity of death-and-resurrection figures, etc.), so that the Christian drama began to seem just one of the many that had long been dismissed as pagan. There was a way to accommodate this in a Christian view, but only through an unmistakable drift in Christian conviction, from Christianity as an historically unique ideal to Christianity as a universal idea, an archetype out of depth psychology. Then the Christian claim might seem to be warranted, as something primordially, *mythically* true, as the Oedipus story has been said to be true. It would not be confounded by its apparent duplication.

Yet, this triumphant transformation of a rationalistic objection into a mystical confirmation may be more gaudy than final. One may, of course, be satisfied that some universal pattern of divine kingship was fulfilled in the Christian mythos; but there always remains, never really dismissed by the Jungian fanfare of *ur*-perennial philosophy, the original question raised by the perception of parallels. Are ancient Near Eastern myth and ritual patterns reflected in Christian soteriology because they were mystically, perennially fulfilled in it, or because they prosaically, historically suggested it? When Christianity is considered a 'universal idea', it may be vindicated, or it may be shaken.[49]

We have already intimated that the ching-t'ien system was once accepted as an ideal part of a uniquely valuable Confucianism, and that it was salvaged by many moderns as a universal idea, confirmed for China by its parallels abroad. This confirmation, too, was bought at the price of a drift in conviction, to a point where Confucianism was undermined by such comparative anthropologizing. For Confucian China was properly the acme of Culture, not a respecter of cultures, and its institutions were certainly not supposed to be avatars, merely local versions of universal things. The ching-t'ien of the Confucianists was unique. Mencius, to them, gave a true record of a particular course of events. But if Mencius, instead, was only tuned in on a wave of meta-history, then traditional history was strangely altered. If it was the 'pattern' that guaranteed ching-t'ien, then even though moderns might conclude that ancient China had known this Confucian experience, it lost its traditional meaning.

For Chinese anti-traditionalists, this had its compensation; they were cheerfully impervious to an attack on their ching-t'ien convictions which was directed (as Hu Shih directed it) against these willingly abandoned old associations. Unlike still-committed Christians, for whom pattern-thinking was potentially a double-edged weapon, post-Confucianists, having nothing Confucian left exposed, had nothing to fear from the inside. Christians depending on parallels and universals for their affirmations of Incarnation or Resurrection had to be, however slightly, uneasy: the status of the Bible had somehow become ambiguous. But Chinese depending on parallels and universals for their affirmations of ching-t'ien could be calmly unconcerned: for them, the status of the Classics was not ambiguous but perfectly clear and acceptable. The Classics were not classics any more (see Ku Chieh-kang *vis-à-vis* Chang Ping-lin and K'ang Yu-wei, in Volume One), but sources for the Chinese branch of universal history.

5. SENTIMENTAL RADICALISM

Hu Shih was left in a somewhat embarrassing stance. Here was the scientific critic of outworn fancies immobilized with his literal Mencius, while sophisticated rebuttalists danced round him (for years), raising a fog of Russian *mirs* and German *marks*, Japanese *shōen* and French demesnes and English manors, something Inca and something Welsh, all to shield a ching-t'ien that he had never meant.[50] But in this bewildering debate there were degrees of license, and from Hu Shih's standpoint the sentimental radical idealism of Liao Chung-k'ai must have been much more exasperating than Hu Han-min's at least internally consistent historical materialism. Having discovered his ching-t'ien as an historical idea, immanent in China and almost everywhere else at a stage in history, Hu Han-min had the grace to leave it there, instead of setting it up as a beacon for modern times. But Liao gave an almost unexampled display of intellectual double-entry. Trading on the materialism which posited an ancient ching-t'ien era, one which had to be superseded as history made its way, Liao claimed it as well for socialism, man's last best hope. Conjectures which others had made to establish ching-t'ien as the primitive-communal or feudal idea, of merely historical and no normative significance, Liao diverted to his own end of non-historical idealization.

Liao, as a socialist enthusiast rather than anything a Marxist would call a 'scientific socialist', embraced a modern ideal and, in the trite fashion long established, found its earlier Chinese model. He wanted to believe in ching-t'ien, to see a

Chinese version of a norm that crossed the ages, and he almost pleaded with Hu Shih, in their published correspondence on the great question, not to disillusion him. Hu Shih had said there was no Santa Claus; Hu Han-min said there was. But, of course, there was a discrepancy, though the name was the same. What Hu Shih denied was a model of blissful harmony. What Hu Han-min affirmed was an iron age of shared but meagre satisfactions. Liao used Hu against Hu, then slipped the jolly image of his own fancy in the place of the worn-out ancient. 'Primitive communism', somehow more credible than Mencius' idyll of settled communities (with their mulberry trees everywhere, and women nourishing silkworms, and each family with its five brood hens and two brood sows), assured Liao that, yes, there was a ching-t'ien. Then the 'primitive' slipped away—at least the 'primitive' of the relativistic materialists, 'primitive' in the sense of rudimentary or first in the stages of progress—and a Rousseauistic 'primitive' was spirited into its place. Ching-t'ien became the natural, the true value, out of history, and the prototype of the true value (release from struggle, to mutual aid and unrestrained fulfilment) of the modern western world.

Liao Chung-k'ai, then, ran the approved course through the landscape of collective ownership and collective use, signposted on the right by familiar proof-texts from the Classics (especially the *Shih-ching*'s hard-worked 'rain on our public fields'—no 'lord's-field' *kung-t'ien* for socialist Liao), and on the left by Marx, Maine, and Emile de Laveleye, Guizot, Vinogradoff, and Henry George. Communal landholding was each people's original system, ching-t'ien marked the passing from a pastoral to an agricultural stage. Consider primitive Germany. Contemplate Anglo-Saxon England. Reflect on ancient Italy, Wales, Java, and the Russian *mir*.[51]

Most of the literature which Liao used, especially de Laveleye (*De la propriété et de ses formes primitives*, Paris, 1874), was tendentious. Its *tendenz* was the discrediting of contemporary inequality by reference to early (i.e. natural, fundamental) communal institutions.[52] This was Liao's polemical purpose, too, and he had to be pulled up short in his

33

utopianist-historical garble. Chi Yung-wu gave him the
weary counsel that communism was communism and the
equal-field concept the equal-field concept—they should
never be mixed in one discussion—and that communal landholding in a tribal society was not the realization of 'ultimate communism'.[53] Another writer, attacking half-baked
westernization, struck Liao at least a glancing blow. He
scorned the travesties of western ideas which Chinese made
when they imagined Yüan Shih-k'ai to represent the
American presidency, Tuan Ch'i-jui the French cabinet
system, or Chou dynasty ching-t'ien Marxist communism.[54]

6. THE CONTEMPORANEITY OF HU SHIH, HU HAN-MIN, AND LIAO CHUNG-K'AI

The three main shades of opinion in the ching-t'ien controversy of the 1920s were equally modern. How, in summary,
did they relate to one another?

The question of the existence of ching-t'ien had to be
asked by Hu Shih, because he meant, by claiming its non-
existence, to reveal it as merely Confucian utopianism. With
the Classics thus stripped of credit as history, minds might
then be liberated and decisions made on a modern pragmatic
basis, without any stress on conformity to unchallenged
tradition. But the question, once put, lent itself to answers
irrelevant to his issue, and the air was filled with answers to
Hu Shih which did *not* avow what he challenged, Confucian
authority, but merely asserted the plausibility of the existence
of something in society which could have been the wraith of
Mencius' creation. Thus Hu Han-min, while accepting the
existence of ching-t'ien or some facsimile, had none of the
attitudes which Hu Shih saw bound up in the ching-t'ien
affirmation. Hu Shih's anti-Confucian scholarship was
matched by a post-Confucian scholarship, i.e. one in which
the question of the validity of Confucian ideals scarcely occurs.

With Liao Chung-k'ai, on the other hand, Hu Shih had a
closer confrontation. Liao treated Mencius as though he
mattered intensely. He treated ching-t'ien, that is, not just
as though it characterized an early phase of Chinese history

34

(though he did that, too), but as though it lived metaphorically in the present. He obviously saw it as metaphor, a concept sharing its spiritual content with a modern ideal, though differing in form—material embodiment: when it came to actual prescriptions for China's needs, Liao's great concerns were industrialization and the nationalism which he hoped would protect it against foreigners' obstruction.[55] Any literal conception of ching-t'ien, a system of land distribution, had nothing to do with this.

Under these circumstances, Hu Shih and Liao Chung-k'ai were like critic and exegete. Neither critic nor exegete takes a text at face value, but they differ in what they do to it. The critic has an air of detachment and uncommitted intellect, and tends to see opaqueness in a text or unintelligibility as a likely sign of corruption. The exegete feels challenged by the text and moved by its problems to draw out of it a truth which the words only partly expose, a truth or essential content which could take form in other words. The critic of Mencius asks what he says, and sees unauthentic history. The exegete of Mencius asks what he means, and sees a prophetic pointer to Marx.[56]

Perhaps, if Liao's exegesis be compared with rabbinic exegesis of the Hebrew Bible, the nature of Liao's relation to his classical tradition can be made clearer. By the tannaim and amoraim, the rabbis of the Mishnah and the Talmud, it was taken for granted that any truths which a dedicated student of Torah could disclose were already made known to Moses on Sinai. Oral traditions were believed to be implied in biblical revelation from the outset. It was held that they could be reconstructed by 'hermeneutic' reinterpretation, methods of rigorous reasoning, as in the ancient and medieval 'seven modes of Hillel', the thirteen modes of Rabbi Ishmael, or the thirty-two modes of Rabbi Eliezer.[57]

Rabbinical Judaism thus relates later values to an original revelation, which lends the later values their absolute validity. Confucianism characteristically had no such revelation (as it had no such infinite and transcendent God, directing and law-giving, on the far side of an abyss from finite man: see Volume Two). K'ang Yu-wei's 'modern-text' radicalism, which would have brought Confucianism nearer than orthodox scholars brought it to the status of religion, came closer to a rabbinical feeling for exegesis; Confucian texts (in appropriate versions) were given a strained authority and modern particulars deduced from them. But Liao Chung-k'ai was a good deal past the 'modern-text' influence, and his 'validation' of socialism by reference to Mencius and ching-t'ien was quite a different proposition. There was no 'hermeneutic' interpretation of the text. Socialism was just made, hopefully, 'Chinese' and authorized *as such*, not as a deduction from absolute ancient authority. This was emotive rhetoric, not rigorous reasoning. The authority flowed backward, not forward.

The connection Liao made between socialism and ching-t'ien was analogous not to rabbinic extension of biblical revelation forward but to the modern rhetorical extension of Marx backward, as in knowing references to 'Jewish messianism' or the 'Prophetic passion for social justice'. If this analogy lets us move for the moment wholly to the western scene, we may be able to set at its true quality a post-Confucian protestation of devotion to a Classic. For no one could more explicitly disavow rabbinic tradition than Karl Marx; and perhaps we may permit him to be his own judge in this, without injecting a 'mere form' demurrer to his insistence on genuine change in content. Dealing high-handedly with Liao, we should have to decline to let him be his own judge: he saw himself in relation to the past as some others so sentimentally and superficially have seen Marx. But Liao was a modern man, with industrial predilections and socialist sympathies, that were something more than classical ching-t'ien attachments, merely formally changed. His ideas, like Marx's—unlike the ideas of Talmudists—had antecedents that were not the classics of their respective ancestral traditions.

7. THE CHANGING STYLE OF CONSERVATISM

It may be easy to accept the idea that Liao Chung-k'ai, a prominent radical of the Kuomintang left, should be beyond the Confucian tradition, even if he did sound loyal to Mencius. Less obviously, perhaps, but just as conclusively, Chinese conservatives of the May Fourth period and after were just as new. As we have seen, Hu Han-min, though politically of the Kuomintang right, was not indulgent to Confucianism and remarkably detached about Marxism. When he said that Marxism was 'not new', he did not say it in the spirit of other conservatives, for whom ching-t'ien anticipated Marx. Hu Han-min made no mention of ching-t'ien here; he was merely referring to the lapse of seventy years since Marx developed his theories, and suggesting that progress had passed him by. And when Hu Han-min said that Marxism was 'not adequate', he did not invoke a Chinese spirit which this alien creed could never satisfy. Rather, he spoke of Marx's devotion to scientific method (of which Hu approved), but mentioned the limitations of his circumstances which made his conclusions scientifically incomplete—his study of only one phase of the economic process (said Hu), with economic data from only one or two European countries.[58]

What of the other conservatives, however, the ones who seemed opposed to modernization in an unequivocal way? When they spoke of industrialism it was with utter distaste,[59] and when they spoke of ching-t'ien they treated it with the literalness of the old believers. There was unblushing use of the traditional vocabulary, no resorting like Liao Chung-k'ai to the language of social science. Mencius and the *Chou-li* were cited without a murmur, and ching-t'ien was traced in good fundamentalist fashion to the sage-kings, called by name, and not with euhemerist intent.[60] Hu Shih might never have written.

Or is that a wrong conclusion? For these traditionalists, ostensibly so literal in their approach to the texts, may well have been no less metaphorical in their treatment of ching-t'ien than Liao. Ching-t'ien spoke to the latter as socialism. The traditionalists took him at his word. They associated ching-t'ien with socialism, too, and ended up with a ching-t'ien not important as its traditional literal self, but as a traditionalistic (a modern) symbol of the mortally threatened traditional way of life. When they agreed that socialism had a Chinese precedent, of course they were not recommending it—any more than 'Six Dynasties' Taoists were recommending Buddhism when they claimed that Buddha had learned it all from Lao-tzu. The modern traditionalists were calling attention to Chinese verities not to encourage new thought but to preclude it; they meant to show the absurdity of cultural apostasy. What they were doing was putting ching-t'ien forward (and *chün-t'ien*, too, to some extent) as the proto-socialist (and superior) guarantors of equality and harmony, and as standing reproaches, therefore, to the shallow pursuers of 'new culture'.[61]

These conservatives, then, were not really taking ching-t'ien as their literal concern. It represented the traditional Chinese culture to which Chinese owed commitment. And in fostering tradition thus, in the 'national essence', non-Confucian way, these defenders of the old were not remote from the modern point of view. When they used the ching-t'ien-socialist argument to confound genuine radicals, they were talking the radicals' language. But in monarchical days, when centralizing officials like Wang An-shih preached ching-t'ien to the conservatives, they were talking the conservatives' language. Ching-t'ien then was a *fable convenue*. These old traditional conservatives might charge their foes with hypocrisy in invoking tradition, with seeking really anti-Confucian ends under a mere guise of loyalty to Confucianism. Yet, no one would then deny that the ching-t'ien tradition was really being invoked.

But modern radicals could charge *their* foes—new, traditionalistic conservatives—with hypocrisy in invoking radicalism, with using ching-t'ien for anti-socialist ends under a guise of correspondence with socialism. What made these conservatives new was a change in the tactical situation: unlike Wang An-shih's well-placed antagonists, modern traditionalists did not set the rules of the game. They were no longer the ones who owned the current great ideas, the ideas whose prestige their rivals had to acknowledge. Mencius' ching-t'ien might be a fable—there were plenty of moderns to say it was—but it was emphatically not agreed on.

Other modern conservatives of a more practical political turn were just as new as these—ostensibly old, but in just as illusory a way. Chiang Kai-shek (b. 1887), for example, also handled ching-t'ien in a pseudo-traditional fashion. His particular tradition was that of the ching-t'ien pessimists, like Chu Hsi, who considered it too disruptive to try to make ching-t'ien work. Chiang wrote (or signed) a discussion of land ownership which purported to prove from history (the failure of Wang Mang's ching-t'ien order of A.D. 9, etc.) that compulsory equalization was bound to fail.[62] But this was not really traditional either; there was none of the poignancy of a Chu Hsi's or a Su Hsün's feeling that one should be restoring a perfect institution. Chiang repeated a long-established pragmatic conclusion against ching-t'ien, without the premises, the 'inner' and 'outer' poles, that gave it the Confucian pathos. For Chiang, as for the more contemplative new conservatives, ching-t'ien stood for something—in their case Chinese culture, in his, social disorder. The literal meaning had long been overlaid.

8. CONFUCIAN SOUND IN A MARXIST SENSE

The social disorder which Chiang deplored came his way. The victorious communists, however, interpreted history as progress, and had no intention of seeing the 'spirit' of their movement in an ancient institution. Chiang Kai-shek might array himself with the Confucian foes of Yen Yüan and other such optimists about a ching-t'ien restoration, but the communists, true to the dialectic, were as far from Yen Yüan as Chiang was from Chu Hsi. A communist's appraisal of Yen Yüan, while generally friendly (Yen was seen as a 'progressive' in his day, with popular affinities and patriotic intent), nevertheless gave short shrift to his ching-t'ien propositions; this zeal for renewing the 'feudal system', the communist biographer wrote, was a great error, a sin against social progress, out of place in the newly emerging world of capitalist and working classes.[63] And Wang Mang, one of the solidest ching-t'ien enthusiasts of all time, and one of the most roundly condemned by Confucianist and Kuomintang alike, nevertheless, in spite of these credentials, failed to impress another communist scholar. He saw Wang as a selfish plunderer, and Hu Shih's references to Wang as a 'socialist emperor' met with contemptuous rejection. For allegedly, Hu was attempting to discredit socialism by fastening the usurper on its back.[64]

Given these premises, the communists were quite distinct, too, from sentimental radicals of the Liao Chung-k'ai variety. Although Liao's widow, in a memoir published in Peking in 1957, wrote loyally of his feelings of nearness to communists whom he knew in Canton in the early 20s—Mao Tse-tung (b. 1893), Chou En-lai (b. 1896), and Li Ta-chao (1888–1927), among others—she could only bring him near, not within that circle.[65] In 1961, a selection of Liao's writings was published under official auspices in Canton. The occasion was the fiftieth anniversary of the revolution of 1911. That was the revolution, 'progressive' but far from ultimate, which the communists offered to Liao's memory.[66] He was not a communist in fact, and his ching-t'ien views show him not a communist in theory, in his mode of interpreting history.

Liao once spoke of the stability of Chinese society and Chinese values from Ch'in unification to western invasion, roughly twenty-two centuries. He granted that there were great changes, social and economic, during the Chou transition from the communal ching-t'ien to a feudal private property system, but after the feudal system met its end in the Ch'in-Han centralization there had been fixity, a dead balance in a self-sufficient economy. This stasis was shattered by the West. 'The invasion of imperialist capitalism is the source of the ten thousand evils.'[67]

Liao could be a good enough Nationalist with such a picture of Chinese history, but Chinese communism said something else again. The communists yielded to none in vituperation against imperialism. Yet, in their eyes, Liao's view of the matter could only seem hyperemphasis. It seemed to have as a corollary the de-emphasis of domestic evil, exploitation by 'feudalists'—whom the communists did *not* see expiring at the end of the classical era. Rather, as both revolutionaries and Chinese, seeking their place in synthesis between a rejected Confucian China and a resisted modern West, the communists needed 'feudal exploitation'; it was something to weigh off even-handedly against foreign exploitation. In itself, Liao's anti-imperialism (anti-westernism of a sort) was quite all right. Without it, one might be revolutionary but alienated from China. Yet, if one were only anti-imperialist, one might be at home in China, but too much at home, alienated from modern revolution.

Thus, when Liao cut off feudalism at the triumph of Ch'in, he cut out the heart of the communist version of Chinese history, a version composed with just that even-handedness: China developed *on its own* through *universal stages*, and accordingly indigenous capitalism would still have emerged (from feudalism, as in the West) had there been no influence of foreign capitalism, no Opium War and aftermath. And a theory like Liao's, which seemed to abort the historical process, naturally (and to the communists, unacceptably) included the view of a ching-t'ien timelessly linked with socialism by identity in essence. This was far from the communist view of ching-t'ien's place in the midst of historical process, and ching-t'ien's link with socialism only by a thread of intervening time.

For ching-t'ien had its place in communist histories. Few indeed were the mainland scholars who dismissed it as Mencius' fantasy.[68] After all, Hu Shih was the original powerful exponent of that view, a fact which made it filth by association, since Hu decided to absent himself from felicity. More than that, while deep down the communists knew that they and the May Fourth liberals like Hu Shih had a common bond in anti-traditionalism ('anti-feudalism' in the communist lexicon), the communists' matching commitment to anti-imperialism also carried weight; therefore Hu's impatience with Confucian authority, which in isolation no communist would think unreasonable, came under the heading of colonialism, mere surrender to cultural aggression. It was not approved as anti-Confucianism but condemned as anti-communism. And so the communists denounced 'Ching-t'ien pien', Hu's original contribution of

1920 to the controversy, as 'reactionary poison', a 'wild treatise', anti-scientific. Impugning the system of communal production on public land, it denies the existence of primitive communism in China, and thus denies the objective laws of social development, and thus attacks communism.[69]

Under the circumstances, one may wonder whether certain literati in the 1950s may not have been keeping their powder dry for a blast at Kuo Mo-jo, Vice-minister of Culture. Kuo, long ago, by his publication of *Chung-kuo ku-tai shih-hui yen-chiu* (Researches into ancient Chinese society) (Shanghai, 1930), laid himself open to identification with Hu Shih on the ching-t'ien issue.[70] Sun Li-hsing, who was so harsh with Hu Shih, did not fail to note in the same invective that Kuo had once been similarly unsound, finding the textual evidence for ching-t'ien very dubious. After the Liberation, Sun noted (perhaps with innuendo: opportunism?), Kuo set aside his scepticism; after the Liberation, historians grasped the laws of social development.[72]

This is to say that (for both generally communist and specially Chinese communist reasons) history as progressive and ordered development became the rule, and the ching-t'ien issue, which had long ago won its way into almost any polemic on ancient history, became enmeshed in the problem of periodization. Ching-t'ien existed. But did this mark the Chou period as slave or feudal?[74]

That is where ching-t'ien rested, in the middle of a question really about something else. Its evocative power, so vivid to centuries of Confucianists and decades of sentimentalists, seemed almost gone—to the extent that a Chinese could blandly identify ching-t'ien with that primitive communal ownership which is attributed in *Das Kapital* to ancient Poland and Rumania—hardly the obvious Chinese choices for centres of civilization.[73] What passion still attached to ching-t'ien *per se* seemed to come from the Hu Shih anathema, and one of Hu's pursuers was even so hot in the chase that he strayed into a sticky thicket. The ching-t'ien system must have existed, he said, because we know from the *Chou-li* its connection with irrigation, in the *kou-hsü* network. And Marx (continues the argument) has pointed out the high importance of waterworks in ancient Oriental agriculture.[74]

Caveat Sun Li-hsing. We may shake our heads at finding him near these deep Wittfogelian waters.[75] Still, though the example may be unusual, there is a nuance here we can well accept as standard for Chinese communists: the *Chou-li* suggests a link between irrigation and ching-t'ien—but Marx is the Classic, not *Chou-li*, which dictates that irrigation must have anciently existed. And where Marx and Mao judge, no Shao is judging yet, no Mencius and no Confucius. *Les poiriers sont coupés.*

Part Two

INTO HISTORY

CHAPTER III

The Placing of the Chinese Communists by Their Studies of the Past

IN the communist version of Chinese history, ching-t'ien lost its Confucian significance. What is the significance of the communist version for the general fate of Confucianism?

There is a theory abroad—partly sentimental (China is 'forever China', the cliché has it) and partly sceptical of dynamic potential in Chinese society—that the Chinese communist is not really a new man. Part of a dominant bureaucracy in a centralized State committed to public works, and with a set of Classics to swear by, he plays a role, allegedly, that Confucianists played for centuries. One of the things that might seem to support this is the dedication of Confucianists and communists alike to the study of history. But the central concern of Marxist historical thinking, of course, is with lineal development through stages, while Confucian thinking was ordinarily concerned not with process but permanence, with the illustration of the fixed ideals of the Confucian moral universe. The communist idea of progress, like Liao P'ing's and K'ang Yu-wei's, is both a break with conventional Confucian conceptions and a means of explaining the break away.

In other words, to put it flatly, traditional Chinese civilization has not been renewed in modern times but unravelled. The intelligentsia, though accordingly losing its Confucian

47

character, naturally repelled any inference that Chinese history was running dry or was simply being diverted into the western stream. And many of its number, therefore, developed a taste for communist views on history. For the latter, without implying an impossible loyalty to systems thought *passé*, yet provided for continuity with the Chinese past; and at the same time it gave assurance of development parallel to western history, not just an unnerving confrontation in modern times. Communist historical premises anywhere are developmental. It was not simply a communist dictatorship which established these premises in China, but the appeal of the premises particularly in China which helped to establish the dictatorship.

I. EQUIVALENCE AND PERIODIZATION

That is why periodization on universal Marxist lines came to seem, in the nineteen-fifties, the favourite task of communist historians. On a world scale, periodization is what they saw as the great theoretical issue engaging capitalist and communist historians in combat.[1] For China alone, it engaged their attention in the highest degree. The situation of ching-t'ien was only a particular instance. In monographs, in the three main periodicals (Peking monthlies) devoted to problems of teaching history, and in the scholarly journals, problems of adjusting the outer limits of primitive, slave, feudal, and capitalist society predominated. In December 1956, a Peking National University seminar made a critique of a new book by Shang Yüeh, *Essentials of Chinese History*; the discussion centred on points of view about transition from slave to feudal society and from feudal to capitalist.[2] That these topics should be singled out from a book of that title shows what such a group regarded as the stuff of Chinese history.

Paradoxically, this passion for equating Chinese history with the West's by periodization, and thus denying to China any highly individual character, was combined with insistence that all the transitions were essentially internal to China. It was not to be supposed that foreign tribal conquest in the

48

second millenium B.C. ushered in the slave-society of the Shang era, nor that Chou conquerors brought in a feudalism not potentially there with Shang. Most important, it must not be thought that capitalism depended on the incursions of the modern West. The 'shoots of capitalism' question was raked over and over again, with constant quoting of Mao Tse-tung's ruling, in 1939, that indigenous capitalism was beginning to grow before the Opium War, and that a Chinese capitalism would still have emerged had there been no influence of foreign capitalism.[3] Late Ming–early Ch'ing (sixteenth to nineteenth centuries) weaving, mining, and shipbuilding—characteristic, according to Marx, of burgeoning capitalism—as well as porcelain-making and other handicrafts, overseas trade, urbanization, division of labour, etc., came frequently under review, and early Ch'ing intellectuals of relatively unorthodox views, like Yen Yüan, Li Kung, and the textual critics of the 'Han Learning', were said to reflect a rise of new, proto-capitalist social forces. Chinese history *on its own* developed in a way *not just its own*. This was the basic communist historical statement (as we noted in the case of Liao Chung-k'ai), with equal weight on subject and predicate; these together established the equivalence of China and Europe.

Open controversy was possible on the issue of whether slave society was Shang only, or Shang and Hsia before it (Hsia, interestingly enough, being the Confucian-traditional 'first dynasty', though archaeologically not yet identified), or Shang and its successor, Western Chou, or even on through Eastern Chou and Ch'in and Han. Evidently no one had to agree with even great names, Fan Wen-lan or Kuo Mo-jo, that slave society began or ended just here or there.[4] When Mao permitted 'contradictions among the people' (as distinct from dangerous counter-revolutionary ideas), he was speaking primarily about political, social, and economic tensions.[5] But intellectually, too, this was the sort of thing he meant. Chien Po-tsan, a most eminent communist historian, granted that there might be a question as to when this or that historical stage existed; critics took him precisely at his word, and rejected his finding of a slave basis for Han agriculture.[6]

However, when Chien went on to say that there could be no question *whether* a stage existed, no one seems to have demurred. 'Slave society is a stage which human society must pass through': this was a flat imperative. And it was unequivocally emphasized that a slave-feudal sequence, however differently men might fix the dates, was not itself in dispute.[7]

When the periodization controversy was set in motion, it was a refreshment, not a threat, to Marxism as 'grand theory'. Scope was given to dissidence and its appropriate emotions, all within the system. It made the latter more truly all-embracing than total authoritarianism, which would flood, chokingly, into every crevice. Here, intellectuals were allowed 'freedom' within the maze. They should never emerge, but they could roam, in tonic exercise. It was hardly serious but a kind of sport, vital in the constraining Marxist framework. But if flexible boundaries of historical periods helped to make Marxism viable in China, the rigorous order of periods ('Oriental despotism', a disturbing joker, omitted) gave Marxism much of its explicitly Chinese appeal.

Parallel histories, Chinese and western, with the same internal dynamic principle (though, of course, with short-run disparities)—this, then, was an article of faith which the literature laboured but would not argue. Liang Sou-ming (b. 1893), a founder of the Democratic League and long-time theorist of comparative cultures, reaffirmed his non-Marxist beliefs in 1951 and boldly insisted that Chinese history was *sui generis*, classless, not feudal from Han to modern times. After the first wave of denunciation he wrote a 'Reply to Some of My Critics', pointing out that the issues seemed frozen: 'Shen, for instance, after bringing up the topic as to whether old China was a feudal society, started by asserting that it was a feudal society, and continued with such casual phrases as, "it being well known to all" . . . .'[8] Liang had caught the tone exactly. In the many disparaging articles still to come, the attack was entirely *ad hominem*. The closest anyone came to discussing his thesis on feudalism was to call him, on the strength of it, a feudal survival himself.[9]

'Feudalism' was the one permitted social tag for ancient

down to modern times—Mao said, some three thousand years, directly from Chou and Ch'in. And yet, while invoking the term was a matter of strict discipline, its definition was remarkably loose. It must be the connotation of process (with the European parallel) which the communists sought in the term, for feudalism was qualified so broadly, with stages within the stage, that it hardly served an analytic purpose. It conveyed almost nothing of specific social character.

The characterization, 'feudal', that is, for Mao's three thousand years did not imply the homogeneity that one might expect. Mao might say 'feudal from Chou and Ch'in', and others repeat it,[10] but only the adjective—*not* the actual social description—bracketed those eras, Chou and Ch'in, together. For the famous 'first emperor' of Ch'in, in 221 B.C., consolidated the State which (in other hands) gave such novel scope to Confucian bureaucracy. Mao knew it, others knew it, they actually described these eras as vastly different, and only an *a priori* assumption made them paste the feudal label over the cracks.

Everything was feudal for a long time, but for Mao and his epigones pre-Ch'in feudal was aristocratic-autonomous, post-Ch'in feudal was autocratic-centralized. Somewhere under this verbiage lay a clear sense of essential transformation. 'From the time that Ch'in Shih Huang united China, it was a unified feudal state.'[11] And what had 'Lord Shang' accomplished, the famous minister of the Ch'in State in the fourth century B.C., before Ch'in won the Empire? He had 'broken the economic influence of the hereditary ruling class';[12] he represented a 'stage in the establishment of the *chün-hsien* system',[13] a stage, that is, of rationalized local government by centrally appointed officials, no longer by regional magnates. Fan Wen-lan (b. 1891) described the repercussions of the Ch'in conquest in terms that would seem to exhaust the vocabulary of qualitative change—the great monarchs of Ch'in and Han unified, reduced the feudal lords, fixed the *chün-hsien* administrative system, organized vast public works, standardized weights and measures and script and system of laws. And yet all this centralization, hardly feudal in implication if the term implies anything at all, still added up to 'feudalism'. For here Fan explicitly disavowed analogy with the West. In Europe, it was early capitalism that he saw leading to centralized monarchies before the French Revolution. But with the strongest rose-coloured glass he could hardly spy a Chinese capitalism this side of eighteen centuries, so the Ch'in and Han Empire must be feudal, 'representing the landlord-class'.[14] Or—the reason why it was feudal is that, being feudal, it stood for the landed interest, which (everything else aside) made it qualify as feudal. Or, once more—if it was pre-capitalist and post-slave, what else could it be put feudal?

If this was intellectually embarrassing, this preternaturally long age of feudalism, then it had to be explained. One historian did it with a diversionary thrust. Russian development, he said, aroused wonder for exactly the contrary reason. For a nation that became visible only in the ninth century A.D., that was approaching capitalism by the middle of the nineteenth century, attaining socialism in 1917, and nearing communism now, the length of each stage was interestingly short. Thus, the rate of social development in Russia exceeded that in England, France, and other western countries. And slave society in Greece and Rome had a longer run, both absolutely and relatively, than in any of these other lands. Why, then, should anyone be quizzical about China? One could say simply that feudal society in China had a long span, compared with its life in other countries.[15]

2. EQUIVALENCE AND MODERNIZATION

When communist historians shifted their sights to relatively recent times, the air of scientific detachment in their discussions of feudalism tended to be dispelled by the passion of involvement, and 'feudal' became an epithet. The short span of history since the Opium War had stages assigned to it, too, by many historians. Most of them used the classic text-book topics—Opium War, Taiping Rebellion, Sino-Japanese War, Reform Movement, Boxer Rising, 1911, May Fourth—as markers, with appropriate references to foreign aggression, people's movements, feudal persistence, and revolutions old-democratic and new-democratic.[16]

But periodization on this shrunken modern scale had quite another character from that of the over-all periodization. It was not assumed, for instance, that there must be western counterparts to the modern Chinese sub-stages. And, similarly, while in the grand design both China and the West were allotted an epoch of capitalism, imperialism, the 'last stage of capitalism', was the West's alone, with China no more than a victim. Though there was considerable talk of rising *bourgeoisie* and nascent proletariat, communist historians wrung little assurance of parallel development from the specifically modern record—at least, parallel with the West. If anything, China's modern history, its revolutionary record, was offered as a prospective parallel to other peoples, *non*-western peoples, seeking liberation. Thus, for the continuum of the recent past, the present, and the future, the gaze was not on a western model for China, but on a Chinese model for the nations which the West had long exploited. They 'will expect to find in Chinese history the key to the solution of their own problems'.[17]

Yet, despite this different approach to modern history—an understandably special, sensitive area—the interest of historians was the same. When feudalism was more a Chinese blemish than a ubiquitous type of society, when imperialism was more a western crime than a universal stage, one could still, with these ingredients and a Marxist flair, create a sense of confidence of equivalence with the West.

What was it in modern history that had jeopardized such confidence? Clearly, the crisis (see Volume One) grew out of a subjugation of the literati's China which began as political and economic and came to be intellectual as well. Intransigent traditionalism could not stand, and no eclectic apologetics could mask the Confucian retreat before foreign standards of value. Where once new ideas had had to face tests of compatibility with received tradition, now Chinese tradition faced tests of compatibility with independently persuasive ideas.

But the tradition was Confucian—or in the communist

lexicon, feudal. Then a Chinese might cut himself away from the doomed tradition by calling it class, not national. He might identify the nation as a 'people's China', quite uncommitted to the feudal culture of landlords, hence emotionally uninvolved in its débâcle. So much for one side of the western-Confucian imbalance.

Yet, the other side, carrying the preponderance of western intellectual influence, had to be righted. In itself, the simple abandonment of Confucianism by an anti-feudal 'people' could never restore the equilibrium implied in self-respect. There was, however, a still point in the centre. For the West, instead of being left in solitary eminence, could be scored off as imperialist, and the last century of Chinese history, with all its invasions and revolutions, could most solacingly be contemplated in a dialectical way.

We have seen this implication in the ching-t'ien argument: anti-feudal and anti-imperialist, between a rejected Confucian China and a resisted modern West, the communists located themselves in synthesis. Historically the iconoclastic May Fourth movement of 1919 remained a great tradition. But one heard it said that its revolutionary thought must be distinguished from its reactionary thought, such as Hu Shih's and Ts'ai Yüan-p'ei's ideas.[18] These were liberal intellectuals, and liberalism seemed culturally off-balance in China, leaning to Europe and America. Communism, on the other hand, was nicely centred between moribund Confucianism and the non-communist West which had discomfited Confucianists in the first place. So communists could denounce liberalism as cultural colonialism, even while they matched liberals in cold scrutiny of the Confucian past. If anti-imperialism was not enough to make a communist (see the limitations of Liao Chung-k'ai), anti-feudalism was not enough either. One needed to fill it out with an anti-imperialist complement.

This could be seen in cultural terms. After the First World War, the 'new literature' in western vein might seem to be revolutionary. But in communist eyes it was basically unpopular, in the fullest sense of the word. A learned, exclusive, hyperaesthetic character was attributed to it. Thus, in its western ('imperialist') form, it had the same essential content as the traditional literature of the feudal gentry in periods of decline.[19] So much for resistance to the West: now for rejection of Confucian standards.

Mao could continue to write poetry in the classical style—to the pure all things are pure. But generally, communist poets were warned off the ancient literary forms, and foreign forms as well. They were led to adopt the 'median' form of the Chinese popular songs.[20]

Historical writing had its median, too. For the red thread running through the whole communist version of modern history was the charge that feudal China and foreign imperialism inevitably came together, each a support for the other against the Chinese people rising against them both. These 'twin enemies' rode with all the communist historians, who wrote of the 1860s, 'Foreign capitalism and the feudal landlord power, which was represented by Tseng Kuo-fan, Li Hung-chang, and Tso Tsung-t'ang, joined forces to press down the Chinese people',[21] or of the 1900s, 'The Ch'ing government and imperialism had a tight alliance, imperialism and feudalism laid heavy oppression on the Chinese people',[22] and 'The abortiveness of 1911s anti-imperialism and anti-feudalism marked out the area of the revolution's failure'.[23] These simplicities from run-of-the-mill historians could be easily matched in the modern studies of Fan Wen-lan or Hua Kang. They coloured all the introductions to the new, rich, multi-volume collections of modern source materials—on such central subjects as the Opium War, the Taiping and Nien and Moslem rebellions, the French and Japanese wars, the Reform Movement, the Boxers, and the revolution of 1911.

Thus, social protest and patriotism were held to belong together, residing in the people, for the feudal oppressors were, first inept, then unwilling in the fight against foreign pressures. If the imperialists outraged Chinese nationalism, and the feudalists, desperate for succour domestically, connived at the outrage, then their common foe, the people, stood for absolute morality. Under the spell of this conception, communist historians often departed from Marxist historical relativism. That is, while there was plenty of communist emphasis on the historical limitations of the Taipings (and of other peasant rebels throughout Chinese history)[24]—allegations, for instance, of internal corruption and eventual 'separation from the masses', all for the lack of a proletariat—there remains also a vast, less technical literature, where the Taipings figure as 'our side' in a paradigm of conflict. The same holds true for Li Tzu-ch'eng (the 'bandit Li' of the older accounts of the fall of Ming) and other leaders of anti-dynastic risings.

3. POPULAR AND UNPOPULAR THEMES

This variant of communist historical insight, wherein the people is seen as eternally poised against the anti-people, brought certain motifs into prominence. Feudal China is literati-China, or the China of formal intellectual expression. Then people's China is the China of material culture—at least the way people lived and the things they used were highly proper themes for the new intelligentsia. For the latter, whom the death of Confucianism orphaned, sought another line of ancestry in the non-literati past; and Marxist historicism, too, which also made the loss of Confucianism easier to take, confirmed by its very premises the rightness of this new line of research. The materialist assumptions of the periodizers accorded rather well with a bias against the former governing classes, the builders of the 'superstructure', Confucianism. Against the latter's literary emphasis, communist historians weighed in heavily with studies of tangible stuff—artefacts from the fascinating archaeological excavations, Chinese military weapons and their history, even something as homely as the use of manure in the Shang period. The purpose was not antiquarian, it was made quite clear, but study of the development of ancient society; that meant unearthing materials which reflected the life of the ancient workers. And it was not amiss to connect the study with contemporary development—to point out that archaeological discovery was coinciding with current economic construction.[25]

It is perhaps this respect for the hard material relics of

the historical past which permitted generous tribute to the memory of Wang Kuo-wei (1877–1927). Wang, a great archaeologist and epigraphist, nostalgically faithful to the Ch'ing imperial house, had drowned himself in despair of his hopes, in K'un-ming Lake, in the Imperial Palace grounds. He might so easily have qualified for the contemptuous 'feudal' dismissal. Yet, with only a passing graceful reference to Wang's 'early death', and tolerant acceptance of his state of mind before it, a communist critic mourned the loss to the world of scholarship.[26]

If material culture was a congenial theme, as a standing reproof to the 'idealism' which communists freely diagnosed as the literati's flaw, natural science had this and more to recommend it. Ancient Chinese inventions or suggestions of the future, like versions of the compass, seismograph, distance-measurement gauge, and armillary sphere, were proudly emphasized as national achievements. The lore of Chinese medicine was especially combed in both an historical and practical spirit, for the enrichment of western medical science.[27] At an earlier day in the communist movement, before its victory and identification with all China dictated a certain delicacy in dealing with the Chinese past, Taoism had been excoriated as superstition (by the communists' favourite, Lu Hsün [1881–1936], for one), as a code of mere escapism. But later its affinities with proto-science, as in Taoist alchemy's place in metallurgy, came to occupy historians. This was a people's tradition in the course of construction. For science, so little esteemed in the Confucian official tradition, was 'people's' by default.

Indeed, the particular effect of victory on communist assessments of the Chinese record is something to ponder. Not only 'people' but certified literati, great names to long generations of Confucianists, were taken into the communist pantheon, at least for a visit. Ssu-ma Ch'ien, 'Grand Historian' of Han China and the whole great tradition, was praised for realism (a highly legitimizing quality in communist judgements) and given outstanding bibliographical attention;[28] Ssu-ma Kuang of the Sung, once consigned by communists to the dust-heap of orthodox historians, came back in 1957 as 'surpassingly great', one who had the crucial realization that history is a matter of objective facts.[29] Even K'ang Yu-wei, the 'modern sage' of a reform Confucianism, who was a radical in the 1890s as a constitutional monarchist and then remained a monarchist, like Wang Kuo-wei, until his own death in 1925—even K'ang, assailed by Sun Yat-sen as a reformist diversionary before 1911 and written off as dead by most republicans well before his time, was forgiven his tie with counter-revolution and accepted (for his Confucian version of social stages) as a 'progressive'.[30] The conclusive and fatal collapse of the old order had released its foes from some of the compulsion to attack, to see famous men of the past as living spokesmen for a still obstructive Confucian order. With the virtual end of that struggle, and also by virtue of the theory of stages, Ssu-ma Kuang and others of his traditional stature could be relativized, as it were, into their own times, and redeemed from absolute censure. The case of Confucius, the greatest case of all, revealed most fully the implications of this position; it provides the subject of the next chapter.

For the near-contemporary scene, not many brands were plucked from the burning like K'ang Yu-wei. The polemical note sounds louder than the broadly theoretical in studies of the Republican era, when communists were themselves involved in the action, or at the very least were struggling to be born. For the more recent non-co-operative non-communists, the Liang Sou-ming treatment was general. As for earlier figures like the some-time strong man and would-be emperor, Yüan Shih-k'ai, his death in 1916, some time before he could oppose the communists as such, did him no good. Though certainly no Buddhists, communists took him to be re-incarnated as Chiang Kai-shek; in tone, at least, it is more than doubtful that Ch'en Po-ta's early tribute (1946), *Introducing the Thief of the Nation, Yüan Shih-k'ai*,[31] will ever be superseded.

On the subject of Chiang and the Kuomintang, there was plenty of opprobrium, but it is possible that the communists wished to play down merely anti-Kuomintang muck-raking, such as any reformist liberal might engage in. Turning from domestic opponents to foreign, communist historians seemed more interested in blackening the United States than Japan or Great Britain, and they reached back for any likely ammunition. The editors of the Opium War source materials collection, while forced by the nature of the documents to give Britain its lion's share of censure, insisted that America had a hand in this aggression. The same point was made in the sister publication on the Sino-Japanese war.[32] A book entitled, *Battles of the Masses Before the Revolution of 1911*, dealing with post-Boxer 'people's patriotic struggles' (while 'the Ch'ing Government sells the nation'), dwelt lovingly on the 'anti-American patriotic movement', the boycott of 1905.[33] And Hu Shih, indicted as a reactionary idealist in his approach to world history, was traced back to William James, 'creator of American imperialist pragmatism', and to John Dewey, who dispensed, allegedly, a pluralistic idealism to counter the Marxist monistic materialism.[34]

Communist publication on foreign history did not go much beyond this sort of reference to essentially Chinese concerns. A Szechwan University history group studied American China Policy, 1945–50, and American 'capitalist class use of scholars' writings on the China question' (the group did, however, investigate also the 'capitalist historians' slanted misconstruction of the North American War of Independence').[35] Anti-imperialism, and the centennial year of 1957, inspired several articles and translations concerning the Indian Mutiny, and foreign policy requirements (at least, before the break on the Himalayan frontier) kept green the grand old subject of Sino-Indian contacts; though the purely religious story was varied with the less-developed and more congenial subject of commercial interchange. The twentieth-century Russian revolutions naturally claimed attention. Japanese research on China had long been all-embracing, but there was little reciprocity, limited mainly to Sino-Japanese relations and radicalism in Japan. For the 'several thousand years old history of China'—not unique, but autonomous—was the real concern. Marxism-Leninism was supposed to assume Chinese features, to cease to be western-centred.[36] Absorbed really in Chinese periodization, communist historians kept their occasional treatments of such miscellaneous problems as ancient Babylonian society, medieval European taxation, and the industrial revolution in England very close to home.

Home, they say, is where the heart is, and in this first decade or so the hearts, the emotions, of historians in Communist China were very much engaged. Mao had laid down the law for China's modern history: imperialism invaded China, opposed Chinese independence, obstructed the development of indigenous capitalism. All the rest was commentary. But where the mainland historians became so committed, outsiders, too, must comment. One may hold that so many Chinese felt so strongly about autonomous generation of their modern values because really this autonomy was doubted. For Chinese communism came to the fore *because* of the foreign invasions—which broke the older civilization and set off the drive for compensation—and not in spite of them, in train of inevitable historical progress. There is a venerable tradition in Marxist matters of intellectual gymnastics. I think Mao should be turned on his head: Chinese history *not* on its own (in modern times, at least) developed in a way *just* its own.

The history that produced the Chinese communist historians was not the history that these historians felt able to produce. History, the events of the past into which they inquired, and history, the inquiry they conducted, could not quite coincide.

CHAPTER IV

The Place of Confucius in Communist China

> The entire area has, in fact, shared in this attention
> to the relics of the Sage since the creation of a special
> commission for the preservation of monuments and
> relics in Kufow . . .
>
> *The Times*, London (July 31, 1961), 9

So far, the Chinese communist historiography seems un-Confucian. It seems, indeed, comprehensible only as a successor to the Confucian. A Confucian theme like ching-t'ien could remain a subject for historians, but their object in treating it was new. Confucius himself could still be of current concern. He was even, apparently, open to approval. Does this confound the ching-t'ien revaluation? Was communist revolution an illusion, after all?

In Chinese communist fashions, by the early nineteen-sixties, Confucius seemed to be 'in'. Earlier, certainly in the twenties, revolutionaries were quite ready to see him out, and even later, in the first decade or so of the People's Republic, there were plenty of people with little patience for the sage of the old intelligence. Indeed, 'despise the old' and 'preserve the national heritage' had been chasing each other down the nineteen-fifties and incipient sixties, and we should perhaps not dwell too seriously on trends *pro* and *anti*, so fore-shortened, if discernible at all, in the foreground of our age. What seems historically significant is the range, not the petty successions, of the later communist options in evaluating Confucius. For all the possibilities were equally modern, all plausible and consistent within a new Chinese view—an essentially anti-Confucian view informing even the pro-Confucius minds.

In the early years of the 1911 Republic, embattled radical iconoclasts, out to destroy Confucius, and romantic conservatives, bent on preserving him, had been equally untraditional (see Volume Two). In the People's Republic of 1949, successor-radicals, with that battle behind them and those foes crushed, might bring the romantic note into their own strain, and celebrate Confucian anniversaries in the name of the national heritage. But the communists who told Confucius happy birthday only swelled the chorus that sounded him down to burial in history.

1. IMPERISHABILITY OF THE CONFUCIAN SPIRIT?

A grand old question: is Confucianism a religion? Certainly the problem of Confucianism is rather different from the problem of Buddhism in the communist era; there was no organized Confucian body whose state could be statistically assessed.[1] Actually, when there was some sort of effort, before the First World War, to conceive of it as a church, Confucianism was at its nadir. As far as communist policy was concerned, Confucianism as a religion was a dead issue. Other questions claim attention. First, did Confucianism enter into communism? Second (and more important here), what of Confucius himself, his current reputation and its meaning?

There have been observers, with a taste for paradox, who felt that the new régime was 'in spirit', in real content, whatever the surface forms of revolution, the old régime eternally returning. This implied a view of continuity in terms not of process but reality; past was related to present not by sequence but by essence. From this point of view, it was enough to remark that (give or take a few degrees) both Communist and Confucian China were institutionally bureaucratic and despotic, intellectually dogmatic and canonical, psychologically restrictive and demanding. And for those who balked at forcing Confucianism and communism to match, there was still the 'Legalist' label for

Mao's China. With this, the principle of 'sinological determinism' might still be defended, a Chinese ideal type still preserved against corrosive historical thinking; and with Mao a Ch'in Shih Huang-ti, Confucianism would still be implicitly there, an alternative or a partner, as in the days of that Legalist 'First Emperor' or of later dynastic autocrats.

If, in such a timeless, noumenal version of continuity, China were 'always China', the place of Confucius in Communist China would be pre-ordained, and empirical inquiry gratuitous or fussily misleading. Yet, if only out of piety to history (or, less grandly, in defense of his occupation), a historian has to assume the authenticity of change, and, in this instance, contemplate not the ideal of a ghostly Confucius in the mere flesh of a modern communist, but the idea of Confucius in the minds of men who published under communist aegis. One of them, Lo Ken-tse (editor of Volumes IV, 1933, and VI, 1938, of *Ku shih pien*, 'Symposium on Ancient History', the famous collection of modern critiques of Classical historical orthodoxy), made a point in discussing Confucius that could seem to assimilate Confucianism to Marxism. What lay behind the appearance?

In some observations about Confucius on poetry, Lo remarked that Confucius had basically philosophical, not literary interests. Knowing that poetry had a lyrical, expressive character, he wanted to impose on it standards of moral orthodoxy, since he valued poetry from a utilitarian, not an aesthetic point of view. Lo spoke of Confucius' practice of *tuan chang chü i* ('cutting off the stanza and selecting the principle'); this had become a traditional method in the literature of Confucianism. For example, it was the way the *Chung-yung* (Doctrine of the Mean) cited the *Shih-ching* (Book of Poetry): to extract moral dicta. Literature was a tool for Confucius, and rhetorical considerations *per se* played no part. That is why, though his doctrine of 'seizing the word' had a great influence on the development of literary criticism, its purport was not 'revise words' but 'rectify names'.[2]

Now, surely not only Lo's subject but his own patrons had a utilitarian, not an 'aesthetic' conception of literature. Mao as well as Confucius viewed literature as the carrier of an ethos. Yet this was no communist version of (or reversion to) Confucian assumptions.

In the nineteen-twenties the 'Creation Society', a body of writers imbued at first with a western-tinged aestheticism, had turned towards Marxist commitment.[3] This might seem a throw-back to the Confucian doctrine of 'literature to convey the *tao*'. But communist impatience with the early aestheticism of the Creation Society was not just one more ideological demand, like the Confucian demand, that literature serve an ethic. The later, the Marxist, commitment of the Society was quite as remote from Confucian premises as the earlier, the aesthetic. Indeed, it was the exhaustion of Confucianism, premises and all, which had deprived aestheticism of its original target. And therefore, 'art for art's sake', though a radical slogan against a vital Confucianism, seemed superfluous at last—to the communist way of thinking, even counter-revolutionary for a *post*-Confucian age.

Lo Ken-tse, some thirty years later, was just as far as that from simply engrossing a Confucian motif in a Marxist one. Rather, when he spoke of Confucius 'imposing standards' on the *Shih-ching*, Lo (rather late in the critical day) meant to release the poems from their Confucian blanket and to reveal them, by restoring their natural, poetic quality, as truly 'popular'. He wanted to save a Classic by redeeming it from purely Confucian associations, thus permitting it to qualify for a communist accolade.

2. THE DWINDLING SHARE OF CONFUCIAN MATTER IN INTELLECTUAL LIFE

But why should communists care about such a salvage job? Would not revolutionaries (once we take them seriously as such) be expected to cancel the old intellectual currency, instead of converting it? At least from a quantitative standpoint, certainly, the old concerns of Confucian scholarship got relatively meagre attention. In 1958 Kuo Mo-jo, in a briskly modern, no-nonsense mood, said that ancient studies had only a slight claim on available Chinese energies.[4]

Even so, a considerable programme of annotation, translation into modern Chinese, and publication of Classics and other early literature was reported for the next two years.[5] But with the development of a paper shortage (undoubtedly real since spring 1961, and already blamed in 1960 for the serious cut in the export of publications), the ancient texts were the first to go.[6] And this is not surprising, since Shanghai publishers—typically, we may suppose—were proclaiming in 1960 the necessity of 'learning about science and technology', 'catching up with science and technology', and 'overtaking science and technology'.[7] These were the twins, not classical arts and letters, that the communists especially fostered in the educational system.

Intellectual training, then, once a Confucian preserve, was now pervaded by a spirit quite alien to the Confucian. Science and technology were there, on the one hand; and on the other, especially after 1958, some sort of material production and physical labour was injected into the curriculum, with the avowed aim of domesticating the intellectuals, destroying any lingering Confucian assumptions about the 'higher life' and its natural claim to prestige.[8]

3. CONFUCIAN MATTER DE-CONFUCIANIZED: (A) MILESTONES TO THE PRESENT

In a society where an anti-classical education set the tone, what could the Classics be used for? In Communist China, where Confucian scholars were invisible, scholars in Confucianism still found employment. Their principal aim was not to extol antiquity, but to illustrate a theory of process.[9]

Accordingly, Classics retained no scriptural authority; far from providing the criteria for historical assessments, they were examined themselves for significance in history. The authority they had was an object of historical study, not its premise.

There was plenty of historical revisionism, turning villains into heroes. But where the Classics were concerned, it was the pattern rather than the praise-and-blame which was markedly revised. True, Kuo Mo-jo could stand an old judgement on its head and rehabilitate Chou Hsin of Yin, whom the *Shu-ching* (Book of History) made the classic example of the 'bad last emperor'. But when Kuo said that the latter was really competent, that he struck blows for the Chinese people's expansion and unification,[10] Kuo was fitting him into the annals of Chinese progress; and it was this orientation to progress, more than the bleaching of a blackened name, which put Kuo in the un-Confucian stream. In communist use of the Classics for making historical points, Marxist process was the governing idea, not, however revalued, a moralistic absolute.

(a) *From Primitive to Slave*

Thus, history teachers should use the Classics in illustrating stages, e.g.: 'For the waning of primitive communism and the coming of slave society, cite the *Li-yün* section of the *Li-chi* (Book of Rites), from "Ta tao chih hsing yeh" to "Shih wei hsiao-k'ang" ' (*Li-chi* VII A, 2–3; Legge, 'When the Grand Course was pursued, a public and common spirit ruled all under the sky . . .').[11] This passage was dear to nineteenth-century innovators and egalitarians, Taiping rebels and K'ang Yu-wei's Reformers.[12] But these groups (though generally far apart in their attitudes toward the Classics) used the *Li-chi* for the validity that a Classic might lend; while communists cited the same text as illustrative, not exemplary—to corroborate a theory, not authenticate a value.

As a matter of fact, some communists saw not only their modern predecessors' *Li-yün* citations, but the *Li-yün* itself, as a falling back on authority. For the *Li-yün* attributes the 'Grand Course' passage to Confucius, though it really dates from some two centuries after his time.[13] There were harsh words for one Comrade Jen Chüan, who seemed to accept the attribution uncritically.[14] And yet, while inviting this attack from a critic who denied that Confucius had any intention of 'abolishing distinctions', Jen Chüan was really not in the business of praising Confucius by raising him out of his time, taking him as a validator of socialism, or socialism as validator of him. Jen Chüan suggested that Confucius (like

K'ang Yu-wei, who revered this *ta-t'ung* side of him) had a vague *kung-hsiang* (fantasy) socialism, impracticable in his day. Therefore, lacking a clear road ahead to his goal, he looked back to primitive communism. Whence, 'Ta tao chih hsing yeh . . .'[15]—or, back to the *Li-yün* as reflector of primitive communism, a superseded stage.

(b) From Slave to Feudal

And so for the next transition, from slave society to feudalism: the Confucian *jen* (human kindness) was said to be progressive in its class base. *Jen* came in with the new relationship of the means of production, as feudal landholding became the general pattern and most of the slaves were freed. *Jen* and *li* (the ritual proprieties) were closely connected. One of the anti-slavery inferences from *jen*, in this reading, was the extension of *li* to the common man (and here Confucius was very different from the *Chou-li*, the 'Rites of Chou'). When Confucius taught, the feudal landholding class was still weak. That is why, though he really spoke for progress, he had to advocate innovation in the form of 'restoring the old'.[16] But progress it really was, reflected textually in the sequence of *I-ching* (Book of Changes) to *I-chuan* (Commentary on Changes—possibly included among the 'Ten Wings', appendices to the *I-ching*). For these texts were equated, respectively, with an early Chou religious idealism (*T'ien-tao*, 'Way of Heaven') and a 'Warring States' materialistic naturalism.[17]

Thus, as materialism is a higher stage of thought than idealism, and naturalism higher than religion, so the 'Warring States' advance of the doctrines of Confucius towards victory was an advance indeed, in the historical sense of the word. For, as a pair of authors interpreted the *Lun-yü* (Analects), Confucius' concept of *jen* was both anti-aristocratic and anti-religious. *Jen*, the special mark of the *chün-tzu*, undercut the nobles by substituting individual quality for blood line in distinguishing *chün-tzu* from *hsiao-jen*, the 'princely man' from the 'small'. And inasmuch as *jen* implied 'esteeming wisdom', this was progressive, too—in its humanist agnosticism, that strain in Confucius that Feuerbach praised when he marked the advance of capitalism on European feudalism, reflected in the attrition of religion.[18]

This proved a popular theme. There was a special Marxist pleasure in the dialectic of eighteenth-century Europe, where the Jesuits praised Confucius for their own religious purposes, only to find him turned against them. For the anti-feudal capitalist class philosophy was materialistic and agnostic, and French and German secularists, pitting philosophy against religion, invoked Confucius. The Germans, being idealistic, used Confucius in making a philosophical revolution. But the materialistic French made the great *bourgeois* political revolution, and they found Confucius pertinent as well.[19]

The Chinese commentator here, expressing this opinion, was neither praising capitalism for itself nor suggesting that on the Chinese scene Confucius was capitalistic. He was only approving progress generally, not capitalism specifically, and Confucian humanism, he felt, was generally progressive, attuned to progress out of feudalism in Europe, progress into feudalism in China. Others, too, appreciated Confucius for the humanism and materialism they sometimes strained to find. One, for example, saw the message of *Lun-yü*, III, xii ('One should sacrifice to a spirit as though that spirit were present'), as 'Gods and ancestral spirits exist only in the mind'. Passages indicating Confucius' preference for non-speculative direct perception, and for enriching the people before teaching them, were cited as materialist, in different senses of the word. Confucius, who opposed excessive concentration of wealth, the fleecing of the poor, accepted the fact that men desired to enrich themselves. Poverty, he knew, was the cause of social disturbance.[20]

This hardly seems especially startling or profound. But at least—and this was its merit in the eyes of the communist commentators—it was not moralistic. If Confucius was to be saved, materialism had to be found as the saving grace. And so Confucius' scepticism about knowing the 'Way of Heaven' (see *Lun-yü*, V, xii) was an appealing thing to emphasize. It was a Way referred to often, superstitiously, by men recorded in the *Ch'un-ch'iu* (The Spring and Autumn Annals), but materialistically doubted in the *Tso-chuan* (the main classical 'commentary' appended to the 'Annals'), Ch'ao-kung 18: 'The Way of Heaven is far, the way of man is near . . .'[21]

As the *Lun-yü* and *Tso-chuan* contributed humanism to the march of progress, so the *Shih-ching* (which we have seen already as 'popular') was said to begin a great tradition of realism, reflecting the creativity which burgeoning feudal society so abundantly released.[22] We know well enough, from modern invective, that feudalism *per se* won no communist admiration. As with capitalism in Europe, with its touch of the Confucian agnostic spirit, it was the progressive stage, not the thing in itself, that was praiseworthy; and a Classic was used for documenting and praised for projecting progress.

Accordingly, possible communist respect for Confucian Classics, as creative expressions of social evolution, did not usually carry over to Confucian classical scholarship. It might be said occasionally that there was much to be learned from one of its practitioners; for example, there was praise of Chia I (200–168 B.C.), a Han official who made a famous critique of Ch'in rule by power alone. Such praise, far from implying communist self-identification with the past through Confucian fellow-feeling, reflected more likely a stung reaction to allegations of 'Legalism'—the hostile way of identifying the Party with the past. What was Chia I's virtue? It was nothing absolute, but relative to process. In what he was, he had to be imperfect: he could not escape the limitations of time and place. His merit lay in where he was going.

His lifetime (so the argument ran) coincided with a great change in feudal society, and Chia I, seeking to construct a programme for a new feudal government, represented the interest of a newly rising commoner landlord class. He had a realistic viewpoint (good), and he paid special attention (very good) to Ch'in and contemporary (early Han) history —which was, for his own day, modern history.[23] Thus, the communist favour went out to modern times, and, among men and events of the past, to the modernizing forces.

For the most part, then, Confucian classical scholarship after the classical age itself was seen as the main line of Chinese feudal culture, the support of feudal monarchy. And feudal society, as distinct from the feudalization of slave society, had no intrinsic virtue. Han Wu-ti (regn. 134–86 B.C.) winnowed the Ju (the Confucianists) from out of the 'Hundred Schools' for special honour, and established their texts as authoritative. Thus, the Classics became the preserve of the feudal landholding, bureaucratic literati. And one of the aims of classical study now was to show how classical study then could serve the feudal interests.[24] The Sung *li-hsüeh* neo-Confucianism—to cite an impressive school of classical scholarship—constrained thought, imposed rote, blocked science; and the 'Han-chien (Chinese traitor) Tseng Kuo-fan' (1811–72), not by chance, was a great patron of *li-hsüeh*.[25]

(c) From Confucian to Marxist

In short, the Marxist approach to the Classics was neither *necessarily* to damn them as feudal (some did), nor to praise them (in the Confucian vein) as timeless. They were subject to scrutiny from a mental world beyond them; they did not govern the mental world (as once they did) themselves. As a Communist *Mencius* study-group expressed it: *They* (traditional intellectuals) used *Mencius* as a vehicle—Chu Hsi did it to carry his neo-Confucianism, Tai Chen (1724–77) did it to correct Chu Hsi; K'ang Yu-wei did it as a 'modern-text' Confucian Reformer, all of them summoning up antiquity to sanction innovation. But *we* use the tool of Marxism-Leninism for an analytic critique.[26]

This meant, of course, that a Marxist commentary on Mencius conveyed Marxism. In this it might seem to be doing, *mutatis mutandis*, just what Chu Hsi, Tai Chen, and K'ang Yu-wei did. Yet, while such Sung and Ch'ing commentators may not, indeed, have been doing what they claimed, expounding Mencius or Confucius 'authentically', still they assumed that only if they did so would their own views be valid. However individual their interpretations, however eccentric they seemed to their opponents, these earlier scholars had to establish—for their own satisfaction as much as for anyone else's—that classical Confucian authority was being duly upheld. But Marxists scouted Confucian authority, considering it a specimen to be analyzed (not idolized) and put in its place in history—a place in the flux of the past, not an eternal place of ever-present judgement.

That is why a communist reversal of older radical textual critiques is comprehensible. It may seem extraordinary that a contemporary scholar in Communist China should take up the traditional Confucian line on the *Tso-chuan*: that it really was compiled by Tso Chiu-ming as a commentary on the *Ch'un-ch'iu* (which was Confucius' own).[27] Yet, despite appearances, decades of 'doubting antiquity' had not quite gone for nothing. For the main point of Confucius, said to be 'rectification of names', was seen as completely feudal and only feudal. And Confucius, while commendably materialistic in some ways, and incomparably important in planting history in Chinese education, was a step behind Ssu-ma Ch'ien, the 'Grand Historian' of the Former Han. Though Confucius did not (as so often advertised) see history as an irredeemable fall from sage-antiquity, he did see eternal oscillation (in the Mencius phrase, 'now order, now chaos'), while Ssu-ma Ch'ien had a sense of historical progress.

We have, then, in this account of Confucius, another avowal of progress (indeed, to see progress *was* progress), not a triumphant return of an old unfaded perennial. If progress went through Confucius (as evinced in his 'Spring and Autumn', which was not the first of its name, but first to deal with 'the Empire' and not just a single state), it also went beyond him. And therefore, without losing his modern identity, a communist might agree now with orthodox Confucianists on the link of *Tso-chuan* to *Ch'un-ch'iu*. What they agreed on was the error of the *Kung-yang* school; and this error was to deny that link, in order to make the specious *Kung-yang* case for Confucius as the ultimate progressive. Same stand, different standpoints; different affects from the same description. For progress mattered in communist theory, while it mattered precious little to the orthodox Confucianist. To the orthodox, the *Kung-yang* Confucius was spurious because Confucius, gratifyingly, was not progressive at all. To communists, the *Kung-yang* Confucius was spurious because Confucius, regrettably, was not progressive enough.

In the communist era, when the thrill of iconoclasm in the field of Classics had worn off—because icons no longer sacred tempted fewer men to break them—old conventional combinations (like the *Ch'un-ch'iu* and the *Tso-chuan*, respectably together) bore no witness at all to the renascence of Confucius.

Thus, praise of Confucius (e.g., for seeing the true relation between 'ideology' and 'reality')[28] tended to be patronizing, not a reverent expression of discipleship. Confucius could not guarantee this truth; he simply decorated the discussion. One pointed up a thesis, perhaps, by referring to the Classics, but legitimacy flowed back from Marx (Lenin, Mao), not forward from Confucius. 'Ideology' and 'reality', in our example, were *wen* and *tao*, luminous classical terms—but here, metaphorical, used clearly in the expectation that no one would misunderstand. And nothing marks so much the relegation of values to the past, to historical significance, as metaphorical drift, when originally literal statements become rhetorical allusions.

When the communist 'collectors, of the 'multi-million poems' (1958) were said to engage in *ts'ai-feng* ('collection of the airs of the states'), they recalled the tradition that glorified Confucius' favourite, the 'Book of Songs', the classical *Shih-ching*.[29] But no literal analogy could stand. For the original *ts'ai-feng* revealed suffering in feudal states; the communist *ts'ai-feng*—no doubts about this—turned up only paeans of joy and thanks to the unitary state. History could not be allowed to repeat, and the classical phrase, which suggested Confucius in a 'decorative' way, was meant to consolidate Mao, and Mao alone.

4. CONFUCIAN MATTER DE-CONFUCIANIZED: (B) GRAVE-STONES FROM THE PAST

On this showing, when writers in Communist China displayed some admiration of Confucius, they were not reproducing the traditional admiration. Therefore, when other contemporary writers sounded unregenerately anti-Confucian, this was no sign of party schizophrenia. For this was the kind of controversy that a Marxist world could contain. If one wanted to put a reactionary construction on Confucius' work (holding that he feared the future and was generally 'anti-people'),[30] this taste in interpretation clashed, to be sure, with the 'progressive' taste, but the tasters, all the same, had a common assumption: that history moves regularly through progressive stages, no matter which stage one sees as dear to Confucius, or to which he seems appropriate. The controversy was tame, like the more general one about when slave society ended and feudal began. As we have seen, within a framework of agreement on the historical reality of these societies in China, in that order, there could be several ideas about their boundaries.

But even if one acknowledges that the relatively pro-Confucius wing of communist opinion was safely communist enough, not Confucian, why did it come into being? Why did it differ not only from traditional conservatism but from traditional (earlier twentieth-century) radicalism? The fact that it could co-exist with hostility to Confucius does not explain how it came to exist at all. It is provocative, surely, that after all the vitriolic treatment of Confucius in the 'Renaissance', the 'New Tide', all the early radical intellectual groupings, we can find a scholar in mainland China, in 1958, with this fine antique allusion: 'The Great Pheasant gives a cry, dawn comes to the world.' Confucius, here no wretched feudal crow, is the 'Great Pheasant'. Galvanizing scholarship, diffusing it in new, non-aristocratic circles, he gives rise to the 'Hundred Schools'. 'This had great significance in the history of Chinese thought and Chinese education. Thereafter, literate men took Confucius as their great ancestral teacher . . .'[31]

(a) From Class to Nation

The big difference between early days and late for the communists and Confucius was the difference between social and national associations. In communist eyes originally, Confucius was simply the idol of the rulers of the old society; if those feudal rulers (or their semi-feudal, semi-colonial successors), for their part, claimed that Confucius embodied the 'national essence', this was only a reactionary fiction, designed to avert the class struggle which would sweep the old away. Ch'en Tu-hsiu saw Confucianism as a spiritual weapon of the anti-revolutionary feudalists. Li Ta-chao reviled it as the rotten fruit of thousands of years ago, the symbol of monarchical despotism, invoked in modern China by crafty scoundrels. Sun Yat-sen, the communists thought, soon after his death, needed to be rescued for the 'World Park', with Marx and Lenin; Kuomintang rightists were trying to make off with him to the 'Confucian Temple', so as to quash the revolution. There was no doubt, really, that Confucius was being overworked in the anti-communist cause. A speaker in 1928 commemorated Confucius (and while he was at it, Yao, Shun, Wen, and Wu) with the whole litany of *li* and *i*, self-cultivation, peace to the *T'ien-hsia*. . . . The communists were madmen, standing for slaughter and burning, for fathers not fathers and sons not sons—not (to put it mildly) respectful to Confucius' admonitions.[32]

Thus, Confucius, in trouble enough just for his traditional distinction, was further compromised by traditionalistic efforts to revive him. At first, in the new Republic after 1911, the old elementary education in Confucian *hsiu-shen tu-ching* (moral culture and classical reading) had fallen into abeyance. The texts of Confucian learning were left to the universities, where a spirit of detachment—knowledge *of*, not knowledge *in*, judgement, not immersion—was expected to prevail. This was one of the developments that made K'ang Yu-wei, the sponsor of Confucianism as national essence and national religion, so disaffected. However, in 1915 Yüan Shih-k'ai, appealing to conservatives with his monarchical movement, put the old formula back in the lower schools. In 1923, *hsiu-shen* slipped once more, supplanted by a blandly modern 'citizenship and hygiene', and *tu-ching* vanished, too, as the literary language, with its Confucian aura, yielded to the colloquial in the primary and high schools.[33] But when Chiang Kai-shek turned to the old pieties, with his '*San-min chu-i* (Three People's Principles) education' for an anti-communist China's destiny, Confucius again turned up in school. Ch'en Li-fu's directives in January 1942 had agriculture as the basis of national life, *Ch'un-ch'iu* and *Li-chi* as the heart of instruction in ethics.[34] (And twenty years later, on Taiwan, Confucius was still being enlisted against the 'alien revolution'.)[35]

What the communists made of this should be easy to imagine. Confucius needed only the curse of Japanese sponsorship to make his exposure complete. Reactionary 'sellers of the nation', the indictment ran, 'revived the old, revered Confucius'. And the predatory buyers, the Japanese fascists, pumped their own gas of 'Confucius and the Kingly Way' into occupied China.[36] 'Yao and Shun reappear in Great Manchuria!' blared a poster at the Great Wall in 1933.[37] Everwhere the sage-kings went, the Sage was sure to go.

This made two things clear. First, Confucius must be anathema to communists as long as he seemed identified with a contemporary Chinese class cause or a Japanese foreign cause: to the communists, by no means always distinguishable. But second, communists, pre-empting the *national* cause, could nationalize Confucius, freeing him of current social associations, taking him out of history from now on—by putting him back into it (in another sense), packing him away in the past as *historically* significant!

For the very fact that their enemies, foreign and domestic, *used* Confucius meant that the defence of Confucius was not their genuine end; and if these enemies, exactly like the communists, were really concerned with present interests, their used Confucius was just as dead as a communist might wish him. A dead man, superseded as a target, could be measured for a monument.

Passing time can bury the ground of controversy, make it entirely 'historical'. In 1924 the great Bengali poet, Rabindranath Tagore, was pilloried in China as anti-materialist, because of his plea for 'Asian spirit'. But in 1957 the People's Literature Publishing House could promise him nine volumes in a projected edition of 'world classics'.[38] His idealism, evidently, was not an active poison now, but only an historical specimen, respectably bound for the shelf. Conceivably, there could have been a move to reconsider publication when Chinese relations with India worsened. But this would mean that his current associations, with India as a national foe, had prejudiced his standing. His *historical* associations in the China of the 1920s—allegedly with the 'imperialist' and 'feudalist' foes of progress—had lost their repulsive force by the 1950s; at the later date Tagore could seem innocuous, an acceptable Asian nominee for greatness, a symbol of a people still more sinned against by imperialists than sinning. And the communists as victors, presiding over the fostering of culture, were ready to be his patrons. In the same spirit, and with greater zeal, they could patronize Confucius, too.

(b) *From Life to Museum*

Publicity for a 'people's tradition' against a 'gentry' (Confucian) tradition[39] was not inconsistent with a restoration of Confucius. Once, during the days of the Paris Commune, the great historian, Jakob Burckhardt, rushed to believe a rumour of something he rather expected, the burning of the Louvre and all its contents;[40] to Burckhardt, the treasures of art and culture seemed destined for ruin in the dawning age of destruction of authority. What should they do, revolutionaries from the lower depths, but destroy the products of the old high culture, symbols of their own subservience?

But Burckhardt might have remembered the first French Revolutionaries' preservation of the Bayeux Tapestry as a national treasure, even though, as a relic of the grandeur of nobles, it had been threatened, like its associates, with destruction.[41] And Burckhardt (in a heroic feat of clairvoyance and broadening of sympathies) might have applied the lesson in envisioning the fate of Confucius: 'the people', without abandoning hostility to bearers of the 'other culture', could conceive of themselves as capturing it. Like 'The Hermitage' in Leningrad, all over China palaces and temples and varied relics—all things in *absolute* terms remote from communist sympathies—were simply appropriated, 'relativized', and materially preserved.[42] And like these materially, Confucius morally did not have to be shattered; he could be preserved, embalmed, deprived of life in a glass case instead of in a cultural holocaust. He could be restored, in short, not as an authentically resurgent Confucianism (or an immanently

Confucian communism) might restore him, but as a museum-keeper restores, his loving attention to 'period' proclaiming the banishment of his object from any living culture. What could be more aggressive than that (new masses *versus* old *élite*), and yet more soporific? Revolutionaries, in a *metaphorical* way, kissing off into the past instead of blowing up in the present, committed the destruction which Burckhardt half-literally expected. As the communists claimed to stand for the whole nation, the ancient mentor of a high, once mighty part was quietly taken over, and given his quietus. Nobody raises his voice in a National Gallery—on either side of the picture frames.

Under the new dispensation, then, Confucius could have one or another class-association, as long as it was ascribed to him *for his own day only*. Make him 'slave' or 'feudal', but only for late Chou. He could then belong to the modern nation by being in its history, or (to say the same thing) by being *for now* de-classed: that is, out of historical action. Thus, 'the feudalist system which set up his name as a symbol has gone for good; but the name of Confucius himself is, and always will be, respected and cherished by the Chinese people'.[43] And another writer, in the same business of extricating Confucius from the past for present admiration, consigned him to the past, too, as a matter of practical influence: "I myself am not a Confucianist, and I think, to speak frankly, that what he taught belongs now irrevocably to history.'[44] A biographer censured Yen Fu (1848–1921) for using Confucius after World War I as a stick for beating western civilization. To a communist, this was using the anti-historical concept of 'Chinese essence' to damn modernization, and he said that Confucius' teaching had the form of the feudal consciousness, which was not for modern China, not for the modern world. But the critic was attacking Yen Fu, a late antagonist, not Confucius, a late, late one. He agreed that the thought of Confucius, *in history*, had a great position and applicability.[45]

To accept literal Confucian influence was wrong; he must be dead to the present. Therefore, even the generally favoured Hung Hsiu-ch'üan, the Taiping ruler, might be scored off for 'traditional feudal superstition' implanted by his youthful Confucian training.[46] But to acknowledge some national Confucian ancestry, over a gulf of time, was right. For this meant continuity, or life to the culture. Thus, an alphabetic script-reformer would preserve against obliteration Confucius and the culture which he dominated, though this culture was enshrined in the script that was marked for discard.[47] And the historian, Ch'en Po-ta (b. 1904), avowing that 'today's China is an extension of historical China', referred to a Mao statement of 1938: 'As we are believers in the Marxist approach to history, we must not cut off our whole historical past. We must make a summing up from Confucius down to Sun Yat-sen and inherit this precious legacy.'[48]

'Broaden the modern, narrow the old,' Ch'en continued, as he made it clear that a line was thrown back to the past not for the sake of the past, but for the present. The tie was for continuity, not constraint. What, to Ch'en, marked off the communist zeal for the modern from that of earlier iconoclasts, with their capitalist world-view and their slogans on the order of, 'Break through the web!' or 'Break down the Confucianists' shop!'? What these men lacked, with their capitalist-reformist mentalities, was scientific detachment regarding ancient thought and culture. Some of their fellows tried superficially to harmonize the old and the new; they themselves went to extremes, and cut off the old from the new absolutely. A new scholarship was needed, and communists would supply it: neither classical, nor Sung neo-Confucian, nor Ch'ing empirical, nor late-Ch'ing reformist. It must be a scholarship fulfilling each earlier type, transcending the accomplishments of all who went before.[49]

Fulfilment—neither dismissal nor resuscitation. For the former would leave an impression of China de-nationalized, the victim of 'cultural imperialism', and the latter would leave her unmodernized, a relic of feudalism. The great aim was to be modern *and* Chinese, that combination so desperately sought through a century of reformist and revolutionary exasperation at a seemingly immobile China and an all-too-kinetic West. Behind apparent banalities ('A new form of brushwork does not mean that we can dispense with tradition. The new technique must grow out of the old, for only so will it retain a Chinese style.')[50] lay a poignant search for identity. Thus, for all the communists' hostility to the reactionary use of Confucius, there was an equal animus against what they saw as the liberal, *bourgeois*, pro-western abuse of Confucius. Ku Chieh-kang (b. 1893), in a new preface (1954) to a 1935 book on Han dynasty scholarship, censured himself for his old unmitigated rejection of the Confucian thought of those days—an error stemming from his failings in historical materialism.[51] And another writer, not baring the culpability as his own but spreading it around, indicted the Chinese *bourgeoisie* for an overweening reverence for western culture and disparagement of Chinese, though Mao had ordained that 'today's China is the extension of historical China'.[52]

Confucius, then, redeemed from both the class aberration (feudal) of idolization and the class aberration (*bourgeois*) of destruction, might be kept as a national monument, un-worshipped, yet also unshattered. In effect, the disdain of a modern pro-western *bourgeoisie* for Confucius cancelled out, for the dialecticians, a feudal class's pre-modern devotion. The communists, driving history to a classless synthetic ful-filment, retired Confucius honourably into the silence of the museum. In a concrete way, this was evident in the very making of museums in Communist China.

For the Confucian temple at Sian was restored, to house an historical museum. The temple and tomb (and environs) of Confucius at Ch'ü-fu were repainted, regilded, and pre-served.[53] In April 1962, over the traditional 'Ch'ing-ming' spring festival for worshipping at graves, streams of visitors were drawn there, in a market-fair atmosphere, officially contrived, along the route of procession from the 'Confucian grove' to the temple.[54] (The *K'ung-lin*, 'Confucian grove', had once been proposed as the Mecca and Jerusalem of Con-fucianism as a religion.)[55] And such acts of piety (consistent with, not confounded by, a 'feudal' identification)[56] con-veyed the communists' sense of synthesis in arresting physical ruin. Products of the old society, which might be (and earlier, were) deemed proper objects of iconoclasm, provocative symbols of a social type which communists ought to attack, nevertheless had suffered neglect and depredation, not loving care, from the society which the communists succeeded.[57] This neglect, combined with foreign plundering, came to the fore as a cultural crime of the old society, overshadowing the inequities of the even older society which made the relics in the first place. If anything, it was the pre-communist neglect which consigned these things to history, which stamped them *non-contemporary*. When the Marxist historicism of the current society relativized its 'restored' Confucius to a remote stage of society—and preserved him for the present through the Museum's trick of dissociating art from any life at all—it only confirmed the action (or inaction: neglect) of the society just before this one. In a satirical fantasy from that Kuomintang era, the 1930s, the novelist Lao She, ultimately quite acceptable to the communists, mordantly pictured two things, perceived as a combination: conservative spirit in clinging to a moribund culture, and material failure to conserve. For the museum in 'Cat City' was empty, its possessions all sold to foreigners.[58]

Any contemporary assault against Confucius, then, while still a sort of ritual exercise for some writers in Communist China, was ideologically superfluous. Sometimes, of course, impatience with mere history before the heady tasks of the present still peeped through. A reporter, praising a cooperative at Ch'ü-fu, declared that in three years, after some two thousand years of poverty, the people of Confucius' village were at last improving their economic and cultural life; this showed the superiority of socialism to the Confucian Classics. People who thronged to see the Confucian temple and the Confucian grove would do themselves no harm if they went out of their way to take a look at this co-operative.[59]

But the animadversion was mild. One could afford to be merely wry and reserved about Confucius' historical standing—just because it was kept historical. The communists knew they had living men to assail, non-communists as modern and post-Confucian as themselves, not the stuffed men from a costume past (whose clothes they were stealing anyway, to display as their 'national heritage'). The stake now was title to the prestige of science. Science, as we have suggested, sets up values alien to the Confucian, and a Confucian challenge on this score could hardly be an issue. But anti-traditionalism of a non-communist variety could not be stripped of a claim on that title so easily. An attack on a biologist for basing himself on Darwin instead of Michurin[60] was a more typical accusation of 'rightism' than an attack on grounds of Sinocentric narrowness. The Confucian literatus, who might have been narrow in that way, was so faint a memory that no one now got credit in heaven, as a new man, just for being a western-trained scientist. The latter was now the old man (the Confucianist was the dead man), and the 'post-*bourgeois*' scientist, the new.

Scientists came to be less harassed by ideologues in a technologically hungry China, but the demand for 'red and expert', the redder the better, had long been heard in the land,[61] and could doubtless be heard again. The question has been raised of a possible affinity between this demand and the Confucian preference for the highly indoctrinated universal man over the specialist.[62] If the affinity existed, then the Confucian spirit might well be thought, in a sense, imperishable. Yet, the 'red and expert' formula could better be taken, perhaps, to prove the opposite: scientific expertise, specialized knowledge, far from being inferior to the general, was indispensable. It was because it was indispensable that it was so important to capture; it must not be seen as independent, or as anything but derived from the Marxist point of view. The communists had to own science—or *they* would appear not indispensable.

A Chinese world in which science had to be owned, to be captured, was the very world in which Confucius could only be captured. He could not be free and dominant. Where science was all-pervasive (even seeping into the rhetoric that described the social system), Confucius was under lock and key and glass. It was the curators, not the creators, who looked to Confucius now. Unlike the Confucius of the Confucianists, the Confucius of the communists had to be entombed to be enshrined. No longer a present incitement to traditionalists, for these had been crushed, Confucius was ready for history.

But not for 'the dustbin of history'. The museum where they posed Confucius may be a storehouse of value and inspiration. And 'museumified' is not 'mummified'. Still, the 'museumified' Confucius does not speak; when he is no longer involved in the handing down of judgements, he is not very much involved in clamorous class struggle. One is neither quartering Botticelli, nor taking his as the last word for a contemporary jury, when one hangs him on the wall, far from the social context of his patronage. The critics, by and large, call him masterly. They also call him *quattrocento*. Confucius, too, is wise today for many revolutionaries, and may grow wiser as his patrons grow deader. But Confucius is also *Chou*.

The first wave of revolution in the twentieth century had virtually destroyed him, and seemed to destroy with him a precious continuity, an historical identity. Many schools have tried to put these together again. The communists had their own part in the search for time lost, and their own intellectual expedient: bring it back, bring him back, by pushing him back in history. It was a long peregrination, from the Confucian *tao*, K'ung's Way, to the past recaptured.

Part Three

HISTORICAL SIGNIFICANCE

'Time,' he said, 'is the best Censor:
Secret movements of troops and guns, even,
Become historical, cease to concern.'

Robert Graves, 'The Censor'

Theory and History

I. THEORY

IN Proust's 'overture' and 'Combray', bits of themes crackle, mingle, flicker into new ones; until finally a single long-breathed tune, swirling out of the rich tone that grounded it and announced it, leads into *Swann's Way* and the great theme of search. Sadly, that music, or anything like it, is fled from this account of modern Chinese history. But a theme is there, anticipated, quoted, in much that has gone before—waiting (like the reader) for release.

Intonation matters, in English as well as Chinese. We may describe an item in the human record as historically (really) significant, or as (merely) historically significant. The distinction is between an empirical judgement of fruitfulness in time and a normative judgement of aridity in the here and now.

The ambiguity of 'historical significance' is a virtue, not a flaw. To resist the taxonomical zeal for precision, the literalist's restriction of one phrase to one concept, is both an intellectual and moral requirement for the historian. For as a whole man he indeed has intellectual and moral require-ments—he must know that he stands on shifting sands, yet he must take a stand—and the tension implicit in 'historical significance', the strain between neutral analysis and com-mitted evaluation, must be acknowledged and preserved if history, the records men make, and history, the records men write, are to come close to correspondence.

(a) Intellectual Significance of the Ambiguity

Historical understanding precludes restriction of the vision to literal meanings. What, for example, does the character *te* 德 (pronounced like the French 'de') denote in a Chinese text? During the many centuries of Confucian and Taoist intellectual prominence in China, *te* suggested a cluster of meanings around the concept 'virtue' or 'power' (of virtue). But when Ch'en Tu-hsiu, a hater of the old intellectual culture in which *te* was profoundly embedded, summoned 'Mr. Science' and 'Mr. Democracy' to root it out, his 'Mr. Democracy' was 'Te Hsien-sheng', Mr. *Te*, the old character drained of its Confucian substance, tamed as a mere phonetic (in a foreign language, at that) to an anti-Confucian purpose.[1] And yet its old associations were still there, significantly so, for they lent the term its sterilizing force, appropriate to its new associations. Virtue, power, were delivered over to an iconoclastic ethic. At one and the same time the old *te*, with the old culture, was being proclaimed merely *historically* significant—i.e. dead to modern men—and historically really *significant*, confirmed as such by its very selection as the literal point of departure for a metaphoric drift.

Historical process is captured in such transitions from literalness to metaphor. As some commentators remarked, Chiang Kai-shek 'lost the mandate' in 1949, when Mao Tse-tung supplanted him as the ruler of mainland China. Reference to the 'mandate of Heaven' would once have had a literal quality, as a live Confucian assumption about dynastic successions. But passing time reduced it to archaism, a metaphor with a period air that would call attention to passing time. One could hardly contemplate Chinese history without realizing how historically significant Confucian political theory had been; and one could hardly seize more surely the fact of its displacement than by savouring 'historical significance' in its full range of meaning—not only the 'real' but the 'mere'. It is historical consciousness that attunes the ear to the changing ring of 'mandate of Heaven': from the ring of current coin, to a knell.

In time, then, words will not stand still. Moralistic theories of history, like the praise-and-blame Confucian, or idealistic theories of anti-history, like the Platonic, dwell on timeless pattern or being, not process, and therefore deal in absolutes. But a concern with process, becoming, ousts the language of fixity for the language of movement—the language of relativism. Absolutism is parochialism of the present, the confusion of one's own time with the timeless, a confusion of the categories of reasonable and rational. This is the confusion one fosters when he judges other times by his own criteria, without acknowledging that he himself, not the culminator of history but the latest comer, has only what his subjects have—ideas, aesthetics, morality that may be reasonable, pleasing, commendable in his own day and age, but not surely rational, beautiful, or mandatory as trans-historical absolutes. No one has the norm of norms.

What, for example, makes a biography historically significant? It has to be written from that standpoint of relativism which rationalists, censoriously, have often ascribed to the historical mode of knowledge. Anti-historical rationalists produce criteria of truth and consistency, inherent rationality. But historians, as such, ask in neutral tones, not whether something is true or good, but why and where and to what end it came to be enacted or expressed. Therefore, an historical biographer goes beyond assessment of his subject's thought as rationally (timelessly and abstractly) perhaps erratic. He proceeds to analyse why, nevertheless, that thought was not ridiculous (an indictment that would be irrelevant to larger historical issues) but reasonable—in spite of or because of imperfect rationality. And the latter problem is eminently relevant to history: reasonableness relates to the questions put by the subject's time (for his ideas are answers), not by his biographer's. In history, relativism is all.

(b) Moral Significance of the Ambiguity

But history is not all. The present is precious in every generation. True, historians meet their subjects through a chastening acceptance of their common relativity, but they all have something else in common, the prerogative to hold their own convictions. The moral dilemma suggested by historical relativism has often been noted: if to explain seems to excuse, an abyss opens. Or as Nietzsche, speaking of value in its aesthetic dimension, sardonically described its dissolution: 'We can feel that one thing sounds differently from another, and pronounce on the different "effects". And the power of gradually losing all feelings of strangeness or astonishment, and finally being pleased with anything, is called the historical sense or historical culture.'[2]

Or, we might add (and not as a contradiction), *not* being pleased at something, at least on its own terms, can sometimes be the consequences of the historical sense. It may prove impossible to surrender oneself to the experience, say, of fourteenth-century music, without awareness of its historical alternatives, its historical *location*. It is not just that history, in the Nietzschean sense, interferes with the philosophical basis of value. Consciousness of history interferes psychologically with the perception of value.

Yet, history and value need not be taken to confront each other so blankly. Abdication of standards, far from being the price of historical insight, precludes it. That is, there is more than one way to diverge from relativism.

One way, the one we have noted as the anti-historical way, is to appraise the past, in so far as it fails to accord with one's own standards, as the product of fools or knaves. (Such was the way, for example, of many early twentieth-century un-historically-minded critics of the traditional literary examinations for the Chinese bureaucracy. These critics, with the modern world's criteria of professionalism, explained as aberrations, from their standpoint, what was actually the triumph of a non-specialized culture's amateur ideal: see Volume One.) But there is another way, safely historical—indeed, indispensable for historical explanation—to take one's own day seriously, retaining the moral need to declare oneself and stand somewhere, not just to swim in time. For the historian's own day is his Archimedean leverage point outside the world of his subject. By judging as best he can (*not* by denying himself, out of intellectually relativist scruples, the right to indulge in judgement), he raises to his consciousness the historically significant question. Why should a generation comparable enough to his own to be judged in his vocabulary not be analogous to his own? Why (since he also should not deny, out of morally absolutist scruples, the right of his subjects to be seen as living out the values of their culture, not aiming at and falling short of his), why should earlier men, who deserve to be taken as seriously as he himself, diverge so far from his standards? He must articulate his own standards in order to find the rationale of his subjects', in order—by raising the question he could never recognize if he lacked his own convictions—to find what made it reasonable for the earlier generation to violate the later historian's criteria of rationality. The relativism which gives the past its due can really be arrived at only by men who give the present its due. Recognition of the historical relativity of one's own standards is not the same as abdication of standards, nor need it be conducive to that. The aim is to be truthful (to aim at truth), even if the truth cannot be known.[3]

Relativism, then, is essential for historical understanding, but it is a relativism which depends on, not banishes, a contemporary acceptance of norms. If it seems merely wilful paradox, a violation of rationality, to suggest that it is proper to be absolutist in order to be properly relativist, that may be because rationalism is not sufficient for historical knowledge. As we indicated at the outset, the basic term for expressing such knowledge, the quality attributed to the subject of the historian's statement—historical significance—has paradox or ambiguity built into it. For on the one hand, many things are granted historical significance without distinction of value: of two eighteenth-century Chinese novels, it is possible to say that *Ju-lin wai-shih* ('The Scholars') is as historically significant as *Hung-lou meng* ('The Dream of the Red Chamber'). Each one yields to the modern reader many insights about eighteenth-century China and the course that lay before it. But 'The Dream', we can say, on the other hand—and here all value-neutrality vanishes—is a splendid work of art. Historical knowledge, knowledge of the conventions of its society, may make it more accessible to moderns and foreigners, but these are simply annotator's aids: it speaks directly to us. Except for historians on duty, the historical status of 'The Dream' is just a detail, irrelevant to the sense of appreciation. Though it comes from long ago and far away, we do not read it *because* of that fact. To say now of 'The Scholars' that it has historical significance is not to link it with 'The Dream' in equivalence—both novels contributing to historians' explanations—but to distinguish it from 'The Dream' and the latter's more than historical, aesthetic significance. 'The Scholars' ' historical significance is 'mere'. The phrase is a phrase of relativism, but the voice is the voice of value.

And so the historian, by abjuring judgement in his ambiguous way, has a chance to be an alchemist. With an even-handed allocation of historical significance, he treats unequal quantities with equal *historical* respect. And thereby he may be converting dross (by his contemporary standards of judgement—which are *not* abjured) into the gold of a work of historical art. The historian's task, his golden opportunity, is to make what seems not valuable into the invaluable. Perhaps his comprehension, when formed into his creation, will make memorable the works and days which value-judgement, unmitigated by historical judgement, would leave neglected. Thus, far from being a relativist in a nihilistic sense, he seeks to create something in the here and now out of the nothing of the *historically* significant. His creativity makes it historically *significant*, and his own creative act, by submitting itself to judgement, confirms judgement as meaningful instead of confounding it as vain.

For creation and value belong together. To judge a work as one of high value is to praise its creator and maintain one's own contemporary standards as the measure; to dismiss a work as of little or no contemporary significance is tantamount to saying that 'history' created it, determined it, making any evaluation superfluous. Something reduced to historical significance, without being granted the quality of transcending its function of helping to explain its time, is left to be explained by its time, since no supra-historical artistry, the proper object of praise, is perceived to inform it.

It is here that historical significance has its relativist associations; in the draining away of the personal element, so that 'history' is the creator, the implied determinism precludes the intrusion of value.

When Marxists speak with the voice of ethical value, there is unmistakably a note of discord with their fundamental historicist determinism. By the labour theory of value, capitalism is blamed for depriving the workers of their social product: a judgement from the standpoint of norms. It has been suggested that this was, psychologically, an ethical backstop for the socialist demand, in case the historicist law of declining rate of profits fell apart.[4] But a backstop is not a logical support, and a human sense of injustice is not a *theoretical* ally of determinism. In historicist, deterministic theory, value is still precluded.

Where Marx and Engels are most historicist, with their emphasis on the inexorable succession of historical ages, they are most purely relativistic in judgements of the past. Where 'progressive' is the overriding term of appreciation, 'reactionary' (anachronistic) is the only strictly permissible pejorative. That is, as 'progressivists', not moralistic meliorists like Voltaire, they could never rest with a moral revulsion from 'medieval priestcraft'; they would *explain*, not indict, a religious institution as a function of the mode of production which characterized a stage. And, 'Without ancient slavery, no modern socialism.'[5] Accordingly, where they seem to be most moralistic is either where they are passionately *contemporary*, shaken by the human cost of the early conquests of capitalism, or where they can see no historical development, so that their historicism seems embarrassed: 'The ancient communes, where they continued to exist, have for thousands of years formed the basis of the most barbarous form of state, Oriental despotism, from India to Russia.'[6] As this 'form of state' is outside process (otherwise, how 'continue to exist'?), so an absolute condemnation breaks out of the determinist frame of thought. (Perhaps this is part of the reason for the unsure, glancing treatment of 'Oriental despotism' in the orthodox Marxist tradition.)

And perhaps, too, this strain between determinism and

value is what gives a grain of meaning to Acton's bromide, 'Power tends to corrupt and absolute power corrupts absolutely'—it expresses the truth that historicism (with relativism attending) is tied to amorality. For really impressive power is the gift of a society sufficiently complex to bear the weight of historical study, and the holder of power, certainly the holder of absolute power, through his very conviction of freedom (however illusory) to affect the destiny of his own milieu, may identify his decisions with the destined course of history.

And yet, to recapitulate, the relativism to which historians of process are drawn does not condemn them to the corrosion of their own values. There is all the difference in the world between acknowledging no creators but history (and thus inviting such corrosion), and valuing creativity, to the effect that relativistic 'historical significance' actually acquires normative significance. For it implies distinguishing—by standards—between those things which, but for the historian's grace, would be only time-ridden, insignificant and lost, and those which live as (relatively) timeless. This is not the relativism, the historical consciousness, which makes the contemporary man impotent, in the Nietzschean sense. Rather, it can free men from the impotence of feeling under the dead hand of the past. Such has been its function in recent Chinese history, from which we have brought up a few details to clothe the theory of historical significance. It is now time to bring theory down to history.

2. HISTORY

(a) Moral Significance of the Ambiguity

An eighteenth-century 'proto-Western' Chinese thinker, Tai Chen, had little influence in his own day. He was taken up, however, and celebrated by Chinese thinkers in the nineteen-twenties.[7] With what shade of meaning was he historically significant?

This latter-day assertion of Tai's historical significance, in our first sense of the phrase, confirmed him as historically significant only in the second sense. Tai's modern admirers, granting his ideas a formal philosophical importance in themselves, dramatized the fact that his ideas had had no effective importance in the history of Chinese thought. Their historical importance really consists in their historical *un-importance*, in the circumstance, that is (provocative to the historian of thinking, but irrelevant to the analyst of thought), that Chinese thinkers of one age should ignore thought which a later age would value. For Tai Chen was endowed with importance only when it was too late for him to have any objective influence, when Chinese intellectual life was being moulded by other, western authority. Twentieth-century Chinese honoured him not really because he was intellectually important to them—it was western thought which had persuaded them to be 'modern'—but just because, in his historical context, he had never been important at all. Had he been thus important, historically *significant* for the future, young Chinese modernists would have inherited their values, and would therefore not have felt pressed to unearth a Chinese precedent, in order to dull their sense of drift from traditional Chinese civilization. Men who were self-evidently heirs would not have had to work so hard to construct an ancestry. Tai Chen was merely *historically* significant. What that drift implied was submission not to his but to an outside intellectual influence, which alone made intellectually possible (and thus made emotionally necessary) the discernment of any significance in a figure like Tai Chen.

And yet, by these moderns, Tai was esteemed, endowed by their own criteria with a value quite the reverse of 'merely historical'. They were trying to raise an historical Chinese utterance to more than historical significance, because they, with so many of their contemporaries, were increasingly deaf to historical Chinese utterances in general. They were unhappily persuaded that, for their own day, harsh judgement of an unreconstructed Chinese culture was required of them. They could not quench the suspicion that, to a disturbing degree, the values coming down to them from Chinese history were of merely historical significance, dead in the modern day, a blight on creativity.

Thus Lu Hsün, most searing and powerful of all Chinese writers in this iconoclastic century, felt that everything new in China had come from abroad. And he put the blame for China's troubles on China herself, not on foreign foes. He saw the famous Confucian classical virtues, *tao*, *te*, *jen*, and *i*, as 'eaters of men', old figures still loathesomely alive, for their partisans were even then the 'establishment'[8] (like Nietzsche's proponents of 'monumental history', with their hidden motto, 'Let the dead bury the . . . living').[9]

Chang and Li are contemporaries. Chang has learned some classical allusions for his writing, and Li has learned them too in order to read what Chang has written. It seems to me that classical allusions were contemporary events for the ancients, and if we want to know what happened in the past we have to look them up. But two contemporaries ought to speak simply, so that one can understand the other straight away, and neither need trouble to learn classical allusions.[10] Some foreigners are very eager that China should remain one great antique for them to enjoy for ever. Though this is disgusting, it is not to be wondered at, for after all they are foreigners. But in China there are people who, not content to form a part of a great antique themselves for those foreigners to enjoy, are dragging our young folk and children with them.[11]

Here was an iconoclasm, then, a bitter value-judgement, expressed as resentment of the absolute presentness of a past which should be relative—or, *historically* significant: let it be a subject of study but not a basis for present action. Though an antiquarian may be described as someone interested in historical fact without being interested in history, the concept of 'antique' implies the historical sense, a feeling for the piquancy of the contrast between antique and the living contemporary. To feel that oneself or one's culture is an antique is to see the self as a means, something to furnish observers with a delicate *frisson*, something used and therefore dead.

When the old culture was indicted as a dead stifler of life, the indictment was moral, with 'historically significant' implied as an epithet in the realm of value, not as a relativist acknowledgement of process. It was a desperate assault on a traditional culture seen as very much too much in being, tragically not becoming something else, or modern.

And yet, the traditional culture which Lu Hsün criticized so absolutely was, in fact, in process; it had become traditionalistic. Men who resisted the new as foreign were adhering to the old in a new way, advancing essentially romantic (relativist) arguments from 'national essence' rather than rationalistic arguments from universal validity. As we have seen in connection with K'ang Yu-wei, these were no longer plain Confucian arguments for conservatism but conservative arguments for Confucianism—the change was the measure of Confucian moribundity. And it was just this moribundity, this death-in-life, which imparted such passion to Confucianism's assailants.

Latter-day Confucianists and their hostile contemporaries were equally modern, symbiotically fitting together, and it was 'historical significance', an ambiguous term but a single term, which both linked them and distinguished them. Together, traditionalistic Confucianists and anti-traditional iconoclasts violated the traditional assumptions of Confucianism, which were anti-relativist in the extreme. Confucianists had always studied the past, but in the conviction of its eternal contemporaneity and world associations, the absolute applicability of the fixed standards and sequences of classical Chinese antiquity. Now, however, modern Confucianists relativized Confucianism to Chinese history alone, and modern anti-Confucianists relativized it to early history alone. The traditional feeling for history as philosophy teaching by example was dissipated equally by the traditionalistic 'history' as organic life and the iconoclastic 'history' as a nightmare from which men should be trying to awake.

But by this same token, the traditionalistic Confucianists and the anti-Confucianists, equally modern, had a genuine confrontation of their own. The radicals, trying to break the grip of the old ideas and institutions, thought in terms of the 'merely' historically significant, and thus devalued history; history, however, was far from being devalued by the romantic conservatives, for whom reason or pragmatism were 'mere'. The evolution of a diffuse, generalized Chinese radicalism to Marxism may be interpreted as a transition of 'historical significance' from normative to relativist usage, in the historicism (hardly a devaluation of history) of the Marxist way of thinking. One turned from escaping history to writing history: that was the escape. To make old Values merely values, with a time and place, not eternity and ubiquity, was to bring understanding to the aid of sentiment. What a modern iconoclast could not accept he could relegate to history, a history comprehended as evolving up, not dictating down, to the present. Marxist historiography, with its periodization, offered a sense of release. Its determinism offered the radicals detachment from the passion of rejection; its sense of inevitable process gave them assurance of succession. When the old values (and the valued elders, Confucius and the rest) became the historian's subjects, they were no longer on the throne.

This transition from a normative to a relativist 'historical significance' came about when fresh history had been made, and could be seen to be made. It was when the hated traditionalistic opponents could seem merely historically significant themselves—that is, broken so completely that living, indeed dominant champions of the old order no longer existed. Iconoclasts in power could do what iconoclasts struggling for power could not do: adopt the relativism of their bested foes, and turn from blasting the old with hatred to explaining it coolly away. Lu Hsün looked forward to that when he inveighed against traditional doctors, yet recognized the salvageable contributions of a Ming *materia medica*. He called for the young to succeed the old—and then to be grateful to the old, if only they would die, filling the holes in the road of youth's advance.[12] From absolute to relative, from passionate to detached, from a moral to an intellectual stance—this was the turning which the radicals made, changing the tone of 'historical significance'. And in this very act of tearing up the Confucian historical premise, which was so fateful for Chinese historical continuity, they made running repairs in this very continuity.

(b) *Intellectual Significance of the Ambiguity*

The modern historically minded conservatives, with their 'national-essence' incantation (covertly anti-traditional) as their final, self-destructive charm against the openly anti-traditional, had the relativism of despair. Their opponents, like Lu Hsün, began by signing out of responsibility for the tradition whose current inanition bred despair; as modern men, they said, they rejected history's claims. Yet, these iconoclasts knew that they were not just modern men but modern Chinese, knew it in the fever of their revulsion—far from intellectual detachment—which bespoke their tie in history to the moorings they longed to slip. They had their own despair, not just the anguish of seeing their triumph deferred or problematical but the anguish of having to seek such a triumph at all.

Under the circumstances, their assessment of traditional values under the aspect of 'historical significance' tended to drift from the normative pole to the relativist, a relativism of compensation for despair. In effect, the collapse of their opponents released the new men from their compulsion to attack—or allowed them, and obliged them, to divert their attack to live enemies, men whom they could see now as modern as themselves.[13] Once an historic Confucian spokesman showed that he knew how to die (or after his death, at least, to lie down), he could be neutrally assigned to his own day—the career of Confucius like the idea of ching-t'ien—and domesticated historically for modern China, even a China vastly removed from the old in spirit.

It was a resolution of an emotional problem (the need to alleviate the pain of a ruthless expression of value) by intellectualizing it; it was the disarming of absolute judgement by relativizing it. All manner of early Chinese achievements fell into place, acceptable as the communist nation's worthy past, no longer necessarily the targets of present revolution. When revolution had shattered the traditional whole, pieces could be salvaged for present contemplation, selections made from a past so truly laid, as *history* (in the sense of superseded), that it could hardly resist dissection. Relativistic history—

admitting the historically *significant* instead of expelling the *historically* significant—was the sweet sterilizer of values, or the cauterizer of the wounds dealt in cutting them out. They had become historical, ceased to concern. Time was the censor.

And so the communist régime restored the old Manchu imperial 'Forbidden City' in Peking, long dilapidated, and the tombs of the Ming emperors, with careful attention to historic décor and design. 'It has been left, strangely enough, to a Communist government, ruling in the name of the People and under the slogans of anti-imperialism to spend a great sum on a most complete and beautifully executed restoration of the tomb of Ming Yung Lo, the founder of Peking, and a wholehearted autocrat.'[14] Is it all so strange? And is it strange that revolutionaries, claiming to shake the country into modern values and attitudes, should vaunt 'ancient Chinese science'?[15]

The last shall be first. It is not strange that 'ancient science' should come under modern communist protection. We have already seen the importance of 'popular' motifs for communist historians, and Chinese science, to just the extent that Confucian 'feudalists' inhibited it, had popular standing. Its original affinities were mainly with popular Taoism, the Taoism which radicals had earlier written off as an excrescence of the old society. But communist victory over 'feudal' society (or 'semi-feudal, semi-colonial') brought the chance, and the need, to soften the tone. Once the grip of the leaders of the old society, at both its higher and lower levels, was broken, the passions of the struggle to break it might cool, and old ideas be relativized to history. The very decay infecting modern Taoism made it acceptable for *historical* rehabilitation, now that its dead hand had been shaken off the present. Commentators on Taoism began to find in it not so much depressing quietism but rousing rebellious action, not just superstitious magic but the seeds, and some of the fruits, of science. It had been quite consistent of Confucianism, looking with such fearful scorn on Taoist religious enthusiasm, to be a drag on science as well. And it was consistent of communism, also, to turn Confucian scorn into communist indulgence.

Indulgence, however, is something that a superior dispenses. There could be no question of Taoism renewing its claims to pre-eminence. For science, the saving title that restored the Taoist reputation, had become an ideal of communists in a context of anti-traditionalism, both anti-Confucian and anti-Taoist. The communists had to feel, first, that they had succeeded in crushing Taoism, that it was now a thing of the past. Then it could have its place in the gallery of national achievements, its *early* place, with *early* science, while Marxists took over the end. When Taoism (and other products of the Chinese past) could be filed away in a carefully tended museum, the communists would own the living present. Only when Taoism was exorcized from history—that is, from a claim to affect the future—could it be put back in history; and then it was really back, to a place of harmless honour in the Chinese people's past. The celebration of 'ancient science', given these associations, was perfectly consistent with the communist drive for the future.

In short, Marxist relativism made Taoism at best a progressive force in an historical stage. It was an anachronism in the present, and the régime suppressed any Taoist claims to be accepted now on grounds of absolute value. Communist policy was quite in line with communist interpretation: contemporary Taoists were given the spades to dig their own grave in history. A Taoist Association was brought into being. What was it to do? It decided in 1961 to compile the history of the Taoist religion.[16] It took charge of Taoist monuments. And so the Taoist temples, no longer active and therefore no longer nests of deceivers, ceased to be 'feudal' as the term was used in moralistic epithet; they were feudal just in the nomenclature of 'scientific history'. A temple was not a disgrace, but an antique. Communists, instead of exhorting the masses to crush the infamy, urged them to preserve the relics. That was crushing enough.

And it is not strange that the republicans of 1912, who claimed metaphorically to be 'restoring the Ming', the native Chinese predecessors of the Manchu conquest-dynasty of Ch'ing, should let the Ming tombs crumble. Factors of social demoralization aside, these early republicans were

really 'engaged' against monarchy, as against a visible, contemporary foe; its monuments were symbols of something
currently provocative. But the communists could 'restore the
Ming' in another metaphorical sense, as museum-keepers
restore. They were freed from the earlier radicals' frustration
at seeming to be museum-dwellers. The communists' act of
restoration was a gesture of release, a recognition of a dead-
ness in monarchy so final that its monuments could be
relativized to historical significance.

It may be suggested, of course, that Mao Tse-tung was
indulgent to the Yung-lo emperor because one good autocrat
deserves another. Is the new Chinese régime just another
dynasty, and yesterday eternal? Do the communists, with
all their concern for process and their apparent superseding
of Confucianists, fall into a timeless Confucian historical
pattern?

Intonation matters: the answer implied is, no. Whatever
the Chinese communists won, it was not the 'mandate of
Heaven'.

3. CONCLUSION

When Confucianism finally passed into history, it was because
history had passed out of Confucianism. Intrinsic classical
learning, the exercise of divining from canonical historical
records how men in general should make history for all time,
lapsed. Extrinsic classical learning came in, divining how a
certain people made history at a certain stage of a master-
process. This was the learning of the 'new' historian, Ku
Chieh-kang, setting out, he said, to 'clarify China's ancient
writings', in response to the May Fourth anti-Confucian
demand to 'revise the national heritage'.[17] Confucianism
became an object of intellectual inquiry (instead of the
condition of it), or else an object of emotional attachment,
an historical monument, eliciting (instead of inculcating) a
piety towards the past. It was in encounter with the modern
western industrial world that Chinese were either shaken
quite clear of traditionalism, the Confucian *sine qua non*, or
confirmed indeed as traditionalists, but of an untraditional
sort.

(a) *Disputation and Vitality*

When Confucius, several centuries after his own time, finally became the master sage of the Chinese intelligence, he testified to the intellectual vitality of late-Chou society, which had nurtured his genius. Did he also testify to a failure of vitality, Han and after, when his eminence, the very acknowledgement of his genius, presumably precluded any vigorous intellectual challenge? First, we must note that the presumption is shaky: Taoism and (later) Buddhism openly, Legalism more covertly (i.e. without organization, without a coherent body of believers) continued to challenge Confucianism (as well as to affect it), and Confucianism itself developed various expressions. The presumption dates in China from the beginning of the twentieth century, when the 'idea of progress' had entered the Chinese world and when Social Darwinism, conceiving of progress as the fruit of struggle, became a very important influence. Still, whatever the modern responsibility for this oversimplification of Confucian history, even from the standpoint of Han and post-Han Confucianists themselves late-Chou China was set apart, as an intellectual mother-country, where their principles rose superior to alternatives in an atmosphere of polemical intensity.

What is the relation of disputation to vitality? Is it simply tautological to suggest any relation at all; are we just saying that where there is action there is life, and that disputation is action? Or do we see vitality precisely in the *result* of disputation, the fact that the late-Chou controversy among the 'Hundred Schools' established Confucianism's title to a long-sustained acceptance? Confucianism owed its long life to its character, and owed its character to the original conditions of combat.

Confucianism, in intellectual character, was a 'middle way'. Confucianists—principally that intelligentsia which became so intimately associated with bureaucracy in the Han and post-Han dynastic state—were, in social character, poised between aristocracy and autocracy (see Volume Two). We may well assume that the 'middle' quality of

Confucianism made it peculiarly fit for perpetuation, made it *vital*, in the impending long-lived bureaucratic society; and what was 'middle' about Confucianism clearly emerges when we see it framed by sets of its late-Chou rivals.

All roads in Taoism pointed to egoism: the self was the Taoist's great concern—or, more literally, the banishment of self, the liberation and salvation of the ego from the fatal, death-directed consciousness of self. This banishment of self was not the Mohist (the Mo-tzu school's) banishment of self by the dictates of universal love; the latter was altruist, not egoist. Between these two lay Confucianism, with its injunction to 'graded love', its feeling for specific, delimited human relationships which countered both the Mohist undiscriminating orientation out to all society and the Taoist quietist transcendence of any social attachments. Confucianism stood for the 'near', midway between the Taoist individual 'here' and the Mohist universal 'far'. It is in this sense that both Chinese family solidarity and Chinese cultural discrimination (not self, not world, but *family* and *culture*) became intimate parts of the typically Confucian world-view.

But, more than Mohism, Legalism was the 'outer', social extreme which paired with Taoism, the 'inner', anti-social extreme, to set off Confucianism, the 'inner-outer' compromising middle (cf. *nei sheng wai wang*—'within, sage; without, king'). The Confucian Classic, *Ta-hsüeh* ('The Great Learning'), an autonomous part of the *Li-chi*, inextricably linked the concepts *hsiu-shen* (self-cultivation) and *p'ing t'ien-hsia* (world-pacification), the virtue of the individual and the government of society. The Confucian ideal was establishment of social order among the governed by radiation of virtue from the governor. The Legalists, however, came down one-sidedly for 'world-pacification' (without the Confucian matching concern for self-cultivation) and for a social order, then, which owed everything to despotic power, exercised or menacingly held in reserve, and nothing to virtue, to a rule neither by force nor law but by example. And the Taoists, as philosophical anarchists, came down on the other side, against government, against social order, for the primal virtue of a self tampered with neither by Legalist despotic manipulators nor by Confucian dispensers of that contrived, denaturing, *social* influence, education.

For the Taoists nature, and, *a fortiori*, human nature, was good; hence education, an artificial gloss from the outside, could only be a blight on the natural. For the Legalists human nature was evil; hence only force could control it. But, for the Confucianists human nature was good (the 'Mencius' strain) and therefore *amenable* to education; or it was evil (the 'Hsün-tzu' strain) and therefore *in need of* education. Either way, this Confucian ambiguity (corresponding to the inner-outer ambiguity, between Taoist 'inner' and Legalist 'outer') was yet another mediant affirmation, with education standing between the Taoists' blissful emptiness of mind and the Legalists' trust in force instead of learning.

The Taoist and Legalist poles have sometimes been said to come together, and in a sense they did, in their common egoism—despotic egoism of the solitary ruler (the one in the state) and anarchic egoism of the solitary hermit (the one in nature). And this common egoism made for a common revulsion from the Confucian social and intellectual discipline, which was a restraint equally on anarchy and despotism. Whereas history was the perennial Confucian study and the appeal to history the favourite Confucian polemical device, Taoism and Legalism, straddling Confucianism, spurned history equally. For the Taoists, partisans of *wu-wei* ('nonactivity'), history was the weary story of action, man's impairment of the state of nature; for the Legalists, the appeal to history, i.e. to precedent, was an unwelcome curb (as any curb would be unwelcome) on power, an impairment of the perfection of the ruler's freedom of action.

Indeed, the Legalist prescriptions were predominantly political, while the Taoist prescriptions, so thoroughly antipolitical, had, as a *constructive* force, predominantly cultural implications (though Taoism could lend itself to political destructiveness). Confucianism was the golden mean in the sense that only Confucianism was oecumenical. Its ideas pervaded both the realm of government (as the Legalist did) and the realm of the imagination (as the Taoist did).

Confucianism and Legalism together made political China in the bureaucratic-imperial post-classical régimes, and Confucianism and Taoism together (with Buddhism still to come) made cultural China. The common term, the middle way, the fulcrum for the balance that stability implies, was *Confucianism*.

What was stability but the power to survive, that power which is vitality? It seems rather a romantic foible of historians to attribute 'health' to the period of quest and struggle, with achievement and victory written off as fatal infections. For Confucian China, the really fatal infection came late, in the nineteenth and twentieth centuries, and from a foreign body.

(b) *Anti-Confucianism and Pseudo-Confucianism: The Change in Historical Consciousness*

Confucianism ceased to have the virtue, the vitality, of centrality when China ceased, even in Chinese eyes, to be the central or Middle Kingdom of the world—or ceased, rather, to be the world. As a nation, China faced the world instead of containing it, even faced the prospect of being contained. The great modern change in Chinese civilization, the change (which was the attrition of Confucianism) in historical consciousness, coincided with a growing awareness of the spectre announced by Ranke, the 'spirit of the Occident subduing the world'.[18] For the spirit of Ranke was subduing the Occident as history seemed to be confirming his inference, that the West had gained for itself a position from which world history and European history could be considered a corporate unity. There was a Chinese correlative to this conclusion: China had lost the position from which it could consider world history and Chinese history as a corporate unity, the *T'ien-hsia*—all-under-Heaven—denoting 'the Empire' and the world.

The confrontation was stark. In European history we find the Christian transcendental sense of divinity and evolutionary sense of history, then the modern secular messianisms with their visions (like Ranke's) of progress in time, in Europe, culminating in progress in space, outwards from

Europe. In Chinese history we find Confucius, for whom 'Heaven does not speak' but rather reflects a cosmic harmony as a model to society, and a model once clothed in ancient historical fact. Against the transcendental and the evolutionary, we must set Confucian immanence and orientation to the past. Nothing repelled the normative Confucianist more than messianic goals and eschatological structures, Christian, Buddhist (Maitreya cult) or popular Taoist. The meaning of history was not in the end-stage of culture but in sage-antiquity.

Modern Chinese syncretisms of western and Confucian ideas finally yielded to the full force of the western oecumenical drive, and there came to be a readiness, in radical circles, to listen to foreign voices without concern for their legitimacy by any Confucian standards. Then, when the environment was no longer a Confucian world but a Chinese nation, when the innovators were condemners of Confucian authority instead of syncretizers invoking it, the anti-iconoclasts commended Confucius in a new way: he and his doctrine represented 'national essence', not supra-national truth. Traditionalism became relativistic, the values it protected were relative to a single organic history. 'Confucianism', shielded by history, by a romantic appeal to it in its aspect of uniqueness, was a far cry from the Confucianism which wielded history, rationalistically, as philosophy by example. The name was hopelessly unrectified.

But the traditionalists were not alone in their defensiveness, nor in their relativism. A simple Chinese anti-traditionalism proved emotionally expensive, for the West was too intrusive. Thus, unadorned, non-Marxist 'May Fourth' iconoclasts may have been indispensable front-runners for communists—front-runners and natural victims. They may have been indispensable in setting out to clear the field of the dead destroyers, Lu Hsün's 'eaters of men', all the Confucian idols. But it was a Pyrrhic victory for the liberals, a vicarious operation; the Marxists took the spoils. For the pangs of self-destruction mingled with the pangs of creativity. This is one great reason why, once the absolute disparagers had carried off the assault, Marxist historical relativism could plausibly claim the field—to heal the wounds of the action. Passionate, disturbing excoriation of the old (the Chinese self) may have seemed necessary, but for most Chinese intellectuals it was not sufficient; some kind of rehabilitation of the self had to be made. And Marxist historicism came to the fore, enabling intellectuals to despatch the old values as live options, but to do so relatively coolly and undisturbed, without the passion of the pioneer iconoclasts, who felt they faced a living infamy. That is why Marxist revolutionaries in power could appear more tender with the Chinese past than May Fourth revolutionaries, Marxist or not and out of power, could be to the past in their generation. Communists could try to have it both ways, killing the past for their own day, yet relativistically fitting it into history, and a history China owned, not a history flowing into the West's. One had to kill to be kind. The kindness was a solace, a relief to the pain of killing; and it was old Drs. Lenin and Marx, not Dr. Dewey, who offered the balm after the common battle of May Fourth.

The new Chinese historical consciousness, in its ravaging of Confucianism, menaced the sense of Chinese historical continuity: this was the menace that China faced while *western* historical continuity seemed to offer the world its modern intellectual constructs. But this historical consciousness, in all its disruptiveness, knitted up, in two ways, the ravelled continuity. On its radical side, it laid down lines to the Chinese past through a supposedly universal (not exclusively western) sequence of historical stages. And on its conservative side, it read into Chinese history a special soul, hopefully impervious to just such corruption as this very reading exemplified. History either integrated China in the world or insulated China from the world. But in neither reading, the post-Confucian Marxist nor the post-Confucian 'Confucian', was China the world itself, or China shrunk to nothing.

What we have, then, in twentieth-century China, is a complicated response to a situation of European expansion and expansiveness. The response to new foreign ideas took place in a new matrix for intellectual controversy. For to say that modern Chinese traditionalists and iconoclasts are all

new men, bound together and severed from the old predominant Confucianism by their relativism, is to see them
in Herder's categories: one, as Herder's vision was one in its
anti-rationalism—but bifurcated, like Herder's historicism,
which had forked out into conservative and revolutionary
branches.

The centrality of Herder was established in his contention
(see Volume One) that every nation and every age holds the
centre of its happiness within itself.[19] What Herder combined,
nation and *age* with their individual geniuses, romantic conservatives and Marxist revolutionaries put asunder. The
former emphasized the genius of the nation and thus confirmed their own traditionalism; this would be impossible
if they granted equal title to the genius of the age, for then
moderns could not be committed (as the Chinese modern
traditionalists were) to defence of the 'national essence', something distilled from the history of the past. Marxists, for their
part, acknowledged the genius (or the 'mode of production')
of the age, and hence their mode of historical thinking was
evolutionary, anti-traditionalist. Appropriately, they rejected
in its fullest romantic flavour the genius of the nation; nations
were assumed to share the prospects of passing time. But the
romantic conservatives and the Marxist revolutionaries truly
drew on the same source. For when Herder praised the folk
genius as creator of the true poetry, in opposition to theories
of rules and sophistication,[20] he was offering 'the people' to
the one and the other. The communists could use them as the
reason and the force for revolution. The conservatives could
use them for their elemental 'spirit'. And the liberals were
lost in the middle.

For in Europe, the earliest liberalism moved, too, from
rationalistic to relativistic assumptions. At first, to strict
liberalism of the utilitarian sort (as in James Mill's *History
of British India*), 'non-progressive' parts of the world seemed
fields to be evangelized; the modern West would bring
regeneration. But by the early twentieth century men of
broadly liberal attitudes (like G. Lowes Dickinson in *Letters
from John Chinaman*) had lost the taste for the imposition of
one culture on another. And this had its part in giving

Marxism, not liberalism, the lead in modern China. Liberalism of the later sort would only confirm instead of supplant the Confucian cultural tradition, and Chinese revolutionaries were in no mood for that brand of relativistic tolerance. Confucianism back in Chinese time was tolerable; Confucianism here in Chinese space was not to be borne. Marxism, however, revived the early liberal assumption that inherited traditions could be changed. But the Marxist school of historicists could assume that the age and not the race determined the state of society. And so they captured the *élan* which liberalism once had known, but which liberals lost when racial smugness, more and more obviously a moral blight, seemed implied in their original zeal to tamper with foreign cultures, to make others just like themselves. With the liberals sunk between them, revolutionaries claimed the age, traditionalists claimed the race.

Herder lives in both these camps of related antagonists, now Chinese as well as European. The Confucianists, anti-relativist to the core, anti-historicist (though profoundly historically minded) were alien to both. When the world (as seen from China) was a Chinese world, Confucian civilization was civilization in the abstract, not *a* civilization in a world with others. But when the world (even as seen from China) seemed a European world (for which read 'modern': i.e. Europe as historically *progressive*), then Confucianism's chances lay with the Chinese 'national essence', a romantic, non-Confucian conception.

Why should Confucianism have withered into this anomaly? Why should it be Europe and not China that has been able to sustain its self-image as a history-maker coterminous with the world—at least in culture, regardless of political recession?

My own suggestion (see Volume One), as a partial answer, is that Confucian civilization was the apotheosis of the amateur, while the genius of the modern age (evil or not) is for specialization. In the modern world the 'middle' character of Confucianism was lost; it was no longer a mean among alternatives, but an opposite, on the periphery, to a new spirit from a new centre of power. Confucian education, perhaps supreme in the world for anti-vocational classicism, sought to create a non-professional free man (*pace* Hegel) of high culture, free of impersonal involvement in a merely manipulative system. Accordingly the mandarin bureaucracy, taking its special lustre as a reflection from the essentially aesthetic, ends-not-means, cultural content of the literati-official examinations, inhibited development in the direction of expertise. Under these circumstances, the Confucian deprecation of specialization implied a deprecation (and deprivation) of science, rationalized and abstractly legalistic economic networks, and the idea of historical progress, all of these bound in the West to specialization in a subtle web, and bringing the West subversively to China. Han dynasty disciples of Confucius, the traditionalist, had made good his achievement as innovator. They had established him as the presiding genius of a new and almost eternal post-feudal, bureaucratic culture. From that time on, no authentic Confucianist had ever had to fight Jonathan Swift's battle of the books, for the ancient against the modern. When the issue arose in China it was post-Confucian, forced in China at last because it had come to the test in Europe first, and Swift had lost.

Conclusion

HAVING concluded roundly, let us conclude squarely, with a concluding conclusion.

I. THE FAILURE OF ANALOGY: COMMUNIST CHINA AND CONFUCIAN CHINA

The race was not to the Swift and the course was not a circle. In the China of May Fourth, which nurtured the communist movement, one could resent foreign political pressure and yet be far from traditional anti-foreignism (which could never harmonize with a May Fourth cultural self-indictment). And there is a corollary: in the China of May Fourth one could resent foreign cultural pressure—that is, resent the anti-Confucian 'new youth', with its 'Mr. Science' and 'Mr. Democracy' and all the rest—and yet be far from traditional Confucianism.

Not so long before, most Confucian literati had resisted the adoption of western procedures in science and technology—resisted, that is, the pretensions of modern science to universal geographical dominion. But by May Fourth, Confucian sympathizers were long past conceiving of opposition to the material, geographical spread of this science to China. The debate had shifted ground, irreversibly, from the terrain of China to the terrain of the mind. It had become a debate on 'science and the philosophy of life' (see Volume One), and what conservatives resisted—the only thing they could resist—was the pretensions of science to universal *intellectual* dominion. Those literati, in earlier years, who accepted scientific innovations had usually filed them away as western *yung*, supplements to the Chinese *t'i* or essence. But after May Fourth, the traditionalists' fight was basically for *t'i* in the abstract, *any* 'spirit' against the aggressive claims of materialism.

Chang Chih-tung, in the eighteen-nineties, had worded the *t'i-yung* dichotomy in this way (among others): 'Chiu-hsüeh wei t'i, hsin-hsüeh wei yung',[1] *old* learning for essence, *new* learning for utility. He still lived in a mental world where *old*, in good Confucian fashion, was superior to *new*; hence, Chinese learning was reaffirmed as the equal of western, to say the least. But in the May Fourth and communist ages the new was precious to China, as the sign of process in time, which China might own as properly as any other nation. The wording used by Chang could do nothing for China now but embarrass it.

When the communists stood for new against old, their 'East' against 'West' meant a new East, not the 'ancient East'. They spoke in the language of cold war, not Confucianism. It is quite in order to point out that both Confucianism and Marxism are all-embracing systems: but it is misleading to suggest that the journey between them is only a passage home. From Christianity to Marxism is just as familiar a passage. Then, Marxism in China may be a particular example of a general yearning for an all-embracing system, not an exclusively Chinese revelation of the deathlessness of the Sage.

If there is one suggestion calculated to confuse the meaning of the communist era in Chinese history, it is the suggestion that the communists were somehow not really revolutionary —form changed, of course, but content much the same. By this reasoning, the new 'cold war' definition of 'West' slips into the place of the old world of western culture. And by this reasoning, the May Fourth movement may be allowed to have been a revolutionary turning toward the West, but communism, the 'anti-West', brought the eternal return to China, a China still indomitably a pillar of 'the East'. May Fourth, then, would be only an aberration, the sport between one idolatry and another, one slavery and another. Such was the purport of Hu Shih's remark, 'Now that the slaves of Confucius and Chu Hsi have decreased in number, the slaves of Marx and Kropotkin have appeared.'[2] This was explaining new departures in China (really, explaining away) by noting their *accordance* with traditional attitudes. It was denying the significance of history, as though history were only appearance, and appearances deceived.

And so they do—if by ignoring historical context one takes likenesses for changelessness.

Did Confucianists and communists inhibit private enterprise with bureaucratic restraints? Then nothing has changed —except that the bureaucratic communists, worshipping dynamism, meant to force history, and the bureaucratic Confucianists, looking backward, made the kind of history that seemed to have to be forced.

Would the Confucian quietistic sage-emperor be at home where the state had 'withered away'?[3] Then nothing has changed—except that Marxists deduced their utopia from theoretical premises, while Confucianists held to theirs in existential situations of tension with historical monarchs.

In 1892, did suspicion race through Manchuria that foreigners were scattering poisoned lice among the people?[4] Then the germ-warface charge during the Korean War was the traditional vilification of foreigners, and there is nothing new under the Chinese sun—except that the earlier indictment, proto-Boxer and xenophobic, could only have been for home consumption. But in current history the indictment was for the world, where a nagging feeling of *possible* truth in the charge could not be banished and might be exploited. For men, by the 1950s, were familiar with ultimate violence, and bacteriological warfare had come to seem not really different in kind from the perfectly plausible (since already historical) use of atomic bombs.

When the British representative came to communist Peking to establish diplomatic ties, did he meet the same haughty indifference as Lord Macartney and Lord Amherst at the courts of Ch'ing emperors? Then nothing has changed —except the quality of awareness. China knew Britain now, and was setting a tone in world politics, not acting politically as though China were the world. A 'Macartney' reference could only be metaphorical, like Chiang 'losing the mandate'.

2. THE FRAGMENTS AND THE WHOLE

Still, the appearance of survivals is by no means just a trick of the eye. Many bricks of the old structure are still around—but not the structure. Fragments may survive because they meet a modern taste, not because (more than the fragments forgotten) they must be conveying the essence of an invincible tradition. And the taste, the language of the culture, cannot be explained as created by the fragment. Rather, the language is being enriched in its vocabulary. We have seen (Volume One) that Europe and pre-modern China, reaching each other only through intellectual diffusion, had only broadened each other's cultural vocabulary—that the Chinese cultural language changed in the nineteenth and twentieth centuries, when social subversion, not just intellectual diffusion, was set off by the West. So, too, when the original social associations were stripped from intellectual creations of the Chinese past, these creations, carrying with them mind but not society, might come down to modern China as vocabulary enrichment, without determining the language.

Therefore, if the ink-painting of the literati persists in Communist China, this does not mean that the former whole, the world of the literati, persists. Just as several centuries ago this *wen-jen hua* (literati-painting), without the Chinese social associations, had been diffused out (as 'bunjinga') to a very different society in Japan, so it has been diffused down to a very different society in China—perhaps as different as Renaissance Rome from ancient Rome, though Michelangelo and Bernini took fragments of their vocabulary from classical antiquity. Of course, Greeks and Romans and much of what they prized appeared in the Renaissance. Sophocles holds the stage today. But Hellenic and Hellenistic culture remain fast in history. And of course Confucius appears in Communist China, as one in a cast of historical characters—maybe a star, certainly historical.

And so once again we go through the turnstile, from the present world outside, into the Museum. To the museum mentality, the exhibits may be 'historically' significant, pointers to a past that does not appeal and does not threaten.[5]

Or they may be 'aesthetically' significant, seen with the eye of value rather than history; then they are carefully abstracted from past to present, shorn away from a total culture to take their part in a new one. In this case, what is (merely) historically significant is what the shears leave behind, the environment, the associations of the works of art at the time of their creation.

That is why, though early Christians might break the images of pagan gods, centuries later the Vatican Museum would shelter its Apollos. The gods no longer signified a living rival in a contemporary struggle. They were historically significant, or, the best of them, aesthetically significant—merely aesthetic, fragments of a vanquished, vanished whole. And that is why a Confucian temple could be restored in Communist China, though the temple was once a centre for Confucian scholarship, Sung to Ch'ing, which was at a high discount in communist appraisals: the restored temple became a recreation centre, for cinema, drama, and games, with cages for monkeys, pythons, leopards[6] (and, metaphorically, Confucius). And the communists protected statues of the villains in the story of Yüeh Fei, tragic hero of the Southern Sung. For a long time these statues had been the targets of patriots' stones. But 'the figures . . . are of historical value'[7]—which is to say that they are 'art', museum-bait, no longer living in their total early context, a natural world without walls.

For art, in one of its qualities, is alienation, the removal of an object from its customary environment, where it might be used, to a special place of preservation, where it might be aesthetically contemplated.[8] And it was still a merely aesthetic object, alienated from its proper function, if used (like the python-Confucian temple) for ends completely at odds with the authentic original purposes. What is a communist doing when he condemns beliefs (as superstitious) which led to the making of tomb figures to bury with the dead—but praises 'the fine traditions of the ancient art'?[9] He is connecting himself with the past (in its wholeness), by containing it in a museum. It is a museum in just the sense that Malraux sees it: the museum that never existed where

the civilization of modern Europe was unknown; that 'tended
to estrange the works from their original functions and to
transform even portraits into "pictures" '; that 'did away
with the significance of . . . Saint and Saviour'; that 'not
only isolates the work of art from its context but makes it
foregather with rival and even hostile works'.[10] And it is a
museum in just the sense that Coomeraswamy sees it: the
museum that exhibits mainly ancient and foreign works of
art '. . . because they no longer correspond to any needs of
our own of which we are actively conscious'; that should
never exhibit living artists, for things are not normally made
simply 'for exhibition'; that is not for the imager 'casting his
bronze primarily for use and not as a mantelpiece ornament
for the museum showcase'; that reveals, in the art it shows,
'not that something has been *gained*, but that we know that
something has been lost, and would fain preserve its
memory'.[11] Confucius, and the traditional values that are still
extant in the latest China, live—in a manner of speaking—in
every clause of these catalogues of insights into museums.

3. THE FAILURE OF ANALOGY: COMMUNIST CHINA AND COMMUNIST RUSSIA

The Museum came into Russia, too, turning slices of life from
the old days, which the Soviets meant to supersede, into
objets d'art, exhibits from an historically significant past. To
restore the beautiful mosques in Samarkand was not to
restore the mullahs, but to ease them out, away from aesthetic
'national treasures'. Or rather, to move them while they
stayed. With their occupations not quite gone but going, they
were passing out of the world of piety, to the picturesque.
And the Orthodox seminary at Zagorsk was still permitted to
function, but in such a way as to divorce itself from function.
Religious objects and religious people, both were left to be
looked at; 'do not touch the icons' seemed figuratively
extended to 'do not feed the worshippers'. And 'do not touch
the icons' seems an extension, not a reversal, of revolutionary
iconoclasm.

But Russians and Chinese—particularly the intellectuals,

the articulate affirmers and rejectors of values—came to their revolutions from different points of departure. Russia was part of Europe; China was all of China.

We have seen, in Chinese communist historiography, the effort to show that Chinese history, culminating in communism, ran parallel to the West's. In Russia, on the other hand, communists saw Russian history not as parallel to the West's, but as that part of western history which leads the whole to culminate in communism. Whatever distinctions between Russia and the West the Slavophiles might make,[12] the Marxists, under Lenin, took Europe's past as their past (something which Mao could never, and would never, do). The French Revolution was an historical ancestor, not an analogue to some event (like the Chinese revolution of 1911) from quite another history.

Pre-communist China and Russia may seem alike, as economically backward (compared with the farther West). By classical Marxist criteria, then, they should both be inappropriate for socialist revolution. But since the Russian intelligentsia could (while the Chinese could not) consider its country a part of 'the West', Russian Marxists could make a virtue of theoretical necessity; they could see their country as peculiarly *appropriate* for socialist revolution, just because it was industrially weak. For they could see themselves as western revolutionaries, attacking, with tactical wisdom, the most vulnerable sector of a broad front, the part of the *bourgeois* West where the *bourgeoisie* was weakest. Thus, they would be contributing to the ultimate communization of not just their laggingly capitalist nation but their ripely capitalist, hence potentially socialist, world.

The Russian intelligentsia, then, was a prevailingly western one, actually created by the influence of western ideas. But the Chinese intelligentsia of the 'Renaissance', 'New Youth', May Fourth stamp was westernizing—which implied a markedly different state of mind.[13] This was the latest branch of an intelligentsia which had originally been created by Chinese ideas, and had spread their influence outward. Now it had to convert *its* world into a nation (see Volume One), and Marxism had its appeal as a compensa-

THE FAILURE OF ANALOGY

tion for the lost values of Confucian civilization, not (like its Russian appeal) as the culmination of a civilization to which the intelligentsia subscribed.

When the Russian intelligentsia emerged in the early nineteenth century its great sorrow was the seeming emptiness of the national past. Like the Chinese intelligentsia in the twentieth century, the Russian became historicist, for the most part. German romantic ideas convinced Russian thinkers that their nation had its own genius, no matter how low it rated on a rationalist scale of values. And the low rating (for the empty past) could be rubbed out, anyway, by the genius of the age. Russia could have the future by coming into history on the crest of revolution.

But to have a crest, there had to be a wave, and the wave was European. Precisely because they deprecated the Russian past as Russians, they had to point towards a future that had Europe behind it; they had to fall in line with European history. Even the revolutionaries of a specially 'Russian' bent, rivals of the Marxists, needed the other parts of Europe in their minds, to set off the 'Russian spirit'.

Though they became historicists, too, none of this applied to the Chinese intellectuals. They had no 'Third Rome' in their past, so they could not—and their past was not empty, but full, so they need not—attempt to ride a western wave of history. What they deplored was their present, not their past. Their radicals looked to revolution to unfreeze a mighty iceberg; frozen, but yet floating from its own impressive base. As their past was much more brilliant than the Russian, their present was more parlous, and their future harder to see as *theirs* in a world of western hegemony.

For the very indictments of the past Russian culture, the past living into the present, had flowed into a superb modern literature, a Russian, European, and world literature that no Russian had to regard with cultural dismay. But the indictments of the present Chinese culture had no comparable effect, that of softening their own harshness. And so in China, as a resolver of the dilemma of cultural malaise, Marxism was really a *deux ex machina*; while in Russia, a Marxist resolution might seem to issue from the logic of the drama.

The drama in China, the tragic history, was the wearing away of Confucian China to historical significance. One of the signs was 'sinology' as the sum of western interest in Confucian civilization. From western sources, on the other hand, Chinese indulged an interest in all the other -ologies, the sciences (in the broadest sense) that have no historical boundaries. The vital quest was for knowledge in the abstract, not knowledge of western thought. In a world where a 'Congress of Orientalists' would regularly convene, the idea of a 'Congress of Occidentalists' had the force of whimsical paradox.

It was whimsy, but not a joke. It was no joke, first, because China indeed had once been able to conceive the idea of 'barbarian experts', much as the modern West conceives of its 'China experts'; that was a time when China could still be thought of, at least at home, as the kind of world to which Europeans like the *philosophes* applied, not in the 'sinological' spirit, but in search of answers to universal questions. And it was not a joke, too, because it was anything but funny. Lu Hsün, for one (and he spoke for more than one), would not see himself as a happy antique. He could not bear to see China as a vast museum. History had to be made there again, and the museum consigned to the dead, as a place of liberation for the living, not a mausoleum for the modern dead-alive.

4. POLITICS AND PROSPECTS

If liberation led to Liberation, we have a lovely Maoist 'contradiction'. What has, in fact, occurred?

In May 1956, when Mao Tse-tung invited the hundred schools to contend, it seemed possible that the curse of absolute conformity and uniformity, particularly heavy on Chinese intellectuals, was about to be lifted. The literary monopoly of socialist realism, for example, was abrogated; the natural sciences were declared free of class character. But by and large the intellectuals, with six years of icy discpline behind them, discreetly declined to blossom. Mao persisted, and with his speech, 'On Contradictions' (February 27, 1957), he laid the groundwork for a moderate independence of views. Distinguishing between 'contradictions' within the nation and 'contradictions' between the nation and its enemies, he indicated that the former type should be brought into the open. Flaws in the execution of state policies did indeed exist, he suggested, and such conflicts, which were not malign, could be solved without the use of force. Criticism, to that end, was solicited.

On April 30 a directive to rectify the approach and methods of officials was issued. Bureaucratism, subjectivism, and sectarianism, the 'Kuomintang style of work', were to be rooted out and public forums encouraged to identify such evils. This time, after some initial caution, at least part of the public found its voice. During May and early June, with almost no official rebuttal, criticism swelled. And then on June 8, an editorial in *Jen-min jih-pao* ('People's Daily'), the organ of authority, proclaimed that certain rightists had exposed themselves as pro-western, longing for the destruction of the Communist Party and socialism. The Anti-Rightist campaign was on, and wherever critics had bloomed and contended, denunciations followed. Here is the recantation of a man reduced to jelly, a demoralized sinner in the hands of an angry god:

The whole nation is demanding stern punishment of me, a rightist. This is what should be done and I am prepared to accept it. I hate my wickedness. I want to kill the old and reactionary self so that he will not return to life. I will join the whole nation in the stern struggle against the rightists, including myself. The great Chinese Communist Party once saved me, it saved me once more today. I hope to gain a new life under the leadership and teaching of the Party and Chairman Mao and to return to the stand of loving the Party and socialism . . .[14]

History imitates fiction.

The record as we have it from the Chinese press for those few weeks of blooming and contending, before the freeze, is an indictment of many features of the régime. Party members and cadres were damned as economic parasites, policemen sowing distrust, perpetrators of waste and inefficiency, warpers of intellectual integrity and creativity. What does the record tell us, not just about the history of the Chinese Communist order, but about its place in Chinese history? One might come to two conclusions, neither of them tenable. First, one might assume that the communist bureaucracy was merely the old Confucian bureaucracy in disguise and China was true to itself, as a perennial 'Oriental despotism'. Some of the charges, like those against officials' nepotism and against their 'Confucian philosophy, "tell them [the masses] what to do, but not why to do it" ', may suggest this. But, second, other charges set the bureaucracy and the intelligentsia apart from each other (which was not the case in traditional China); these charges might seem to imply that, though a revolution had taken place, the intelligentsia was unimplicated, for it sustained a continuity with traditional literati. 'Our Party's massacre of the intellectuals and the mass burying alive of the literati by the tyrant, Ch'in Shih-huang' (ran a letter to Mao from a Hankow professor) 'will go down in China's history as two ineradicable stigmas.'[15]

And yet, whatever affinity the communists might have with the ancient Ch'in anti-Confucian 'Legalists', the modern intelligentsia was clearly post-Confucian, far from the old literati in values and role. Disenchantment with the communists gave witness not to the vitality of historic Chinese conservative values, but to their lifelessness. There was no static body in Chinese history, the intelligentsia, on which the communists simply worked. True, the Communist Party imposed ideas, but there were reasons for its rise to such imposing power, and the reasons moved intellectuals directly. Throughout these volumes we have seen some of these reasons, working against the chances of a liberal commitment. Traditional ethnocentric culturalism had to go, but a simple 'western' avowal made a very weak successor. And whatever it was that hampered the liberal modernists hastened the day of the communists, when Marxism became the official way of breaking with (by tying to) the past.

But '*bourgeois* intellectuals', though denounced by the Party, had broken with the past, too. If they lived in a State in which intellectuals were tools, merely used (and therefore subject to harassment) by the rulers, the State with intel-

lectuals as ends, the Confucian State, had been deserted by
intellectuals just like these. They were not a perennial
element in Chinese society, unmoving, whose fate in the
newest China was settled solely by State directives.

Far from seeing the new régime as simply alien, even its
opponents could be morally involved with it. The insistent
communist claims of material success might be scouted. But
if they were admitted at all, then strain and tension were
admitted into the mind. There was not just the pressure of
outside force against liberal sentiments, but a genuine
questioning of liberal sentiments. A nagging doubt might
intrude; were these sentiments hollow, while material
achievement was 'real'? This was the inner schism that
seemed to corroborate the communist charge of '*bourgeois
egoism*'—the schism expressed in feeling that what might be
good for China was hell to me. The psychological implications of 'thought-reform' must be taken seriously. For intellectuals were not outside the system, resisting or bending to
force; their character helped to account for the system's
existence, and was then affected by the system's operation.

Therefore, at the time of the 'Hundred Flowers', Mao
seems to have had some confidence that he possessed the
intellectuals. He was convinced of the underlying unity of
the Chinese people, a unity divined during the nineteen-
thirties and expressed in the politics of United Front. Paradoxically, the 'Hundred Flowers' revelation of a 'Democratic
League' restlessness within the United Front proved Mao
both right in his premise and wrong in his conclusion.

That is, what was described as 'the storm in the universities' confirmed rather than impugned the broad scope of
the communists' victory. The old Confucian intelligence,
whose moribundity (with the social reasons behind it) had
led to communist success, was now so dead that alliance
against it—of all the new men in China, non-communist
nationalist and communist together—no longer had to be
preserved. Since the 'Hundred Flowers' critics of communism
were as far from old China as the communists themselves,
their hostility to the communists could not be expressed in a
mood of restoration. And while the old seemed to persist,

such hostility to the communists was inhibited: if communists and liberals were to be able to acknowledge the gulf between them, their common foe, who had fused them into a common short-term interest, had to expire.

Mao believed that 'antagonistic' contradictions had been resolved by the communist victory and that only 'non-antagonistic' contradictions remained, non-crucial tensions which might relax in an atmosphere of 'blooming and contending'. It is not likely that Mao, with his metaphor, simply intended a trap. Why was he so surprised by the virulence of the critics?

Perhaps, to explain it, we need a mirror-image of Mao's theory of contradictions. 'Non-antagonistic' contradictions, in a context of shared interest, existed *before* the communist victory—not after—among all men disaffected with the Kuomintang and tradition. It was the communist victory itself which opened the way to a new, modern antagonism. For victory made the cleavage in the anti-Kuomintang side, not small (compared with the great gulf between new and old), but visible and rending.

Modern liberalism made little headway while traditionalism was the main alternative defining it, enforcing some arrangement between liberalism and communism. Traditionalism had to be put down—by victory of the communists—before definition by the new alternative could restore a modern non-communist faith to a possible field of action, in a new phase of history. The possibility, one must wryly observe, was only metaphysical; the practical restraints, if anything, were more severe. But an 'inner' viability was restored, even when 'outer' repression was enhanced.

The repression, the communist monopoly of rule and expression, are all that we see now. When or whether some new non-communist cause (surely not the old) may come to flower is a matter for speculation. No one writing in early 1963 can say he sees it, and no historian needs to chart the future. This is not the time to start work on *Communist China and Its Modern Fate*.

But the broad conditions of whatever history is likely to be made have been laid down.

China will have a Chinese past as Russia has a Russian past and England has an English past: past. That is, China's past will be kept in mind and fragments from its world of values valued. No radical westernization will put an end to the historical significance of China.

Yet, the spread of a common technology, though it may destroy the world materially, may actually create that Hegelian fantasy, a world-spirit. And China, then, would differ from Russia and England not as the Confucian civilization differed from the Christian, but as nations, in keeping their own historical *personae*, differ from one another —yet exist in a single many-coloured, more-than-national civilization.

The sageliness of Confucius may still be felt in China (or felt again), like Socrates' in Europe. But Confucian civilization would be as 'historical' as Greek, and modern Chinese culture as cosmopolitan as any, like the western culture that reaches now, in paper-back catholicity, to 'The Wisdom of Confucius'. In a true world history, when all past achievements are in the museum without walls, everyone's past would be everyone else's; which implies that quite un-Confucian thing, the loss of the sense of tradition. 'To us today the sense of tradition is not strong, not so much because we have no tradition but because we have mixed so many traditions. . . .'[16]

'The figure of Ch'in Shih Huang-ti ought to be as familiar to the cultivated Frenchman as that of Alexander the Great. . . .'[17] That is, all pasts are 'ours'. And since for the cultivated Chinese the same principle holds, all pasts are 'theirs'. Or, the distinction between 'ours' and 'theirs' itself, the basis for single histories, is on the way to being past. Then what of the possibility that 'the traditional culture of China is called upon to disappear as Egypt's disappeared in its time'? This is not the spectre. But to distinguish China from dead Egypt is not to endow *Confucian* China and ancient values with immortality. Nothing proves this, least of all the recognition that even revolutionaries, with their 'honour to archaeology' and 'editions of the Classics', 'have not denied the heritage of the past'. If the museum is not the mummy case, it still encloses a still, still life—which is open to all to see (passports and visas permitting) in a cosmopolitan world of interchangeable exhibits.

Ancient Egyptian culture, mummies and all, has also filled museums. But foreigners (including the modern Arabic-speaking, non-hieroglyphic Egyptians) are the curators. There lies the difference between the Pharaohs and Confucius. By making their own museum-approach to traditional Chinese culture, the Chinese kept their continuity without precluding change. Their modern revolution—against the world to join the world, against their past to keep it theirs, but past—was a long striving to make their museums themselves. They had to make their own accounting with history, throwing back a new line, and holding fast to it, while heading in quite the opposite direction.

There is a parable from another culture that tells us something of what history-writing does to extend a history. Preserving the past by recounting it, or displaying its bequests, is not perpetuating it. But it does preserve. When cultures change by becoming historically significant, historical remembering is a kind of compensation for forgetting. There has been so much forgetting in modern Chinese history. The current urge to preserve, the historical mood, does not bely it. If the forgetting, and this special remembering, have really taken place because in our unfolding cosmopolitan world, with its revolutionary impact on China, 'we (they, and everyone) have mixed so many traditions', it should not be amiss to conclude a story of China with a tale of the Hasidim:

'When the Baal Shem had a difficult task before him, he would go to a certain place in the woods, light a fire and meditate in prayer—and what he had set out to perform was done. When a generation later the "Maggid" of Meseritz was faced with the same task he would go to the same place in the woods and say: We can no longer light the fire, but we can still speak the prayers—and what he wanted done became reality. Again a generation later Rabbi Moshe Leib of Sassov had to perform this task. And he, too, went into the woods and said: We can no longer light a fire, nor do we know the secret meditations belonging to the prayer, but we do know the place in the woods to which it all belongs—and that must be sufficient; and sufficient it was. And when another generation had passed and Rabbi Israel of Rishin was called upon to perform the task, he sat down on his golden chair in his castle and said: We cannot light the fire, we cannot speak the prayers, we do not know the place, but we can tell the story of how it was done.'[18]

Notes

CHAPTER I

1. Wu Chia-mou, *Ching-yen chih* (Gazetteer of Ching-yen) (n.p., 1900), ch. 23. 7a.

2. These biographical data come from Liao P'ing, 'Lü li' (Personal chronicle), *Ssu-i-kuan ching hsüeh ts'ung-shu* (Collection of classical studies published by Liao P'ing) (Chengtu, 1886), ts'e 14, 1a–2b; Yang Chia-lo, *Min-kuo ming-jen t'u-chien* (Biographical dictionary of eminent men of the Chinese Republic) (Nanking, 1937), 1, 1.12–13; Onogawa Hidemi, *Seimatsu seiji shisō kenkyū* (Studies in late-Ch'ing political thought) (Kyoto, 1960), 155; Yang Yin-shen, *Chung-kuo hsüeh-shu chia lieh-chuan* (Biographies of Chinese scholars) (Shanghai, 1939), 482; Morimoto Chikujō, *Shinchō Jugaku shi gaisetsu* (A general survey of the history of Confucian learning in the Ch'ing dynasty) (Tokyo, 1931), 322–3; Ojima Sukema, 'Ryō Hei no gaku' (Liao P'ing's learning), *Geibun*, VIII, No. 5 (May, 1917), 426; Shimizu Nobuyoshi, *Kinsei Chūgoku shisō shi* (History of modern Chinese thought) (Tokyo, 1950), 422; Fukui Kojun, *Gendai Chūgoku shisō* (Recent Chinese thought) (Tokyo, 1955), 24; Naitō Torajirō, *Shinchō shi tsūron* (Outline of Ch'ing history) (Tokyo, 1944), 162–3; Liao P'ing 'Chung-wai pi-chiao kai-liang pien hsü' (Preface to a comparative listing of Chinese and foreign reforms), *Liu-i-kuan ts'ung-shu* (Chengtu, 1921), ts'e 8, 25a.

3. Ojima, 435–6; Fukui, 23; Liang Ch'i-ch'ao (Immanuel C. Y. Hsü, tr.) *Intellectual Trends of the Ch'ing Period* (Cambridge, Mass., 1959), 92; Yang Chia-lo, 1.13; Yang Yin-shen, 482; Naitō, 162–3; Shimizu, 442; Hashikawa Tokio, *Chūgoku bunkakai jimbutsu sōkan* (General directory of intellectuals of the Chinese Republic) (Peking, 1940), 661–2; Morimoto, 323, 332; Fung Yu-lan (Derk Bodde, tr.), *A History of Chinese Philosophy: Volume Two, The Period of Classical Learning* (Princeton, 1953), 709; Kung-ch'üan Hsiao, 'K'ang Yu-wei and Confucianism', *Monumenta Serica*, XVIII (1959), 126–31; Ch'ien Mu, *Chung-kuo chin san-pai nien hsüeh-shu*

shih (History of Chinese scholarship in the last three hundred years) (Taipei, 1957), II, 642-6.

The invidious reflection on K'ang is rejected by Chang Hsi-t'ang, editor of Liao P'ing, *Ku-hsüeh k'ao* (On the 'ancient text' learning—first published, 1894) (Peiping, 1935), on the inconclusive grounds that Liao's work was published after K'ang's and seems in two places to refer to K'ang's opinions as independently relevant. See preface, 1; 19, 29; colophon, 2.

4. Ojima, 444.

5. 'Hui-shih chu-chüan' (Essays, copied out in red, of successful candidates at the metropolitan examinations), *Ssu-i-kuan ching-hsüeh ts'ung-shu*, ts'e 14, 1a-1b.

6. Liang, 92; Ch'ien, II, 651.

7. Liu Shih-p'ei, 'Chih Liao Chi-p'ing lun T'ien jen shu' (Letter to Liao P'ing on Heaven and man), *Chung-kuo hsüeh-pao*, No. 2 (February, 1916), 1a.

8. Detailed accounts of the changes in Liao's thought may be found in Fung, 705-19, and in two articles by Ojima, the one already cited, in *Geibun*, VIII, no. 5 (May 1917), 426-46, and 'Rokuhen seru Ryō no gakusetsu' (Six stages in the development of Liao P'ing's theories), *Shinagaku*, II, no. 9 (May 1922), 707-14. For the early Liao (of the *Chin ku hsüeh-k'ao* exploited by K'ang), with his *chin-wen*, *ku-wen* distinction between emphases, respectively, on Confucius and the Duke of Chou, the elder Confucius and the younger Confucius, the *Wang-chih* (section of *Li-chi*) and the *Chou-li*, the *Ch'un-ch'iu* and the *Chou-li*, prescription for change and for following Chou tradition, Confucian authorship of Classics and Confucian transmission of older histories, see Uno Tetsujin (tr. Ma Fu-ch'en), *Chung-kuo chin-shih Ju-hsüeh shih* (History of Chinese Confucian learning in modern times) (Taipei, 1957), II, 431-4.

9. Fukui, 9.

10. *Ibid.*, 29, 116.

11. Tung Chung-shu, *Ch'un-ch'iu fan-lu* (Luxuriant dew from the *Spring and Autumn Annals*), in Ch'ang Chih-ch'un, ed; *Chu tzu ching-hua lu* (Record of the splendours of varieties of philosophers) (Shanghai, 1924), ch. 4, 3b.

12. Liao P'ing, 'Lun Shih hsü' (On the preface to the *Shih-ching*), *Chung-kuo hsüeh-pao*, No. 4 (April 1916), 1a-2b. In 'Fu Liu Shen-shu shu' (Reply to Liu Shih-p'ei), *Chung-kuo hsüeh-pao*, No. 2 (Feb. 1916), 1a. Liao wrote: 'The *Shih-ching* is related to the *I-ching* as *t'i* to *yung*'.

13. Ch'ien, II, 644.

14. Hsüeh Fu-ch'eng, 'Yung-an wen-pien' (Collection of Hsüeh Fu-ch'eng's writings), *Yung-an ch'üan-chi* (Collected works of Hsüeh Fu-ch'eng) (1884–98), ts'e 1, ch. 1.20a–20b.

15. Hsüeh Fu-ch'eng, 'Ch'ou yang ch'u-i' (Rough discussion on the management of foreign affairs), *Yung-an ch'üan-chi*, ts'e 15, 13a–16a, esp. 15a.

16. And Ch'in was Britain, and Lu was Japan, etc. See Ojima, 'Ryō Hei no gaku', 437–8.

17. Liao P'ing, 'Yü K'ang Ch'ang-su shu' (Letter to K'ang Yu-wei), *Chung-kuo hsüeh-pao*, No. 8 (June 1913), 19.

18. Liao P'ing, 'Ta-t'ung hsüeh-shuo' (The theory of the Great Harmony), *ibid.*, 1–2, 10–11; Ojima, 'Ryō Hei no gaku', 438.

19. Ojima, 'Ryō Hei no gaku', 436–7.

20. For 'empty words' as the proper medium of the providentially 'throneless king', see *ibid.*, 434.

21. Liao, 'Yü K'ang Ch'ang-su shu', 19.

22. See Joseph R. Levenson, *Liang Ch'i-ch'ao and the Mind of Modern China* (London, 1959).

23. K'ang Yu-wei, 'Chung-kuo hsüeh-pao t'i-tzu' (The thesis of the *Chung-kuo hsüeh-pao*), *Chung-kuo hsüeh-pao*, No. 6 (Feb. 1913), 3.

CHAPTER II

1. Ezra Pound, *The Classic Anthology Defined by Confucius* (Cambridge, Mass., 1955), 8.

2. James Legge, tr., *The Chinese Classics*, Vol. II (*The Works of Mencius*) (Oxford, 1895), 245.

3. See Uchino Kumaichirō, 'Minkoku sho chūku no keigaku kan' (Views on classical studies in the early and middle years of the Chinese Republic), *Nihon Chūgoku gakkai hō*, No. 9 (1957), 1–9.

4. For the *kou-hsü* system, see *Chou-li* (Ssu-pu ts'ung-kan ed.) (Shanghai, 1942), ts'e 6, ch. 12, 18b, and Edouard Biot, tr., *Le Tcheou-li ou Rites des Tcheou* (Paris, 1851), II, 566.

Chu Hsi, it is true, maintained that the *Chou-li* made a distinction between the *ching-t'ien* and *kou-hsü* systems. It was the rival Yung-chia school of Chekiang (oriented more to questions of 'rites' and 'music' than to his own great concerns of 'mind' and 'human nature'), he said, which was currently amalgamating the two systems in its discussion of land problems; see Chu Hsi,

'Li i: *Chou-li*' ('Rituals' ≠ 1: *Chou-li*), *Chu-tzu ch'üan-shu* (Complete works of Chu Hsi), ed. Li Kuang-ti (1714), ts'e 15, ch. 37.12b. For a modern expression of scepticism about the link between ching-t'ien and *kou-hsü*, see Tazaki Masayuki, *Shina kōdai keizai shisō oyobi seido* (Economic thought and systems in Chinese antiquity) (Tokyo, 1925), 495–511. But, notwithstanding Chu Hsi's disclaimer and his presentation of the issue as a matter of contemporary polemic, ching-t'ien and *kou-hsü* were generally linked together in Confucian scholarship, e.g., in the Sung works, Su Hsün, 'T'ien-chih' (Land systems), *San Su wen-chi* (Collection of writings of the three Su worthies) (Shanghai, 1912), ts'e 1, ch. 6.6a; and Ma Tuan-lin, *Wen-hsien t'ung-k'ao* (Che-chiang shu-chü ed., 1896), ts'e 2, ch. 1.4a–9a, 33b–34b, 36b–37a. Su Hsün and Ma Tuan-lin wrote, respectively, before and after Chu Hsi's time.

5. Hu Shih, 'Ching-t'ien pien' (The ching-t'ien dispute), *Hu Shih wen-ts'un* (Selected essays of Hu Shih) (Shanghai, 1927), 249. For a near-contemporary comment on the ching-t'ien issue as Hu raised it, see P. Demiéville, review of 'Hou Che wen ts'ouen', 4 volumes (1921), *Bulletin de l'Ecole Française d'Extrême-Orient*, XXIII (1923), 494–9.

6. Kao Yün-hui, 'Chou-tai t'u-ti chih-tu yü ching-t'ien' (The Chou period's land system and ching-t'ien), *Shih-huo*, I, No. 7 (March 1, 1935), 12. Cf. Ting Tao-ch'ien, 'Yu li-shih pien-tung lü-shuo tao Chung-kuo t'ien-chih ti "hsün-huan" ', (From theories of legal change in history to 'recurrence' in Chinese land systems), *Shih-huo*, V, No. 3 (Feb. 1, 1937), 46, for a modern comment on Ssu-ma Ch'ien's (145–90 B.C.) often-quoted assertion that Shang Yang (390?–338 B.C.), Legalist minister of the Ch'in state, destroyed the ching-t'ien system; Ting maintained that there had never actually been any ching-t'ien in Ch'in, either in form or in fact. He distinguished between ching-t'ien as a system (non-existent) and as a socio-political conception, and saw only the latter reflected in any remarks about traces of ching-t'ien in Ch'in.

7. James Robert Hightower, tr., *Han Shih Wai Chuan: Han Ying's Illustrations of the Didactic Application of the Classic of Songs* (Cambridge, Mass., 1952), 138–9.

8. See W. Theodore de Bary, 'A Reappraisal of Neo-Confucianism', *Studies in Chinese Thought*, ed. Arthur F. Wright (Chicago, 1953), 103–4, and Carsun Chang, *The Development of Neo-Confucian Thought* (New York, 1957), 188, for discussions of

the tension between adherence to Mencius' prescription of ching-t'ien (the stance of Chang Tsai, 1020–17, and Wang An-shih) and revulsion from coercion (Ch'eng Hao, 1032–85; Ch'eng I, 1033–1107; and Chu Hsi).

9. Su Hsün, ts'e 1, ch. 6.6a.

10. Shōji Sōichi, 'Chin Ryō no gaku' (The thought of Ch'en Liang), *Tōyō no bunka to shakai* (Far Eastern culture and society), V (1954), 98.

11. Ma Tuan-lin, ts'e 1, preface, 5a–5b; see also Chen Huan-chang, *The Economic Principles of Confucius and His School* (New York, 1911), II, 528.

12. C. Martin Wilbur (translating from *Ch'ien Han shu*), *Slavery in China During the Former Han Dynasty, 206 B.C.–A.D. 25* (Chicago 1943), 452–3.

13. H. R. Williamson, *Wang An Shih: A Chinese Statesman and Educationalist of the Sung Dynasty* (London, 1935), I, 27.

14. See Wang An-shih, *Chou kuan hsin i* (New interpretations of the government system of Chou) (Shanghai, 1937), I, 84 (deriving from *Chou-li*, ts'e 2, ch. 3.23a–23b; Biot, I, 226–7) for his elaborate formal pyramid of units of administration, beginning with 'nine *fu* make a *ching*', up to 'four *hsien* make a *tu*'—which also appears elsewhere in *Chou-li*; see note 3 above.

15. Williamson, II, 301. See *Chu-tzu ch'üan-shu*, t'se 15. ch. 37.10a, for Chu Hsi's arguments against a father and son named Hu, who maintained that Wang Mang ordered Liu Hsin (d. 23 A.D.) to compose it. Chu Hsi reaffirmed the orthodox tenet that it was handed down by the Duke of Chou.

16. Hung Jen-kan 'Tzu-cheng hsin-p'ien' (New essay to aid in government), *T'ai-p'ing T'ien-kuo* (The Heavenly Kingdom of Great Peace), ed. Hsiang Ta et al. (Shanghai, 1952), II, 524.

17. de Bary, W. T., 'Chinese Despotism and the Confucian Ideal: a Seventeenth-century View', *Chinese Thought and Institutions*, ed. John K. Fairbank (Chicago, 1957), 188–9.

18. Ku Yen-wu, *Jih-chih lu* (Record of knowledge day by day) (Shanghai, 1933), I, ch. 3.12; Mencius, IIIA, iii, 9 (Legge, 242).

19. Yen Yüan, 'Ts'un chih pien', *Yen Li ts'ung-shu* (1923), ts'e 4, 1b–4b. Li Kung (1659–1733) explicitly echoed Yen, his master and colleague, on reinstitution of ching-t'ien; see Li Kung, *Yüeh shih hsi shih* (Shanghai, 1937), ch. 4.47–48.

20. Yen Yüan, *Hsi-chi chi-yü* (Shanghai, 1936), ch. 1.10.

21. Su Hsün, ts'e 1, ch. 6.5.

22. See Chu Hsi, 'Meng-tzu chi-chu' (Annotation of Mencius),

Ssu-shu chang-chü chi-chu (Piecemeal annotation of the 'Four Books')
(Shanghai, 1935), ch. 5.67, where he discusses Mencius IIIA, iii,
15 (Legge, 244): 'I would ask you, in the remoter districts,
observing the nine-squares division, to reserve one division to be
cultivated on the system of mutual aid, and in the more central
parts of the kingdom, to make the people pay for themselves a
tenth part of their produce.' Chu Hsi says that this method of land
division and of payment is the means whereby the countrymen
(*yeh-jen*) are governed and the superior men (*chün-tzu*) supported.
Here the concern is very much for the gentleman who toils not,
and ching-t'ien is a regularized system providing for his thoroughly
proper support. Cf. *Mencius* IIIa, iv, 6 (Legge, 249–50): 'Hence
there is the saying, "Some labour with their minds, and some
labour with their strength. Those who labour with their minds
govern others; those who labour with their strength are governed
by others. Those who are governed by others support them; those
who govern others are supported by them." This is a principle
universally recognized.' On the last part of *Mencius* IIIA, iii, 19
(Legge, 245: 'And not till public work is finished may they
presume to attend to their private affairs. This is the way by which
the countrymen are distinguished *from those of a superior grade*'),
Chu Hsi emphasizes that the *kung-t'ien*, 'public field', provides the
chün-tzu's emolument, and that the priority of public field over
private field marks the distinction between *chün-tzu* and *yeh-jen*.

23. Rinji Taiwan kyūkan chōsakai dai-ichi-bu hōkoku (Temporary commission of the Taiwan Government-general for the
study of old Chinese customs, report of the First Section),
Shinkoku gyōseihō (Administrative laws of the Ch'ing dynasty),
kan 2 (Kobe, 1910), 232.

Wang An-shih had provided the precedent for this agricultural
military ching-t'ien effort. In 1070 he had established a militia
system with ching-t'ien assumptions of collective responsibility.
According to T'ao Hsi-sheng, Wang saw ching-t'ien and his
nung-ping (farmer-soldier) systems as inseparably tied together.
See T'ao Hsi-sheng, 'Wang An-shih ti she-hui ssu-hsiang yü
ching-chi cheng-tse' (The social thought and economic policies
of Wang An-shih), *She-hui k'o-hsüeh chi-k'an* ('Social Sciences
Quarterly'), V, No. 3 (Sept. 1935), 126.

For a modern expression of dogged confidence in ching-t'ien—
an insistence that the Yung-cheng ching-t'ien was not merely a
Confucian archaism but a plausible specific for a social ill, which
failed to cure not because of ching-t'ien's inherent hopelessness

but because of the defective class-character of the bannermen—
see Wei Chien-yu, 'Ch'ing Yung-cheng ch'ao shih-hsin ching-
t'ien chih ti k'ao-ch'a' (A study of the ching-t'ien experiment
during the Yung-cheng reign of the Ch'ing period), *Shih-hsüeh*
nien-pao ('Yenching Annual of Historical Studies'), I, No. 5
(Aug. 1933), 125–6.

24. Chen Huan-chang, II, 526.

25. Ma Tuan-lin, ts'e 2, ch. 1.39a, quoting another Sung
scholar and concurring with him.

26. Su Hsün, ts'e 1, ch. 6.6a.

27. For Chang Tsai, who believed like Wang in the viability
of the *Chou-li* and who saw no ultimate peace if the empire were
not governed on the basis of *ching* landholding, which he defined
by saying, 'The way of Chou is only that of *chün-p'ing*', see Ch'ien
Mu, *Kuo-shih ta-kang* (The main outlines of the national history)
(Chungking, 1944), II, 415, and Ting Tao-ch'ien, 49 (citing his
biography in *Sung-shih*). For Wang An-shih's *chün-p'ing* objective
as the main emphasis in one of his *Chou-li: ching-t'ien* discussions,
see Wang An-shih, I, 98.

28. E.g., Tung Chung-shu to the Han Emperor Wu (134–86
B.C.): 'Although it would be difficult to act precipitately [in a
return] to the ancient land system ching-t'ien, it is proper to make
[present usage] draw somewhat nearer to the old [system]. Let
people's ownership of land be limited in order to sustain [the
poor],' in Nancy Lee Swann, *Food and Money in Ancient China: Han*
Shu 24 (Princeton, 1950), 183; and a *chün-t'ien* memorial to
Emperor Ai (6 B.C.–1 A.D.): 'Of the ancient sage-kings, there was
none who did not establish ching-t'ien, and henceforward their
governing made for peace . . .,' in Teng Ch'u-min, 'T'u-ti kuo-
yu wen-t'i' (The question of land nationalization), *Tung-fang*
tsa-chih ('The Eastern Miscellany'), XX, No. 19 (Oct. 10, 1923),
14. For testimony to the modern coupling of *chün-t'ien* with
ching-t'ien, from a scholar who sees *chün-t'ien* as originally a tax
system with 'levelling' connotations for later men but who sees
ching-t'ien as a purely feudal exploitation of serfs by nobles, and
who criticizes his contemporaries for what seems to him a widely
believed error—the characterization of ching-t'ien as a Confucianist prototype of egalitarian *chün-t'ien*—see Liang Yüan-tung,
'Ku-tai chün-t'ien chih-tu ti chen-hsiang' (What the ancient
chün-t'ien system was really like), *Shen-pao yüeh-k'an* ('The Shun
Pao'), V, No 4 (May 15, 1935), 65–66; and Liang Yüan-tung,
'Ching-t'ien chih fei t'u-ti chih-tu shuo' (Exposition of the ching-

t'ien system as not a land system), *Ching-chi hsüeh chi-k'an* ('Quarterly Journal of Economics of the Chinese Economic Society'), VI, No. 3 (Nov. 1935), 51–53.

29. Almost all discussions of ching-t'ien history accused the fourth-century B.C. minister, Shang Yang, of this policy of destruction; see note 6 above. Yen Yüan put the responsibility on Ch'in Shih Huang-ti himself, the 'First Emperor', who united the Empire in 221 B.C.

30. For emphasis, in the ching-t'ien discussion of the 1920s and later, on *chün-t'ien* as the concomitant of private ownership, see Hu Han-min, 'Hu Han-min hsien-sheng ta Hu Shih-chih hsien-sheng ti hsin' (Hu Han-min's answer to Hu Shih's letter), 1920, in Chu Chih-hsin, et al., *Ching-t'ien chih-tu yu-wu chih yen-chiu* (A study of whether there was or was not a ching-t'ien system) (Shanghai, 1930), 45; Liu Ta-tiao, 'Chung-kuo ku-tai t'ien-chih yen-chiu' (An investigation of ancient Chinese land systems), 685; and Liang Yüan-tung, 'Ching-t'ien chih fei t'u-ti chih-tu shuo', 51. For a corollary identification of ching-t'ien with the *feng-chien* ('feudal') system which had yielded to Ch'in establishment of general alienability of land and unification of the Empire—so that Ch'in Shih Huang-ti, his triumph inseparable from these policies, could not have a ching-t'ien revival (which the author poses as a hypothetical wish), since this would have to occur in isolation from its former and necessary context)—see Hu Fan-jo, 'Chung-kuo ching-t'ien chih yen-ko k'ao' (On the overthrow of the ching-t'ien system in China), *K'o-hsüeh* ('Science'), X, No. 1 (May 1925), 139–40. On the other hand, for a communist identification of *chün-tien* not with a post-ching-t'ien régime of private ownership but precisely with the very ching-t'ien system allegedly destroyed by the expansion of private ownership, see Fan I-t'ien, 'Hsi-Chou ti she-hui hsing-chih—feng-chien she-hui' (The nature of Western Chou society—feudal society), *Chung-kuo ku-shih fen-ch'i wen-t'i lun-ts'ung* (Collection of essays on the question of the periodization of ancient Chinese history) (Peking, 1957), 234.

31. Ming-shih, ch. 226, quoted in Ch'en Po-ying, *Ching-kuo t'ien-chih ts'ung-k'ao* (General survey of Chinese land systems) (Shanghai, 1935), 233.

32. Laurence G. Thompson, tr., *Ta T'ung Shu: the One-World Philosophy of K'ang Yu-wei* (London, 1958), 137 and 211. For essentially the same statement on slavery by a disciple of K'ang, see Chen Huan-chang, II, 374 (though more conventionally, he attributed ching-t'ien to sage-kings and the Duke of Chou; *ibid.*,

I, 82). This work by Chen, incidentally, though appearing first in English, as a dissertation for Columbia University, has been considered enough of a primary source for its publication to be noted in a Japanese chronicle of events in Confucian history; see Imazeki Hisamaro, *Sung Yüan Ming Ch'ing Ju-chia hsüeh nien-piao* (Chronological tables of Sung, Yüan, Ming, and Ch'ing Confucianism) (Tokyo, 1920), 217 (in Chinese).

33. Liang Ch'i-ch'ao, 'Chung-kuo chih she-hui chu-i' (China's socialism), *Yin-ping shih ho-chi* (Shanghai, 1936), chuan-chi 2: 2.102.

34. T'an Ssu-t'ung, 'Jen-hsüeh' (Study of benevolence), *T'an Ssu-t'ung ch'üan-chi* (Collected works of T'an Ssu-t'ung) (Peking, 1954), 69.

35. Wang K'an, *Pa shan ch'i chung*, quoted in Ch'en Po-ying, 18.

36. (a) Hu Han-min, with Sun Yat-sen's endorsement, wrote in *Min-pao* (1906) that socialism would be easy enough for China, since her ancient ching-t'ien system was a socialist model long in the Chinese mind: quoted in Robert A. Scalapino and Harold Schiffrin, 'Early Socialist Currents in the Chinese Revolutionary Movement: Sun Yat-sen versus Liang Ch'i-ch'ao', *Journal of Asian Studies*, XVIII, No. 3 (May 1959), 326.

(b) Sun called ching-t'ien ('the best land system of Chinese antiquity') essentially the same as his own socialist principle of equalizing land rights—'similar in idea (*i*) but different in method (*fa*)': Ch'en Cheng-mo, 'P'ing-chün ti-ch'üan yü Chung-kuo li-tai t'u-ti wen-t'i' (Equalization of land rights and the land question through Chinese history), *Chung-shan wen-hua chiao-yü kuan chi-k'an* ('Quarterly Review of the Sun Yat-sen Institute for Advancement of Culture and Education'), IX, No. 3 (Autumn 1937), 889–90, 911. Note that the *i-fa* dichotomy, an old one in Chinese rhetoric, always implies the 'mereness' of *fa*, which, as 'method', is tantamount to the empirically observable historical event; while *i*, 'principle', is precisely the essence which metaphor shadows forth.

(c) In 1906, in *Hsin-min ts'ung-pao*, Liang Ch'i-ch'ao wrote condescendingly of Sun that the latter failed to understand that his 'socialism' was only ching-t'ien, not the real thing (Scalapino and Schiffrin). At this time Liang was no longer a 'modern-text' Confucianist and was reacting against his own former practice of finding classical precedents for the latest things. But in 1916 Liang was bromidic again: 'Socialist economic theories, which the West thinks so advanced, were fore-shadowed by the ching-t'ien system'; see Liang Ch'i-ch'ao, 'Lun Chung-kuo ts'ai-cheng-hsüeh pu fa-ta chih yüan-yin chi ku-tai ts'ai-cheng hsüeh-shuo chih i-pan' (On the reason for the lack of progress in Chinese study of finance, and a miscellany of ancient financial theories), *Yin-ping-shih ho-chi*: wen-chi 12:33.92–93.

(d) Though Sun, as a matter of fact, disapproved of this suggestion, Huang Hsing in 1907 proposed a revolutionary flag for the *T'ung-meng hui*, with the character *ching* as a symbol of socialism; see Chün-tu Hsüeh, *Huang Hsing and the Chinese Revolution* (Stanford, 1961), 50–51.

(e) Feng Tzu-yu, old Kuomintang stalwart, while acknowledging that the socialism at issue today came from modern European thought, held that the ching-t'ien system, 'practiced by ancient sages and famous monarchs of high antiquity', was early Chinese socialism; see Feng Tzu-yu, *She-hui chu-i yü Chung-kuo* (Socialism and China) (Hong Kong, 1920), 2.

(f) 'Although modern socialism stems from Europe, yet there were early shoots of this type of thought in ancient China . . . Western missionaries of the seventeenth and eighteenth centuries brought ancient Chinese thought to Europe, and this may well have been one of the sources of modern socialist thought . . . Mencius' intellectual spirit was such that he ought to be regarded as a very great unveiler to latter-day socialists': Leng Ting-an, *She-hui chu-i ssu-hsing shih* (History of socialist thought) (Hong Kong, 1956), 9–13.

37. See Hu Shih, 248–9, for his call to a scientific attitude on ching-t'ien. He suggests that the ancient Chinese feudal system (which should be compared with European and Japanese) was not what Mencius and the *Chou-li* describe. He feels that to a scientific, modern mentality the burden of proof is on the ancients; he does not so much prove the ching-t'ien account false, as reject as too slight such affirmative proofs as *Shih-ching* offers (again, 265). Mencius himself offers no proof (269). For *Kung-yang chuan*, *Ku-liang chuan*, Ho Hsiu commentary, *Ch'un-ch'iu*, and *Wang-chih* section of *Chou-li* (all traditional sources for corroboration of ching-t'ien) as being late dependents on a tainted common source, or simply crudely misapplied to the problem, see 271–2, 278–81.

38. See *ibid.*, 270, for his impatience (irrespective of the question of the historical validity of texts) with those who take the ching-t'ien of Mencius' description as having anything to do with communism.

39. *Ibid.,* 281.

40. Viz., *Ching-t'ien chih-tu yu-wu chih yen-chiu,* Appendix I, 83, where Chi Yung-wu concurs with Hu in doubting that the Chinese, with their long experience in history well into Chou, should not have developed private ownership of land.

Also, Kao Yün-hui, 13, where the author notes that one cannot have it all ways: if the *Shih-ching* is cited to prove the existence of ching-t'ien (as, following Mencius, every ching-t'ien apologist cites it), and ching-t'ien is equated with 'primitive communism', we must note that the *Shih-ching* reflects a culture obviously long evolving to sophistication. It hardly represents the rude culture which must be supposed to characterize primitive communism.

41. Kao Yün-hui, 12.

42. Liang Ch'i-ch'ao also, as a settled anti-communist in the post-War period, did not revert to his earlier occasional practice of grouping ching-t'ien and socialism together (as in note 36 above). He called the ching-t'ien question a dead issue, pertaining to the Chou dynasty, not to modern times; see Liang, 'Hsü-lun shih-min yü yin-hsing' (Supplementary discussion of citizens and banks), *Yin-ping-shih ho-chi,* wen-chi 13: 37.40.

For Hu Han-min's role as a spokesman for the uniqueness of Sun Yat-sen's 'three people's principles' and their superiority to communism as well as their distinction from communism, see Hu Han-min 'P'ing-chün ti-chüan ti chen-i chi t'u-ti fa yüan-tse ti lai-yüan' (The true meaning of equalization of landed power and the provenance of the basic rule of the land law), in Shih Hsi-sheng, ed., *Hu Han-min yen hsing lu* (Biography of Hu Han-min), part 3, 119–21; and Hu Han-min, 'San-min-chu-i chih jen-shih' (Knowledge of the Three People's Principles), in Huang-pu chung-yang chün-shih cheng-chih hsüeh-hsiao te-pieh tang-pu (Special Kuomintang party council, Whampoa Academy), ed., *Chiang Hu tsui chin yen-lun chi* (Most recent collected discourses of Chiang Kai-shek and Hu Han-min) (Canton?, 1927), Part II, 1–12, esp. 5–6 where the three principles are explained as defining one another, in such fashion as to be superior to the three envisioned alternatives, nationalism (i.e., *kuo-chia chu-i,* not the Sun principle of *min-tsu chu-i*), anarchism, and communism.

43. Hu Han-min, *Wei-wu shih-kuan yü lun-li chih yen-chiu* (A study of the materialist interpretation of history and ethics) (Shanghai, 1925), 155–6.

44. Hu Han-min, "P'ing-chün ti-chüan . . .', 117–28. For Sun in 1921, maintaining that the principles of the ching-t'ien

system coincided with the intentions of his 'equalization of landed power', see Hsiao Cheng, 'P'ing-chün ti-chüan chen-ch'üan' (The true interpretation of equalization of landed power), *Ti-cheng yüeh-k'an* ('The Journal of Land Economics'), I, No. 1 (Jan. 1933), 10.

45. Hu Han-min, *San-min-chu-i ti lien-huan-hsing* (The cyclical character of the 'Three People's Principles') (Shanghai, 1928), 65–66.

46. See Hu Han-min, *Wei-wu shih-kuan yü lun-li chih yen-chiu*, 74, for his discussion of the critical population factor; Hu bases it on Han Fei-tzu (cited in very 'Malthusian' vein, emphasizing the geometrical rate of natural increase). Hu considers also the factor of the development of exchange and the power of merchants relative to farmers.

47. *Ibid.*, 73.

48. Western scholarship on ancient China, naturally unaffected by the emotional overtones of the ching-t'ien controversy, and accordingly more directly concerned with construction of a history than destruction of the authority of the letter of a text, tends toward this view, which metaphorizes the ching-t'ien of Mencius. See Demiéville, note 5 above, and Henri Maspero, *La Chine antique* (Paris, 1927), 108–10. Among others following Maspero, J. J. L. Duyvendak, *The Book of Lord Shang: a Classic of the Chinese School of Law* (London, 1928), 41–44, declines to follow Hu Shih in dismissing ching-t'ien as mere utopianism. They see it as a system of dependents and lord in a time of slash-and-burn cultivation, before individual property was possible. As soon as families became more settled on more or less definitely allotted land, say Maspero and Duyvendak, the tendency to develop individual property began.

According to a notice in *T'oung Pao*, XXIX, Nos. 1–3 (1932), 203–4, a serious Russian work, M. Kokin and G. Papayan, '*Czin-Tyan*', *agrarnyi stroi drevnego Kitaya* (The ching-t'ien agrarian system of ancient China) (Leningrad, 1930), also follows Masepro closely.

For early modern Japanese scholarship on this subject, see Hashimoto Masuyoshi, 'Shina kodai densei kō' (Examination of the land system of Chinese antiquity), *Tōyō gakuhō*, XII, No. 1 (1923), 1–45; XII, No. 4 (1923), 481–94; XV, No. 1 (1925), 64–104. Hashimoto relates the Chinese factions to Japanese schools of interpretation: Hu Han-min, Liao Chung-k'ai, and Chu Chih-hsin with Katō Shigeru in the pre-private property school, Hu Shih and Chi Yung-wu with Fukube Unokichi in the school critical of Mencius. Part One, 15.

49. For this question, see S. G. F. Brandon, 'The Myth and Ritual Position Critically Considered', *Myth, Ritual, and Kingship: Essays on the Theory and Practice of Kingship in the Ancient Near East and in Israel*, ed. S. H. Hooke (Oxford, 1958), 280.

50. Examples from pre-1949 period (official communist scholarship to be treated below):

(a) For ching-t'ien as 'primitive communism' or 'communal village society' or 'natural socialism' (the ching-t'ien age being characterized by small population, no economic exchange, no free competition, no capital, and an institution of landownership either tribal or village-based or non-existent; the ching-t'ien system being analogous in social organization and technical development with early 'Gemeineigentum' and systems of collectivist organization elsewhere; being established by the ontological necessity of something in the real historical past to account for Mencius' idea of it; and being undeserving of Hu Shih's sweeping scepticism), see, successively, Pang Li-shan, 'She-hui chu-i yü she-hui cheng-ts'e' (Socialism and social policy), *Tung-fang tsa-chih*, XXI, No. 16 (Aug. 25, 1924), 20; Ni Chin-sheng, 'Ching-t'ien hsin ch'eng pieh-lun' (Another discussion of new clarifications of ching-t'ien), *Shih-huo*, V, No. 5 (March 1, 1937), 22 and 25; Chang Hsiao-ming, *Chung-kuo li-tai ching-ti wen-t'i* (The land question in Chinese history) (Shanghai, 1932), 20–22 and 365; Chu Hsieh, 'Ching-t'ien chih-tu yu-wu wen-t'i chih ching-chi shih shang ti kuan-ch'a' (Examination from the standpoint of economic history of the question of the existence of the ching-t'ien system), *Tung-fang tsa-chih*, XXXI, No. 1 (Jan. 1, 1934), 187–90. Yü Ching-i, 'Ching-t'ien chih-tu hsin-k'ao' (New examination of the ching-t'ien system), *Tung-fang tsa-chih*, XXXI, No. 14 (July 16, 1934), 163–5, 168–72; Cheng Hsing-sung, 'Ching-t'ien k'ao' (Examination of ching-t'ien, part one, *Ching-chi hsüeh chi-k'an*, V, No. 2 (Aug. 1934), 58–59, 61; Hsü Chung-shu, 'Ching-t'ien chih-tu t'an-yüan' (An enquiry into the ching-t'ien system), *Chung-kuo wen-hua yen-chui hui-k'an* ('Bulletin of Chinese Studies'), IV, Part 1 (Sept. 1944), 153–4—these studies, like the ones which follow, often incapsulating other studies of the 1920's and later.

(b) For ching-t'ien as feudal or affiliated with feudalism (*kung-t'ien* being 'noble's field' not 'public field' as anachronistically later understood; the system idealized by Confucianists but with rough outlines of an actual feudal system behind it; a servile basis of land-cultivation—the peasantry being the lord's 'oxen and horses'—rather than an egalitarian or 'public-ownership' basis; ching-t'ien as possibly a fossil form of Shang communalism in a Chou feudal context; *Chou-li* suggesting manorial practice; Japanese affinities; 'mutual aid' as corvee), see summary of Li Chien-nung, *Chung-kuo ching-chi shih kao* (Draft economic history of China) in Lien-sheng Yang, 'Notes on Dr. Swann's "Food and Money in Ancient China",' *Studies in Chinese Institutional History* (Cambridge, Mass., 1961), 93–94; Niu Hsi, 'Tzu Shang chih Han-ch'u she-hui tsu-chih chih t'an-t'ao' (Inquiry into social organization from Shang to the beginning of Han), *Ch'ing-hua chou-k'an* ('Tsing Hua weekly'), XXXV, No. 2 (March 1921), 26–27; Liu Ta-tiao, 683; Chao Lin, 'Ching-t'ien chih-tu ti yen-chiu' (Investigation of the ching-t'ien system), *Shih ti ts'ung-k'an* (History and geography series), No. 1 (1933), 7–9, 17; Lü Chen-yü, 'Hsi-Chou shih-tai ti Chung-kuo she-hui' (Chinese society in the Western Chou period), *Chung-shan wen-hua chiao-yü kuan chi-k'an* ('Quarterly Review of the Sun Yat-sen Institute for Advancement of Culture and Education'), II, No. 1 (Spring, 1935), 120–6; Wang I-sun, 'Chung-kuo she-hui ching-chi shih shang chün-t'ien chih-tu ti yen-chiu' (Investigation of the *chün-t'ien* system in Chinese social and economic history), *Tung-fang tsa-chih*, XXXIII, No. 14 (July 16, 1936), 53–54; Kao Yün-hui, 12, 15–17; Hsü Hung-hsiao, 'Ch'in Han she-hui chih t'u-ti chih-tu yü nung-yeh sheng-ch'an' (Land systems and agricultural production in Ch'in and Han society), *Shih-huo*, III, No. 7 (March 1, 1936), 13; Ch'i Ssu-ho, 'Meng-tzu ching-t'ien shuo-pan' (Mencius' theory of shing-t'ien), *Yen-ching hsüeh-pao* ('Yen-ching Journal of Chinese Studies'), No. 35 (Dec. 1948), 107, 120–1, 127; Shao Chün-p'u, 'Ching-ti chih-tu k'ao' (On the *ching* land system), *Ling-nan hsüeh-pao* ('The Lingnan Journal'), IX, No. 2 (June 1949), 199–200. This last study, 200, and Wei Chü-hsien, 'Ching-t'ien ti ts'ai-liao' (The character of ching-t'ien), *Hsüeh-i* ('Wissen und Wissenschaft'), XIV, No. 4 (May 15, 1935), 17 are among the few to inject a note of historical geography into the essentially textual argument for the feudal origins of some actual ching-t'ien land arrangement; they note the present-day topographical character of certain villages, with their regular dimensions in diked fields and waterways—persisting, it is suggested, notwithstanding changes in the economics of land-tenure, from feudal antiquity.

51. Liao Chung-k'ai, 'Ta Hu Shih chih lun ching-t'ien shu' (In answer to Hu Shih's writings on ching-t'ien), *Liao Chung-k'ai chi* (A Liao Chung-k'ai collection) (Taiyuan, 192?), 87–93.

52. Harold J. E. Peake, 'Village Community', *Encyclopaedia of the Social Sciences* (New York, 1935), XV, 253–4.

53. *Ching-t'ien chih-tu yu-wu chih yen-chiu*, Appendix I, 103.

54. Chien Hu, ' "Ou-hua" ti Chung-kuo' ('Europeanized' China), *Tung-fang tsa-chih*, XX, No. 4 (Feb. 25, 1923), 1.

55. Liao Chung-k'ai, 'Chung-kuo shih-yeh ti hsien-chung chi ch'an-yeh lo-hou ti yüan-yin' (The present condition of Chinese industry and the root cause of backwardness in production), *Chung-kuo Kuo-min-tang shih-yeh chiang-yen* (Chinese Nationalist Party lectures on industry) (Shanghai, 1924), 54.

56. For this distinction between critic and exegete, see Arthur A. Cohen, *Martin Buber* (New York, 1957), 60; also, Bernard M. Casper, *An Introduction to Jewish Bible Commentary* (New York and London, 1960), 113.

57. Salo W. Baron and Joseph L. Blau, *Judaism: Postbiblical and Talmudic Period* (New York, 1954), 101–2.

58. Hu Han-min, 'San-min-chu-i chih jen-shih', 7.

59. E.g., Hsü Shih-ch'ang, *Ou-chan hou chih Chung-kuo: ching-chi yü chiao-yü* (China after the European War: economics and education) (Shanghai, 1920), 58–59; Hsü praised the 'Chinese national spirit', based on agriculture and education in *tao* and *te*, held tenaciously for thousands of years, incomparable in the world. He saw commerce and industry as 'captivating' but very thinly based; they were the rivals of agriculture, as 'practical education' was the rival alternative to cultivation of *tao* and *te*. But Europe's flourishing was just a matter of a recent century or two, while Chinese culture was early and rich. Hsü resented the vaunting of science and material efficiency against *tao-te*, and the slur on agriculture as a 'feudal' association. He only knew, he said, that the ancients revered virtue and laid stress on agriculture.

60. For reference to ching-t'ien as the 'golden age' land régime of the *san-tai*, founded by the Yellow Emperor, reconstituted by Yü the Great after the great flood, etc., see *ibid.*, 56; Tsou Chou-li, 'She-hui chu-i p'ing-i' (A balanced consideration of socialism), *Hsüeh-heng* ('The Critical Review'), No. 12 (Dec. 1922), 6; Teng Ch'u-min, 'Tu-ti kuo-yu wen-t'i' (The question of land nationali-zation), *Tung-fang tsa-chih*, XX, No. 19 (Oct. 10, 1923), 13–14; Hsiang Nai-ch'i, 'Tzu Ma-k'o-ssu nung-yeh li-lun chih fa-chan lun tao wo kuo t'u-ti wen-t'i' (A discussion of the land problem

in China from the standpoint of the development of Marxist theories on agriculture), *She-hui k'o-hsüeh chi-k'an* ('Social Sciences Quarterly'), V, Nos. 1–2 (Jan.–June 1930), 15.

One would be hard put to distinguish these accounts of the origins and nature of ching-t'ien from such a traditional account as that of Ch'ien T'ang (1735–90) in 'Kai-t'ing shu-ku lu', *Huang-Ch'ing ching-chieh* (1829), ts'e 195, ch. 718.1a. Cf. Ch'en Chao-k'un, 'Chung-kuo ku-tai t'ien-fu hsing-ko lun-lüeh' (An outline of land-tax innovation in ancient China), *She-hui k'o-hsüeh chi-k'an (new series)*, II, No. 2 (Summer 1943), 1–2, for a euhemerist identification of the Yellow Emperor's establishment of ching-t'ien (cited from the *T'ung-tien* of Tu Yu, 735–812), with the transition in Chinese history from successive hunting and pastoral stage to the agricultural stage, the latter having delimitation of land as its novel requirement.

61. Hsü Shih-ch'ang, 58; Tsou Cho-li, 1, 6, 10; Teng Ch'u-min, 16; Hsiang Nai-ch'i, 14–15.

62. Chiang Kai-shek, *'China's Destiny'* and *'Chinese Economic Theory'*, ed. Philip Jaffe (New York, 1947). The reference is from the latter work, published in 1943.

63. Yang P'ei-chi, *Yen Hsi-chai yü Li Shu-ku* (Yen Yüan and Li Kung) (Wuhan, 1956), 84–85.

64. Li Ting-fang, *Wang Mang* (Shanghai, 1957), 50, 2. Hu Shih published articles on 'China's socialist emperor' in 1922 and 1928.

65. Ho Hsiang-ning, *Hui-i Sun Chung-shan ho Liao Chung-k'ai* (Recollections of Sun Yat-sen and Liao Chung-k'ai) (Peking, 1957), 33. When she wrote this, Mme. Liao herself was near but not within—as Vice-chairman of one of the mainland minority parties, the 'Revolutionary Committee of the Kuomintang".

66. *Liao Chung-k'ai wen-chi* (Essays of Liao Chung-k'ai) (Canton, 1961). A companion volume, *Chu Chih-hsin wen-chi*, was published on the same occasion.

67. Liao Chung-k'ai, 'Nung-min yün-tung so tang chu-i chih yao-tien' (Important points which the peasant movement should take into account), in Cheng Wu, ed., *Tang kuo hsien-chin yen-lun chi* (Discourses of Kuomintang elders) (Changsha, 1938), 144.

68. One such was Li A-nung, *Chung-kuo ti nu-li chih yü feng-chien chih* (Slave régime and feudal régime in China) (Peking, 1954), 75.

69. Sun Li-hsing, 'P'i-p'an Hu Shih ti "Ching-t'ien pien" chi ch'i-t'a' (Criticism of Hu Shih's 'The ching-t'ien dispute', etc.),

Hu Shih ssu-hsiang p'i-p'an (Critique of Hu Shih's thought), VI (Peking, 1955), 160–4. Similarly, for an insistence that 'science' (i.e., precisely the 'objective laws of social development') demands rejection of the idea that ching-t'ien was simply a utopian vision of Mencius', see Kao Heng, 'Chou-tai ti-tsu chih-tu k'ao' (On the Chou land-tax system), *Chung-kuo ku-shih fen-ch'i wen-t'i lun-ts'ung*, 30.

70. For a description of Kuo Mo-jo as using arguments similar to Hu Shih's against the actual existence of ching-t'ien, with rich and seemingly convincing evidence from bronze inscriptions, showing among other things that land could be given away in the Chou period, see Wolfram Eberhard, 'Zur Landwirtschaft der Han-Zeit', *Mitteilungen des Seminars für Orientalische Sprachen zu Berlin*, XXXV, Part I (Ostasiatische Studien) (1932), 81.

71. Sun Li-hsing, 166–7.

72. The literature on this question is already enormous. Sun Li-hsing, 166–7, records the agreement of the great majority of scholars that some system of communal production on public land (and it seems to have come down to the alternatives of calling this ching-t'ien or something else of the same name) existed in Chinese antiquity. Kao Heng, 63–64, concludes that the Chou period was feudal, but (29) he deems a ching-t'ien system compatible with any of the possible definitions of pre-Ch'in society. However, two interpretations, by and large, have divided the field, (a) that this system was one of a village agricultural communal society, and (b) that it was a feudal manorial system. If (a), then Chou was a slave society (on the authority of B. K. Nikorsky's *History of Primitive Society*, which said that agricultural village communal society is the backwash of primitive society in the first class society, i.e., slave); if (b), then Chou was feudal.

Kuo Mo-jo, in *Nu-li Chih shih-tai* (The slave era) (Shanghai, 1952), 23, showed his conversion to acceptance of ching-t'ien by repeating as a statement of fact the famous *Shih-chi* description of the influence of Shang Yang, to the effect that in 350 B.C. Ch'in Hsiao-kung 'did away with ching-t'ien, opened public roads'. And in *Shih p'i-p'an shu* (Ten critiques) (Peking, 1954), 324, Kuo wrote that in Shang Yang's period Ch'in society was in a transitional phase from slave to feudal. Thus Kuo Mo-jo sees ching-t'ien ultimately in a context of slave society; see Jan Chao-te, 'Shih lun Shang Yang pien-fa ti hsing-chih' (On the nature of Shang Yang's reforms), *Li-shih yen-chiu* (Historical Research) [hereafter LSYC] (1957), No. 6, 44, and Lien-sheng Yang, 100–3. Hou

Wai-lu, likewise, in 'Lun Chung-kuo feng-chien chih ti hsing-cheng chi ch'i fa-tien hua' (On the form of the Chinese feudal régime and its legal development), LSYC (1956), No. 8, 24, called the Ch'in Hsiao-kung action against ching-t'ien (above) a 'shoot' of feudalism, thus relating it and Chou society to slavery.

Other writers, e.g., Fan Wen-lan, interpret Shang Yang (hence ching-t'ien as well) differently, seeing his day as transitional from one sort of feudalism to another; see Jan Chao-te, 43. Like Yang Hsiang-k'uei, 'Shih lun hsien-Ch'in shih-tai Ch'i-kuo ti ching-chi chih-tu' (Tentative discussion of the economic system of the pre-Ch'in state of Ch'i), *Chung-kuo ku-shih fen-ch'i wen-t'i lun-ts'ung*, 88, Wang Yü-che, 'Yu kuan Hsi-Chou she-hui hsing-chih ti chi-ke wen-t'i' (Some problems relating to the social character of the Western Chou dynasty), LSYC (1957), No. 5, 87–88, notes that the famous *kung-t'ien—ssu-t'ien*, 'public fields' and 'private fields' distinction of the *Shih-ching* and Mencius is a 'characteristic of the first phase of feudalism', hence should not be dismissed. However, he notes further (an old observation: see note 50 above) that *kung* in *Shih-ching* signifies not 'public' in the sense of belonging to the collectivity but only in the sense of belonging to the nobles, the governing class. Indeed, according to Ch'en Ming-lin, who was a slave-society theorist not on 'village-communal' grounds but on grounds of scepticism about servile land-tenure, *ssu-t'ien* as well as *kung-t'ien* was nobles' land. The *kung-t'ien* was distinguished by being, after the fall of Shang, royal domain retained by the ruling house during the process of infeudation; by extension of this principle of classification down through the system, progressively minor nobles' land was known as *kung-t'ien* when it was retained by the superior during the process of sub-infeudation. See Ch'en Ming-lin, 'Kuan-yü Hsi-Chou she-hui hsing-chih wen-t'i' (Questions relative to the character of Western Chou society), *Chung-kuo ku-shih fen-ch'i wen-t'i lun-ts'ung*, 208.

As is natural in a communist exposition, for which feudalism—whatever the permissible dispute about the date of its inception—must not be assumed to have been superseded until fairly recent times, there is no interpretation of this semantic problem here like that in Fung Yu-lan, *A History of Chinese Philosophy: the Period of the Philosophers (from the Beginnings to circa 100 B.C.,* tr. Derk Bodde (Peiping, 1937), 118–19 (first published in Chinese, Shanghai, 1931): Fung saw the original ching-t'ien system as contrived to benefit the noble class. Mencius, in a typically Confucian act of creation by transmission of traditional forms, converted it into an 'economic institution having socialistic implications', *kung* shifting in connotation from 'noble' to 'public'.

73. Ho Tzu-ch'üan, 'Kuan-yü Chung-kuo ku-tai she-hui ti chi-ko wen-t'i' (Some questions relating to ancient Chinese society), *Chung-kuo ku-shih fen-ch'i wen-t'i lun-ts'ung*, 135–6.

74. Sun Li-hsing, 162.

75. The reference is to the theory of despotic 'hydraulic society', supposed to apply to the bulk of Chinese history. This theory, which is anathema in Communist China, has been most elaborately worked out by Karl A. Wittfogel, in *Oriental Despotism: a Comparative Study of Total Power* (New Haven, 1957) and elsewhere.

CHAPTER III

1. 'Ssu-te-k'o-erh-mo ti shih-i tz'u kuo-chi li-shih hsüeh-chia ta-hui shang ti lun-cheng' (Discussion-war of the Eleventh International Congress of Historians at Stockholm), *Jen-min jih-pao* [hereafter JMJP] (Feb. 26, 1961), 5.

2. Pei-ching ta-hsüeh li-shih hsi, Chung-kuo ku-tai shih chiao-hen shih (Peking University history department, seminar on the teaching and study of the ancient history of China), '*Chung-kuo li-shih kang-yao* t'ao-lun hui chi-lu' (Minutes of the conference on *Essentials of Chinese history*), LSYC (1957), No. 4, 43–77.

3. Mao Tse-tung, *Chung-kuo ko-ming yü Chung-kuo kung-ch'an-tang* (The Chinese revolution and the Chinese Communist Party) (Hong Kong, 1949); see especially Hou Wai-lu, *Chung-kuo tsao-ch'i ch'i-meng ssu-hsiang shih* (History of the early modern Chinese enlightment) (Peking, 1956), with its title employing explicitly, significantly, the current Chinese term for the French intellectuals' eighteenth century. For the complexities of this issue, see Albert Feuerwerker, 'Chinese History in Marxian Dress', *American Historical Review*, LXVI, No. 2 (Jan. 1961), 327–30.

4. Chung-shan ta-hsüeh li-shih hsi (History department of Sun Yat-sen University), 'Tui Fan Wen-lan *Chung-kuo t'ung-shih* chien-pien hsiu-ting pen ti-i-pien ti i-chien' (Opinions on the first edition of Fan Wen-lan's simplified and revised *General History of China*), LSYC (1955), No. 1, 111–14. See also critiques of Fan's work by Wu Ta-k'un, Chao Kuang-hsien, and Wang Yü-che in LSYC (1954), No. 6, 45–71.

5. A Doak Barnett, *Communist China and Asia: Challenge to American Policy* (New York, 1960), 30.

6. Chien Po-tsan, 'Kuan-yü liang-Han ti kuan-ssu nu-pi wen-t'i' (Concerning the question of public and private slaves during the two Han), LSYC (1954), No. 4, 1; Wang Ssu-chih, Tu Wen-k'ai, and Wang Ju-feng, 'Kuan-yü liang-Han she-hui hsing-chih wen-t'i ti t'an-t'ao—chien-p'ing Chien Po-tsan hsien-sheng ti "Kuan-yü liang-Han ti kuan-ssu nu-pi wen-t'i" ' (An inquiry concerning the question of the nature of society in the two Han—a joint critique of Mr. Chien Po-tsan's 'Concerning the question of public and private slaves during the two Han'), LSYC (1955), No. 1, 19–46.

7. Hsü Chung-shu, 'Lun Hsi-Chou shih feng-chien-chih she-hui—Chien-lun Yin-tai she-hui hsing-chih' (On the Western Chou's being a feudal society—together with a discussion of the nature of the society of the Yin dynasty), LSYC (1957), No. 5, 55; Wang Ssu-chih, et al., and the reply of Yang Wei-li and Wei Chün-ti, 'Han-tai shih nu-li she-hui hai-shih feng-chien she-hui?' (Was the Han dynasty a slave society or a feudal society?), LSYC (1956), No. 2, 31–49.

8. Liang Sou-ming, 'Changes I have Undergone in the Past Two Years', tr. from *Kuang-ming jih-pao* [hereafter KMJP] (Nov. 2, 1951); 'Reply to Some of My Critics', tr. from KMJP, Jan. 10, 1952, in 'The Case of Liang Shu-ming', *Current Background*, No. 185 (Hong Kong: American Consulate-General), June 16, 1952.

9. See, for instance, articles on Liang by Liu Ta-nien, LSYC (1955), No. 5, 1–27; and Hou Wai-lu, LSYC (1956), No. 1, 6–29.

10. E.g., Yang P'ei-chih, 80. Mao's essay, which Yang quotes verbatim and without acknowledgement (thus confirming its status as revealed truth, not just the opinion of an authority), is 'The Chinese Revolution and the Chinese Communist Party' (see note 2 above).

11. Fan Wen-lan, 'Shih-lun Chung-kuo tzu Ch'in-Han shih ch'eng-wei t'ung-i kuo-chia ti yüan-yin' (A tentative exposition of the reasons for China's having become a unified state from the Ch'in-Han period), LSYC (1954), No. 3, 15.

12. Yang K'uan, *Shang Yang pien-fa* (The reforms of Shang Yang) (Shanghai, 1955), 63.

13. Hou Wai-lu, *Chung-kuo ku-tai she-hui shih lun* (Discussion of the history of ancient Chinese society) (Peking, 1955), 63.

14. Fan, 19–21.

15. Lü Chen-yü, *Shih-hsüeh yen-chiu lun-wen chi* (Collection of essays on historical research) (Shanghai, 1954), 107.

16. Cf. *Chung-kuo chin-tai-shih fen-ch'i wen-t'i t'ao-lun chi* (A collection of discussions of the question of periodization in modern Chinese history) (Peking, 1957), *Li-shih yen-chiu* essays from 1954 to 1957.

17. Kuo Mo-jo, 'K'ai-chan li-shih yen-chiu ying-chieh wen-hua chien-she kao-hu' (Develop historical research to meet the high tide of cultural reconstruction), LSYC (1954), No. 1, 3.

18. See Volume One, 141.

19. Jaroslav Prusek, 'The Importance of Tradition in Chinese Literature', *Archiv Orientalni*, XXVI, No. 2 (1958), 218-19.

20. Patricia Guillermaz, *La poésie chinoise contemporaine* (Paris, 1962), 15.

21. Shao Hsün-cheng, 'Hsin-hai ko-ming ch'ien wu-shih-nien chien wai-kuo ch'in-lüeh-che ho Chung-kuo mai-pan-hua chün-fa kuan-liao shih-li ti kuan-hsi' (The relationship between foreign aggressors and China's "comprador-ized" warlord and bureaucratic forces during the fifty years before the revolution of 1911), LSYC (1954), No. 4, 53. See also Hu Sheng, 'Chung-kuo chin-tai li-shih te fen-ch'i wen-t'i (The problem of periodization in contemporary Chinese history), LSYC (1954), No. 1, 110, and Kuo Mo-jo, 'K'ai-chan li-shih yen-chiu', 2, for rapprochement in the latter part of the nineteenth century between 'capitalist aggressors' from the outside and domestic feudal forces.

22. Ting Yüan-ying, 'I-chiu-i-ling nien Ch'ang-sha ch'ün-chung ti "ch'iang-mi" feng-ch'ao' (The 'rice-plunder' uprising of the masses at Changsha in 1910), China Academy of Science, Historical Research Section, Third Section, *Collection 1* (1954), 198.

23. Li Shih-yüeh, *Hsin-hai ko-ming shih-ch'i liang-Hu ti-ch'ü ti ko-ming yün-tung* (Revolutionary movements in the Hupei-Hunan area during the period of the *hsin-hai* revolution) (Peking, 1957), 29. Li, after running through the primer about primitive, slave, feudal, and 'shoots of capitalism', all developing in China *independently*, emphasizes Mao's dictum about imperialism interfering with the inevitable dissolution of feudalism. See 4 et seq.

24. Feuerwerker, 325-6.

25. Hsia Nai, 'Shih nien lai ti Chung-kuo k'ao-ku hsin fa-hsien' (New discoveries in Chinese archaeology in the last ten years), KMJP (Oct. 15, 1959), 3.

26. Chang Shun-hui, *Chung-kuo shih lun-wen chi* (Collected essays on Chinese history) (Wuhan, 1956), 163-4.

27. See, for instance, Jen Chi-yü, 'Chung-kuo ku-tai i-hsüeh

ho che-hsüeh ti kuan-hsi' (The relation between medical studies and philosophical studies in ancient China), LSYC (1956), No. 5, 59-74; *Hsin Hua pen-yüeh-k'an* (New China Fortnightly), No. 145 (Dec. 1958), 106-7; Ling Yang, 'Integrating Chinese and Western Medicine', *Peking Review*, No. 43 (Dec. 23, 1958), 21-23; Gerald Clark, *Impatient Giant: Red China Today* (New York, 1959), 130; Leo A. Orleans, *Professional Manpower and Education in Communist China* (Washington, 1961), 137; *Communist China Digest*, No. 26 (Oct. 18, 1960), 92-93; *Survey of China Mainland Press*, No. 2475 (April 13, 1961), 18.

A different line is taken in Pa Chin and others, *A Battle for Life: a full record of how the life of steel worker, Chiu Tsai-kang, was saved in the Shanghai Kwangtze Hospital* (Peking, 1959), foreword, 6. Here, western medicine is 'bourgeois', and its authority is to be shaken by a popular Chinese medicine which is socialist, mass co-operative, rather than a fund of inherited lore.

28. Chi Chen-huai, *Ssu-ma Ch'ien* (Shanghai, 1955), 128. See also Hou Wai-lu, 'Ssuma Chien: Great Ancient Historian', *People's China*, No. 12 (June 16, 1956), 36-40, and Cheng Ch'üan-chung, *Shih-chi hsüan-chiang* (Selected comments on the *Shih-chi*) (Peking, 1959), 10-11.

29. Ch'en Ch'ien-shün, 'Lun *Tzu-chih t'ung-chien*' (On the *Tzu-chih t'ung-chien*), LSYC (1957), No. 7, 40.

30. Sung Yün-pin, *K'ang Yu-wei* (Peking, 1955).

31. Ch'en Po-ta, *Ch'ieh-kuo ta-tao Yüan Shih-k'ai* (re-published Peking, 1954).

32. Ch'i Ssu-ho, et al., ed., *Ya-p'ien chan-cheng* (The opium war) (Shanghai, 1954); Shao Hsün-cheng, et al., ed., *Chung-Jih chan-cheng* (The Sino-Japanese War) (Shanghai, 1956).

33. Li Chu-jan, *Hsin-hai ko-ming ch'ien ti ch'ün-chung tou-cheng* (Peking, 1957).

34. Ch'i Ssu-ho, 'P'i-p'an Hu Shih-p'ai tui-yü shih-chieh shih ti fan-tung wei-hsin kuan-tien' (A criticism of the Hu Shih clique's reactionary idealist point of view toward world history), LSYC (1956), No. 6, 23-41.

35. T'ang Chia-hung, 'Ssu-ch'uan ta-hsüeh li-shih hsi ti chiao-hsüeh ho yen-chiu kung-tso' (The instruction and research work of the history department of Szechwan University), LSYC (1956), No. 2, 50.

36. Donald S. Zagoria, 'Khrushchev's Attack on Albania and Sino-Soviet Relations', *The China Quarterly*, No. 8 (Oct.-Dec. 1961), 4.

CHAPTER IV

1. Cf. Holmes Welch, 'Buddhism under the Communists', *The China Quarterly*, No. 6 (April–June, 1961), 1–14.

2. Lo Ken-tse, *Chung-kuo wen-hsüeh p'i-p'ing shih* (History of Chinese literary criticism) (Shanghai, 1957), 39, 48–49.

3. Chow Tse-tsung, *The May Fourth Movement: Intellectual Revolution in Modern China* (Cambridge, Mass., 1960), 284–7, 309–10.

4. Kuo Mo-jo, 'Kuan-yü "hou-chin po-ku" wen-t'i' (On the 'broaden the new, narrow the old' question), JMJP (June 11, 1958), 7. For the 'pressure of the present on all Chinese historiography' see Albert Feuerwerker and S. Cheng, *Chinese Communist Studies of Modern Chinese History* (Cambridge, Mass., 1961), 4.

5. *Daily Report: Foreign Radio Broadcasts*, No. 248 (Dec. 22, 1960), BBB, 10–11.

6. CCS report (July 1961).

7. *Weekly Report on Communist China*, No. 28 (June 3, 1960), 26.

8. Orleans, 18.

9. For description and analysis of the use of Classics as sources in communist periodization of history, see (together with Chapters Two and Three above) Feuerwerker, 336–40, and Feuerwerker and Cheng, 2–9, 21–26, 209–13.

10. Kuo Mo-jo, 'Kuan-yü nu-ch'ien li-shih yen-chiu chung ti chi-ke wen-t'i' (Several problems concerning present-day historical research), *Hsin chien-she* (April, 1959), 5.

11. Wang Chih-chiu and Sung Kuo-chu, *Chung-hsüeh li-shih chiao-shih shou-ts'e* (Handbook for history teachers in middle schools) (Shanghai, 1958), 56.

12. As noted, with context of 'primitive communism' in Feng Yu-lan, 'K'ang Yu-wei ti ssu-hsiang' (The thought of K'ang Yu-wei), in *Chung-kuo chin-tai ssu-hsiang shih lun-wen chi* (Collection of essays on modern Chinese intellectual history) (Shanghai, 1958), 120.

13. *Chung-kuo ta-t'ung ssu-hsiang tzu-liao* (Materials in Chinese utopian thought), ed. Chinese Academy of Sciences, philosophical research department, history of Chinese philosophy section (Peking, 1959), 1. For an endorsement of this position, see Ku Ti, 'K'ung-tzu ho "ta-t'ung" ssu-hsiang' (Confucius and utopian thought), KMJP (May 24, 1961), 2.

14. Ku Ti, 2, referring to Jen Chüan, 'K'ung-tzu Li-yün "ta-t'ung" ssu-hsiang' (Confucius' *Li-yün* utopian thought),

KMJP (May 12, 1961), 4. Ku Ti maintained that Confucius was unconnected with *ta-t'ung* ('Great Harmony') utopianism. His article insisted that in the *Lun-yü* (Analects), in large part a reliable source for Confucius' thought, there is no shred of *ta-t'ung* doctrine; and Ku Ti declined to accept the two *Lun-yü* extracts in the Academy of Science volume (note 13) as specimens of *ta-t'ung*, on the ground that the *Lun-yü* has non-utopian class-distinction (viz., between *jen* and *min*) built into it.

15. Jen Chüan, 4.

16. Chung Chao-p'eng, 'Ts'ung *jen* ho *li* k'an K'ung-tzu ssu-hsiang ti chieh-chi hsing' (From *jen* and *li*, to look at the class nature of Confucius' thought), KMJP (Dec. 12, 1961), 3; Liu Tse-hua, 'Shih-lun K'ung-tzu ti fu-min ssu-hsiang' (Consideration of Confucius' thought on enriching the people), KMJP (June 22, 1962), 4.

17. Wang Ming, '*I-ching* ho *I-chuan* ti ssu-hsiang t'i-hsi wen-t'i' (The problem of *I-ching* and *I-chuan* systems of thought), KMJP (June 23, 1961), 4.

18. Kuan Feng and Ling Yü-shih, 'Lun K'ung-tzu ti "jen" ho "li" ' (A discourse on Confucius' *jen* and *li*), JMJP (July 23, 1961), 5; for *jen* as humanistic base of *li*, liberating thought from an original superstitious theology, see also Chi Wen-fu, *Ch'un-ch'iu Chan-kuo ssu-hsiang shih-hua* (Historical discourses on the thought of the 'Spring and Autumn' and 'Warring States' periods) (Peking, 1958), 20–22, and 'Chung-nan ti-ch'ü shih-hsüeh-chieh tsai Kuang-chou chü-hsing hsüeh-shu t'ao-lun-hui' (The historical society of the Chung-nan region holds a scholarly discussion meeting in Canton), KMJP (May 19, 1961), 2.

19. Chu Ch'ien-chih, 'Shih-ch'i-pa shih-chi hsi-fang che-hsüeh-chia ti K'ung-tzu kuan (Western philosophers' views on Confucius during the seventeenth and eighteenth centuries), JMJP (March 9, 1962), 5.

20. Chang Tai-nien, *Chung-kuo wei-wu-chu-i ssu-hsiang chien-shih* (A brief history of Chinese materialist thought) (Peking, 1957), 22; Li Shou-yung, 'Kuan-yü K'ung-tzu ti "chün" ti ching-chi ssu-hsiang ti t'an-t'ao' (An enquiry into Confucius' economic thought on 'equalization'), KMJP (March 12, 1962), 4; Liu Tse-hua, 4.

21. Chang Tai-nien, 20. For a more cautious discussion, locating Confucius between materialism and idealism, since he professed neither belief nor disbelief in 'Heaven's decree' or 'spirits', cf. Kuo Shao-yü, *Chung-kuo ku-tien wen-hsüeh li-lun p'i-p'ing*

shih (A critical history of classical Chinese literary doctrines) (Peking, 1959), 28.

22. Jen-min wen-hsüeh ch'u-pan she pien-chi-pu, ed., *Shih-ching yen-chiu lun-wen chi* (Collection of research papers on the *Shih-ching*) (Peking, 1959), 1; Yu Kuan-ying, 'China's Earliest Anthology of Poetry', *Chinese Literature*, 1962, No. 3, 109, 111. Cf. Kuo Shao-yü, 16, for Confucius recognizing the *Shih-ching's* realism.

23. 'T'an-t'ao Chia I ssu-hsiang ho *Hsin-shu* chen-wei wen-t'i' (An inquiry into Chia I's thought and the question of the authenticity of the *Hsin-shu*), JMJP (Oct. 5, 1961), 7.

24. Chou Yü-t'ung and T'ang Chih-chün, 'Wang Mang kai-chih yü ching-hsüeh chung ti chin-ku-wen hsüeh wen-t'i' (Wang Mang's reform and the problem of modern and ancient texts in classical scholarship, KMJP (May 16, 1961), 2; Chou Yü-t'ung and T'ang Chih-chün, 'T'an-t'ao Chung-kuo ching-hsüeh wen-t'i' (An inquiry into the problem of Chinese classical scholarship), JMJP (May 31, 1961), 7.

25. Hsü Lun, *Shen-mo shih feng-chien she hui?* (What is feudal society?) (Shanghai, 1954), 69.

26. *Meng-tzu i-chu* (*Mencius*: translation and commentary), ed., Lanchow University Department of Chinese Literature, Mencius-annotation sub-section (Peking, 1960), 13; and similarly, 'Chung-kuo Jen-min Ta-hsüeh che-hsüeh-hsi t'ao-lun Meng-tzu p'ing-chiai wen-t'i' (The Philosophy Department of the Chinese People's University discusses the problem of evaluating Mencius), KMJP (July 28, 1961), 1. Cf. the call for a scientific study, through Marxism-Leninism, of intellectual history from Confucius to Sun Yat-sen, in 'Hou Wai-lu t'an ju-ho tui-tai Chung-kuo che-hsüeh-shih i-ch'an' (A talk by Hou Wai-lu on how to treat the heritage of the history of Chinese philosophy), KMJP (May 6, 1961), 1.

27. For this reference and others in this paragraph and the next, see Shu Shih-cheng, 'K'ung-tzu *Ch'un-ch'iu*' (Confucius' *Spring and Autumn*), LSYC (1962), No. 1, 47–50, 55, 57.

28. T'ai Shih-chien, 'Wen yü tao' (*Wen* and *tao*), JMJP (Jan. 21, 1962), 5.

29. S. H. Chen, 'Multiplicity in Uniformity; Poetry and the Great Leap Forward', *The China Quarterly*, No. 3 (July–Sept. 1960), 5.

30. Examples: For Confucius (a) loving the old, specifically to inculcate conservatism, cf. Chu Tung-jun, ed., *Tso-chuan hsüan*

(Selections from the *Tso-chuan*) (Shanghai, 1956), 8. (b) On the side of a declining class of masters of slaves, or a tool (with Classics) of reactionary feudal class against the people, cf. 'Chung-nan ti-ch'u shih-hsüeh-chieh . . .' (note 18 above), 2; 'Of Confucius, Fung Yu-lan and Others', *China News Analysis*, No. 398 (Nov. 24, 1961), 3, 5, 7; *Communist China Digest*, No. 17 (June 6, 1960), 83; Jen Chi-yü, 'Ho Ch'i Hu Li-yüan ti kai-liang chu-i ssu-hsiang' (The reformist thought of Ho Ch'i and Hu Li-yüan), *Chung-kuo chin-tai ssu-hsiang shih lun-wen chi* (Collected essays on the history of modern Chinese thought) (Shanghai, 1958), 86. (c) As an idealist and a religionist, fostering anti-materialist, anti-scientific thought, unholding traditional supersition through the doctrine of the 'Will of Heaven', with its implication that the fate of society is determined from outside society, cf. Ch'en Po-ta, 'P'i-p'an ti chi-ch'eng ho hsin ti t'an so' (A critical inquiry into heritage and novelty), *Hung-ch'i* (Red Flag), No. 13 (1959), 44; Kuo Shao-yü, 19; Kuan Feng and Lin Yü-shih, 'Lun K'ung-tzu' (On Confucius), *Che-hsüeh yen-chiu* (Philosophical Research), IV (July 25, 1961), 54–56 (some points in this article and others in similar vein summarized in 'Of Confucius, Fung Yu-lan and Others'), 5; Feng Yuan-chun, *A Short History of Classical Chinese Literature* (Peking, 1958), 39; A. A. Petrov (Li Shih, tr.), *Wang Ch'ung— Chung-kuo ku-tai ti wei-wu-chu-i che ho ch'i-meng ssu-hsiang-chia* (Wang Ch'ung—an ancient Chinese materialist and enlightened thinker) (Peking, 1956), iii, 73–75. (d) As a reformist, basically conservative, seeking to harmonize class contradictions and prevent the rising of the poor against the governming class, cf. Ho-nan Ta-hsüeh li-shih-hsi, ed., *Chung-kuo t'ung-shih tzu-liao hsüan-chi* (Compilation of materials for a general history of China) (Kaifeng, 1953), 40; Kuan Feng and Lin Yü-shih, 'Lun K'ung-tzu', 46–47; Kuan Feng and Lin Yü-shih, 'Lun K'ung-tzu ti "jen" ho "li" ', 5.

It is significant that in many of these references (e.g., the last, with which compare purport of note 18), criticism of Confucius is combined with respect: both idealist *and* materialist elements, conservative *and* progressive, etc., are often noted. Cf. 'Review of Reviews', *China New Analysis*, No. 410 (March 2, 1962), 3, for summary of yet another article on Confucius and *jen* and *li*, with Confucius being granted at least a relative merit while at the same time his limitations (as a member of the dominant class) are noted; and 'Hsü Chung-shu lun K'ung-tzu cheng-chih ssu-hsiang' (Hsü Chung-shu discusses Confucius' political thought), KMJP (Dec. 13, 1961), 1, where Confucius, dependent like his disciples (none of them peasants) on the nobility, yet has a progressive side, while he basically tries to sustain the feudal *chün-ch'en* class system and the Western Chou *tsung-fa* organization of lineage.

31. Chi Wen-fu, 16–17. Cf. also Tu Shou-su, *Hsien-Ch'in chu tzu ssu-hsiang* (The thought of the pre-Ch'in philosophers (n.p., n.d.), 6, and Chang Tai-nien, 20, for Confucius as more than the progenitor of the *Ju* school—as the first spokesman for open, public instruction in the history of Chinese education. For an account of others' emphasis on Confucius as a pioneer non-discriminatory educator, characterized by the spirit of study and eagerness for knowledge, cf. 'Of Confucius, Fung Yu-lan and Others', 2–3; and for a more grudging respect for Confucius as mildly progressive in his own day, an opinion clinched by reference to his disciples 'propagating knowledge', cf. Feng Yuan-chun, 26–27.

32. Huang Sung-k'ang, *Lu Hsün and the New Culture Movement of Modern China* (Amsterdam, 1957), 10; Chang Chün-yen, 'Li Ta-shao yü hsin wen-hua yün-tung' (Li Ta-chao and the new-culture movement), LSYC (1959), No. 8, 3–4; Mary Clabaugh Wright, *The Last Stand of Chinese Conservatism: the Tung-chih Restoration, 1862–1874* (Stanford, 1957), 304; 'Lu Ti-p'ing yen-shuo tz'ü' (Speech by Lu Ti-p'ing), *Shih-chieh shu-kuang chih Chung-hua wen-hua* (Chinese culture, the world's dawning light) (Changsha, 1928), 99.

33. Chiao-yü pu, ed., *Ti-erh-tz'u Chung-kuo chiao-yü nien-chien* (The second Chinese educational yearbook) (Shanghai, 1948), 205–6, 209; Hsiao Kung-ch'üan, 101.

34. *Ibid.*, 5, 8, 12, 355.

35. Cf. *Shih-chieh jih-pao* (The Chinese World), San Francisco (April 14, 1962), 1, for Chiang Kai-shek blessing a commorative effort of the 'Confucius-Mencius Society' and urging everyone to study the Sages, restore the Chinese ethic, and thereby sweep the communists aside.

36. Wu Yü-chang, *Chung-kuo li-shih chiao-ch'eng hsü-lun* (Introduction to the teaching pattern for Chinese history) (Shanghai, 1950), 1 (preface), 8. For another suggestion, from the outside, of an appropriate link between the pro-Confucian and anti-national causes (or the anti-Confucian and anti-fascist), cf. Ezra Pound, *Impact: Essays on Ignorance and the decline of American Civilization* (Chicago, 1960), 139; 'Lady Hosie's introduction in a recent reprint tells us that the Four Classics have been relegated

to University study and are no longer the main preoccupation of Chinese schools. She dates the essay 1937, which year brought the natural consequence of unusual idiocy in the form of Japanese invasion. If China had got to this point, naturally there would be an invasion, and quite naturally some Chinese would, as they do, hold the view that such an invasion is to be welcomed.'

37. Nakayama Hisashirō, 'Manshūkoku to Kōshikyō no shin shimei' (Manchukuo and the new mission of Confucianism), *Shibun*, XV, No. 8 (Aug. 1933), 1–12.

38. *Chinese Literature* (1958), No. 1, 162.

39. For reference to Mao and Lenin on these 'two cultures', cf. Miu Yüeh, 'Chiang-shou Chung-kuo li-shih tui-yü wen-hua pu-fen ju-ho ch'u-li' (How to handle the cultural portions in lecturing on Chinese history), KMJP (May 30, 1961), 2–3.

40. Alexander Dru, ed., *The Letters of Jacob Burckhardt* (New York, 1955), 24.

41. Frank Rede Fowke, *The Bayeux Tapestry: a History and Description* (London, 1913), 6–7.

42. For examples, see *Communist China Digest*, No. 8 (Jan. 15, 1960), 15, and No. 20 (July 26, 1960), 8; *Survey of China Mainland Press*, No. 2471 (April 7, 1961), 16, and No. 2483 (April 26, 1961), 14–15; *Glimpses of China* (Peking, 1958); *Guide to Hangchow* (n.p., n.d.); and below, note 53. Cf. Lu Hsün, inveighing in 1932 against the canards of 'imperialists and their lackeys'—'No libraries or museums have been blown up in Leningrad or Moscow': 'We Can No Longer Be Duped', *Selected Works of Lu Hsun*, III (Peking, 1959), 153.

43. 'Of Confucius, Fung Yu-lan and Others', 2.

44. *Ibid.*, 5.

45. Wang Shih, *Yen Fu chuan* (Biography of Yen Fu) (Shanghai, 1957), 96.

46. 'Ho-nan shih-hsüeh-chieh t'ao-lun Hung Hsiu-ch'üan ti ssu-hsiang yü Ju-chia ti kuan-hsi wen-t'i' (The Historical Society of Honan discusses the thought of Hung Hsiu-ch'üan and the problem of its relationship to Confucianism), KMJP (June 1, 1961), 1.

47. Ni Xaishu (Ni Hai-shu), *'Lunjy' Syanji* ('Lun-yü' hsüan-i) (Selected translation from the *Lun-yü*) (Shanghai, 1954), 1–2.

48. Ch'en Po-ta, 37. For Mao's remarks, cf. 'The Role of the Chinese Communist Party in the National War', *Selected Works of Mao Tse-tung* (London, 1954), II, 259–60. For another reference to Mao in this vein ('learn from the people—and learn from the

ancients'), cf. Tang Su-shih, 'A Brief Discussion on Comrade Mao Tse-tung's Contribution to Marxist Literary Style', translated in *Communist China Digest*, No. 17 (June 6, 1960), 84–85.

49. Ch'en Po-ta, 37–38.

50. Hua Hsia, 'The Paintings of Shih Lu', *Chinese Literature* (Jan. 1962), 96.

51. Ku Chieh-kang, *Ch'in Han ti Fang-shih yü Ju-sheng* (Taoist, and Confucianists of the Ch'in and Han Periods) (Shanghais 1955), 15.

52. Li Shu, 'Mao Tse-tung t'ung-chih ti "Kai-tsao wo-men ti hsüeh-hsi" ho Chung-kuo li-shih k'o-hsüeh' (Comrade Mao Tse-tung's 'Reform our learning' and Chinese historical science), JMJP (June 8, 1961), 7.

53. Joseph Needham, 'An Archaeological Study-tour in China, 1958', *Antiquity*, XXXIII, No. 130 (June 1959), 116–17.

54. JMJP (April 8, 1962), 2; *Hua-chiao jih-pao* (China Daily News), New York (April 16, 1962), 1; *Shih-chieh jih-pao* (April 24, 1962), 1. The latter account cites Hong Kong speculation to the effect that, with a shortage of seeds for spring plowing, Mao prefers to divert attention to the Confucian associations of spring. (This does not seem to be a very powerful analysis.)

55. Ch'en Huan-chang, *K'ung-chiao lun* (On the Confucian religion) (Shanghai, 1912), 27.

56. Cf. *Glimpses of China*: 'Confucius (551–469 B.C.) was a famous thinker of ancient China. His teachings held sway in feudal society. Temples dedicated to him were built in various places. The one in Chufu, his native town, is the largest and houses a large number of precious cultural objects and relics.'

57. For impressions of this neglect of monuments, see K. M. Panikkar, *In Two Chinas: Memoirs of a Diplomat* (London, 1955), 34, 99–100.

58. Cyril Birch, 'Lao She: the Humourist in his Humour', *The China Quarterly*, No. 8 (Oct.–Dec. 1961), 48–49. Cf. the considerable leakage from the Imperial Palace collection in the early years of the Republic, when the ex-emperor P'u-i was left in possession (until 1924); Na Chih-liang, *Ku-kung po-wu-yüan san-shih nien chih ching-kuo* (Thirty years of the Palace Museum) (Hong Kong, 1957), 2.

59. *Chung-kuo nung-ts'un ti she-hui chu-i kao-ch'ao* (The high tide of socialism in the Chinese village) (Peking, 1956), 475.

60. Roderick MacFarquhar, *The Hundred Flowers Campaign and the Chinese Intellectuals* (New York, 1960), 90.

61. Cf. Franklin W. Houn, *To Change a Nation: Propaganda and Indoctrination in Communist China* (Glencoe, Ill: Free Press, 1961), 7.

62. Mary C. Wright, 'The Pre-Revolutionary Intellectuals of China and Russia', *The China Quarterly*, No. 6 (April–June 1961), 179.

CHAPTER V

1. Fukui, 115.

2. Friedrich Nietzsche, *The Use and Abuse of History* (New York, 1957), 45.

3. Cf. Isaiah Berlin, 'History and Theory: the Concept of Scientific History', *History and Theory*, I, No. 1 (1960): 'This kind of imaginative projection of ourselves into the past, the attempt to capture concepts and categories not altogether like ours by means of concepts and categories that cannot but be our own, is a task that we can never be sure that we are even beginning to achieve, yet are not permitted to abjure . . . and nothing counts as an historical interpretation unless it attempts to answer the question of how the world must have looked to individuals or societies if their acts and words are to be taken as the acts and words of human beings neither wholly like ourselves nor so different as not to fit into our common past.'

4. Lewis S. Feuer, 'Marxism as History', *Survey*, No. 41 (April, 1962), 182.

5. Friedrich Engels, *Herrn Eugen Dührings Umwälzung der Wissenschaft* (Berlin, 1954), 221.

6. *Ibid.*, 221. Cf. Lü Chen-yü, *Shin-hsüeh yen-chui lun-wen chi*, 108, for Mao on the cause of the very slow emergence of China from the feudal stage. Mao speaks moralistically of the extreme cruelty of the landlords, which deepened peasants' poverty and robbed their strength, so that productive forces were hindered. Here again we have the equation: the less perception of process, the less moral relativism.

7. See Liang Ch'i-ch'ao, 'Tai Tung-yuan sheng-jih erh-pai nien chi-nien hui yüan-ch'i' (The origins of the conference to commemorate the two hundredth anniversary of the birth of Tai Chen), *Yin-ping-shih ho-chi, wen-chi*, 14: 40.38–40.

8. See Lu Hsun, 'Some Thoughts on Our New Literature', *Selected Works*, III, 153; Harriet C. Mills, 'Lu Hsün and the Communist Party', *The China Quarterly*, No. 4 (Oct.–Dec. 1960), 24; Lu Hsün, 'A Madman's Diary', *Selected Works*, I (Peking, 1957), 8–21.

9. Nietzsche, 17.

10. Lu Hsun, 'Random Thoughts (47)', *Selected Works*, II, (Peking, 1957), 47.

11. Lu Hsun, 'Sudden Notions (6)', *Selected Works*, II, 112–23.

12. Lu Hsün, 'Tui-yü "Hsin Ch'ao" i-pu-fen ti i-chien' (A fragmentary opinion on *Hsin Ch'ao*), *Lu Hsün san-shih-nien chi* (Thirty years' collected works of Lu Hsün) (n.p., 1947), III, 28; Lu Hsun, 'Experience', *Selected Works*, III, 271; Lu Hsun, 'Random Thoughts (49)', *Selected Works*, II, 42.

13. Cf. Huang, 121, for Lu Hsün in 1927 (after Chiang Kai-shek's rightist coup), renouncing his old denunciations of the old and his appeals to 'save the children'; for it seemed now that those who killed the young were mostly also the young.

14. C. P. Fitzgerald, *Flood Tide in China* (London, 1958), 20–21.

15. For surprise at this development, see Suzanne Labin, *The Anthill: the Human Condition in Communist China* (New York, 1960), 113.

16. 'Popular Beliefs—Taoism—Christianity', *China News Analysis*, No. 439 (Sept. 28, 1962), 4–5.

17. Ku Chieh-kang, *Ku shih pien* (Symposium on ancient history), Vol. III (Shanghai, 1931), 5. Cf. the perceptive reaction of the Orthodox Rabbi Samson Raphael Hirsch to the 'Wissenschaft des Judentums' in nineteenth-century Germany: 'In fact this learning does not want the practicing Jew . . .' because of its 'separation of science from faith and life . . .'; Louis Jacobs, *Jewish Values* (London, 1960), 29.

18. Gerhard Masur, 'Distinctive Traits of Western Civilization: Through the Eyes of Western Historians', *American Historical Review*, LXVII, No. 3 (April, 1962), 600.

19. *Ibid.*, 596.

20. Erich Auerbach, 'Vico and Aesthetic Historism', *Scenes from the Drama of European Literature* (New York, 1959), 185.

CONCLUSION

1. Fujiwara Sadame, 'Seimatsu shisō no kōryū', (Late Ch'ing intellectual currents), *Kindai Shina shisō* (Modern Chinese thought), ed. Sanetō Keishu (Tokyo, 1942), 77.

2. Chow, 242.

3. Cf. the promise and prophecy of August 1958, that the state would be limited in function to protecting the country from

external aggression, and that it would play no role internally; Barnett, 26.

4. Paul A. Varg, *Missionaries, Chinese, and Diplomats: the American Protestant Missionary Movement in China, 1890–1952* (Princeton, 1958), 38.

5. Cf. Kurt W. Marek, *Yestermorrow: Notes on Man's Progress* (New York, 1961), 85, for the opinion, *contra* museums of modern art, that the original and only proper function of the museum is to store the testimony of the past.

6. Li Tien, 'Gay Life on the Chinhuai', *China Reconstructs*, XII, No. 1 (Jan. 1963), 40.

7. *Guide to Hangchow*, 49.

8. Cf. Marek, 88–89.

9. Lo Shu-tzu, 'Terracotta Tomb Figures', *Chinese Literature*, No. 2 (Feb. 1962), 105.

10. André Malraux, *The Voices of Silence* (New York, 1953), 13-14.

11. Ananda K. Coomaraswamy, *Why Exhibit Works of Art?: Collected Essays on the traditional or 'normal' view of Art* (London, 1943), 7–8, 69, 99.

12. Cf. Wlodzimierz Baczkowski, 'Perspective I: World History', *Bear and Dragon*, ed. James Burnham (New York, 1960), 10–11, where Slavophile spiritual leanings toward Asia are taken to corroborate the 'Oriental Despotism' theory of social kinship between Czarist and Soviet Russia together and Confucian and Communist China.

13. See Mary C. Wright, 'Revolution from Without?' (A Commentary on "Imperial Russia at the Turn of the Century: the Cultural Slope and the Revolution from Without", by Theodore Von Laue)', *Comparative Studies in Society and History*, IV, No. 2 (Jan. 1962), 247–8, for comment on the Russian Revolution as, by contrast with China, a revolution from within. She suggests that pre-revolutionary Russian culture was a European sub-culture, different from nineteenth century upper class culture, but no more different than Irish, southern Italian, or Greek. Russia should be seen as the last major western country, not as the first non-western country, to struggle with modernization.

14. MacFarquhar, 288.

15. *Ibid.*, 95.

16. Richard McKeon, 'Moses Maimonides, the Philosopher', *Essays on Maimonides*, ed. Salo Wittmayer Baron (New York, 1941), 8.

NOTES: CONCLUSION, *pp.* 123-125

17. For this and the other phrases in quotation marks in this paragraph, see Paul Demiéville, 'Présentation', *Aspects de la Chine: Langue, histoire, religions, philosophie, littérature, arts* (Paris, 1959), I, 9.

18. Gershom G. Scholem, *Major Trends in Jewish Mysticism* (New York, 1946), 349.

Bibliography

A. CHINESE AND JAPANESE

Chang Chün-yen, 'Li Ta-chao yü hsin wen-hua yün-tung' (Li Ta-chao and the new-culture movement), *Li-shih yen-chiu* (1959), No. 8, pp. 1–19.

Chang Hsiao-ming, *Chung-kuo li-tai ching-ti wen-t'i* (The land question in Chinese history) (Shanghai, 1932).

Chang Shun-hui, *Chung-kuo shih lun-wen chi* (Collected essays on Chinese history) (Wuhan, 1956).

Chang Tai-nien, *Chung-kuo wei-wu-chu-i ssu-hsiang chien-shih* (A brief history of Chinese materialist thought) (Peking, 1957).

Chao Lin, 'Ching-t'ien chih-tu ti yen-chiu' (Investigation of the *ching-t'ien* system), *Shih-ti ts'ung-k'an* (History and geography series), No. 1 (1933), pp. 1–17.

Ch'en Chao-k'un, 'Chung-kuo ku-tai t'ien-fu hsing-ko lun-lüeh' (An outline of land-tax innovation in ancient China), *She-hui k'o-hsüeh chi-k'an* (new series) ('Social Sciences Quarterly'), II, No. 2 (Summer, 1943), pp. 1–12.

Ch'en Cheng-mo, 'P'ing-chün ti-ch'üan yü Chung-kuo li-tai t'u-ti wen-t'i' (Equalization of land rights and the land question through Chinese history), *Chung-shan wen-hua chiao-yü kuan chi-k'an* ('Quarterly Review of the Sun Yat-sen Institute for Advancement of Culture and Education'), IX, No. 3 (Autumn, 1937), pp. 889–911.

Ch'en Ch'ien-chün, 'Lun *Tzu chih-t'ung-chien* (On the *Tzu-chih t'ung-chien*), *Li-shih yen-chiu* (1957), No. 7, pp. 27–40.

Ch'en Huan-chang, *K'ung-chiao lun* (On the Confucian religion) (Shanghai, 1912).

Ch'en Ming-lin, 'Kuan-yü Hsi-Chou she-hui hsing-chih wen-t'i' (Questions relative to the character of Western Chou Society), *Chung-kuo ku-shih fen-ch'i wen-t'i lun-ts'ung* (Collection of essays on the question of the periodization of ancient Chinese history) (Peking, 1957), pp. 196–215.

Ch'en Po-ta, *Ch'ien-kuo ta-tao Yüan Shih-k'ai* (Introducing the thief of the nation, Yüan Shih-k'ai) (Peking, 1954).

159

'P'i-p'an ti chi-ch'eng ho hsin ti t'an so' (A critical inquiry into heritage and novelty), *Hung-chi* (Red flag), No. 13 (1959), pp. 36–49.

Ch'en Po-ying, *Chung-kuo t'ien-chih ts'ung-k'ao* (General survey of Chinese land systems) (Shanghai, 1935).

Cheng Ch'üan-chung, *Shih-chi hsüan-chiang* (Selected comments on the *Shih-chi* (*Peking*, 1959).

Cheng Hsing-sung, 'Ching-t'ien k'ao' (Examination of *ching-t'ien*), part one, *Ching-chi hsüeh chi-k'an* ('Quarterly Journal of Economics or the Chinese Economic Society'), V, No. 2 (Aug. 1934), pp. 57–62.

Chi Chen-huai, *Ssu-ma Ch'ien* (Shanghai, 1955).

Chi Wen-fu, *Ch'un-ch'iu Chan-kuo ssu-hsiang shih-hua* (Historical discourses on the thought of the 'Spring and Autumn' and 'Warring States' periods) (Peking, 1958).

Ch'i Ssu-ho, 'Meng-tzu ching-t'ien shuo-pan' (Mencius' theory of *ching-t'ien*), *Yen-ching hsüeh-pao* ('Yenching Journal of Chinese Studies'), No. 35 (Dec. 1948), pp. 101–27.

'P'i-p'an Hu Shih-p'ai tui-yü shih-chieh shih ti fan-tung wei-hsin kuan-tien' (A criticism of the Hu Shih clique's reactionary idealist point of view toward world history), *Li-shih yen-chiu* (1956), No. 6, pp. 23–41.

Ch'i Ssu-ho, et al., ed., *Ya-p'ien chan-cheng* (The opium war) (Shanghai, 1954).

Chiao-yü pu, ed., *Ti-erh-tz'u Chung-kuo chiao-yü nien-chien* (The second Chinese educational yearbook) (Shanghai, 1948).

Chien Hu, ' "Ou-hua" ti Chung-kuo' ('Europeanized' China), *Tung-fang tsa-chih* ('The Eastern Miscellany'), XX, No. 4 (Feb. 25, 1923), p. 1.

Chien Po-tsan, 'Kuan-yü liang-Han ti kuan-ssu nu-pi wen-t'i' (Concerning the question of public and private slaves during the two Han), *Li-shih yen-chiu* (1954), No. 4, pp. 1–24.

Ch'ien Mu: *Chung-kuo chin san-pai nien hsüeh-shu shih* (History of Chinese scholarship in the last three hundred years) (Taipei, 1957).

Kuo-shih ta-kang (The main outlines of the national history) (Chungking, 1944).

Ch'ien T'ang, 'Kai-t'ing shu-ku lu', *Huang-Ch'ing ching-chieh* (1829), ts'e 195, ch. 717–18.

Chou-li (Ssu-pu ts'ung-kan ed.) (Shanghai, 1942).

Chou Yü-t'ung and T'ang Chih-chün, 'Wang Mang kai-chih yü ching-hsüeh chung ti chin-ku-wen hsüeh wen-t'i' (Wang Mang's reform and the problem of modern and ancient texts in classical scholarship), *Kuang-ming jih-pao* (May 16, 1961), p. 2.

'T'an-t'ao Chung-kuo ching-hsüeh wen-t'i' (An inquiry into the problem of Chinese classical scholarship), *Jen-min jih-pao* (May 31, 1961), p. 7.

Chu Ch'ien-chih, 'Shih-ch'i-pa shih-chi hsi-fang che-hsüeh-chia ti K'ung-tzu kuan' (Western philosophers' views on Confucius during the seventeenth and eighteenth centuries), *Jen-min jih-pao* (March 9, 1962), p. 5.

Chu Hsi, 'Li i: *Chou-li*' ("Rituals" #1: *Chou-li*), *Chu-tzu ch'üan-shu* (Complete works of Chu Hsi), ed., Li Kuang-ti (1714), ts'e 17, ch. 37, 9b–27b.

'Meng-tzu chi-chu' (Annotation of *Mencius*), *Ssu-shu chang-chü chi-chu* (Piecemeal annotation of the 'Four Books') (Shanghai, 1935).

Chu Hsieh, 'Ching-t'ien chih-tu yu-wu wen-t'i chih ching-chi shih shang ti kuan-ch'a' (Examination from the standpoint of economic history of the question of the existence of the *ching-t'ien* system), *Tung-fang tsa-chih* ('The Eastern Miscellany'), XXXI, No. 1 (Jan. 1, 1934), pp. 183–91.

Chu Tung-jun, ed., *Tso-chuan hsüan* (Selections from the *Tso-chuan* (Shanghai, 1956).

Chung Chao-p'eng, 'Ts'ung *jen* ho *li* k'an K'ung-tzu ssu-hsiang ti chieh-chi hsing (From *jen* and *li*, to look at the class nature of Confucius' thought), *Kuang-ming jih-pao* (Dec. 12, 1961), p. 3.

'Chung-kuo Jen-min Ta'hsüeh che-hsüeh-hsi t'ao-lun Meng-tzu p'ing-chiai wen-t'i' (The Philosophy Department of the Chinese People's University discusses the problem of evaluating Mencius), *Kuang-ming jih-pao* (July 28, 1961), p. 1.

Chung-kuo nung-ts'un ti she-hui chu-i kao-ch'ao (The high tide of socialism in the Chinese village) (Peking, 1956).

Chung-kuo ta-t'ung ssu-hsiang tzu-liao (Materials in Chinese utopian thought), ed. Chinese Academy of Sciences, philosophical research department, history of Chinese philosophy section (Peking, 1959).

'Chung-nan ti-ch'ü shih-hsüeh-chieh tsai Kuang-chou chü-hsing hsüeh-shu t'ao-lun-hui' (The historical society of the Chung-nan region holds a scholarly discussion meeting in Canton), *Kuang-ming jih-pao* (June 22, 1962), p. 4.

Chung-shan ta-hsüeh li-shih-hsi (History department of Sun Yat-sen University), 'Tui Fan Wen-lan *Chung-kuo t'ung-shih* chien-pien hsiu-ting pen ti-i-pien ti i-chien' (Opinions on the first edition of Fan Wen-lan's simplified and revised *General History of China*), *Li-shih yen-chiu* (1955), No. 1, pp. 111–14.

Fan I-t'ien, 'Hsi-Chou ti she-hui hsing-chih—feng-chien she-hui' (The nature of Western Chou society—feudal society), *Chung-kuo ku-shih fen-ch'i wen-t'i lun-ts'ung* (Collection of essays on the question of the periodization of ancient Chinese history) (Peking, 1957), pp. 217–54.

Fan Wen-lan, 'Shih-lun Chung-kuo tzu Ch'in-Han shih ch'eng-wei t'ung-i kuo-chia ti yüan-yin' (A tentative exposition of the reasons for China's having become a unified state from the Ch'in-Han period), *Li-shih yen-chiu* (1954), No. 3.

Feng Tzu-yu, *She-hui chu-i yü Chung-kuo* (Socialism and China) (Hong Kong, 1920).

BIBLIOGRAPHY

Feng Yu-lan, 'K'ang Yu-wei ti ssu-hsiang' (The thought of K'ang Yu-wei), *Chung-kuo chin-tai ssu-hsiang shih lun-wen chi* (Collection of essays on Chinese intellectual history) (Shanghai, 1958), pp. 110–27.

Fujiwara Sadame, 'Seimatsu shisō no kōryū' (Late Ch'ing intellectual currents), in Sanetō Keishu, ed., *Kindai Shina shisō* (Modern Chinese thought) (Tokyo, 1942), pp. 54–97.

Fukui Kojun, *Gendai Chūgoku shisō* (Recent Chinese thought) (Tokyo, 1955).

Hashikawa Tokio, *Chūgoku bunkakai jimbutsu sōkan* (General directory of intellectuals of the Chinese Republic) (Peking, 1940).

Hashimoto Masuyoshi, 'Shina kodai densei kō' (Examination of the land system of Chinese antiquity), *Tōyō gakuhō*, XII, No. 1 (1923), pp. 1–45; XII, No. 4 (1923), pp. 481–94; XV, No. 1 (1925), pp. 64–104.

Ho Hsiang-ning, *Hui-i Sun Chung-shan ho Liao Chung-k'ai* (Recollections of Sun Yat-sen and Liao Chung-k'ai) (Peking, 1957).

Ho Tzu-ch'üan, 'Kuan-yü Chung-kuo ku-tai she-hui ti chi-ko wen-t'i' (Some questions relating to ancient Chinese society), *Chung-kuo ku-shih fen-ch'i wen-t'i lun-ts'ung* (Collection of essays on the question of the periodization of ancient Chinese history) (Peking, 1957), pp. 117–69.

'Ho-nan shih-hsüeh-chieh t'ao-lun Hung Hsiu-ch'üan ti ssu-hsiang yü Ju-chia ti kuan-hsi wen-t'i' (The Historical Society of Honan discusses the thought of Hung Hsiu-ch'üan and the problem of its relationship to Confucianism), *Kuang-ming jih-pao* (June 1, 1961), p. 1.

Ho-nan Ta-hsueh li-shih-hsi, ed., *Chung-kuo t'ung-shih tzu-liao hsüan-chi* (Compilation of materials for a general history of China) (Kaifeng, 1953).

Hou Wai-lu, *Chung-kuo ku-tai she-hui shih-lun* (Discussion of the history of ancient Chinese society) (Peking, 1955).
  Chung-kuo tsao-ch'i ch'i-meng ssu-hsiang shih (History of the early modern Chinese enlightment) (Peking, 1956).
  'Lun Chung-kuo feng-chien chih ti hsing-cheng chi ch'i fa-t'ien hua' (On the form of the Chinese feudal régime and its legal development), *Li-shih yen-chiu* (1956), No. 8.

'Hou Wai-lu t'an ju-ho tui-tai Chung-kuo che-hsüeh-shih i-ch'an' (A talk by Hou Wai-lu on how to treat the heritage of the history of Chinese philosophy), *Kuang-ming jih-pao* (May 6, 1961), p. 1.

Hsia Nai, 'Shih nien lai ti Chung-kuo k'ao-ku hsin fa-hsien' (New discoveries in Chinese archaeology in the last ten years), *Kuang-ming jih-pao* (Oct. 15, 1959), p. 3.

Hsiang Nai-ch'i, 'Tzu Ma-k'o-ssu nung-yeh li-lun chih fa-chan lun tao wo kuo t'u-ti wen-t'i' (A discussion of the land problems in China from the standpoint of the development of Marxist theories on agriculture), *She-hui k'o-hsüeh chi-k'an* ('Social Sciences Quarterly'), V, Nos. 1–2 (Jan.–June 1930), pp. 1–32.

Hsiao Cheng, 'P'ing-chün ti-ch'üan chen-ch'üan' (The true interpretation of equalization of landed power), *Ti-cheng yüeh-k'an* ('The Journal of Land Economics'), I, No. 1 (Jan. 1933), pp. 3–28.

Hsin Hua pan-hüeh-k'an (New China fortnightly), No. 145 (Dec. 1958.)

Hsü Chung-shu, 'Ching-t'ien chih-tu t'an-yüan' (An inquiry into the *ching-t'ien* system), *Chung-kuo wen-hua yen-chiu hui-kan* ('Bulletin of Chinese Studies'), IV, part 1 (Sep. 1944), pp. 121–56.

'Lun Hsi-Chou shih feng-chien-chih she-hui—chien-lun Yin-tai she-hui hsing-chih' (On the Western Chou's being a feudal society—together with a discussion of the nature of the society of the Yin dynasty), *Li-shih yen-chiu* (1957), No. 5, pp. 55–78.

'Hsü Chung-shu lun K'ung-tzu cheng-chih ssu-hsiang' (Hsü Chung-shu discusses Confucius' political thought), *Kuang-ming jih-pao* (Dec. 13, 1961), p. 1.

Hsü Hung-hsiao, 'Ch'in Han she-hui chih t'u-ti chih-tu yü nung-yeh sheng-ch'an' (Land systems and agricultural production in Ch'in and Han society), *Shih-huo*, III, No. 7 (March 1, 1956), pp. 10–29.

Hsü Lun, *Shen-mo shih feng-chien she-hui?* (What is feudal society?) (Shanghai, 1954).

Hsü Shih-ch'ang, *Ou-chan hou chih Chung-kuo: ching-chi yü chiao-yü* (China after the European War: economics and education) (Shanghai, 1920).

Hsüeh Fu-ch'eng, *Ch'ou yang ch'u-i* (Rough discussion on the management of foreign affairs), *Yung-an ch'üan-chi* (Collected works of Hsüeh Fu-ch'eng) (1884–98), ts'e 15.

'Yung-an wen-pien' (Collection of Hsüeh Fu-ch'eng's writings), *Yung-an ch'üan-chi* (Collected works of Hsüeh Fu-ch'eng) (1884–98), ts'e 1–4.

Hu Fan-jo, 'Chung-kuo ching-t'ien chih yen-ko k'ao' (On the overthrow of the *ching-t'ien* system in China), *K'o-hsüeh* ('Science'), X, No. 1 (May 1925), pp. 132–40.

Hu Han-min, 'Hu Han-min hsien-sheng ta Hu Shih-chih hsien-sheng ti hsin' (Hu Han-min's answer to Hu Shih's letter), in Chu Chih-hsin, et al., *Ching-t'ien chih-tu yu-wu chih yen-chiu* (Investigation into the existence or non-existence of the *ching-t'ien* system) (Shanghai, 1930), pp. 37–46.

'P'ing-chün ti-chüan ti chen-i chi t'u-ti fa yüan-tse ti lai-yüan' (The true meaning of equalization of landed power and the provenance of the basic rule of the land law), in Shih Hsi-sheng, ed., *Hu Han-min y en hsing lu* (Biography of Hu Han-min), part 3, pp. 117–28.

Hu Han-min, 'San-min-chu-i chih jen-shih' (Knowledge of the Three People's Principles), in Huang-pu chung-yang chün-shih cheng-chih hsüeh-hsiao te-pieh tang-pu (Special Kuomintang party council, Whampoa Academy) ed., *Chiang Hu tsui chin yen-lun chi* (Most recent collected discourses of Chiang Kai-shek and Hu Han-min) (Canton?, 1927), Part II, pp. 1–12.

San-min-chu-i ti lien-huan-hsing (The cyclical character of the 'Three People's Principles') (Shanghai, 1928).

Wei-wu shih-kuan yü lun-li chih yen-chiu (A study of the materialist interpretation of history and ethics) (Shanghai, 1925).

Hu Sheng, 'Chung-kuo chin-tai li-shih te fen-ch'i wen-t'i' (The problem of periodization in contemporary Chinese history), *Li-shih yen-chiu* (1954), No. 1, pp. 5–15.

Hu Shih, 'Ching-t'ien pien' (The *ching-t'ien* dispute), *Hu Shih wen-ts'un wen-ts'un* (Selected essays of Hu Shih) (Shanghai, 1927), pp. 247–84.

Hua-chiao jih-pao (China Daily News), New York (April 16, 1962).

'Hui-shih chu-chüan' (Essays, copied out in red, of successful candidates at the metropolitan examinations), *Ssu-i-kuan ching-hsüeh ts'ung-shu*, ts'e 14.

Hung Jen-kan, 'Tzu-cheng hsin-p'ien' (New essay to aid in government), *T'ai-p'ing T'ien-kuo* (The Heavenly Kingdom of Great Peace), ed. Hsiang Ta et al. (Shanghai, 1952), II, pp. 522–41.

Imazeki Hisamaro, *Sung Yüan Ming Ch'ing Ju-chia hsüeh nien-piao* (Chronological tables of Sung, Yüan, Ming, and Ch'ing Confucianism) (Tokyo, 1920) (In Chinese).

Jan Chao-te, 'Shih lun Shang Yang pien-fa ti hsing-chih' (On the nature of Shang Yang's reforms), *Li-chih yen-chiu* (1957), No. 6, pp. 43–63.

Jen Chi-yü, 'Chung-kuo ku-tai i-hsüeh ho che-hsüeh ti kuan-hsi' (The relation between medical studies and philosophical studies in ancient China), *Li-shih yen-chiu* (1956), No. 5, pp. 59–74.

'Ho Ch'i Hu Li-yüan ti kai-liang chu-i ssu-hsiang' (The reformist thought of Ho Ch'i and Hu Li-yüan), *Chung-kuo chin-tai ssu-hsiang shih lun-wen chi* (Collected essays on the history of modern Chinese thought) (Shanghai, 1958), pp. 75–91.

Jen Chüan, 'K'ung-tzu Li-yün "ta-t'ung" ssu-hsiang' (Confucius' *Li-yün* utopian thought), *Kuang-ming jih-pao* (May 12, 1961), p. 4.

Jen-min wen-hsüeh ch'u-pan she pien-chi-pu, ed., *Shih-ching yen-chiu lun-wen chi* (Collection of research papers on the *Shih-ching*) (Peking, 1959).

K'ang Yu-wei, 'Chung-kuo hsüeh-pao t'i-tz'u' (The thesis of the *Chung-kuo hsüeh-pao*), *Chung-kuo hsüeh-pao*, No. 6, (Feb. 1931).

Kao Heng, 'Chou-tai ti-tsu chih-k'ao' (On the Chou land-tax system), *Chung-kuo ku-shih fen-ch'i wen-t'i lun-ts'ung* (Collection of essays on the question of the periodization of ancient Chinese history) (Peking, 1957), pp. 26–64.

Kao Yün-hui, 'Chou-tai t'u-ti chih-tu yü ching-t'ien' (The Chou period's land system and *ching-t'ien*), Shih-huo, I, No. 7 (March 1, 1935), pp. 10–20; I, No. 12 (May 16, 1935), pp. 1–7.

Ku Chieh-kang, *Ch'in-Han ti Fang-shih yü Ju-sheng* (Taoists and Confucianists of the Ch'in and Han periods) (Shanghai, 1955).

Ku shih pien (Symposium on ancient history), III (Shanghai, 1931).

Ku Ti, 'K'ung-tzu ho "ta-t'ung" ssu-hsiang' (Confucius and utopian thought), *Kuang-ming jih-pao* (May 24, 1961), p. 2.

Ku Yen-wu, *Jih-chih lu* (Record of knowledge day by day) (Shanghai, 1933).

Kuan Feng and Lin Yü-shih, 'Lun K'ung-tzu' (On Confucius), *Che-hsüeh yen-chiu* (Philosophical Research), IV (July 25, 1961), pp. 42–70.

'Lun K'ung-tzu ti "jen" ho "li" ' (A discourse on Confucius' *jen* and *li*), *Jen-min jih-pao* (July 23, 1961), p. 5.

Kuo Mo-jo, 'K'ai-chan li-shih yen-chiu ying-chieh wen-hua chien-she kao-hu' (Develop historical research to meet the high tide of cultural reconstruction), *Li-shih yen-chiu* (1954), No. 1, pp. 1–4.

'Kuan-yü "hou-chin po-ku" wen-t'i' (On the 'broaden the new narrow the old' question), *Jen-min jih-pao* (June 11, 1958), p. 7.

Kuo Mo-jo, 'Kuan-yü mu-ch'ien li-shih yen-chiu chung ti chi-ke wen-t'i' (Several problems concerning present-day historical research) *Hsin chien-she* (April 1959), pp. 1–5.

Nu-li chih shih-tai (The slave era) (Shanghai, 1952).

Shih p'i-p'an shu (Ten critiques) (Peking, 1954).

Kuo Shao-yü, *Chung-kuo ku-tien wen-hsüeh li-lun p'i-p'ing shih* (A critical history of classical Chinese literary doctrines) (Peking, 1959).

Leng Ting-an, *She-hui chu-i ssu-hsiang-shih* (History of socialist thought) (Hong Kong, 1956).

Li A-nung, *Chung-kuo ti nu-li chih yü feng-chien chih* (Slave régime and feudal régime in China) (Peking, 1954).

Li Chu-jan, *Hsin-hai ko-ming ch'ien ti ch'ün-chung tou-cheng* (Battles of the masses before the revolution of 1911) (Peking, 1957).

Li Kung, *Yüeh shih hsi shih* (Shanghai, 1937).

Li Shih-yüeh, *Hsin-hai ko-ming shih-ch'i liang-Hu ti-ch'ü ti ko-ming yün-tung* (Revolutionary movements in the Hupei-Hunan area during the period of the *hsin-hai* revolution) (Peking, 1957).

Li Shou-yung, 'Kuan-yü K'ung-tzu ti "chün" ti ching-chi ssu-hsiang ti t'an-t'ao' (An enquiry into Confucius' economic thought on 'equalization'), *Kuang-ming jih-pao* (March 12, 1962), p. 4.

Li Shu, 'Mao Tse-tung t'ung-chih ti "Kai-tsao wo-men ti hsüeh-hsi" ho Chung-kuo li-shih k'o-hsüeh' (Comrade Mao Tse-tung's 'Reform our learning' and Chinese historical science), *Jen-min jih-pao* (June 8, 1961), p. 7.

Li Ting-fang, *Wang Mang* (Shanghai, 1957).

Liang Ch'i-ch'ao, 'Chung-kuo chih she-hui chu'i' (China's socialism), *Yin-ping shih ho-chi* (Shanghai, 1936), chuan-chi 2: 2.101–2.

'Hsü-lun shih-min yü yin-shing' (Supplementary discussion of citizens and banks), *Yin-ping shih ho-chi* (Shanghai, 1936), wen chi 13: 37. pp. 34–41.

'Lun Chung-kuo ts'ai-cheng-hsüeh pu fa-ta chih yuan-yin chi ku-tai ts'ai-cheng hsüeh-shuo chih i-pan' (On the reason for the lack of progress in Chinese study of finance, and a miscellany of ancient financial theories), *Yin-ping-shih ho-chi* (Shanghai, 1936), wen-chi 12: 33. pp. 90–94.

'Tai Tung-yüan sheng erh-pai nien chi-nien hui yüan-ch'i' (The origins of the conference to commemorate the two hundredth anniversary of the birth of Tai Chen), *Yin-ping-shih ho-chi* (Shanghai, 1936), wen-chi 14: 40. pp. 38–40.

Liang Yüan-tung, 'Ching-t'ien chih fei t'u-ti chih-tu shuo' (Exposition of the *ching-t'ien* system as not a land system), *Ching-chi hsüeh chi-k'an* ('Quarterly Journal of Economics of the Chinese Economic Society'), VI, No. 3 (Nov. 1935), pp. 51–56.

'Ku-tai chün-t'ien chih-tu ti chen-hsiang' (What the ancient *chün-t'ien* system was really like), *Shen-pao yüeh-k'an* ('The Shun Pao'), V, No. 4 (May 15, 1935), pp. 65–73.

Liao Chung-k'ai, 'Chung-kuo shih-yeh ti hsien-chung chi ch'an-yeh lo-hou ti yüan-yin' (The present condition of Chinese industry and the root cause of backwardness in production), *Chung-kuo Kuo-min tang shih-yeh chiang-yen* (Chinese Nationalist Party lectures, on industry) (Shanghai, 1924), pp. 32–54.

'Nung-min yün-tung so tang shu-i yao-tien' (Important points which the peasant movement should take into account), in Cheng Wu ed., *Tang kuo hsien-chin yen-lun chi* (Discourses of Kuomintang elders) (Changsha, 1938), pp. 142–9.

'Ta Hu Shih chih lun ching-t'ien shu' (In answer to Hu Shih's writings on *ching-t'ien*), *Liao Chung-k'ai chi* (A Liao Chung-k'ai collection), Taiyan, 192?, pp. 85–93.

Liao Chung-k'ai wen-chi (Essays of Liao Chung-k'ai) (Canton, 1961).

Liao P'ing, 'Chunh-wai pi-chiao kai-liang pien hsü' (Preface to a comparative history of Chinese and foreign reforms), *Liu-kuan ts'ung-shu* (Chengtu, 1921), ts'e 8, 25a–25b.

'Fu Liu Shen-shu shu' (Reply to Liu Shih-p'ei), *Chung-kuo hsüeh-pao*, No. 2 (Feb. 1916).

Ku-hsüeh-k'ao (On the 'ancient text' learning) (Peiping, 1935).

'Lun Shih hsü' (On the preface to the *Shih-ching*), *Chung-kuo hsüeh-pao*, No. 4 (April 1916).

'Lü li' (Personal chronicle), *Ssu-i-kuan ching-hsüeh ts'ung-shu* (Collection of classical studies published by Liao P'ing) (Chengtu, 1886), ts'e 14.

'Ta-t'ung hsüeh-shuo' (The theory of the Great Harmony), *Chung-kuo hsüeh-pao*, No. 8 (June 1913).

'Yü K'ang Ch'ang-su shu' (Letter to K'ang Yu-wei), *Chung-kuo hsüeh-pao*, No. 8 (June 1913).

Liu Shih-p'ei, 'Chih Liao Chi-p'ing lun T'ien jen shu' (Letter to Liao P'ing on Heaven and man), *Chung-kuo hsüeh-pao*, No. 2 (Feb. 1916).

Liu Ta-tiao, 'Chung-kuo ku-tai t'ien-chih yen-chiu' (An investigation of ancient Chinese land systems), *Ch'ing-hua hsüeh-pao* ('The Tsing Hua Journal'), III, No. 1 (July 1926), pp. 679–85.

Liu Tse-hua, 'Shih-lun K'ung-tzu ti fu-min ssu-hsiang' (Consideration of Confucius' thought on enriching the people), *Kuang-ming jih-pao* (June 22, 1962), p. 4.

Lo Ken-tse, *Chung-kuo wen-hsüeh p'i-p'ing shih* (History of Chinese literary criticism) (Shanghai, 1957).

Lu Hsün, 'Tui-yü "Hsin Ch'ao" i-pu-fen ti i-chien (A fragmentary opinion on *Hsin Ch'ao*), *Lu Hsün san-shih nien chi* (Thirty years' collected works of Lu Hsün) (n.p., 1947), III, pp. 28–29.

'Lu Ti-p'ing yen-shuo tz'u' (Speech by Lu Ti-p'ing), *Shih-chieh shu-kuang chih Chung-hua wen-hua* (Chinese culture, the world's dawning light) (Changsha, 1928).

Lü Chen-yü, 'Hsi-Chou shih-tai ti Chung-kuo she-hui' (Chinese society in the Western Chou period), *Chung-shan wen-hua chiao-yü kuan chi-k'an* ('Quarterly Review of the Sun Yat-sen Institute for Advancement of Culture and Education'), II, No. 1 (Spring, 1935), pp. 113–32.

Shih-hsüeh yen-chiu lun-wen chi (Collection of essays on historical research) (Shanghai, 1954).

Ma Tuan-lin, *Wen hsien t'ung-k'ao* (Che-chiang shu-chü ed., 1896).

Mao Tse-tung, *Chung-kuo ko-ming yü Chung-kuo kung-ch'an-tang* (The Chinese revolution and the Chinese Communist Party) (Hong Kong, 1949).

Meng-tzu i-chu (*Mencius*: translation and commentary), ed. Lanchow University Department of Chinese Literature, Mencius-annotation sub-section (Peking, 1960).

Miu Yüeh, 'Chiang-shou Chung-kuo li-shih tui-yü wen-hua pu-fen ju-ho ch'u-li' (How to handle the cultural portions in lecturing on Chinese history), *Kuang-ming jih-pao* (May 30, 1961), pp. 2–3.

Morimoto Chikujō, *Shinchō Jugaku shi gaisetsu* (A general survey of the history of Confucian learning in the Ch'ing dynasty) (Tokyo, 1931).

Na Chih-liang, *Ku-kung po-wu-yüan san-shih nien chih ching-kuo* (Thirty years of the Palace Museum) (Hong Kong, 1957).

Naitō Torajirō, *Shinchō shi tsūron* (Outline of Ch'ing history) (Tokyo, 1944).

Nakayama Hisashirō, 'Manshūkoku to Kōshikyō no shin shimei' (Manchukuo and the new mission of Confucianism), *Shibun*, XV, No. 8 (Aug. 1933), pp. 1–12.

Ni Chin-sheng, 'Ching-t'ien hsin ch'eng pieh-lun' (Another discussion of new clarifications of *ching-t'ien*), *Shih-huo*, V, No. 5 (March 1, 1937), pp. 22–25.

Ni Xaishu [Ni Hai-shu], '*Lunjy* Syanji ['Lun-yü hsüan-i] (Selected translations from the Lun-yü) (Shanghai, 1954).

Niu Hsi, 'Tzu Shang chih Han-ch'u she-hui tsu-chih chih t'an-t'ao' (Inquiry into social organization from Shang to the beginning of Han), *Ch'ing-hua chou-k'an* ('Tsing Hua weekly'), XXXV, No. 2 (March 1921), pp. 75–92.

Ojima Sukema, 'Rokuhen seru Ryō Hei no gakusetsu' (Six stages in the development of Liao P'ing's theories), *Shinagaku*, II, No. 9 (May 1922), pp. 707–14.

'Ryō Hei no gaku' (Liao P'ing's Learning), *Geibun*, VIII, (May 1917) pp. 426–46.

Onogawa Hidemi, *Seimatsu sei*[i] *shisō kenkyū* (Studies in late-Ch'ing political thought) (Kyoto, 1960).

Pang Li-shan, 'She-hui chu-i yü she-hui cheng-ts'e' (Socialism and social policy), *Tung-fang tsa-chih* ('The Eastern Miscellany'), XXI, No. 16 (Aug. 25, 1924), pp. 19–29.

Pei-ching ta hsüeh li-shih hsi, Chung-kuo ku-tai shih chiao-yen shih (Peking University history department, seminar on the teaching and study of the ancient history of China), '*Chung-kuo li-shih kang-yao* t'ao-lun hui chi-lu' (Minutes of the conference on *Essentials of Chinese history*), *Li-shih yen-chiu* (1957), No. 4, pp. 43–77.

Petrov, A. A. (Li Shih, tr.), *Wang Ch'ung—Chung-kuo ku-tai ti wei-wu-chu-i che ho ch'i-meng ssu-hsiang-chia* (Wang Ch'ung—an ancient Chinese materialist and enlightened thinker) (Peking, 1956).

Rinji Taiwan kyūkan chōsakai dai-ichi-bu hōkoku (Temporary commission of the Taiwan Government-general for the study of old Chinese customs, report of the First Section), *Shinkoku gyōseihō* (Administrative laws of the Ch'ing dynasty), kan 2 (Kobe, 1910).

Shao Chün-p'u, 'Ching-ti chih-tu k'ao' (On the *ching* land system), *Ling-nan hsüeh-pao* ('Lingnan Journal'), IX, No. 2 (June 1949), pp. 175–200.

Shao Hsün-cheng, 'Hsin-hai ko-ming ch'ien wu-shih-nien chien wai-kuo ch'in-lüeh-che ho Chung-kuo mai-pan-hua chün-fa kuan-liao shih-li ti kuan-hsi' (The relationship between foreign aggressors and China's 'comprador-ized' warlord and bureaucratic forces during the fifty years before the revolution of 1911), *Li-shih yen-chiu* (1954), No. 4.

Shao Hsün-cheng, et al., ed., *Chung-Jih chan-cheng* (The Sino-Japanese War) (Shanghai, 1956).

Shih-chieh jih-pao (The Chinese World), San Francisco (April 14, April 24, 1962).

Shimizu Nobuyoshi, *Kinsei Chūgoku shisō shi* (History of modern Chinese thought) (Tokyo, 1950).

Shōji Sōichi, 'Chin Ryō no gaku' (The thought of Ch'en Liang) *Tōyō no bunka to shakai*, IV (1954), pp. 82–100.

Shu Shih-cheng, 'K'ung-tzu *Ch'un-ch'iu*' (Confucius' 'Spring and Autumn'), *Li-shih yen-chiu* (1962), No. 1, pp. 46–57.

'Ssu-te-k'o-erh-mo ti shih-tz'u kuo-chi li-shih hsüeh-chia ta-hui shang ti lun-cheng' (Discussion-war at the Eleventh International Congress of Historians at Stockholm), *Jen-min jih-pao* (Feb. 26, 1961), p. 5.

Su Hsün, 'T'ien-chih' (Land systems), *San Su wen-chi* (Collection of writings of the three Su worthies) (Shanghai, 1912), ts'e 1, ch. 6, 4b–6a.

Sun Li-hsing, 'P'i-p'an Hu Shih ti "Ching-t'ien pien" chi ch'i-t'a' (Criticism of Hu Shih's 'The *Ching-t'ien* dispute', etc.), *Hu Shih ssu-hsiang p'i-p'an*, VI (Peking, 1955), pp. 160–7.

BIBLIOGRAPHY

Sung Yün-pin, *K'ang Tu-wei* (Peking, 1955).

T'ai Shih-chien, 'Wen yü tao' (*Wen* and *tao*), *Jen-min jih-pao* (Jan. 21, 1962), p. 5.

T'an Ssu-t'ung, 'Jen-hsüeh' (Study of Benevolence), *T'an Ssu-t'ung ch'üan-chi* (Collected works of T'an Ssu-t'ang) (Peking, 1954).

'T'an-t'ao Chia I ssu-hsiang ho *Hsin-shu* chen-wei wen-t'i' (An inquiry into Chia I's thought and the question of the authenticity of the *Hsin-shu*), *Jen-min jih-pao* (Oct. 5, 1961), p. 7.

T'ang Chia-hung, 'Ssu-ch'uan ta-hsüeh li-shih hsi ti chiao-hsüeh ho yen-chiu kung-tso' (The instruction and research work of the history department of Szechwan University), *Li-shih yen-chiu* (1956), No. 2, p. 50.

T'ao Hsi-sheng, 'Wang An-shih ti she-hui ssu-hsiang yü ching-chi cheng-tse' (The social thought and economic policies of Wang An-shih), *She-hui k'o-hsüeh chi-k'an* ('Social Sciences Quarterly'), V, No. 3 (Sept. 1935), pp. 103–26.

Tazaki Masayuki, *Shina kōdai keizai shisō oyobi seido* (Economic thought and systems in Chinese antiquity) (Tokyo, 1925).

Teng Ch'u-min, 'T'u-ti kuo-yu wen-t'i' (The question of land nationalization), *Tung-fang tsa-chih* ('The Eastern Miscellany'), XX, No. 19 (Oct. 10, 1923), pp. 13–20.

Ting Tao-ch'ien, 'Yu li-shih pien-tung lü-shuo tao Chung-kuo t'ien-chih ti "hsün-huan"' (From theories of legal change in history to 'recurrence' in Chinese land systems), *Shih-huo*, V, No. 3 (Feb. 1, 1937), pp. 41–51.

Ting Yüan-ying, 'I-chiu-i-ling nien Ch'ang-sha ch'ün-chung ti "ch'iang-mi" feng-ch'ao' (The 'rice-plunder' uprising of the masses at Changsha in 1910), China Academy of Science, Historical Research Section, Third Section, *Collection* 1 (1953).

Tsou Cho-li, 'She-hui chu-i p'ing-i' (A balanced consideration of socialism), *Hsüeh-heng* ('The Critical Review'), No. 12 (Dec. 1922), pp. 1–11.

Tu Shou-su, *Hsien-Ch'in chu tzu ssu-hsiang* (The thought of the pre-Ch'in philosophers) (no place, no date).

Tung Chung-shu, *Ch'un-ch'iu fan-lu* (Luxuriant dew from the *Spring and Autumn Annals*), in Chang Chih-ch'un, ed., *Chu tzu ching-hua lu* (Record of the splendours of varieties of philosophers) (Shanghai, 1924), ch. 4.

Uchino Kumaichirō, 'Minkoku sho chūki no keigaku kan' (Views on classical studies in the early and middle years of the Chinese Republic), *Nihon Chūgoku gakkai hō*, No. 9 (1957), pp. 1–9.

Uno Tetsujin, *Chung-kuo chin-shih Ju-shüeh shih* (History of Chinese Confucian learning in modern times) (Taipei, 1957).

Wang An-shih, *Chou kuan hsin i* (New interpretations of the government system of Chou) (Shanghai, 1937).

Wang Chih-chiu and Sung Kuo-chu, *Chung-hsüeh li-shih chiao-shih shou-ts'e* (Handbook for history teachers in middle schools) (Shanghai, 1958).

Wang I-sun, 'Chung-kuo she-hui ching-chi shih shang chün-t'ien chih-tu ti yen-chiu' (Investigation of the *chün-t'ien* system in Chinese social and economic history), *Tung-fang tsa-chih* ('The Chinese Miscellany'), XXXIII, No. 14 (July 16, 1936), pp. 53–61.

Wang Ming, '*I-ching* ho *I-chuan* ti ssu-hsiang t'i-hsi wen-t'i' (The problem of *I-ching* and *I-chuan* systems of thought), *Kuang-ming jih-pao* (June 23, 1961), p. 4.

Wang Shih, *Yen Fu chuan* (Biography of Yen Fu) (Shanghai, 1957).

Wang Ssu-chih, Tu Wen-k'ai, and Wang Ju-feng, 'Kuan-yü liang-Han she-hui hsing-chih wen-t'i ti t'an-t'ao—chien-p'ing Chien Po-tsan hsien-sheng ti "Kuan-yü liang-Han ti kuan-ssu nu-pi wen-t'i" ' (An inquiry concerning the question of the nature of society in the two Han—a joint critique of Mr. Chien Po-tsan's 'Concerning the question of public and private slaves during the two Han'), *Li-shih yen-chiu* (1955), No. 1, pp. 19–46.

Wang Yu-che, 'Yu kuan Hsi-Chou she-hui hsing-chih ti chi-ke wen-t'i' (Some problems relating to the social character of the Western Chou dynasty), *Li-shih yen-chiu* (1957), No. 5, pp. 79–101.

Wei Chien-yu, 'Ch'ing Yung-cheng ch'ao shih-hsing ching-t'ien chih ti-k'ao-ch'a' (A study of the *ching-t'ien* experiment during the Yung-cheng reign of the Ch'ing period), *Shih-hsüeh nien-pao* ('Yenching Annual of Historical Studies'), I, No. 5 (Aug. 1933), pp. 113–26.

Wei Chü-hsien, 'Ching-t'ien ts'ai-liao' (The character of *ching-t'ien*), *Hsüeh-i* ('Wissen und Wissenschaft'), XIV, No. 4 (May 15, 1935), pp. 15–22.

Wu Chia-mou, *Ching-yen chih* (Gazetteer of Ching-yen) (n.p., 1900).

Wu Yü-chang, *Chung-kuo li-shih chiao-ch'eng hsü-lun* (Introduction to the teaching pattern for Chinese history) (Shanghai, 1950).

Yang Chia-lo, *Min-kuo ming-jen t'u-chien* (Biographical dictionary of eminent men of the Chinese Republic) (Nanking, 1937).

Yang Hsiang-k'uei, 'Shih lun hsien-Ch'in shih-tai Ch'i-kuo ti ching-chi chih-tu' (Tentative discussion of the economic system of the pre-Ch'in state of Ch'i), *Chung-kuo ku-shih fen-ch'i wen-t'i lun-ts'ung* (Collection of essays on the question of the periodization of ancient Chinese history) (Peking, 1957), pp. 83–116.

Yang K'uan, *Shang Yang pien-fa* (The reforms of Shang Yang) (Shanghai, 1955).

Yang P'ei-chih, *Yen Hsi-chai yü Li Shu-ku* (Yen Yüan and Li Kung) (Wuhan, 1956).

Yang Wei-li and Wei Chün-ti, 'Han-tai shih mu-li she-yui hai-shih feng-chien she-hui?' (Was the Han dynasty a slave society or a feudal society?), *Li-shih yen-chiu* (1956), No. 2, pp. 31–49.

Yang Yin-shen, *Chung-kuo hsüeh-shu chia lieh-chuan* (Biographies of Chinese scholars) (Shanghai, 1939).

Yen Yüan, *Hsi-chai chi-yü* (Shanghai, 1936).

'Ts'un chih pien', *Yen Li ts'ung-shu* (1923), ts'e 4, 1a–14a.

BIBLIOGRAPHY

Yü Ching-i, 'Ching-t'ien chih-tu hsin k'ao' (New examination of the
ching-t'ien system), *Tung-fang tsa-chih* ('The Eastern Miscellany'),
XXXI, No. 4 (July 16, 1934), pp. 163–75.

B. WESTERN

Auerbach, Erich, 'Vico and Aesthetic Historism', *Scenes from the Drama of
European Literature* (New York, 1959), pp. 183–200.

Baczkowski, Wlodzimierz, 'Perspective I: World History', *Bear and
Dragon*, ed. James Burnham (New York, 1960), pp. 9–13.

Barnett, A. Doak, *Communist China and Asia: Challenge to American Policy*
(New York, 1960).

Baron, Salo W. and Blau, Joseph L., *Judaism: Postbiblical and Talmudic
Period* (New York, 1954).

Berlin, Isaiah, 'History and Theory: the Concept of Scientific History',
History and Theory, I, No. 1 (1960), pp. 1–31.

Biot, Edouard, tr., *Le Tcheou-li ou Rites des Tcheou* (Paris, 1951).

Birch, Cyril, 'Lao She: the Humourist in His Humour', *The China Quarterly*, No. 8 (Oct.–Dec. 1961), pp. 45–62.

Brandon, S. G. F., 'The Myth and Ritual Position Critically Considered',
*Myth, Ritual, and Kingship: Essays on the Theory and Practice of
Kingship in the Ancient Near East and in Israel*, ed. S. H. Hooke
(Oxford, 1958), pp. 261–291.

Casper, Bernard M., *An Introduction to Jewish Bible Commentary* (New York
and London, 1960).

Chang, Carsun, *The Development of Neo-Confucian Thought* (New York
1957).

Chen Huan-chang, *The Economic Principles of Confucius and His School*
(New York, 1911).

Chen, S. H., 'Multiplicity in Uniformity: Poetry and the Great Leap
Forward', *The China Quarterly*, No. 3 (July–Sep. 1960), pp. 1–15,

Chiang Kai-shek, *China's Destiny and Chinese Economic Theory*, ed. Philip
Jaffe (New York, 1957).

Chinese Literature (1958), No. 1.

Chow Tse-tsung, *The May Fourth Movement: Intellectual Revolution in
Modern China* (Cambridge, Mass., 1960).

Clark, Gerald, *Impatient Giant: Red China Today* (New York, 1959).

Cohen, Arthur A., *Martin Buber* (New York, 1957).

Communist China Digest, No. 8 (Jan. 15, 1960); No. 17 (June 6, 1960);
No. 20 (July 26, 1960); No. 26 (Oct. 18, 1960).

Coomaraswamy, Ananda K., *Why Exhibit Works of Art?: Collected Essays
on the traditional or 'normal' view of Art* (London, 1943).

Daily Report: Foreign Radio Broadcasts, No. 248 (Dec. 22, 1960).

de Bary, W. Theodore, 'A Reappraisal of Neo-Confucianism', *Studies in
Chinese Thought*, ed. Arthur F. Wright (Chicago, 1953), pp. 81–111.
    'Chinese Despotism and the Confucian Ideal: A Seventeenth-Century

BIBLIOGRAPHY

View', *Chinese Thought and Institutions*, ed. John K. Fairbank (Chicago, 1957), pp. 163–203.

Demiéville, Paul, 'Présentation', *Aspects de la Chine: Langue, histoire, religions, philosophie, littérature, arts* (Paris, 1959), pp. 7–10.

Review of 'Hou Che wen ts'ouen', 4 volumes (1921), *Bulletin de l'Ecole Française d'Extrême-Orient*, XXIII (1923), pp. 489–99.

Dru, Alexander, ed., *The Letters of Jacob Burckhardt* (New York, 1955).

Duyvendak, J. J. L., *The Book of Lord Shang: A Classic of the Chinese School of Law* (London, 1928).

Eberhard, Wolfram, 'Zur Landwirtschaft der Han-Zeit', *Mitteilungen des Seminars für Orientalische Sprachen zu Berlin*, XXXV, Part I (Ostasiatische Studien) (1932), pp. 74–105.

Engels, Friedrich, *Herrn Eugen Dührings Umwälzung der Wissenschaft* (Berlin, 1954).

Feng Yuan-chun, *A Short History of Classical Chinese Literature* (Peking, 1958).

Feuer, Lewis S., 'Marxism As History', *Survey*, No. 41 (April 1962), pp. 176–85.

Feuerwerker, Albert, 'China's History in Marxian Dress', *American Historical Review*, LXVI, No. 2 (Jan. 1961), pp. 323–53.

Feuerwerker, Albert and Cheng, S., *Chinese Communist Studies of Modern Chinese History* (Cambridge, Mass., 1961).

Fitzgerald, C. P., *Flood Tide in China* (London, 1958).

Fowke, Frank Rede, *The Bayeux Tapestry: a History and Description* (London, 1913).

Fung Yu-lan, *A History of Chinese Philosophy: the Period of the Philosophers (from the Beginnings to circa 100 B.C.)*, tr. Derk Bodde (Peiping, 1937).

A History of Chinese Philosophy: Volume Two, The Period of Classical Learning, tr. Derk Bodde (Princeton, 1953).

Glimpses of China (Peking, 1958).

Guide to Hangchow (n.p., n.d.).

Guillermaz, Patricia, *La poésie chinoise contemporaine* (Paris, 1962).

Hightower, James Robert, tr., *Han Shih Wai Chuan: Han Ying's Illustrations of the Didactic Application of the Classic of Songs* (Cambridge, Mass., 1952).

Hou Wai-lu, 'Ssuma Chien: Great Ancient Historian', *People's China*, No. 12 (June 16, 1956), pp. 36–40.

Houn, Franklin W., *To Change a Nation: Propaganda and Indoctrination in Communist China* (Glencoe, Ill., 1961).

Hsiao Kung-ch'üan, 'K'ang Yu-wei and Confucianism', *Monumenta Serica*, XVIII (1959), pp. 96–212.

Hsüeh Chün-tu, *Huang Hsing and the Chinese Revolution* (Stanford, 1961).

Hua Hsia, 'The Paintings of Shih Lu', *Chinese Literature* (Jan. 1962), pp. 91–97.

Huang Sung-k'ang, *Lu Hsün and the New Culture Movement of Modern China* (Amsterdam, 1957).

Jacobs, Louis, *Jewish Values* (London, 1960).

Labin, Suzanne, *The Anthill: the Human Condition in Communist China* (New York, 1960).

Legge, James, tr., *The Chinese Classics*, Vol. II (*The Works of Mencius*) (Oxford, 1895).

Levenson, Joseph R., *Liang Ch'i-ch'ao and the Mind of Modern China* (Cambridge, Mass., 1953).

Li Tien, 'Gay Life on the Chinhuai', *China Reconstructs*, XII, No. 1 (Jan. 1963), pp. 40–42.

Liang Ch'i-ch'ao, *Intellectual Trends in the Ch'ing Period*, tr. Immanuel C. Y. Hsü (Cambridge, Mass., 1959).

Ling Yang, 'Integrating Chinese and Western Medicine', *Peking Review*, No. 143 (Dec. 23, 1958), pp. 21–23.,

Lo Shu-tzu, 'Terracotta Tomb Figures', *Chinese Literature*, No. 2 (Feb. 1962), pp. 98–105.

Lu Hsun, 'A Madman's Diary', *Selected Works of Lu Hsun*, I (Peking, 1957), pp. 8–21.

'Experience', *Selected Works of Lu Hsun*, III (Peking, 1959), pp. 271–3.

'Random Thoughts (47)', *Selected Works of Lu Hsun*, II (Peking, 1957), pp. 39–40.

'Random Thoughts (49)', *Selected Works of Lu Hsun*, II (Peking, 1957), pp. 41–42.

'Some Thoughts on Our New Literature', *Selected Works of Lu Hsun*, III (Peking, 1959), pp. 153–5.

'Sudden Notions (6)', *Selected Works of Lu Hsun*, II (Peking, 1957), pp. 121–3.

'We Can No Longer Be Duped', *Selected Works of Lu Hsun*, III (Peking, 1959), pp. 153–5.

MacFarquhar, Roderick, *The Hundred Flowers Campaign and the Chinese Intellectuals* (New York, 1960).

Malraux, André, *The Voices of Silence* (New York, 1953).

Mao Tse-tung, 'The Role of the Chinese Communist Party in the National War', *Selected Works of Mao Tse-tung* (London, 1954), II, pp. 244–61.

Marek, Kurt W., *Yestermorrow: Notes on Man's Progress* (New York, 1961).

Maspero, Henri, *La Chine antique* (Paris, 1927).

Masur, Gerhard, 'Distinctive Traits of Western Civilization: Through the Eyes of Western Historians', *American Historical Review*, LXVII, No. 3 (April, 1962), pp. 591–608.

McKeon, Richard, 'Moses Maimonides, the Philosopher', *Essays on Maimonides*, ed. Salo Wittmayer Baron (New York, 1941), pp. 2–8.

Mills, Harriet C., 'Lu Hsün and the Communist Party', *The China Quarterly*, No. 4 (Oct.–Dec. 1960), pp. 17–27.

Needham, Joseph, 'An Archaeological Study-tour in China, 1958', *Antiquity*, XXXIII, No. 130 (June 1959), pp. 113–19.

Nietzsche, Friedrich, *The Use and Abuse of History* (New York, 1957).

'Of Confucius, Fung Yu-lan and Others', *China News Analysis*, No. 398 (Nov. 24, 1961), pp. 1–7.

Orleans, Leo A., *Professional Manpower and Education in Communist China* (Washington, 1961).

Pa Chin and others, *A Battle for Life: a full record of how the life of steel worker, Chiu Tsai-kang, was saved in the Shanghai Kwangtze Hospital* (Peking, 1959).

Panikkar, K. M., *In Two Chinas: Memoirs of a Diplomat* (London, 1955).

Peake, Harold J. E., 'Village Community', *Encyclopaedia of the Social Sciences* (New York, 1935), XV, pp. 253–4.

'Popular Beliefs—Taoism—Christinaity', *China News Analysis*, No. 439 (Sept. 28, 1962).

Pound, Ezra, *Impact: Essays on Ignorance and the Decline of American Civilization* (Chicago, 1960).

The Classic Anthology Defined by Confucius (Cambridge, Mass., 1955).

Prusek, Jaroslav, 'The Importance of Tradition in Chinese Literature', *Archiv Orientalni* 26, No. 2 (1958), pp. 212–22.

'Review of Review', *China News Analysis*, No. 410 (March 2, 1962), pp. 1–7.

Scalapino, Robert A., and Schiffrin, Harold, 'Early Socialist Currents in the Chinese Revolutionary Movement: Sun Yat-sen versus Liang Ch'i-ch'ao', *Journal of Asian Studies*, XVIII, No. 3 (May 1959), pp. 321–42.

Scholem, Gershom G., *Major Trends in Jewish Mysticism* (New York, 1946).

Survey of China Mainland Press, No. 2471 (April 7, 1961); No. 2475 (April 13, 1961); No. 2483 (April 26, 1961).

Swann, Nancy Lee, *Food and Money in Ancient China: Han Shu 24* (Princeton, 1950).

'The Case of Liang Shu-ming', *Current Background*, No. 185 (Hong Kong: American Consulate-General), June 16, 1952.

Thompson, Laurence G., tr., *Ta T'ung Shu: the One-World Philosophy of K'ang Yu-wei* (London, 1958).

Varg, Paul A., *Missionaries, Chinese, and Diplomats: the American Protestant Missionary Movement in China, 1890–1952* (Princeton, 1958).

Weekly Report on Communist China, No. 28 (June 3, 1960).

Welch, Holmes, 'Buddhism under the Communists', *The China Quarterly*, No. 6 (April–June, 1961), pp. 1–14.

Wilbur, C. Martin, *Slavery in China During the Former Han Dynasty, 206 B.C.– A.D. 25* (Chicago, 1943).

Williamson, H. R., *Wang An Shih: a Chinese Statesman and Educationalist of the Sung Dynasty* (London, 1935).

Wittfogel, Karl A., *Oriental Despotism: A Comparative Study of Total Power* (New Haven, 1957).

Wright, Mary C., 'Revolution from Without? (A commentary on "Imperial Russia at the Turn of the Century: the Cultural Slope and the Revolution from Without", by Theodore Von Laue)',

Comparative Studies in Society and History, IV, No. 2 (Jan. 1962), pp. 247–52.

The Last Stand of Chinese Conservatism: the T'ung-chih Restoration, 1862–1874 (Stanford, 1957).

'The Pre-Revolutionary Intellectuals of China and Russia', *The China Quarterly*, No. 6 (April–June 1961), pp. 175–9.

Yang Lien-sheng, 'Notes on Dr. Swann's "Food and Money in Ancient China" ', *Studies in Chinese Institutional History* (Cambridge, Mass., 1961), pp. 85–118.

Yu Kuan-ying, 'China's Earliest Anthology of Poetry', *Chinese Literature*, No. 3 (March 1962), pp. 99–111.

Zagoria, Donald S., 'Khrushchev's Attack on Albania and Sino-Soviet Relations', *The China Quarterly*, No. 8 (Oct.–Dec. 1961), pp. 1–19.

Index

Abelard, Peter, I: 7, 169
Académie Francaise, II: 57, 83
Acton, Lord, III: 92
Ai (duke of Lu), I: 90
Ai Ching, I: 135
Ai Ssu-chi, I: 135
Alexander the Great, III: 123
amateurism, I: 15—43, 52; II: 33, 34, 48, 56, 57, 59, 62, 63, 67 111, 115, 126, 127; III: 81, 109
Amherst, Lord, III: 112
An Lu-shan Rebellion, II: 38
Analects, see *Lun-yü*
'ancient-text', see *ku-wen*
Annals, see *Ch'un-ch'iu*
"anti - feudal, anti - imperialist" synthesis, I: 140—145; III: 41, 53—55, 76, 78
Aristotle, I: 66
Arnold, Matthew, I: 18, 19, 32
Augustus, II: 96
Avicenna, I: 135

Bacon, Francis, I: 7—9, 169—71
Balázs, Etienne, I: 15, 16
Baldwin, James, I: 167, 168
Ball, John, II: 79
Bayeux Tapestry, III: 76
Bernini, Giovanni Lorenzo, III: 113
Boas, Franz, I: 167
Book of Changes, see *I-ching*
Book of History, see *Shu-ching*
Book of Poetry, see *Shih-ching*
Book of Rites, see *Li-chi*
Boxers, I: vii, 72, 96, 105, 150, 194; II: 7; III: 55, 112
Buddha, III: 38
Buddhism, I: 5, 9, 10, 23—6, 29, 32, 35, 68, 82, 119, 124, 144, 158, 161, 176, 202, 203; II: viii, 13, 26, 49, 67, 78, 87—9, 144—5; III: 14, 38, 62, 100, 104—5
Burckhardt, Jakob, II: xi, 119; III: 76—7
Burke, Edmund, I: 128, 198
Burlington Art Exhibition, I: 142

Calvin, Jean, II: 96
Cassirer, Ernst, I: 166, 167
Castiglione, Giuseppe, I: 158, 202
Cézanne, Paul, I: 30
Chan-kuo ts'e, III: 10
Ch'an, I: 5, 23—5, 27, 29, 32, 44, 176, 179
Chang Chien, II: 127
Chang Chih-tung, I: 60, 61, 65, 67—70, 77, 106, 107, 116, 186; III: 5, 111
Chang Chung-li, I: 184
Chang Hsi-t'ang, III: 127
Chang Hsien-chung, II: 89
Chang Hsueh-ch'eng, I: 91, 92, 192, 193; II: 149
Chang Hsun, II: 161
Chang Keng, I: 181
Chang Ping-lin, I: 88—91, 93, 94, 96, 194; II: 122—3; III: 32
Chang Shao-tseng, II: 162
Chang Tsai, I: 111; III: 24, 130, 132
Chao Erh-sun, II: 5
Chao Meng-fu, II: 62
Chao Po-chü, I: 175
Chao Po-su, I: 175
Charlemagne, II: 94—5
Charles I, II: 95

177